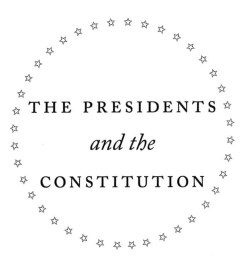

THE PRESIDENTS

*and the*

CONSTITUTION

# The Presidents

## *and the*

# Constitution

A LIVING HISTORY

*Edited by*
Ken Gormley

NEW YORK UNIVERSITY PRESS
New York

NEW YORK UNIVERSITY PRESS
New York
www.nyupress.org

References to Internet websites (URLs) were accurate at the time of writing. Neither the author nor New York University Press is responsible for URLs that may have expired or changed since the manuscript was prepared.

Library of Congress Cataloging-in-Publication Data
Names: Gormley, Ken, editor.
Title: The Presidents and the Constitution : a living history / edited by Ken Gormley.
Description: New York : New York University Press, 2016. | Includes index.
Identifiers: LCCN 2015043555 | ISBN 9781479839902 (cl : alk. paper)
Subjects: LCSH: Executive power—United States—History. |
Presidents—United States—History. | Constitutional history—United States.
Classification: LCC KF5053 .P75 2016 | DDC 342.73/062—dc23
LC record available at http://lccn.loc.gov/2015043555

New York University Press books are printed on acid-free paper, and their binding materials are chosen for strength and durability. We strive to use environmentally responsible suppliers and materials to the greatest extent possible in publishing our books.

Manufactured in the United States of America

Also available as an ebook

This book is dedicated to the law students, graduate students, and undergraduates at the authors' respective universities and colleges whose interest in, and enthusiasm for, the topic of American presidents and the Constitution has inspired the telling of this important story. The editor additionally dedicates this book to his wife, Laura Kozler Gormley, their children—Carolyn, Luke, Becca, and Maddy—and their two puppies, Gracie and Simba, who endured years' worth of boxes piled up in the study, along with nights and weekends listening to nonstop stories about obscure presidents, as the book took shape. It may not be the same as serving as president of the United States, but being co-chief executive of this wonderful family—albeit with limited powers, in a much smaller white house in Pittsburgh—is the greatest honor imaginable.

—KEN GORMLEY

Pittsburgh, Pennsylvania, February 2015

# CONTENTS

Introduction: An Unfinished Presidency   1
KEN GORMLEY

## PART I. THE FOUNDING ERA

1. George Washington . . . . . . . . . . . .17
RICHARD J. ELLIS

2. John Adams . . . . . . . . . . . . . . . .34
LOUIS FISHER

3. Thomas Jefferson . . . . . . . . . . . . .47
CLIFF SLOAN, LOUIS FISHER,
AND MOSHE SPINOWITZ

4. James Madison . . . . . . . . . . . . . .61
RALPH KETCHAM

5. James Monroe . . . . . . . . . . . . . .75
GARY HART

6. John Quincy Adams . . . . . . . . . . .89
JONATHAN L. ENTIN

## PART II. THE AGE OF JACKSON

7. Andrew Jackson . . . . . . . . . . . . .103
MARK A. GRABER

8. Martin Van Buren . . . . . . . . . . .116
MICHAEL J. GERHARDT

9. William Henry Harrison . . . . . . . 126
DAVID MARKS SHRIBMAN

10. John Tyler. . . . . . . . . . . . . . . . . 136
ROBERT J. SPITZER

11. James K. Polk . . . . . . . . . . . . . . 149
FRANK J. WILLIAMS

PART III. THE PRE–CIVIL WAR ERA

12. Zachary Taylor . . . . . . . . . . . . . 161
PAUL FINKELMAN

13. Millard Fillmore. . . . . . . . . . . . 173
JOSEPH F. RISHEL

14. Franklin Pierce . . . . . . . . . . . . . 181
PAUL FINKELMAN

15. James Buchanan . . . . . . . . . . . . 194
THOMAS A. HORROCKS

PART IV. CIVIL WAR AND RECONSTRUCTION

16. Abraham Lincoln. . . . . . . . . . . . 211
WILLIAM D. PEDERSON

17. Andrew Johnson. . . . . . . . . . . . . 227
MICHAEL LES BENEDICT

18. Ulysses S. Grant . . . . . . . . . . . . 239
JOHN F. MARSZALEK

## PART V. THE GILDED AGE

19. Rutherford B. Hayes............253
MICHAEL A. ROSS

20. James A. Garfield.............266
THOMAS C. SUTTON

21. Chester A. Arthur.............276
THOMAS C. SUTTON

22. Grover Cleveland, First Term.....288
DONALD GRIER STEPHENSON JR.

23. Benjamin Harrison............297
ALLAN B. SPETTER

24. Grover Cleveland, Second Term...308
DONALD GRIER STEPHENSON JR.

25. William McKinley............316
THOMAS C. SUTTON

## PART VI. THE PROGRESSIVE ERA

26. Theodore Roosevelt...........331
WILLIAM D. BADER

27. William Howard Taft..........343
FRANCINE SANDERS ROMERO

## PART VII. WORLD WAR I AND THE GREAT DEPRESSION

28. Woodrow Wilson.............357
SALADIN M. AMBAR

29. Warren G. Harding ...........371
JAMES D. ROBENALT

30. Calvin Coolidge ..............385
JOHN W. JOHNSON AND DALE E. P. YURS

31. Herbert Hoover ..............395
JOHN Q. BARRETT

CONTENTS

## PART VIII. THE NEW DEAL AND WORLD WAR II

32. Franklin Delano Roosevelt......409
WILLIAM D. PEDERSON

33. Harry S. Truman.............427
JAMES N. GIGLIO

## PART IX. THE CIVIL RIGHTS ERA

34. Dwight D. Eisenhower.........443
RICHARD V. DAMMS

35. John F. Kennedy.............459
BARBARA A. PERRY

36. Lyndon B. Johnson...........473
JOHN L. BULLION

## PART X. THE WATERGATE ERA AND REFORM

37. Richard M. Nixon ...........491
STANLEY KUTLER

38. Gerald R. Ford.............507
JEFFREY CROUCH

39. Jimmy Carter ..............521
SCOTT KAUFMAN

## PART XI. NEW CONSERVATIVES, NEW DEMOCRATS, AND POLARIZATION

40. Ronald Reagan.............539
KENNETH W. STARR

41. George H. W. Bush ..........557
LORI COX HAN

42. William Jefferson Clinton ......570
KEN GORMLEY

## PART XII. NATIONAL SECURITY ERA: POST-9/11

43. George W. Bush . . . . . . . . . . . . . .589
BENJAMIN A. KLEINERMAN

44. Barack Obama . . . . . . . . . . . . . .605
MICHAEL J. GERHARDT


Conclusion:
An Evolving American Presidency  623
KEN GORMLEY


*Acknowledgements* . . . . . . . . . . . . .657

*About the Contributors* . . . . . . . . . .659

*Photo Credits* . . . . . . . . . . . . . . . .667

*Index* . . . . . . . . . . . . . . . . . . . . . .671

# Introduction

*An Unfinished Presidency*

KEN GORMLEY

The presidency of the United States is the most powerful position in the American system of government, and perhaps in the world. As Woodrow Wilson once wrote, the chief executive "is the vital place of action in the system, whether he accepts it as such or not, and the office is the measure of the man—of his wisdom as well as his force."[1] Yet the Constitution dedicates surprisingly little space to defining the duties or powers of the president; instead, it leaves the contours of that high office to be sketched out in real time, as history plays itself out over distinctive eras in American life.

Article II of the Constitution, which barely contains a thousand words, is the provision in which most of the power of the American presidency is housed. In one sense, the article is vast and awesome in scope. After all, in the period following the Revolutionary War, the framers created a new model of a chief executive—a model that had no precise parallel in world history. The office of presidency was designed to maximize the good—and temper the bad—characteristics of executive power known to the framers in the 1780s. This constitutional office thus helped to create a shining new form of republican government and a bold invention in the history of democracy. In this sense, Article II of the Constitution represents one of the great triumphs of American ingenuity. As two prominent presidential scholars have noted: "The president would not be a king or sovereign. Instead, he would swear to protect and defend a higher authority: the Constitution."[2]

At the same time, if the framers knew they were creating a revolutionary type of chief executive who would play a central role in the life of the nation, they put surprisingly little meat on the bones of this key figure. Article II, Section 1, vests the "executive Power" in the president, but does nothing to define the powers that lie at the heart of the chief executive's office. Section 2 states that the president shall be "Commander in Chief of the Army and Navy," yet it does nothing to clarify the president's authority in commanding the military. Nor does it untangle the president's authority from Congress's separate power to "declare War" (Article I, Section 8, Clause 11), leaving that sticky wicket for another day. Article II, Section 2, empowers the president "with the Advice and Consent of the Senate" to make treaties, appoint federal judges, ambassadors, and certain "inferior Officers," and to seek advice from "principal Officers" in the executive branch. The language is ostensibly packed with power, yet it is surrounded by a mist of uncertainty: If the president must secure the advice and consent of the Senate to *appoint* certain officials, must he or she also obtain permission from the Senate to *remove* these officials? What about "inferior officers" in the executive branch—how much control does the president have over these figures if Congress is empowered (as is often the case) to create them in the first place? And if the president plays a central role in appointing ambassadors and making treaties with foreign nations, does this mean that under the Constitution, the president is the chief actor in foreign affairs, more generally?

Even in areas where the president's powers seem to be clearest, gaps and instances of constitutional silence abound: For example, the Constitution gives the president a seemingly sweeping power to grant "Reprieves and Pardons" for all federal offenses (Article II, Section 2). Another provision gives the president authority to deliver a "State of the Union" address to Congress so that he or she can propose legislation (Article II, Section 3). Interestingly, one of the president's most potent powers—to veto legislation that he or she finds objectionable (Article I, Section 7)—is wedged into the Constitution's opening article rather than with the other key presidential powers in Article II. Taken together, these provisions seem to crown the president with extraordinary power vis-à-vis Congress. Yet the Constitution is silent as to when, and for what reasons, the president can trump Congress where there is overlap in authority—which occurs frequently. It is almost as if the Constitution assumes that the president and Congress will have to duke it out, battling over the parameters of their respective powers.

The same is true with respect to the judicial branch. Ever since Chief Justice John Marshall in *Marbury v. Madison* (1803) confirmed the power of judicial review over other branches of government, presidents are subject to being checked by the courts. Thus, the Constitution creates an uneasy dynamic between all three branches.

And when the president goes too far or seeks to defy another branch of government, there is the looming presence of Article II, Section 4, which states that he or she "shall be removed from Office on Impeachment for, and Conviction of, Treason, Bribery, or other high Crimes and Misdemeanors." To heighten the drama, impeachments will be initiated in the House of Representatives and tried before the Senate, with the chief justice of the United States presiding over the proceedings (Article I, Section 3, Clause 6). Thus, the other two branches of government, often at odds with the president as they skirmish for authority, have the final power to extinguish his or her time in office, a provision that hangs over the head of each president like a constitutional sword of Damocles.

And who, exactly, is the vice president? This ill-defined official is barely mentioned in the Constitution. His or her only official duty is to preside over the Senate, and this individual does not even have a vote except for ties (Article I, Section 3, Clause 4). What exactly did the framers intend to do when the president could no longer function? Did they envision that this weak vice president would have a temporary role as an acting chief executive who merely exercised "the Powers and Duties" of his or her predecessor for a brief time (Article II, Section 6)? Or was the purpose to fully empower this individual to become the new president? On this point, the Constitution remained silent.

The framers were not unaware of the ill-defined nature of the new presidential office they were creating. Indeed, they reached a consensus in Philadelphia only by leaving many of the bedeviling details to be worked out over time.[3] Records of the Constitutional Convention and other historical sources suggest that the provisions dealing with the presidency were purposely left sketchy, with the intention that the presidents themselves (starting, the framers expected, with George Washington) would fill in that sketch.

Yet certain common goals no doubt undergirded the drafting of the provisions of the Constitution dealing with the presidency. During the heated ratification debates, James Madison wrote in *The Federalist* No. 47 that "the accumulation of all powers, legislative, executive, and judiciary, in the same hands, whether of one, a few, or many, and whether hereditary, self-appointed, or elective, may justly be pronounced the very definition of tyranny."[4] Consequently, the principle of separation of powers lay at the heart of the new form of republican government being constructed by the framers. It was derived from the work of writers like Montesquieu, who had spelled out the essentials of the doctrine in 1748 in his famous treatise *The Spirit of Laws.*[5]

As the drafting of the Constitution progressed, it became clear that the principal fear of the Federalists was that the *legislature* would gain too much power and become oppressive. Ironically, during the colonial period, the foremost perceived enemy was the chief magistrate: King George III had ruled like a despot, and British governors in the colonies were forever taxing the colonists and running roughshod over them.[6] With fresh memories of unscrupulous and unpopular governors, the first state constitutions, beginning with Virginia's in 1776, had created weak chief executive positions and placed the lion's share of power in the legislative bodies.[7] Yet the experience of the post-Revolutionary period taught new lessons. Under the newly adopted state constitutions, legislative bodies in some states had run away with seemingly unchecked power and left governors as impotent figureheads. Additionally, Shays' Rebellion in 1787 demonstrated the folly of the Articles of Confederation, which had established a system of government with no chief executive—that crisis escalated because there was no central figure who could take command and quell domestic crises. Indeed, Secretary of Foreign Affairs John Jay wrote to George Washington in 1787 and asked: "Shall we have a king?"[8] States like New York, whose constitution had been adopted in 1777, had established strong governors in their state constitutions, and these executives seemed surprisingly successful.[9] James Wilson of Pennsylvania, the chairman of the Committee of Detail at the Constitutional Convention, therefore led the fight for a single, vigorous chief executive. He favored "a single magistrate, as giving most energy, dispatch, and responsibility to the office." Wilson also believed that a strong chief executive was necessary to blunt unwelcome acts of the legislature. "Without such a defense specifically a veto power," he declared, "the legislature can at any moment sink it [the executive branch] into non-existence."[10]

Thus, although the framers were wary of monarchs after the period of British oppression, they had become even warier of a runaway legislative branch. As Madison noted in *The Federalist* No. 47, the legislature possessed "an intrepid confidence in its own strength" and an ability to overpower other branches of government.[11] Madison sharpened this point in *The Federalist* No.48, reasoning that the three departments had to be "blended" and interlaced to achieve the desired separation of powers.[12] Additionally, the framers concluded that the Constitution had to include an elaborate system of checks and balances, so that each branch of government was in a position to limit or check the powers of the other competing branches.

The chief executive's place in this new weblike scheme was the subject of considerable debate as different versions of the Constitution were being drafted and subject to negotiation. A central notion that ultimately gained acceptance, as articulated by Alexander Hamilton in *The Federalist* No. 70, was linked to the idea of the president as a force of energy and action in the tripartite system of government. In Hamilton's words, "energy in the executive is the leading character in the very definition of good government."[13] Or, as Hamilton argued in *The Federalist* No. 69, "a feeble execution is but another phrase for a bad executive; and a government ill executed, whatever it may be in theory, must be, in practice, a bad government."[14]

Tench Coxe, a delegate from Pennsylvania, would later write that there was a great advantage to having a democratically selected president over a king who ruled merely by hereditary right. The president, said Coxe, would hold office by virtue of having been selected by the people and "cannot be an idiot, [and] probably not a knave or tyrant, for those whom nature makes so, discover it before the age of thirty-five."[15]

When the delegates of the Constitutional Convention gathered in Philadelphia, in May 1787, they were purportedly assembling "for the sole and express purpose of revising the Articles of Confederation." Yet it quickly became clear that their task was to draft a wholly new constitution. The wrangling that took place before they decided on the type of chief executive they wanted in the Constitution is instructive, because it discloses what options they *rejected*.

Several issues dominated the debate as the American presidency took shape. First, some delegates favored having more than one chief executive.

John Rutledge of South Carolina declared that "unity in the Executive magistracy" was "the foetus of monarchy."[16] In contrast, as described above, James Wilson pressed hard for a unitary chief executive. His argument won the day; the delegates ultimately approved the notion of incorporating a single, unitary head of the executive branch.[17]

The second big decision facing the convention delegates was how the chief executive would be selected. At various times during the debate, they considered having the president chosen by the national legislature, directly by the people, or through a complex scheme of electors (originally, these electors would be selected by the state legislatures).[18] Early in its deliberations, the convention leaned toward a provision that would have the president selected by the national legislature (i.e., Congress) for a single term of seven years.[19] As the summer progressed, however, the framers concluded that election by Congress was too dangerous. Respected delegates such as James Wilson, John Rutledge, and Edmund Randolph of Virginia argued that this system would give the national legislature—specifically the Senate—a disproportionate amount of power. It would vest that chamber of Congress with "such an influence . . . over the election of the President in addition to its other powers, [as] to convert that body into a real & dangerous Aristocracy."[20]

The novel Electoral College ended up being the compromise solution, designed to keep the president from being co-opted by the legislative branch. At the same time, this solution also (at least in theory) kept the electoral process at arm's length from the general citizenry so that the president did not become "tribune of the people" and so that the job of selecting the president was placed in the hands of "men of special discernment."[21] In many ways, the complex, untested Electoral College system that was ultimately adopted mimicked the Connecticut Compromise—it dispersed electoral votes among the states in a fashion that took account of population, while also recognizing the basic equality of each state in the new union. While the Electoral College relied on specially elected "electors," as a practical matter it largely mirrored the will of the general electorate. Thus, populism made its way back into the mix, albeit in a slightly diluted fashion.

A hidden piece of the new Electoral College scheme, however, would leave a dubious imprint on the new nation for nearly a century. Article I, Section 2, Clause 3, provided that slaves would count as three-fifths of persons for purposes of determining population and hence the number of each state's representatives in the U.S. House of Representatives.²² This provision, also known as the federal ratio, had been a nonnegotiable condition imposed by the Southern states before they would agree to ratify the Constitution. It guaranteed that Southern states would indefinitely hold the whip hand over Northern states in electing members of Congress. It also gave the South a clever advantage in selecting presidents: Article II, Section 2, mandated that the number of electors would be determined by the number of senators and representatives to which each state was entitled in Congress. Thus, slave owners—and slave-owning states—received a whopping over-vote in the Electoral College. The three-fifths provision therefore skewed the results in favor of the South even though the slaves themselves, whose numbers affected the outcome, "had no more will in the matter than 'New England horses, cows, and oxen.'"²³ Thus, the Electoral College system itself, combined with the insidious Three-Fifths Clause, played a direct role in shaping the U.S. presidency for a century, ensuring that the slavery issue would inevitably come to a head in the new nation.

A third issue confronting the Constitutional Convention was whether to create a "council of revision"—similar to that established by the first New York Constitution—to allow a joint executive-judicial council to override repugnant acts of Congress.²⁴ The idea was to enable the weaker two branches of government to band together and invalidate "unjust and pernicious laws" enacted by the legislature.²⁵ In the end, this idea was scrapped on the assumption that the separation of powers built into the Constitution would allow the executive and judicial branches to fend off encroachments by the legislative branch. Yet the death of the council of revision gave birth to an important new presidential power: a limited veto power over congressional legislation. While some delegates (particularly Wilson and Hamilton) were prepared to give the chief executive an absolute veto, this idea was scuttled because it might allow power-hungry presidents to cripple Congress by cutting legislation to ribbons. The limited veto power, on the other hand, contained a safety valve: It permitted Congress to override the veto with a two-thirds vote of both chambers. This was viewed as a prudent middle ground that sufficiently shored up the president's place in the system of government.²⁶

As the completed Constitution was being debated prior to its ratification, those who harbored doubts about the potentially powerful and largely undefined office of the presidency were mollified, to a certain extent, by the understanding that George Washington would be the likely first occupant of the office. Thus, the details of the presidency could be hashed out, at least initially, with an honorable man in the chief executive's post. As Hamilton noted at the conclusion of the Constitutional Convention, the fact that Washington was the presumptive choice for the nation's first president "will insure a wise choice of men to administer the government and a good administration." Moreover, Hamilton said, the choice "will conciliate the confidence and affection of the people and perhaps enable the government to acquire more consistency than the proposed constitution seems to promise."[27] Another delegate wrote after the Convention: "I am free to acknowledge that his powers [the president's] are full great, and greater than I was disposed to make them. Nor, *entre nous*, do I believe they would have been so great had not many of the members cast their eyes towards George Washington as President; and shaped their ideas of the powers to be given to a President by their opinions of his virtue."[28]

As reduced to parchment in the new U.S. Constitution, the presidency was therefore a uniquely American office. More than any other branch of government delineated in the first three articles of the Constitution, the executive branch was left intentionally incomplete. As Professor Akhil Reed Amar has written in his magnificent biography of the Constitution: "The evident openness of the text [in Article II] reflected the framers' genuine uncertainty as they struggled to invent a wholly new sort of executive."[29] Some of the blanks would be filled in during the expected presidency of George Washington; he could guide the way through the fog for future occupants of that office. The rest of the blanks would be left to history itself. The new American presidency would be defined by the Constitution but also would be allowed to play itself out, gradually giving definition to the sparse words of the written document.

For all of the flexibility built into the presidency by the framers, the office has remained remarkably stable. Some of this stability was made possible because presidents—starting with George Washington—voluntarily stepped down from office after two terms to ensure that the office did not transform itself into a monarchy. (President Franklin D. Roosevelt, of course, broke the two-term tradition—a decision that led to the passage of the Twenty-Second Amendment.) Some of the stability of the office also related to the willingness of losing presidential candidates—beginning with defeated President John Adams after the election of 1800 and most recently with Vice President Al Gore in the contested election of 2000— to step aside and transfer power peacefully to the new chief executive.

Some of the stability, as well, can be traced to the physical location of the chief executive. In over 225 years, the home of U.S. presidents has remained remarkably fixed. When George Washington took office in 1789, he initially conducted his executive business from the four-story private mansion on Cherry Street in New York City. That home had been used by the president of the Continental Congress, because there was not yet a permanent seat of government for the new nation.[30] In late 1790, Congress and President Washington both moved to Philadelphia; that city then served as the temporary capital for a decade while the newly planned Federal City (which would come to be named Washington, D.C.) was being built on a swampland along the Potomac River, between Maryland and Virginia. For the duration of his two terms, then, Washington leased a spacious three-story house on Market Street in Philadelphia that belonged to his close friend (and fellow delegate at the Constitutional Convention) Robert Morris. Finally, in 1800, John and Abigail Adams moved into the grand neoclassical White House situated behind wrought-iron gates on Pennsylvania Avenue in Washington, D.C., becoming the first chief executive and spouse to occupy that mansion.

For over two centuries, American presidents have taken up residence in that same structure—with only a brief hiatus during the presidency of James Madison in the midst of the War of 1812: When the British burned the White House in 1814, the Madisons lived temporarily in the Octagon House on New York Avenue. (Newly elected President James Monroe moved back into the refurbished White House in 1818.) Thus, the office has enjoyed remarkable stability, even in terms of its domicile.

Yet bricks and mortar only constitute a backdrop for the story. The study of American presidents and the Constitution is primarily animated by events that must be placed into an historical context. Individual presidents and their personalities, as the framers like Alexander Hamilton had hoped, "energize" the office. Unexpected events in American history play out across the landscape of a president's term in office, creating breezes, strong winds, and at times tornadoes, buffeting around the actors and squeezing out meaning from the sparse words of the Constitution that define the chief executive's role.

This book seeks to bring to life the rich story of forty-four (and still counting) presidents, as they have interfaced with the Constitution, and to tell their stories in the context of American history. (Grover Cleveland served two noncontiguous terms as president; for this reason, the book consists of forty-four chapters rather than forty-three.) This is not meant to be a book solely, or even primarily, about famous Supreme Court cases defining presidential power. Nor does it follow the pattern of traditional books on presidential power, which examine groups of cases and other material dealing with specific topics, such as presidential power as commander in chief, in foreign affairs, in domestic matters, and so on. Even the most astute reader cannot simply peruse neat folders of material, organized by topic, to get the full picture. The fast-moving events of history that propel presidents into office and animate their time in public life are equally important—or more important—if one is to understand the unique interplay between the American presidency and the Constitution. Thus, this book chronicles the people and events that have pushed, tugged at, lit fires under, made heroes of, or destroyed American presidents as they carried out their duties in office.

The framers constructed the American presidency with an elaborate web of strings attached and affixed these tightly to the legislative and judicial branches. The more one observes the arc of the story over time, the more one can appreciate that all three branches of government are bound together inextricably in this saga. Indeed, the framers ensured this by building into the Constitution the Federalist notion of *separation of powers* and *checks and balances*, so that the three branches of government would remain in a constant state of tension, each guarding its own turf.[31] The events that have most poignantly defined presidential authority under the Constitution—from President George Washington through President Barack Obama—have thus been played out like a stage drama featuring all three branches of government. When one actor performs, the other two step forward or recede accordingly. In this fashion, animated by real people and competing institutions of government and unexpected historical forces, the presidents' roles vis-à-vis the Constitution have sprung to life.

Simultaneously, the framers constructed a system of *federalism*, by which the national government regularly vies with the states for authority.[32] Even as presidents wield enormous power as the chief executive in one of the world's most powerful nations, they must be respectful of dozens of independent sovereignties (in the form of fifty states) nipping at their heels. Federalism thus provides another source of drama and presidential energy.

The goal of capturing all U.S. presidents in action is admittedly an ambitious one. The American presidents have been a busy and lively bunch of political figures. As Franklin D. Roosevelt once stated: "All of our great presidents [have been] leaders of thought at a time when certain ideas in the life of the nation had to be clarified."³³ Constitutional issues, during the presidents' respective times in office, swirl around like thunderstorms and become relevant only at unpredictable moments. How is it possible to produce forty-four chapters that say something meaningful about each president, especially when some have held office for as little as thirty-one days? (See the chapter on William Henry Harrison.)

The authors selected to write these chapters are experts uniquely suited to answer that question. They are historians, political scientists, judges, legal scholars, and journalists who rank among the nation's leading presidential experts. Their challenge in each case was to create a short, readable chapter that created a colorful portrait of the president and shone a light on constitutional issues that confronted the president, helped to shape the president's time in office, or gave birth to a piece of constitutional precedent during the president's tenure in office. Chapters were then edited and rewritten countless times to weave together an interconnected historical account.

If this were an exhaustive collection of presidential biographies, it would require forty-four volumes. Yet this was not the goal. Nor was the book designed as an assortment of unconnnected essays. It is an ongoing narrative that continues to evolve each time the American citizenry elects a new president and as new elements of the story come to life.

Illuminating the elements that span the divide across presidential administrations makes this a particularly fascinating and worthwhile endeavor. Consider the story of Woodrow Wilson, who in 1914 sought to force a *New York Tribune* city editor named George Burdick to testify in front of a federal grand jury about allegations that a Treasury Department employee was illegally leaking information to the press. President Wilson decided to outsmart Burdick by having a pardon waiting for him so that the editor could not invoke the Fifth Amendment and assert that he might be subjected to criminal prosecution for his testimony. Yet the president was thwarted by the Supreme Court, when it handed down its decision in *Burdick v. U.S.* in 1915, declaring that a pardon "carries an imputation of guilt; acceptance a confession of it," and held that Burdick could not be forced to accept that pardon.³⁴

Now, consider Gerald R. Ford in 1976, when he made the politically risky decision to pardon his predecessor, Richard M. Nixon, for all crimes relating to the Watergate scandal. In doing so, Ford sent a young lawyer named Benton Becker to President Nixon's home in California carrying a copy of the *Burdick* case in his briefcase. At Ford's insistence, the former president was informed that if he accepted the pardon, it would constitute a legal admission of guilt. (It turns out that, for this reason, President Nixon at first refused to accept the pardon, although the American public was generally unaware of this fact.) President Ford was therefore prepared to consummate the pardon deal only because he believed that he was getting from the disgraced former president what the American people most wanted—a formal admission of wrongdoing. Yet only if one connects the dots back to President Wilson's foiled attempt to use the pardon power in 1914 can one properly appreciate President Ford's action in 1976—an action that was tied to Ford's understanding of the Constitution and that helped extinguish his own political career.

Similarly, one needs to place events in an historical context to properly analyze the decisions made by George W. Bush and Barack Obama as they confronted the recent War on Terror, set up military tribunals in Guantanamo, and unleashed drones in Pakistan. Specifically, one must understand the decisions faced by Abraham Lincoln during the Civil War, the role played by new technology (telephones and telegraphs) during the presidency of William McKinley in the Spanish-American War, and the failed effort by Harry S. Truman to exert his commander-in-chief powers in seizing the nation's steel mills during the Korean War, to make sense of such modern-day executive actions.

How will scholars and American citizens assess the fitness of individuals to step into this high office, when it comes time to elect new presidents? How will they judge the records of past, present, and future presidents on dramatic constitutional issues that inevitably define the nation? Only by peering through a specially crafted historical lens can one see links between and among presidents, from George Washington to present-day leaders— links that would otherwise be obscured by a web of distant events.

By helping to untangle this web, this book aims to bring to life a story as unique as the American presidents themselves.

### NOTES

1. Woodrow Wilson, *Constitutional Government in the United States* (New York: Columbia University Press, 1908), 73.
2. Michael A. Genovese and Robert J. Spitzer, *The Presidency and the Constitution: Cases and Controversies* (New York: Palgrave Macmillan, 2005), 5.

3. James Madison, just weeks before the delegates arrived in Philadelphia, confided to George Washington that when it came to the chief executive position, he had "scarcely ventured to form my own opinion either of the manner in which it ought to be constituted or of the authorities with which it ought to be cloathed." Madison to Washington, April 16, 1787, in *The Papers of Madison*, ed. William T. Hutchinson et al. (Chicago and Charlottesville, VA: 1962–1991), 9:385, quoted in Jack Rakove, *Original Meanings: Politics and Ideas in the Making of the Constitution* (New York: Vintage Books, 1997), 255.

4. James Madison, Federalist No. 47, in *The Federalist Papers*, ed. Clinton Rossiter (New York: New American Library, 1961), 301.

5. For a complete text of the work, see Montesquieu, *Spirit of the Laws*, trans. and ed. Anne M. Cohler, Basia C. Miller, and Harold S. Stone (Cambridge: Cambridge University Press, 1989).

   Montesquieu wrote: "When the legislative and executive powers are united in the same person, or in the same body of magistrates, there can be no liberty; because apprehensions may arise, lest the same monarch or senate should enact tyrannical laws, to execute them in a tyrannical manner.

   "Again there is no liberty, if the judiciary power be not separated from the legislative and executive. Were it joined with the legislative, the life and liberty of the subject would be exposed to arbitrary control; for the judge would be then the legislator. Were it joined to the executive power, the judge might behave with violence and oppression." Philip B. Kurland and Ralph Lerner, eds., *The Founder's Constitution* (Chicago: University of Chicago Press, 1987), book 11, chap. 6, 1:624–625, available at http://press-pubs. uchicago.edu/founders/documents/v1ch17s9.html. A slightly different text version appears in ibid., 157.

6. Edward S. Corwin, *The President: Office and Powers, 1787–1984* (New York: NYU Press, 1984), 5–6; Donald L. Robinson, *To the Best of My Ability: The Presidency and the Constitution* (New York: W.W. Norton, 1987), 37–39.

7. Corwin, *President: Office and Powers*, 6–7.

8. Genovese and Spitzer, *Presidency and the Constitution*, 4.

9. Robinson, *To the Best of My Ability*, 46–47.

10. Max Farrand, ed., *Records of the Federal Convention of 1787*, rev. ed. (New Haven, CT: 1937; repr. 1966), 1:65, 68–69, 98, cited in Corwin, *President: Office and Powers*, 11.

11. Madison, Federalist No. 47, 300–308.

12. James Madison, Federalist Paper No. 48, in *The Federalist Papers*, ed. Clinton Rossiter (New York: New American Library, 1961), 308–313.

13. Alexander Hamilton, Federalist Paper No. 70, in *The Federalist Papers*, 423–431.

14. Alexander Hamilton, Federalist Paper No. 69, in *The Federalist Papers*, 415–423.

15. Tench Coxe, "An American Citizen," *Philadelphia Independent Gazetteer*, September 26, 1787, Doc. Hist., 13:249–251, quoted in Rakove, *Original Meanings*, 276.

16. John Rutledge, quoted in Rakove, *Original Meanings*, 257.

17. Farrand, *Records*, 1:66–69, quoted in Rakove, *Original Meanings*, 257.

18. For selection by national legislature, see Rakove, *Original Meanings*, 260. For selection by the people or by electors, see Corwin, *President: Office and Powers*, 12.

19. Rakove, *Original Meanings*, 260.

20. Farrand, *Records*, 2:501–502, 511–513, quoted in Rakove, *Original Meanings*, 265.

21. For "tribune of the people," see Genovese and Spitzer, *Presidency and the Constitution*, 5. This reference refers to tribunes of Roman times. But see Akhil Reed Amar, *America's Constitution: A Biography* (New York: Random House, 2005), 151–155 (noting that the notion of populism was emphasized by leading Federalists during the ratification debates). For "men of special discernment," see Corwin, *President: Office and Power*, 13.

22. Gary Wills, *Negro President: Jefferson and the Slave Power* (Boston: Houghton Mifflin, 2003), 1–5; Amar, *America's Constitution: A Biography*, 87–98.

23. Albert F. Simpson, "The Political Significance of Slave Representation, 1787–1821," *Journal of Southern History* 71 (1941): 321, quoted in Wills, *Negro President*, 2.

24. Peter J. Galie, *Ordered Liberty: The Constitutional History of New York* (New York: Fordham University Press, 1996), 44–46. There was also some similarity to the Council of Censors created by the Pennsylvania Constitution.

25. Farrand, *Records*, 2:78 (Mason), 52 (Morris, July 19), 30 (Wilson, July 17), cited in Rakove, *Original Meanings*, 261.

26. Rakove, *Original Meanings*, 258.

27. Alexander Hamilton, *Conjectures About the Constitution: September*, in *The Documentary History of the Ratification of the Constitution* (Madison: State Historical Society of Wisconsin, 1981), 13:277–278, cited in Rakove, *Original Meanings*, 287.

28. Pierce Butler to Weedon Butler, quoted in Genovese, *Presidency and the Constitution*, 6 (emphasis added).

29. Amar, *America's Constitution: A Biography*, 197.

30. President Washington also lived briefly at the Alexander Macomb House on Broadway, before moving to Philadelphia.

31. The separation of powers doctrine, premised on the notion that the sum total of governmental power should not reside in one individual or body, is embedded in the structure and provisions of the Constitution. Pursuant to this doctrine, government is divided into three distinct branches—the legislative, the executive, and the judicial—and each is given its own sphere of power. At the same time, the Constitution provides each branch with the means to check and balance the others and thus further prevent the abuse of power. Keith E. Whittington, "The Separation of Powers at the Founding," in *Separation of Powers: Documents and Commentary*, ed. Katy J. Harriger (Washington, DC: CQ Press, 2003), 1–12.

32. The Constitution's scheme of federalism recognizes that sovereignty exists at the national and state levels. Thus, power is exercised concurrently by the U.S. government and by the governments of the individual fifty states. Willi Paul Adams, *The First American Constitutions* (Chapel Hill: University of North Carolina Press, 1980), 276–291.

33. Arthur M. Schlesinger Jr., Introduction to *George Washington*, by James McGregor Burns and Susan Dunn (New York: Times Books, 2004), xvii; *New York Times*, November 13, 1932, quoted in Corwin, *President: Office and Powers*, 313.

34. Burdick v. United States, 236 U.S. 79, 94–95 (1915).

# PART I

# The Founding Era

# 1

# George Washington

RICHARD J. ELLIS

*No other president in American history faced so many decisions about the scope of his constitutional powers as did George Washington. Keenly aware that his interpretations of the fundamental charter would set precedent for future generations, and reluctant to appear that he was gathering power like a king, Washington was extremely cautious as chief executive. Throughout his two terms in office, he was especially careful to shore up the notion of separation of powers, ensuring that each branch of government retained its own independent sphere of authority under the new Constitution. Through careful, restrained exercise of power, Washington paradoxically helped to build a strong and respected American presidency.*

## Introduction

When it comes to the presidency, the Constitution of the United States is a document of remarkably few words. Most presidents navigate their way around the silences of the Constitution by emulating, rejecting, or modifying the actions of their predecessors. In the unique case of George Washington, who served as the nation's first president from 1789 until 1797, there were no presidential precedents to help him figure out what the Constitution required or allowed. There was, of course, the British monarchical model, but few Americans—least of all Washington—wanted the president to be a king. There were also the diverse examples supplied by state governors, but the nation's first president never understood his role to be that of a glorified governor. Washington shouldered the additional burden of knowing that his every step could become a precedent for his successors. Remarkably, the nation trusted this extraordinary power to shape the constitutional meaning of the presidential role to a relatively uneducated career military man whose direct experience in politics was limited to a few months as a delegate to the First and Second Continental Congresses during the mid-1770s.

Born in February 1732, George Washington grew up a farm boy in Virginia's Tidewater region, where the crop of choice was tobacco and the workforce was largely slaves. Washington's father was a hard-edged, upwardly mobile businessman who acquired acreage by the thousands. When Washington was eleven years old, his father died suddenly, leaving the family in a precarious position.[1] At sixteen, with the family's finances at a nadir and desirous of escaping from his exacting mother's control, Washington took up surveying as a career, a fortuitous choice that would allow him to serve some of the wealthiest and best-connected landholders in Virginia. His knowledge of the backwoods of Virginia, acquired from his time as a surveyor, made him invaluable to the British military, and he spent much of his twenties distinguishing himself in the French and Indian War. His marriage to the widow Martha Dandridge Custis at age twenty-six helped make Washington one of the wealthiest men in Virginia. By the time he became president, Washington owned five farms totaling eight thousand acres, which were worked by three hundred slaves and were worth about half a billion in today's dollars.[2]

Washington emerged from his twenties a very rich man but not a well-educated one. Unlike almost all the other famous founding fathers (John Adams, Thomas Jefferson, James Madison, and Alexander Hamilton), he neither went to college nor studied law. Washington may have been, as historian Gordon S. Wood writes, "a man of few words and no great thoughts," but even as a relatively young man, he possessed the commanding bearing, self-discipline, and mature judgment that made him a leader whom other men were willing to follow.[3]

When the American Revolution broke out in 1775, the Second Continental Congress chose Washington to serve as commander in chief of the Continental Army, a post he held until the defeat of the British in 1783. General Washington was hailed as an exemplar of republican virtue for relinquishing military power the moment victory was assured.

In the spring of 1787, Washington came out of retirement to preside over the Constitutional Convention in Philadelphia. Seated on a raised platform in front of the other delegates, he managed to appear detached from the convention's often-rancorous debate. However, he consistently voted with those delegates, like his fellow Virginian James Madison, who favored a strong national government and an independent executive branch. Although the prospect of a strong executive conjured up images of monarchy and despotism among many of the delegates, a majority of the fifty-five convention delegates ended up supporting the creation of a single, independent chief executive. That support probably owed a great deal to the knowledge that the new office would be filled first by Washington.[4]

On September 17, 1787, four months after the convention had begun, the delegates approved the new Constitution and sent it to the states for ratification. After a prolonged debate between those in favor of the Constitution, who referred to themselves as "Federalists," and the "Anti-Federalists," who opposed it, the Constitution was ratified by the requisite number of states. On September 13, 1788, the Congress of the Confederation certified the new Constitution and set the date (March 4, 1789) for the first meeting of the new government. Washington had anxiously monitored the ratification process from Mount Vernon, knowing that he would certainly be selected the nation's first president. True to form, each of the sixty-nine presidential electors cast his ballot for Washington in the nation's first presidential election.

## Presidency

Washington was acutely aware that fears of executive power remained a potent part of American political culture. He also knew that the leading statesmen in the new nation remained jealously solicitous of legislative prerogatives. Washington understood that building support for the new Constitution and fostering trust in the presidency required him to exercise great self-restraint, particularly in his interactions with the legislative branch.

### Relationship with Congress

Washington's self-restraint was evident in the cautious approach he took toward the veto power granted him by Article I, Section 7, of the Constitution. He admitted to a friend that he signed "many Bills" with which he disagreed. Indeed, during eight years as president, Washington vetoed only two bills. The first, at the end of his first term, was an apportionment bill, which Washington vetoed at the insistence of his secretary of state, Thomas Jefferson. Not only did Jefferson believe that the bill was unconstitutional, he also feared that "non-use" of the veto was beginning "to excite a belief that no President will ever venture to use it." Washington did not exercise his next and last veto—of a bill that disbanded two dragoon companies—until four days before he was to leave office.[5]

Washington also cooperated with Congress when it requested information, even some embarrassing information related to military policy. When the House of Representatives requested War Department documents relating to General Arthur St. Clair's humiliating defeat at the hands of American Indians in November 1791, Washington could easily have stonewalled. The Constitution, after all, did not specify what information the president was required to divulge to Congress. Well aware, however, that his response might "become a precedent" and that Congress might in the future request papers "of so secret a nature as that they ought not to be given up," Washington gave the House investigating committee all the information it requested.[6]

Washington's public communications with Congress were unfailingly deferential. His speeches and messages were never scolding or confrontational. In his inaugural address, he chose to avoid altogether any "recommendation of particular measures." Instead, he paid "the tribute that is due to the talents, the rectitude, and the patriotism . . . [of the legislators] selected to devise and adopt them." In his first annual message, he dutifully drew Congress's attention to the issues that he believed required legislative action, yet he was careful to avoid specifying what legislation he thought should be adopted.

Behind the scenes, however, President Washington was not entirely passive in shaping legislation, particularly on matters relating to national defense. For instance, his first annual message vaguely referenced the need to establish a "uniform and well-digested plan" for a militia, yet Washington had already drawn up a more specific plan and instructed Secretary of War Henry Knox to work it "into the form of a Bill with which to furnish . . . Congress." It turned out that the First Congress did not share the president's sense of urgency and took no action on the administration's bill. Although deeply disappointed, Washington bore the setback stoically and did not attempt to lobby legislators on behalf of his preferred plan.[7]

Washington had strategic reasons for wishing to avoid being drawn too deeply into the legislative process. For one, taking sides in fractious legislative debates would jeopardize his carefully cultivated reputation as a president above party and faction. In addition, he believed that attempting to influence Congress would be counterproductive because doing so could trigger charges of executive usurpation and arouse legislative resentment. Finally, Washington feared that by intervening in the legislative process, he could damage the prestige of his own presidency and that of future presidents.[8]

However, Washington's restraint was more than just a tactical or political calculation. It also reflected his strict interpretation of the separation of powers embodied in the newly adopted Constitution. Washington believed that the Constitution required the executive not to encroach on legislative powers just as much as it commanded the legislature not to encroach on executive powers. When he thought Congress had trespassed on executive powers, Washington was quick to protest. For instance, when the House of Representatives passed a resolution congratulating the French on adopting their new constitution, Washington complained to Jefferson that the legislature was "endeavoring to invade the executive." At the same time, Washington showed a principled regard for legislative prerogatives. When Attorney General Edmund Randolph suggested an administrative fix to a troublesome law, Washington demurred, insisting that the Constitution "must mark the line of [the president's] official conduct." Washington informed Randolph that he "could not justify . . . taking a single step in any matter, which appeared to . . . require [the legislature's] agency, without its being first obtained." Congress and the president, in Washington's view, properly occupied separate spheres of action under the Constitution.[9]

## Debating Washington's Neutrality Proclamation

As a practical matter, the decision about what fell within the executive sphere and what belonged in the legislative sphere was often not so simple. One of the great constitutional debates of the Washington administration erupted over the question of whether the president or the Congress had the power to declare neutrality vis-à-vis other countries. Article I of the Constitution unambiguously gave Congress the power to "declare war." At the same time, Article II just as clearly gave the president the power to receive ambassadors and the power—with the advice and consent of the Senate—to make treaties. Nowhere did the Constitution mention who had the power to declare neutrality.

This constitutional silence took on tremendous urgency when France—having guillotined its king, Louis XVI—declared war on Great Britain in February 1793. Taking sides in a war between the world's two superpowers was clearly not in the interests of a fledgling nation with no navy and a tiny regular army. Making matters more vexing was that the French—with whom the Americans had signed a treaty of "perpetual alliance" in 1778—wanted the United States to aid them. Many Americans, having just concluded a revolutionary war with the British, sympathized with the French cause. Indeed, a special envoy from France was actively urging American citizens to seize British trading ships off the Atlantic coast and to join the fight against the Spanish (with whom France was also at war) in the territories of Florida and Louisiana.[10]

These events alarmed Washington, who worried that private citizens heeding the French call might provoke the British to declare war on America. Washington asked each member of his cabinet two questions: First, should he call Congress into session? Second, should he issue a proclamation to prevent "interferences of the Citizens of the United States in the War between France and Great Britain?" The cabinet—which included Treasury Secretary Alexander Hamilton and Secretary of State Thomas Jefferson—agreed that Congress did not need to be called back into session. The cabinet also agreed that Washington should issue a proclamation that made it clear that the United States would not take sides in the war between France and Britain and that the U.S. government would criminally prosecute American citizens who violated this proclamation.[11]

Issued on April 22, 1793, Washington's Proclamation of Neutrality was generally well received. Nobody wanted another war, least of all with Britain. And yet for many Jeffersonian Republicans, who loathed Britain and sympathized with the French republic, strict neutrality was, as Jefferson said, "a disagreeable pill." They asked, how could the American republic be neutral in a contest that pitted republican liberty against monarchy, or how could the republic ignore the duties it owed France under the Treaty of Alliance it had signed in 1778? And what gave the president the right to declare peace without consulting Congress?

Republican newspapers' attacks upon the proclamation provided Hamilton the excuse he needed to enter the fray. In seven tightly argued essays penned under the pseudonym Pacificus, Hamilton vindicated both the president's policy of neutrality and the president's constitutional authority to declare neutrality. Hamilton argued that the Constitution made the president "the organ of intercourse between the United States and foreign nations." According to Hamilton, it was the president's job to declare "the existing condition of the nation with regard to foreign powers." Hamilton found this authority partly in specific grants of constitutional power— the power to receive ambassadors, the power to make treaties with the advice and consent of the Senate, the Commander in Chief Clause, and the power to execute the laws. But he also found authority in the Vesting Clause in Article II, Section 1, Clause 1, which declared that "the executive power shall be vested in a president of the United States." In Hamilton's reading, whereas the Constitution enumerated the legislative powers that were granted to the Congress, the Constitution did not enumerate "all the cases of executive authority." Thus, anything that was in its nature an executive power belonged to the president, except where the Constitution explicitly specified a role for Congress, as it did in granting the legislature the power to declare war and giving the Senate a role in the appointment of officers and the making of treaties.[12]

Hamilton's expansive reading of presidential power appalled Jefferson, who urged James Madison to join the argument: "For god's sake, my dear Sir, take up your pen, select the most striking heresies, and cut him to pieces in the face of the public."[13] Under the pseudonym Helvidius, Madison took up Jefferson's challenge with gusto. Madison rejected

Hamilton's argument that the powers to declare war and to make treaties were inherently executive powers—only those with their "eyes too much on monarchical government" could believe such a proposition. The "natural province" of the executive was to *execute* laws, Madison reasoned. Nothing about making a treaty or declaring war involved the execution of laws. To bolster his case, Madison invoked Hamilton himself, who in *Federalist* No. 75 had proclaimed that the treaty-making power, although neither strictly legislative nor executive, partook "more of the legislative than of the executive character."[14]

While Madison effectively exposed the inconsistency in Hamilton's position, he was less effective in explaining why Washington's proclamation unconstitutionally encroached on Congress's power to declare war. After all, nothing in Washington's proclamation prevented Congress from declaring war on Britain or France. In arguing that the Constitution lodged the powers of making war and peace almost entirely in the legislative branch, Madison did as much violence to the framers' intent as Hamilton did in claiming that the Vesting Clause gave the president a near-limitless reservoir of powers to decide questions of war and peace.[15]

In the end, neither Madison's nor Hamilton's reading of the Constitution had much effect on Washington's decision making. Although Washington may have sympathized with Hamilton's expansive reading of Article II, he steered a prudent course that avoided an institutional showdown with Congress. He sided with Jefferson and against Hamilton in deciding not to abrogate the 1778 treaty with France, and when Congress convened in December 1793, he offered to leave it to "the wisdom of Congress to correct, improve, or enforce" the policy he had announced in his Proclamation of Neutrality. Congress responded by passing the Neutrality Act of 1794, which enabled the administration to successfully prosecute violators of the proclamation, thereby accomplishing President Washington's goal.[16]

### Washington's Supreme Court

As the nation's first president, Washington was granted an opportunity not offered to any subsequent president: the chance to pack the Supreme Court with justices entirely of his own choosing. It was an opportunity that he seized.

The Constitution specified that there should be a Supreme Court and "such inferior Courts as the Congress may from time to time ordain and establish" (Article III, Section 1). However, the document did not prescribe the size of the highest court or the number of lower courts. In the Judiciary Act of 1789, Congress supplied the missing pieces. The Supreme Court was to have six members: five associate justices and a chief justice. In addition, there were to be thirteen district courts—roughly one per state—and three regional circuit courts, which could hear appeals from the district courts.

On the same day that Washington signed the Judiciary Act, he submitted his six Supreme Court nominees to the Senate. Two days later, the Senate confirmed all six by voice vote. Washington said he had picked the "fittest characters to expound the Laws and dispense Justice," and his six picks were certainly a distinguished bunch. But legal talent and judicial temperament were not the only criteria that Washington applied. He also sought geographic diversity—his six nominees hailed from six states, three Southern, three Northern. He also picked exclusively from among those who had "strongly supported" the new Constitution. Indeed, three of his six picks—James Wilson of Pennsylvania, John Rutledge of South Carolina, and John Blair of Virginia—had a hand in drafting the Constitution. The Senate's speedy and unanimous approval of Washington's six nominees was a tribute to the distinguished characters the president had selected, but it was also a sign of the Senate's deference to Washington and the absence of organized political parties.[17]

If this was the way the framers always hoped it would be, those hopes were shattered with Washington's choice of John Rutledge to succeed Chief Justice John Jay, who resigned in the summer of 1795 to become governor of New York. Rutledge himself had quit the Court in 1791 after being elected chief justice of South Carolina's state supreme court. The resignations of both Jay and Rutledge serve as reminders that U.S. Supreme Court positions in the early republic were not necessarily seen as more important or desirable than state posts. What made the job especially grueling was the responsibility under the Judiciary Act of 1789 for "riding circuit." That is, Supreme Court justices were responsible not only for hearing cases in the nation's capital but also for traveling thousands of miles on often-poor roads to hear cases in one of the three circuits (Eastern, Middle, and Southern) to which each justice was assigned.[18]

Washington received Jay's resignation after Congress had already adjourned for the year. Not wishing to leave the chief justice's seat vacant for another six months, Washington used a recess appointment to appoint Rutledge (who had already served on the Court) to serve as chief on an interim basis until Congress returned to the capital. However, Rutledge became enveloped by the fierce partisan disagreement over the Jay Treaty—a treaty that Jay had secretly negotiated with Britain while he was still chief justice.

The terms of the Jay Treaty, which addressed trade disputes and other unresolved issues relating to the American Revolution, were publicly unveiled on July 2, 1795, the day after Washington appointed Rutledge. The treaty divided the country along partisan lines: Federalists urged its ratification, whereas Republicans condemned the treaty for forging closer ties with monarchical England at the expense of America's revolutionary ally, France. At a public meeting in Charleston, South Carolina, Rutledge thrust himself into the center of the partisan debate by speaking out against the treaty.[19]

In *Federalist* No. 76, Hamilton had predicted that the Senate's role in judicial appointments would generally be limited to a "silent" role of discouraging presidents from nominating cronies or plainly "unfit characters." Now, however, Hamilton orchestrated a noisy campaign to keep Rutledge off the bench. Undeterred, Washington submitted Rutledge's name to the Senate for approval as soon as Congress reconvened in December. Five days later, with Hamilton lobbying furiously against the supposedly "insane" Rutledge, the Senate voted along party lines to reject Rutledge.[20]

Washington got the message. In place of Rutledge, he nominated a stalwart Federalist, Oliver Ellsworth, to serve as chief justice. As a U.S. senator, Ellsworth not only had enthusiastically backed the Jay Treaty, but also had been, in the words of John Adams, "the firmest pillar" of the Washington administration's policies. From the outset of the republic, then, partisanship was an inseparable part of the process by which presidents nominated and the Senate approved Supreme Court justices.[21]

Moreover, the early Court, which Washington had packed with Federalists, set precedents that strengthened the power of the federal government and ultimately paved the way for the Court's even more expansive assertion of federal power under Chief Justice John Marshall.[22]

*Making the First Executive Departments, Convening the First Cabinet*

If the Constitution said nothing about judicial review and next to nothing about how the courts should be constituted, it was only marginally
less unhelpful when it came to organizing the presidency. The framers did
clearly anticipate the creation of executive departments, headed by a "principal officer" (Article II, Section 2, Clause 1), but they left it to Congress to
enumerate those departments as well as the principal officers' duties.

During the summer of 1789, Congress created the departments of
foreign affairs, war, and treasury. Each department was to be directed
by a department head, whose role in advising the president nevertheless
remained unclear. Article II, Section 2, stipulated only that the president
could require department heads to provide a written opinion "on any subject relating to the duties of their respective offices." Washington soon
discovered that following a literal reading of this clause did not allow him
"always to compare the opinions of those in whom I confide with one
another."[23]

While Washington initially consulted with cabinet members individually rather than collectively, in the final year of his first term Washington began to experiment with a new advisory structure. Instead of relying
solely on written opinions and private conversations, the president convened meetings with the three department heads and the attorney general.
The gang of four—which Washington now dubbed his "cabinet"—met
frequently during the spring of 1793 as the president struggled to forge a
policy that would keep the United States out of the war between France
and Britain. During these meetings, Jefferson and Hamilton were, according to Jefferson, "daily pitted in the cabinet like two cocks." Although
Washington took no pleasure in watching his two chief advisers gouge
each other, he found the frank exchange of views invaluable and continued
to hold cabinet meetings regularly for the remainder of his time in the
presidency.[24]

*Seeking the Senate's "Advice and Consent"*

The Constitution provided that the chief executive had to obtain the
"advice and consent" of the Senate before acting on treaties and certain
appointments (Article II, Section 2, Clause 2). Nonetheless, much was left
for the first president to interpret. Washington assumed that he should

seek the Senate's advice about treaties in person, because their complexities required the give-and-take of discussion. To communicate in writing would be "tedious without being satisfactory," Washington reasoned. The president put this theory into practice in August 1789, when he visited the Senate chamber for advice and consent on a treaty with the Creek people.[25]

The experiment did not go well. The vice president, John Adams, was asked to read the document the president had prepared, including seven questions on which the president sought the Senate's advice and consent. The noise from the street combined with Adams's rushed delivery prevented the chamber's twenty-two senators from hearing much of what had been read, requiring Adams to reread it. Even then, when Adams asked, "Do you advise and consent?" nobody was quite sure what to say. The awkward silence was only broken by Senator William Maclay's request that previous treaties and other relevant documents also be read so that senators would be better informed. After that information was read aloud, discussion rapidly degenerated into an extended meditation on the process. When it was suggested that the president's document should be referred to a select committee, an exasperated Washington (according to Maclay) "started up in a violent fret," declaring that "this defeats every purpose of my coming here."[26]

It was a rare outburst of anger from a president who was generally the picture of composure. Washington quickly cooled down, however, and both president and Senate agreed to postpone the deliberations for forty-eight hours. Upon returning to the Senate chamber on Monday morning, Washington, his demeanor now "placid and serene," patiently endured a long and sometimes tedious debate over the various questions he had put to the senators. The Senate ultimately approved the instructions with only minor modifications, but a chastened Washington had learned his lesson. Never again would he—or any other president—seek the Senate's advice in person. In the future, senatorial advice on treaties would be transmitted to the president unofficially, through private conversations and consultations, or through communications between committee chairs and department secretaries.[27]

### *A Failed Experiment: The Supreme Court as Advisory Council*

For a brief time, Washington considered the Supreme Court an ex offi-cio advisory council since Congress clearly could not fulfill that role. The Court was blessed with men whose judgment Washington trusted greatly, none more so than Chief Justice John Jay. Washington had wanted Jay to be his secretary of state but had reluctantly deferred to Jay's desire to be the nation's first chief justice. Yet this did not stop Washington from seek-ing Jay's advice, or Jay from giving it. Neither Washington nor Jay saw this relationship as inappropriate, particularly in view of the several proposals made at the Constitutional Convention, including a proposal by the Com-mittee on Detail (chaired by John Rutledge) to include the chief justice as a member of the council of state.

However, in the first year of Washington's second term, the Court rebuffed his request for advice on legal issues connected to the Proclama-tion of Neutrality.[28] This reluctance to get involved may have stemmed from the justices' awareness that the president was asking them to ref-eree a political dispute between Secretary of State Thomas Jefferson and Treasury Secretary Alexander Hamilton over the U.S. treaty obligations to France. Or perhaps the justices were slyly playing partisan politics: Rec-ognizing the strength of Jefferson's legal position, they could best advance Hamilton and Washington's policy of neutrality by declining to answer the twenty-nine questions the president had put to them. Or perhaps the Court sincerely believed, as Jay told Washington, that "the lines of separation, drawn by the Constitution between the three departments of the government," prevented the Court from rendering advisory opinions to the president. Whatever the justices' motives, their refusal cut off the judiciary as another potential channel of advice and strengthened Wash-ington's (and future presidents') reliance on their own executive branch officials for advice.[29]

### Conclusion

Convinced that the new Constitution was firmly established, Washington chose to exit the public stage in 1796 rather than to seek a third term in office. Although no law required him to do so, Washington believed it was important to show, in the words of political scientist Thomas Cronin, that "the new political system did not depend on any individual."[30]

Washington returned to Mount Vernon, where he spent the final two years of his life with his family, tending to his estate and occasionally accepting an assignment in public service. Besides his voluntary return to private life, Washington has other lessons to teach us as well, lessons that are too often obscured by the heroic myths with which we envelop his memory. Remarkably, the real President Washington little resembles the ideal of presidential greatness that has become embedded in national folklore. One of the great canards of the heroic narrative is that the greatest presidents boldly did what was right, regardless of whether it was popular.[31] Yet no president was more solicitous of his public reputation than Washington. Almost every action Washington took, including running for president, was made with an eye on how it would be perceived by his countrymen and how it would affect his reputation as a paragon of virtue.

Nor does Washington's behavior fit the standard storyline about great presidents fearlessly testing the boundaries of presidential power. Instead, Washington exercised his powers with enormous caution and self-restraint. Washington built presidential authority not through daring defiance of Congress or bold, unilateral action, but through carefully building trust in the competence and judgment of the executive branch.

In fact, Washington was among the most cautious and circumspect of all American presidents. Before making decisions, he consulted broadly and deliberated with excruciating care. Jefferson rightly remarked that "the strongest feature" in Washington's character "was prudence, never acting until every circumstance, every consideration, was maturely weighed." On this one matter, even Jefferson's nemesis Alexander Hamilton was in full agreement. Washington was temperamentally suited to the presidency, Hamilton explained, because the nation's first president "consulted much, pondered much, resolved slowly, resolved surely."[32] What others called bold, Washington regarded as foolish and rash.

Washington's understanding of the Constitution—and the president's role within it—bears little resemblance to the view adopted by most contemporary presidents. Modern presidents are inclined to follow Woodrow Wilson in reading the Constitution as a license that gives a president enormous latitude and leaves the chief executive "at liberty, both in law and in conscience, to be as big a man as he can." Today, deference to other constitutional actors is typically interpreted as a sign of weakness, the restrained use of power a failure of nerve. Washington, in contrast, filled the Constitution's silences with prudent judgments and the careful, restrained exercise of power. For him, building a strong presidency and a respected government required neither bold, unilateral executive action nor strident bullying of Congress. Rather, it depended upon a sober reckoning of the political, legal, and constitutional constraints on presidential power.

NOTES

1. Ron Chernow, *Washington: A Life* (New York: Penguin Press, 2010), 5–7, 9–10.

2. Ibid., 18–28, 31–32; "The Ten Richest U.S. Presidents," *24/7 Wall St. Wire*, February 17, 2012, http://247wallst.com/2012/02/17/the-ten-richest-u-s-presidents/.

3. Gordon S. Wood, *Revolutionary Characters: What Made the Founders Different* (London: Penguin Books, 2006), 33.

4. Chernow, *Washington*, 521, 524, 529, 531, 543, 537, 549.

5. Washington to Edmund Pendleton, September 23, 1793, in *The Writings of George Washington*, ed. Worthington Chauncey Ford (New York: G.P. Putnam's Sons, 1891), 12:327; Robert J. Spitzer, *The Presidential Veto: Touchstone of the American Presidency* (Albany: State University of New York Press, 1988), 28.

6. James Thomas Flexner, *George Washington and the New Nation, 1783–1793* (Boston: Little, Brown, 1970), 301; Chernow, *Washington*, 668.

7. George Washington, First Annual Message, January 8, 1790, in *The Diaries of George Washington*, ed. Donald Jackson and Dorothy Twohig (Charlottesville: University Press of Virginia, 1979), 5:507–508.

8. George Washington, Communication of Sentiments to Benjamin Hawkins, in *The Writings of George Washington*, ed. Worthington Chauncey Ford (New York: G.P. Putnam's Sons, 1891), 12:72–73; Leonard D. White, *The Federalists: A Study in Administrative History* (New York: Macmillan, 1948), 55.

9. White, *The Federalists*, 55, 53. See also Flexner, *George Washington and the New Nation*, 221.

10. Forrest McDonald, *The American Presidency: An Intellectual History* (Lawrence: University Press of Kansas, 1994), 236. See also Stanley Elkins and Eric McKitrick, *The Age of Federalism: The Early American Republic* (New York: Oxford University Press, 1993), 333–335.

11. Martin S. Flaherty, "The Story of the Neutrality Controversy: Struggling Over Presidential Power Outside the Courts," in *Presidential Power Stories*, ed. Christopher H. Schroeder and Curtis A. Bradley (New York: Foundation Press, 2009), 25.

12. Pacificus (Alexander Hamilton), *Pacificus No. 1*, available at the Online Library of Liberty, http://oll.libertyfund.org/. See also Richard J. Ellis, ed., *Founding the American Presidency* (Lanham, MD: Rowman and Littlefield, 1999), 174–175.

13. Jefferson to Madison, July 7, 1793, in *The Papers of Thomas Jefferson*, volume 26, *May 1793 to August 1793*, ed. John Catanzariti et al. (Princeton, NJ: Princeton University Press, 1995), 444.

14. Madison also objected to Hamilton's claim that specific grants of executive power in Article II, particularly the power to receive ambassadors, made the president "the organ

of intercourse" with other nations. Madison argued that this language did not give presidents the power to conduct foreign policy on their own. For support, Madison again appealed to Hamilton's own words, this time in *Federalist* No. 69. Here, Hamilton had argued that the power to receive ambassadors and other public ministers was merely a recognition that it would be inconvenient to convene the legislature every time a foreign minister arrived in the country. Helvidius (James Madison), *Helvidius No. 1 and No. 3*, available at the Online Library of Liberty, http://oll.libertyfund.org/. See also Ellis, *Founding the American Presidency*, 176–179.

15. *Federalist* No. 75.

16. Louis Fisher, *Presidential War Power*, 2nd ed. (Lawrence: University Press of Kansas, 2004), 28; Flaherty, "Story of the Neutrality Controversy," 43, 48.

17. John Anthony Maltese, *The Selling of Supreme Court Nominees* (Baltimore: Johns Hopkins University Press, 1995), 24–25.

18. Under the 1789 act, each circuit court consisted of three judges—two Supreme Court justices and the local district court judge. In 1793, Congress eased somewhat the Court's burden by reducing each circuit court to two judges—one Supreme Court justice and a district court judge. Circuit riding by Supreme Court justices continued until 1891. For a history of circuit riding—and an unorthodox argument that the Supreme Court should resume the practice—see David R. Stras, "Why Supreme Justices Should Ride Circuit Again," *Minnesota Law Review* 91 (June 2007): 1710–1751.

19. Washington himself had doubts about the terms of the treaty, but believed it was necessary to avoid a war with Great Britain and to achieve a compromise that allowed the two nations to resume peaceful trade.

20. Maltese, *Selling of Supreme Court Nominees*, 19, 26–31.

21. Adams to James Lloyd, January 1815, in *The Works of John Adams*, ed. Charles Francis Adams (Boston: Little, Brown, 1856), 10:112.

22. As early as 1796, the Court took tentative steps into the realm of judicial review, paving the way for the landmark case of *Marbury v. Madison*. The first case in which it confronted a direct challenge to an act of Congress was the little-known case of *Hylton v. United States*. Although the Court unanimously concluded that the law in question (placing a "duty" on privately owned carriages used for transportation) did not violate the Constitution, the case nonetheless was important because it was the first decision to explicitly recognize that the Court could act as a check on the actions of another branch of government. Hylton v. United States, 2 U.S. (3 Dall.) 171, 173 (1796). See also Julius Goebel Jr., *History of the Supreme Court of the United States*, vol. 1, *Antecedents and Beginnings to 1801* (New York: Macmillan, 1971), 778.

23. Flexner, *George Washington and the New Nation*, 401. The Department of Foreign Affairs was established in July 1789 and renamed the Department of State a few months later.

24. Thomas Jefferson to Doctor Walter Jones, March 5, 1810, *The Works of Thomas Jefferson* (G.P. Putnam's Sons, 1904–1905; 12 vols.), available at the Online Library of Liberty, http://oll.libertyfund.org/; Flexner, *George Washington and the New Nation*, 400; Richard F. Fenno Jr., *The President's Cabinet* (Cambridge, MA: Harvard University Press, 1959), 17–18.

25. Elkins and McKitrick, *Age of Federalism*, 56; Flexner, *George Washington and the New Nation*, 216; "Conference with a Committee of the United States Senate," August 8, 1789, in *The Papers of George Washington, Presidential Series*, ed. Dorothy Twohig (Charlottesville: University Press of Virginia, 1979), 3:401.

26. Elkins and McKitrick, *Age of Federalism*, 56–57; Flexner, *George Washington and the New Nation*, 216.

27. Elkins and McKitrick, *Age of Federalism*, 57–58; William Maclay, *Journal of William Maclay*, entry of August 24, 1789, http://memory.loc.gov/ammem/amlaw/lwmj.html.

28. For a discussion of the Court's role in the neutrality debate, as well as the related correspondence between Washington's administration and the Supreme Court, see Maeva Marcus, *The Documentary History of the Supreme Court of the United States, 1789–1800*, vol. 6, *Cases: 1790–1795* (New York: Columbia University Press, 1998), 296–311, 743–758.

29. McDonald, *The American Presidency*, 227. Glenn A. Phelps, "George Washington: Precedent Setter," in *Inventing the American Presidency*, ed. Thomas E. Cronin (Lawrence: University Press of Kansas, 1989), 272; James Willard Hurst, *The Growth of American Law: The Law Makers* (Boston: Little, Brown, 1950), 181; Fenno, *The President's Cabinet*, 15–16.

30. Thomas E. Cronin, "Pro: Resolved, the Twenty-Second Amendment Should Be Repealed," in *Debating the Presidency: Conflicting Perspectives on the American Executive*, 2nd ed., ed. Richard J. Ellis and Michael Nelson (Washington, DC: CQ Press, 2010), 52; Chernow, *Washington*, 752. Although Washington was the first president to step down after two terms, he did not necessarily intend to establish a two-term tradition for other presidents to follow. As Michael Korzi and others have shown, Thomas Jefferson has the best claim to being the intellectual "founder" of the two-term tradition. Michael J. Korzi, *Presidential Terms Limits in American History: Power, Principles, and Politics* (College Station: Texas A&M University Press, 2011), 43–50. But even then, the two-term tradition was always more tenuous than is sometimes believed. It was challenged in the nineteenth and early twentieth century not only by a robust one-term tradition but also by a few presidents who pressed for a third term, notably Ulysses S. Grant in 1880 and Theodore Roosevelt in 1912. The two-term tradition was ultimately broken in 1940, with the election of Franklin D. Roosevelt for a third term. A couple of years after FDR's reelection for a fourth term, Congress passed and the states ratified the Twenty-Second Amendment, which limited all presidents to two terms.

31. Thomas E. Cronin and Michael A. Genovese, *The Paradoxes of the American Presidency*, 2nd ed. (New York: Oxford University Press, 2004), 84.

32. Ron Chernow, *Alexander Hamilton* (New York: Penguin, 2004), 290, 510.

# 2

# John Adams

LOUIS FISHER

*In testing the scope of the president's power in the field of foreign affairs under the Constitution, John Adams quickly learned that an aggressive approach to exercising executive power could backfire. He found himself caught in a political tug-of-war between the Federalists and the Jeffersonian Republicans over foreign affairs. Adams became involved in the Quasi-War against France, signed the repressive Alien and Sedition Acts, and was ousted from office after one term. Although some believed that the president was the exclusive voice of government in the sphere of foreign relations under the Constitution, John Adams's presidency would prove such a belief to be a misconception.*

## Introduction

The second president of the United States (1797–1801), John Adams, was born on October 19, 1735, in the village of Braintree, near Boston. Although his family means were modest, his parents were determined to send him to private schools and provide him with assistance from tutors. Adams attended Harvard to become a clergyman and graduated at age nineteen, impressing professors with his intellectual dedication. Instead of becoming a clergyman, however, Adams preferred to teach and became active in public life. Studying in the law office of James Putnam, he was admitted to the Boston Bar on November 7, 1758.[1]

In 1770, Adams defended British soldiers accused of killing and wounding Americans in the Boston Massacre, winning the acquittal of all except two found guilty of manslaughter. Adams focused on the extent to which the British soldiers were intimidated and provoked by the crowd.

Elected as a delegate to the Continental Congress in 1774 and 1775, Adams published a pamphlet titled *Thoughts on Government* in 1776, which identified key principles for a republican government and was widely read.[2] In 1779, he was chosen to represent Braintree in the Massachusetts constitutional convention, where he drafted much of the final document that became the first Massachusetts Constitution. After serving as minister to negotiate peace with Great Britain, Adams then became the first American minister to the Court of St. James's in London.

Over the next decade, Adams continued to live abroad and was often separated from his family for long stretches of time. When the newly constituted government of the fledgling United States was being put into operation, however, Adams returned home with a keen interest in serving in that government. Fully aware that George Washington would be the overwhelming favorite to become president, Adams sought the vice presidency. In 1789, as Washington won the unanimous vote of the Electoral College, Adams received the second-largest number of votes and was selected as the nation's first vice president.

Adams's eight years as vice president under President Washington were often uncomfortable, because Adams was not considered a member of the president's cabinet and was excluded from its meetings. The Constitution said very little about this ill-defined official, other than to state that he was to preside over the Senate and only cast a vote in the event of a tie (Article I, Section 3, Clause 4). Indeed, the vice president was often regarded during these early years of the republic as primarily a legislative officer, given his role in the Senate, and not even legally a part of the executive branch.[3] Yet Adams maintained a reasonable amount of visibility. In 1791, for instance, he published *Discourses on Davila*, warning against extremist, unchecked political developments in France. In other ways, Adams found ways to engage himself in governmental matters and to express his general support of the Federalist position in favor of a strong national government.

## Presidency

At the end of President Washington's two terms, John Adams was viewed as the natural successor to Washington. Nonetheless, the results of the election of 1796 were quite unusual. As expected, with the support of the Federalists, Adams won the most electoral votes: seventy-one. Yet the individual selected to be his vice president, Thomas Pinckney, failed to garner the second-largest number of electoral votes. Instead, Thomas Jefferson—a rival of Pinckney's—secured the second-place position. At this early stage of American history, political parties had not yet emerged with any clarity. Nonetheless, Adams was unmistakably associated with the Federalists (who favored a strong and energetic president), and Jefferson with the Democratic-Republicans (who sought to constrain the power of the executive branch). Although Jefferson held a different set of political views, he was nevertheless selected as Adams's vice president under then-prevailing rules.[4] From the start, therefore, Vice President Jefferson was viewed as a national force capable of challenging President Adams for the presidency four years later.

Adams occupied the President's House in Philadelphia, a stately brick mansion located at Sixth and Market Streets, after George Washington and his family moved out and returned to Mount Vernon. Here, Adams conducted official business in the second-floor private office and entertained guests with First Lady Abigail Adams, hosting elegant receptions and dinners. Throughout his presidency, Adams considered Abigail his confidante and sought her opinions on matters of state. He also gathered his cabinet members in the executive mansion; they vigorously debated issues that swiftly confronted his administration.

## *The XYZ Affair*

The principal tension inside the Adams administration was between the Federalist political commitment to England and the Republican-Jeffersonian support for France. Adams's inaugural address on March 4, 1797, gave Federalists great concern that the president would not support their cause in this important tug-of-war. He spoke of "a personal esteem for the French nation," which had helped America gain its independence, and "a sincere desire to preserve the friendship which has been so much for the honor and interest of both nations."[5] Yet Adams's interest in peacefully settling differences with France hit a snag quickly. Within months of his taking office, French naval vessels and privateers began to attack American ships. On May 16, 1797, President Adams called Congress into joint session to announce that France had broken off commercial relations; he simultaneously ordered Charles Cotesworth Pinckney, American minister to France, to leave Paris. Adams urged Congress to authorize harbor fortifications and to purchase a dozen vessels to be armed and equipped for naval duty.[6]

In those early months, Adams faced a rebellion within his own ranks. Attorney General Charles Lee remained loyal. Yet other members of his cabinet—Secretary of State Timothy Pickering, Treasury Secretary Oliver Wolcott Jr., and War Secretary James McHenry—were determined to protect the commitment to England and opposed any friendly or diplomatic overtures to France. Alexander Hamilton, although he was no longer in government after serving as treasury secretary in the Washington administration, still maintained a strong influence on these cabinet officials as a leader of the Federalist movement.

Adams appointed three individuals to travel to France to seek a peaceful resolution of the conflict: John Marshall, Pinckney, and Elbridge Gerry. In March 1798, Adams announced that the peace mission had failed and his envoys had been treated with disrespect; they had even been subjected to attempted bribes or extortion from three individuals identified as X, Y, and Z. On June 21, 1798, in light of the so-called XYZ Affair, Adams said that "the negotiation may be considered at an end." He declared that he would never send another minister to France "without assurances that he will be received, respected, and honored as the representative of a great, free, powerful, and independent nation."[7] Congressional and public pressure was now building for military action against France.

## *The Quasi-War*

Adams concluded that military action against France was necessary, but he never claimed authority to act unilaterally. Instead, he asked Congress to provide the authority. Deciding against a formal declaration of war, lawmakers enacted several statutes to prepare the country for aggressive military action against France. These statutes clearly authorized war, laying the groundwork for further action. During debate on one of these bills in 1798, Representative Edward Livingston (New York) made clear that he considered the country "now in a state of war; and let no man flatter himself that the vote which has been given is not a declaration of war."[8] Congress took the additional step of establishing the Department of the Navy and the Marine Corps, while also increasing the size of the regular army. Many of the Federalists saw these new agencies as an opportunity to create a standing army, a policy that Adams had consistently opposed.

The Federalist majority in Congress next passed the Alien and Sedition Acts of 1798, a series of four statutes that increased the naturalization period from five to fourteen years, authorized the president to deport aliens the executive considered a risk to national security, and provided criminal penalties against those who criticized the three branches of the national government. The Sedition Act applied to both aliens and citizens. Fines and sentences awaited anyone who wrote or uttered anything about Congress or the president deemed "false, scandalous and malicious" with intent to "defame" those political institutions or bring them into "contempt or disrepute," "to excite" any hatred against them, or "stir up" sedition to oppose or resist federal laws or any presidential act to implement those laws.[9] The Federalist government now used this statutory authority for partisan purposes, invoking these laws to act against Republican critics.[10]

While not playing a prominent role in promoting these statutes, Adams did help shape the climate of opinion that justified and supported this controversial legislation.[11] The Sedition Act was particularly criticized as violating the First Amendment, which had been added to the Constitution in 1791 and prohibited Congress from enacting any law abridging the freedoms of speech or press.[12] Both the president and his party paid a price for their action. The severity of these laws, particularly the use of the Sedition Act to fine and imprison those who spoke out against the administration, seriously damaged the Federalist Party and contributed to its eventual decline as a political force. Indeed, the party gained a reputation for being hostile to popular government, public debate, free press, dissent, civil liberties, and immigrants. Although the Sedition Act ultimately expired in 1801, it embodied the overreach of the Federalist Party during this time of conflict abroad and was partly responsible for President Adams's political undoing.

Lacking experience in military affairs, Adams turned to the former president to take command of U.S. forces as the country geared up for action against France. On July 2, 1798, President Adams nominated Washington "to be Lieutenant-General and Commander in Chief of all the armies raised or to be raised in the United States."[13] Washington replied that he wished that the choice "had fallen upon a man less declined in years and better qualified to encounter the usual vicissitudes to war." He agreed to accept the commission "with the reserve only that I shall not be called into the field until the Army is in a situation to require my presence or it becomes indispensable by the urgency of circumstances."[14] Moreover, Washington insisted that Adams appoint Hamilton as the second-in-command, a step that delighted the Federalists. Adams deeply regretted this turn of events, given Hamilton's prominence as leader of the Federalist cause. However, the president felt he had no choice but to acquiesce to Washington's request.[15]

The country was now moving toward an undeclared war against France. The so-called Quasi-War was a not a full-fledged war. Instead, military actions were limited to naval operations against French ships. Hamilton and other Federalists wanted to use the French military threat to justify a large standing army, a commitment that Adams regarded as a costly expense that would require increased taxes and would pose a threat to popular government. Fortunately for Adams, a victory by Admiral Horatio Nelson over the French at the Battle of the Nile, on August 1, 1798, substantially undercut the argument for this standing army.[16]

When Elbridge Gerry returned from Paris in October 1798, he advised Adams that the so-called XYZ Affair was overblown. There was no evidence, he said, that the French foreign minister knew of or condoned the actions of anonymous individuals who attempted to extract bribes from American negotiators. More importantly, France wanted a peaceful settlement. Although Adams was ready to explore that possibility, it was clear that some Federalists regarded Gerry "as a fool, a traitor, or both."[17] Nonetheless, Adams met privately with Gerry and listened to his report with respect. The willingness of Adams to again seek peaceful negotiations with France convinced High Federalists (the most militant, pro-war faction) that he was too weak a leader to merit the support of their party.[18] By the summer of 1799, High Federalists concluded that Adams had to be replaced in the coming presidential election. They first appealed to Washington to run for a third term, but he refused.[19] Still determined to dump Adams, the Federalists searched for other alternatives. They also sought a declaration of war against France because existing statutes were not sufficiently broad. When Adams sent another peace commission to Paris, even his own secretary of state, Timothy Pickering, expressed outrage that American envoys would be dispatched to the "execrable government of France."[20] Indeed, Adams ended up dismissing Pickering because of their disagreements—an early instance of a president's dismissing a cabinet officer.[21]

## Threat of Censure or Impeachment

By early 1800, the presidential campaign had begun in earnest, with Republicans eager to push Adams out of the White House and replace him with Thomas Jefferson. Amid this heightened partisan atmosphere, in February the Republicans began an effort to either censure or impeach Adams for handing over to the British an individual named "Jonathan Robbins." Although Robbins claimed to be American, in fact he was an Englishman whose real name was Thomas Nash. This unlikely political martyr had been charged with committing mutiny and murder on a British ship, HMS *Hermione*, before being arrested in South Carolina. Because the case was already pending in an American court, some lawmakers accused President Adams of encroaching on the judiciary and violating the doctrine of separation of powers by injecting himself into the matter. A House resolution on February 20, 1800, described Adams's decision to turn the prisoner over to the British as "a dangerous interference of the Executive with Judicial decisions."[22]

U.S. District Judge Thomas Bee, when asked to release the prisoner so that Nash could be handed over to the British, agreed with President Adams. Nash was extradited to Jamaica and was subsequently tried and hanged. Political opponents of Adams now loudly criticized the decision, claiming that Nash was really an American sailor who had been persecuted by the British. They charged that Adams had improperly interfered with the jurisdiction of the American courts and thwarted justice. Representative Edward Livingston of New York introduced a bill seeking to censure the president.[23] After listening to a lengthy debate on the House floor, Representative John Marshall of Virginia took the floor to say there were no grounds to rebuke President Adams, either by censure or by impeachment. Marshall—who would soon find himself on the Supreme Court—defended Adams's authority to carry out an extradition treaty with England. The treaty included murder as a criminal offense that authorized one nation to transfer to another nation a person charged with that crime. Marshall declared that by implementing Article 27 of the Jay Treaty— entered into by the Washington administration and Great Britain in 1794 to resolve issues after the Revolutionary War and to reestablish relations between the two countries—Adams had executed one of the supreme laws of the land, which he was constitutionally bound to observe and carry into effect.[24]

Marshall's speech so meticulously defended the actions of Adams that the drive for censure or impeachment faded away. A year later, on January 31, 1801—just before Adams completed his term in office—John Marshall took his seat as chief justice of the Supreme Court. In that capacity, he consistently argued that the making of foreign policy was a joint exercise by the executive and legislative branches, through treaties and statutes, and not a unilateral or exclusive power of the president or Congress.[25]

Ironically, Marshall's defense of President Adams on the floor of Congress has occasionally been misinterpreted to suggest that the president is the "sole organ" of the nation when it comes to foreign affairs. Marshall's speech said no such thing; he never proclaimed that Adams was the "sole organ" in making foreign policy. Rather, Marshall said, the president was the sole organ in *implementing* foreign policy, in this case carrying out a treaty ratified by the Senate. It was the duty of Adams to comply with the constitutional command that he "take Care that the Laws be faithfully executed" (Article II, Section 3). President Adams learned the hard way that his powers in foreign affairs were not nearly as sweeping as some presidents and judges would later suggest.[26]

## Reelection Effort in 1800

On June 3, 1800, John Adams moved to Washington and became the first president to reside in the new capital city. While his wife, Abigail, remained at their home in Quincy, Massachusetts, preparing for the move, President Adams was forced to live temporarily at a tavern until the new President's

Mansion (later called the White House) was ready to be occupied on November 1, 1800. At this time, Adams and the First Lady moved into the still-unfinished white structure designed by architect James Hoban. They would not occupy the building for long, however.

In April 1800, Alexander Hamilton had outwardly supported the ticket of President Adams and Charles Cotesworth Pinckney (from South Carolina) as the best strategy to protect the country from the "fangs of *Jefferson*."[27] The Democratic-Republican ticket consisted of Thomas Jefferson and Aaron Burr. Nonetheless, Hamilton made quiet yet concerted efforts to shift electoral votes so that Pinckney would be president and Adams his vice president.[28] Adams, aware of these machinations, referred to "the unreasonable conduct of the jacobins and insolent Federalists."[29]

By May 1800, President Adams was prepared to turn against some of the disloyal members of his own administration. He confronted War Secretary McHenry for taking directions from Hamilton. When McHenry denied the charge, Adams told him: "I know it, sir, to be so. You are subservient to him."[30] McHenry submitted his resignation the next day. The next target for forced resignation was Secretary of State Pickering. After Pickering refused to step down voluntarily, President Adams said: "You are hereby discharged from any further service as Secretary of State."[31] John Marshall, who had so ardently supported Adams in Congress, became secretary of state.

In August, Hamilton now decided to publicly charge that Adams was unfit to be president. He published a pamphlet excoriating Adams and titled "A Letter from Alexander Hamilton, Concerning the Public Conduct and Character of John Adams, Esq., President of the United States." Jefferson, conducting his own campaign from Monticello, described the internal Federalist quarrels as "wonderful."[32]

Adams labored against many disadvantages in the presidential campaign of 1800. Taxes had risen to pay for the military, and the cost of operating the federal government had nearly doubled during his four years in office. Moreover, the Sedition Act, openly used to punish Republicans, had energized the followers of Jefferson. Because of these myriad problems, the Federalist Party was severely weakened. Accordingly, Jefferson and his running mate, Aaron Burr, received the highest number of votes—tied at seventy-three. With the two Republican candidates each having the same number of electoral votes, the Federalist-dominated House of Representatives was left to select a new president. Some Federalists mulled over selecting Burr to spite Jefferson. However, in an ironic turn of events, Jefferson's archrival, Alexander Hamilton, persuaded the Federalists that Burr posed a greater threat to the Republic than did Jefferson. Jefferson defeated Burr on the thirty-sixth ballot in the House and was declared the third president of the United States.

## Conclusion

On Inauguration Day, March 4, 1801, Adams decided to leave the nation's capital at an early hour to travel to Baltimore and, from there, to Quincy to rejoin Abigail.[33] He chose not to appear at Jefferson's inauguration to witness the transfer of national power to the opposing party. Yet this quiet transfer of power to his successor (to a person of a different party) was noteworthy because it was not marked by resistance or violence, but was instead a peaceful and respectful transition of leadership.

During his single term in office, President Adams had struggled to establish the power of the presidency, not always successfully. After stepping down as chief executive, he saw some of his actions taken during the Quasi-War come before the Supreme Court. He was not always vindicated in these decisions. In one noteworthy case, *Little v. Barreme*, decided in 1804, the Court ruled on a conflict between what Congress had provided by statute—in authorizing the capture of vessels during the Quasi-War with France—and a proclamation issued by Adams that went beyond the statute. In a unanimous decision, the Court held that in this sphere, national law was established by Congress, not by a presidential proclamation contrary to the statute. In an added twist, the person who wrote that opinion had been placed on the Court by Adams himself: Chief Justice John Marshall.[34]

Beset by divisions in his party, Adams was ushered out of office after a single term. Yet his exodus as chief executive was itself historic for the nation. Sometimes referred to as the Revolution of 1800, it established a vitally important precedent for the young democracy.[35] There was no bloodshed. The outgoing president readily relinquished power. His political rival, Jefferson, made a famous conciliatory statement during his address, declaring, "We are all republicans, we are all federalists," and helping to unite the country after the bitter partisan battle that had defined the election.[36] Rather than take steps to undermine his successor, Adams acknowledged that the constitutional electoral process had worked, and he quietly returned to private life. This custom of respect for the incoming president continues to this day.

Adams enjoyed a long and fulfilling retirement. He and his wife Abigail had suffered great personal hardship because of Adams's service to the nation. They had endured years of painful separation, although both viewed this sacrifice as a patriotic necessity. After leaving Washington, Adams lived out his remaining years happily with his beloved wife. During this time, he also repaired and renewed his friendship with Jefferson. The two exchanged many letters of warmth, intellectual inquiry, and mutual appreciation. In March 1825, Adams's son, John Quincy Adams, became the sixth president of the United States, the first son of a former president to attain that office. Sixteen months later, in 1826, the senior Adams died at his home in Quincy, having reached the age of ninety. For someone who had dedicated his life to America's break with England and the pursuit of self-government, his death came on a fitting day: July 4, exactly fifty years after the signing of the Declaration of Independence. It was the same day his friend, Thomas Jefferson, died hundreds of miles away at Monticello.

Thus, despite his mixed successes and failures as president, John Adams helped to shape the office and the nation that he had devoted his entire career to creating.

## NOTES

1. For a historical narrative of John Adams's life, see David McCullough, *John Adams* (New York: Simon & Schuster, 2001).

2. Other notable publications include John Adams, *A Dissertation on the Canon and Feudal Law* (1765); and John Adams, *A Defence of the Constitutions of Government of the United States*, 3 vols. (1786–1787).

3. The main substantive reference to the vice president in the Constitution is not contained in Article II, which relates to the president, but in Article I, covering Congress: "The Vice President shall be President of the Senate, but shall have no Vote, unless they be equally divided." In Article II, both the president and the vice president are mentioned in the system of electors. Article II also provides that in case the president is removed from office because of death, resignation, or inability to discharge official duties, "the Same shall devolve on the Vice President."

4. This result would no longer be possible after the adoption of the Twelfth Amendment in 1804, which required each member of the Electoral College to vote separately for president and vice president, rather than providing that the two highest vote-getters became president and vice president, respectively.

5. Arthur M. Schlesinger Jr. and Fred L. Israel, eds., *My Fellow Citizens: The Inaugural Addresses of the Presidents of the United States, 1789–2009* (New York: Facts on File, 2010), 12.

6. James D. Richardson, ed., *Messages and Papers of the Presidents* (Washington, DC: Bureau of National Literature, 1916), 1:223–229.

7. Ibid., 256.

8. 8 Annals of Congress 1507 (1798).

9. 1 Stat. 596–597, sec. 2 (1798).

10. Louis Fisher, *The Constitution and 9/11: Recurring Threats to America's Freedoms* (Lawrence: University Press of Kansas, 2008), 72–81.

11. James Morton Smith, *Freedom's Fetters: The Alien and Sedition Laws and American Civil Liberties* (Ithaca, NY: Cornell University Press, 1956), 20.

12. Sidney M. Milkis and Michael Nelson, *The American Presidency: Origins and Development, 1776–2011*, 6th ed. (Washington, DC: CQ Press, 2012), 94–95.

13. Richardson, *Messages and Papers of the Presidents*, 1:257.

14. Ibid., 257–258.

15. Ralph Adams Brown, *The Presidency of John Adams* (Lawrence: University Press of Kansas, 1989), 63–70.

16. Alexander DeConde, *The Quasi-War: The Politics and Diplomacy of the Undeclared War with France, 1797–1801* (New York: Charles Scribner's Sons, 1966), 161.

17. Brown, *Presidency of John Adams*, 81.

18. Adams's response to "Fries's Rebellion" also angered the High Federalists. By the spring of 1799, resentment over the direct property taxes that the federal government had levied to fund the anticipated war against France had spread across the county. Opposition to the taxes was especially pronounced in the rural counties of Pennsylvania. When federal authorities imprisoned several individuals in Bethlehem, Pennsylvania, for refusing to pay the tax, John Fries, a county auctioneer, gathered a group of armed farmers and forced the release of the prisoners. Fries and two of his cohorts were arrested, tried for treason in federal court, and sentenced to death. They petitioned President Adams for a pardon. After familiarizing himself with the legal principles regarding treason and the circumstances presented, Adams determined that Fries was a hot-headed man who had endangered the public order, but not a traitor. Although several members of Adams's cabinet argued against the pardons, Adams decided otherwise. He issued the pardons and granted a general amnesty to all those involved in the incident. Ibid., 127–129.

19. DeConde, *The Quasi-War*, 259–260.

20. Pickering offered these recriminations to William Vans Murray on October 25, 1799. Brown, *The Presidency of John Adams*, 112–123.

21. John Ferling, *John Adams: A Life* (New York: Oxford, 2010), 613. In fact, Adams also forced the resignation of his secretary of war, James McHenry. Ibid. See also Edward L. Larson, *A Magnificent Catastrophe: The Tumultuous Election of 1800; America's First Presidential Campaign* (New York: Free Press, 2007), 125–127. President George Washington had established a precedent of sorts in this regard: He had confronted his secretary of state, Edmund Randolph, in front of the entire cabinet and demanded an explanation for a letter Randolph had written, indicating that he had divulged sensitive information to the French, causing Randolph to resign on the spot. Mary K. Bonsteel Tachau, "George Washington and the Reputation of Edmund Randolph," *Journal of American History* 73 (1986): 15. See also Akhil Reed Amar, *America's Unwritten*

*Constitution: The Precedents and Principles We Live By* (New York: Basic Books, 2012), 320. In its famous 1789 decision, Congress had acknowledged the president's implied power under the new Constitution to remove cabinet members at will. Saikrishna Prakash, "New Light on the Decision of 1789," *Cornell Law Review* 91 (2006):1021. See generally Louis Fisher, *Constitutional Conflicts Between Congress and the President*, 6th ed. (Lawrence: University Press of Kansas, 2014), 57–62.

22. 10 Annals of Congress 533 (1800).

23. Ibid., 515.

24. Ibid., 613–614. Representative Marshall's speech was later popularized in 1936, when Justice Sutherland in the *Curtiss-Wright* case cited this particular sentence: "The President is the sole organ of the nation in its external relations, and its sole representative with foreign nations." United States v. Curtiss-Wright Corp., 299 U.S. 307, 319 (1936). Taking Marshall's speech wholly out of context, Sutherland used it as a source of presidential power in foreign affairs—a power not grounded in authority delegated by Congress, either by statute or by treaty. Sutherland cited the speech to promote presidential powers that are inherent, independent, plenary, and exclusive. Marshall never argued for that type of executive power. Adams was not attempting to make foreign policy single-handedly. Rather, he was carrying out a treaty made jointly by the president and the Senate. In 2015, the U.S. Supreme Court narrowed the expansive language in *Curtiss-Wright* by clarifying that *Curtiss-Wright* did not hold that the president is free from Congress's lawmaking power in the field of international relations. Zivotofsky v. Kerry, 135 S.Ct. 2076, 2090 (2015). Rather, as the Court pointed out, even though the president "does have a unique role in communicating with foreign governments, as then Congressman John Marshall acknowledged," it is "still the Legislative Branch, not the Executive Branch, that makes the law [whether the realm is foreign or domestic."]. Ibid.

25. Louis Fisher, "The 'Sole Organ' Doctrine," *Law Library of Congress*, August 2006, available at http://loufisher.org/docs/pip/441.pdf.

26. For additional analysis of the erroneous sole-organ dicta in *Curtiss-Wright*, see Louis Fisher, amicus brief submitted to Supreme Court in the *Zivotofsky* case, July 17, 2014, www.loufisher.org/docs/pip/Zivotofsky.pdf.

27. Brown, *Presidency of John Adams*, 177.

28. Ibid., 181–185.

29. Ibid., 179–180 .

30. DeConde, *The Quasi-War*, 271.

31. Ibid., 272.

32. Ibid., 277–278.

33. Adams's son, Charles, had just recently died of alcoholism, and this event left the outgoing president saddened and depressed.

34. Little v. Barreme, 6 U.S. (Cranch) 170, 179 (1804).

35. See, for example, James Horn, Jan Ellis Lewis, and Peter S. Onuf, eds., *The Revolution of 1800: Democracy, Race, and the New Republic* (Charlottesville: University of Virginia Press, 2002).

36. Thomas Jefferson's First Inaugural Address is available at http://avalon.law.yale.edu/19th_century/jefinau1.asp.

# 3

# Thomas Jefferson

CLIFF SLOAN, LOUIS FISHER, AND MOSHE SPINOWITZ

*Thomas Jefferson displayed a rich, complex, and sometimes contradictory view of the Constitution. Among early presidents, Jefferson was the leading advocate of limited federal power, instead favoring strong authority for the states. Nevertheless, as president, he oversaw the vast expansion of the nation through the Louisiana Purchase, despite the lack of explicit statutory or constitutional authority for this initiative. A fierce defender of individual liberties under the Constitution, Jefferson nevertheless attacked the Supreme Court's claim to supremacy on constitutional interpretation, expressing contempt for Chief Justice John Marshall's landmark decision in Marbury v. Madison (1803). During his two terms as president, Jefferson discovered that the practicalities of the office required certain compromises and other adjustments. His constitutional philosophy thus turned out to be both visionary and pragmatic.*

## Introduction

Thomas Jefferson left a unique imprint on the nation. He drafted the Declaration of Independence and advocated an enumeration of individual rights—a concept that evolved into the Bill of Rights.[1] He also championed free speech and free press and fiercely defended the freedom of religion.[2]

Known for his lasting contributions as an architect of a nation dedicated to safeguarding "Life, Liberty and the pursuit of Happiness," Jefferson also engaged in extensive battles regarding the proper allocation of power between the federal and state governments. Federalism animated Jefferson's constitutional philosophy throughout his tenure in public office. His life experiences produced a man of brilliant ideas and firm convictions; yet, like most master politicians, he learned he could not always apply his philosophy consistently.

Born in 1743, Jefferson enjoyed a childhood of comfort and social position. His father, Peter Jefferson, was a prosperous surveyor, landowner, and slaveholder. His mother, a Randolph, belonged to one of the most prominent families in Virginia. He was raised on sprawling agrarian estates and idolized his father, who died when Thomas was fourteen—a loss that haunted him throughout his life.[3]

Two years after his father's death, Jefferson entered the College of William and Mary. He completed his schooling in three years and began studying and then practicing law. In 1769, at twenty-six, he was elected to the Virginia House of Burgesses. At the same time, he began building Monticello, a plantation estate near Charlottesville, Virginia. He would live at Monticello for his entire life, except for periods when he was engaged outside Virginia in public service.[4]

In 1772, Jefferson married Martha "Patty" Wayles Skelton, a member of a wealthy, landowning Virginia family. Both were avid readers and loved music. Jefferson played the violin; his wife played the piano. In one of the great tragedies of Jefferson's life, Martha died suddenly in 1782, at the age of thirty-four, shortly after giving birth to the last of their six children, only two of whom survived. Jefferson would never remarry, a promise he had made to his wife as she lay on her deathbed. However, he subsequently became engaged in a long-term relationship with Sally Hemings, one of his many slaves. According to historical research, he fathered several children with Sally, who was Martha's half-sister; they had the same father. Jefferson's relationship with Hemings was not unusual. Indeed, it exemplified a common practice among many wealthy Southern planters in the early 1800s.

As a young politician in Virginia, Jefferson would argue against the expansion of slavery into the frontier territories; as president, he would sign into law a bill ending the transatlantic slave trade. Yet, throughout his life, he owned over six hundred slaves and profited from their labor. Moreover, he never came to terms with the notion of freed slaves and whites living together in harmony.[5] Unlike George Washington, Jefferson did not free his slaves in his will. Thus, perhaps because of these contradictory views, Jefferson failed to alter the nation's dependence on slavery (as well as his own) in any meaningful way.

In 1775, Jefferson was selected as the youngest member of Virginia's delegation to the Second Continental Congress in Philadelphia. Although he was junior to the more prominent figures on the delegation, which included George Washington and Patrick Henry, the congress tapped Jefferson to draft the Declaration of Independence. Thus, his seminal articulation of the commitment to "Life, Liberty and the pursuit of Happiness" would endure as a polestar of American values.

Jefferson returned to his home state to serve in the legislature during the Revolutionary War and became governor of Virginia in 1779. During his brief two-year tenure as a wartime governor, he moved the state capital from Williamsburg to Richmond. Yet Jefferson suffered public humiliation in 1781 when he fled Richmond in the face of approaching British troops who subsequently burned the state capital to the ground.[6]

In 1784, still distraught over the recent death of his wife, Jefferson joined Benjamin Franklin and John Adams in Paris as a member of the American delegation to France. He remained in Paris for five years, serving as minister to the French court from 1785 until 1789. During his time in Paris, Jefferson developed an enduring admiration and affinity for France, a defining feature of his worldview that would set him apart from Adams and the Federalists, who continued to identify strongly with England.

Thomas Jefferson was in France when the Constitution was drafted; he therefore played no direct role in the historic Constitutional Convention. However, Jefferson managed to express his constitutional views in a number of key areas before he became president.

## Secretary of State: The National Bank

President Washington appointed Jefferson the nation's first secretary of state, in 1790. Thereafter, deep divisions emerged between Jefferson (who was assisted by his ally Congressman James Madison) and both Vice President John Adams and Secretary of Treasury Alexander Hamilton. One major rift between Jefferson's Democratic-Republicans (or Republicans) and Adams's Federalists involved the basic structure of government. Jefferson and Madison favored a limited federal government while Adams and Hamilton supported an assertive federal role under the new Constitution. Jefferson came to view the Federalists as anti-republican monarchists. Federalists saw Jefferson as an ambitious Francophile who was unduly loyal to the agrarian interests of the South.[7]

Jefferson frequently expressed his opposition to a powerful federal government. In 1791, Secretary of the Treasury Hamilton urged that the government charter a national bank to provide fiscal stability. As was his custom, President Washington consulted his cabinet and asked Secretary of State Jefferson for his constitutional views. Jefferson duly informed Washington that he opposed the bank because it went beyond federal authority. He argued that the creation of a national bank was not among the enumerated powers granted Congress in Article I, Section 8, of the Constitution. Nor was the bank "necessary" to the execution of any of the federal government's enumerated powers under the Necessary and Proper Clause. To Jefferson, if the federal government could act in this area, it would wreak havoc because "for a shade or two of *convenience*, more or less, Congress [would] be authorized to break down the most ancient and fundamental laws of the several States."[8] Washington decided to embrace Hamilton's broad interpretation of congressional power under the Necessary and Proper Clause, rejecting Jefferson's view. Decades later, in *McCulloch v. Maryland*, the Supreme Court upheld the bank's constitutionality according to a generous interpretation of the Necessary and Proper Clause.[9]

Jefferson left the government in January 1794. Despite his strong desire to return to private life at Monticello, Jefferson's retirement turned out to be short-lived. In 1796, he narrowly lost the presidency to John Adams. As the second-highest recipient of Electoral College votes, Jefferson became vice president.[10] During this period, his opposition to the Federalist agenda intensified.

## *Vice Presidency: The Alien and Sedition Acts*

Jefferson's commitment to a federal government of narrowly limited powers emerged in his strong opposition to the Alien and Sedition Acts, which Congress enacted in 1798 during his time as vice president. The Federalists used the legislation to prosecute and silence Republican critics, including journalists and politicians. The fact that the statutes were being used to suppress political views angered and offended Jefferson because of his deep commitment to the principles underlying self-government and the new First Amendment.

Although he was vice president, Jefferson secretly drafted the Kentucky Resolutions to oppose the Alien and Sedition Acts; James Madison drafted similar Virginia Resolutions. Jefferson warned that if the federal government exceeded its constitutional authority, "annihilation of the state governments, and the erection upon their ruins, of a general consolidated government, will be the inevitable consequence."[11] He even raised the controversial prospect of state nullification of federal law as a possible solution, a theory that would later haunt the nation as it headed toward civil war.

## Presidency

Jefferson challenged President John Adams a second time in 1800 and this time decisively won. However, Jefferson and his running mate, Aaron Burr, received the same number of electoral votes. After thirty-six ballots, intense intrigue, and great national uncertainty, the House of Representatives selected Jefferson—only two weeks before the scheduled inauguration of the new president.

The Revolution of 1800, as the transfer of power from the Adams administration to the Jefferson administration came to be known, occurred because Adams readily relinquished power. Moreover, Jefferson, in his inaugural address ("we are all republicans, we are all federalists"), demonstrated respect for those who had supported his rivals, and he called for reconciliation between the political parties.

### *The Louisiana Purchase*

Jefferson's constitutional commitment to limited national power was severely strained during his presidency. One test was the opportunity to greatly expand the country by acquiring the Louisiana Territory, which Spain had ceded to France. Congress provided $2 million to be applied toward the purchase of New Orleans and the Floridas, but Napoléon Bonaparte, needing money for another likely war with England, offered to nearly double the size of the land offered. Jefferson supported negotiations for this acquisition, knowing he would exceed the funds initially agreed to by Congress.

Initially, Jefferson believed the deal could not be consummated without a constitutional amendment, because the U.S. Constitution did not explicitly give him this authority. He felt the purchase was "an act beyond the Constitution" and would require "an additional article to the Constitution, approving and confirming an act which the nation had not previously authorized."[12] Nevertheless, when it appeared that delay might endanger the deal, he urged Congress to approve the acquisition. In this case, given the exigencies of the situation, Jefferson endorsed a broad federal power (in complete contrast to his previous positions) even though that power was not explicitly enumerated in the Constitution.

In providing this leadership, Jefferson understood he could not succeed by presidential power alone. He needed to convince Congress to appropriate additional funds and secure Senate support for the treaty, which he was able to do. By a treaty signed on April 30, 1803, the United States purchased from France the Louisiana Territory for 60 million francs, or about $15 million. On October 20, the Senate agreed to the treaty by a vote of twenty-four to seven, and on October 31, Congress passed legislation enabling President Jefferson to take possession of the territories ceded by France to the United States.[13] The Louisiana Purchase turned out to be one of Jefferson's greatest accomplishments. It revealed a more pragmatic Jefferson—an executive who, without explicit constitutional authority, was willing to exercise broad presidential power to secure long-term benefits to the country.

## Marbury v. Madison

Jefferson's commitment to a limited national government included opposition to a strong federal judiciary. His belief that judicial power promoted oppressive government crystallized during the experience with the Alien and Sedition Acts. Jefferson knew that federal judges, including Supreme Court justices, willingly assisted the prosecution of government critics during the Adams administration, a practice he described in 1798 as "the reign of witches."[14]

After the Alien and Sedition Acts expired on March 3, 1801, Jefferson used his pardon power to discharge every person prosecuted and punished under the sedition law, which he considered "a nullity, as absolute and as palpable as if Congress had ordered us to fall down and worship a golden image."[15] Congress later determined that the Sedition Act "was unconstitutional, null, and void" and appropriated funds to reimburse those who had been fined under the statute.[16] A century and a half later, the Supreme Court would acknowledge that the Sedition Act had been rejected not by a court of law but by the "court of history."[17]

The scope of federal judicial power loomed large in the Jefferson administration. During the waning days of Adam's presidency, the lame-duck Federalist Congress enacted the Judiciary Act of 1801 to create new courts with appellate powers and sixteen additional judgeships, as well as legislation creating other new positions. In the weeks before Jefferson's inauguration, Adams feverishly nominated the judges, and the Federalist Senate confirmed them. These "midnight judges," as they came to be known, ensured that, despite the sweeping Republican electoral victory, the judiciary would remain a Federalist "stronghold," as Jefferson himself put it.

Adams's flurry of judicial nominations set the stage for one of the best-known Supreme Court decisions in American history—*Marbury v. Madison*, a case with Jefferson's secretary of state, James Madison, serving as the defendant.[18] *Marbury v. Madison* is viewed as one of the great constitutional landmarks in American history. The traditional view is that *Marbury* established the principle that the Supreme Court could exercise "judicial review" and thus decide the constitutionality of legislation passed by Congress. *Marbury* is indeed the first case in which the Supreme Court struck down an act of Congress as unconstitutional.

The situation that gave rise to *Marbury* was a direct result of President Adams's midnight appointments. Adams appointed William Marbury as a justice of the peace of the District of Columbia during the final days of his administration. However, in Adams's rush to fill the vacancies with his Federalist appointees, a batch of commissions, including Marbury's, failed to be delivered. Jefferson discovered this oversight soon after becoming president. Deeply affronted by Adams's last-minute maneuver, Jefferson ordered that the commissions not be delivered. Marbury and three other justices of the peace who likewise failed to receive their commissions sought a writ of mandamus in the Supreme Court, asking the Court to compel Madison to deliver their commissions.

Meanwhile, the Supreme Court had a new chief justice. Adams had elevated John Marshall, his secretary of state, to serve as chief justice, taking advantage of a lame-duck appointment in January 1801. As fate would have it, Jefferson and Marshall detested each other, even though they were fellow Virginians and distant cousins (Jefferson's grandfather and Marshall's great-grandfather were brothers). Marshall viewed Jefferson as disloyal to Marshall's hero and mentor, George Washington. The chief justice also seemed to view Jefferson as self-absorbed and aloof, caustically referring to Jefferson as the "great lama of the mountains."[19] Jefferson, in turn, thought Marshall was guilty of "profound hypocrisy" and was not to be trusted.[20]

Beyond this intense personal animosity, significant ideological differences separated the two men. Marshall believed strongly in the national government. During the Revolutionary War and his service as aide to George Washington, he came to see himself as an American first and a Virginian second.[21] Marshall had served in Congress and in the Adams administration as a loyal Federalist. Jefferson, in contrast, had been deeply skeptical of a strong national government to the point that he galvanized a new political party against Adams and the Federalists in 1796 and 1800.

This clash of personalities set the stage for the Supreme Court's landmark decision in *Marbury v. Madison*, on February 24, 1803. Chief Justice Marshall wrote the Court's unanimous opinion. The opinion had many twists and turns. Marshall first sharply criticized the Jefferson administration for withholding the commission from the duly appointed Marbury. Moreover, Marshall said that Marbury was entitled to a remedy for the wrong that had been done to him. But Marshall was careful to avoid a dramatic confrontation with the Jefferson administration. His opinion declared that the Court could not rule for Marbury, because the law that allowed Marbury to file his case directly in the Supreme Court was unconstitutional. Under Article III, Marshall reasoned, the Supreme Court was an appellate court, not a court of first resort, with very limited exceptions. Thus, the act of Congress giving Marbury a right to file a mandamus action in the Supreme Court could not stand. As Marshall's opinion stated in often-quoted words about the role of the judiciary, "it is emphatically the province and duty of the judicial department to say what the law is."

As a result, Marbury lost the case. At the same time, however, the Court subjected Jefferson and Madison to the most severe criticism of a presidential administration that had ever appeared in a Supreme Court opinion up to that point. And *Marbury* became the symbol for judicial review as the cornerstone of the American rule of law.

Some commentators believe that judicial review was well understood from the beginning of the nation's history. They point out that, in 1796, the Court reviewed a congressional statute that imposed a tax on carriages and decided that the law was constitutional. In this early case, *Hylton v. U.S.*, Justice Samuel Chase (writing for himself) said it was unnecessary to determine whether the Court possessed the power to declare an act of Congress void, but if the Court exercised such power, "I am free to declare, that I will never exercise it, but in a very clear case." Two years later, the Court similarly upheld the constitutionality of another congressional act, this time involving the process of constitutional amendment. On the other hand, Republican critics of the Federalist judiciary during the Jefferson administration argued that federal judicial power was sharply limited, and even argued that federal courts lacked the power to decide constitutionality. Whether or not the principle of judicial review was widely accepted before *Marbury v. Madison*, the decision came to be seen by many jurists and scholars as "the linchpin of our constitutional law" for its role as the first decision to invalidate an act of Congress on the ground that it violated the Constitution.[22]

Jefferson abhorred the *Marbury* decision. He sharply disagreed with its conclusion that his administration had violated the law; he later castigated Marshall for saying anything other than that the Court lacked jurisdiction to hear the case. He also rejected the Court's premise that the Supreme Court was somehow superior to the elected branches in deciding constitutional issues. Jefferson declared that each branch of government had an "equal right to decide for itself what is the meaning of the Constitution submitted to it for its action."[23] He expressed his opposition to *Marbury* forcefully and repeatedly—writing to Abigail Adams in 1804, for example: "The opinion which gives to the judges the right to decide what laws are constitutional, and what not, not only for themselves, in their own sphere of action, but for the legislature & executive also, in their spheres, would make the judiciary a despotic branch."[24] So strong were Jefferson's feelings about *Marbury v. Madison* that he instructed the U.S. attorney in one prominent case not to cite the decision, because he, President Jefferson, wished to see the opinion "denounced as not law."[25]

*Second Term*

Thomas Jefferson was reelected to a second term by a landslide in November 1804. In this election, he dropped Aaron Burr from the ticket and chose New York's governor, George Clinton, as his running mate. The Twelfth Amendment, adopted in 1804, now directed electors to cast separate votes for president and vice president. Yet, despite his heavy margin of victory over the embattled Federalist Party, Jefferson's second term was defined by ongoing struggles.

In 1804, Burr and Alexander Hamilton became involved in an exchange of letters that led to a duel with pistols in Weehawken, New Jersey. Burr's shot hit Hamilton above his right hip, passed through his liver, and settled in his spine, leading to Hamilton's death the next day.[26] Facing prosecution in both New Jersey and New York, Burr decided to leave the East Coast and travel westward to the Louisiana Territory.

The criminal charges against Burr for dueling were eventually dropped. However, he was tried in 1807 on a charge for treason brought by the Jefferson administration; the charge was unrelated to the duel with Alexander Hamilton. This sensational trial stemmed from Burr's alleged role in a conspiracy to seize lands that had been part of the Louisiana Purchase and to form an independent nation. Although Burr was later acquitted of all charges, the case became the subject of an important controversy with the executive branch. Chief Justice Marshall, who sat on the Burr trial in Richmond, Virginia, as he rode circuit, was confronted with the issue of whether he could direct a subpoena to President Jefferson for documents that Burr and his attorneys insisted were necessary for his defense.[27] Jefferson invoked the principle of executive privilege, proclaiming that he reserved "the necessary right of the President of the U.S. to decide, independently of all other authority, what papers, coming to him as President, the public interests permit to be communicated [and] to whom."[28] Marshall determined that the court could, as a general rule, issue a subpoena for documents to the president just as it could to anybody else.[29] Ultimately, Jefferson voluntarily provided the documents, apparently concluding that it was not necessary to withhold them.[30]

Jefferson used every power available to him in his effort to convict Burr. In the president's message to Congress on January 22, 1807, he acknowledged that "a mixture of rumors, conjectures, and suspicions" made it difficult to determine the actual facts. However, Jefferson identified the "prime mover" as Aaron Burr, and declared that "[his] guilt is placed beyond question."[31] In pursuit of Burr, Jefferson tolerated violations of the writ of habeas corpus, publicly charged Burr with a crime before trial, and even misused the pardon power to induce witnesses to testify against Burr. Moreover, Jefferson relied on information provided by General James Wilkinson, including a letter allegedly written by Burr. The letter proposed stealing land from the Louisiana Purchase, but turned out to be in Wilkinson's handwriting. In the end, however, George Hay, the U.S. attorney who prosecuted the case, was convinced that it was a mistake to rely on Wilkinson's testimony. Hay confided to Jefferson: "My confidence in him is shaken, if not destroyed."[32] After Burr was acquitted, he fled to Europe, his career as a politician and statesman ruined.

When it came to foreign affairs, Jefferson's policy was increasingly dictated by the unstable political situation in Europe, coupled with the young nation's limited ability to project power on the global stage.[33] Late in Jefferson's second term, these two factors began to converge dangerously as British aggression toward American ships threatened the fledgling U.S. economy. Eventually, Jefferson was forced to institute a deeply unpopular embargo against both Britain and France during the Napoleonic Wars.[34] The embargo, intended to punish Great Britain, served also to damage the economic interests of American businesses. To enforce the embargo, Jefferson resorted to stopping and searching any ship owned by American citizens without warrants or court process. These actions and others collided with Jefferson's earlier reputation for safeguarding individual rights against arbitrary government.[35] When Jefferson turned over the presidency to his handpicked successor, James Madison, the country was on the brink of war with Great Britain.

In March 1809, Jefferson bid farewell to his public career, which had spanned forty years, and returned to Monticello. During the War of 1812, the British burned Congress and destroyed its library. To refurbish this collection, Jefferson sold his vast personal library of 6,487 volumes to the federal government, making him the de facto founder of the Library of Congress.[36] Funds raised by this sale helped alleviate some of Jefferson's financial distress at the time. In his final years, he devoted his energy to founding the University of Virginia through a long and arduous process that was ultimately successful.[37] Jefferson died on July 4, 1826, at the age of eighty-three. His death came on the same day that his political rival and friend, John Adams, died and fifty years to the day after the signing of the Declaration of Independence that Jefferson had drafted.

## Conclusion

Many elements of Jefferson's constitutional vision continue to resonate: his commitment to a limited national government of enumerated powers, his skepticism about the unelected federal judiciary, his articulation of a "wall of separation" between church and state, and his reverence for freedom of speech and vigorous debate. At the same time, the apostle of limited national government embraced the expansive Louisiana Purchase, and the drafter of the Declaration of Independence bitterly condemned the Supreme Court's decision in *Marbury v. Madison*, which gave life to the American rule of law. As in other areas of his intellectual, political, and personal life, Jefferson's constitutional perspective is rich, provocative, original, complex, sometimes contradictory, and deeply influential.

### NOTES

1. Jon Meacham, *Thomas Jefferson: The Art of Power* (New York: Random House, 2012), 214. Jefferson wrote a letter to James Madison—a member of the First Congress—in December 1787, stating that the failure to include a Bill of Rights in the Constitution was a major blunder. He believed the Constitution should include a declaration of rights to guarantee "freedom of religion, freedom of the press, protection against standing armies, restriction against monopolies, the eternal and unremitting force of the habeas corpus laws, and trial by jury." Ibid. However, Jefferson's role in the drafting and adoption of the Bill of Rights was limited, because he was stationed in Paris for much of the time.

2. Jefferson described the Free Exercise Clause and the Establishment Clause as "building a wall of separation between Church and State." Thomas Jefferson to the Danbury Baptist Association, January 1, 1802, reprinted in *The Papers of Thomas Jefferson* (Princeton, NJ: Princeton University Press, 2009), 36:258. Throughout his career, Jefferson was proud of his contributions in this area. Indeed, he chose to include among the three items listed on his tombstone at Monticello his authorship of the Virginia Statute of Religious Freedom. The other two were the authorship of the Declaration of Independence and the founding of the University of Virginia.

3. Joseph J. Ellis, *American Sphinx* (New York: Vintage Books, 1998).

4. Ibid.

5. Meacham, *The Art of Power*, 48, 55, 124, 146, 216–219.

6. Ellis, *American Sphinx*, 77–78. Jefferson was nearly captured at Monticello not long after. Ibid.

7. R. B. Bernstein, *Thomas Jefferson* (New York: Oxford University Press, 2003), 89–95.

8. Thomas Jefferson, "Opinion on the Constitutionality of a National Bank" (1791), reprinted in *The Papers of Thomas Jefferson* (Princeton, NJ: Princeton University Press, 1974), 19:275 (emphasis in original).

9. McCulloch v. Maryland, 17 U.S. (4 Wheat.) 316 (1819).

10. U.S. Const. art. II, § 1. This provision was replaced in 1804 by the Twelfth Amendment.

11. Kentucky Resolutions of 1799, reprinted in Jonathan Elliot, ed., *Debates in the Several State Conventions, on the Adoption of the Federal Constitution, as Recommended by that General Convention at Philadelphia, in 1787*, 2nd ed. (Philadelphia: Lippincott, 1888), 4:544–545.

12. Thomas Jefferson to John C. Breckinridge, August 12, 1803, reprinted in *The Works of Thomas Jefferson*, ed. Paul Leicester Ford (New York: G. P. Putnam's Sons, 1905), 9:7 n. 1.

13. On the Senate vote, see 13 Annals of Cong. 308 (1803). On the authority to President Jefferson to take possession, see 2 Stat. 245 (1803).

14. Thomas Jefferson to John Taylor, June 4, 1798, reprinted in *The Papers of Thomas Jefferson* (Princeton, NJ: Princeton University Press, 2003), 30:387.

15. Thomas Jefferson to Mrs. John Adams, July 22, 1804, *The Writings of Thomas Jefferson* (Lipscomb-Bergh ed., 1904), 11:43–44.

16. H. Rept. No. 86, 26th Cong., 1st Sess. (1840), 2; 6 Stat. 802, ch. 45 (1840).

17. New York Times Co. v. Sullivan, 376 U.S. 254, 276 (1964).

18. Marbury v. Madison, 5 U.S. (1 Cranch) 137 (1803).

19. John Marshall to Joseph Story, September 18, 1821, in *The Papers of John Marshall*, ed. Charles F. Hobson (Chapel Hill: University of North Carolina Press, 1998), 9:183.

20. Thomas Jefferson to James Madison, November 26, 1795, in *The Papers of Thomas Jefferson* (Princeton, NJ: Princeton University Press, 2000), 28:539.

21. Cliff Sloan and David McKean, *The Great Decision: Jefferson, Adams, Marshall, and the Battle for the Supreme Court* (New York: Public Affairs, 2009).

22. William H. Rehnquist, *The Supreme Court* (New York: William Morrow & Co., 1987), 114.

23. Sloan and McKean, *The Great Decision*, 168–169.

24. Thomas Jefferson to Abigail Adams, September 11, 1804, in *The Writings of Thomas Jefferson* (Paul L. Ford, ed., 1897), 310.

One week after *Marbury*, the Supreme Court issued a brief decision in *Stuart v. Laird* on whether Congress possessed constitutional authority to repeal the statute creating federal appellate courts. The judges had already been appointed and were deciding cases. Congress had constitutional authority to impeach and remove federal judges, but could it eliminate courts? The Supreme Court concluded that "there are no words in the constitution to prohibit or restrain the exercise of legislative power" in adjusting the appellate process, and thus the repeal was not unconstitutional. By abolishing the appellate courts, moreover, Supreme Court justices would have to perform that function by again "riding circuit," a task all of them greatly disliked. Reflecting on the fact that justices had ridden circuit from 1789 to the end of the Adams administration without anyone raising a constitutional objection, the Court said in *Stuart*: "It is sufficient to observe, that practice and acquiescence under it for a period of several years, commencing with the organization of the judicial system, affords an irresistable [*sic*] answer, and has indeed fixed the construction." The acceptance represented "a contemporary interpretation of the most forcible nature. This practical exposition is too strong and obstinate to be shaken or controlled." Stuart v. Laird, 5 U.S. (1 Cranch.) 299, 309 (1803). The opinion in sustaining the repeal statute was unanimous. After invalidating an act of Congress for the first time in *Marbury*, the Supreme Court in *Stuart v. Laird* showed that it would use that power sparingly.

25. Thomas Jefferson to George Hay, June 2, 1807, in *The Papers of Thomas Jefferson*, www.gutenberg.org/files/16784/16784-h/16784-h.htm#link2H_4_0044. This correspondence took place in the trial of Aaron Burr, discussed above.

26. Nancy Isenberg, *Fallen Founder: The Life of Aaron Burr* (New York: Viking, 2007), 164–166, 257–269.

27. For a detailed account of the Burr trial, see Dumas Malone, *Jefferson the President*, vol. 5 of *Jefferson and His Time* (Boston: Little Brown and Co., 1974), 332–370.

28. Ibid., 320.

29. United States v. Burr, 25 F. Cas. 30 (No. 14,692d) (C.C.D. Va. 1807).

30. Louis Fisher, "Jefferson and the Burr Conspiracy: Executive Power Against the Law," *Presidential Studies Quarterly* (March 2015): 169.

31. 16 Annals of Cong. 39–40 (1807).

32. Milton Lomask, *Aaron Burr: The Conspiracy and Years of Exile, 1805–1836* (New York: Farrar, Straus, Giroux, 1982), 289. For further details on Jefferson's efforts to convict Burr, see Fisher, "Jefferson and the Burr Conspiracy."

33. Meacham, *The Art of Power*, 413–414, 423.

34. Embargo Act of 1807, 2 Stat. 451 (1807). See also Meacham, *The Art of Power*, 425–435.

35. Leonard W. Levy, *Jefferson and Civil Liberties: The Darker Side* (New York: Quadrangle, 1973).

36. Dumas Malone, *The Sage of Monticello*, vol. 6 of *Jefferson and His Time* (Boston: Little Brown and Company, 1981), 199.

37. For a full account of Jefferson's role in the founding of the University of Virginia, see John S. Patton, *Jefferson, Cabell, and the University of Virginia* (New York: Neale Publishing, 1906).

# 4

# James Madison

RALPH KETCHAM

*James Madison, "Father of the Constitution" and a member of the First Congress, was devoted to the concept of a strong union. Madison is seldom considered an adept or successful president. Yet he viewed compromise and attention to the public good as means of keeping the Union intact, even if it meant a diminution of the president's power. He was the first president to urge Congress to formally declare war. And, although the War of 1812 nearly destroyed his presidency and the seat of government, he survived and continued to work with Congress, recognizing that a separation of powers did not mean absolute separation, but meant respectful coopera-tion. Madison believed that the president and Congress each needed to work within the parameters of the Constitution, and if additional powers were required, the two branches of government had to secure this author-ity through the amendment process.*

## Introduction

James Madison (1751–1836), planter, constitutional theorist, legislator, and fourth president of the United States, was born in Port Conway, King George County, Virginia. His ancestors, probably all from England and tradesmen and farmers at first, quickly acquired more lands and soon were among "the respectable though not the most opulent class," as Madison himself described them. He lived all his life in Orange County, Virginia, on Montpelier, a 5,000-acre plantation that produced tobacco and grains and was worked by perhaps a hundred slaves. Though he abhorred slavery and had no use for the aristocratic airs of Virginia society, Madison remained a Virginia planter. This meant that he depended all his life on a slave system that he could never square with his republican beliefs. Indeed, throughout his public life, Madison avoided the question of slavery. The issue put him in a paradoxical position he was reluctant to discuss—championing liberty and the inalienable rights of all persons on the one hand, but, as a slave owner, holding men and women in bondage on the other.[1]

Madison received fundamental instruction at home and then went away to preparatory school before entering the College of New Jersey at Princeton. He received his bachelor of arts degree in 1771 and considered law and divinity as vocations, but never entered either profession. The political thought he acquired at Princeton rested on the moral standards of John Locke's *Second Treatise on Civil Government*, primarily the principle that reason requires that all men be esteemed free and equal. This principle left a profound impression on a young Madison.

Another foundation for Madison was the Christian tradition. Down through his graduation from college, every one of his teachers was either a clergyman or a devoutly orthodox Christian layperson. From the Christian tradition, he inherited a sense of the prime importance of conscience, a strict personal morality, an understanding of human dignity as well as depravity, and a conviction that vital religion could significantly contribute to the quality of citizenship and to the public good.

Madison's understanding of public affairs developed during the decade of colonial resistance to British measures, from 1765 to 1775. In 1776, at age twenty-five, he was elected to the Virginia convention that both declared the colony independent from Britain and drafted a new state constitution. There he strengthened the clause guaranteeing religious "toleration" to proclaim "liberty of conscience for all." Elected to the governor's council in 1777, he lived in Williamsburg for two years, dealing with the routine problems of the Revolutionary War under two governors, Patrick Henry and Thomas Jefferson. Madison was elected in 1780 to the Continental Congress, where he served for nearly four years. He became one of the leaders of the so-called nationalist group, which believed that the goals of the revolution could only be achieved under a strong central government.

## Father of the Constitution

During his three years in the Virginia legislature, from 1784 to 1786, Madison worked to enact Thomas Jefferson's bill for religious freedom and other reform measures. In his *Memorial and Remonstrance Against Religious Assessments*, Madison proclaimed: "No man's right in matters of Religion is abridged by the institution of civil society." When Jefferson's Virginia Statute for Religious Freedom passed, Madison wrote to Jefferson that he hoped Virginia "had extinguished forever the ambitious hope of making laws for the human mind."

Madison was soon convinced, as well, that a new frame of government was needed to replace the Articles of Confederation. At the Constitutional Convention of 1787 in Philadelphia, he offered the Virginia plan, which would give taxing and law enforcement powers to the national government. He also worked with James Wilson and other nationalists to support a strengthened executive, a broadly based House of Representatives, lengthy terms in the Senate, an independent judiciary, and other devices designed to enhance national power.

Because of his key role in guiding the federal Constitution to completion, James Madison would later be called the "Father of the Constitution." With Alexander Hamilton, he formulated a strategy for supporters of the Constitution and wrote portions of the *Federalist Papers*, in which he and Hamilton defended the supreme power of federal courts throughout the Union. In a dramatic and ultimately successful debate with Patrick Henry at the Virginia ratifying convention in June 1788, Madison asserted that "controversies affecting the interest of the United States ought to be decided by their own [federal] judiciary."

## Influential Statesman

As a member of the first U.S. Congress representing Virginia's Fifth District in the House of Representatives, James Madison sponsored the all-important addition of the Bill of Rights. He also drafted President Washington's inaugural address and helped the new president make the precedent-setting appointments of his first term.

Madison broke ranks with the Washington administration, however, in opposing the proposed national bank, believing that such an institution gave a privileged position to commerce and wealth. Fearful that this power could overwhelm and sometimes even control the organs of government, Madison concluded that Secretary of the Treasury Hamilton's proposed national bank was unconstitutional.[2] Along with Thomas Jefferson, Madison broke with Hamilton and the newly dubbed Federalist Party, helping to form the Republican Party (later called the Democratic-Republican Party).

In the realm of foreign affairs, Madison bitterly opposed the Jay Treaty (1795), which sought to resume peaceful trade between the United States and Great Britain.[3] He believed that the treaty made the United States too dependent on England and tied America to the corrupt power politics of the Old World. In his opinion, the new nation needed to establish both its national independence and the beginnings of a new, more humane system of international relations. Politically discouraged after the enactment of Jay's Treaty in April 1796, Madison left Congress in 1797.

As the United States and France moved perilously close to war, Congress passed the Alien and Sedition Acts, which Madison believed violated the new First Amendment and severely threatened free government.[4] In protest, he drafted two documents while serving in the Virginia legislature: the Virginia Resolutions of 1798 and a report defending his position in 1800. In these writings, Madison stated most fully his concern about protecting state's rights, yet he advocated neither nullification of the offensive federal alien and sedition laws nor secession (despite later assertions to the contrary). Rather, Madison defended civil liberties against encroachments by the federal government and displayed an evolving constitutional philosophy that insisted on a respectful adherence to both federal law and the Constitution in unison.

Appointed secretary of state in 1801 by President Thomas Jefferson, Madison became a key figure in the new republic. Along with Jefferson and Secretary of Treasury Albert Gallatin, he became part of the republic's triumvirate that essentially guided the nation for eight years.[5]

In this capacity, Madison also played a key role in the saga of *Marbury v. Madison*.[6] Like President Jefferson, he abhorred Chief Justice John Marshall's ultimate ruling, which established a sweeping power of judicial review over acts of Congress.[7] Indeed, the historic *Marbury v. Madison* opinion also represented the first of Marshall's many decisions that strained his relationship with Madison; the decision had ramifications well into Madison's presidency.

## Presidency

As President Jefferson completed his second term in office, he supported the decision of Madison to run for president in 1808.[8] Despite an effort by the now-weakened Federalist Party to mount a challenge, Madison won a decisive victory as the Democratic-Republican candidate, defeating Charles Cotesworth Pinckney of South Carolina.[9]

Madison, a longtime bachelor, had pleasantly surprised friends when he married a vivacious young widow, Dolley Payne Todd, in 1794. Dolley Madison had already become a popular social figure in Washington and had periodically assisted President Jefferson in entertaining guests at official functions at the White House. Now, as First Lady, she continued to captivate visitors there.

### Ineffective Political Leadership

Yet as James Madison assumed the duties of office, the productive relationship that Jefferson had cultivated with the legislature dissolved under Madison's less charismatic leadership. This political weakness was especially debilitating and dangerous when Madison sought, after the failure of the embargo on Europe, to find other paths to peace with honor as the Napoleonic Wars reached their climax. The belligerents paid little heed to Madison's efforts at commercial retaliation; they saw no need to respect a distant republic that was both disunited and virtually disarmed.

Madison's weakened political position as the new president, in 1809, foreshadowed complications and difficulties he would face in making both executive and judicial appointments. A powerful group in the Senate, claiming to be the true Republicans, forced Madison to make weak

appointments in the State Department and elsewhere.[10] Madison continued to act essentially as his own secretary of state, even down to writing
the dispatches that could not be entrusted to the unqualified appointee.
Political necessity also dictated similarly weak appointments in the War
and Navy Departments.

As the prospect of a new war with Great Britain became imminent,
Madison also became entangled with issues surrounding judicial appointments. The problem was further exacerbated by his concerns over Chief
Justice Marshall's decision in *Fletcher v. Peck*, handed down on March 16,
1810. This controversial case involved a lawsuit by Robert Fletcher against
John Peck for breach of contract, relating to land that Fletcher had purchased along the Yazoo River (later part of Mississippi and Alabama). The
state of Georgia had taken the land from Native Americans and sold it off
to land companies. The Georgia legislature had overwhelmingly approved
this Yazoo Land Act sale. Later, however, evidence surfaced that the deal
had been forged through widespread bribes and corruption among the
Georgia legislators; the state legislature was forced to repeal the law and
void these transactions.[11]

In an unexpected decision written by Chief Justice Marshall, the U.S.
Supreme Court ruled that the Georgia legislature's repeal of the Yazoo
Land Act sale was unconstitutional under the Contract Clause of the U.S.
Constitution.[12] The sale of land, declared the Court, constituted a contract
that legally bound future buyers and sellers.[13] *Fletcher v. Peck* was important because it was the first case in which the Court flexed its muscles and
demonstrated its ability to invalidate state laws that were contrary to the
U.S. Constitution pursuant to the Supremacy Clause in Article VI, Section 2.[14]

However, *Fletcher v. Peck* created deep suspicions in President Madison
and his predecessor, Thomas Jefferson. In the minds of both men, the decision confirmed Marshall's political hostility.[15] President Madison seemed
to discount Marshall's basic and most important constitutional motiva-
tion in this case—to assert federal court supremacy over state legislative
action, with which Madison would generally have agreed.[16] Instead, Jefferson convinced Madison that the chief justice was up to no good.[17] The
former president was carefully watching a potentially devastating civil case
filed against him in federal court in Virginia, which alleged that Jefferson had illegally voided the ownership interests of his now rival, Edward

Livingston, in valuable land along the Mississippi River batture in New Orleans while in public office.[18]

Jefferson worried that Marshall might exert his "biases" against him to strip him of his life savings. Jefferson wrote to Madison in alarm, saying that Marshall's "twistifications" in *Fletcher v. Peck* and other cases "show how dexterously he can reconcile law to his personal biases."[19]

Jefferson went so far as to seek to convince his successor to appoint figures to the Supreme Court who would not do Marshall's bidding. Yet Madison eventually ignored Jefferson's admonitions and appointed Joseph Story (whom Jefferson opposed, asserting that Story was "unquestionably a Tory" and "too young").[20] The appointment turned out to be one of Madison's most significant contributions as president.[21]

## War of 1812

Another defining aspect of Madison's presidency related to the War of 1812—a piece of his legacy that was not altogether flattering. In November 1811, with the support of newly elected "War Hawks" in Congress, Madison decided the nation should move toward war with Britain unless the British ceased their assaults on American ships and seamen. With his own party splintering over the proposed war against Great Britain and his pro-French posture, Madison still managed to receive the nomination of the Democratic-Republicans for a second term, although some party leaders boycotted the nominating caucus. With no sign of conciliation from Britain, Madison finally asked for and received a declaration of war from Congress, in June 1812.

Madison struggled with growing factions within his own party and a determined opposition in New England—an opposition that, excited by preachers and politicians who decried the declaration of war, reached proportions the president regarded as nearly hysterical and treasonous. In a series of meetings referred to as the Hartford Convention, New England Federalists challenged Madison's actions. Though Madison thought the calling of the Hartford Convention was unwise and unhelpful, he believed it lawful and clearly within the bounds of free, republican politics, even in wartime. He did, though, post a loyal militia near Hartford in case the convention began some extra-legal venture. He received the convention's resolutions silently in Washington, without response.

On the battlefield, Madison hoped that American zeal and the vulnerability of Canada—a colony of Great Britain—would lead to a swift victory. However, the surrender of one American army at Detroit, the defeat of another on the Niagara frontier, and the disgraceful retreat of yet another blasted these hopes. The chaos of American financial matters, the bungled efforts of French military leader Napoléon Bonaparte in Europe, and yet another fruitless military campaign in New York State left Madison disheartened. Attorney General Richard Rush wrote to former president John Adams: "[The nation] seems to fight for nothing but disaster and defeat; and I dread to add, disgrace. . . . I am sick at heart at the view of our public affairs." "Have we, Sir," Rush demanded, "ever seen worst times, and survived them?"[22]

The summer of 1814 brought to America thousands of battle-hardened British troops. They fought American armies to a standstill on the Niagara frontier and appeared at the Chesapeake Bay, intent on capturing the capital city of Washington. A small but well-disciplined British force defeated the disorganized Americans at Bladensburg, Maryland, as Madison watched from a nearby hillside. His humiliation was complete when he saw the Capitol and White House—two sacred buildings that symbolized the newly formed U.S. government—engulfed in flames as he fled across the Potomac River. (According to some reports, Dolley Madison was responsible for saving the portrait of George Washington in the White House, so that it was not destroyed or desecrated by the British.)[23] Publicists in England and the United States ridiculed what they saw as the naive idealism of "Mr. Madison's War."

When Madison returned to Washington after three days, he was encouraged by word of the British defeat in Baltimore Harbor and of the repulse of a British army coming down Lake Champlain. When, in late October, the Duke of Wellington and other British leaders learned of the setbacks, they decided that the American war was not worth the strenuous efforts necessary for victory. Instead, they decided to seek peace. But Madison did not know this, and with a powerful British force menacing New Orleans, he had to prepare his disordered and disunited nation for more war. Sectional strains grew as Federalist leaders denounced the war and gathered for the so-called Hartford Convention, at which they aired their grievances against Madison and his Republican Party.

As gloom settled over the makeshift quarters in Washington and Madison was positioning forces to meet a possible rebellion in New England, events unknown to him were moving in the nation's favor. On Christmas Eve, diplomats in Ghent, Belgium, had negotiated a peace with Britain, restoring prewar boundaries and ensuring American independence. Next, Major General Andrew Jackson won a stunning victory over the British in the Battle of New Orleans on January 8, 1815. When news of both Jackson's victory and the peace treaty reached Washington in February, Madison exulted and the city celebrated.[24]

With the threat of disunion ended and the nation's institutions vindicated, Madison's last two years as president were triumphant. Responding to the nationalist mood, he proposed to guide and stimulate the economy by recommending a re-charter of the national bank and by ensuring federal support for roads and canals that would "bind more closely together the various parts of our extended confederacy." He also recommended the establishment of a national university and defense measures strong enough to deter future potential enemies. In urging a variety of measures "best executed under the national authority," Madison cast aside republican dogma about weak government and was willing to let a free people use their representative institutions to fulfill national objectives as long as the objectives remained faithful to the Constitution.

Indeed, Madison revealed a great deal about his constitutional philosophy when he spoke to the issue of using federal power to accomplish "internal improvements" in the aftermath of the War of 1812. Madison urged Congress in 1815 to pay attention "to the great importance of establishing throughout our country the roads and canals which can best be executed under national authority." He added, however, that Congress was obligated to remain within its constitutional powers in achieving this goal. When Congress passed a bill providing for a national program of internal improvements, without amending the Constitution, Madison promptly vetoed it on his last day in office, March 3, 1817. He declared that "such a power is not expressly given by the Constitution, . . . [and] could not be deduced from any part of it without an inadmissible latitude of construction . . . and that the success of the Constitution depends on a definite partition of powers between the General and State Governments." Madison certainly understood "the benefit of such measures." Yet he believed that Congress was required to press for a constitutional amendment before it expanded its powers in this fashion.[25]

Madison thus remained true to his belief in a balance of powers between the state and federal governments, as he had explained in the *Federalist*

*Papers* in 1787–1788. At the same time, he recognized the need for constitutional change where this might accomplish a "signal advantage to the general prosperity."

Similarly, Madison's handling of the national-bank issue as president showed the evolution of his constitutional principles. Albert Gallatin's long and brilliant service as secretary of the treasury had convinced Gallatin (and the president) of the national bank's great utility in managing the nation's finances. Yet because of Madison's unwillingness to make public his strict constructionist opposition to the bank in 1791, he avoided taking part in the re-charter effort in 1811. His lack of endorsement for the effort led to its defeat by one vote in each house of Congress. By then, however, Madison believed that "requisite evidence of the national judgment and intention" of the bank had rendered it constitutional. Now, in 1816, after seeing the federal government weakened during the War of 1812 due to the lack of a stable currency, Madison approved the bank's re-charter without requiring a constitutional amendment, satisfied that twenty years of use, and the strengthening of the nation's political system, made the bank a constructive rather than a dangerous part of the government.[26]

## Conclusion

James Madison happily retired to his Virginia plantation in 1817, along with his wife Dolley. There, Madison practiced scientific agriculture, helped Thomas Jefferson found the University of Virginia, advised President James Monroe on foreign policy, arranged his papers for posthumous publication, and maintained a wide correspondence. He returned officially to public life only to take part in the Virginia Constitutional Convention of 1829–1830. There, he sought both to diminish the power of slave owners in the Tidewater region by altering Virginia's system of apportionment from one based on counties and election districts to one based on population in which every slave was counted as three-fifths a person, and to extend the right to vote to "house keepers and heads of families."[27] His efforts fell in the wake of pressure from proslavery forces to preserve their dominance by keeping a district-based system. Nonetheless, Madison continued to display a desire to keep state government in check, maintaining the proper balance that he regarded as essential for the federal system.

In retirement, Madison contemplated the issue of slavery more openly than he did while in public life, pondering how slavery could be eradicated from the country.[28] Madison did not fully embrace a then-popular pro-posed strategy that the expansion of slavery, rather than its restriction, would diminish the institution's harmful consequences. Moreover, unlike Washington and other prominent Virginians, Madison rejected the idea of individuals freeing their own slaves as the answer to the conundrum. Ulti-mately, Madison supported the solution known as colonization and envi-sioned a federal project whereby freed slaves would be transported back to and resettled in Africa.[29]

Still a prominent national figure, Madison did not shirk from contro-versy. He wrote a public letter in 1830 repudiating South Carolina nullifiers who sought to block federal tariff laws, and he argued passionately that the interests of the Union had to prevail over state issues of this sort. Madi-son's public stance earned him great praise, including that from the elderly Chief Justice Marshall, with whom Madison had periodically clashed dur-ing his career. In old age, it turned out, the two men became great admirers of each other.[30]

When it came to the Constitution that he helped craft, Madison was an unwavering believer that a strong central government was essential to the success of this grand experiment in democracy. In fact, his whole career and his most profound political thought rested on securing for the United States the benefits of a union. Madison's final publication, *Advice to My Country*, offered guidance that he envisioned as "issuing from the tomb, where truth alone can be respected and the happiness of man alone con-sulted.... The advice nearest to my heart and deepest in my convictions is that the Union of the States be cherished and perpetuated. Let the open enemy to it be regarded as a Pandora with her box opened, and the dis-guised one as the Serpent creeping with his deadly wiles into Paradise."[31]

Although Madison was not a politically nimble or charismatic pres-ident, he kept his beloved Union intact and embraced a flexibility that allowed the components of the Union to achieve a semblance of harmony.

He died at age eighty-five on June 28, 1836, at his beloved estate at Montpelier, Virginia, the last prominent survivor of the founding of the American republic.

NOTES

1. Richard Brookhiser, *James Madison* (New York: Basic Books, 2011), 231.
2. Madison viewed republican government as resting on the virtue of the people, sus-tained by the self-reliance and moral vigor of an agricultural economy and the benefits

of public education. Government itself, he believed, should remain "mild" and responsive to grassroots impulses. Moreover, Madison himself had proposed that Congress be given a general power to issue charters of incorporation. However, at the Constitutional Convention, this power was not included in the list of powers granted Congress in Article I, Section 8. For this reason as well, Madison was convinced that Congress did not possess the power to charter a bank, absent a constitutional amendment granting it this power. Richard S. Arnold, "How James Madison Interpreted the Constitution," *New York University Law Review* 72, no. 2 (May 1997): 274–275.

3. Irving Brant, *James Madison: Secretary of State 1800–1809* (Indianapolis: Bobbs-Merrill, 1953), 440. In 1794, President George Washington sent Chief Justice John Jay to London to negotiate a treaty that would tie up several loose ends after the American Revolution. Among the items addressed in the treaty were British seizures of American shipping; outstanding American debts to British creditors; American trade with the British West Indies; and continued British occupation of forts on the American frontier. The Jay Treaty was initially signed in secret out of fear that most Americans would dislike the terms, but the benefits it conferred eventually won over much of the public. Brookhiser, *James Madison*, 123–127.

4. David McCullough, *John Adams* (New York: Simon & Schuster 2001), 493–499.

5. These individuals sought to lead in accordance with the ideals of limited government, personal and political freedom, and ordered pursuit of the public good—all ideals that Jefferson had outlined in his first inaugural address. See Chapter 3, "Thomas Jefferson."

6. Lawrence Goldstone, *The Activist: John Marshall, Marbury v. Madison, and the Myth of Judicial Review* (New York: Walker & Co. 2008), 208–210; Robert Allen Rutland, *James Madison: The Founding Father* (Columbia: University of Missouri Press, 1987), 175–176.

7. Marbury v. Madison, 5 U.S. (1 Cranch) 137, 138 (1803). See also Cliff Sloan and David McKean, *The Great Decision: Jefferson, Adams, Marshall, and the Battle for the Supreme Court* (New York: Public Affairs 2009), 154–165.

8. Brant, *James Madison*, 419–426.

9. Dumas Malone, *Jefferson and His Time*, vol. 4, *Jefferson the President, First Term, 1801–1805* (New York: Little, Brown & Co. 1970), 433–437; Brant, *James Madison*, 467–468.

10. These were led by Senator Samuel Smith of Maryland and Senator William B. Giles of Virginia. Senator Giles coveted the State Department for himself, while Senator Smith wanted the position for his brother, Robert Smith. Ultimately, Madison was forced to appoint Robert Smith to that department though the appointee was widely acknowledged to be lazy, incompetent, and largely ignorant of foreign affairs.

11. Fletcher v. Peck, 10 U.S. (6 Cranch) 87 (1810); C. Peter Magrath, *Yazoo, Law and Politics in the New Republic: The Case of Fletcher v. Peck* (Providence, RI: Brown University Press 1966), 5–19, 53–54.

12. U.S. Const. art. I, § 10, cl. 1.

13. *Fletcher*, 6 U.S. at 136–139.

14. Ware v. Hylton, 3 U.S. (3 Dall.) 199 (1796), was a precursor of sorts for *Fletcher*. In *Ware*, basing its ruling on the Supremacy Clause (Article VI, Clause 2), the Supreme Court invalidated a Virginia statute as inconsistent with federal law, the 1783 Treaty of Peace.

15. Evidence does show that Madison certainly disliked Marshall, and the two frequently disagreed, even after Madison's presidency. Irving Brant, *James Madison: Commander in Chief 1812–1836* (Indianapolis: Bobbs-Merrill, 1961), 98, 432–434.

16. Henry Abraham, *Justices Presidents, and Senators* (New York: Rowman & Littlefield, 1985), 87–90; George Lee Haskins, *History of the Supreme Court of the United States*, vol. 2, part 1, "States Rights and the National Judiciary" (New York: Macmillan), 336–353. Neither of these works, however, mentions the complications raised by Jefferson's Louisiana batture case and his paranoid fear of Marshall's "twistifications" and "biases," which had been brought so persistently to Madison's attention.

17. Magrath, *Yazoo*, 60–62. Jefferson was never shy about his disdain for his cousin, the chief justice. Merrill D. Peterson, *Thomas Jefferson and the New Nation: A Biography* (New York: Oxford University Press, 1970), 601.

18. Thomas Jefferson to James Madison, 25 May 1810, in *The Papers of Thomas Jefferson Digital Edition, Retirement Series, vol. 2: 16 Nov. 1809 to 11 Aug. 1810*, ed. Barbara B. Oberg and J. Jefferson Looney (Charlottesville: University of Virginia Press, 2008), 416–417.

19. Jefferson also feared that Chief Justice Marshall's decision in *Fletcher v. Peck* might foreshadow a decision that deferred too much to state governing bodies, however misguided those bodies' actions.

20. Jefferson to Madison, May 25 and October 15, 1810, in *The Republic of Letters: The Correspondence Between Thomas Jefferson and James Madison*, ed. James M. Smith (New York: Norton, 1995), 3:1631–1747.

21. For instance, in the aftermath of the revolution, the state of Virginia had attempted to take control of all property formerly belonging to the Church of England. In Terrett v. Taylor, 13 U.S. (9 Cranch) 43 (1815), Justice Story invalidated Virginia's claim to these lands, citing the proposition that "all men are equally entitled to the free exercise of religion according to the dictates of conscience." Madison was certainly pleased with Justice Story's decision for the Court in *Terrett*. Indeed, the quoted statement had been incorporated into the Virginia Bill of Rights by Madison himself in 1776. Joseph Tussman, ed., *The Supreme Court on Church and State* (New York: Oxford University Press, 1962), 3–4.

22. Richard Rush to Charles J. Ingersoll, February 28, 1812, and October 20, 1813, Historical Society of Pennsylvania, Philadelphia; Richard Rush to John Adams, October 23, 1814, in *Pennsylvania Magazine of History and Biography* 61 (1937): 41–43.

23. In the years following the War of 1812, Dolley advocated for and worked to improve the welfare of orphaned children in Washington, DC. The practice of a first lady working for social cause during her husband's presidency was first adopted by Dolley Madison and continues to this day. Miller Center of the University of Virginia, "Dolley Madison," in *American President: A Reference Resource*, accessed August 23, 2014, http://millercenter.org/president/madison/essays/firstlady.

24. The French minister, who had been close to Madison throughout the war, observed that "three years of warfare have been a trial of the capacity of [American] institutions to sustain a state of war, a question . . . now resolved in their advantage." Charles Serurier to Talleyrand, February 21, 1815, noted in Irving Brant, *James Madison* (Indianapolis: Hackett, 1941–1961), 6:378.

25. James Madison, Annual Message, December 5, 1815, and "Veto Message," March 3, 1817, in *Selected Writings of James Madison*, ed. Ralph Ketcham (Indianapolis: Hackett, 2006), 298–299, 302.

26. Irving Brant, *James Madison the President, 1809–1812* (Indianapolis: Bobbs-Merrill, 1956), 269–272.

27. Gaillard Hunt, ed., *The Writings of James Madison*, vol. 9, *1819–1836* (New York: G.P. Putnam's Sons, 1910), 358–364; Brookhiser, *James Madison*, 234–235.

28. Brookhiser, *James Madison*, 232.

29. Ibid., 232–233.

30. In a meeting five months before Marshall's death and a year before Madison's, the sociologist and writer Harriet Martineau reported that when she mentioned Madison to Marshall, the old chief justice "instantly sat upright in his chair, and with beaming eyes began to praise Mr. Madison." When Martineau visited Madison a few days later at Montpelier, she noted: "Madison received the mention of Marshall's name in just the same manner." Harriet Martineau, *Retrospect of Western Travel* (London: Saunders and Otley, 1838), 2:189.

31. Ralph Ketcham, ed., *Selected Writings of Madison* (Indianapolis: Hackett, 2006), 362.

# 5

# James Monroe

GARY HART

*President James Monroe recognized that as the United States matured, it had to convey forcefully what the nation's place in the world would be. In articulating the Monroe Doctrine, the fifth president declared that the new democratic republic would refrain from seeking to exert control over other nations, yet it would also protect itself from foreign governments that sought to interfere with the American continents. President Monroe thus demonstrated the power of a president to speak for the nation in a way that—although lacking the force of law—created foreign policy that remains potent nearly two centuries later.*

## Introduction

L ong minimized as the "last of the Virginia dynasty," after Washington, Jefferson, and Madison, James Monroe played a much greater role in defining America's role in the world of the nineteenth century and beyond than he is traditionally given credit for. And in playing that role, he advanced the notion of a powerful executive beyond the bounds of either his Republican or his Federalist predecessors. He dealt with an ambitious military leader, Andrew Jackson, in a manner that forecast struggles over the role of the commander in chief up to and including the twentieth-century confrontation between President Harry Truman and General Douglas MacArthur. He managed the increasingly thorny issue of slavery in newly minted states through the Missouri Compromise. He was the first national security president. And, most definitively, he issued the Principles of 1823, better known as the Monroe Doctrine, that decreed European noninterference and therefore implicit U.S. hegemony, in the entire Western hemisphere—a decree that would echo down to the Cold War of the twentieth century.

The son of Spence Monroe, who was both a furniture maker and a farmer, and Elizabeth (Jones) Monroe, who was the daughter of an architect, James Monroe was born on April 28, 1758, in Westmoreland County, Virginia. His uncle Joseph Jones, known as "Judge" for his background on the judicial bench, claimed a "confidential" friendship with George Washington and close friendships with Thomas Jefferson and James Madison. James Monroe attended Parson Campbell's school, the elite Campbelltown Academy, where his time overlapped with a slightly older friend, John Marshall, future chief justice of the U.S. Supreme Court. Marshall would later join Monroe at the College of William and Mary and then in entering the Continental Army. During the war, a detachment of the Third Virginia Regiment— under the command of Captain William Washington and assisted by his lieutenant, an eighteen-year-old Monroe—played a key role in securing a crossroads north of Trenton, New Jersey, in the early hours of December 26, 1776, following George Washington's famous crossing of the Delaware River. This action helped guarantee the successful surprise attack on the Hessian garrison at Trenton. For his bravery, James Monroe was immortalized by the painter Emmanuel Leutze some seventy-five years later as the young uniformed officer holding the flag in the painting, now hanging in the nation's capitol, of *Washington Crossing the Delaware*. He was the last veteran of the American Revolution to serve as president.

Like his Virginian predecessors, Monroe arrived at the presidency after many years in a variety of assignments on behalf of the still-new nation. He served as a member of the Virginia Assembly and was elected to the Continental Congress. Although he was not a delegate to the Constitutional Convention in Philadelphia, Monroe served as a member of Virginia's state ratification convention. Here, he joined others, like George Mason, who opposed the proposed Constitution because it did not contain a bill of rights. After the Bill of Rights was added (Monroe lobbied James Madison to accomplish this end), Monroe became an ardent supporter of the finished Constitution.[1] By 1790, Monroe had been appointed to the U.S. Senate from Virginia and established himself as a leader in the Republican faction in the new U.S. Congress. Following Jefferson's example, he became minister to revolutionary France during the complex period produced by the Jay Treaty, after which he served as governor of the Virginia Commonwealth. He returned to Paris, then London and Madrid, as envoy extraordinaire tasked with resolving the complications raised by the Louisiana Purchase.[2] Monroe then served as secretary of state during the Madison administration in the run-up to the War of 1812 and thereafter as acting secretary of war (thus occupying two powerful cabinet positions simultaneously).

Ultimately, with his Federalist opponents in disarray, James Monroe was easily elected president in 1816. His success in presiding over an "Era of Good Feeling," in which partisan disputes gave way to a push for national unity, caused him to be overwhelmingly reelected in 1820. Indeed, all but one of the 232 electors voted for him in what one historian described as the "least-contested presidential race since Washington's unanimous election was decided."[3] Though none of Monroe's major decisions and controversies required Supreme Court adjudication, a number of significant events put him at the center of an evolving definition of executive authority under the Constitution.

## Presidency

### *General Jackson and the Florida Campaign*

For many years, slave owners in Georgia and other Southern states had lost slaves who managed to escape to the Florida swamps, where the fugitive slaves were protected by the Seminole and Creek people. Together, the Natives and the slaves periodically conducted cross-border raids on nearby plantations. Spain had refused to cede this territory to the United States. Therefore, President Monroe and his cabinet ordered the U.S. Army, in the form of the hero of New Orleans, General Andrew Jackson, to halt these activities and to pursue hostile Seminoles who were taking sanctuary at Spanish garrisons within the Florida Territory.[4] This Jackson did with dispatch and proceeded, on his own recognizance, to execute two British soldiers of fortune, then continued to Pensacola to drive the Spanish governor and his garrison from West Florida, as if single-handedly trying to seize the Florida Territory for the United States. Neither the British nor the Spanish, with both of whom the United States had complex relations, were amused by Jackson's brash actions.

These nations, along with some in Monroe's cabinet, insisted that General Jackson be censured for exceeding his orders. Even Secretary of War John Calhoun declared that Jackson had disobeyed orders. Yet Jackson stood firm, claiming that his orders authorized him to take the action he took. Monroe's secretary of state and eventual successor, John Quincy Adams, sided with Jackson on the grounds that communications from the field were slow (true) and that Jackson had acted from necessity based on the realities he encountered in his engagements (partly true). Given Jackson's widespread popularity, President Monroe walked a fine line between diplomacy and politics. Monroe tried to smooth over the dispute by suggesting that the orders were imprecise and that perhaps Jackson had misinterpreted them, even as Jackson maintained that he was absolutely correct in taking the actions in question.[5] Months after these incidents, Monroe sent Jackson a letter that stated: "In transcending the limit prescribed by those orders [limited to driving out the pirates] you acted on your own responsibility, on facts and circumstances which were unknown to the Government when the orders were given . . . and which you thought imposed on you the measure, as an act of patriotism, essential to the honor and interest of your country."[6] Thus, the message was being communicated to the British and Spanish: "He disobeyed orders and acted on his own." To Jackson and his public supporters, the message was different: "We understand that you thought you were acting in the national interest."

This bifurcated approach was probably reasonable, except that the United States, principally in the form of Secretary of State Adams, was negotiating with the Spanish to legitimately acquire Spain's interest in

East and West Florida and to expand the U.S. boundaries on the southern and western edges of the Louisiana Purchase to include the territory known as Texas. That Adams was able to proceed with these negotiations even as General Jackson continued to expand his operations in Florida was a tribute to the secretary's diplomatic skills. It was also, more importantly, a testament to the slowness of communications from the field in that day.

Andrew Jackson, being something of a national monument, at least to his followers, managed to keep the controversy between himself and Monroe active throughout the lives of both men. He wanted credit for his military successes without accepting the blame for exceeding his authority. Eventually, the United States successfully acquired the Floridas and, following the War with Mexico, Texas.

In the realm of U.S. foreign policy, President Monroe—like most of the chief executives who preceded him—faced major challenges. These included not only the Seminole Wars and the Louisiana Purchase boundary but also the eventual acquisition of Florida from the Spanish, the resolution of U.S. and Russian interests in the Northwest, and the multiple republican revolutions in South America.

Yet the controversy with Andrew Jackson was an early, if not the earliest, test of the president's authority as commander in chief. Indirectly, it was also a test of Congress's authority under the Constitution to wage war. Both episodes would echo down the halls of U.S. history even to today. As the Monroe-Jackson drama was playing out, however, the shadow of slavery was looming over the nation ever more ominously.

## The Missouri Question

Writing to Jefferson in early 1820, before his reelection, Monroe used the phrase: "The Missouri question, absorbs by its importance, & the excit'ment it has produc'd, every other & there is little prospect, from present appearances of its being soon settled."[7] In Monroe's time, the expanding nation was forced—by the application of the Missouri Territory for statehood in 1819—to confront an important issue purposely unresolved in the Constitution: What would the future of the country look like, in terms of the continuation of slavery? More specifically, could Congress require a territory to prohibit "the further introduction of slavery" within its borders as a condition of its admission into the Union?[8] Jefferson, among others, had foreseen the awful consequences this latent political and social time bomb represented. However, he chose not to try to resolve it, in the interest of first forming a constitutional republic delicately composed of a proslavery South and an antislavery North. The issue now was whether the West, in the expanding Union, would become pro- or antislavery.

The consensus of historians is that Monroe failed to demonstrate national leadership on the explosive slavery question, which was presented for resolution on the eve of his reelection in 1820. Despite being a son of slave-owning Virginia, Monroe had long since adopted the mantle of a national patriot, and his political and moral instincts placed the welfare of the nation first. For that reason, he believed that a resolution was required. And that resolution—later known as the Missouri Compromise—was presented to Monroe for his approval in the form of a compromise forged in the House of Representatives by Speaker Henry Clay (Kentucky) in February 1820. (Clay himself had mixed feelings; he publicly opposed slavery on moral grounds but continued to own slaves himself.)[9]

The Missouri Compromise admitted Maine to the Union as an antislavery state, admitted Missouri to the Union as a state at liberty to adopt or reject slavery, and prohibited slavery in all other parts of the Louisiana Purchase north of the 36-degree, 30-minute latitude, a westward extension of Missouri's southern border.

Monroe's initial, informal indication of support for the Missouri Compromise almost triggered revolt within Virginia's political establishment. He was advised by family and friends that if he signed the compromise, people in Virginia and throughout the South would "look for a new president" in 1820. Monroe therefore submitted to his cabinet the question of whether Congress had the authority under the Constitution to restrict slavery in new states. Monroe himself believed that Article IV, Section 3, of the Constitution established specific requirements for the admission of new states, and anything beyond that was unconstitutional.[10] The cabinet concluded unanimously, however, that the proposed compromise bill fell within Congress's authority. It turned out that Monroe's approval of the Missouri Compromise, which he signed on March 6, 1820, was a major factor in holding the Union together until the eve of the dreaded Civil War, some forty years later.

## Invoking the Constitution as a Symbol of Unity

Monroe placed a high priority on healing the divisions that had led to political strife under prior administrations. He often pointed to the Constitution as a symbol of national unity, urging fellow citizens to rally around it. In a speech delivered in Providence, Rhode Island, in June 1817, Monroe declared: "Living under a Constitution which secures equal civil, religious and political rights to all, it is a great consolation in administering it, that the people have formed so just an estimate of its value, and from a rational conviction and not from blind prejudices, are sincerely devoted to its preservation."[11]

Monroe himself exhibited a disciplined approach in interpreting, and adhering to, the Constitution. In 1822, when Congress passed an act for the collection of tolls for the maintenance of the National Road, Monroe vetoed it. Indeed, he wrote a lengthy essay explaining his veto. Collecting tolls, he believed, was beyond the proper function of the federal government. Private individuals and businesses, historically, had built toll roads and collected such fees. Monroe went so far as to send copies of his essay to justices on the Supreme Court. One response, from Justice William Johnson, opined that if the U.S. government had the power to build the road, it had the power to collect tolls to pay for it. Indeed, Johnson argued, the government already collected fees for many similar purposes (e.g., postage fees). Collecting tolls for toll roads was no different. Moved by the logic of this argument, President Monroe softened his position. When Congress later enacted laws appropriating funds for the construction and improvement of the National Road, the president signed them.[12] Thus, Monroe displayed the same open-mindedness and respect for the Constitution that he asked of all citizens.

## The Supreme Court

President Monroe made only one appointment to the Supreme Court— Justice Smith Thompson of New York, who joined the Court in 1823. Throughout Monroe's presidency, the Court continued to be dominated by Chief Justice John Marshall, who solidified his legacy with landmark decisions. One such opinion was *McCulloch v. Maryland*, decided in 1819, in which Marshall declared that Congress had the power to create a federal bank, even though the Constitution did not explicitly set forth that power.[13] The case arose when the state of Maryland sought to undermine the Bank of the United States by imposing a state tax on all bank notes not chartered within Maryland. Marshall recognized the threat to federal authority posed by the tax: "The power to tax involves the power to destroy."[14] To get around Maryland's assertion that the bank was unconstitutional, Marshall devised an ingenious opinion: He wrote that although the Constitution did not explicitly grant Congress the power to establish a bank, the Constitution did grant Congress the power to tax and spend and raise armies, and Congress's establishment of a bank was "necessary and proper" to exercise its taxing and spending and national defense power.[15]

Although Monroe generally disagreed with Marshall's decisions that limited state power, *McCulloch* was a notable exception.[16] While serving as James Madison's secretary of state during the War of 1812, Monroe had been the last cabinet member to leave Washington, D.C.—just before the British invaded and set fire to the Capitol Building and the White House. Upon returning to the city, Monroe had witnessed firsthand the destruction that had resulted from America's underfunded military. Because of this experience, both Madison and Monroe became convinced that America's military might was dependent on a strong national bank. They further believed that creating a bank was within Congress's powers, because the financial institution had operated without a problem for twenty years. After decades of national debate on this issue, Marshall and the rest of the Supreme Court ultimately endorsed this view in *McCulloch*.[17] Monroe, a lifelong friend of Marshall's, did not always agree ideologically with the chief justice.[18] On this issue of national importance, however, they found common ground.

## Monroe's Historic Doctrine

Though the Monroe Doctrine relating to European ventures in the Western Hemisphere has never been enshrined in law, it has dominated and guided American foreign policy since the time it was adopted more than any formalized treaty. Also known as the Principles of 1823, it declared the dominant interest of the United States not only in North America but in all of Latin America as well. This statement was prompted by the rise of republican revolutions throughout much of Latin America in the early 1800s, in which Spanish colonial leaders and puppets were overthrown throughout much of the continent.

The Monroe Doctrine would come to define America's role in the world for almost two centuries, if not longer. Moreover, this period provides a fascinating study in idealism versus realism. The South American colonies struggling for their freedom looked to the United States as the hope and beacon of democracy and liberty. But they did so at a time when the United States was deeply engaged in negotiations with the Spanish, as well as with the French and British, over acquiring their territories and limiting their ambitions on the North American continent. Thus, if American leaders had wished to side with the idealism of the emerging postcolonial people and their republican aspirations, the leaders would have taken sides against the established European powers whose goodwill the United States was seeking for a large number of significant purposes.

What the South American revolutionaries wanted was U.S. diplomatic recognition and protection of their fledgling democracies. Public sentiment in the United States was strongly in favor of these revolutions. In recognition of the moral dimensions of the dilemma, Monroe sent a letter to Congress, which stated: "With respect to the [South American] Colonies, the object has been to throw into their scale, in a moral sense, the weight of the United States, without so deep a commitment as to make us a party to the contest. . . . By taking this ground openly and frankly, we acquit ourselves to our own consciences."[19]

The Transcontinental Treaty with Spain, ratified by the United States in 1821, gave the United States full possession of Florida and extended the southern boundary of the Louisiana Purchase all the way to present-day Oregon. With that matter resolved, Monroe and the U.S. government were free to follow their conscience fully in South America. As early as 1821, Adams had notified the Russian minister in Washington that the "American continents are no longer subjects for any new European colonial establishments" and later proclaimed that, with the exception of the British presence in Canada, "the remainder of both the American continents must henceforth be left to the management of American hands."[20]

When Great Britain proposed in the summer of 1823 a joint effort to prevent Spain and its allies from seeking to reestablish their authority over the newly independent countries in Latin America, President Monroe asked his friends and predecessors, Jefferson and Madison, for their advice. Monroe was already mulling over what would become of the Principles of 1823. Jefferson responded to Monroe's query: "The question presented by the letters you have sent me, is the most momentous which has been ever offered to my contemplation since that of Independence . . . that made us a nation. This sets our compass and points the course which we are to steer thro' the ocean of time."[21]

In his seventh message to Congress, on December 2, 1823, President Monroe provided a declaration of national principles that would guide U.S. policy in this hemisphere, but that would never be formally codified in any treaty, statute, or proclamation. These principles were contained in three central paragraphs of the message, the first of which read: "The American continents, by the free and independent condition which they have assumed and maintained, are henceforth not to be considered as subjects for future colonization by any European power."[22]

The second principle was contained in a longer paragraph asserting U.S. resistance to being drawn into European wars, if for no other reason than that the European powers were monarchies and the United States was a republic. It continued: "We should consider any attempt on [the European nations'] part to extend their system to any portion of the hemisphere as dangerous to our peace and safety."[23]

The third major principle was a restatement of traditional American attitudes toward European powers and the "wars which have long agitated that quarter of the globe." Simply stated, the message was this: The United States would not interfere in the internal concerns of any powers, but rather would recognize existing governments and "cultivate friendly relations with them."[24]

Reduced to a single proposition today, the Monroe Doctrine could be summarized as follows: The United States will resist hegemony without seeking hegemony.[25] Within two years, Henry Clay, by then President John Quincy Adams's secretary of state, would cite the Principles of 1823 as established gospel; Daniel Webster would do the same shortly thereafter. Indeed, well into the twentieth century, the Spanish diplomat Salvador de Madariaga summarized it as follows: "The Monroe Doctrine is not a doctrine but a dogma . . . not one dogma but two, to wit: the dogma of the infallibility of the American President and the dogma of the immaculate conception of American foreign policy."[26]

The American historian Arthur Schlesinger Jr. later noted that the Monroe Doctrine was neither self-enforcing nor congressionally ratified: "Still, the Monroe Doctrine, if neither authorized nor ratified, was a notable and unchallenged national commitment."[27] As much as any of his four predecessors in the presidency, James Monroe, with strong support from Secretary of

State John Quincy Adams, who succeeded him in the White House, solidified the authority of the executive over foreign policy and established the definition of America's role in the world. Monroe did not request congressional approval of these principles. He told Congress what they were, and these pronouncements came to be recognized as American gospel.

The durability of James Monroe's signature achievement could be seen over a century later during a tense moment during the Cold War. Warning the United States to keep its hands off Cuba in 1960, the Soviet Union pronounced the doctrine "dead." The U.S. Department of State issued this sharp statement in response: "The principles of the Monroe Doctrine are as valid today as they were in 1823 when the Doctrine was proclaimed."[28]

Thus, even though the power of the president to declare and establish foreign policy is nowhere expressly set forth in the Constitution, Monroe carried out that power in a bold and forward-thinking fashion, forever changing the American presidency.

## Conclusion

Among Southern Republicans like James Monroe, it was an article of faith, based on classic republican theory from the time of ancient Athens forward, that a standing army was a danger to a republic. Yet, as president, Monroe increased America's military fortifications and doubled the size of the standing army. As a second-generation founder, he fully appreciated the emerging importance of the United States in world affairs. Having witnessed U.S. vulnerabilities during the War of 1812, he was determined not to let his nation be invaded or threatened by European powers. Further, if the United States were to declare the entire Western Hemisphere, excepting Canada, off-limits to foreign intervention, he believed the country must be prepared to enforce that principle. Thus, the Monroe Doctrine represented a decisive step for the new nation.

The Monroe presidency, from 1816 through 1824, was also historic in its consolidation of the Louisiana Purchase and other lands all the way to the Pacific as the American continent. In addition to adding East and West Florida and extending the reach of the Louisiana Purchase to the Pacific, President Monroe laid claim to the Oregon Territory beyond the Columbia River by pushing Russian outposts northward of the 54th parallel.

Monroe lacked Thomas Jefferson's incredibly diverse mind and James Madison's brilliant understanding of political theory. However, his one great insight was his grasp of the historic difference between Europe's dedication to monarchy and America's unprecedented commitment to the creation of a republic on a scale never before realized. To complete that experiment, the United States, even as it increased trade and commerce with Europe and the rest of the world, had to partition itself off politically from Europe. Monroe's actions illustrate that he understood that monarchy was an infectious virus to a republic and had to be quarantined on its side of the Atlantic.

Few national political figures of the day could have read the compass so accurately and guided the ship of state as surely in these rapidly shifting currents. Yet James Monroe managed to do this despite his ostensible lack of the kind of genius that marked his Virginia predecessors. For his efforts, he deserves higher marks for his leadership in the nation's critical formative years than he has traditionally been given.

Like his three predecessors to occupy the presidency—Washington, Jefferson, and Madison—James Monroe opted to serve only two terms, paving the way for his secretary of state, John Quincy Adams, to win the presidential election of 1824. Because of his wife Elizabeth's illness, Monroe stayed in the White House for three weeks after the inauguration, until his wife was fit to travel. In his later years, after Elizabeth's death in 1830, Monroe moved to New York City to reside with his daughter and her family. Although his own health was failing, he continued to entertain guests and maintained a keen interest in the affairs of government.

James Monroe died in New York City five years to the day after his friend and mentor, Thomas Jefferson, died at Monticello. The date was Independence Day—July 4, 1831.

NOTES

1. Harry Ammon, *James Monroe: The Quest for National Identity* (Charlottesville: University of Virginia Press, 1990), 68–73.
2. In his capacity as envoy extraordinaire, Monroe had to deal with Robert Livingston, then U.S. minister to France, in conducting negotiations to acquire the Floridas. Livingston pressed the unlikely argument that the French had possessed the Floridas as part of its ownership of Louisiana and therefore that the United States had already acquired the Floridas in the Louisiana Purchase. Henry Adams, *History of the United States During the Administrations of Thomas Jefferson* (New York: Library of America, 1986), 292.
3. Noble E. Cunningham, *The Presidency of James Monroe* (Lawrence: University Press of Kansas Press, 1996), 106.

4. W. P. Cressen, *James Monroe* (Chapel Hill: University of North Carolina Press, 1946), 301–308.

5. Ibid., 311–317.

6. James Monroe to Andrew Jackson, in James Lucier, ed., *The Political Writings of James Monroe* (Washington, DC: Regnery, 2001), 502–506.

7. James Monroe to Thomas Jefferson, February 7, 1820, in Lucier, *Political Writings*, 516–517.

8. Robert Forbes, *The Missouri Compromise and Its Aftermath* (Chapel Hill: University of North Carolina Press, 2007), 327.

9. David S. Heider, *Henry S. Clay: The Essential American* (New York: Random House, 2010).

10. See generally Forbes, *The Missouri Compromise and Its Aftermath*.

11. Samuel Putnam Waldo, *The Tour of James Monroe, President of the United States, in the Year 1817* (Hartford, CT: F.D. Bowles & Company, 1818), 122.

12. Cressen, *James Monroe*, 385–398; William Johnson to James Monroe, undated, Monroe Papers, Library of Congress, June 1822 folder. Two bills that Monroe signed relating to the National Road were dated February 28, 1823 (Statutes at Large, 3:728), and March 3, 1825 (Statutes at Large, 4:128).

13. McCulloch v. Maryland, 17 U.S. (4 Wheat.) 316 (1819).

14. Ibid., 431.

15. Ibid., 413–417.

16. Harlow Giles Unger, *The Last Founding Father: James Monroe and a Nation's Call to Greatness* (Cambridge, MA: Da Capo Press, 2009), 264. Although Monroe ideologically opposed limits on state authority, he took advantage of the expansive view of federal power heralded in by the Marshall Supreme Court, using it to increase American prosperity during the Era of Good Feelings. Ibid.

17. Cunningham, *Presidency of James Monroe*, 3, 81–82. See also Chapter 4, "James Madison," for a discussion on President Madison's views on the constitutionality of the bank.

18. The two men had been childhood neighbors, then continued their friendship at the College of William and Mary, and also in the Continental Army during the American Revolution. Despite their ideological differences, the two remained close through the years (late in life, Monroe would treasure a letter from Marshall congratulating the former president on his retirement and his illustrious career as a public servant). Gary Hart, *James Monroe* (New York: Times Books, 2005), 12, 147–148.

19. Harry Ammon, *James Monroe: The Quest for National Identity* (Charlottesville: University of Virginia Press, 1990), 481–482. It is instructive for modern-day Americans to keep in mind that during the Cold War, the United States supported more than a few dictators in various parts of the world, for the simple reason that they opposed the communist bloc. To use Jefferson's famous "head and heart" analogy, America's posture in world affairs has swung from head (realism) to heart (idealism) and back quite often, with the head winning more bouts than the heart.

20. Cunningham, *Presidency of James Monroe*, 149–163.

21. Thomas Jefferson to James Monroe, October 24, 1823, in Lucier, *Political Writings*, 633.

22. Lucier, *Political Writings*, 649.

23. Ibid., 650.

24. Ibid.

25. For a more detailed dissection of the three basic principles, see Hart, *James Monroe*, 123.

26. Salvador de Madariaga, *Latin America Between the Eagle and the Bear* (New York: Praeger, 1962), quoted as an epigraph in Donald Marquand Dozer, *The Monroe Doctrine: Its Modern Significance* (New York: Alfred A. Knopf), 1965.

27. Arthur Schlesinger Jr., *The Imperial Presidency* (Boston: Houghton Mifflin, 1973), 27.

28. Dozer, *The Monroe Doctrine*, 18.

# 6

# John Quincy Adams

JONATHAN L. ENTIN

*John Quincy Adams, the son of the second president, is generally viewed as a failed chief executive. A respected diplomat who became secretary of state under President James Monroe, JQ Adams won the contested 1824 election with the support of Speaker Henry Clay, whose endorsement led to Adams's selection by the House of Representatives under the Twelfth Amendment. The so-called corrupt bargain haunted him throughout his presidency. Although his time in the White House was largely uninspired, JQ Adams went on to gain election to the House of Representatives, where he ultimately faced censure for his strong antislavery views. The only president to serve in the House of Representatives after leaving the White House, Adams collapsed during a roll call on the House floor, after calling out an objection to the Mexican War, and died two days later.*

## Introduction

John Quincy Adams had several distinctions: the first president whose father had held the office; the first president who had not obtained even a plurality of the popular vote; the last president chosen by the House of Representatives; and the only president to serve in the House of Representatives after leaving the White House.[1] In many ways, Adams can fairly be viewed as a less-than-successful chief executive. Yet he had an extraordinary career in public service and confronted important constitutional issues at several stages of that career.

Adams seemed destined for public service. He was born on July 11, 1767, in what is now Quincy, Massachusetts (then part of Braintree), the second child and first son of John and Abigail (Smith) Adams. The seven-year-old Johnny watched the Battle of Bunker Hill in June 1775 from a Quincy hillside.[2] Before long, he would be more deeply affected by events surrounding the American Revolution.

Early in 1778, the ten-year-old boy accompanied his father to Paris on a diplomatic mission. John Adams returned to Massachusetts in 1780. Shortly thereafter, when the Continental Congress sent the elder Adams back to Paris, the twelve-year-old son accompanied his father again. At age fourteen, young Adams went to St. Petersburg to serve as secretary to Francis Dana, an American representative in Russia; the boy's fluency in French, the language of diplomatic discourse, made him indispensable to Dana. In late 1782, young Adams rejoined his father in Paris, where the youth performed secretarial duties during the negotiations that resulted in the treaty that ended the Revolutionary War.[3]

Returning home in 1785, John Quincy Adams gained admission to Harvard with advanced standing and graduated second in the class of 1787.[4] He thereafter opened a law office in Boston after being admitted to the bar in July 1790.

### Beginnings of a Political Career

But Adams's heart was not really in pursuing that profession. In 1791, he published the *Letters of Publicola*, a response to Thomas Paine's *The Rights of Man*, which defended the virtues of republicanism over the excesses of democracy exemplified by the French Revolution. Then, beginning in the summer of 1793, Adams published another set of pseudonymous letters defending President Washington's Proclamation of Neutrality and strongly criticizing French minister Edmond Genêt's pointed attacks on Washington for the proclamation.[5]

These letters gained wide attention and led to diplomatic appointments in the Netherlands, London (where Adams met and married Louisa Catherine Johnson, daughter of the American consul), and Portugal. Before JQ Adams could take up the latter assignment, the incoming chief executive, President John Adams, appointed his son as minister to Prussia.[6] Young Adams remained in this post until after the 1800 election, when his father, defeated for reelection, recalled the son from Europe so that the diplomat could avoid the embarrassment of being replaced by a Jefferson appointee in the wake of the contentious presidential campaign.[7]

In April 1802, a few months after his return home, John Quincy Adams was elected to the Massachusetts State Senate. After he made an unsuccessful run for Congress, the legislature in 1803 chose him as a U.S. senator. Although he was a Federalist, Adams broke with his party to support the Louisiana Purchase and in other ways bucked his party. When it became clear that the Federalist-controlled Massachusetts legislature would not renew his position, Adams resigned in June 1808, nearly a full year before his term expired.[8]

During his time in the Senate, Adams also developed a critique of the three-fifths compromise that counted slaves (euphemistically described as "all other Persons" in Article I, Section 2, Clause 3, of the U.S. Constitution) for purposes of apportioning seats in the House of Representatives and direct taxes. Foreshadowing his post–White House years in Congress, Adams argued that this compromise enhanced the political power of the slave states and that the South's rigid opposition to the imposition of direct taxes undercut the rationale for the compromise.[9]

In law practice, JQ Adams's most notable case was *Fletcher v. Peck*, a leading case on the Contracts Clause of the Constitution, which forbade states from passing laws that "impair the Obligation of Contracts."[10] A few days after his appearance at the initial argument in the Supreme Court, the newly inaugurated President Madison appointed Adams the first minister to Russia.[11] Adams so much enjoyed his diplomatic work that he declined an appointment to the Supreme Court in 1811.[12] He remained in St. Petersburg as the War of 1812 broke out less than a week before Napoléon invaded Russia. President Madison then named Adams to head the American delegation that negotiated the Treaty of Ghent, which ended the war with Great Britain, and next to serve as minister to London, a position that Adams held until incoming President James Monroe appointed him secretary of state.[13]

In this capacity, Adams played a pivotal role in the development of the Monroe Doctrine. As early as his 1821 Fourth of July address, Adams emphasized that the Western Hemisphere was not open to colonization by European or other powers. Monroe's cabinet extensively discussed these ideas, which the president included in his own 1823 Annual Message to Congress.[14]

In addition, while Adams played no direct role in the debate over the Missouri Compromise, he followed the debate as a member of the cabinet and began to develop his own views on the subject. Ambivalent about slavery but not yet committed to abolition, he feared that the nation eventually would go to war over the issue. Nevertheless, he supported the Missouri Compromise as an expedient that might put off the day of reckoning.[15]

## The Contested Election of 1824

The 1824 election turned out to be a crucial test of the Twelfth Amendment's new system for choosing the president.[16] Adopted in 1804, the amendment provided for the separate election of the president and vice president by the Electoral College and provided that if no candidate for president attained a majority of votes, the House of Representatives would select the president.

Four principal rivals had vied to succeed the outgoing President James Monroe: General Andrew Jackson; Secretary of Treasury William H. Crawford; Speaker of the House Henry Clay; and Secretary of State JQ Adams. No candidate received a majority of either the popular vote or the Electoral College vote. Thus, pursuant to the Twelfth Amendment, the presidential contest was thrown into the House of Representatives, with each state casting one vote. Because only the top three candidates in the Electoral College could be considered by the House, Clay was eliminated. Ironically, this made Clay the kingmaker; the remaining candidates now jockeyed to pick up the powerful Speaker's support.[17] Although the legislature in Clay's home state of Kentucky strongly endorsed Jackson, Clay threw his support to Adams after the two men held a private meeting. In early February, the House chose Adams as the new president on its first ballot. Jackson and his supporters were outraged, claiming that Adams and Clay had entered into a "corrupt bargain." Their outrage increased after Adams appointed Clay as secretary of state, seemingly confirming that the Speaker had effectively sold his support to gain the office.

## Presidency

### The Role of the Federal Government

Adams had an expansive view of federal authority when it came to promoting internal improvements that went beyond building roads, canals and bridges. This outlook was evident in his first State of the Union message to Congress, near the end of his first year in the White House. Adams proposed a federal bankruptcy statute, a naval academy, a national university, a national astronomical observatory, a separate department of the interior, and a reformed patent law.[18] None of these proposals came to fruition during his administration.[19] The U.S. Naval Observatory was established in 1830, a new patent act in 1836, the U.S. Naval Academy in 1845, the Department of the Interior in 1849, and the first bankruptcy code was not adopted until 1898.

Although these proposals languished, the Adams administration still undertook widespread internal improvements, believing these to be within the scope of the federal government's constitutional powers. Among these initiatives were the extension of the National Road into Ohio, the construction of new canals (including the Ohio Canal and the Chesapeake & Ohio Canal), and the development of railways (notably the Baltimore & Ohio Railroad).[20] In this respect, Adams embraced a capacious view of the chief executive's (and the federal government's) power, even in a sphere many believed should be reserved for the states.

### Presidential Removal Power

The scope of executive power has been a hardy perennial of American law and politics. While Article II of the Constitution speaks to the president's power to appoint certain government officials, it makes no express mention of the president's power (if any) to remove them.

In his inaugural speech, President John Quincy Adams promised to rely on "talents and virtue alone" in constructing his administration.[21] Accordingly, Adams sought to avoid the appearance of partisanship in his appointments. Moreover, he removed only a dozen officials during his single term in the White House. Although so few removals might conceivably reflect a limited view of the executive's constitutional power of removal, Adams's reluctance to remove appointed officials more likely confirms that he felt himself personally constrained from doing so. Having been chosen by the House of Representatives and seen by many as owing his office to the "corrupt bargain" with Clay, Adams believed that using the removal power too aggressively would confirm suspicions that his seemingly patrician commitment to merit was hypocritical. But his reluctance to use removals to impose his stamp on the administration left him in the awkward position of tolerating many people who did not support him, including at least one cabinet member and numerous lower-level appointees in other agencies. Moreover, when Adams did engage in party-building activities on behalf of what ultimately became the National Republican Party, he was denounced as a political hack. Critics in what came to be called the Democratic-Republican Party (including supporters of Andrew Jackson) emphasized the unsavory deal with Clay that put Adams into the White House.[22]

## The Tariff Issue

The so-called National Republicans lost control of both houses of Congress in the 1826 election. They supported protective tariffs, while the South traditionally opposed them. The Democratic-Republicans sought to embarrass President Adams by proposing a tariff bill containing features that the North would oppose, thereby casting blame for the rejection on the region that traditionally supported tariffs. The 1828 Tariff Act was indeed a Jacksonian political ploy.[23] The Jacksonians apparently miscalculated, however. Although the bill was full of provisions that everyone disliked, it also contained enough attractive features that the "Tariff of Abominations" passed both the House and the Senate. Adams found many of the bill's provisions objectionable but declined to veto the bill and signed it into law. He believed that a presidential veto exercised under Article I, Section 7, of the Constitution could be justified only if a measure was unconstitutional; this one, in his view, was only unwise and foolish.[24]

Thus, Adams apparently maintained an old-fashioned view of the president's veto power, eschewing political calculations and sticking strictly to constitutional appraisals of the bill at hand.

## Post-Presidency: Congressional Career

John Quincy Adams lost the 1828 election to Andrew Jackson, with Jacksonians campaigning on the "corrupt bargain" that Adams had entered with Clay to capture the presidency. Jackson extracted his revenge, with 56 percent of the popular vote, winning the South and West overwhelmingly.[25] Although Adams (like his father) became a one-term president, his sojourn in private life was brief. He did what no previous president had done and sought a position of public service in Congress after leaving the White House. (Indeed, Congress was viewed as the most powerful branch of the new American government.) In November 1830, Adams was elected to the House of Representatives, where he served for the next seventeen years, the only former president to serve in this capacity.

Representative Adams took a leading role on several issues with important constitutional implications. No sooner had he taken his seat in 1831 than he was appointed to chair the Committee on Manufactures, which had jurisdiction over tariff and trade issues. With the bitterness over the so-called Tariff of Abominations still fresh in memory, the committee produced a compromise bill that lowered tariffs on British textiles containing large amounts of U.S. cotton. Yet some cotton growers in the South objected to any tariff at all. A special convention in South Carolina declared that both the Tariff of Abominations and the new 1832 tariff act were unconstitutional and that the state would exercise its power to nullify these oppressive federal measures. In light of the Supremacy Clause contained in Article VI of the Constitution, Representative Adams strongly rejected nullification of federal law by states, as did President Jackson, who threatened military force to uphold federal law.[26]

It was with regard to slavery, however, that Adams made his most important mark in Congress. On his first day in the House, he presented petitions from some Pennsylvania Quakers seeking to end slavery in the District of Columbia. This move violated an implicit norm of silence on the subject of abolition. Although he disliked slavery, Adams was no abolitionist. Now, in the final stage of his public career, he decided to make abolition his signature issue.[27]

Initially, Adams sought only to present petitions but did not openly express support for abolition. Even the thought of having the topic anywhere on the congressional agenda, however, was too much for many Southerners. When the House subjected slavery-related petitions to an effective gag rule in 1836, Adams's views about slavery became more pronounced.[28] No longer content simply to present antislavery petitions, he actively sought to curtail the peculiar institution. In late 1840, he agreed to help represent fifty-three Africans who had been held as slaves in Cuba. They mutinied against the crew of a ship called *Amistad* but were brought to American shores, where a complex set of proceedings culminated in the Africans being set free. Adams played an important role in that case, presenting a powerful argument against slavery to the Supreme Court, although the case was resolved on narrower grounds than what Adams had advanced.[29] Adams thus established himself as a leading voice in the United States on the subject of slavery (see Chapter 8, "Martin Van Buren").

Meanwhile, his continuing opposition to the gag rule eventually bore fruit. The first time he challenged the rule, in February 1837, he was stymied but won something of a Pyrrhic victory. When he attempted to introduce a petition from a group of slaves but was cut off under the gag rule, one avid slavery defender demanded that Adams be censured. This move backfired, because under House rules, Adams was able to speak on his own behalf on the censure motion (even though he could not discuss the slavery petition that gave rise to the motion). Through Adams's eloquent defense of his own actions, the attempted censure failed.[30]

Adams faced a second censure motion in January 1842 after introducing a petition from residents of Haverhill, Massachusetts, calling for the dissolution of the Union. An outraged Kentuckian moved to censure Adams for treasonously presenting the petition. The debate on the censure motion eventually included extensive discussion of slavery because one supporter of the censure motion defended the practice. After two weeks of debate, Adams acquiesced in a motion to table, which carried, thereby ending the second censure effort but leaving the gag rule in place.[31] The gag rule was eventually rescinded in December 1844, on Adams's motion.[32]

## Conclusion

John Quincy Adams died in Washington on February 23, 1848, two days after collapsing on the House floor during a roll call.[33] Adams is widely viewed as a failed president, but he had an extraordinary public career that spanned nearly six decades as a diplomat, legislator, and chief executive. As the only president to pursue an active career in Congress after his tenure in the White House, Adams became an early and influential voice against the institution of slavery in the United States and died in office while standing up for his deeply held principles. He is buried next to his father—the second president of the United States—beneath the Quincy, Massachusetts, church where the Adams family worshipped.

### NOTES

1. The only other president's son to occupy the White House was George W. Bush, whose father was George H. W. Bush. The younger Bush also lost the popular vote. The only other elected president who failed to receive at least a plurality of the popular vote was Rutherford B. Hayes, who was chosen by a special commission that awarded him the disputed electoral votes of three Southern states. The only former chief executive to serve in the Senate was Andrew Johnson, who died a few months after taking his seat in 1875.
2. Fred Kaplan, *John Quincy Adams: American Visionary* (New York: Harper, 2014), 12–14; Harlow Giles Unger, *John Quincy Adams* (Boston: Da Capo Press, 2012), 14–17.
3. Marie B. Hecht, *John Quincy Adams: A Personal History of an Independent Man* (New York: Macmillan, 1972), 19–36; Paul C. Nagel, *John Quincy Adams: A Public Life, a Private Life* (New York: Alfred A. Knopf, 1997), 12–26, 31–32; Unger, *John Quincy Adams*, 24–54.
4. Hecht, *A Personal History*, 43–58; Nagel, *A Public Life*, 39–56, 62–68; Unger, *John Quincy Adams*, 61–67, 69.
5. Hecht, *A Personal History*, 62–68, 71–73; Nagel, *A Public Life*, 70, 73–76; Unger, *John Quincy Adams*, 71–79 .
6. Lynn Hudson Parsons, *John Quincy Adams* (Madison, WI: Madison House, 1998), 55–57.
7. Hecht, *A Personal History*, 76–137; Nagel, *A Public Life*, 77–126; Unger, *John Quincy Adams*, 82–119.
8. Hecht, *A Personal History*, 142–145, 147–149, 176–181; Kaplan, *American Visionary*, 187–190, 193–196, 197–200, 237–246; Nagel, *A Public Life*, 135–140, 144–145, 171–172, 174–180; Unger, *John Quincy Adams*, 122, 126–131, 140–144.
9. Hecht, *A Personal History*, 153–154; Kaplan, *American* Visionary, 214–116.
10. Fletcher v. Peck, 10 U.S. (6 Cranch) 87 (1810). For a comprehensive analysis of the case, see C. Peter Magrath, *Yazoo: Law and Politics in the New Republic* (Providence, RI:

Brown University Press, 1966). For "impair the Obligation of Contracts," see U.S. Const. art. I, § 10, cl. 1.

11. Hecht, *A Personal History*, 182–184; Kaplan, *American* Visionary, 250–253; Nagel, *A Public Life*, 182–183; Unger, *John Quincy Adams*, 145–147.

12. Kaplan, *American Visionary*, 270–271; Nagel, *A Public Life*, 198–199; Unger, *John Quincy Adams*, 157.

13. Kaplan, *American Visionary*, 276–277, 291–295, 302, 318; Nagel, *A Public Life*, 205–207, 217, 232–233; Unger, *John Quincy Adams*, 163–164, 167, 174–177, 190.

14. Kaplan, *American Visionary*, 380–385; Nagel, *A Public Life*, 269–271; Unger, *John Quincy Adams*, 217–219.

15. Kaplan, *American Visionary*, 353–355; William Lee Miller, *Arguing About Slavery: The Great Battle in the United States Congress* (New York: Alfred A. Knopf, 1995), 182–193; Nagel, *A Public Life*, 265–266; Unger, *John Quincy Adams*, 210–215.

16. The discussion in this section is based on Kaplan, *American Visionary*, 385–393; Nagel, *A Public Life*, 286–289, 291–294; Unger, *John Quincy Adams*, 229–233, 235–236.

17. Adding to the irony, John Q. Adams had opposed the Twelfth Amendment while a senator. If that amendment had not passed, the number of finalists would have remained at five, and most historians believe that Henry Clay—not Adams—would have been elected. Parsons, *John Quincy Adams*, 171.

18. John Quincy Adams, First Annual Message, December 6, 1825, in *Messages and Papers of the Presidents*, ed. James D. Richardson (Washington, DC: Government Printing Office, 1897), 865, 869, 876, 878–881.

19. Adams believed that the Constitution also empowered the president and Congress to advance moral and intellectual improvements as well. Parsons, *John Quincy Adams*, 179–180.

20. Mary W. M. Hargreaves, *The Presidency of John Quincy Adams* (Lawrence: University Press of Kansas, 1985), 173–180.

21. John Quincy Adams, Inaugural Address, March 4, 1825, in *Messages and Papers of the Presidents*, ed. James D. Richardson (Washington, DC: Government Printing Office, 1897), 860, 863.

22. Stephen Skowronek, *The Politics Presidents Make: Leadership from John Adams to George Bush* (Cambridge, MA: Belknap Press of Harvard University Press, 1993), 120–126.

23. Act of May 19, 1828, ch. LV, 4 Stat. 270 (repealed 1832). The 1828 Tariff Act ultimately precipitated the nullification crisis that Jackson confronted as president.

24. Hargreaves, *The Presidency of John Quincy Adams*, 190–196; Kaplan, *American* Visionary, 433–434; Robert V. Remini, *John Quincy Adams* (Times Books, 2002), 112–116.

25. Hargreaves, *Presidency of John Quincy Adams*, 295; Kaplan, *American Visionary*, 433; Nagel, *A Public Life*, 321.

26. Kaplan, *American Visionary*, 458–460, 461–462; Remini, *John Quincy Adams*, 132–133; Unger, *John Quincy Adams*, 269–270, 271.

27. Miller, *Arguing About Slavery*, 197; Unger, *John Quincy Adams*, 266–267.

28. Kaplan, *American Visionary*, 490–491; Miller, *Arguing about Slavery*, 140–149, 209–210; Unger, *John Quincy Adams*, 273–274. Ironically, the gag rule was not part of Pinckney's original proposal. In fact, Pinckney faced intense condemnation and ultimately lost his

seat for failing to characterize congressional interference with slavery in the District of Columbia as unconstitutional. Miller, *Arguing About Slavery*, 145–146.

29. United States v. The Amistad, 40 U.S. (15 Peters) 518 (1841). Parsons, *John Quincy Adams*, 239–240. Unfortunately, Adams did not submit a written version of his "able and interesting argument," so it does not appear in the report of the case. Ibid., 566. For detailed accounts of the case, see Howard Jones, *Mutiny on the Amistad: The Saga of a Slave Revolt and Its Impact on American Abolition, Law, and Diplomacy* (New York: Oxford University Press, 1987); Marcus Rediker, *The Amistad Rebellion: An Atlantic Odyssey of Slavery and Freedom* (New York: Viking, 2012). On Adams, see Jones, *Mutiny on the Amistad*, 145–148, 155–160, 175–182; Rediker, *The Amistad Rebellion*, 188, 189–190.

30. Kaplan, *American Visionary*, 493–494.

31. Ibid., 540–541; Nagel, *A Public Life*, 385–386; Unger, *John Quincy Adams*, 298–302.

32. Miller, *Arguing About Slavery*, 476.

33. Parsons, *John Quincy Adams*, xiii–xiv; Kaplan, *American Visionary*, 450–452, 569–570; Nagel, *A Public Life*, 336, 414; Unger, *John Quincy Adams*, 262, 308–310.

PART II

# The Age of Jackson

# 7

# Andrew Jackson

MARK A. GRABER

*Andrew Jackson ushered in a new age, in which populist democracy (at least for white males) was favored over the more deferential politics of an earlier era. During Jackson's presidency, the country stopped doing business with the Bank of the United States and left the business of internal improvements largely to the states, but it condemned Southern states that sought to ignore federal protective tariffs and it threatened military action against them. Jackson relied on public support in national elections to justify expansive presidential powers. All told, the Jackson era ended the founding notion that the presidency was above politics and joined the two, indissolubly.*

## Introduction

Andrew Jackson was the first president who was neither a founder nor personally connected to the founders. George Washington, John Adams, and Thomas Jefferson were members of the Continental Congress. Washington and James Madison played crucial roles in the convention that drafted the Constitution. James Monroe and Madison were members of the Virginia ratification convention. John Quincy Adams was the son of a founder and personally connected to other prominent New England founders. Andrew Jackson was too young at the time to participate meaningfully in either the Revolution or any constitutional convention, and he lacked personal, professional, or political associations with any prominent revolutionary or framer.

In any nation, second-generation political leaders must decide whether to accept, reject, or modify the constitutional commitments of the first generation. The average national constitution lasts seventeen years or about one generation of political leadership, in part because second-generation leaders in many countries prefer new constitutions that reflect their distinctive perspectives.[1] President Jackson, by comparison, insisted that constitutional fidelity was the key to national prosperity. His 1837 farewell address asserted this point: "Our Constitution is no longer a doubtful experiment and at the end of nearly half a century we find that it has preserved unimpaired the liberties of the people, secured the rights of property, and that our country has improved and is flourishing beyond any former example in the history of nations."[2]

Yet Jackson's observations undeniably played a major role in what James Madison described as the "particular discussions and adjudications" that helped to "ascertain" the meaning of the Constitution before the Civil War.[3] Jackson initiated a distinctive generational perspective on the American constitutional order, one that his immediate successors expanded and his later successors, after the Civil War, decisively abandoned.[4] Whether Jackson was constitutionally faithful, as he claimed, or a constitutional usurper, as Whigs such as Henry Clay insisted, remains open to debate.

Jackson was born on March 15, 1767, in Waxhaw, South Carolina. During his youth, he fought as an underage soldier in the Revolution, read law, and dueled. In 1788, Jackson moved to Nashville, Tennessee, where in the

1790s he twice married Rachel Donelson Robards, the second marriage being necessary because Robards may not have been legally divorced from her first husband when she and Jackson first married.

Jackson prospered economically and politically in Tennessee. He gained national attention during the War of 1812 for his victories over Native American tribes and for his stunning victory over British forces in January 1815 in the Battle of New Orleans. Jackson solidified both his national military repudiation and his reputation for playing fast and loose with legalities from 1818 to 1820 during the Seminole Wars in Florida.

Jackson soon parlayed his military cachet into a political career. He served a very short term as territorial governor of Florida and then represented Tennessee in the U.S. Senate from 1823 to 1825. Jackson received a plurality of both the electoral and popular votes in the 1824 presidential election, but he failed to obtain the majority of electoral votes mandated by the Constitution. As described in an earlier chapter, the election was thrown into the House of Representatives, where Henry Clay, a rival candidate, threw his support to John Quincy Adams. Clay's support proved sufficient for the latter to triumph. Charging that a "corrupt bargain" had been struck, Jackson and his supporters were vindicated when Jackson easily defeated Adams in their 1828 rematch.

## Presidency

Jackson's political and constitutional positions were unclear when he took office in 1829. His supporters in 1828 included persons for and against almost every popular proposal in early American constitutional politics. Future president Martin Van Buren, a prominent opponent of the Second Bank of the United States, and future president James Buchanan, then a prominent supporter of the bank, both cast their ballots for Jackson.[5] The only policy that may have united the vast majority of Jacksonians in the mid-1820s was a commitment to removing Native American tribes in the southeast and resettling them to west of the Mississippi River, a commitment achieved when Jackson pushed the Removal Act of 1830 through Congress.

Jackson's first inaugural address, which set out his "principles of action," hardly clarified his positions on the main constitutional controversies of the day.[6] With respect to federalism, Jackson promised to take "care not to confound the powers [states] have reserved to themselves with those they have granted to the Confederacy."[7] Most of the aspirants for the presidency in the early Jacksonian era could have made the same assertion. Similarly, Jackson's commitment to "secure to us the rights of persons and of property, liberty of conscience and of the press" did not exactly distinguish him from any other mainstream political actor of the 1820s.[8]

### Vetoes

Jackson's presidency first acquired specific constitutional character when he vetoed the Maysville Road Bill on May 27, 1830. Up until that time, the presidential veto had been largely limited to legislation the president regarded as unconstitutional.[9] Starting with the Maysville Road Bill, Jackson used the veto to make public policy as well as articulate a presidential commitment to a narrow construction of congressional powers under Article I of the Constitution.[10]

The Maysville Road was part of the controversial national highway system that Congress had been sporadically building since the Jefferson administration. Proponents of the road insisted that the Constitution gave Congress the power to build post roads and otherwise make internal improvements that facilitated interstate commerce. President James Monroe (for the most part) and many members of Congress insisted that no such constitutional power existed, that Congress had no power beyond designating which existing roads should be used by the post office, and that internal improvements were matters reserved for the states.[11]

Jackson's veto message on the Maysville Road Bill distinguished between federal internal improvements that did not require permission from the host state and federal financial support for state internal improvement projects. Jackson insisted the Constitution did not permit federal internal improvements if they had not been approved by the states in which those projects were located: "The power to this extent has never been exercised by the Government in a single instance. It does not, in my opinion, possess it."[12] He also asserted that the Maysville Road Bill was constitutionally different from those internal improvements sanctioned by previous administrations. The crucial paragraph of the veto maintained that the federal government could only finance internal improvements that promised substantial national benefits. The Maysville Road, Jackson believed, failed this test: "[Past] grants have always been professedly under the control of the general principle that the works which might be thus aided should be 'of a general, not local, national, or State,' character. A disregard of this distinction would of necessity lead to the subversion of the federal system."[13]

Jackson's July 10, 1832, veto of the Bill Reauthorizing the Bank of the United States even more decisively set out a narrow view of federal powers. Proponents of the national bank insisted that the Supreme Court's decision in *McCulloch v. Maryland* firmly established the constitutionality of that institution.[14] Jackson disagreed. In his veto message, he insisted that precedent provided no support for the constitutional power to incorporate a national bank: "If the opinion of the Supreme Court covered the whole ground of this act, it ought not to control the coordinate authorities of this Government. The Congress, the Executive, and the Court must each for itself be guided by its own opinion of the Constitution."[15]

Jackson then claimed that even if the Supreme Court's opinion in *McCulloch* had some constitutional force, Congress had final say over the issue of whether a national bank was "necessary" within the meaning of the Constitution. *McCulloch*, he asserted, made clear that "the 'degree of [the national bank's] necessity,' involving the details of a banking institution, is a question exclusively for legislative consideration."[16] Jackson concluded that the bill incorporating the national bank was not a "necessary and proper" exercise of any power enumerated in the Constitution of the United States. "Many of the powers and privileges conferred on [the bank]," he declared, "can not be supposed necessary for the purposes for which it was proposed to be created, and are not, therefore, means necessary to attain the end in view, and consequently not justified by the Constitution."[17]

Jackson's bank veto played a major role in the political realignment of the 1830s. The president's opponents in Congress had hoped that the national bank bill would create an issue for the 1832 presidential election. Jackson's veto, to their surprise, proved popular and propelled the incumbent into a landslide victory over Henry Clay. Jackson held himself out as the champion of average white Americans. As Akhil Reed Amar has written, Jackson was "more welcoming of mass democracy" and "more open to lowborn and unpropertied (white) men than other presidents."[18] He favored popular election of the president within each state, and many Jacksonians in the states fought for universal white male suffrage. Such Jacksonian leaders as Martin Van Buren cast the rebuilt Democratic Party as the people's party, which they contrasted to a Whig Party they claimed was elitist and bent on restoring such discredited Federalist policies as the national bank. (Whigs, unsurprisingly, insisted that they were the proper heirs to the Jeffersonian tradition.) Jackson's decisive win set American constitutional politics on a course of narrow federal powers and national expansion—a course that would not be altered until the Civil War.

## Removing Deposits from the National Bank

After the 1832 election, Jackson's determination to destroy the political influence of the Second Bank of the United States immediately embroiled him in a separation-of-powers controversy. Against the advice of most members of his cabinet, the president sought to remove all federal moneys from the national bank. This action was inconsistent with a recent congressional resolution that federal moneys were secure in the bank. It was also inconsistent with the bank's charter, which provided that the secretary of treasury, rather than the president, had the authority to remove the deposits. Undeterred, Jackson asked his secretary of the treasury, William Duane, to remove all federal funds from the bank. When Duane refused this request, Jackson removed him from office and appointed the then attorney general, Roger Taney, to head the Treasury Department. When Taney removed the deposits, the anti-Jackson majority in the Senate was enraged. Led by Henry Clay of Kentucky, the Senate passed a resolution censuring Jackson for treating his cabinet as mere subordinates with no responsibility to Congress. Jackson reacted just as strongly. In protesting the censure resolution, he defended presidential control of the cabinet and condemned all efforts short of impeachment to sanction the president.

Jackson's "Paper on the Removal of the Deposits" (1833) strongly challenged the founding vision of a presidency above politics, a vision already shaken by Jackson's use of the veto in his first term to promote a partisan political agenda. In Jackson's view, national elections were vehicles for deciding pressing constitutional issues rather than simply identifying worthy public officials. Having used the bank veto to achieve victory in the 1832 national election, he went on to ask: "Can it now be said that the question of a re-charter of the bank was not decided at the election which ensued?" "Whatever may be the opinions of others," Jackson continued, "the President considers his reelection as a decision of the people against the bank."[19] Senator Henry Clay was aghast. He informed Congress: "No such conclusions can be legitimately drawn from (Jackson's) re-election." Advancing the more traditional view of elections as turning on the "presumed merits generally" of presidential candidates, Clay stated: "The people had no idea, by the exercise of their suffrage, of expressing their approbation of all the opinions which the President held."[20]

Jackson's "Message to the Senate Protesting Censure Resolution" (1834), however, asserted exclusive presidential responsibility for control over his subordinates in the executive branch, including members of the cabinet. Responding to Clay's charge that the secretary of the treasury had independent duties that he owed to Congress, Jackson insisted otherwise: "The whole executive power being vested in the President, who is responsible for its exercise, it is a necessary consequence that he should have a right to employ agents of his own choice to aid him in the performance of his duties, and to discharge them when he is no longer willing to be responsible for their acts."[21]

In addition to this argument from the constitutional text, Jackson insisted that constitutional precedent was on his side. Consistent with his Maysville Road and national bank vetoes, Jackson emphasized legislative and executive precedents, rather than judicial decisions (of which there were none), regarding the removal power of the president. "The power of removal was a topic of solemn debate in the Congress of 1789," he maintained, "and it was finally decided that the President derived from the Constitution the power of removal so far as it regards the department for whose acts he is responsible."[22] Jackson was referring to the famous Decision of 1789, when the First Congress tackled the cabinet-removal issue during the Washington presidency while enacting three departmental acts. The language that Congress used in creating the first cabinet departments did not expressly recognize that the president had the constitutional power to remove an executive officer without congressional approval, but presidents almost immediately interpreted the legislation in question as conceding the president's implied and unilateral power under the Constitution to remove cabinet members at will.[23] President Washington thereafter established informal precedent when he confronted his secretary of state, Edmund Randolph, in front the entire cabinet. When the president demanded that Randolph explain a letter the secretary had written that indicated he had divulged sensitive information to the French, Randolph resigned on the spot.[24]

The combination of Jackson's belief that all executive branch officials could be removed for any cause by the president and his claim that ordinary people were perfectly capable of holding virtually any government office resulted in the unprecedented development of the spoils system.[25] Over time, the excessive use of patronage as a means of maintaining partisanship—a practice made famous by Jackson—would become the impetus for the civil service reforms Congress instituted in the late nineteenth century.[26]

Jackson's message to the Senate also denied that the Senate had the power to censure the president. Such resolutions, he maintained, had no constitutional authorization and perverted the constitutional process for impeachment: "The Constitution makes the House of Representatives the exclusive judges, in the first instance, of the question whether the President has committed an impeachable offense." The Senate had become simultaneously "accusers, witnesses, counsel and judges." This, he asserted, created an "appalling spectacle" and a usurpation of powers reserved for the lower chamber of Congress.[27] Unsurprisingly, the Jacksonian majority in the House of Representatives had no interest in impeaching, censuring, or disapproving, in any way, Jackson's behavior in the so-called bank war. (Even John Quincy Adams—now a U.S. congressional representative—whom Jackson had displaced as president, voted against the censure.)[28] Shortly after Democrats gained control of the Senate in the 1834 national election, the Senate voted to expunge the censure resolution against Jackson, handing him a great symbolic victory.

## The Proclamation on Nullification

Jackson's Proclamation on Nullification in December 1832 surprised many of his followers and confounded others.[29] The proclamation condemned South Carolina's attempt to declare federal protective tariffs null and void within that state. The political alliances that resulted from this bold action differed from those that formed in response to the vetoes of internal improvements and the national bank. Many committed Jacksonians were appalled by what they perceived as a betrayal of states' rights and the compact theory of the Constitution. Soon-to-be Whigs, such as Daniel Webster, loudly cheered Jackson's nationalistic assertions. Some observers thought a realignment of parties was in the offing.

Jackson's powerful assertion of national supremacy was particularly surprising. The Maysville and bank vetoes spoke of limited federal powers and state prerogatives. While not explicitly rejecting the common view that the

Constitution was a compact between states, Jackson's Proclamation on Nullification sharply denied every common implication of that theory:

> Each State, having expressly parted with so many powers as to constitute, jointly with the other States, a single nation, can not, from that period, possess any right to secede, because such secession does not break a league, but destroys the unity of a nation; and any injury to that unity is not only a breach which would result from the contravention of a compact, but it is an offense against the whole Union.[30]

States that lacked independent sovereign status, the president declared, lacked the power to nullify federal laws: "The power to annul a law of the United States, assumed by one State, (is) *incompatible with the existence of the Union, contradicted expressly by the letter of the Constitution, unauthorized by its spirit, inconsistent with every principle on which it was founded, and destructive of the great object far which it was formed.*"[31] Thus, states aggrieved by federal laws could either bring a case before the Supreme Court or seek a constitutional amendment.[32]

At Jackson's urging, Congress passed the Force Bill in March 1833, giving the president the authority to use military force in South Carolina and other states to force compliance with the federal tariffs.[33]

The Proclamation on Nullification and the Force Bill were not necessarily inconsistent with the rest of Jackson's constitutional opus.[34] Jackson was a states' rights nationalist who believed that Congress's powers under Article I should be narrowly construed. That was the theme of his major vetoes. Yet like Lincoln after him, Jackson believed that the Constitution vested national officials with the authority to determine the balance of power between the federal government and the states. Jackson thought the federal judiciary played an important role in this process, but the ultimate constitutional authorities were nationally elected officials, most notably the president.

This analysis of Jackson's constitutional authority may be too neat, attributing a sophisticated constitutional theory to a political person who had no previous reputation as a stickler for legal niceties. During the War of 1812, Jackson imposed martial law in New Orleans on dubious legal and constitutional grounds.[35] During his later escapades fighting Native Americans, Jackson gained a reputation for ignoring (or at least creatively interpreting) executive orders. This lack of concern with legality also characterized President Jackson's relationship with the Supreme Court. As president, he made little effort to encourage states to abide by the Marshall Court's 1832 decision in *Worcester v. Georgia*, the controversial case in which the Court concluded that the Cherokee people constituted a sovereign nation that could not be subjected to Georgia criminal laws.[36] In a famous (or infamous) response to that decision, Jackson purportedly declared: "John Marshall has made his decision; now let him enforce it."[37]

This history suggests that the only common pattern in all of Jackson's legal arguments, from the War of 1812 to his farewell address, may be that all such arguments promoted the power of Andrew Jackson.

## Conclusion

Despite his popularity, Jackson adhered to tradition and did not seek a third term. After his presidency, he retired to the Hermitage, his estate outside Nashville. Although he was ill for most of the last decade of his life, Jackson continued to play a major role in Democratic Party politics. Indeed, his disapproval of his former Vice President Martin Van Buren's reluctance to annex Texas later doomed Van Buren's chance to recapture the White House in 1844, setting the United States on a rapid course of national expansion.[38] However, Jackson did not live to see the fruits of these political activities. Battered by tuberculosis, heart disease, and a wound from a past duel, he died on June 8, 1845.

As president, Jackson left behind a philosophy and style of governance that would largely define the office, at least until the eve of the Civil War. The union he forged between the express constitutional powers of the chief executive and the political authority derived from the will of the people is still evident in the modern American presidency. Presidents after 1836, following Jackson's example, claimed electoral mandates to advance favored policy and no longer presented themselves as apolitical stewards of the public good.

NOTES

1. Zachary Elkins, Tom Ginsburg, and James Melton, *The Endurance of National Constitutions* (New York: Cambridge University Press, 2009).
2. Andrew Jackson, "Farewell Address," in *A Compilation of the Messages and Papers of the Presidents 1789–1897*, ed. James D. Richardson (Washington, DC: Library of Congress, 1899), 3:293.

3. In Federalist No. 37, Madison observed that the framers had not fully settled the constitutional powers of and limits on the national government: "All new laws are considered as more or less obscure and equivocal, until their meaning be liquidated and ascertained by a series of particular discussions and adjudications." Alexander Hamilton, James Madison, and John Jay, *The Federalist Papers* (New York: Oxford University, 2008), 177.

4. Gerard N. Magliocca, *Andrew Jackson and the Constitution: The Rise and Fall of Generational Regimes* (Lawrence: University Press of Kansas, 2007).

5. Mark A. Graber, "James Buchanan as Savior? Judicial Power, Political Fragmentation, and the Failed 1831 Repeal of Section 25," *Oregon Law Review* 88 (2009): 137–142.

6. Andrew Jackson, "First Inaugural Address," in *A Compilation of the Messages and Papers of the Presidents 1789*, ed. James D. Richardson (Washington, DC: Library of Congress, 1899), 2:37.

7. Ibid.

8. Ibid., 438.

9. Magliocca, *Andrew Jackson and the Constitution*, 30–31.

10. Jackson used the veto formally twelve times and issued several pocket vetoes. By comparison, the six presidents before him issued eight formal vetoes (Washington, two; Adams, none; Jefferson, none; Madison, five; Monroe, one; and John Quincy Adams, none). Ibid., 438 n.78.

11. James Monroe, "Veto Message," in *A Compilation of the Messages and Papers of the Presidents 1789*, ed. James D. Richardson (Washington, DC: Library of Congress, 1899), 2:711–712. Monroe later softened his view on the constitutionality of such congressional action, however. W. P. Cressen, *James Monroe* (Chapel Hill: University of North Carolina Press, 1946) 385–398. See also Chapter 5, "James Monroe."

12. Jackson, "Veto Message, May 27, 1830," in *Messages and Papers*, 2:485.

13. Ibid. Of the Maysville Road project, Jackson stated: "I am not able to view it in any other light than as a measure of purely local character. . . . It has no connection with any established system of improvements; is exclusively within the limits of a State, starting at a point on the Ohio River and running out 60 miles to an interior town, and even as far as the State is interested conferring partial instead of general advantages."

14. McCulloch v. Maryland, 17 U.S. (4 Wheat.) 316 (1819).

15. Looking to Congress, Jackson pointed out that two Congresses had voted in favor of the bank and two against. State precedent, he said, also mattered. Jackson observed: "If we resort to the States, the expressions of legislative, judicial, and executive opinions against the bank have been probably to those in its favor as 4 to 1." Andrew Jackson, "Veto Message, July 10, 1832," in *Messages and Papers*, 2:582.

16. Ibid., 583.

17. Ibid. Among the provisions in the national bank bill that Jackson did not consider constitutionally necessary were provisions granting the bank exclusive privileges to market U.S. bonds, permitting foreigners to own stock in the national bank, authorizing the bank to decide where to locate local branches, and providing the bank with a bonus for performing certain national functions. Jackson also regretted that Congress had failed to permit states to tax the private business transactions of the national bank.

18. Akhil Reed Amar, *America's Constitution: A Biography* (New York: Random House, 2006), 159.

19. Andrew Jackson, "Message Read to the Cabinet on Removal of the Public Deposits," September 18, 1833, in *Messages and Papers*, 3:6–7.

20. *Register of Debates in Congress*, 23rd Cong. 1st Sess. 66.

21. Andrew Jackson, "Protest," in *Messages and Papers*, 3:79–80.

22. Ibid., 80.

23. Congress, by comparison, remained divided between those who thought the president had constitutional power to remove executive brand officials at will and those who believed the president had no such inherent constitutional power, but could be given statutory authority to remove executive branch officials at will. A few members of Congress insisted that impeachment was the only constitutional means for removing executive branch officials. David Alvis, Jeremy D. Bailey, and F. Flagg Taylor IV, *The Contested Removal Power, 1789–2010* (Lawrence: University Press of Kansas, 2013), 16–47.

24. Mary K. Bonsteel Tachau, "George Washington and the Reputation of Edmund Randolph," *Journal of American History* 73, no.1 (1986): 15.

25. Sidney M. Milkis and Michael Nelson, *The American Presidency: Origins and Development, 1776–2011*, 6th ed. (Washington, DC: CQ Press, 2012), 136.

26. Melvin I. Urofsky, *The American Presidents* (New York: Garland Publishing, 2000), 85–86.

27. Ibid., 76.

28. Fred Kaplan, *John Quincy Adams: American Visionary* (New York: Harper, 2014), 461.

29. For a good account of the Nullification Crisis, see Richard E. Ellis, *The Union at Risk: Jacksonian Democracy, States' Rights and the Nullification Crisis* (New York: Oxford University Press, 1987).

30. Andrew Jackson, "Proclamation," in *Messages and Papers*, 2:648.

31. Ibid., 643 (emphasis in original).

32. Ibid., 647.

33. Jon Meacham, *American Lion* (New York: Random House, 2008), 239–241.

34. Matthew S. Brogdon, "Defending the Union: Andrew Jackson's Nullification Proclamation and American Federalism," *Review of Politics* 73 (2011), has made the strong case that Jackson was a states' rights nationalist who had more in common with Abraham Lincoln than with James Buchanan.

35. Matthew Warshauer, *Andrew Jackson and the Politics of Martial Law: Nationalism, Civil Liberties, and Partisanship* (Knoxville: University of Tennessee Press, 2006).

36. Worcester v. Georgia, 31 U.S. (6 Peters) 515 (1832). This case, as well as Cherokee Nation v. Georgia, 30 U.S. (5 Peters) 1 (1831), decided a year earlier, comprised the Court's response to the Indian Removal Act of 1830. The act, which was the first (and only) major piece of legislation passed at Jackson's behest during his presidency, altered the relationship between Indian tribes and the states by declaring that the tribes were no longer considered sovereign and, therefore, were required to succumb to state law. John Marshall's opinion in *Worcester*, however, rejected this view. Magliocca, *Andrew Jackson and the Constitution*, 21–29, 37–47.

37. Even if Jackson never used these exact words, the statement accurately represents his position. The Court's opinion in *Worcester*, issued at the end of its term, was directed to the Georgia courts for enforcement. Although Georgia did nothing in response to Marshall's ruling, Jackson's authority to enforce the decision had not yet been triggered, because the Court was in recess and could not immediately render a "final judgment" under the Judiciary Act of 1789. In reality, however, Jackson supported Georgia's efforts to remove the Cherokees, and therefore his failure to act resulted from his own sympathies and not from a desire to adhere to the letter of the law. For more on this dispute in a broader historical context, see Jon Meacham, *American Lion: Andrew Jackson in the White House* (New York: Random House, 2008), 203–205.

38. Van Buren was defeated in 1844 by James K. Polk, another Jackson protégé.

# 8

# Martin Van Buren

MICHAEL J. GERHARDT

*President Martin Van Buren, a Jacksonian Democrat, did his best to project a strong executive image, like that of his predecessor. However, the Panic of 1837 crippled Van Buren's economic plan. His effort to influence the courts in the Amistad case—involving a group of Africans who had staged a revolt from their Spanish captors on the high seas—only fueled his abolitionist opponents. And Van Buren's effort to prevent Congress from having any supervisory role with respect to the postmaster general chipped away at the power of the executive branch and cemented his reputation as an ineffective president.*

## Introduction

Martin Van Buren, the first president to be born a citizen of the United States, came from modest beginnings. He was born on December 5, 1782, in the small village of Kinderhook, New York, to a tavern keeper and farmer.[1] Van Buren did not attend college, but he learned the law as an apprentice to one of the town's lawyers and established a thriving law practice. He married his childhood sweetheart, Hannah Hoes, in 1804 and fathered four sons.

Van Buren launched his political career by joining and working tirelessly for the state Democratic-Republican Party. He proved quite adept at politics and rose quickly in the ranks, becoming a state senator in 1812 and then New York's attorney general in 1815. He was elected to the U.S. Senate in 1821 and, once in Washington, aligned himself with Andrew Jackson, who was then the popular war hero dedicated to the return of Jeffersonian principles of a limited federal government and state rights.[2] In 1828, Van Buren returned to New York, where he was elected governor.

With Van Buren's assistance, Jackson carried New York in the presidential election of 1828. In recognition of Van Buren's service and support, Jackson named him secretary of state. Van Buren became a member of Jackson's inner circle and ultimately became one of Jackson's closest advisers.[3] Van Buren was the nation's vice president during Jackson's second term.

In May 1836, the Democrats unanimously chose Van Buren as their nominee for president; he was opposed by three candidates running as Whigs. Promising to carry on Jackson's policies and to protect the states from federal overreaching, Van Buren won the election. Unfortunately for him, just as he assumed the office of the presidency, the U.S. economy, which had been booming, began a slow downturn that eventually culminated in the nation's first great depression.[4]

## Presidency

### The Panic of 1837

The severity of the economic downturn the United States faced during the Panic of 1837 was unprecedented. So was the constitutional challenge that Van Buren confronted in having to determine the parameters of the federal government's power to address an economic crisis of national proportions. The teetering economy was the result of the convergence of both domestic and foreign factors. U.S. banks, especially in the South and West, had engaged in speculative lending practices. Across the ocean, England had retracted its credit, which had been the financing source of the nation's economic growth for the preceding two decades. Finally, Jackson's Specie Circular order of 1836 required that all purchases of federal land be made in gold or silver.[5] When, in May 1837, New York banks could not meet continuing demands for specie and refused to convert paper money into gold or silver, panic ensued. In short order, a third of the nation's banks folded, unemployment soared, credit became unavailable, the price of cotton fell dramatically, and food prices escalated.[6]

Van Buren had to decide what, if anything, the federal government would do to alleviate the nation's economic woes. He could refuse to veer from the Jacksonian principle of limited federal government—a principle Van Buren had promised to uphold while campaigning for the presidency—and take a hands-off approach. Or, he could argue for federal intervention and support the creation of the Third Bank of the United States, abandon the Specie Circular, which critics blamed for the economic chaos, and agree to the establishment of a uniform national currency.[7] The latter were policies that the opposing party, the Whigs, insisted were essential to stopping the country's economic downward spiral. According to the Whigs, Congress had the power to advance these measures under the Necessary and Proper Clause (Article I, Section 8, Clause 18), as interpreted by the Supreme Court in *McCulloch v. Maryland*; the Commerce Clause (Article I, Section 8, Clause 3); and the Coinage Clause (Article I, Section 8, Clause 5).

Reiterating the Jeffersonian conviction that it was not for the federal government to rescue the states or people in economic distress, Van Buren opposed the rechartering of the national bank, maintained the Specie Circular, and rejected any notion that the federal government, separate from the states and the private sector, could manage money and other fiscal affairs. Reaffirming the statements he made in his inaugural address regarding his duty to adhere strictly to "the letter and spirit of the Constitution as it was designed by those who framed it" and to prevent the federal government from interfering in matters left to the states, Van Buren declared: "All communities are apt to look to government for too much.

If, therefore, I refrain from suggesting to Congress any specific plan for regulating the exchanges of the country, relieving mercantile embarrassments, or interfering with the ordinary operations of foreign and domestic commerce, it is from a conviction that such measures are not within the constitutional province of the General Government."[8]

Nevertheless, Van Buren did not reject all possible avenues of federal intervention to combat the crippling depression.[9] Since the Constitution empowered Congress to "coin money" (Article I, Section 8, Clause 5), Van Buren believed that Congress had some authority, albeit limited, to remedy the evils of "depreciated paper currency" and to reform the banking system.[10] In an effort to provide stability and predictability to America's financial system, Van Buren proposed that federal funds be deposited in and controlled by an independent treasury system and not the state banks, as had been the case since Andrew Jackson's second term.[11] Van Buren's proposal was immediately met with congressional resistance from all sides.[12] The fight lasted for three years, but in 1840, an independent treasury bill was finally passed.[13] This enactment, as modest as it was, set a constitutional precedent that Van Buren himself might have found troubling, in light of his view that the federal government did not belong in the business of addressing the country's economic problems. Indeed, the treasury bill established that the federal government would intervene in and institute solutions to a national economic crisis. The depression, however, continued, and the failure of Van Buren's plan to help the nation underscored the ineffectiveness of this president's narrow construction of federal power. Ultimately, it was one of the reasons the electorate denied Van Buren a second term in the White House.

## *The* Amistad *Case*

In his inaugural address, Van Buren announced that he would resist any efforts by Congress to interfere in slavery where it existed: "I must go into the Presidential chair the inflexible and uncompromising opponent of every attempt on the part of Congress to abolish slavery in the District of Columbia against the wishes of the slaveholding states, and also with a determination equally decided to resist the slightest interference with it in the States where it exists."[14] In fact, Van Buren went so far as to support a resolution, known as the gag rule, that prohibited petitions pertaining to slavery from being introduced in the House or formally acknowledged in any other way.[15] While the Whigs criticized the resolution as a political ploy that demonstrated Van Buren's willingness to silence free speech in the hopes of winning reelection, the Democrats defended him as a man of principle whose first priority was preserving the intended constitutional order of the Union.

The issue of slavery came to preoccupy Van Buren most unexpectedly, when the *Amistad* case, one of the most famous federal cases of the nineteenth century, was litigated on his watch. For sheer human drama, the case was beyond compare. In 1839, hundreds of native Africans were captured by Spanish slave traders in the Africans' homeland near Sierra Leone. They endured a journey on a slave ship to the Spanish colony at Havana, Cuba, and were fraudulently sold there as Cuban-born slaves. Some fifty-three of them were put aboard the cargo schooner *La Amistad*, which set sail for another part of the island. Three days into the journey, the Africans staged a revolt and seized control of the vessel. After killing the captain and the cook, they ordered the two Spanish slave dealers on board to guide the ship east toward Africa. The Spaniards secretly changed course and sailed toward Long Island, New York. When *La Amistad* entered U.S. waters, the schooner, its cargo, and the Africans were seized by the U.S. surveying brig *Washington* and towed to New London, Connecticut. There, the Africans were jailed. They were charged with mutiny, piracy, and murder and claimed as salvaged property, along with the vessel.

The case went to trial in federal district court, with the United States intervening on behalf of the queen of Spain, who asserted Spain's right to the Africans as Spanish property under the Treaty of 1795. Highly organized abolitionist groups in Connecticut spearheaded a defense. The Africans argued that they were not slaves and had been kidnapped in clear violation of international law.

As Van Buren was not in Washington when *La Amistad* entered U.S. waters, the decision to involve the federal government on the side of Spain's treaty claims was made by three of his cabinet members. When he returned to Washington, Van Buren took charge.[16] He secured from his attorney general an opinion supporting the cabinet members' interpretation of the Treaty of 1795 and instructed his secretary of state, John Forsyth, to direct the U.S. district attorney in Connecticut to keep the matter out of court and under the executive branch's control. When, against the president's wishes, a case was filed in federal district court, Van Buren took the position that the treaty took precedence. He wanted the court to declare that Spain's claim to the ship and the Africans was legitimate. Having appointed the presiding judge to the bench, Van Buren expected a favorable ruling and ordered the navy to prepare to transport the Africans to Cuba.[17]

Much to Van Buren's dismay, things did not go as planned. The district court found in favor of the Africans and ordered that they be returned home. Van Buren responded by instructing his attorney general to appeal to the Supreme Court. The Amistad Committee, composed of leading abolitionists, enlisted former President John Quincy Adams of Massachusetts to argue the case in the High Court on behalf of the Africans. Partly blind and seventy-two years of age, Adams delivered a stirring defense of the Africans' right to freedom, in the process "decrying President Van Buren's illegal attempts to influence the judicial system and circumvent the Constitution."[18]

The Supreme Court agreed, concluding that the Africans were not slaves, but free men and, accordingly, were not property within the meaning of the treaty. Therefore, the Court held, the Africans did not have to be restored to Spain. Justice Joseph Story wrote:

> It is plain beyond controversy, if we examine the evidence, that these negroes never were the lawful slaves of Ruiz or Montez or of any other Spanish subjects. They are natives of Africa, and were kidnapped there, and were unlawfully transported to Cuba in violation of the laws and treaties of Spain and the most solemn edicts and declarations of that government.[19]

Thus, by stating that Spaniards had never lawfully owned the Africans, Justice Story sidestepped the more explosive question of slavery itself, while sending a clear signal that the days of the institution of slavery in the United States might be numbered. (While several of the Africans died in prison or at sea, thirty-five of them returned to their homeland in Sierra Leone, along with American missionaries. There, they helped propel forward the independence of Sierra Leone from Great Britain and served as further inspiration to the abolitionist movement in the United States.)[20]

To his credit, President Van Buren did not follow Andrew Jackson's reputed example of defying the Court's unfavorable ruling.[21] Instead, he quietly took his lumps. In the process, the *Amistad* case reinforced the principle that a president must enforce final judgments rendered by the Supreme Court, even if he disagrees with them.[22]

## The Executive Branch, Supreme Court Review, and Congressional Oversight

Van Buren suffered another major defeat in the Supreme Court in pressing the constitutional question of how far the president could go in controlling executive agencies created by Congress. Amos Kendall was Van Buren's postmaster general. Contractors who transported the U.S. mail under a contract entered with the previous administration made a claim against Kendall's department. Congress enacted legislation that authorized the solicitor of the Treasury Department to make a final settlement and adjustment of the claim. The solicitor awarded the contractors the sum of $39,462.43. Kendall, however, refused to pay the claim—with the support of President Van Buren—relying on the independent authority of the executive branch.[23]

In *Kendall v. United States*, the Supreme Court again slapped the hand of the Van Buren administration.[24] The Court acknowledged that Article II, Section 1, of the Constitution vested the president with executive power and that the president was "beyond the reach of any other department" (except for impeachment proceedings).[25] Yet the Court made clear that executive officers such as the postmaster general—who were (after all) creatures of Congress—were not under the president's exclusive control and could be subject to Congress's statutory direction. Further, the Court upheld Congress's power to direct executive officials (other than the president) to carry out "ministerial" acts such as abiding by the duly enacted statute creating a mechanism to settle the claim.[26] Additionally, the Court upheld the federal circuit court's authority to issue the writ of mandamus and reaffirmed the duty of an official, like the postmaster general, to abide by the circuit court's order, declaring that this authority did not create a conflict between the executive and judicial branches.

*Kendall* constituted a dramatic pronouncement that would have ripple effects into future presidencies. First, it chipped away at the unitary executive theory—at least the most extreme forms of this theory—which suggested that the Constitution gave the president complete control over the executive branch and the exercise of executive power. Instead, *Kendall* made clear that Congress—in creating executive agencies and delegating to them certain authority—shared in that power. As Chief Justice Roger Taney stated in concurrence with the *Kendall* decision:

The office of postmaster general is not created by the constitution; nor are its powers or duties marked out by that instrument. The office was created by act of congress; and wherever congress creates such an office as that of postmaster general, by law, it may unquestionably, by law, limit its powers, and regulate its proceedings; and may subject it to any supervision or control, executive or judicial, which the wisdom of the legislature may deem right.[27]

The pronouncement in *Kendall* would have a far-reaching impact on the American presidency. It made clear that a sweeping array of agencies and positions created by Congress—even those housed in the executive branch—were nonetheless subject to congressional supervision.[28] Thus, the web of shared powers between Congress and the president—a web that had been identified only generally in the Constitution—was given more substance because of Van Buren's actions. In the end, the Supreme Court's unambiguous pronouncement only shored up insistence that his postmaster general was not free from congressional oversight, giving support to the legislative branch's authority at the expense of the executive branch's constitutional power.

## Conclusion

Van Buren won the Democratic nomination for a second term, but he and his party faced an uphill battle to win the presidential election of 1840. The country remained mired in economic distress, and the Whig candidate, William Henry Harrison, ran a masterful campaign, presenting himself as a no-nonsense military hero who could get things done and Van Buren as a fussy, "lily-fingered aristocrat" who could not.[29] Van Buren lost the election so badly that he even failed to carry New York. He left the office as a loser, a perception that he was unable to shake for the rest of his life. Van Buren retired to Lindenwald, his Kinderhook estate. Although he was the leading contender after the first ballot at the 1844 Democratic convention, he ultimately lost the nomination to James K. Polk and resolved never to seek elective office again. Van Buren died at Lindenwald on July 24, 1862, at the age of seventy-nine.

If there was a lesson to be learned from the Van Buren presidency, it was that a rigid adherence to a constitutional point of view could lead to political ruin for a chief executive. Although Van Buren entered office with noble goals, he ultimately eroded the powers of the president for future occupants of that office and ruined his chances for reelection by projecting an image of weakness rather than strength. Ultimately, President Martin Van Buren showed how Congress and the Supreme Court could gain the upper hand over an inflexible chief executive.

NOTES

1. Melvin I. Urofsky, *The American Presidents* (New York: Garland Publishing, 2000), 100.
2. Ibid., 101.
3. Ibid., 103.
4. Michael J. Gerhardt, *The Forgotten Presidents* (New York: Oxford University Press 2013), 3–4.
5. Urofsky, *The American Presidents*, 105.
6. Gerhardt, *The Forgotten Presidents*, 4.
7. Ibid., 4–5.
8. Martin Van Buren, Inaugural Address, March 4, 1837, in *Inaugural Addresses of the Presidents of the United States from George Washington 1789 to George Bush 1989* (Washington, DC: U.S. Government Printing Office, 1989), 69–78; Martin Van Buren, Special Message to Congress, September 4, 1837, quoted in Gerhardt, *The Forgotten Presidents*, 5.
9. Gerhardt, *The Forgotten Presidents*, 7.
10. Major L. Wilson, *The Presidency of Martin Van Buren* (Lawrence: University Press of Kansas, 1984), 88 (citations omitted).
11. Urofsky, *The American Presidents*, 106.
12. The Whigs, who were persuaded that the reestablishment of a national bank was the means to secure the country's financial sector, opposed the plan, as did members of Van Buren's own party, who were committed to state prerogatives.
13. Gerhardt, *The Forgotten Presidents*, 10.
14. Van Buren, Inaugural Address, 69–78.
15. Gerhardt, *The Forgotten Presidents*, 12.
16. Ibid., 13.
17. Ibid., 14.
18. National Park Service, *Amistad: Seeking Freedom in Connecticut*, National Park Service National Register of Historic Places, accessed May 27, 2015, www.nps.gov/nr/travel/amistad/intro.htm.
19. U.S. v. Amistad, 40 U.S. 518, 593 (1841).
20. Ibid.
21. Gerhardt, *The Forgotten Presidents*, 15.
22. William Baude, "The Judgment Power," *Georgetown Law Journal* 96 (2008): 1818–1828. The notion that the executive branch had no power to overturn final judgments was evident at the country's founding. Ibid., 1815–1819. As president, James Madison defended the power of the judiciary to issue binding judgments. When Madison was asked by the governor of Pennsylvania to stop the enforcement of a federal judgment, Madison responded in no uncertain terms that the president was not authorized to interfere with the execution of a decree of the U.S. Supreme Court. Ibid., 1825.

23. Gerhardt, *The Forgotten Presidents*, 21. The contractors requested and were issued a writ of mandamus from the local circuit court, ordering that Kendall satisfy the award. Kendall, again, refused, and Van Buren directed that an appeal be taken to the Supreme Court.

24. Kendall v. United States, 37 U.S. (12 Peters) 524 (1838).

25. Ibid., 610. This ruling can be contrasted with the Court's later decision in Myers v. United States, 272 U.S. 52 (1926), holding that the president could remove a postmaster without first seeking the advice and consent of Congress. For a discussion of the *Myers* case, see Chapter 30, "Calvin Coolidge."

26. *Kendall*, 37 U.S. at 613.

27. Ibid., 626 (Taney, C. J., concurring).

28. Some of the ground the executive branch lost in *Kendall* was arguably made up two years later in Paulding v. Decatur, 39 U.S. (14 Peters) 497 (1840). In that case, the widow of a naval hero requested that the secretary of the navy, James Paulding, pay her a pension from a general statute granting pension benefits to the widows of naval officers and a separate law granting a special pension to her. Paulding, authorized to make decisions on pension entitlement, advised her that she was entitled to one pension, of her choosing, but not to both. The widow filed for a writ of mandamus from the federal circuit court and was refused. On appeal, the Supreme Court limited the Court's holding in *Kendall* to "mere ministerial" acts. Ibid., 521. The Court held that the judiciary did not have the authority to entertain an appeal from an executive official's performance of a duty that required the exercise of his judgment and discretion. Thus, *Paulding* provided an argument to subsequent presidents seeking insulation of executive decision-making from legislative direction or judicial review.

29. Alan Brinkley and Davis Dyer, *The American Presidency* (Boston: Houghton Mifflin, 2004), 113.

# 9

# William Henry Harrison

DAVID MARKS SHRIBMAN

*President William Henry Harrison died after only thirty-one days in office, the shortest term served by any American president. A celebrated military hero who had defeated Native American tribes at the Battle of Tippecanoe, Harrison delivered an inaugural address that lasted nearly two hours. He developed pneumonia and expired before his wife, Anna, had even left Ohio to move to Washington. Harrison's death triggered a scramble to determine the constitutional meaning of succession. Thus, William Henry Harrison's principal legacy related not to his contributions as chief executive, but to his death in office.*

## Introduction

William Henry Harrison is one of the least-known presidents in history. This unlikely American symbol of rustic simplicity and rural rectitude was territorial governor of Indiana at the opening of the nineteenth century. He was the principal negotiator of the 1809 Treaty of Fort Wayne—an agreement that ceded three million acres of American Indian land to the United States. Two years later, Harrison was lauded for battling the heroic Shawnee leaders Tecumseh and the Prophet at Tippecanoe Creek. His grandson, Benjamin Harrison of Indiana, became president in 1889, making William Henry Harrison the only president to have a grandchild rise to the same high office. Ironically, the elder Harrison is remembered, if at all, as a presidential afterthought; in fact, however, he is more significant as a presidential forethought. Chosen in 1840 in the first political campaign to employ the media, he served but a month in office, leaving an often-forgotten legacy worthy of a Shakespearean drama: Nothing became of his administration except the result of his leaving it.

President Harrison delivered the longest and perhaps the only fatal inaugural address of American history. Had he lived, his thoughts in that address on the presidential veto—the word appears five times in his remarks, a reflection of the pertinence of the veto issue as midcentury approached—might have shaped American constitutional history. Indeed, Jacksonians suspected that Harrison, a political novice, had been persuaded by the Whigs to mount a challenge to the expansion of executive power that had taken place under Andrew Jackson and to delegate the powers of the presidency to Congress.[1]

But whether it was from a case of pneumonia possibly contracted at the frosty ceremony or from another cause, the new Whig president died a month into office. The circumstances were made all the more remarkable for the vital constitutional issue prompted by his demise and by the ascendancy of John Tyler, who was then the youngest man to become president and who also happened to succeed the then-oldest man to occupy the White House.

The phenomenon of the dark-horse chief executive—the rise of a political figure from obscure origins, with minimal public exposure and limited civic experience—was thoroughly unknown in the first half century of

American life. The ninth president of the United States was no exception. An accomplished military man and colorful fighter of American Indians from the romantic frontier of America and beyond, Harrison was well known—and his record was well celebrated. Besides George Washington and Andrew Jackson (the two earlier generals to ascend to the presidency), Harrison was very likely the most vibrant and radiant candidate for high office in early American political history. The other figures elected to the presidency before him—from John Adams and Thomas Jefferson to John Quincy Adams and Martin Van Buren—were men more of philosophical and legal reasoning than of physical daring and combat courage. Harrison was a man of action, shaped more by the battlefield than by the cabinet room or the legislative chamber.

Like Washington and Jackson, he was a figure of lore and legend and indeed was the prototype of a certain brand of American politician, not so much a creature of a homespun background but the creation of mythologists who celebrated a log-cabin background that was pure fiction—but purely American in its appeal. Indeed, both Harrison and his Tyler-too running mate, John Tyler, who figures significantly in the Harrison legacy, were products of elite backgrounds and grand childhood homes—both, it turns out, part of the rich Tidewater upland that created the patrician planter-and-merchant society of Virginia. The two men produced the renowned 1840 "Log Cabin and Hard Cider" campaign that was more fable than campaign.

Harrison, the last British subject to become president, was born on February 9, 1773, on the Berkeley Plantation in Charles City County, Virginia. He emerged from a prominent family; his father had signed the Declaration of Independence and served as governor of Virginia. Although young Harrison was the scion of a slaveholder family, he nonetheless joined an abolitionist society at age eighteen to, as he put it, "ameliorate the condition of slaves and procure their freedom *by every legal means.*"[2] This abolitionist sympathy separated him in temperament and outlook from his running mate Tyler, a slaveholder and an ardent supporter of the institution. So, too, did his military experience. As a young man, Harrison earned early notice as a soldier of unusual imagination and courage, so much so that he was cited in Major General "Mad" Anthony Wayne's official action report at the 1794 Battle of Fallen Timbers. Harrison's conduct was impressive enough that Lieutenant Thomas J. Underwood, Wayne's recording secretary, was moved to add that "if he continues a military man he will be a second Washington."[3]

Despite his Virginia origins, much of Harrison's life was rooted in what is now regarded as the Middle West, then more Western in tone than middle in character. He served in various Northwest Territory administrative capacities, defeated celebrated American Indian forces in ferocious fighting at Tippecanoe Creek, and chased the British and Indians into Canada during the War of 1812. After marrying Anna Symmes in 1795, Harrison settled down in North Bend, Ohio, where he acquired a large piece of land from his bride's father. Here, Harrison settled easily and unobtrusively into a series of political positions, including the U.S. House of Representatives and the Ohio and U.S. Senates. He did, however, have a difficult tenure as U.S. minister to Colombia, where he clashed with that country's leader, Simón Bolívar. Harrison, described in a hagiographic 1840 campaign biography as "a plain, Republican farmer," held the unassuming position of clerk of courts in Hamilton County, Ohio, when he won the Whig nomination for president at a convention that adopted no platform.[4] He defeated incumbent Martin Van Buren, running on his stellar war record and pointing to the wrecked economy caused by the Panic of 1837 under his opponent's watch. Before long, however, the man known as "Tippecanoe" would become a Fallen Timber himself.

## Presidency

### Death of a President

By April 3, 1841, a mere thirty days after his inauguration, Harrison told a medical attendant, "I am ill, very ill, much more so than they think me."[5] At ten o'clock that night, Harrison's secretary wrote to his own father that the president was "drawing his last breath," suggesting that "in a few minutes he will doubtless be among the dead" and adding, "He now is as low as possible."[6] Within hours, Fletcher Webster, the son of Secretary of State Daniel Webster, would be on horseback, racing through the night to Williamsburg, Virginia, where he would rap on the door of Vice President Tyler and deliver the news that had upended the country and would soon catapult Tyler into a new role and new controversy.

## A Great Constitutional Question

For the first fifty-two years of the young nation's existence, through eight presidents, no American chief executive had died in office, and so when Harrison expired, one of the principal unanswered questions of the American Constitution—what to do at the death of a president?—moved urgently and unavoidably from the theoretical to the practical. Harrison's last words, perhaps uttered for the benefit of his vice president, offered little guidance for the road ahead: "Sir, I wish you to understand the principles of the Government. I wish them carried out. I ask nothing more."[7]

In the conventional telling of this story, Tyler, importuned in nightshirt and cap, is portrayed as unready but resolute. And yet there is ample reason to believe that the vice president had given substantial thought to becoming president. He knew Harrison was sixty-eight years old and not in robust health, and Tyler had been warned that the president's condition was deteriorating. "I should not be surprised to hear by tomorrows [sic] mail," James Lyon, a Richmond attorney who was a Tyler associate, wrote to the vice president, "that General Harrison is no more."[8]

Indeed, the notion that he would become president and not interim president or, in the awkward construction used by the Harrison cabinet that awaited his arrival in the capital, "Vice-President, acting President," was Tyler's immediate inclination and, before long, his strong conviction.[9] Like many vice presidents, Tyler had been selected to balance the presidential nominee on the party ticket, in his case as a Southern states' rights running mate and an ally of Henry Clay, the powerful Whig from Kentucky, to complement a National Republican Whig from the North. Tyler had few natural allies in the Harrison circle or indeed among establishment politicians generally. He knew he had to move decisively if he were to have the prestige and the power of the presidency, both of which he calculated he needed in Whig Washington.

Tyler's frantic 230-mile transformation from obscurity into history—the journey from Williamsburg to Washington by horse, steamboat, and train constituting a portrait of 1841 America captured in its varied modes of transportation—has become seared into American folklore: a man without a settled title racing across the countryside for fifty-three hours to govern a sorrowed and leaderless nation. The Harrison cabinet had agreed that, in the words of Nathan Sargent, a Whig journalist who would later correspond with Abraham Lincoln on political matters, "Mr. Tyler must, while performing the functions of President, bear the title of Vice-President, acting President."[10] Two days after the president's death, his successor, who until that moment had been regarded as a strict constructionist of the Constitution, was preparing to assert his right to Harrison's title as well as his duties. He was determined to become president—and to set a precedent.

That was the crux of the crisis, prompted by the ambiguity of the framers and compounded by the imprecise drafters of the Twelfth Amendment, which was ratified in 1804. The amendment provided for filling the presidency if the House of Representatives had not settled a contested election: "The Vice-President shall act as President, as in the case of the death or other constitutional disability of the President." This statement only confused the matter, which was muddled from the start. Article II, Section 1, Clause 6, of the Constitution stated that "in the case of the removal of the President from office, or of his death, resignation, or inability to discharge the powers and duties of said office, the same shall devolve on the Vice President."

So, after the death of Harrison, the debate in the nation's capital centered on the constitutional phrase "the same." The question was whether by those two words the framers meant that the office devolved on the vice president—or that only the *duties* devolved on the vice president. Left unanswered, too, was what the person who had been elected vice president would be called after the change in status.

Though Supreme Court Justice Joseph Story had argued in 1833 that vice presidents could succeed to the presidency, the country clearly was drifting in uncharted waters. As the crisis deepened, Secretary Webster asked Chief Justice Roger B. Taney for advice. But the jurist declined, apparently not wishing to wade across the separation-of-powers divide to influence what he regarded as a purely executive-branch matter. In such a constitutional vacuum, the decisive one decides, which is what Tyler did, in a series of deliberate and precisely orchestrated maneuvers. His actions settled forever a matter that would appear in fraught moments of tragedy or sadness many more times in American history.

First, Tyler rejected the prevailing political ethos of the Harrison cabinet. In the Harrison administration, the chief executive and the six members of his cabinet had equal votes. "I beg your pardon, gentlemen," Tyler said. "I am very glad to have in my cabinet such able statesmen as you have proved yourselves to be. And I shall be pleased to avail myself of your counsel and advice. But I can never consent to being dictated to. I am the President and I shall be responsible for my administration."[11] The meaning of that statement was clear—Harrison was gone, Tyler was in charge—and the choice of the phrases "I am the President" and "my administration" made clear the larger point: Tyler would act as president rather than as acting president. Moreover, as a Southern politician with views incongruent with the Harrison Whigs, he understood that he could not govern as mere regent, imprisoned by the personnel and governing philosophy set in place by his predecessor. Otherwise, Harrison would in effect rule from the grave. That, in fact, is what Henry Clay, the dominant Whig in Washington and a man with eyes on the presidency in 1844, plainly had in mind.[12] But Tyler foiled Clay and the other Whig grandees, swiftly consolidating his position with defiance and deftness.

Webster suggested that Tyler should take the oath of office. The Virginian, who already had argued that he was president by virtue of Harrison's death, did not think this step was necessary. But he agreed to do so because he believed it would leave no doubt as to his status. The oath was administered in the parlor of Brown's Indian Queen Hotel in Washington on April 6 by William Cranch, chief judge of the U.S. Circuit Court of the District of Columbia. The presence of the Harrison cabinet at the proceedings served to underline Tyler's position. Judge Cranch later issued a sworn statement saying that though Tyler felt the oath superfluous, "yet as doubts may arrive, and for greater caution, [he] took and subscribed the . . . oath before me."[13]

The new president then delivered a set of remarks that are often referred to as his inaugural address, though he did not describe it that way. In these formal comments, Tyler set forth what he called "a brief exposition of the principles which will govern me in the general course of my administration," another deliberate use of the phrase "my administration."[14] This was intended to couple the political acknowledgment of his new position with a public declaration of his new role. In these inaugural remarks, punctuated with references to himself as "Chief Magistrate" or "President" and designed to fortify his position among voters, he asserted: "The person elected to the vice presidency of the United States has had devolved upon him the presidential office."[15] In addition, by calling himself president, Tyler claimed the salary for the president set forth in Article II, Section 9, of the Constitution.[16] Not only was Tyler's presidential salary considerably higher than his vice presidential salary, but because it was fixed by the

Constitution for the entirety of a president's term, it was also insulated from a Congress that might be inclined to tamper with it.[17]

Though Tyler consolidated his position by moving into the White House on April 14, doubts lingered. As late as May 31, when a special congressional session was convened, Representative Henry A. Wise, a Virginia Whig, offered an otherwise-unremarkable resolution stating that Congress was ready to receive communications from "the President of the United States."[18] When that language was challenged, Wise argued that Tyler believed "he was by the Constitution, by election and by the act of God, President of the United States."[19] But Representative John McKeon, a Democrat from New York, then offered an amendment to make the resolution read "Vice-President, now exercising the duties of President." That measure, however, did not carry.[20] The matter thus was settled in the House.

The next test came in the Senate, where William Allen, an Ohio Democrat, proposed describing Tyler as "the Vice-President, on whom by the death of the late President, the powers and duties of the office of President have devolved."[21] His amendment was defeated 38 to 8, and by June 25, one of Tyler's greatest critics, John Quincy Adams—who earlier had described the Virginian as "a political sectarian, of the slave-driving, Virginian, Jeffersonian school, with all the interests and passions and vices of slavery rooted in his moral and political constitution"—was referring to Tyler as "the President."[22] Politically and constitutionally, the matter was settled.

## Conclusion

In the years and decades that followed, assassinations (Abraham Lincoln, William A. Garfield, William McKinley, and John F. Kennedy), illnesses (Zachary Taylor and Warren G. Harding), and resignation (Richard M. Nixon) would thrust vice presidents into the White House. Thus, because of Tyler's decisive actions in 1841, Millard Fillmore, Andrew Johnson, Chester A. Arthur, Theodore Roosevelt, Calvin Coolidge, Lyndon B. Johnson, and Gerald R. Ford seamlessly took office as president. Indeed, Tyler's movement into the presidency was transformed from phenomenon to precedent in 1850, when Millard Fillmore told the Zachary Taylor cabinet upon the president's unexpected death in 1850, "I shall avail myself of the earliest moment to . . . appoint a time and place for taking the oath of office prescribed to the President of the United States."[23] By 1967, the Twenty-Fifth Amendment codified the tradition: "In the case of the removal of the President from office or of his death or resignation, the Vice-President shall become President."

The Tyler Precedent, as it is known today, assures a smooth transition at the top of a government that is immensely bigger, more complex, and more engaged in the world than it was when Harrison died. Moreover, the administering of the oath of office to a new chief executive after the office is vacated in the middle of a term is regarded not only as customary but also as constitutionally valid. In modern time, such ceremonies in Air Force One on the Love Field tarmac after the assassination of President John F. Kennedy in Dallas and in the White House after the resignation of President Richard M. Nixon in the wake of the Watergate scandal have become sturdy symbols of continuity in crisis. Thus, in death, William Henry Harrison gave continuing life to the presidency he had occupied for only one month.

## NOTES

1. Sidney M. Milkis and Michael Nelson, *The American Presidency: Origins & Development, 1776–2011* (Washington, DC: CQ Press, 2012), 140–141.
2. Henrik V. Booraem, *A Child of the Revolution: William Henry Harrison and His World, 1773–1798* (Kent, Ohio: Kent State University Press, 2012), 32. Emphasis in original.
3. Robert M. Owens, *Mr. Jefferson's Hammer: William Henry Harrison and the Origins of American Indian Policy* (Norman: University of Oklahoma Press, 2007), 25.
4. Samuel Jones Burr, *Life and Times of William Henry Harrison* (New York: L. W. Ransom, 1840), 263.
5. Freeman Cleaves, *Old Tippecanoe: William Henry Harrison and His Time* (Port Washington, NY: Kennikat Press 1969), 342.
6. Henry Harrison to Benjamin Harrison, April 4, 1841, "William Henry Harrison Announces Harrison's Impending Death," Shapell Manuscript Foundation, accessed May 27, 2015, www.shapell.org/manuscript.aspx?william-henry-harrison-death.
7. Gail Collins, *William Henry Harrison* (New York: Times Books 2012), 123.
8. Edward P. Crapol, *John Tyler: The Accidental President* (Chapel Hill: University of North Carolina Press, 2006), 8.
9. Norma Lois Peterson, *The Presidencies of William Henry Harrison and John Tyler* (Lawrence: University of Kansas Press, 1989), 45.
10. Robert J. Morgan, *A Whig Embattled: The Presidency Under John Tyler* (Lincoln: University of Nebraska Press 1954), 7.
11. Gary May, *John Tyler* (New York: Times Books, 2008), 7.
12. Henry Clay's ambition was no secret. Harrison understood that Clay expected to wield the power of the presidency behind the scenes. In fact, Harrison had to remind Clay that it was he, not Clay, who had been elected president. Alan Brinkley and Davis Dyer, eds., *The American Presidency* (Boston: Houghton Mifflin, 2004), 119.

13. Morgan, *A Whig Embattled*, 8.

14. Peterson, *Presidencies of William Henry Harrison and John Tyler*, 42.

15. Ibid.

16. U.S. Const. art. II, § 9, cl. 7, states: "The President shall, at stated Times, receive for his Services, a Compensation, which shall neither be increased nor diminished during the Period for which he shall have been elected."

17. Akhil Reed Amar, "Presidents Without Mandates (With Special Emphasis on Ohio)," *University of Cincinnati Law Review* (winter 1999): 378–379.

18. Morgan, *A Whig Embattled*, 13.

19. Crapol, *John Tyler: The Accidental President*, 13.

20. Morgan, *A Whig Embattled*, 13.

21. Oliver Perry Chitwood, *John Tyler: Champion of the Old South* (New York: Russell & Russell, 1964), 206.

22. Ibid., 207; Morgan, *A Whig Embattled*, 17.

23. Crapol, *John Tyler: The Accidental President*, 15

# 10

# John Tyler

ROBERT J. SPITZER

*John Tyler, despite his adroitness in establishing that he had inherited complete presidential power when his predecessor died in office, became a weak and maladroit chief executive during his own time in the White House. Yet, Tyler was not afraid to exercise his authority. First, he stared down an insurrection in Rhode Island, leaving it to the political processes to settle that feud. Second, he wielded enormous power in the form of his presidential vetoes, whittling away at Congress's previously supreme authority and establishing that there was no limit to the number of, or reasons for, presidential vetoes. A clumsy one-term president who left office politically emasculated, he nonetheless opened the door for a more muscular presidency—in relation to Congress—that would benefit future chief executives.*

## Introduction

John Tyler will never make the list of best or greatest American presidents—nor should he. Yet Tyler's presidency proved to be one of the most important in framing, resolving, and advancing constitutionally based executive power. Tyler was a man of principle, of intelligence and learning, of courage, and of extensive political experience—all traits venerated as indispensable to a successful president. But Tyler proved himself a maladroit political leader who managed to infuriate supporters and opponents in equal measure, undercut his own already-precarious standing, and ultimately precipitate the nation's first impeachment crisis. As one biographer noted, Tyler's career was "one of American failure and tragedy."[1] Despite all this, his presidency managed to extend executive power no less than other presidents extolled for their greatness in office.

John Tyler was born into an influential family in Charles City County, Virginia, on March 29, 1790. He was only seventeen when he graduated from the College of William and Mary in 1807 and entered the study of law. He won admission to the Virginia Bar in 1809 at the age of nineteen. A mere two years later, he was elected to the Virginia House of Delegates, where he served on and off for the succeeding three decades. In 1816, Tyler won election to the U.S. House of Representatives, where he served until 1821. He also served as Virginia governor from 1825 to 1827 and U.S. senator from 1827 to 1836. By the account of one biographer, Tyler possessed a degree of "training in the art and science of government unmatched by any other American President before or since."[2] While this account is arguably an overstatement, Tyler without question possessed as extensive, lengthy, and varied a political résumé as that of anyone ever elected to the presidency to that point.

Tyler's political leanings emerged early on. He opposed the Missouri Compromise of 1820 during the presidency of James Monroe, believing that slavery should be allowed to exist without restriction. To this Southern slave-owning aristocrat, the compromise constituted unwelcome federal meddling in the matter. Tyler was also an early opponent of "nationalist" policies, including calls for a national bank, the expansion of the electorate to include all white males, and the imposition of import tariffs.

Tyler's career was significantly shaped by his disdain of the populist Andrew Jackson. In the presidential election of 1824, Tyler endorsed Northerner John Quincy Adams as the less odious alternative, but supported Jackson in 1828 in the vain hope that Jackson harbored states' rights proclivities. Jackson's attacks on the Bank of the United States were enough to rally Tyler behind him, but after Jackson's smashing reelection in 1832, Tyler broke with him over the nullification controversy and Jackson's threat to use military force if South Carolina tried to secede from the Union. Again in 1833, Tyler gave a fiery Senate speech denouncing Jackson and was the only Democrat to vote against the compromise Force Bill, which gave the president authority to use the army and navy to carry out the law—in that case, to enforce federal tariffs. That dispute in turn helped precipitate the formation of the Whig Party. Tyler swiftly abandoned the Democrats and joined the Whigs.[3] When Tyler was instructed by the Virginia state legislature to vote in favor of a U.S. Senate measure to rescind the Senate's earlier censure vote against Jackson (the effort to rescind succeeded), Tyler resigned from his seat in protest.

By 1840, the nation had been staggering for over three years under the economic collapse that followed shortly after the election of Martin Van Buren to the presidency. The economic downturn opened the door wide to Whig ambitions to capture the presidency. The Whigs' choice, former general and military hero William Henry Harrison, selected Tyler as his running mate, primarily because Tyler was a Southerner (Harrison was from Ohio, although he was born in Virginia) and firmly supported states' rights.[4] The well-known slogan promoting the ticket—"Tippecanoe and Tyler Too"—accurately suggested that Tyler was nearly an afterthought.[5] Less than a month after his inauguration, Harrison was dead of pneumonia, and Tyler was president. On the day of his inauguration as the tenth president, Tyler was fifty-one years old, the youngest man to have assumed the office up to that time.[6]

## Presidency

Tyler's term thus began with a constitutional imbroglio about his status (see Chapter 9, "William Henry Harrison"). Some observers, like former president John Quincy Adams, argued that the imprecise language of the Constitution meant only that the vice president should acquire the powers of the presidency—but not the office itself.[7] Thus, Adams opined that

Tyler should be known as the "Vice-President acting as President."[8] Some even thought that a special election would be required to fill the position. Yet, from the moment Tyler assumed the office, he made clear that he would be assuming the office no less than the powers and formally took the presidential oath of office on April 6, 1841, to ratify his claim. Thereafter, Tyler would not accept any salutation unless it was "Mr. President," and refused to acknowledge anyone who addressed him as "Mr. Acting President." For the rest of his presidency, however, Tyler would be dogged by the derisive moniker "His Accidency," even though both houses of Congress ultimately passed resolutions recognizing his decision.[9]

Yet, Tyler shored up the political and constitutional viability of such "accidental" administrations. His determination on this issue ensured that such future occupants of the White House would not become mere placeholders who were less powerful or less legitimate than a popularly elected chief executive.[10]

### The Dorr Rebellion

In 1842, early in Tyler's presidency, a constitutional crisis with national implications, and sparked by a rebellion in Rhode Island, came to a head. Unlike the other states, Rhode Island continued to be governed under its colonial charter dating back to 1663. The document, among other things, allowed the state's General Assembly to control the qualifications for voting and office holding. The legislature continued to limit voting to white male property owners (the property ownership requirements had been generally abolished by the 1820s in the rest of the states). Dissatisfaction finally reached a boiling point when attorney Thomas Dorr issued a plea asking the legislature to call a state convention to revise the archaic document. The General Assembly of Rhode Island flatly rejected the request and ignored the growing unrest. In response, Dorr and other reformists organized a rump state convention in 1841. The convention introduced significant reforms in a "people's Constitution," which was then adopted in a statewide referendum of all white adult males. The existing state government formulated its own more modest set of reforms, but when the reforms were put to the vote of the smaller, officially recognized electorate, they were narrowly defeated.[11]

Early in 1842, Thomas Dorr and his followers then set up their own state government in Rhode Island, selecting Dorr as an alternate governor.

The ever-escalating tensions seemed to presage an outbreak of violence, prompting the incumbent governor, Samuel Ward King, to ask President Tyler for federal military intervention to stave off violence and rebellion. Governor King invoked Article IV, Section 4, of the U.S. Constitution, which states: "The United States shall guarantee to every State . . . a Republican Form of Government, and shall protect each of them against invasion; and on Application of the Legislature, or of the Executive (when the Legislature cannot be convened) against domestic Violence."

Tyler's vehement opposition to both Andrew Jackson's threat of military force against South Carolina in 1833 and the resulting Force Bill suggested that President Tyler's response would be more circumspect than Jackson's, and indeed it was. In an April 11 letter to the state's governor, Tyler expressed concern for the situation in Rhode Island, but denied the governor's request for federal involvement. He stated that "no power is vested in the executive of the United States to *anticipate* insurrectionary movements against the government of Rhode Island." Rather, he said, before federal military authority could be invoked "there must be an actual insurrection."[12] Moreover, Tyler emphasized that Congress had already settled the question, in effect, by seating the representatives and senators from the existing (charter) government. Thus, the president stated, Congress had recognized the qualifications of the senators and House members from the original charter government as the legitimate "Republican Form of government"; there was nothing more for him to do.[13]

Soon after the president's proclamation, Dorr and followers attempted to seize state offices, prompting Governor King to declare martial law. Tyler again demurred, urging the governor to be conciliatory toward the rebellious forces. After sending an envoy to the state, however, President Tyler exercised his authority and ordered the rebels to cease, warning that if they failed to do so, he would call on the governors of two neighboring states to send in militias to restore order.[14] This final threat ended the rebellion.

In the aftermath of these events, in 1843, the state government in Rhode Island called a proper state convention, which approved universal white male suffrage. Of equal importance, the Dorr episode also prompted a major U.S. Supreme Court case, *Luther v. Borden* (1849), in which the Court was confronted with, but ducked, the Article IV issue (relating to what constituted a valid "Republican Form of Government").[15] In siding with the existing Rhode Island government's lawyer, Daniel Webster, the Court ruled that the issue was a "political question" that was "non-justiciable," meaning that it was not within the Court's purview to resolve this issue. The Supreme Court thus sidestepped the central question of which of the two competing state governments in Rhode Island was legitimate. In articulating the "political questions" doctrine, the Court determined that, under the Constitution, it was within the province of Congress and the president, as the political branches of government elected by the people, to determine whether the guarantee of a republican form of government had been upheld in Rhode Island, rather than the courts. The Court also held that President Tyler's recognition of the incumbent governor as the lawful executive and the president's declaration that he would take "measures to call out the militia" if the rebels did not cease their insurrection, were valid as a means to quell the uprising.[16]

Tyler's approach was surely consistent with his narrow view of federal and executive power. Was his reluctance to commit federal troops a sign of weakness or commendable restraint? Would the logjam in Rhode Island have been broken sooner if Tyler had issued a Jackson-like threat? If nothing else, this incident proved that Rhode Island's intransigent governor and legislature were on the wrong side of the march toward greater democratization and universal suffrage. Of equal importance, however, the standoff in Rhode Island gave birth to the political-questions doctrine, which continues to caution the Supreme Court to stay out of certain sensitive political issues, leaving them to Congress and the president.

### Controversial Veto Use

Congressional Whigs, led by the ambitious and frustrated presidential aspirant Senator Henry Clay of Kentucky, had initially expected Tyler to be deferential to Congress as they pushed Clay's American System agenda. The agenda included federally financed internal improvements, protective tariffs, and a national bank. Tyler was not obliging, however. On August 16, 1841, he vetoed the Whig-backed bank bill. While he clearly had consistently harbored doubts about the bank and while this veto came as no real surprise to Clay Whigs, Tyler had mostly kept his views to himself and was reluctant to communicate his views directly to members of Congress. Tyler's propensities in this regard magnified congressional outrage.[17] Even so, the veto was sustained in the Senate.

Clay Whigs immediately set about to draft a new bank bill that responded to Tyler's objections, which had been specified at least in part in

Tyler's veto message. Congress worked rapidly, and the new bill was sent to the president in early September. Tyler knew that his political position was weak, but he paid little heed to the advice of others; "for the most part, he followed his own counsel."[18] At first, the president signaled that the bill should go ahead, but then he asked that it be postponed in Congress. (It was not.)[19] On September 9, and without consulting with his cabinet, Tyler again vetoed the bank bill. In his second veto message, he stated that he had exercised his veto "with extreme regret" and "great pain," and that it was a power to be "most cautiously exerted."[20] He declared that presidents bore an obligation to use the power when circumstances dictate.

Tyler's statement of veto principles stood on firm constitutional grounds, but his vacillation and reticence to address the bank issue publicly or more forthrightly only infuriated his opponents. In response to the veto, Tyler's entire cabinet—except for Secretary of State Daniel Webster—resigned on September 11, 1841.[21] In addition, the Whigs expelled him from the party. Congress's fury extended to an effort in both the House and the Senate to consider a constitutional amendment to lower the veto override from two-thirds to a simple majority.[22] To Tyler opponents such as Representative Samson Mason of Ohio, the veto was "his royal prerogative" that too easily became "an engine of the most odious tyranny."[23]

## Impeachment Effort

On June 29, Tyler issued his third veto, this time of a provisional tariff bill. Though this veto was expected, it set off a howl of protest and a flood of debate, both in Congress and throughout the country. One Whig newspaper called Tyler a "corrupt fool and knave who pretends to act as President of the United States" but who "ought to be shot down in his tracks, as he walks along."[24] Debate in Congress was no more civil. Representative James Cooper of Pennsylvania called Tyler "a stupid yet perfidious devil amongst those cast out of heaven," further comparing Tyler to "Judas Iscariot, who sold his Master for thirty pieces of silver. He was both a traitor and an ingrate. Thus the parallel between him and the President starts fair; but to assert that it continues throughout, would be doing injustice to the memory of Judas, who repented, returned the money, and hung himself."[25] Strident rhetoric notwithstanding, Tyler's veto was sustained in the House.

Tyler's fourth veto also rejected a tariff bill, which had been enacted to generate desperately needed revenue. Issued on June 29, Tyler's veto message was nearly obsequious. He stated that he was returning the bill to Congress "with unfeigned regret." He went on: "Nothing can be more painful to any individual called upon to perform the Chief Executive duties under our limited Constitution than to be constrained to withhold his assent from an important measure adopted by the Legislature."[26] By now, Tyler's opponents were talking openly of impeachment.[27]

On January 10, 1843, Representative John Minor Botts of Virginia introduced articles of impeachment in the House. Among the articles' nine charges, the two central charges were "withholding his assent to laws indispensable to the just operations of Government" and "an arbitrary, despotic and corrupt abuse of the veto power."[28] An additional count condemned Tyler for his so-called fifth veto (it was not actually a veto), in which he signed a bill into law, but recorded his objections questioning the law's constitutionality.[29] A vote to refer the impeachment articles to committee failed, ending the first impeachment effort against a president in American history.[30]

Undaunted, Tyler issued four more vetoes during his presidency, for a total of ten in four years. His last veto, of a bill pertaining to revenue vessels and steam cutters, came in February 1845 and faced the first successful congressional override up to that time. Yet it was Tyler's first four vetoes that fell like hammer blows in Congress and in much of the country. By one account, "Tyler's rejection of the bank and tariff bills represented the height of the veto power . . . because they destroyed the very foundation of the Whig political program."[31] Political scientist Richard Pious later concluded that Tyler "had demonstrated conclusively that a president without a shred of popular or party support could wield prerogative power and by doing so reduce his congressional opponents to complete ineffectiveness in policymaking."[32]

Tyler's use of the veto enraged his foes, undercut what little political capital he had, and doomed his presidency. Moreover, his failure to lay the proper groundwork for this exercise of political powers insured the political hurricane that followed. Yet, the net result of the maelstrom over Tyler's veto use ended up turning the balance in favor of the president.

From 1841 to 1843, Congress debated at length whether Tyler was abusing executive power and, if so, to what extent he was doing so. Many in Congress argued that the veto was itself a monarchical, undemocratic, and abusive power, especially if used more than rarely; that the founders meant for the power to be used rarely or under limited circumstances; and that the veto constituted improper executive influence over the legislative process. Although such congressional debates filled literally hundreds of pages in the *Congressional Globe*, they marked the end of a bitter struggle between Congress and the chief executive. In this case, Tyler and his few strident defenders finally established that, constitutionally, presidents operate under no limits on the number of, or reasons for, vetoes.[33] While excessive or otherwise unskilled use of the veto is politically costly for a president, the failed Tyler presidency ultimately won for the institutional presidency the right to unconstrained veto use. Even more significantly, the enhanced veto power became the leading edge for greater executive influence over the legislative process, opening the door to the modern legislative presidency of the twentieth century.[34]

To modern political sensibilities, the idea that even a president's most vehement opponents would bring impeachment charges against a president for the exercise of four vetoes would seem a frivolous, if not absurd charge. Yet in the early nineteenth century, presidential involvement in legislative matters was generally limited and circumspect. Indeed, it was generally assumed that Congress functioned as the first branch of government. Andrew Jackson had managed to challenge Congress on many fronts, survive a censure vote, and pursue an activist presidency, yet his ability to do so was possible largely because he was the beneficiary of two large electoral mandates.

Tyler, on the other hand, was a politically artless president without a mandate, a power base, or even a party. His veto actions were, in many respects, no less significant for the future of the American presidency than Jackson's were. However, Tyler riled Congress with his aggressive veto use, and he had scant political capital to ward off the ensuing attacks.

## Texas Annexation and Second Term

Tyler continued to harbor aspirations to win a second term, and he hoped that his support for the annexation of Texas might be the vehicle for such a minor political miracle. Texas had won independence from Mexico in 1836 but functioned as an independent country. Sentiments favoring its annexation to the United States were strong, but Texas recognized slavery, so its admission would complicate the delicate balance between free and slave state representatives in Congress. Since Tyler was an outcast from both parties, he hoped to form a new party, the Democratic Republicans, around Texas annexation. The new party held a brief convention in May 1844, at the same time that the Democrats were holding theirs, yet Tyler's hope that the Democrats might turn to him if the Democratic convention deadlocked never materialized.[35] In yet another awkward move, Tyler appointed John C. Calhoun as his secretary of state in 1844. Calhoun would then assume responsibility for negotiations with the nation of Texas. Yet, Calhoun was a fervent and vocal supporter of slavery, which was enough to sink the annexation treaty in the Senate. Tyler shifted tactics, however. He viewed the 1844 election of James K. Polk as an endorsement of Texas annexation, so in his December 1844 message to Congress, he focused mainly on the Texas question and submitted to Congress a measure to approve annexation by joint resolution, which required only a simple majority vote of both houses to win passage. The House passed an amended version in January 1845, but the matter stalled in the Senate. Yet thanks at least in part to President-elect Polk's personal efforts, the Senate relented and approved the bill, which Tyler signed on March 1. Even though Tyler's hopes of riding the Texas question to another term had long passed, he could at least claim the annexation as a final accomplishment.

### Supreme Court Nominations

As if to cement his legacy as a presidential and constitutional failure, Tyler holds the unenviable record of fewest Senate confirmations of his Supreme Court nominees.[36] When a seat on the High Court opened in 1843 on the death of Justice Smith Thompson, Tyler nominated his treasury secretary, John C. Spencer, but Clay's animus toward the nominee ended Spencer's chances. Tyler then nominated a New York attorney for the post, but before the Senate could act, another vacancy occurred with the death of Justice Henry Baldwin. Tyler offered that post to future president James Buchanan, who declined the offer. With this scrambled set of events, Tyler then nominated a prominent Philadelphia lawyer, but by now Tyler opponents seized the chance to delay both nominations until after the 1844 elections. His hands tied, lame duck Tyler withdrew both nominations after the November election and offered one post to New York Chief Judge Samuel Nelson, who was rapidly confirmed in early 1845. When Tyler nominated another prominent lawyer for the second vacancy, the Senate adjourned without taking action, leaving the nomination to Tyler's successor, James K. Polk, as a final slap in the face of the outgoing president.

## Conclusion

After his presidency, Tyler and his young second wife (whom he married in 1844 after his first wife died of a stroke) retired to his Virginia plantation. They lived quietly until 1860, when threats of a civil war drew Tyler back into politics in a vain effort to stave off war. In 1861, he presided over the Peace Convention in Richmond, Virginia, which sought to fashion a compromise to prevent war. Tyler then embraced the Southern cause and won election to the Confederate House of Representatives. Many in the North and several native-born, prominent Virginians who remained loyal to the Union condemned Tyler as a treasonous turncoat.[37] Tyler died in 1862, days before he was to take his seat.[38]

Even taking into account the circumstances under which Tyler became president, there is little doubt that his clumsy political actions only weakened his position; keener judgment on his part "would quite probably have saved him grave political embarrassment."[39] Yet here was a man who, on paper at least, had superb political credentials and the personal traits most highly valued in political leaders: courage, confidence, intelligence, experience, and a strong adherence to principle. Nonetheless, these leadership traits proved to be less of a boon and more of a boondoggle. Courage may too easily become foolhardiness; confidence and experience may become arrogance; intelligence can become rigidity; principles may become ideological blinders. What Tyler lacked was a key trait that too often fails to appear on the list of desired skills: political sense.

Despite his failings, Tyler contributed importantly to the evolution of the constitutional presidency, especially in affirming the full powers of vice presidents who find themselves presidents and in ending the debate over constitutionally based limitations of the veto power. These contributions were not purely accidental, but they were largely inadvertent. Tyler's weak and failed presidency—and it was both—also ultimately extended executive power for the presidential institution.

NOTES

1. Edward P. Crapol, *John Tyler: The Accidental President* (Chapel Hill: University of North Carolina Press, 2006), 2.
2. Robert Seager II, *And Tyler Too: A Biography of John & Julia Gardiner Tyler* (New York: McGraw-Hill, 1963), 147.

3. Oliver Perry Chitwood, *John Tyler: Champion of the Old South* (New York: Russell & Russell, 1964), 112–115.

4. Norma Lois Peterson, *The Presidencies of William Henry Harrison and John Tyler* (Lawrence: University Press of Kansas, 1989), 26–27.

5. Tippecanoe was identified with Harrison, as he won fame for commanding American forces in the 1811 battle of Tippecanoe, in which government forces defeated an attacking force of Native Americans near the Tippecanoe River.

6. For good, basic sources of general information about the Tyler presidency, see "[John Tyler]: Life Before the Presidency," in *America President: A Reference Resource*, Miller Center at the University of Virginia, accessed May 27, 2015, http://millercenter.org/president/tyler/essays/biography/2; and "John Tyler's Presidency," *The History Channel*, accessed May 27, 2015, www.history.com/topics/john-tyler.

7. U.S. Const. art. II, § 1 stated that if the office of president were to become vacant, "the Same shall devolve on the Vice President."

8. Peterson, *William Henry Harrison and John Tyler*, 48. Harrison's cabinet members came to the same conclusion when they hurriedly met to discuss the situation before Tyler's arrival in the nation's capital. Ibid., 45. Constitutional and presidency scholar Edward S. Corwin, *The President: Office and Powers* (New York: NYU Press, 1957), 345, concluded that "it was the intention of the Framers that the Vice-President, for whatever reason he 'succeeded' the President, should remain Vice-President unless and until he was elected President." Assuming Corwin to be correct, the framers' judgment on this issue differed significantly from what later occupants of the office of vice president decided.

9. For more on the controversy engendered by Tyler on his handling of succession, see Robert J. Morgan, *A Whig Embattled: The Presidency under John Tyler* (Lincoln: University of Nebraska Press, 1954), 6–12.

10. In addition to Tyler, vice presidents who succeeded to the presidency through means other than independent election include Millard Fillmore, Andrew Johnson, Chester Arthur, Calvin Coolidge, Harry Truman, Lyndon Johnson, and Gerald Ford.

11. Peterson, *William Henry Harrison and John Tyler*, 108–112.

12. Lyon G. Tyler, *The Letters and Times of the Tylers*, 3 vols. (New York: Da Capo Press, 1970), 2:195 (emphasis added).

13. Michael J. Gerhardt, *The Forgotten Presidents: Their Untold Constitutional Legacy* (New York: Oxford Press, 2013), 65.

14. The use of militias of other states was not without precedent. Connecticut and New York assisted the Massachusetts government to suppress Shays' Rebellion in 1787. David P. Szatmary, *Shays' Rebellion: The Making of an Agrarian Insurrection* (Amherst: University of Massachusetts Press, 1980), 116–117.

15. Luther v. Borden, 48 U.S. 1 (1849).

16. Ibid.

17. Chitwood, *John Tyler*, 225; Peterson, *William Henry Harrison and John Tyler*, 71–72.

18. Peterson, *William Henry Harrison and John Tyler*, 81.

19. Ibid., 92.

20. James D. Richardson III, *Messages and Papers of the Presidents*, 11 vols. (Washington, DC: Bureau of National Literature, 1913), 3:1921–1922.

21. Secretary Webster was in the midst of negotiations with the British over issues involving the Maine-Quebec border. Once those negotiations were settled, he too resigned from Tyler's cabinet.

22. Robert J. Spitzer, *The Presidential Veto: Touchstone of the American Presidency* (Albany: SUNY Press, 1988), 42–47.

23. Samson Mason, "Objections of the President to the Bill to Establish a Fiscal Corporation" (delivered in the House of Representatives), *National Intelligencer*, September 10, 1841.

24. Carlton Jackson, *Presidential Vetoes, 1792–1945* (Athens: University of Georgia Press, 1967), 66.

25. Rep. Cooper, *Congressional Globe*, July 1, August 4, 1842: appendix, 867, 803.

26. Richardson, *Messages and Papers of the Presidents*, 3:2036–2037.

27. Peterson, *William Henry Harrison and John Tyler*, 102–103.

28. *Journal of the House of Representatives of the United States*, January 10, 1843, 15–59.

29. This action was an early instance of what is now known as a signing statement, an otherwise uncontroversial action by presidents that, in controversial instances, questions (or even repudiates) a law's constitutionality, even though presidents sign the bills in question into law. Robert J. Spitzer, "Liberals and the Presidency," in *Contending Approaches to the American Presidency*, ed. Michael A. Genovese (Washington, DC: CQ Press, 2012), 87–90; Louis Fisher, *Defending Congress and the Constitution* (Lawrence: University Press of Kansas, 2011), 55.

30. The impeachment effort occurred during the lame duck session of the Twenty-Seventh Congress (1841–1843). The Whigs had lost control of Congress in the 1842 midterm election, and the Democrats had no desire to press impeachment against a president who had done so much to thwart the Whigs.

31. Jackson, *Presidential Vetoes*, 72.

32. Richard Pious, *The American Presidency* (New York: Basic Books, 1979), 64.

33. Spitzer, *The Presidential Veto*, 17–21.

34. Robert J. Spitzer, *President and Congress: Executive Hegemony at the Crossroads of American Government* (New York: McGraw-Hill, 1993), 27–39.

35. Peterson, *William Henry Harrison and John Tyler*, 224.

36. Kermit L. Hall, ed., *The Oxford Companion to the Supreme Court of the United States* (New York: Oxford University Press, 1992), 884–885.

37. Crapol, *John Tyler: The Accidental President*, 275–277.

38. As of 2014, Tyler had two living grandsons—remarkable, given that the tenth president was born 224 years earlier.

39. Morgan, *A Whig Embattled*, 27.

# 11

# James K. Polk

FRANK J. WILLIAMS

*James K. Polk, who believed it was the nation's "Manifest Destiny" to expand its boundaries and rebuild western lands in its own image, swiftly led America into war with Mexico. Polk claimed that Mexican forces had killed American soldiers on American soil, yet this claim was viewed with skepticism by members of Congress, including Representative Abraham Lincoln. Whether Polk had usurped Congress's power under the Constitution was a question that would stamp his presidency with a lingering question mark. Yet under Polk's leadership, the country grew by more than a third (more than one million square miles) and was for the first time bounded by two oceans. Polk thus set out to use his constitutional powers to become an expansionist president and accomplished that goal.*

FRANK J. WILLIAMS

## Introduction

James Knox Polk, the nation's eleventh president, was an unlikely candidate for that post, entering into the 1844 presidential race only after matters of foreign policy, namely, the U.S. expansion, became the dominant campaign issue. The young Tennessean and Jackson protégé nicknamed "Young Hickory" took office in 1845. He had a penchant for westward expansion and, just over a year later, informed Congress that the nation was at war with Mexico. It was this declaration that would cause Polk's critics to raise issues of constitutional dimension, challenging the president's authority to set such a policy. Despite such criticism, when Polk's term of office ended in 1849, he left a dramatically different nation from that which he inherited.

Polk was born on January 2, 1795, in Mecklenburg County, North Carolina, on his family's farm.[1] When he was ten years old, his family relocated to the Tennessee wilderness, where he learned to farm. At the age of twenty, the studious and ambitious Polk set aside his rural training and returned to North Carolina to complete his education. He graduated with honors from the University of North Carolina in 1818.[2] After graduation, he returned to Tennessee, where he studied for, and took up, the practice of law.[3] Like many young lawyers of his day, Polk became active in politics, serving seven terms in the Tennessee legislature and acting as the Speaker of the U.S. House of Representatives between 1835 and 1839 before his election as governor of Tennessee. In 1841, he was defeated in his bid for reelection as governor, but the loss would not end his political career.[4] Three years later, the presidential election of 1844 would bring to the forefront issues that propelled Polk into the presidency.

The dominant issue during the campaign of 1844 concerned the annexation of Texas. The issue "exploded just in time to take effect on the two great nominating conventions and their platforms."[5] In fact, by the time the subject of annexation rose to the forefront, the parties already had their favored presidential nominees. The Whig nomination was expected to go to Henry Clay, and the Democratic nomination to Martin Van Buren. Recognizing that Texas's annexation was the dominant issue, Clay and Van Buren expressed their views on the matter on the same day, both opposing immediate annexation of Texas. Yet public opinion was growing against this position; as a result, Van Buren lost the nomination. With Van Buren

[ 150 ]

out, the door was opened for a dark horse—a new name on the ballot, that of James Knox Polk—to be considered at the Democratic convention. When Polk's name appeared for consideration, many party members were left asking, "Who is Polk?"[6]

Unlike Van Buren and Clay, Polk argued that Texas should be "re-annexed" and all of Oregon "re-occupied." Polk's support of this extensive expansion of the nation throughout North America became known as Manifest Destiny. Indeed, this position earned him the Democratic nomination. At the urging of close advisers, when Polk accepted the nomination, he pledged that, if elected, he would not seek a second term.[7] This promise was consistent with a mantra of the Whigs, who called on all presidential candidates to take such a pledge and even demanded a constitutional amendment limiting chief executives to a single four-year term.[8] The one-term pledge served Polk well. It denied the Whigs, who raised the prospect of eight more years of another Jackson and tried to insist that a one-term presidency was essential to limited executive government, two of their more potent campaign rallying cries. It also prompted Democrats, who harbored their own presidential aspirations, to place their ambitions on hold and unite behind Polk.[9] Polk won the election with 62 percent of the Electoral College vote.

Thus, the dark-horse candidate prevailed, to the surprise of many seasoned politicians. Among other things, Polk's victory in the 1844 presidential election was perceived as a strong message that the people of the United States wanted to annex Texas.[10]

## Presidency

When he assumed the presidency on March 4, 1845, Polk was forty-nine years old and then the youngest person to hold this office. The young president's penchant for westward expansion had led to his election; before he could even take office, Congress passed a joint resolution offering annexation to Texas.[11] This action, however, nearly guaranteed a dispute, if not a war, with Mexico over the nation's borders. However, war did not ensue on that account and would not erupt until more than a year later.

Throughout the earliest days of his presidency, Polk remained committed to his campaign platform and his firm belief in expansion. The former farmer and lifelong slaveholder believed that expansion would open up more land for agriculture. Polk's focus was on the country's expansion—not the growing controversy over slavery. Like many in his party, he considered slavery a side issue. In Polk's view, the issue could only distract his administration from its political goals, which included consolidation of the nation's position on the North American landmass.[12] With continued westward expansion in mind, after the Texas annexation, Polk focused his energies on acquiring from Mexico the area of California, which he considered an access point for trade with Asia. This foreign-policy goal would thrust Polk into a constitutional dilemma that would become a lasting part of his legacy.

President Polk, a "strict constitutionalist" in at least domestic affairs, ironically believed that the government did not have the authority to perform any functions not clearly spelled out in the Constitution.[13] He preferred less government and believed that the national government should have limited powers.[14] In his inaugural address, he invoked the Constitution and spoke to that point:

> It will be my first care to administer the Government in the true spirit of that instrument, and to assume no powers not expressly or clearly implied in its terms. The Government of the United States is one of delegated and limited powers; and it is by a strict adherence to the clearly granted powers, and by abstaining from the exercise of doubtful or unauthorized implied powers, that we have the only sure guarantee against the recurrence of those unfortunate collisions between the Federal and State authorities which have, occasionally, so much disturbed the harmony of our system, and even threatened the perpetuity of our glorious Union.[15]

Although absolute in his beliefs on the limited domestic powers that came with the office of the president, Polk nevertheless led the country into war with Mexico, and as a result, he was criticized by some for usurping Congress's constitutional war-making powers.

### War with Mexico

Less than a year into his presidency, amid turmoil over the U.S. desire to purchase California and New Mexico from Mexico, on October 16, 1845, President Polk ordered General Zachary Taylor and his troops to the Rio Grande, the territory that was in dispute between Texas and Mexico. Seven months later, Polk received word that Mexican forces had crossed the Rio Grande and killed eleven American soldiers. Some critics argued that Polk provoked the violence by ordering General Taylor to move his troops to the edge of this area that the United States claimed for Texas and that Mexico claimed for itself.[16] Others have cast doubt over whether the slayings actually took place on American soil.[17] Nevertheless, with that bloodshed as a justification, on May 11, 1846, Polk delivered a message to Congress, stating that Mexico had "invaded our territory and shed American blood upon the American soil. She has proclaimed that hostilities have commenced, and that the two nations are now at war."[18] Polk pleaded with Congress to act swiftly: "In further vindication of our rights and defense of our territory, I invoke the prompt action of Congress to recognize the existence of the war, and to place at the disposition of the Executive the means of prosecuting the war with vigor, and thus hastening the restoration of peace."[19]

Congress overwhelmingly approved the declaration of war, yet some senators and representatives sharply criticized President Polk.[20] Senator John Calhoun (D-SC) objected, asserting that simply because a president says there is a war, "there is no war according to my sense of the Constitution." In his view, there was a distinction between hostilities and war. "The President is authorized to repel invasion without war. But it is *our* sacred duty to make war, and it is for *us* to determine whether war shall be declared or not."[21] Congressman Alexander H. Stephens (D-GA) urged a similar interpretation of the Constitution in an address to Congress:

> The Constitution gives Congress the sole power to declare war. Perhaps some gentlemen may suppose that clause in the Constitution simply means that when the President gets us into war, it is the business of Congress to make it known—to declare it—or recognize the fact. This, however, is not my understanding of it. Congress alone has the right and power to engage in war. The President has the right to repel hostilities; but not by his policy with other nations to bring on and involve the country in a war without consultation with Congress.[22]

As one recent commentator has noted, the observations made by Polk's critics turned out to be correct. In the case of the Mexican-American conflict during the Polk administration, Congress did not set the policy on war. The legislature only affirmed the president's actions and the policy he set.[23]

In his second annual message to Congress, President Polk defended his decisions, explaining that the "existing war with Mexico was neither desired nor provoked by the United States. . . . After years of endurance of aggravated and unredressed wrongs on our part, Mexico, in violation of solemn treaty stipulations, and of every principle of justice recognised [*sic*] by civilized nations, commenced hostilities, and thus, by her own act, forced the war upon us."[24]

## The Spot Resolutions

The Whig constituency, however, demanded that Polk provide evidence to support his claims that Mexico had invaded U.S. territory. On December 22, 1847, Abraham Lincoln, who was then a brand-new member of Congress from the frontier West, introduced the Spot Resolutions, which questioned Polk's claim that American blood had been shed by Mexicans on U.S. soil.[25] The resolutions demanded that Polk both submit evidence to Congress of the exact "spot" where the attack had taken place and show that "Mexico herself became the aggressor by invading our soil in hostile array."[26] The president did not respond to the obscure new representative's demand; nor did Congress adopt the Spot Resolutions. As a result, Lincoln earned the nickname "Spotty Lincoln." Weeks later, however, Lincoln voted in favor of a resolution introduced by Whig Congressman George Ashmun of Massachusetts; it stated that the war had been "unnecessarily and unconstitutionally" initiated by the president.[27]

Lincoln later argued in a letter to his third and youngest law partner, William H. Herndon, that President Polk had exceeded his authority under the Constitution. Herndon had argued that "if it shall become necessary, to repel invasion, the President may, without violation of the Constitution, cross the line, and invade the teritory [*sic*] of another country; and that whether such necessity exists in any given case, the President is to be the sole judge."[28] In response, Lincoln argued:

> Allow the President to invade a neighboring nation, whenever he shall deem it necessary to repel an invasion, and you allow him to do so, whenever he may choose to say he deems it necessary for such purpose—and you allow him to make war at pleasure. . . . The provision of the Constitution giving the war-making power to Congress, was dictated, as I understand it, by the following reasons. Kings had always been involving and impoverishing their people in wars, pretending generally, if not always, that the good of the people was the object. This, our Convention understood to be the most oppressive of all Kingly oppressions; and they resolved to so frame

the Constitution that no one man should hold the power of bringing this oppression upon us. But your view destroys the whole matter, and places our President where kings have always stood.[29]

Such comments are surprising from the man who would later become president and, like Polk, would find the need to exercise powers that many believed exceeded what the framers had envisioned for the chief executive.

Regardless of whether conflict had broken out on U.S. soil, the nation had become embroiled in a war with Mexico, because of Polk's representation. In September 1847, General Winfield Scott captured Mexico City, and General Taylor was victorious in several battles in northern Mexico. While these victories did not result in Mexico's surrender, against this backdrop Mexico agreed to Polk's peace terms set forth in the Treaty of Guadalupe Hidalgo, which officially ended the war on February 2, 1848.[30] Under that treaty, Mexico lost 1.2 million square miles to the United States and was thus reduced to half its size. As a result, the United States gained what would become California, Nevada, Utah, most of Arizona, and parts of New Mexico, Colorado, and Wyoming.[31] The treaty also represented a formal recognition of Texas's annexation.

Despite President Polk's staunch adherence to the position that American blood had been shed on U.S. soil, after the war's conclusion in July 1848, Polk did finally concede that Texas had "never conquered or reduced to actual possession . . . that part of New Mexico lying east of the Rio Grande, which she claimed to be within her limits. On the breaking out of the war, we found Mexico in possession of this disputed territory."[32] Thus, Polk hinted at some level of potential error in initiating the war.

Whether it was constitutional or not, under Polk's leadership, the two-year war with Mexico extended the U.S. boundaries to the Pacific Ocean. His presidency was also successful in lowering tariffs, establishing an independent federal treasury, and issuing the first postage stamp.[33] His administration also began two significant construction projects that became important landmarks in the United States—the Washington Monument and the Smithsonian Institution, both in Washington, D.C.[34]

Less than a year later, his four-term presidency ended, and Polk, remaining true to his one-term pledge, did not seek reelection. To discourage efforts by some Democrats to convince him to renege on his promise, and to end speculation that he might run again, Polk sent a letter to the Democratic convention, making explicit that he would not accept the party's nomination for a second term.[35] Three months after leaving the White House, Polk contracted cholera in New Orleans and died at Polk Place, his Nashville home that he had purchased for his retirement.

## Conclusion

Whether intentional or not, Polk's misstatement that American blood had been shed on American soil resulted in the Mexican-American War. The constitutionality of his declaration and Congress's subsequent endorsement of war would be debated for decades to come. The spirit of the Constitution may have authorized the war, *if* it was in fact necessary for the protection and welfare of the nation. This argument, however, was not developed in Polk's day. Ironically, it would be developed when Lincoln, the proponent of the so-called Spot Resolutions, faced a similar predicament as president when he inherited a nation on the brink of war.

### NOTES

1. James K. Polk, *The Diary of James J. Polk During His Presidency, 1845 to 1849* (Chicago: A.C. McClurg & Co., 1910), xxiv.
2. Ibid.
3. Ibid., xxv.
4. Ibid.
5. Ibid., xxvii.
6. Ibid., xxviii.
7. Robert W. Merry, *A Country of Vast Designs* (New York: Simon & Shuster, 2009), 103–105.
8. William Henry Harrison, the only successful Whig candidate for president up to that point, had taken such a one-term pledge both when he accepted his party's nomination and again in this inaugural address. Walter R. Borneman, *Polk: The Man Who Transformed the Presidency and America* (New York: Random House, 2008) 113.
9. Ibid., 112–113. Significantly, Polk's pledge did not, in his view, commit his party to the one-term principle. Rather, it simply articulated his own political intentions. Ibid., 115.
10. George Pierce Garrison, *Westward Extension 1841–1850* (New York: Harper & Brothers, 1906), 136–137.
11. Ibid., 141–155.
12. Merry, *A Country of Vast Designs*, 128–130. Whether Polk, a lifelong slave owner, supported the expansion of slavery into Texas is disputed. However, many Southern planters strongly favored the annexation of Texas because they believed that it would become a slave state. Paul H. Bergeron, *The Presidency of James K. Polk* (Lawrence: University Press of Kansas, 1987), 51–53.

13. Carl Cavanagh Hodge and Cathal J. Nolan, *US Presidents and Foreign Policy* (Santa Barbara, CA: ABC-CLIO, 2007), 91.

14. Mark Eaton Byrnes, *James K. Polk: A Biographical Companion* (Santa Barbara, CA: ABC-CLIO, 2001), 106.

15. William Chauncey Fowler, *The Sectional Controversy; or, Passages in the Political History of the United States, including the Causes of the War Between the Sections, with Certain Results* (New York: Charles Scribner and Company, 1868), 137.

16. Michael S. Green, *Politics and America in Crisis: The Coming of the Civil War* (Santa Barbara, CA: ABC-CLIO, 2010), 5.

17. Louis Fisher, "The Mexican War and Lincoln's 'Spot Resolutions,'" *Law Library of Congress*, August 18, 2009, available at http://loc.gov/law/help/usconlaw/pdf/Mexican. war.pdf.

18. Byrnes, *James K. Polk: A Biographical Companion*, 257.

19. Ibid.

20. Arthur H. Garrison, *Supreme Court Jurisprudence in Times of National Crisis, Terrorism, and War* (Lanham, MD: Lexington Books, 2011), 27.

21. Cong. Globe, 29th Cong., 1st Sess. 784 (1846) (emphasis in original).

22. Henry Cleveland, *Alexander H. Stephens in Public and Private: With Letters and Speeches* (Philadelphia: National Publishing Company, 1866), 304.

23. Garrison, *Supreme Court Jurisprudence*, 27.

24. James K. Polk, *Message from the President of the United States to the Two Houses of Congress* (Washington, DC: Ritchie & Heiss, 1846), 3.

25. Harold Holzer, *Lincoln on War* (Chapel Hill: Algonquin Books of Chapel Hill, 2011), 27.

26. Ibid.; Doris Kearns Goodwin, *Team of Rivals: The Political Genius of Abraham Lincoln* (New York: Simon & Schuster, 2005), 121.

27. Goodwin, *Team of Rivals*, 121.

28. Abraham Lincoln, *The Collected Works of Abraham Lincoln*, ed. Roy P. Basler (New Brunswick, NJ: Rutgers University Press, 1953–1955), 1:451–452.

29. Ibid.

30. Eugene Irving McCormac, *James K. Polk: A Political Biography* (Berkley: University of California Press, 1922), 487–555.

31. John DiConsiglio, *Living Through the Mexican American War* (Chicago: Heinemann Library, 2012).

32. James K. Polk, "Message from the President of the United States to the House of Representatives," July 24, 1848, in *American Quarterly Register and Magazine* 1 (1848): 562.

33. Wayne Cutler, ed., *Correspondence of James K. Polk* (Knoxville: University of Tennessee Press, 1993), 8:104.

34. Carol H. Behramn, *James K. Polk* (Minneapolis: Lerner Publications, 2005), 95.

35. Polk's decision against standing for reelection contributed to a split in the Democratic Party; the split paved the way for Zachary Taylor, a Whig candidate, to succeed Polk as president. Sam W. Haynes, *James K. Polk and the Expansionist Impulse* (New York: Pearson Longman, 2006), 201–202.

# PART III

# The Pre–Civil War Era

# 12

# Zachary Taylor

### PAUL FINKELMAN

*Zachary Taylor, a professional soldier and sugar planter with no previous political experience, held the office of president for barely sixteen months before dying of acute gastroenteritis. A war hero before moving into the White House, he immediately confronted a rogue effort (supported by Southern slave owners and politicians) to seize Cuba and had to address issues involving slavery in the new territories acquired from Mexico, demands for a new fugitive-slave law, and petitions for the admission of New Mexico and California as free states. A patriotic nationalist with a steady hand, Taylor was prepared to allow slavery where it existed, but was also ready to halt its expansion and face down Southern extremists. His death likely extinguished the nation's last hope for tamping down the fierce disagreements developing between North and South.*

## Introduction

Zachary Taylor was born in Virginia in 1784, but was raised in rural Kentucky, where his father, a Revolutionary War officer and minor Virginia politician, moved in 1785. Through his mother, Taylor was related to both James Madison and Robert E. Lee. In addition, before her untimely death, Taylor's daughter was married to Jefferson Davis. Thus, early in Taylor's life, he was also the father-in-law of the president of the future Confederacy. Accordingly, Taylor's familial connection to the Constitution was to its primary author, to a traitorous general who tried to destroy it, and to the West Point–trained former U.S. officer and former U.S. officer and former senator who led a treasonous rebellion against the Constitution he had sworn to support. Taylor came from a long line of planters, and throughout his life, he accumulated land and slaves. By the time he was elected president, in 1848, Taylor was an enormously wealthy man with sugar plantations in Louisiana and more than 140 slaves. While in the White House, he purchased another plantation with about 90 slaves.

Yet, Taylor's main occupation was always soldiering. Taylor joined the army when he was twenty-three, working his way up to captain. In 1812, President Madison elevated him to brevet major for his heroic and skilled defense of Fort Harrison in Indiana.[1] Taylor next served in Florida during the Second Seminole War, rising to the rank of brevet brigadier general. In May 1846, while he was serving in Mexico, President Polk promoted him to brevet major general, which later became his permanent rank.[2] Taylor returned from Mexico as a popular war hero and in July 1848 became the commanding general of the Western Division of the U.S. Army. He would retain that position until shortly before his inauguration.

Even before he left Mexico in December 1847, politicians were sizing up Taylor as a possible presidential candidate. Henry Clay of Kentucky, who barely lost the presidential election in 1844, considered himself the Whig frontrunner for 1848, but the aging Kentuckian had already failed to win the presidency in three elections (1824, 1832, and 1844). Many Whigs wanted a fresh face rather than a three-time loser. In December 1876, seven relatively young Whig congressmen who had previously supported Clay came out for Taylor.[3]

Taylor had never even voted in a presidential election. Like many military officers at the time, Taylor avoided electoral and partisan politics.[4] Supporters of Taylor compared him to Washington, the nonpartisan general, hero, and patriot. Taylor's candidacy also reminded Americans of Andrew Jackson and William Henry Harrison, military heroes who became presidents.[5]

At the Whig Convention in June 1848, Taylor received the most votes on the first ballot; by the fourth ballot, he had captured the nomination.[6] Clay, certain he would win the nomination in 1848, was stunned and bitter when the Whigs turned to a war hero with no formal political experience. After the election, Clay returned to the Senate, determined to take control of his party and fully prepared to undermine a president of his own party. Meanwhile, Taylor had become commanding general of all of the western armies of the United States, which raised interesting constitutional questions about the relationship between civilian authority and the military in a constitutional democracy.[7]

As was the custom of the age, Taylor did not personally campaign for the office, leaving that role to surrogates. Nor did he comment on the great issues surrounding the election; most of the issues concerned the new territories acquired from Mexico, slavery, or a combination of the two. He spent most of the campaign in Baton Rouge, serving as commander of the army's Western Division and using that military post to dodge the major questions of the campaign. Antislavery Democrats and others teamed up to create the nation's first viable antislavery political organization, the Free-Soil Party. Running former Democratic President Martin Van Buren, the Free-Soilers won nearly 300,000 popular votes. In Van Buren's home state of New York, he siphoned off about 120,000 votes from the Democratic candidate, Lewis Cass. This splitting of the party vote gave Taylor a victory in New York and the election.[8]

Taylor was the only person to be elected president while retaining a full-time commission in the army.[9] On December 21, 1848, more than a month after the election, he tendered his resignation from the army, effective February 28—less than a week before his inauguration. With a variety of conflicts brewing when he took office in March 1849, Taylor seemed to be the perfect leader to address the troublesome issues that faced the nation.

## Presidency

The new Congress, elected at the same time as Taylor, would not be in session until December 1849. Taylor hoped to deal with some of the most pressing issues before the new Congress convened. However, the most urgent ones—involving governments for the new territories and Southern demands for a new fugitive-slave law—ultimately required congressional action. Unfortunately for the new president, the disgruntled Clay immediately tried to deal with these issues in Congress without cooperating with Taylor or even consulting him. Clay, the lifelong leader of the Whig Party, essentially challenged the leadership of his own party's president, determined that he, Clay, and not the chief executive, should be both party leader and the de facto head of state. As a result, most of the issues that the new president faced would be unresolved and remain festering until Taylor's unexpected death sixteen months after he took office.

### The Fugitive-Slave Issue

In Article IV, Section 2, Clause 3, the U.S. Constitution provided that states could not emancipate slaves escaping into their jurisdictions, but instead had to return those slaves on the demand of the owner. This was not a particularly important issue when the Constitution was drafted in 1787; at that time, slavery was legal in every state but Massachusetts and New Hampshire.[10] The Fugitive Slave Act of 1793 authorized all American judges—federal, state, and local—to conduct a summary proceeding and then issue a certificate of removal to allow a master to bring a fugitive slave home.[11] Because there were very few federal judges at the time, enforcement was only possible with the cooperation of state and local judges. Starting in the 1820s, most Northern states had passed so-called personal liberty laws, which required state judges to impose a higher standard of evidence than the federal law for the return of a fugitive slave. Southerners claimed that these laws frustrated their attempts to recover their slave property. Northerners insisted such laws were necessary to prevent the kidnapping of free blacks. In *Prigg v. Pennsylvania* (1842), the U.S. Supreme Court had declared that these state laws unconstitutionally interfered with the power of Congress to enforce the Fugitive Slave Clause of the Constitution.[12]

Justice Joseph Story's majority opinion in *Prigg* had urged state officials to enforce the federal law as a matter of constitutional obligation and comity. However, applying a concept that is today known as unfunded mandates, Story also held that because Congress did not pay the salaries of state officials, Congress could not require them to enforce the federal law. Many free-state legislatures responded by prohibiting their officials from taking part in the return of fugitive slaves, and many Northern judges simply refused to act in fugitive-slave cases. Enforcement was thus left entirely up to the federal government. But with few federal judges or marshals available and no national police force in existence, the lack of state involvement severely limited the ability of slave owners to recover fugitive slaves. By 1849, when Taylor took office, Southerners were demanding a new federal law to vindicate their constitutional right to recover runaway slaves. Taylor, however, did not see this as a pressing issue and thought any discussion of it should be deferred until after California (with nearly one hundred thousand settlers) was admitted to the Union.

## Halting Illegal "Filibustering" in Cuba

Shortly after taking office, Taylor faced another constitutional issue, with both domestic and international implications. The matter arose from attempts by American citizens to seize the island of Cuba from Spain and to secure its annexation by the United States. During the summer of 1848, Narciso López, a former Spanish general and a Cuban landowner, who had fled to the United States because of his opposition to continued control of Cuba, began to organize an invasion force largely composed of Southerners from the United States. With this army, López planned to invade Cuba and overthrow Spanish rule. Known as filibustering, such expeditions were illegal under both American and international law.[13] Support for López came from Southerners—including some politicians—who wanted to acquire new lands for slavery and new sources of slaves. With more than three hundred thousand slaves, Cuba offered the opportunity for Americans to increase their slaveholding while providing the new land—and ultimately a new slave state—to support this most important institution.

López boldly approached various prominent men with experience in the Mexican War, including Jefferson Davis, Captain Robert E. Lee, and General William J. Worth, hoping they would help him with his effort to seize Cuba. None showed the slightest interest in this harebrained scheme that violated American laws dating from the Neutrality Act of 1794. Nevertheless, López recruited six hundred men, many of them veterans of the Mexican War. Most of the Americans in his putative army were from Mississippi and Louisiana, while others were Cuban refugees living in New York. López chartered three ships to transport his soldiers to Cuba. In August 1849, President Taylor issued a proclamation denouncing "an enterprise to invade the territories of a friendly nation" as "the highest degree criminal" and warning he would "prevent by all lawful means any such enterprise."

The administration swiftly moved to stop the expedition. The U.S. attorney in New Orleans investigated the plot while authorities in New York seized two of the vessels López had chartered. Authorities in New Orleans seized the third vessel while a U.S. Navy ship blockaded Round Island in the Gulf of Mexico, where the recruits were awaiting transportation to Cuba. Thus, Taylor skillfully used his law enforcement powers and his power as commander in chief to avoid an international incident and to prevent a major violation of American law.

López, however, was undeterred. He recruited more men for a second invasion in May 1850. This time, he received aid from John A. Quitman, the governor of Mississippi. López sailed into the gulf under the watchful eyes of the American navy with Quitman's help and by falsely asserting that his expedition was headed to California. The former Spanish general managed to invade Cuba, but after suffering significant casualties, he headed back to the United States, where he was arrested. Spanish authorities captured two other ships, arresting the bulk of the invasion force. Taylor pushed for the prosecution of López, Quitman, and other leaders of the plot, while at the same time negotiating with the Spanish to secure the return of the hapless adventurers captured and taken to Cuban prisons. This round of prosecutions proved futile, however, as juries in New Orleans would not convict these proslavery adventurers. Taylor's response to López illustrated his intolerance of the reckless use of military force, his opposition to American expansion against weaker neighbors, and his willingness to use the powers of his office to enforce the law. The response also showed his opposition to an expansion of slavery or aggressive proslavery schemes. He applied this same view to dealing with the newly acquired southwestern territories.

## The Texas Border

A significant constitutional challenge loomed over the exact size and shape of the state of Texas. Before 1836, Tejas had been the most northeastern state in Mexico. Under Mexican law and international agreements dating from the administration of James Monroe, the southern boundary of Tejas was the Nueces River (which ran through Corpus Christi, Texas). In 1836, Texas declared its independence from Mexico and claimed that its boundary extended about two hundred miles further south, to the Rio Grande. This disputed territory had been one of the causes of the Mexican War after the United States annexed Texas in 1845. When the war ended, the state government in Austin declared that its boundaries extended not only to the Rio Grande in the south but also to Santa Fe (in what is today New Mexico), some eight hundred miles west of Austin. With no territorial bill coming out of Congress and no civilian government in New Mexico, the governor of Texas was pushing to seize all the land between Austin and Santa Fe for his state. This development set the stage for a confrontation between federal troops and the Texas militia. Zachary Taylor had no intention of backing down. Instead, his goal was to develop a plan to organize the new territories while avoiding a huge debate over slavery. Thus, he decided to deal firmly with the Texas dispute while confronting issues in the territories with an equally firm hand.

## A Plan to Address Slavery in the Territories

By the late 1840s, some Southerners wanted to repeal the Compromise of 1820 (the Missouri Compromise) adopted during the presidency of James Monroe. As part of this compromise, Congress had admitted Missouri into the Union as a slave state, while banning slavery in all the territories directly west or north of Missouri. Some Southern critics of the compromise argued that all American citizens should have access to the federal territories and should be able to bring their property (including slave property) with them. The acquisition of vast new western land, gained through President Polk's aggressive war with Mexico—increasing the size of the nation by about 25 percent—had heightened the debate over the problem of slavery in the territories. Many Northerners who wanted to ban slavery in the new territories argued that the war with Mexico itself was part of a Southern plot to add new slave territory to the nation.

This claim threatened Northern Democrats in Congress, who might not be reelected if they became entangled in this issue. Representative David Wilmot of Pennsylvania attempted to solve the problem with a rider to an appropriations bill—known as the Wilmot Proviso—which sought to prohibit slavery in any territories acquired from Mexico. The House of Representatives, which had a large Northern majority, passed the Wilmot Proviso several times on an overwhelmingly sectional vote. In the Senate, however, a few Northerners voted with the South to defeat the proviso. This difference between the two houses of Congress led to stalemate, with no possibility of passing any legislation to govern the new territories.

Southerners had supported Taylor because they assumed he favored the spread of slavery into the West. As the historian David Potter noted, they "regarded Taylor as their man," and "trusting him as a southerner, they had not even asked him to state his position on the territories."[14] Yet, despite his Southern roots and his status as a slave owner, Taylor thought expanding slavery into the territories was politically counterproductive and economically pointless. Having seen the new territories, he did not believe they were suited to an agrarian economy or slavery.

When the congressional session began, Senator Henry Clay introduced a series of resolutions that together became known as the Omnibus Bill. Still smarting from not being nominated in 1848, Clay proposed this bill without any consultation with Taylor. Under Clay's bill, California would be admitted to the Union without "any restriction in respect to the exclusion introduction of slavery"; the remaining territories acquired from Mexico would be organized without any reference to slavery. This shrewd maneuver would have opened up the rest of the Mexican Cession to slavery. Central to Clay's proposal was a new fugitive-slave law. Clay's resolutions omitted the details of this law, but the eventual law would be among the most vicious bills ever passed by Congress. Not only would it deny alleged fugitives the right to a jury trial, but it would also prohibit them from even testifying on their own behalf. The law threatened the liberty of some two hundred thousand free blacks in the North, while obligating Northern militias to help enforce the act and providing huge fines and jail sentences for anyone helping an alleged fugitive slave. The bill also gave some new land to Texas (but not nearly what Texas would eventually be given under the Compromise of 1850) and authorized the federal government to bail out the Lone Star State by paying off all its pre-statehood debts.[15]

Taylor opposed all efforts to open the territories to slavery, but he also opposed the Wilmot Proviso as unnecessary and politically divisive. He also insisted on the immediate admission of California as a free state. Thus, Taylor refused to support any measure that held California hostage to other bills.

Taylor believed that the best way to resolve the political crisis over the territories was to avoid creating territorial governments and instead to move swiftly to statehood. He planned to allow the people of the entering states to decide the slavery issue for themselves, without Congress's interference. Once California was admitted, he planned to turn to the speedy admission of New Mexico. In this sense, his position mirrored that of the Democrats who were arguing for what would become known as popular sovereignty. However, there was a difference. The Democrats favored territorial organization without resolving (or mentioning) the slavery issue; this approach could allow slavery to take root in the territory at some future time. Taylor rejected this approach. Mexico had banned slavery some two decades before the war with the United States. Thus, there were virtually no slaves in California or New Mexico. By moving quickly on statehood—and avoiding any territorial government—Taylor hoped to annex both places as free states. To the shock of Southern politicians, Taylor also made it clear that he would sign a bill banning slavery in the new U.S. territories, if Congress passed such a bill.

Indeed, Taylor seemed prepared to stand up to the most powerful pro-slavery political leaders. Southern radicals like Senator John C. Calhoun of South Carolina ranted about the need for a new fugitive-slave law. Unconvinced of its necessity, Taylor refused to consider such a bill until after California and New Mexico were dealt with. He remained adamant, moreover, that he would not allow for an expansion of Texas into what had traditionally been part of New Mexico. This expansion, he believed, was unconstitutional. After the governor of Texas threatened to invade New Mexico and seize much of the territory, Taylor declared that he would personally sign an order authorizing the U.S. Army commander there to resist such an incursion with whatever force was necessary.[16] Thus, President Taylor repeatedly demonstrated his resolve as a leader and his willingness to stand firm in the face of crises and challenges—even when his positions did not suit his own party.

## Conclusion

On July 4, 1850, Taylor ate large quantities of fresh fruit and vegetables and drank a great deal of milk while participating in a sweltering Fourth of July ceremony at which the cornerstone was laid for the Washington Monument. By the end of the day, he was suffering from sunstroke and gastroenteritis. He might have recovered from both, but could not recover from his medical treatment, which included calomel (which is made from mercury), opium, and induced bleeding. On July 9, 1850, barely sixteen months after he had taken the oath of office, President Zachary Taylor died.[17]

A war hero, patriotic nationalist, and Southern slave owner, Taylor had the right background to lead the nation through the crisis after the Mexican War. He was prepared to face down Southern extremists, while at the same time protecting slavery where it existed. Had he lived, Taylor might have succeeded in reducing sectional tensions, in part by the sheer force of his will and prestige. His death, however, left the nation in the hands of Millard Fillmore, a Lilliputian president more concerned with winning the next election than with the large issues the nation faced. Indeed, Fillmore would undo most of Taylor's carefully laid plans to admit new territories as free states and to resist a land grab by Texas.[18] In contrast to Taylor, who led with firmness and vision, Fillmore would compromise freedom at every turn in hopes of winning his own term in the White House. President Taylor was probably the nation's last hope for defusing the sectional crisis that led to the war between the North and the South, while his successor helped bring the nation much closer to that self-destructive Civil War.[19]

### NOTES

1. Taylor's promotion, the first brevet promotion in the history of the army, was considered an honor. However, it also had constitutional implications, since the promotion evaded the congressionally imposed limitation on the number of majors in the army.
2. This promotion occurred about a month later, when Congress authorized the creation of a second major general for the army. Supplementary War Act, June 18, 1846, 9 Stat. 17.
3. The leader of these "Young Indians," as they called themselves, was Alexander Stephens of Georgia, who would later become the Confederate vice president. One of the two Northerners was Abraham Lincoln, serving his only term in Congress. Privately, Taylor began to tell friends he would accept a presidential nomination, but publicly, he vacillated, saying that he would not even consider a political future until the war in

Mexico ended. Taylor also stated that he would run only as a "non-party" candidate and that he was a supporter of Henry Clay.

4. Along with Ulysses S. Grant and Dwight David Eisenhower, Taylor is the only president who had never held an appointive or elective civilian office before entering the White House. However, unlike Grant and Eisenhower, he also lacked civilian experience as an adult, except for his private ownership of plantations, which he did not personally supervise.

5. Taylor's lack of experience as a civilian officeholder did not mean, however, that he lacked political experience. As the highest-ranking officer in the army, along with Winfield Scott, he was well acquainted with leaders in Congress and political powers outside of Congress. He understood how to maneuver across political parties and with congressional committees. At various times, he lobbied Congress for promotions and corresponded with members on military matters. While not a not an elected official (or even a voter), he was certainly an adept politician.

6. Significantly, the Whig convention in Kentucky refused to endorse Clay, and Senator Crittenden had maneuvered to send a delegation to the national convention that would support Taylor.

7. The only other similar event was the appointment of Secretary of Treasury Alexander Hamilton as a major general during the Whiskey Rebellion.

8. Van Buren probably siphoned off enough antislavery Whig votes to give the Democrats a victory in Ohio.

9. In 1852, General Winfield Scott ran for president while still retaining his commission. When Senator Barry Goldwater ran for president in 1964, he still held a reserve commission as an air force general. He was later forced to resign that position as a violation of the constitutional prohibition on multiple office holding.

10. Even the three states that were gradually ending slavery (Pennsylvania, Rhode Island, and Connecticut) had passed laws to facilitate the return of fugitive slaves. For background on the adoption of the Fugitive Slave Clause of Article IV, see Paul Finkelman, *Slavery and the Founders: Race and Liberty in the Age of Jefferson*, 3rd ed. (Armonk, NY: M.E. Sharpe, 2014), chap. 1 and 4.

11. An Act respecting fugitives from justice, and persons escaping from the service of their masters, Act of February 12, 1793, 1 Stat. 302 (1793).

12. Prigg v. Pennsylvania, 41 U.S. (16 Peters) 539 (1842).

13. The term comes from the Spanish *filibustero* for a pirate, which came from the Dutch *vrijbuiter*, which is a freebooter—someone who takes loot or "booty" from someone else.

14. David M. Potter, *The Impending Crisis, 1848–1861* (New York: Harper and Row, 1976), 86.

15. Clay balanced this proslavery bill by including a provision admitting California immediately as a free state and prohibiting slave markets in the District of Columbia. The first was a meaningless offer, since there were virtually no slaves in California and the vast majority of settlers—almost one hundred thousand of them—were opposed to slavery. The second offer would eliminate the embarrassment of auctioning off slaves

in the shadow of the U.S. Capitol, but would not prevent private sales or prevent masters from crossing into Virginia to buy and sell human beings.

16. Elbert B. Smith, *The Presidencies of Zachary Taylor and Millard Fillmore* (Lawrence: University of Kansas Press, 1988), 155.

17. John S. D. Eisenhower, *Zachary Taylor* (New York: Times Books, 2008), 132–134.

18. Fillmore would sign the Fugitive Slave Law of 1850 and aggressively enforce it, ignoring provisions that seemed patently unconstitutional to many Northerners. Similarly, he would endorse legislation giving a large portion of New Mexico to Texas, while refusing to pass on to Congress a constitution written by citizens in New Mexico to bring that place into the union as a free state. Paul Finkelman, *Millard Fillmore* (New York: Times Books, 2011).

19. Paul Finkelman, "The Cost of Compromise and the Covenant with Death," *Pepperdine Law Review* 38 (2011): 845–888; Paul Finkelman, "The Appeasement of 1850," in *Congress and the Crisis of the 1850s*, ed. Paul Finkelman and Donald R. Kennon (Athens: Ohio University Press, 2012), 36–79.

# 13

# Millard Fillmore

JOSEPH F. RISHEL

*Millard Fillmore, who fell into the presidency when Zachary Taylor died unexpectedly, is often regarded as a weak leader and a failed chief executive. Eager to show that he could heal the rift between North and South, Fillmore reversed some of Taylor's cautious policies. He zealously supported the controversial Compromise of 1850, which some historians believe worsened the sectional divide; others, however, insist that it successfully postponed the Civil War for a decade. Failing to win his own term and watching helplessly as the Whig Party fell apart in the process, Fillmore receded into obscurity, where he remains today.*

## Introduction

In virtually every ranking of U.S. presidents, Millard Fillmore is rated near the bottom. Yet Fillmore faced a complex set of historical forces. He was catapulted from the relative obscurity of the vice presidency after the death of the illustrious President Zachary Taylor and forced to deal with the issue of slavery then consuming the nation. His undistinguished place in history is doubtless influenced by his support for the Compromise of 1850 with its infamous Fugitive Slave Act and the supposed betrayal of his own Whig Party principles. Fillmore, in part, was thrust into difficult circumstances. He was neither incompetent nor unintelligent. Indeed, when he first embarked on a career in public service, he was viewed as a man who had risen from modest circumstances to create for himself a bright political future. Yet history did not cooperate with that plan.

The second of nine children, Millard Fillmore was born on January 7, 1800, in a log cabin in Cayuga County, New York, to Nathaniel and Phoebe Millard Fillmore, descendants of Scottish Presbyterians and English dissenters. Later in life, the future president would become a Unitarian. The family lived on what was then the New York frontier on a farm too small to support the Fillmores.

Following a brief apprenticeship as a cloth maker at age fourteen, the young Fillmore, who had taught himself to read, enrolled at the New Hope Academy in 1819. After half a year of study, he left to begin serving as a law clerk for a judge in nearby Montville, New York, and later in Buffalo. Fillmore was admitted to the New York Bar in 1823 and, in 1826, married Abigail Powers, his former New Hope Academy teacher, who was the daughter of a Baptist minister.

Becoming a member of the newly formed Anti-Masonic Party, Fillmore was elected to the New York State Assembly in 1828. Thereafter, he won election to the U.S. House of Representatives as a Whig.[1] In the House, Fillmore generally supported Henry Clay's nationalism (i.e., internal improvements and a protective tariff). In 1844, Fillmore ran for governor of New York but was defeated by 10,000 votes out of 480,000 cast and returned to his law practice. Four years later, he founded a private medical school, the University of Buffalo, and became its first chancellor. The following year, he was elected comptroller of New York, a post equivalent to the state's chief financial officer.

In the presidential election of 1848, it was not at all certain that General Zachary Taylor would carry the populous state of New York with its thirty-six electoral votes, largely because Taylor was a slave owner who angered abolitionists. He had also refused to endorse Whig economic policies. After a good deal of maneuvering, Millard Fillmore was selected as the Whig vice presidential candidate, owing to his New York roots and his well-known commitment to Whig economic programs that Taylor had refused to embrace. Fillmore's inclusion on the ticket was meant to give balance and to stave off a defection by the Whig Party's Northern constituency. It was an odd match for both Taylor and Fillmore. They did not even meet until after the election, and when they did meet, they did not particularly like one another.

After Taylor and Fillmore squeaked by as the winning candidates, Fillmore was excluded from any meaningful decision-making role as vice president.[2] Specifically, he was kept out of discussions about the simmering conflict between the North and South and whether slavery should be permitted in newly added territories and states.

Suddenly, on July 9, 1850, President Taylor died of gastroenteritis, days after participating in an Independence Day celebration. The following day, Fillmore succeeded to the presidency, taking the oath of office in the House of Representatives.

## Presidency

The newly inaugurated president was soon faced with the escalating border dispute between the State of Texas and the New Mexico Territory. The governor of Texas had sent a letter addressed to Fillmore's predecessor, President Taylor, demanding that the United States recognize that Texas's boundary extended all the way to Santa Fe.[3] Although Texas's claim had no legal basis and Fillmore himself voiced the importance of upholding the integrity of the borders of a federal territory against such a claim, he faced opposition even from antislavery Whig enemies. Repeating his predecessor's threat to send in federal troops to Santa Fe if Texas tried to annex it, Fillmore made it clear to Texas that its expansionist efforts would not be tolerated. He then worked to persuade Congress to enact a compromise that was acceptable to Texas, a maneuver that neutralized many of his critics.[4]

*The Compromise of 1850*

While he was considering the Texas issue, Fillmore indicated his support for the other separate bills that constituted the so-called Compromise of 1850. Largely written by Senator Henry Clay of Kentucky, the bills presumably were designed to prevent an open conflict between the slave states and the free states. Although the Taylor administration had vigorously opposed this legislation, Fillmore now worked with Senator Stephen A. Douglas, a Democrat from Illinois, and the newly appointed secretary of state, Daniel Webster (a Whig), to push the pieces of the compromise through. On September 20, 1850, Fillmore signed all of the bills into law. The Compromise of 1850, as finalized, provided for the following:

1) California, with its modern borders, was to be admitted as a free state with no companion slave state, thus ending the equal slave-state and free-state balance in the Senate.
2) The Utah and New Mexico territories were to be established, and under the concept of popular sovereignty, the people of those territories would decide if they wanted to be slave or free territories.
3) Texas was given more land than proposed in Clay's original bill, but was to be scaled down in size to its present boundaries. The United States was to assume the Texas public debt after the Mexican-American War.
4) The slave trade, but not slavery itself, was to be ended in the District of Columbia.
5) A new Fugitive Slave Act of 1850 was to be implemented, taking enforcement from the state courts and placing it in the hands of U.S. commissioners. Under this law, a slave catcher could make an affidavit and the commissioners could make a decision without obligation to hear the opposing side in the case. Any alleged fugitives were specifically forbidden to testify on their own behalf. Those aiding fugitives were to be subject to fine and imprisonment, with civil damages paid to the slave owner.

The Fugitive Slave Act of 1850, which was tacked onto the Compromise of 1850 in the late stages of the debate, was viewed by abolitionists as repugnant to basic Anglo-Saxon concepts of civil liberty. In response, the states of Connecticut, Rhode Island, Massachusetts, Michigan, Ohio, and Wisconsin enacted new "personal liberty laws" to prevent the act's enforcement. These aggressive state laws made it illegal to seize a fugitive slave without proof in a jury trial. They also provided a lawyer for the accused fugitive, made it illegal to use state jails for arrested fugitives, made it illegal to use state officials to return fugitives, and imposed heavy fines for kidnapping "free Negroes."[5] The personal liberty laws enacted in Massachusetts even went so far as to effectively disbar any attorney who represented a claimant under the Fugitive Slave Act. Ultimately, these laws produced a series of direct confrontations in the courts.[6] For now, the Compromise of 1850—which Fillmore had embraced to forestall a battle between North and South over the slavery issue—achieved that goal temporarily. However, it also contributed to the rapid disintegration of the Whig Party; Northern Whigs thought it gave the South too much, while Southern Whigs felt undermined by the deal. As a result, the party was fractured irreversibly.

## The Supreme Court

Fillmore made a single appointment to the Supreme Court when Levi Woodbury, a Polk appointee and a Democrat, died in 1851. On the recommendation of Secretary of State Daniel Webster, Fillmore named Benjamin Curtis, making him the Supreme Court's first and only Whig justice and the first justice ever to have earned a formal law degree. (Curtis had graduated from Harvard Law School in 1831.)[7]

A number of important decisions were rendered during the Fillmore administration, primarily related to the festering slavery issue. One decision, *Strader v. Graham* (1851), preceded the infamous *Dred Scott v. Sandford* case (in which Justice Curtis would issue a strong dissent), foreshadowing its holding.[8] Christopher Graham, a resident of the slave state of Kentucky, owned three slaves who performed as musicians in the neighboring free states of Ohio and Indiana. In 1841, the slaves traveled to Ohio on a steamboat owned by Jacob Strader for the ostensible purpose of performing. Instead, they continued on to Canada. Making use of a Kentucky law that held steamboat operators liable for any escaping slaves, Graham sued Strader. The Kentucky Supreme Court found in favor of Graham. Strader appealed to the U.S. Supreme Court on the grounds that the slaves became free by virtue of travel in a free state. The boat owner also argued that the Northwest Ordinance made any slaves brought into that area free persons. As the Kentucky decision under review did not implicate a federal law, the Court ruled that it was without jurisdiction and dismissed the case. Nonetheless, Chief Justice Roger Taney, writing for the Court, stated in dicta that Kentucky had the right to determine "the status, or domestic and social condition" of the persons domiciled within its territory (i.e., Kentucky could determine who was free or not free). Nothing in the U.S. Constitution, said the Court, limited state law on the subject. Additionally, Taney asserted that the Northwest Ordinance was no longer in effect, because the Northwest Territory had become part of the Union.[9]

A year later, in 1852, the Supreme Court ruled on an important interstate commerce issue, tangentially related to the bugbear of slavery. A Pennsylvania law required a local pilot to guide ships in the waters of the port of Philadelphia as a safety measure. Aaron Cooley refused to comply with the law and was sued by the Board of Port Wardens in state court. Having lost there, he appealed to the Supreme Court in the case of *Cooley v. Board of Port Wardens of Philadelphia*, arguing that the Constitution's Commerce Clause (Article I, Section 8, Clause 3) superseded state legislation and left the matter entirely to federal laws governing such interstate movement of vessels. In ruling against Cooley, Justice Curtis wrote for the six-to-two majority: "The mere grant to Congress of the power to regulate commerce did not deprive the States of the power to regulate commerce . . . and that although Congress had legislated on this subject, its legislation manifests an intention, with a single exception, not to regulate this subject but to leave its regulation to the several states."[10] In a decision that would have ramifications for more than a century, the *Cooley* case made clear that—in the absence of federal laws to the contrary—states were free to pass laws that affected interstate commerce, when the subject in question was local rather than national in scope. This holding, in turn, indirectly related to the issue of slavery. After all, the interstate movement of slaves—and the legal ramifications of their movement from state to state—was increasingly becoming a source of strong disagreement between North and South. *Cooley* thus left open the possibility that individual states could maintain control over certain forms of interstate commerce—presumably including the movement of slaves from state to state—if these forms of commerce were local in nature and did not require a single national rule to ensure uniformity.

## Conclusion

Millard Fillmore, who served only thirty-two months from the time he took office after Zachary Taylor's death, pressed to implement the Fugitive Slave Act of 1850 to the fullest, even though he did not personally agree with that legislation. The push for implementation angered many in Fillmore's own Whig Party, which did not nominate him for a full term in 1852. Consequently, he sat out the general election. Four years later, in the presidential election of 1856, Fillmore was nominated by the nativist, anti-Catholic, anti-immigrant American Party, the political organ of the Know-Nothing Movement. He finished last behind James Buchanan (Democrat) and John C. Fremont (of the newly formed Republican Party), garnering only 22 percent of the popular vote. This election ended Fillmore's political career. It also earned him the dubious honor of being the last Whig president.

Fillmore's wife, Abigail, developed pneumonia at Franklin Pierce's outdoor inauguration in 1853 and died shortly thereafter. After a five-year bereavement, Fillmore remarried. He and his second wife, Catherine McIntosh, relocated to Buffalo, where he watched in distress as the Civil War arrived. Although old age had dampened his interest in politics, he actively supported the Union cause.[11] His later opposition of Lincoln and support for Andrew Johnson, however, further damaged his reputation as a statesman. Millard Fillmore died of a stroke on March 8, 1874, in Buffalo. The then-sitting president, Ulysses S. Grant, issued only a brief statement at the time of Fillmore's death; the American public barely noted his passing.[12]

Millard Fillmore was a president who lacked the political judgment and moral suasion to move the North and South off a collision course with each other. It is frequently claimed by some that the Compromise of 1850 delayed the coming of the Civil War by more than a decade. That said, Fillmore's support of the compromise helped cause the eventual collapse of the Whig Party and contributed to making a North-South war nearly inevitable. For that and other missteps, history has been his unforgiving judge.[13]

### NOTES

1. Fillmore served in that body from 1833 to 1835, and again from 1837 to 1843.
2. The results were as follows: Zachary Taylor and Millard Fillmore (Whig) 1,360,235 (47.28%), 163 electoral votes; Lewis Cass and William O. Butler (Democratic) 1,222,353 (42.49%), 127 electoral votes; Martin Van Buren and Charles F. Adams (Free-Soil)

291,475 (10.13%), 0 electoral votes. Susan B. Carter et al., ed., *Historical Statistics of the United States* (New York: Cambridge University Press, 2006); Joseph G. Rayback, *Free Soil: The Election of 1848* (Lexington: University Press of Kentucky, 1970).

3. Paul Finkelman, *Millard Fillmore* (New York: Times Books, 2011), 78–79.

4. Michael F. Holt, *The Rise and Fall of the American Whig Party: Jacksonian Politics and the Onset of the Civil War* (New York: Oxford University Press, 2003), 529–543. See also Melvin I. Urofsky, *The American Presidents* (New York: Garland Publishing, 2000), 140.

5. Holman Hamilton, *Prologue to Conflict: The Crisis and Compromise of 1850* (Lexington: University Press of Kentucky, 1964). A classic political history and an authority in the field is David M. Potter, *The Impending Crisis, 1848–1861* (New York: Harper, 1976).

6. See, for example, Ableman v. Booth, 62 U.S. (21 How.) 506 (1859); Kermit L. Hall, ed., *Oxford Guide to the United States Supreme Court* (New York: Oxford University Press, 2002). This case concluded once and for all that states could not, consistent with the Supremacy Clause contained in Article VI of the Constitution, "nullify" federal laws with which they disagreed.

7. All of his predecessors either "read law" in a kind of apprenticeship then common or attended law school without graduating.

8. The discord caused by Curtis's dissent was so great that he resigned soon thereafter, making him the first justice to resign over a matter of principle. Richard H. Leach, "Benjamin R. Curtis: Case Study of a Supreme Court Justice" (Ph.D. diss., Princeton University, 1951).

9. Strader v. Graham, 51 U.S. (10 How.) 82 (1851). Although the decision was unanimous, two justices did not agree with Chief Justice Taney's opinion that the Northwest Ordinance was no longer in force.

10. Cooley v. Board of Port Wardens of Philadelphia, 53 U.S. (12 How.) 299 (1852); Hall, *Oxford Guide*.

11. Robert J. Rayback, *Millard Fillmore: Biography of a President* (Buffalo, NY: Henry Stewart, 1959), 415–430.

12. Miller Center of the University of Virginia (Michael F. Holt, contrib. ed.), "American President: Millard Fillmore," in *Essays on Millard Fillmore and His Administration: Impact and Legacy*, accessed May 27, 2015, http://millercenter.org/president/fillmore/essays/biography/9.

13. Holt, *Rise and Fall of the American Whig Party*.

# 14

# Franklin Pierce

PAUL FINKELMAN

*President Franklin Pierce took steps to build new commercial relationships abroad, revamp the military, and restructure the federal courts. After an unprecedented landslide in the 1852 presidential election gave him supermajorities in the House and Senate, Pierce seemed poised for a productive presidency. Yet, as a Northerner with Southern sympathies, he was wedded to the notion that citizens of the new territories should be able to determine the issue of slavery for themselves—what was then known as popular sovereignty. Pierce ended up supporting the Kansas-Nebraska Act, which destroyed the thirty-four-year-old compromise on slavery in the federal territories and led to Bleeding Kansas, a series of bloody confrontations and a small civil war between pro- and antislavery settlers in Kansas Territory. With this violence forever stamped on his presidency, Pierce was ushered out of office.*

## Introduction

Few presidential candidates were less qualified or less prepared for the office than Franklin Pierce was in 1852. His entire political career consisted of four years in the New Hampshire legislature, two utterly unremarkable terms in the U.S. House of Representatives, a partial term as U.S. senator, and a few years as the U.S. attorney in New Hampshire. Pierce's only other experience was as a practicing attorney (where he was quite successful), a leader of the Democratic Party in New Hampshire, and as a minor and utterly unimportant brigadier general in the Mexican War. With his father the governor of New Hampshire, perhaps young Pierce gained some political knowledge as he grew up, but it is hard to imagine a person less well prepared to be president.

Despite his utter lack of qualifications, Pierce won a stunning and overwhelming victory as a dark-horse candidate in 1852. He carried more electoral votes than those won by any other president up to then and a greater percentage of electoral votes than any other president except George Washington and James Monroe had carried. Pierce won a greater popular majority than any other president since Andrew Jackson. This landslide victory permanently destroyed the Whig Party and left the Democrats in complete control of the government. Pierce's party held 62 percent of the Senate and 67 percent of the House.

Against this backdrop, the popular, handsome, and personable Pierce should have had a successful presidency, using his huge margins in Congress and his unprecedented electoral victory as a mandate to govern and to heal the nation. At that time, the nation was still coping with the sectional divisions caused by the Compromise of 1850, which left many in the North and the South unhappy. Yet his ardent support of the Kansas-Nebraska Act and other extreme proslavery measures exposed his true colors. Within two years, he would squander his political capital and end up being one of the least successful and least respected presidents in American history.

Pierce came from a politically successful and prominent family. His father, Benjamin, who had served in the Twenty-Seventh Massachusetts Regiment during the American Revolution, was personally decorated by Washington and later served two terms as governor of New Hampshire.

Young Franklin graduated in the middle of his class from Bowdoin College. Although capable of studying hard and getting good grades, which he did in his last year, Pierce was mostly remembered as a hard-drinking fellow, with a well-earned and well-documented reputation for drunkenness that would affect his whole career. Among others passing through the school when he was enrolled were future U.S. senators from Maine, William Pitt Fessenden and James Bradbury; a future U.S. Senator from New Hampshire, John P. Hale; Henry Wadsworth Longfellow; and his lifelong friend, Nathaniel Hawthorne.[1] Pierce then studied law under Levi Woodbury, a future Supreme Court justice.

In 1827, at age twenty-two, Pierce became a lawyer and entered politics as an avid Jacksonian Democrat. At twenty-four, he won a seat in the state legislature and served two terms in the U.S. House of Representatives, where he supported the 1836 gag rule to immediately table without consideration all antislavery petitions sent to the House. His endorsement of the gag rule was the beginning of his long career opposing abolitionists and supporting slavery and the South. Pierce did not support a plan of outright rejection of such petitions, as the most hard-core proslavery legislators wanted. But the gag rule served the purpose of silencing abolitionists. The rule was, of course, a significant constitutional issue, because many Northerners in the House, including former president John Quincy Adams, argued that tabling the petitions without reading them violated the right to petition guaranteed in the First Amendment.

Later in 1836, the New Hampshire legislature elected Pierce, at age thirty-two, to the U.S. Senate.[2] With the election of Harrison in 1840, along with a Whig majority in the Senate, he found politics less interesting. Pierce resigned from the Senate in 1842 and returned to New Hampshire, vowing he would never run for office again, in part because he hated the long separations from his family.[3] He then started a highly successful private law practice, served briefly as U.S. attorney under Polk, and served as chairman of the New Hampshire Democratic Party, helping to turn the party into the most successful Democratic Party in the North.[4] As the New Hampshire Democratic Party chair, he "would not tolerate any criticism of slavery or slaveholders, and he had the clout to impose his intolerance on the state Democratic organization."[5] Pierce's purging of John P. Hale from the Democratic Party because of Hale's antislavery views in 1844 led to Hale's election to the Senate in 1846 by a combination of Whigs and antislavery Democrats.

The Hale episode illustrated how Pierce's obsession with party unity (defining the Democratic Party as he saw fit) and his almost fanatical hatred of antislavery actually undermined the success of the party in his own state. Although he was a native of New England, Pierce never seemed to understand the overwhelming hostility to slavery in the region. Furthermore, he could never grasp why many men in New Hampshire and the rest of the North, while not committed abolitionists, were willing to support antislavery candidates and would oppose blatantly proslavery Northerners like himself.

Pierce supported President Polk's invasion of Mexico in 1846, even though most New Englanders opposed the policy. Many in the region—but not Pierce, of course—considered it an illegal and unconstitutional war of aggression and part of a proslavery conspiracy to add new territory for the expansion of slavery. In February 1847, President Polk (whom Pierce had known in Congress), appointed him as a colonel in a newly formed regiment and, then, a few weeks later, a brigadier general. Pierce was initially a successfully commander, but in his first real battle, he was thrown from his horse and lost consciousness. Many of his troops believed he had passed out from fear, and others believed that the notoriously hard-drinking Pierce was drunk at the time. He was later sick and absent from the front when his brigade helped to storm Chapultepec. After this battle, he remained in Mexico, where he was sometimes seen drunk in public. After six months in Mexico, he returned home, a local hero who had done nothing heroic.

For a short time, Pierce had been an able and conscientious commander, but in the end, he was unconscious, sick, or drunk for much of the time in the war zone and added little to the war effort. He did write in his journal about his distaste for war: "There can be no such thing as a profound sense of justice, the sacredness of individual rights and the value of human life connected with human butchery."[6] But ironically, he focused much of his early attention as president on building up the army and at least indirectly threatened to use military force to seize Cuba for the United States.

By 1848, he was back in politics, turning out a large popular victory in New Hampshire for the Democratic presidential nominee, Lewis Cass, who lost the election to the Whig Zachary Taylor. The 1852 Democratic Convention was a deadlocked disaster for thirty-four ballots, with Lewis Cass, James Buchanan, and Stephen A. Douglas fighting for the nomination. On the thirty-fourth ballot, the Virginia delegation cast its votes for

Pierce, who up to this time had not been in the running. On the forty-ninth ballot, Pierce, shockingly, was nominated. Charming and handsome, with no record to run on—but more importantly, no record to run against—Pierce won a stunning victory over General Winfield Scott, a true hero of the Mexican War who was nevertheless uncharismatic and whose party was fractured and unable to mount a solid campaign.[7]

Sadly, the excitement of Pierce's triumph was stolen by personal tragedy on January 6, when his eleven-year-old son, Benjamin, died after a train derailment. His wife, Jane, was "crushed to the earth by fearful bereavement."[8] Earlier in their marriage, the couple had lost two other children. Jane suffered from prolonged depression and grief after the death of Benjamin, spending days in her room while writing long letters to her now-dead children. During this period of grieving, she told Pierce she would never live in Washington.[9] Shortly after Benjamin's death, the president-elect confided to Jefferson Davis: "How shall I be able to summon my manhood and gather up my energies for the duties before me, it is hard for me to see."[10] His son's death and his wife's deep grief eviscerated Pierce's personal happiness and undermined his ability to function as president.

## Presidency

In his inaugural address on March 4, 1853, Pierce supported new territorial expansion in the aftermath of the Mexican War, a revamped army, and greater world trade, without the impediments of excessive tariffs. He favored territorial expansion while encouraging international free trade.[11] Shortly after he took office, Pierce authorized Secretary of State William L. Marcy to negotiate trade agreements and free trade with Great Britain (including its colony Canada), Brazil, Paraguay, and Argentina. Marcy attempted to buy Alaska from Russia and offered Mexico $50 million for most of northern Mexico and Baja California.[12] Instead, in 1853, he ended up acquiring only a tiny strip of land along the southern boundary of the New Mexico territory. This small acquisition was known as the Gadsden Purchase.

Pierce was seen as a classic doughface—a Northern man with Southern principles, whose face was made of bread dough and could be shaped in any way the Southerners wanted. Thus, the doughface Pierce sought to protect slavery at every turn and to do everything in his power to suppress antislavery politicians and activists. Pierce actively sought the acquisition of Cuba.[13] Such an acquisition, of course, was a major goal of the South, because Cuba would provide land for the expansion of slavery and because about a half million slaves already lived there. In October 1854, Pierce sent three diplomats to meet with Spanish officials in Ostend, Belgium, to discuss acquiring Cuba. Two were aggressively proslavery Southerners, Pierre Soulé and John Y. Mason, and the third diplomat was the Northern proslavery doughface Democrat, James Buchanan. After the meeting, the envoys issued a report, known as the Ostend Manifesto, which argued that the administration should seize Cuba by force if necessary. Pierce rejected the use of force to take Cuba. Nevertheless, when the Ostend Manifesto became public, it undermined Pierce's presidency and confirmed to Northerners that his foreign policy—which was generally considered the constitutional bailiwick of the executive branch—was as proslavery as his domestic policy.

Pierce reveled in his role as commander in chief and proudly traded on his brief stint as a general, even though his military career had been disappointing, short, and not very successful. Unlike the nation's previous military presidents—Washington, Jackson, and Harrison—Pierce was no hero and had no glory attached to his war record. Yet, the new commander in chief argued that the military should be expanded and modernized so that "in every time of need the strength of our military power may be readily formed into a well-disciplined and efficient organization."[14] This policy seemed odd, since less than a decade before, the nation had won a resounding victory against Mexico, and there were no military threats on the horizon. Nevertheless, Pierce emphasized the importance of a first-rate military science education. In addition, he took steps to upgrade the nation's military. At Pierce's direction, his secretary of war, Jefferson Davis, working with Colonel Robert E. Lee, the superintendent of West Point, proposed a comprehensive restructuring of the armed forces.[15] Thus, the future president of the Confederacy and his most famous general reshaped and modernized the military just in time to help defeat the Confederacy a decade later. The choice of an aggressively proslavery Southern nationalist like Davis for such a sensitive position illustrated Pierce's own commitment to slavery. Ironically, Pierce's pro-Southern, proslavery policies helped set the stage for secession and the war that followed.

Pierce supported legislation to restructure and expand the federal court system.[16] He entered the office with one Supreme Court vacancy. In a highly unusual (and what would today be considered completely improper) move, two justices, John Catron and Benjamin R. Curtis, wrote to Pierce recommending John A. Campbell, of Alabama. Pierce nominated Campbell about two weeks after taking office, and the Senate confirmed the Alabama man on March 23. It seems likely that a more experienced politician, who better understood how the national government worked, would have ignored, on principle, the inappropriate letters from Catron and Curtis. Campbell's jurisprudence would be consistently proslavery and deeply supportive of states' rights, at least when it supported the South and slavery. In *Dred Scott*, he would vote to deny Congress the right to ban slavery in any territory; he would hold that slavery was a constitutionally protected form of property and agree with Chief Justice Roger B. Taney that blacks, even when free, had no rights under the Constitution. On the other hand, Justice Campbell would support a strong national government in cases involving the Fugitive Slave Law of 1850, when Northern states asserted their states' rights to protect blacks (free and fugitive) living in them. Consistent with his generally proslavery, pro-Southern positions, in 1861, Campbell would be the only justice from a seceding state to resign from the Court (two others did not). He then returned to the South to become an assistant secretary of war for the Confederacy, fighting against the government and nation he had previously served.[17]

In his first year or so in office, Pierce did little to incite much praise or criticism. His administration tilted toward the South on issues of foreign and domestic policy and consistently favored slavery over freedom. But with an impressive majority in Congress, Pierce accomplished little, even when he pursued an initiative. For example, in the Gadsden Purchase, his envoys to Mexico negotiated for a substantially larger purchase of land than what Congress approved. By late 1853, whatever promise Pierce's administration once enjoyed had begun to come apart over his aggressive enforcement of the Fugitive Slave Law of 1850, his support for allowing slavery in all the federal territories, and his obsessive opposition to antislavery.[18] Consistent with his support for the South, he opposed homestead legislation, which Southerners feared would lead to Northerners settling the West. He also vetoed a popular bill to use federal land to support mental institutions. Believing that this bill would violate states' rights, he also understood that if the national government could pass social legislation, it might eventually use laws to undermine slavery. Notably, of course, Pierce would see no states' rights issues when he ordered federal troops into the states to support fugitive-slave returns.

## *Fugitive Slaves*

Pierce had entered the White House with an enormous gift from his Whig predecessor, Millard Fillmore. In the summer of 1850, Fillmore, the second accidental president, had overseen the passage of a series of laws that collectively became known as the Compromise of 1850. The compromise had been a huge victory for the South. It allowed slavery in all of the new territories acquired from Mexico (except California, which entered the Union as a free state) and provided a harsh fugitive-slave law with federal enforcement—including the use of the military—to bring fugitive slaves back to the South. The laws expanded the boundaries of Texas, making the state an even greater empire for slavery, while giving vast sums of money to Texas to bail it out from its enormous debt. One compromise measure banned the public sale of slaves—but not slavery—in the District of Columbia. This law was a meaningless, cosmetic sop to the North, because masters could easily buy and sell slaves across the river in Arlington and Alexandria, Virginia. The compromise did bring California into the Union as a free state, giving the North a one-state majority in the Senate. But with numerous Northern Democrats willing to vote with the South to protect slavery, the one-state margin did not affect Southern control of the Senate.

The Compromise of 1850 infuriated opponents of slavery. Among Northerners who had previously been uninvolved in debates over human bondage, the Fugitive Slave Law would eventually erode support for national compromises over slavery. But in 1852, there was relatively strong support for the Compromise of 1850 nationwide. In the South, proto-secessionists had been defeated by mainstream politicians who supported the compromise, while high cotton prices created a positive atmosphere. Pierce generally ran on upholding the compromise, and his sweeping victory suggested that the compromise was a model for continued sectional peace.

As part of the Compromise of 1850, Pierce had inherited the recently enacted Fugitive Slave Law of 1850. The statute created new federal commissioners in every county in the country. Along with federal judges, the commissioners would enforce the law throughout the nation and oversee the return of fugitive slaves. The law denied alleged fugitives the right to jury trial, the right to a writ of habeas corpus, or the right even to testify in their own defense. The return of fugitives was to be a summary affair, with no due-process protections. Federal commissioners and judges were authorized to call out the army and navy, as well as state militias, to enforce the law. Pierce, always seeking to placate the South, supported an aggressive enforcement of the law. It 1854, for example, he used the army and the coast guard to return the fugitive slave Anthony Burns from Boston to Virginia. The cost for trying Burns and removing him has been estimated at just under $100,000 (about $2.8 million today).[19] Burns was later sold for about $1,200. The case paralyzed Boston for a week and made a mockery of due process.

The Pierce administration did everything it could to support the law, and at the same time, Pierce made war on any Democrats in Massachusetts (and elsewhere) who questioned his support for slavery.[20] Meanwhile, Pierce appointed aggressively proslavery men to office, such as Davis as secretary of war, Soulé as ambassador to Spain, and Campbell to the Supreme Court.

## The Kansas-Nebraska Act

Pierce is most remembered as the president who signed the Kansas-Nebraska Act, which set the stage for what came to be known as Bleeding Kansas. In 1820, Congress had set rules for accommodating slavery in the territories—rules that would work for thirty years. Under the Missouri Compromise, slavery was permanently banned from the territory north and west of Missouri. By 1850 (if not before), Southerners believed that this compromise was unfair. They wanted access to the Great Plains, where slaves could be used to clear land, build farms, grow wheat and corn, and raise hogs and cattle. Furthermore, Southern politicians wanted new slave states to enter the Union to increase the South's political power in Congress.

Meanwhile, Stephen A. Douglas of Illinois, a leader of the Democratic Party in the Senate, wanted to promote a transcontinental railroad that would begin in Chicago and would pass through Missouri. To gain Southern support for his scheme, Douglas proposed a repeal of the Missouri Compromise, to be replaced with popular sovereignty, which meant that the settlers of the territory would decide for themselves if they wanted slavery.[21] Pierce enthusiastically supported this program. He met with Southern senators and congressmen at the White House to hammer out language to repeal the Missouri Compromise and allow for the establishment of slavery in the territories that would eventually make up the states of Kansas, Nebraska, Wyoming, and the Dakotas and portions of Montana and Colorado.

The new law, which Pierce signed, had three immediate consequences. First, the law led to a mini Civil War in Kansas as armed proslavery settlers and terrorists who crossed over from Missouri (the "Border Ruffians") attacked settlements of Northerners determined to make Kansas a free state. Senator William Seward of New York said the North was prepared to compete to make Kansas a free state: "We will engage in competition for the virgin soil of Kansas, and God give victory to the side which is stronger in numbers as it is in right."[22] But he viewed this competition in terms of settlers and voters, not armed conflict. Similarly, the New England Emigrant Aid Society was created to assemble abolitionists who would go west and settle in Kansas. Senator David Rice Atchison of Missouri, on the other hand, penned articles calling for Southerners to eradicate abolitionists from Kansas "by any means necessary."[23] Northerners came to Kansas with law books, plows, and printing presses, prepared to debate the issue and win elections. Southerners, as Atchison suggested, came with guns. Eventually, Northern settlers would be armed as well. For example, the sons of the Ohio abolitionist John Brown moved to Kansas to farm and then wrote to their father, asking for guns to protect themselves from armed attacks by Southerners.[24] Piece's territorial governors did little to stop the violence and usually supported proslavery men in disputes. Pierce would forever be remembered for his failed and bloody Kansas policy.

The policy at least temporarily destroyed the Democratic Party in the North. In 1854 and 1855, Northern Democrats were slaughtered in congressional and gubernatorial elections. Sitting Democrats lost governorships in New York, Pennsylvania, Iowa, and Michigan, while more than two-thirds of Northern Democrats in the House of Representatives—sixty-six out of ninety-one—lost their seats. The Democrats lost every congressional race in Ohio, Connecticut, Massachusetts, Rhode Island, and, most significantly, Pierce's home state of New Hampshire. Of the forty-four Northern House members who had voted for the Kansas-Nebraska Act, only seven were reelected.[25] The successful politicians ran as Whigs, Free-Soilers, members of the anti-Catholic Know-Nothing Party, or members of the emerging new party, initially called the Anti-Nebraska Party, but later renamed the Republican Party. Both antislavery Democrats and

Democrats who had tried to avoid the slavery issue left their party and abandoned Pierce.

Supporting "Free Soil, Free Labor, Free Speech, and Free Men," the main plank of the newly emerging party was a ban on slavery in the West. In 1856, the Republican Party would sweep through the North, carrying eleven of the sixteen free states (including Pierce's own New Hampshire), and in 1860, the Republicans would capture the White House. Republicans, like Abraham Lincoln, referred to popular sovereignty as "squatter sovereignty" and saw it as part of a conspiracy to nationalize slavery.

Rarely, if ever, has a political party gone from such success—its sweeping victory in 1854—to such failure in the next two years. Pierce's constitutional theory—that the national government should both ignore the issue of slavery in the territories and at the same time support proslavery settlers—was an abject failure. Pierce believed in popular sovereignty as a concept of constitutional self-government. But his administration did not actually support popular sovereignty or free elections. Pierce's first territorial governor, Andrew H. Reeder, postponed elections in Kansas until March 1855, in part to help proslavery forces organize. On Election Day, hundreds of armed terrorists, known as Border Ruffians, crossed into the territory from Missouri. They commandeered polling places, fraudulently voted, prevented free-state settlers from voting, and stuffed ballot boxes to insure a proslavery territorial legislature. The Pierce administration backed these patent frauds. The new legislature made it a capital offense to distribute antislavery literature and passed numerous other proslavery laws, despite the fact that the First Amendment to the Constitution, which applied to all federal territories, guaranteed freedom of speech and freedom of the press.

Pierce supported all these proslavery measures. In 1856, antislavery settlers, who were unquestionably the majority in the state, created their own legislature in Topeka. However, when Pierce ordered the army to disperse the lawmakers, the soldiers aimed their cannons at unarmed legislators trying to actually implement popular sovereignty. In other instances, the army did nothing to stop the cold-blooded murder of antislavery men in the territory, in one case standing idly by while a proslavery minister who was serving as a guide for the army shot and killed an unarmed Northern settler. When a proslavery mob attacked the free-state city of Lawrence and burned much of it, Pierce's territorial governor did nothing. Yet when Free-Soilers retaliated, the governor and the army pursued them.

## Conclusion

Pierce's legacy would be Bleeding Kansas, his corruption of the democratic process and his obtuse proslavery positions. He also left an impact through his support of men like Jefferson Davis and John Campbell, both of whom would later become traitors, making war on their own country. When President Lincoln would try to preserve the Union that Pierce had so undermined, the former president would openly denounce Lincoln. Pierce opposed the Union effort and emancipation. Probably only his status as a former president saved him from being arrested during the Civil War for disloyalty or treason (even though his opposition to the Lincoln administration did not actually constitute treason). After the war, Pierce resumed drinking, became reclusive, and was largely forgotten by the American public. The former president died in Concord, New Hampshire, in 1869, at the age of sixty-four.

NOTES

1. Roy Franklin Nichols, *Franklin Pierce: Young Hickory of the Granite Hills* (Philadelphia: University of Pennsylvania Press, 1931), 27.
2. Some sources on Pierce assert he was the youngest U.S. senator up to then. This is not correct. At least fifteen other men, including Andrew Jackson and Henry Clay, were younger than Pierce when they were elected to the Senate.
3. Pierce to James Knox Polk, September 18, 1846, in *The Papers of Franklin Pierce: Presidential Documents and Diaries*, Manuscripts Division, Library of Congress.
4. Pierce was nonetheless twice offered his party's nomination for governor, was proposed for another Senate term, and was offered the position of attorney general by President James Polk, but he declined all these offers. Ibid.
5 Michael F. Holt, *Franklin Pierce* (New York: Times Books, 2010), 23.
6. Franklin Pierce, Journal Entry, July 22, 1847, in *Pierce Papers*.
7. Taylor, *Book of the Presidents*, 159–160; Nichols, *Young Hickory of the Granite Hills*, 198–204.
8. Franklin Pierce, quoted in Hudson Strode, *Jefferson Davis: 1808–1861* (New York: Harcourt, Brace, & World, 1955), 247.
9. William Seale, *The President's House: A History* (Washington, DC: White House Historical Society, 1986), 308.
10. Franklin Pierce, quoted in Strode, *Jefferson Davis: 1808–1861*, 248.
11. James D. Richardson, ed., *A Compilation of the Messages and Papers of the Presidents* (Washington, DC: Bureau of National Literature and Art, 1897), 2730.
12. Ibid., 5:197–203.
13. David M. Potter, *The Impending Crisis 1848–1861* (New York: Harper & Row Publishers, 1976), 188–189.
14. Franklin Pierce, Inaugural Address, March 4, 1853, Richardson, *Compilation*, 6:2730.

15. For Pierce's belief in the importance of military science, see ibid. For Pierce's efforts to upgrade the military, see Strode, *Jefferson Davis: 1808–1861*, 260–261.

16. Franklin Pierce, "First State of the Union Message to Congress," in Richardson, *Compilation*, 5:867.

17. "Administration Designs Foreshadowed in Inaugural," *New York Daily Times*, March 31, 1853, 2.

18. In early 1854, newspaper columnist Benjamin Perely Poore remarked that the president was "the man of the time, his cabinet . . . an aggregation of the wisdom of the country, his policy the very perfection of statesmanship. Even the Whigs did not utter a word of discontent." Seale, *President's House: A History*, 322.

19. Peter H. Lindert and Richard Sutch, "Consumer Price Indexes, for All Items: 1774–2003," table Cc1–2, in *Historical Statistics of the United States, Earliest Times to the Present: Millennial Edition*, ed. Susan B. Carter et al. (New York: Cambridge University Press, 2006), http://dx.doi.org/10.1017/ISBN-9780511132971.Cc1–65.

20. Holt, *Franklin Pierce*, 66.

21. While the term "popular sovereignty" was invoked regularly in the period leading up to the Civil War and linked by its proponents to the principle of self-government, its precise origin in the Constitution was left ambiguous. Christopher Childers, "Interpreting Popular Sovereignty: A Historical Essay," *Civil War History* 57 (2011): 48. Some proponents tried to anchor popular sovereignty in the Tenth Amendment, which reserves to the states the powers not delegated to the United States, and secondarily in the Ninth Amendment (which states that the enumeration of certain rights in the Constitution does not deny or disparage others retained to the people). Justice Campbell, concurring in *Dred Scott*, specifically invoked the Ninth and Tenth Amendments in supporting the notion of popular sovereignty in the territories and in declaring that Congress could not regulate slavery in the territories or in the new states that chose to permit it. Dred Scott v. Sandford, 60 U.S. (19 How.) 292, 511 (1856) (Campbell, J., concurring). It is not surprising that Abraham Lincoln, during the famous Lincoln-Douglas debates in 1858 and his Cooper Union address in 1860, challenged this notion of popular sovereignty and criticized the Supreme Court's decision in *Dred Scott*. See Henry S. Cohn, review of *Lincoln and the Constitution*, by Brian R. Dirck, *Federal Lawyer* 59 (November 2012): 66. In reality, popular sovereignty turned into a proslavery refrain, invoked to provide a reason to allow newly admitted states like Kansas to choose slavery without the federal government's having to dictate this result. In this manner, those favoring slavery could press the issue without infuriating Northern abolitionists.

22. Major L. Wilson, "The Repressible Conflict: Seward's Concept of Progress and the Free Soil Movement," *Journal of Southern History* 37, no. 4 (1971): 539.

23. Roy D. Bird and Douglas W. Wallace, *Witness of the Times: A History of Shawnee County* (Topeka, KS: H. M. Ives and Sons, 1976), 9.

24. Paul Finkelman, ed., *His Soul Goes Marching On: Responses to John Brown and the Harpers Ferry Raid* (Charlottesville: University Press of Virginia, 1995); Paul Finkelman and Peggy A. Russo, eds., *Terrible Swift Sword: The Legacy of John Brown* (Athens: Ohio University Press, 2005).

25. Holt, *Franklin Pierce*, 85.

# 15

# James Buchanan

### THOMAS A. HORROCKS

*President James Buchanan, who believed that the Republican Party and the abolitionists were destroying the nation, personally lobbied the Supreme Court in the Dred Scott case, hoping it would get him (and the Democratic Party) off the hook on the slavery question. The decision, however, only intensified the conflict over the question. Buchanan was a man of contradictions. A professed strict constructionist, he nonetheless used his presidential powers aggressively when faced with a "rebellion" of Mormons in Utah. Yet, he stood paralyzed and powerless when Southern states began seceding from the Union; he claimed that the Constitution gave him no authority to intervene. Although he would spend the rest of his life denying responsibility, some historians would view the Civil War that ensued as "Mr. Buchanan's War."*

## Introduction

On June 4, 1868, three days after his death at his beloved estate in Lancaster, Pennsylvania, former president James Buchanan was buried by family, friends, and neighbors. His funeral, attended by a crowd of more than twenty thousand, included several speakers who reminded mourners of Buchanan's achievements and his many years of devoted public service to the nation. One orator even compared the former president to his successor, Abraham Lincoln, claiming that two barefoot boys had "climbed to the highest office in the world."[1] Comparisons of these two men would continue to be made in the future, but usually with the intention of identifying differences rather than similarities. While historians and the American people consistently rate Lincoln as one of America's two or three greatest presidents, Buchanan is typically rated among the nation's two or three worst. After all, Buchanan and Lincoln could not have been more different, especially in their approaches to the constitutional powers of the presidency in a time of national crisis. Buchanan was considered by many observers in 1856 to be the right man for the presidency; he boasted a sterling résumé that included stints as a congressman, senator, and diplomat. Yet the prediction was not fulfilled. Entering office at a time that required strong national leadership, Buchanan, despite his years of political experience, failed to provide this leadership, partly because of his narrow interpretation of the Constitution.

James Buchanan, the fifteenth president of the United States, was born in Cove Gap, a small village near Mercersburg, Pennsylvania, on April 23, 1791. His parents were James Buchanan, an immigrant from County Donegal, Ireland, and Elizabeth Speer, a native Pennsylvanian.[2] The second-oldest child and eldest son among eleven children, he attended Old Stone Academy, entered Dickinson College in nearby Carlisle at age sixteen, and graduated with honors two years later. Buchanan decided to pursue a legal career, moving to Lancaster, at that time the state capital, to begin an apprenticeship with James Hopkins, the town's leading attorney. Buchanan became one of the state's most prominent lawyers, earning more than $11,000 a year in legal fees (a fortune back then) by the time he was thirty.[3]

Buchanan was involved in a romantic relationship that ended in tragedy, when in 1819, his twenty-two-year-old fiancée Ann Coleman, the daughter of a wealthy iron manufacturer, became distraught over their relationship.

Soon thereafter, she died suddenly of "hysteria" (some speculated it was suicide). Deeply distressed by this loss, Buchanan never married.[4]

In 1820, the Federalist Party nominated Buchanan, who had served two terms in the Pennsylvania legislature, to represent Lancaster and two other counties in the U.S. Congress. Elected easily, he served in that body for ten years, during which time he continued to drift away from the dying Federalist Party. In 1828, having supported Andrew Jackson for president twice, Buchanan formally joined the Democratic Party.[5]

As a Democrat, Buchanan became a staunch advocate of states' rights, minimal central government, and a strict construction of the Constitution.[6] Buchanan also developed strong pro-Southern views, especially regarding the issue of slavery. Though personally opposed to the institution, he viewed abolitionists and politicians who agreed with them as radical extremists bent on destroying the Union. He firmly believed that the institution of slavery was protected by the Constitution. His pro-Southern sympathies dictated virtually every position he took on major issues, both domestic and diplomatic. His attachment to the South only went so far, however. A devoted Unionist, Buchanan ardently opposed the emerging radical Southern view of secession.

After a brief hiatus in which he served as minister to Russia in the Jackson administration, in late 1833, Buchanan won an open U.S. Senate seat as a Democrat.[7] He continued to serve Pennsylvania with distinction in that body until 1845.[8] A committed expansionist, he espoused America's manifest destiny, especially the annexation of Texas.

Buchanan planned to run for president in 1844, but withdrew from the race for the Democratic nomination when he failed to secure full backing of the Pennsylvania delegation.[9] When he then served as secretary of state under President James Polk, the position raised Buchanan's popularity in Pennsylvania and his profile as a potential presidential candidate. He lost the Democratic Party nomination in 1848, and again in 1852, when he lost out to dark horse Franklin Pierce of New Hampshire on the forty-ninth ballot of the Baltimore convention.[10] During this time, Buchanan acquired Wheatland, a country estate in Lancaster, but his retirement was short-lived. President Pierce appointed Buchanan to serve as minister to Great Britain, where the dignified and urbane Buchanan worked hard on several issues of critical importance to both countries.

In 1855, Buchanan returned to a country that was wracked by political turmoil over the issue of slavery in the territories. The Kansas-Nebraska

Act destroyed the Whig Party, gave birth to the Republican Party, and inflamed sectional tensions.[11] Untainted by this controversial law, Buchanan won the nomination for president at the Democratic Party's convention in May 1856. He and the vice presidential nominee, John C. Breckinridge of Kentucky, ran on a platform that endorsed popular sovereignty in the territories as embodied in the Kansas-Nebraska Act; supported the Compromise of 1850, including the Fugitive Slave Law and federal noninterference with slavery; and otherwise sought to reshape the Democratic brand.[12] Well funded by wealthy Northern merchants who were worried that a Republican victory would disrupt commerce with the South, Democrats carried every Southern state except Maryland and several key Northern states, including Indiana and Pennsylvania.

## Presidency

Buchanan vowed to serve only one term as president in order to devote his full attention to easing sectional tensions and destroying the Republican Party and the abolition movement, which he saw as the same and believed were dividing the nation. However, he failed to assemble a cabinet that reflected the various factions constituting the Democratic Party, ignoring Northern Free-Soilers and popular sovereignty advocates who had supported his rivals. The bachelor president (his niece Harriet Lane served as First Lady) had few close friends. For his cabinet, he chose four Southerners and three Northerners who, like himself, were Southern sympathizers and who were compatible with him socially and ideologically. Thus, Buchanan began his presidency isolated from points of view that challenged his own.

In his inaugural address, Buchanan shared with the American people the two main goals of his administration: the resolution of the slavery issue in the North and the destruction of sectional political parties (meaning the Republican Party). Concerning the slavery issue in the territories, the new president argued that it would soon be resolved by the Supreme Court's decision in the *Dred Scott* case. Indeed, he claimed, it was "a matter of little practical importance" because "it is a judicial question, which legitimately belongs to the Supreme Court of the United States" and will be "speedily and finally settled." Like all good citizen-politicians, Buchanan pledged to "cheerfully" abide by the Court's decision.[13] Yet he had a plan to steer that decision to its desired outcome.

## *The* Dred Scott *Case*

The *Dred Scott v. Sandford* case dated back to 1846, when the enslaved Scott began his quest to gain freedom for himself, his wife, and their two daughters. Scott had been born a slave in Virginia around 1800 and lived in the slave state of Missouri. He was purchased by John Emerson, an army surgeon, and went with Emerson to places outside Missouri, including Illinois (a free state) and an army base in the Wisconsin Territory (now Minnesota), where slavery was banned by the Missouri Compromise of 1820. Scott married (as only a free man could, and with his former master's blessing) and returned to Missouri with Emerson. When Emerson died in 1846, his widow took ownership, and her brother, John Sanford (a New York citizen, whose name was misspelled "Sandford" in court records), sought to maintain her property rights in the slaves. Scott sued for his freedom and that of his family in state court, arguing that he was a free man by virtue of the fact that he lived on free soil. Scott won his case in the local trial court, but the Missouri Supreme Court declared that he remained a slave under state law. Scott brought a diversity-of-citizenship claim in federal court. The lower federal court ruled that it was bound to accept the decision of Missouri's highest court as to Scott's slave status. Scott filed an appeal to the U.S. Supreme Court.

Wishing to have the matter resolved early in his term, thus eliminating the Republican Party's dominant issue while easing sectional tensions, Buchanan blatantly intervened in the deliberations of the Supreme Court just weeks before his inauguration. In early February, he wrote to his old friend, Justice James Catron of Tennessee, inquiring if a decision would be rendered before the inauguration. In subsequent communications, Justice Catron informed Buchanan that the Court's decision against Scott probably would be along sectional lines and that the Court was split on whether to address the larger issue of slavery in the territories. Catron suggested that the president-elect, if he desired a definitive decision on the issue, should make his wishes known to his friend and fellow Pennsylvanian, Justice Robert Grier. Buchanan did so directly. Grier responded that he, Grier, and Chief Justice Roger B. Taney "fully appreciate and concur in your views . . . of having an expression of the opinion of the court of this troublesome question."[14]

On March 6, 1857, two days after Buchanan's inauguration, the Supreme Court, by a vote of seven to two, ruled against Scott. The majority opinion, written by Chief Justice Taney and joined by Justice Grier, was based on two conclusions. First, it held that blacks were not citizens of the United States regardless of their status (free or enslaved), pursuant to the U.S. Constitution. Therefore, they possessed no legal right to sue in a federal court of law and the Court was without diversity-of-citizenship jurisdiction. Second, the Court concluded that Scott's time in a free territory had no legal significance, because the ban on slavery in the Missouri Compromise of 1820 was unconstitutional. The Court reasoned that the ban violated the property rights of slave-owners—rights that were guaranteed by the federal Constitution, and could not be taken away pursuant to the Fifth Amendment without due process of law.[15]

When Buchanan announced that he would "cheerfully" submit to the Supreme Court's decision, he likely already knew the outcome of the case, because of his ex parte discussions with the justices. Despite his strict interpretation of the Constitution, therefore, Buchanan ignored the separation of powers among the three branches of the federal government, injecting himself directly into the *Dred Scott* case. That now-infamous decision, however, did not defuse sectional tensions as Buchanan had hoped. To the contrary, *Dred Scott* only emboldened the Southern Democrats. It also angered the Republican Party, which, fearing that slavery could now be extended anywhere in the North, convinced party leaders that they needed to fight pro-slavery states head-on. The decision also weakened Northern Democrats who had believed that popular sovereignty might allow North and South to peacefully coexist.

## Mormon Uprisings

In addition to the uproar caused by *Dred Scott*, Buchanan faced a Mormon uprising in Utah and an economic panic during his first year in office. Although the Mormon troubles predated his presidency and had been "botched" by his predecessor, President Franklin Pierce, Buchanan was determined to address them forcefully.[16] Founded in 1830 in Upstate New York by Joseph Smith, the Church of Jesus Christ of Latter-Day Saints attracted suspicion and condemnation everywhere its members settled, partly because of their practice of polygamy. Viewed by many as fanatics practicing a strange and immoral religion, Mormons moved to the West to establish their religious kingdom. In 1846, Smith's successor, Brigham Young, built a community in the Salt Lake region of Utah, where he was appointed governor in 1850 by President Millard Fillmore, shortly after Congress established the territory. Seeing himself as accountable to no one but God and viewing the territory as a religious kingdom independent of federal control, Young regularly challenged U.S. government officials and laws. He wrote his own laws and raised a militia that threatened and fought with federal agents and harassed non-Mormon emigrants passing through Utah Territory.

As reports of escalated violence in Utah arrived, President Buchanan, claiming that he "had no alternative but to adopt vigorous measures for restoring the supremacy of the Constitution and its law," decided to "supersede" (or replace) Young as governor and appoint several officials to take charge of the territory.[17] In addition, without informing Congress, the president ordered twenty-five hundred troops—nearly one-third of the U.S. Army—to accompany and protect the newly installed governor, Alfred Cumming. (Cumming had been Buchanan's last choice after numerous men had turned the president down.)[18] In his annual message to Congress, Buchanan defended this use of military force, claiming that the Mormon troubles represented "the first rebellion which has existed in our Territories; and humanity itself requires that we should put it down in such manner that it shall be the last."[19]

Buchanan's handling of the Utah War was far from stellar. The massive number of federal troops sent to Utah appeared to be excessive, prompting Young to proclaim the forces an armed mob. The religious leader consequently dispatched Mormon raiders to burn army supply wagons and set fire to grasslands, forcing federal troops to spend a cold winter at Fort Bridger outside Salt Lake City and causing soldiers to die of the adverse conditions. Moreover, Congress had received only spotty information about the so-called rebellion in Utah; some representatives called for an investigation of the matter.[20]

In the end, Buchanan issued a proclamation on April 6, 1858, commanding all citizens of the Territory of Utah to abide by federal law and offering a free pardon to all who had participated in the "rebellion" if they agreed to these terms. Shortly thereafter, Young formally surrendered his title as governor and accepted the pardon, but the Mormon leader continued to insist that Utah had never rebelled from the United States. By June, Buchanan announced that peace had been restored in Utah. Yet some critics from the press dubbed this "Buchanan's Blunder," and the entire episode was widely viewed as a mishandled mission.

President Buchanan's threat of military action and his willingness to bypass Congress in ordering troops to Utah in the face of a "rebellion" showed that he was willing to use the power of his office during what he perceived to be a time of crisis. However, when facing a more serious rebellion at the end of his term, Buchanan used the Constitution as an excuse to *avoid* taking action.

## The Kansas Debacle

Buchanan's emotional attachment to the South ended up clouding his judgment in his handling of the Kansas controversy. Since 1854, both free- and slave-state advocates had engaged in a bloody conflict in Kansas Territory. To Buchanan, the admission of Kansas as a Democratic-controlled state, with or without slavery, was the primary objective. He appointed a Southerner and former secretary of the treasury, Robert Walker, to serve as the new territorial governor with the promise that he, the president, would only support a state constitution that was submitted to the people of the territory for approval. Walker soon turned to the president for help when free-state men (who opposed slavery) refused to participate in an 1857 election to send delegates to a convention held in the town of Lecompton. The free-staters' action left a proslavery minority controlling the convention. Not surprisingly, this minority group produced a constitution that permitted slavery and prohibited any changes to the document until 1865.

Fully aware that a majority of Kansans opposed slavery, Walker looked to Buchanan to fulfill the president's pledge to reject a constitution that was not approved in its entirety by a popular referendum. Although Walker had been a U.S. senator from Mississippi and supported slavery, he had accepted the post as territorial governor only on Buchanan's assurances that the popular will of the citizens of Kansas would not be subverted. But under intense pressure from Southern congressmen and governors threatening secession if slavery was not permitted in the territory, Buchanan decided to accept the Lecompton constitution, submitting it to Congress with his full support. Buchanan's decision outraged Walker, who resigned; it even angered Senator Stephen A. Douglas and his followers (members of Buchanan's own party), who believed that the Lecompton constitution repudiated the principle of popular sovereignty enshrined in the Democratic platform of 1856.

The Lecompton bill passed the Senate, but was defeated in the House even though Buchanan tried to cobble together votes by using the power of his office, threatening the removal of Douglas officeholders, awarding contracts to wavering congressmen, and offering patronage jobs.[21] Compromise legislation, which permitted a popular referendum on the constitution, eventually passed both houses of Congress. Not only was the proposed Kansas constitution overwhelmingly defeated when both factions voted, but Buchanan's vigorous support of the Lecompton bill shattered his credibility as a national leader and worsened the split in his own party. The Republicans, on the other hand, profited from Buchanan's Kansas debacle, reaping significant gains in the 1858 elections and garnering enough support in Congress to appoint a committee to investigate Buchanan's use of cash incentives and patronage on behalf of the Lecompton bill. The "strict constructionist" president, it turned out, seemed to have no qualms about interfering with the legislative process when it came to the slavery issue, and this contradiction of word and deed was exposed.

Party divisions and revelations of corruption within the Buchanan administration severely damaged the Democrats' chances in the 1860 presidential election. Riddled with in-fighting and other problems, the party nominated two candidates in 1860, with Northern Democrats choosing Senator Stephen A. Douglas and a platform endorsing popular sovereignty, and Southern Democrats nominating Buchanan's vice president, John C. Breckinridge, on a platform advocating a national slave code to protect the institution. Buchanan, who made no attempt to heal the rift within his party, endorsed his vice president. His war against the Democratic Party's Northern wing helped to drive the final nail into the coffin of the Democratic Party. The election was won by the opposing party's candidate, Abraham Lincoln, the Republican candidate from Illinois who campaigned on an antislavery platform. Simultaneously, Buchanan ended up dealing a devastating blow to the objectives he set for himself and his own presidency.[22]

### Secession

States from the lower South, led by South Carolina, began to secede in response to Lincoln's election. Blaming northern antislavery agitation for the crisis, Buchanan called for constitutional amendments to protect slavery in the territories and in the South and for strict enforcement of fugitive-slave laws in the North. Despite his sympathy for the South, however, Buchanan drew the line at secession. Devoted to the Union, he refused to recognize the legality of secession, yet he believed that the Constitution prevented him from stopping it. As Buchanan read the Constitution, the president had no authority, apart from executing the laws, to change the relationship between the federal government and a seceding state. Any attempt on the part of the president to assume such responsibility, he declared, "would be a naked act of usurpation." Thus the president, who was quick to take military action against rebellious Mormons without congressional approval, took no action as South Carolina, Mississippi, and state after state seceded.[23]

As the secession movement gained momentum, the status of federal property and forts in rebellious states, especially South Carolina, became points of contention. Fort Sumter in Charleston Harbor, with its small garrison and dwindling supplies, a location surrounded by batteries controlled by South Carolina forces, was particularly vulnerable. After initially wavering, Buchanan decided not to vacate the fort, profoundly disappointing—and losing the backing of—many of his Southern supporters. Following the advice of his new, pro-Unionist cabinet, Buchanan decided to send an unarmed vessel, the *Star of the West*, to reinforce Fort Sumter. The ship, however, was turned away by heavy fire from harbor batteries. Buchanan, determined to avoid a war, did not respond to the attack. The lame-duck president who had warned South Carolina officials that he would defend "by such means as I may possess" if there were hostile attacks against Fort Sumter, took no further actions to reinforce the fort, preferring to let his successor deal with the crisis.[24]

## Conclusion

On March 4, 1861, Buchanan turned the office of chief executive over to Abraham Lincoln. While Buchanan was pleased to relinquish the duties of the presidency, he made no apologies about his tenure in office, confident that had done everything within his power to prevent a civil war, despite receiving angry letters accusing him of fomenting the civil strife and bloodshed. He devoted most of his retirement years to writing a memoir, *Mr. Buchanan's Administration on the Eve of a Rebellion*, which was published in 1866 and which defended his actions as president. He supported the Union cause in the Civil War only because he supported the goal of a reunited North and South, but adamantly opposed Lincoln's Emancipation Proclamation, believing it to be unconstitutional. Up until his death in June 1868 at his Wheatland estate, where he had lived out his final years in political isolation, Buchanan clung to the belief that abolitionists and the Republican Party were responsible for the Civil War.

Despite his extensive political and diplomatic experience, Buchanan failed to provide strong executive leadership in a time of crisis. His failure as president cannot be attributed solely to a lack of political will or a tendency to vacillate, as some historians have suggested. Attached to a narrow, antiquated Jacksonian political philosophy of decades past, Buchanan seemed oblivious to the economic and cultural changes occurring in Northern society. He was insensitive to the growing antislavery movement in the North and never understood the difference between those who wanted to prevent the spread of slavery and those who wanted to abolish it.

Emotionally attached to the South, Buchanan consistently showed favoritism toward the region, and his partiality compromised his credibility as a national leader. His strict constructionist view of the Constitution, though occasionally broadened when it suited him, prevented Buchanan from effectively using the powers of the presidency in a time of crisis. He entered the White House with noble intentions of restoring harmony to a divided nation. However, he failed to see that his actions as president dealt a final, devastating blow to the objectives he had set for himself when he assumed that high office.

NOTES

1. Philip Shriver Klein, *President James Buchanan: A Biography* (State College: Pennsylvania State University Press, 1962), 427–428.
2. Klein's 1962 biography remains the definitive study of the life and presidency of Buchanan. Whereas Klein's work is sympathetic toward its subject, more recent studies, including Elbert Smith, *The Presidency of James Buchanan* (Lawrence: University Press of Kansas, 1975); Jean H. Baker, *James Buchanan* (New York: Henry Holt, 2004); and Thomas A. Horrocks, *President James Buchanan and the Crisis of National Leadership* (Hauppauge, NY: Nova, 2012), offer negative assessments. Frederick Moore Binder, *James Buchanan and the American Empire* (Selinsgrove, PA: Susquehanna University Press, 1994), presents a comprehensive overview of Buchanan's diplomatic career, from his time as President Andrew Jackson's minister to Russia through his presidency. Michael J. Birkner, ed., *James Buchanan and the Political Crisis of the 1850s* (Susquehanna

University Press, 1996), examines Buchanan's presidency within the context of the political upheaval of the 1850s. Essential to studying Buchanan and his presidency is John Bassett Moore, ed., *The Works of James Buchanan Comprising His Speeches, State Papers, and Private Correspondence*, 12 vols. (New York: Antiquarian Press, 1960). George Ticknor Curtis, *Life of James Buchanan, Fifteenth President of the United States*, 2 vols. (New York: Harper & Brothers, 1883), is useful for correspondence not included in Moore's edition. For Buchanan's defense of his presidency, see James Buchanan, *Mr. Buchanan's Administration on the Eve of the Rebellion* (New York: D. Appleton and Company, 1866).

3. Jean H. Baker, "James Buchanan: Strict Constructionist," in *America's Lawyer Presidents: From Law Office to Oval Office*, ed. Norman Gross (Evanston, IL: ABA Museum of Law, Northwestern University Press, 2004), 118.

4. There is no evidence that Buchanan ever had a sexual relationship with any woman. The most intimate relationship he is known to have had with anyone was with Senator William R. King of Alabama, a lifelong bachelor known for his flamboyant style and extravagant dress. King and Buchanan roomed together for several years when the latter served in the House of Representatives and later in the Senate. Because the two appeared inseparable, fellow politicians referred snidely to them as "Buchanan and wife." His close relationship with King has led some historians and writers to speculate about Buchanan's possible homosexuality. Among his contemporaries, there were occasional whispers and derogatory comments as well. Unless credible evidence comes to light, Buchanan's sexuality will remain a mystery. All that one can say with any certitude is that he was this nation's only bachelor president. Baker, *James Buchanan*, 25–26; Sean Wilentz, *The Rise of American Democracy: Jefferson to Lincoln* (New York: W.W. Norton, 2005), 699; John W. Forney, *Anecdotes of Public Men* (Harper & Brothers, 1873), 65.

5. Buchanan soon became one of Pennsylvania's leading political figures, assembling a coalition of former Federalist farmers in the northern part of the state, along with Philadelphia artisans and Scotch-Irish farmers from the western region.

6. During his tenure as chair of the House Judiciary Committee, he argued against the repeal of Section 25 of the Judiciary Act of 1789, which granted the Supreme Court powers to review and reverse certain decisions of state courts. Buchanan believed that there had to be a higher judicial authority than that of the sovereign states. Baker, *James Buchanan*, 121.

7. By 1830, Buchanan saw his political career at a dead end and decided to retire from Congress. Soon after announcing his intentions, he was asked by President Andrew Jackson to serve as minister to Russia. Here, he successfully negotiated with the Russian government a commercial treaty that ensured the principle of reciprocity and most-favored-nation status while promoting American trade in the Black Sea. The treaty lowered U.S. tariff rates on Russian hemp and iron, and in return, the U.S. was allowed to move sugar and other raw materials into Russia via the Black Sea. John Belohlavek, *"Let the Eagle Soar!" The Foreign Policy of Andrew Jackson* (Lincoln: University of Nebraska Press, 1985), 86–87; Binder, *James Buchanan and the American Empire*, 20–25.

8. As a senator, Buchanan remained a loyal party man, supporting Jackson's policies, including the president's stand against nullification and his war on the Bank of the United States.

9. The party instead nominated James Knox Polk of Tennessee for president and Buchanan's archrival from Pennsylvania, George Mifflin Dallas, for vice president.

10. In 1848, Buchanan lost to Lewis Cass of Michigan, who was in turn defeated by the Mexican-American War hero, General Zachary Taylor, the standard-bearer of the Whig Party.

11. This law was passed in 1854 by Congress with the strong endorsement of President Pierce. It repealed the Missouri Compromise of 1820, which had banned slavery in the northern portions of the Louisiana Purchase, instead allowing residents of the future states of Kansas and Nebraska to decide the slavery issue for themselves.

12. The Republican Party, holding its first national convention, nominated John C. Frémont of California for president. The party's platform opposed the extension of slavery and promoted internal improvements, such as a Pacific railroad and river and harbor initiatives. Former president Millard Fillmore was nominated for president by the Know-Nothing Party, a secret organization born out of fear and bigotry in the face of growing numbers of immigrants, especially Irish Catholics.

13. James Buchanan, Inaugural Address, March 4, 1857, in Moore, *Works of James Buchanan*, 10:105–109.

14. Don E. Fehrenbacher, *The Dred Scott Case: Its Significance in American Law and Politics* (New York: Oxford University Press, 1978), 307–312; Baker, *James Buchanan*, 85. For Catron's February 19, 1857, letter to Buchanan and Grier's February 23, 1857, letter to Buchanan, see Moore, *Works of James Buchanan*, 10:106–108

15. Dred Scott v. Sandford, 60 U.S. (19 How.) 393, 427, 450–451 (1856). See Paul Finkelman, *Dred Scott v. Sandford: A Brief History with Documents* (New York: Bedford Books, 1997), 1. Several concurring opinions were filed in the case, including one by Justice Campbell. He emphasized the power of the states to determine matters related to slavery. Citing the Ninth and Tenth Amendments as supportive of the majority's result, Justice Campbell's concurring opinion suggested the doctrine of popular sovereignty, which was being offered at the time by proponents of slavery to argue that issues regarding slavery were not questions for the federal government's consideration, but were reserved for the people of the states and territories to decide. *Dred Scott*, 60 U.S. at 511 (Campbell, J., concurring). See also Christopher Childers, "Interpreting Popular Sovereignty: a Historical Essay," *Civil War History* 57 (2011): 48.

16. William P. MacKinnon, "Prelude to Armageddon: James Buchanan, Brigham Young, and a President's Initiation to Bloodshed," in *James Buchanan and the Coming of the Civil War*, ed. John W. Quist and Michael J. Birkner (Gainesville: University Press of Florida, 2013), 46–85.

17. James Buchanan, *Mr. Buchanan's Administration on the Eve of the Rebellion* (D. Appleton and Company, 1866), 232.

18. MacKinnon, "Prelude to Armageddon," 61–62.

19. James Buchanan, First Annual Message, December 8, 1857, in Moore, *Works of James Buchanan*, 10:15–54.

20. MacKinnon, "Prelude to Armageddon," 65–68.

21. Baker, *James Buchanan*, 103; Smith, *Presidency of James Buchanan*, 44.

22. In his inaugural address, Buchanan said that to address the critical issues facing the country, unencumbered by the influence of politics, he would not "become a candidate for reelection." Moore, *Works of James Buchanan*, 10:105.

23. James Buchanan, Fourth Annual Message, December 3, 1860, Moore, *Works of James Buchanan*, 11:17–19.

24. To the South Carolina Commissioners, December 31, 1860, Moore, *Works of James Buchanan*, 11:84.

# PART IV

# Civil War and Reconstruction

# 16

# Abraham Lincoln

## WILLIAM D. PEDERSON

*Abraham Lincoln, who began his career as an unsophisticated frontier lawyer, became the first successful presidential candidate of the fledgling Republican Party. As the nation splintered into a civil war, Lincoln wielded his constitutional authority with an inspired wisdom and effectiveness. Author of the Emancipation Proclamation; "Lincoln's Code," which established laws of war; and the Gettysburg Address, Lincoln transformed himself into one of the greatest leaders and statesmen in American history. He also greatly expanded presidential powers as he grappled with the exigencies of an unprecedented war among the states. Despite his death by an assassin's bullet five days after the Confederates surrendered at Appomattox, Abraham Lincoln helped define the concept of democratic self-government—not just in the United States but around the world—perhaps more so than any American president.*

## Introduction

According to polls of scholars, Abraham Lincoln usually ranks first among American presidents—surely as the greatest nineteenth-century president.[1] Yet these polls do a disservice because other data suggests that he is one of the greatest democratic political leaders in world history. More books have been written about him than about any other political leader.[2] Moreover, there are more memorials dedicated to him around the world than any other American president or world leader. His name appears on schools, streets, and businesses on every continent save Antarctica, and his image on stamps, paintings, and sculptures are equally ubiquitous.[3] Even his definition of democratic government appears in several constitutions of other nations. He is the symbol of democratic government.

Lincoln's political and legal achievements are impressive in that they were accomplished during a major civil war in hardly more than one presidential term in office (March 1861 to April 1865). He realized these accomplishments with less than a total year of formal schooling, without travel experience abroad, and without prior executive experience.

Lincoln transformed himself from a frontier hick into a lawyer-statesman who constitutionally transformed a slave society into a free one. Though he spent nearly a quarter century practicing law, Lincoln spent more years seeking or serving in political office.[4] Indeed, politics sustained and personally fulfilled him even during the Civil War. He enjoyed people and working on public-policy issues. In a sense, his wartime presidency involved a series of constitutional issues that suited his personality and background. Not surprisingly, scholars typically rank him as one of the top ten lawyers in American history.[5]

Abraham Lincoln had little formal education. He was born in the border state of Kentucky and moved to the Indiana frontier and then Illinois. Raised on a farm, he suffered tragedy early in his life, losing his mother when he was nine to a mysterious illness called milk sickness. Life was hard on the frontier, and the days long and taxing. Perhaps because he was so tall and gangly, the young Lincoln avoided physical labor at any cost. He especially despised farming, his father's occupation, so he dabbled in many other areas in search of an occupation. Lincoln tried his hand at being a carpenter, riverboat man, store clerk, soldier, merchant, postmaster, blacksmith, and surveyor. In the end, he settled on law and politics after concluding he couldn't make an honest living doing anything else.[6]

Formal schooling wasn't an option for Lincoln, which was true for most country lawyers at that time. Most men aspiring to enter the legal profession apprenticed with an established attorney and learned the law through that experience. Lincoln could not even afford to do this. Instead, he borrowed legal texts like Blackstone's *Commentaries* from friends and taught himself enough law to become a lawyer. By 1861, Lincoln had handled over five thousand cases, had appeared three hundred times in front of the Illinois Supreme Court, and had a successful practice in federal court as well.[7] In 1849, he even made it to the U.S. Supreme Court in a case called *Lewis v. Lewis*, which involved a land dispute governed by an Illinois statute of limitations.[8] Ironically, Chief Justice Roger Taney, who decided against Lincoln in the case, would later issue the infamous opinion in *Dred Scott v. Sandford* and become Lincoln's main foil on the Court during the Civil War.

All the while, Lincoln was active in Whig, and later, Republican politics. He held congressional office from 1847 to 1849 and suffered close defeats in numerous other campaigns. The most stinging of these losses came in the 1858 U.S. Senate race in Illinois at the hands of Stephen Douglas after the famous Lincoln-Douglas debates. Because of his lack of experience as an elected official, Lincoln was viewed as a political novice when he won the presidency in 1860. Indeed, the victory was hardly convincing. He defeated the other three candidates by netting just 40 percent of the popular vote. Meanwhile, the Union was beginning to fracture along the Mason-Dixon Line. Thus, expectations were low as Lincoln embarked on the presidency.[9]

## Presidency

Clearly, presidents are never solely responsible for their successes, especially in the area of legislation. In Lincoln's case, both the Republican Party platform and Congress played a significant role in his successes.

### Social and Economic Legislation

The relationship between the president and Congress was particularly important for the passage of the Land Grant College Act (Morrill Act) that James Buchanan had vetoed in 1860 as beyond the Constitution's scope. Lincoln was quick to sign this bill into law on July 2, 1862. Before then, education was seen as a state issue and higher education was largely left to private religious colleges. The new legislation encouraged a partnership between the federal government and the states. In many ways, it was the first congressional legislation designed for a social purpose—to provide higher education for the middle and working classes. It would eventually transform higher education in the United States and become one of the nation's most successful experiments.[10]

Similarly, the Republican platform in 1860 had called for the Homestead Act, which President Buchanan had vetoed in 1860; Lincoln now signed it into law on May 15, 1862. For a mere $10 registration fee and a promise to live on the 160 acres of prairie land, a family head or an adult male could acquire an essentially free farm. The act attracted thousands of immigrants and helped push America's settlement further west. In less than two decades, more than half of the new farms were homestead ventures by former landless English, Irish, German, Swedish, Danish, Norwegian, and Czech immigrants.[11]

The Republican platform of 1860 had also emphasized the importance of a transcontinental railroad. As a longtime representative and champion of railroads (Lincoln had turned down a lucrative position with a railroad to seek the presidency), the president readily signed the Pacific Railway Act on July 1, 1862. Indeed, in 1864, he persuaded Congress to increase subsidies for railroads—a position that would help establish the transcontinental railroad. As the world's first major engineering feat of the nineteenth century, the railway helped bind the nation closer together and encouraged further economic development.[12]

These key legislative initiatives provided Lincoln with the political and social capital to expand his agenda while the South persisted in political revolt. Lincoln was prepared to transform himself into a genuine lawyer-statesman.

### The Emancipation Proclamation

The hostilities between the North and South over the slavery issue bubbled over soon after Lincoln took office, erupting into Civil War. In early 1861, seven Southern slave states seceded from the Union and formed the Confederacy. Then, on April 12, 1861, Confederate forces led by General P.

G. T. Beauregard, under the direction of Confederate president, Jefferson Davis, fired on Fort Sumter, an important Union fort at Charleston Harbor along the coast of South Carolina. As additional slave states rushed to join the Confederacy, President Lincoln established control over the border states and set up a naval blockade that virtually crippled the Southern economy. With hostilities rapidly escalating, a bloody Civil War ensued. It would last four years and leave over three-quarter million soldiers dead on the battlefield.

Lincoln's "containment" policy of slavery, which he had advocated during the Lincoln-Douglas debates of 1858, dramatically changed after the South seceded from the Union and fired on Fort Sumter. Moderates became radicals in seeking to crush the rebellion. As a traditional Whig lawyer, Lincoln recognized that the U.S. Constitution protected slavery; the issue was an essential compromise at the Constitutional Convention of 1787. Yet, as president, he became strongly influenced by William Whiting, a solicitor in the War Department. Whiting's *War Powers of the President* (1862) argued that as commander in chief, the president possessed the war power to emancipate slaves because they were considered property that could be seized from the enemy.

Lincoln drafted such a proclamation in June 1862.[13] His cabinet was stunned after he read it to them on July 22. Heeding the advice of Secretary of State William Seward, Lincoln postponed announcing the new policy until after a battlefield victory. Five days after Antietam, he issued the preliminary Emancipation Proclamation on September 22, 1862, providing that slaves in states that had not rejoined the Union by January 1, 1863, would be free.[14]

Though critics point out that the proclamation did not formally free slaves since it only applied to areas that were not yet in control of Union forces, the Emancipation Proclamation nonetheless sent a clear moral message to the slaves, the nation, and the rest of the world, including Europe. Even if European monarchs and conservative elites viewed the proclamation with skepticism or even disdain, the working class voiced its support. The Irish were the first to name a street for Lincoln outside the United States.

The Great Emancipator, as a consummate politician, was maneuvering the nation from a slave state to a free society. Fearful that his wartime measure might be overturned, Lincoln took unprecedented steps in lobbying Congress to pass the Thirteenth Amendment (banning involuntary servitude) and in seeking to stack the Supreme Court with justices who might support his policies. To the surprise of many, Lincoln appointed Salmon P. Chase to succeed the ailing Chief Justice Roger B. Taney, who died on October 12, 1864. Chase, a former U.S. senator and governor of Ohio, served as Lincoln's secretary of treasury and was a founder of the Free-Soil Party. He was also a prominent figure in the new Republican Party and an outspoken opponent of slavery. Chase had thought the Emancipation Proclamation was too restrained.

## The Sioux Uprising of 1862

At the end of his second year in the presidency, with the Civil War raging in the South, Lincoln faced a delicate situation regarding American Indians in the North. During the late summer and early fall of 1862, the Sioux Uprising (Dakota War) took place in western Minnesota. Several hundred men (primarily German immigrants too old for military service), along with women and babies, were slaughtered. After the uprising was quashed, an equal number of the Sioux were tried in military proceedings, and over three hundred were sentenced to death. A local Episcopal bishop appealed to the president on behalf of those found guilty.[15]

Lincoln had many reasons not to intervene. His own paternal grandfather had been scalped by an Indian, and the young Lincoln had served as a volunteer in the Illinois Militia during the Black Hawk War (1832). Moreover, neither the Civil War nor the off-year election had shown progress for Republicans. But despite all these reasons, he chose to intervene rather than stay out of what could have easily been avoided as a mere state matter. Lincoln reviewed the records of the condemned and tried to determine the ringleaders. He commuted most of the death sentences to lesser terms; as a result, only thirty-eight of those charged were hanged. Lincoln used his constitutional pardoning power in this instance and, throughout his presidency, to achieve justice. Moreover, he issued the second-largest number of amnesties in American history.[16]

## Wartime Precedents and International Influence

Though Lincoln may have been a frontier lawyer from Illinois, he understood the idea of self-government in sweeping terms. He recognized the Civil War as a "people's contest" and was willing to rely on those who might help him to formulate "the law of war" in a fashion that would shape the nation and the world. In late 1862, Lincoln's secretary of war, Edwin Stanton, and his general in chief, Henry W. Halleck, a lawyer and an author of a volume on international law, appointed Francis Lieber as the only civilian on a board created by the War Department to review the rules of war. At that time, Lieber was the most important American political scientist since James Madison.[17]

By May 1863, Lieber's revised draft was issued by Lincoln as General Orders No. 100, "Instructions for the Government of Armies of the United States in the Field." Lieber's Code, as the document came to be known, was consistent with Lincoln's own principles, which were based on the Declaration of Independence and reflected in the Emancipation Proclamation. It not only set down rules that would govern soldiers and military leaders in the Civil War, but also created rules that would apply to international conflicts abroad.[18] Among other things, the finished Lincoln's Code (consisting of 157 articles) sought to mark off "the outer boundaries of morally acceptable behavior."[19] It prohibited the use of poison, torture, and other practices that had previously been tolerated by military leaders.

Part of Lincoln's impetus for drafting the code stemmed from his fear that newly freed slaves, who were permitted to fight for the North, would be butchered rather than treated as prisoners of war by the Confederates. Indeed, as demonstrated by bloody massacres in Saltville, Virginia, and Fort Pillow, Tennessee, in which black Union soldiers were "murdered on the spot," some laws of war had to be established.[20] In that sense, Lincoln's Code was directly aimed at implementing the Emancipation Proclamation. At the same time, the code gave enormous power to the president as commander in chief. As Lieber, who soon became one of Lincoln's closest military advisers, wrote: "To save the country is paramount to all other considerations."[21] Thus, Abraham Lincoln, who had virtually no military experience before becoming president, relied on his knowledge of the rule of law to create a framework for decision making in wartime.

Because of Lincoln's vision, General Orders No. 100 became the first code of law for land warfare and served as the basis for the revised code of laws of war at the Hague Conventions of 1899 and 1907, as well as for the Geneva Conventions of 1929 and 1949. In a similar vein, Lincoln had advocated even earlier for what became the first modern usage of the centuries-old practice of binding international arbitration. His approach became the basis for the international arbitration of the *Alabama* Claims by a five-nation tribune of arbitration in December 1871.[22] Thus, Lincoln's careful implementation of his constitutional authority had a profound effect on international matters, even though he did not live to see this influence manifest itself.

## The Gettysburg Address

In early July 1863, Union forces dealt a major blow to the Confederacy in the Battle of Gettysburg. Up until this point, Lincoln had struggled with his generals and their incompetence on the battlefield. This reality, combined with a string of Southern victories, emboldened General Robert E. Lee to embark upon his first (and only) military campaign well into the North. However, after three days of fighting at Gettysburg, Lee's Army of Northern Virginia was in retreat. This decisive victory for the Union troops—a victory that up until that point had eluded Lincoln and his generals—was a major turning point in the Civil War. Yet, this triumph came at a heavy cost: All told, over fifty thousand men were killed, wounded, or missing during the three-day battle.[23]

On November 19, 1863, Lincoln visited the battlefield and delivered the most famous and eloquent two-page speech in world history.[24] The president was in Gettysburg to take part in the ceremony dedicating the cemetery where Union soldiers who died in the battle were buried. He worked on the Gettysburg Address both on the train from Washington and in his room the night before the ceremony. Although he initially believed that the speech was a failure, it was apparent to many in attendance that Lincoln had seized the opportunity and recast the war as part of a larger global struggle for equality and freedom.[25] Though he had essentially been saying the same thing throughout his entire political career, Lincoln never had said it so poetically. He put the U.S. Constitution within the natural law framework of the Declaration of Independence and set the new standard for what would constitute democratic government ("of, by and for the people"). His words have resonated with freedom-seeking peoples worldwide ever since.[26] Indeed, Lincoln's definition of democratic government is found near the opening of the French Constitution, and the words of the Gettysburg Address became the anthem for those fighting for democratic principles around the globe.[27] In this sense, Lincoln evolved from being the emancipator of slaves to setting the standard for constitutional democracy throughout the world.

## Confronting the Supreme Court

Perhaps more than any other American president before him, Lincoln was forced to come to grips with a paradox: Wartime required a set of overarching, governing laws at the same time that it produced such vast, unexpected dangers that the chief executive had to exercise enormous, often-unplanned powers. Nowhere was Lincoln's understanding of this incongruity more evident than in his exercise of unwritten presidential authority to suspend the writ of habeas corpus and to establish a blockade of Southern ports without a formal declaration of war by Congress.

Though Lincoln's inclination was to do justice when exercising the extraordinary powers he had concluded were available to a wartime president, he could also count the votes that might be cast against him by justices on the Supreme Court. Thus, he understood the danger that the Supreme Court held for his policy. He faced opposition from one of the dozen greatest justices in American history: Chief Justice Roger B. Taney. A Democrat who had served as attorney general under President Andrew Jackson, Taney had replaced John Marshall in 1835 as chief and served in this role for nearly thirty years. Whether from ill health, old age, or sympathy for Southern plantation owners, Taney failed to understand the Republican Party and Abraham Lincoln.[28] In fact, despite Taney's talent in supporting Jacksonian democracy, the chief justice's blatant judicial activism in *Dred Scott v. Sandford* had sparked Lincoln's challenge. In *Dred Scott*, Taney wrote the infamous decision for the Supreme Court, declaring that blacks were not "citizens" pursuant to the U.S. Constitution and that slave owners did not lose their property rights in slaves simply by moving them into a free state or territory.[29]

Taney was clearly looking for a way to block the inexperienced new president from the very beginning. After all, Lincoln was the dark-horse candidate who had won the presidency only by virtue of a fractured vote (39 percent). Moreover, he clearly lacked executive and military experience except for a brief stint in the Illinois Militia. Taney was not alone in considering the Rail Splitter to be an amateur. Ironically, Taney proved to be the amateur with bad timing while Lincoln steadily established himself as the consummate politician. Whereas Lincoln took his time in dealing with the chief justice, Taney jumped the gun again in an effort to stop the new president, and failed miserably in his effort.

Facing the potential destruction of the Union, Lincoln had suspended the near-sacred provision that the framers had placed in the Constitution, the writ of habeas corpus (Article I, Section 9). The writ requires a governmental official to hand over a prisoner to the courts to determine if the custody is lawful.[30] He had suspended the provision without first seeking congressional approval. Taney's native state of Maryland posed a serious threat to the nation's capital because the state was located directly adjacent to Washington. Determined to eliminate that threat, Lincoln wrote to his general in chief, Winfield Scott, a native Virginian, giving him permission to suspend the writ. Lincoln did this in the form of a letter rather than an executive order. The suspension was aimed at those who posed an immediate danger to the military rather than to accomplish the arrest of political dissidents.

John Merryman, a Marylander who was potentially Taney's judicial deus ex machina, provided the vehicle for Lincoln to act. A farmer from near Baltimore, Merryman served in a Confederate militia. Federal troops had arrested him by the end of May 1861 and imprisoned him in nearby Fort McHenry. Taney seized on the incident shortly after Merryman filed a writ of habeas corpus in federal court. In *Ex Parte Merryman*, the chief justice (who was riding the Maryland Circuit at the time) sided with his fellow Marylander and condemned Lincoln's "arbitrary arrests," taking the position that Congress possessed the sole authority to declare and wage war, including the power to suspend habeas corpus.[31]

After this decision, some thought Taney had violated his own notion of the political question doctrine, which should have counseled in favor of judicial restraint, as he had advocated in *Luther v. Borden*.[32] However, Lincoln refused to be outmaneuvered. Fort McHenry's commanding general ignored Taney's ruling, as did the president. At the same time, Lincoln fully understood that his actions in suspending the writ could be checked more directly by Congress. In July, the president delivered his classic defense to Congress regarding his decision to suspend habeas corpus without even mentioning Taney or Merryman: "Are all the laws, *but one*, to go unexecuted," he asked, "and the government itself go to pieces, lest one be violated?"[33]

Even after Lincoln essentially ignored the federal court's ruling in *Merryman*, Taney's willingness to challenge the president posed a serious threat to the war effort. Lincoln recognized that he needed time to pack the Court with his own appointees to block Taney's influence. He worked methodically, as some previous presidents (such as Thomas Jefferson) had done. Moreover, with the help of Republican allies in Congress, Lincoln succeeded in adding a Tenth Circuit Court to the federal court system on March 3, 1863, after the admission of California and Oregon to the Union. Lincoln then added another associate justice, Stephen Field, to the High Court in December 1863. These appointments soon proved crucial in the Prize Cases, regarding Lincoln's bold decision in April 1861 to blockade Southern ports, and to his war measures generally.[34]

In those consolidated cases, four ships with their cargoes had been captured by the Union Navy as blockade prizes. The owners sued the federal government over Lincoln's order to establish the blockade and the alleged misuse of his commander-in-chief powers because Congress had failed to formally declare war. The Court decided the case on March 10, 1863, in a five-to-four decision written by Justice Robert C. Grier of Pennsylvania. The opinion, joined by Lincoln's three 1862 appointees (Justices Noah Swayne, Samuel Miller, and David Davis) and Justice James M. Wayne, turned out to be the most important holding during the Civil War.

In assuming a broad statement of presidential war powers, the Court upheld Lincoln's blockade even before Congress officially authorized the action. Justice Grier wrote that "civil war is never publicly proclaimed" and that it was the president's primary duty to fulfill his constitutional oath of office. Moreover, the ruling gave the president flexibility in responding to national emergencies. It allowed the administration to simultaneously treat the conflict as an international war without recognizing the Confederate government as a domestic insurrectionist. This meant that the Confederacy would be considered to constitute a belligerent deserving a legal blockade. The decision also seemed to suggest that the Emancipation Proclamation and the suspension of habeas corpus were constitutional, especially after Congress had belatedly approved the measures.

The Great Emancipator had prevailed over the chief justice. Indeed, if the vote had gone the other way, it would have severely undermined Lincoln's ability to provide leadership during the military conflict and America's history might have been written differently.

Although Lincoln would not live to see the Supreme Court's decision in *Ex Parte Milligan* (1866), that case would ultimately vindicate the president with respect to his suspension of the writ of habeas corpus, holding that the suspension was lawful in states that did not have civilian courts in operation at the time.[35] Although the Court in *Milligan* also declared that the president could not use military tribunals to try U.S. citizens when civilian courts were available for such trials, Lincoln had managed to do this throughout the war.[36] Thus, Lincoln successfully used the military commissions to prosecute a wide range of offenses "under the common law of war" throughout his tenure as president.[37] As a result, Lincoln could circumvent both Congress and the courts in prosecuting U.S. citizens in these tribunals.[38] Indeed, during the Civil War, the Supreme Court explicitly acquiesced in this practice by unanimously giving Lincoln its blessing in the case of *Ex parte Vallandigham* by declining to review Vallandigham's arrest and trial by military tribunal.[39] Thus, President Lincoln managed to exercise extraordinary wartime powers throughout the Civil War, even though some of these powers receded after the war ended. Moreover, as with other aspects of his presidency, Lincoln's use of special military tribunals created a blueprint for the expansion of presidential power beyond the logical limits of the Constitution—a template that would later be utilized by twenty-first-century presidents fighting new, previously unimagined types of war.

## The Second Inaugural Address

Lincoln never hesitated in proceeding with the 1864 election in the midst of the American Civil War, despite his near-certain belief that he would lose reelection. However, General William Tecumseh Sherman's Atlanta Campaign changed the odds for Lincoln. During the hot summer of 1864, Sherman led a bold Union assault on Atlanta, capturing the city and driving a knife into the heart of the Confederacy. This gave Lincoln the opportunity to outline his reconstruction philosophy in his second inaugural address on March 4, 1865, the shortest (at three pages) inaugural speech by an American president to that time.[40] Much like the Gettysburg Address, the second inaugural address was in keeping with Lincoln's core values, though it was even more thoughtful and eloquent. The speech defined his lawyer-statesman view of the American legal structure. Crucially, Lincoln did not blame the South for the war, but instead focused on the mutual loss and his hope for a better future. Rather than a statement of victor's justice, Lincoln's policy represented a reflection of his lifelong philosophy, embodied in the words "with malice toward none."[41]

## Conclusion

In a sense, Abraham Lincoln—who traveled down the Mississippi River twice as a youth—became a Huck Finn with a law license. Rather than ending up as Captain Vere in *Billy Budd*, the Great Emancipator steered the ship of state toward achieving justice for all, while upholding the constitutional processes for democratic government.

And then, the ship suddenly lost its rudder, on April 4, 1865—just five days after General Robert E. Lee's surrender. Lincoln was shot while he and his wife, Mary Todd, were attending a comedy at Ford's Theater in the nation's capital. In the short run, John Wilkes Booth (1838–1865) achieved his immediate goal in assassinating America's sixteenth president. It was the first successful presidential assassination in the nation's history. Booth was not deranged. It was a planned political assassination by a Confederate sympathizer attempting to avenge the South's defeat. He was a successful actor from a distinguished family of actors. Yet actors make bad assassins in real life.[42]

Research suggests that the historical reputation of such presidents is actually enhanced by such events. In fact, presidential deaths, unlike deaths of other political figures, are viewed by the public as almost the same as a death in one's immediate family. Citizens tend to remember the date and even their own activities at the time of a presidential death.[43]

The assassination at a comedy became a Shakespearean tragedy that echoed the Civil War. Booth may have broken a leg in the theater and was soon trapped in a barn near Bowling Green, Virginia, where he was killed. His coconspirators—including Mary Surratt (1820–1865), the first woman in American history to be executed—were tried and hanged in the nation's capital. Yet Lincoln's death scene far surpassed Booth's fate. The president was carried across the street from Ford's Theatre to the William Peterson house and then died the next morning on Easter Sunday. Regardless of whether Edwin M. Stanton, Lincoln's secretary of war, uttered the famous sentence, "Now he belongs to the ages," the assassination turned the table on Booth. America's most criticized president, martyred on Good Friday, was instantly transformed into a saint. The Great Emancipator had not only freed the slaves, the South, and the nation but had also preserved the idea of democratic self-government in the world. He had reconciled the U.S. Constitution with the Declaration of Independence.

NOTES

1. A. M. McLaurin and William D. Pederson, "Dimensions of the Rating Game," in *Rating Game in American Politics*, ed. William Pederson and Ann McLaurin (New York: Irvington, 1987), 1–7.
2. Peter Dickson, "Experts' Picks," *Book World* 29, no. 37 (September 12, 1999).
3. William D. Pederson, "Lincoln's Legacy Goes Beyond U.S. Borders," *Washington Times*, October 5, 2002, B3; Richard Carwardine, "The Surprising Global Reach of Lincoln," *Wall Street Journal*, May 7, 2011.
4. Richard Hofstadter, *American Political Tradition* (New York: Knopf, 1948), 86; Thomas M. Green and William D. Pederson, "Behavior of Lawyer-Presidents," in *"Barberian" Presidency*, ed. W. D. Pederson (New York: Peter Lang, 1989), 153–168.
5. Bernard Schwartz, *A Book of Legal Lists* (New York: Oxford University Press, 1997), 221–223.
6. David Herbert Donald, *Lincoln* (New York: Simon & Schuster, 1996), 19–20, 26, 38–41.
7. Ibid., 53, 100.
8. Lewis v. Lewis, 48 U.S. (7 How.) 776 (1849).
9. Donald, *Lincoln*, 109–115, 228, 255–256.
10. Dennis W. Johnson, *The Laws That Shaped America* (New York: Routledge, 2009), 98–104.
11. Ibid., 79–91.
12. David H. Bain, *Empire Express* (New York: Viking 1999), 115, 663.
13. Abraham Lincoln, *Great Speeches* (New York: Dover, 1991), 98–100.
14. William D. Pederson, "President Lincoln: The International Lawyer," in *Abraham Lincoln, Esq.*, ed. Roger Billings and Frank Williams (Lexington: University Press of Kentucky, 2010), 232, 237.
15. Hank H. Cox, *Lincoln and the Sioux Uprising of 1862* (Nashville, TN: Cumberland House, 2005), 164–165.
16. William D. Pederson, "Amnesty and Presidential Behavior," in *The "Barbarian" Presidency: Theoretical and Empirical Readings*, ed. William D. Peterson (New York: Lang, 1989), 118–119.
17. Pederson, "President Lincoln: The International Lawyer," 239.
18. John Fabian Witt, *Lincoln's Code: The Laws of War in American History* (New York: Free Press, 2012), 2–3.
19. Ibid., 7, 371.
20. Ibid., 256–257.
21. Ibid., 4.
22. The *Alabama* Claims arbitration was the result of a U.S. government demand that Great Britain pay damages for providing war ships to the confederate government during the Civil War. The tribunal successfully resolved the dispute in 1872, with Britain paying $15.5 million in restitution. U.S. v. Great Britain, 29 R.I.A.A. 125 (1872). An electronic version of the final order can be accessed at http://legal.un.org/riaa/cases/vol_XXIX/125–134.pdf.

23. Confederate casualties were estimated at twenty-eight thousand (nearly one-third of Lee's army). Union losses were over twenty-three thousand. Doris Kearns Goodwin, *Team of Rivals* (New York: Simon & Schuster, 2005), 532–533.

24. Lincoln, *Great Speeches*, 103–104.

25. Edward Everett, former Harvard president, gave a long-winded address to commemorate the battle before Lincoln delivered his own remarks. The following day, Everett wrote to Lincoln, saying, "I should be glad if I could flatter myself that I came as near to the central idea of the occasion, in two hours, as you did in two minutes." Goodwin, *Team of Rivals*, 586.

26. Jyotirmaya Tripathy, Sura Prasad Rath, and William D. Pederson, eds., *Abraham Lincoln without Borders: Lincoln's Legacy outside the United States* (Delhi: Pencraft International, 2010). American composer Aaron Copland later set Lincoln's words to music in the *Lincoln Portrait* (1942). When the work was performed in Caracas, Venezuela, in 1957, the audience chanted the words in unison and drove its longtime dictator not only from the audience, but soon from power. Similarly, the Gettysburg Address was recited on Free Hungarian Radio by Hungary's freedom fighters in 1965. It was the final broadcast before the Soviets crushed the 1956 uprising. Pederson, *Breaking Boundaries*; Harold Holzer "Prized in Every Liberty-Loving House," in *Lincoln Seen and Heard* (Lawrence: University Press of Kansas, 2000), 7–33; R. Fornieri, "Global Significance of Abraham Lincoln's View of American Mission," *International Abraham Lincoln Journal* 2, no. 1 (2001): 21.

27. Henry P. de Vries, Nina Galston, and Regina Loening, *French Law and Selective Legislation* (New York: Matthew Bender, 1983), 2–9. The phrase was also waved on banners by Chinese students at Tiananmen Square. Fornieri, "Global Significance," 1:26.

28. William D. Pederson and Frank J. Williams, "Roger B. Taney: A Jacksonian Chief Justice Who Favored 'Dixie' on the Bench," in *Leaders of the Pack*, ed. William D. Pederson and N. W. Provizer (New York: Peter Lang, 2003), 51–59.

29. Dred Scott v. Sandford, 60 U.S. (19 How.) 393 (1857).

30. U.S. Const. art. I., § 9, cl. 2, provides: "The privilege of the Writ of Habeas Corpus shall not be suspended, unless when in Cases of Rebellion or Invasion the public Safety may require it."

31. Ex Parte Merryman, 17 F. Cas. 144 (D. Md. 1861).

32. Luther v. Borden, 48 U.S. (7 How.) 1 (1849). Don E. Fehrenbacher, *Slavery, Law, and Politics: The Dred Scott Case in Historical Perspective* (New York: Oxford Press, 1981), 116. See also Chapter 10, "John Tyler."

33. Lincoln, *Great Speeches*, 68 (emphasis in original).

34. The Prize Cases, 67 U.S. (2 Black) 635 (1863).

35. Ex Parte Milligan, 71 U.S. (4 Wall.) 2 (1866). See also Witt, *Lincoln's Code*, 308–309.

36. For the ruling, see *Milligan*, 71 U.S. at 130–132. Milligan was an Indiana citizen who was detained by federal forces in 1864 after being accused of conspiring against the United States. He was convicted and sentenced to death on these charges by a military commission. However, after the war, a civilian grand jury found no grounds to even issue an indictment against Milligan. Despite the civilian court's findings, the federal government still sought to execute him according to his conviction in the military tribunal.

The Supreme Court's intervention prevented the execution, finding that Milligan should have been tried in an Article III court on criminal charges because he was a citizen of a nonrebellious state and had never served in the military. The military commissions, which tried forty-five hundred cases during the war, were separate and distinct from the more familiar courts martial. The latter were intended to prosecute Union soldiers, whereas the commissions focused on any other offense even tangentially related to the war.

37. Both combatants and noncombatants were charged with "violating the laws of war." That terminology was significant because, unlike political prisoners, noncombatant military prisoners could be tried and convicted in the tribunals rather than the federal court system.

38. Witt, *Lincoln's Code*, 264–271.

39. Ex Parte Vallandigham, 68 U.S. (1 Wall.) 243 (1864). This case, decided during the Civil War, is an example of the Supreme Court's approval of Lincoln's wartime military commissions. In this case, Vallandigham, a very outspoken critic of the war, was arrested and tried in a military tribunal for making a series of public declarations against the U.S. government and the war effort. Vallandigham was found guilty of these crimes by the military tribunal and rendered a prisoner of war for the duration of the conflict. After reviewing the case, the Supreme Court held that it lacked jurisdiction over the matter because the matter was within the province of Lincoln's military courts based on the "common law of war."

40. Lincoln, *Great Speeches*, 106–108.

41. Lincoln's desire that the country put the trauma of the Civil War behind it was likewise reflected in the offer of pardon he extended some seven days after his second inaugural address to those who had deserted the Union Army. Abraham Lincoln, "Proclamation 124: Offering Pardon to Deserters," March 11, 1865, *The American Presidency Project*, ed. Gerhard Peters and John T. Woolley, www.presidency.ucsb.edu/ws/?pid=70073.

42. James W. Clarke, *American Assassins* (Princeton, NJ: Princeton University Press, 1892), 19–25.

43. Robert D. Hess and David Easton, "Child's Changing Image of the President," *Public Opinion Quarterly* 24, no. 4 (winter 1960): 642–643.

# 17

# Andrew Johnson

MICHAEL LES BENEDICT

*President Andrew Johnson succeeded to the presidency suddenly, when Abraham Lincoln was killed by an assassin. Confronted with the prospect of Reconstruction—bringing the Union back together after a prolonged Civil War—Johnson tolerated harsh treatment of former slaves in Southern states, believing that it was up to the states to determine their status. Johnson clashed with the Republican-led Congress, which favored complete equality for African Americans as part of Reconstruction. He became the first president ever impeached by the House of Representatives, primarily for defying the Tenure of Office Act in seeking to circumvent Congress's Reconstruction Acts. Johnson barely escaped conviction in the Senate and continued to criticize Congress's Reconstruction plan until he left office.*

## Introduction

A ndrew Johnson became the seventeenth president of the United States upon the assassination of Abraham Lincoln. Born in poverty in North Carolina, Johnson moved to Tennessee, where he became a successful tailor and a Democratic politician. Elected U.S. representative, governor, and U.S. senator, he defended slavery but was a strong Jacksonian unionist. During the secession crisis, he was the only senator from a seceding state who did not resign his seat. In 1862, Lincoln appointed him military governor of Tennessee. In 1864, the Union party, a coalition of Republicans and War Democrats, nominated Johnson for the vice presidency to balance Abraham Lincoln's Northern Republican and Whig antecedents.[1] On April 15, 1865, just weeks after he had begun service as vice president, Johnson received word that President Lincoln had been shot, and Johnson rushed to Lincoln's bedside.[2] (It was later discovered that a coconspirator had plotted to assassinate Johnson too, but the plan had unraveled.) Shortly after Lincoln died, Chief Justice Salmon P. Chase administered the presidential oath of office to Johnson in the Kirkwood Hotel, in the presence of somber cabinet members and several members of Congress.

## Presidency

Succeeding the martyred Lincoln just as the last of the Confederate armed forces were surrendering, Johnson had to deal with the profound constitutional issues of Reconstruction. Among these was the question of the constitutional status of the seceding states and what constitutional authority the federal government had over them. A second question was how to treat those who had supported the rebellion. Both of these issues raised a third question: Which branch of the federal government had the power to decide all these matters—the president, Congress, or the judiciary? The fourth question was the status of African Americans. As slaves, the vast majority of them had been considered property with only the barest legal right even to life. The rights and citizenship of free African Americans had been in doubt everywhere, North and South. What were these rights once slavery was abolished? Fifth was the question of what constitutional power the federal government possessed to protect the rights of African Americans, whatever those rights were, against hostile government officials and private individuals. This question was quickly transformed into, What power did the federal government have to protect the rights of anyone within the jurisdiction of the United States? The resolution of these constitutional issues led to a bitter conflict between the president and Congress—a conflict that would eventually culminate in President Johnson's historic impeachment.[3]

### Johnson's Reconstruction Program

As president, Johnson brought not only deeply held Jacksonian constitutional convictions to the issues at hand but also a Jacksonian inclination to favor strong presidential leadership, in contrast to Whigs who had organized to oppose Jackson's "usurpations."[4] Many Republicans had chafed under Lincoln's aggressive use of presidential war powers.[5] The relations between Johnson and the Republican-controlled Congress, each claiming to represent the American people, would grow more and more strained as their deep disagreement over Reconstruction policy became evident.

Johnson was fiercely committed to states' rights in handling the Reconstruction question. He had come to condemn slavery as the cause of the war. Yet beyond its abolition, he wanted to maintain the federal system—the balance between state and federal authority—as understood by state-rights Democrats like himself. In the words of an insightful historian, Johnson's purpose "was to restore the constitutional order, not to transform it."[6] In Johnson's view, the day-to-day regulation of local affairs, including determining the kinds of rights and responsibilities accorded to various types of people—ranging from basic property rights to those associated with citizenship like the right to vote, hold office, sit on juries, and bear arms—were local matters that the Constitution reserved to the judgment of individual states.

Johnson wanted to restore the Southern states to their normal place and rights in the Union as quickly as possible.[7] A Southerner sensitive to Southern attitudes and politics, he wanted to foster a renewed loyalty among its white population and a recognition that they had been misled by their aristocratic leaders. To promote his vision, Johnson continued Lincoln's policy of giving amnesty to those who would take an oath of future loyalty to the United States and abide by the Emancipation Proclamation.

But he created a different rule for the political leaders and the wealthy elite, who had to apply for presidential pardons individually. Pointing to the Guarantee Clause of the Constitution (Article IV, Section 4), Johnson then issued proclamations appointing provisional governors to administer a process leading to restoration in each state that had seceded. Southerners had to elect delegates to constitutional conventions that would frame constitutions banning slavery. These new constitutions would be submitted for ratification to the voters, who would also elect new state officials to govern under the new rules. However, Johnson limited voting to those who qualified under the rules in force immediately prior to secession. That provision excluded black Southerners from the process. Meanwhile, Johnson appointed federal civil officers and judges, restoring the operation of the federal government in the South. In both these appointments and when naming the provisional governors, Johnson ignored the law limiting federal offices to those who could take the so-called Ironclad Amnesty Oath that they had never supported the rebellion. Presidential amnesty or pardon removed all disabilities, he believed.

Johnson further insisted that each state declare its secession ordinance null and void, repudiate the debts incurred to support the rebellion, and ratify the proposed Thirteenth Amendment. But he said nothing about what status or rights the states should accord the freed people. In the *Dred Scott* decision, the Supreme Court had ruled that no person of African descent was a U.S. citizen.[8] Moreover, nowhere in the slave South had free African Americans been treated as citizens of the states where they resided. This attitude persisted. The new state legislatures in the Deep South passed harsh, so-called Black Codes designed to keep freed slaves as an exploitable agricultural labor force. In the Upper South, the legislatures passed milder, less openly discriminatory codes, but none of them established equality in personal and civil rights for black people or granted African Americans the civic and political rights associated with citizenship. Throughout the region, judges and law enforcement officers complemented the hostile laws with discriminatory enforcement.[9] Sharing the racial prejudices of most white Southerners and believing these to be state rather than national questions, Johnson raised no objections.[10]

President Johnson carried out his Reconstruction program as an exercise of executive authority. He did not call Congress into special session to deal with the issue. When Congress finally met in December 1865, Johnson presented the legislature with the results: Once the Thirteenth

Amendment was ratified through their action, he stated in his first annual message to Congress, "it would remain for the States . . . to resume their places in the two branches of the National Legislature, and thereby complete the work of restoration." Johnson conceded that it was up to the House and Senate "to judge . . . the elections, returns, and qualifications of your own members" as the Constitution mandated.[11] But while conceding that Congress had the final say over admitting individual representatives and senators, Johnson insisted that this authority "can not be construed . . . to shut out in time of peace any State from the representation to which it is entitled by the Constitution."[12]

### *Johnson and the First Congressional Reconstruction Program*

Congressional Democrats, who during the war had argued that the Southern states were entitled to restoration whenever they gave up the struggle, endorsed Johnson's position. But only a very few Union Party congressmen did so. Most insisted that Congress had the final say over Reconstruction policy.[13] Congress, they said, would not simply restore the rights of states with Black Codes that seemed to relegate freed people to a status somewhere between slavery and citizenship. Instead, the House and Senate created a Joint Committee on Reconstruction to consider further action. Meanwhile, Congress renewed the mandate of the Freedmen's Bureau, a military agency designed to protect former slaves in the transition to freedom. To settle the status of African Americans, Congress then passed the Civil Rights Act of 1866. It declared all persons born in the United States and subject to its authority to be citizens both of the United States and of the states where they resided, with the exception of Native Americans not subject to taxation. This law then went on to specify that citizens in every state and territory had the same right as white people to full and equal protection of the law in their personal and property rights and were subject to the same criminal laws and procedures.

President Johnson vetoed the Freedmen's Bureau Bill, complaining that it extended a pervasive federal machinery into the Southern states rather than allowing labor relations between freed people and employers to evolve naturally. Then he vetoed the Civil Rights Act. Johnson opposed recognizing African Americans as citizens, but he was even more adamant that the definition of their status and rights were matters for the states alone to decide. The bill, he declared, was "an absorption and assumption of power by the General Government which . . . must sap and destroy our federative system of limited powers and break down the barriers which preserve the rights of the States."[14] With this veto, Johnson broke decisively with the party that had elected him vice president. With barely any dissent, Unionist congressmen—now more and more reverting to their identity as Republicans—voted to override it, the most significant override of presidential veto up to that time.

Johnson was equally adamant in his opposition to the program the joint committee proposed as a means to settle Reconstruction: namely, a Fourteenth Amendment to the Constitution that the Southern states would be required to ratify before being restored to normal relations. The proposed amendment's first section restated the Civil Rights Act's definition of citizenship and forbade states to abridge citizen's rights; to deprive anyone of life, liberty, or property without due process of law; or to deny anyone the equal protection of the laws. Another provision eliminated the Three-Fifths Clause contained in Article I, Section 2, which had given the Southern states an advantage in electing representatives to Congress and electors to the Electoral College. As described earlier (see the Introduction), the amendment replaced the clause with a provision basing representation on the proportion of men allowed to vote. Other provisions repudiated debts incurred in support of the rebellion, disqualified from holding federal or state office anyone who had taken an oath to support the Constitution and then violated it by aiding the rebellion, and gave Congress power to enforce the provisions. Johnson denounced the proposed amendment as undermining the federal-state balance.

Johnson and his supporters took the constitutional issues to the people of the North in the congressional elections of 1866, blasting Congress's assault on states' rights and the legislature's effort to mandate racial equality. Congress represented only Northern voters, Johnson charged, implying that he, rather than Congress, represented *all* American people. But the voters decisively repudiated the candidates who backed Johnson in the midterm elections, electing an overwhelming majority of Republicans.[15] Still, Johnson would not give up. He urged the state legislatures of the unrestored states to reject the Fourteenth Amendment despite the results of the election—a policy of "masterly inactivity"—and they took his advice.[16] Johnson was sure that after a period of stalemate, Northern voters would come around to his position.

## The Tenure of Office Act

To strengthen his supporters, Johnson began to purge the federal civil service of Republicans. Congress responded by passing the Tenure of Office Act, which precluded the removal of federal officeholders until their replacements were confirmed by the Senate. Although the president could suspend officials while Congress was adjourned, pursuant to this law he would have to send his reasons to the Senate, which could reject them and restore the officials to their positions. Johnson vetoed this bill as an unconstitutional intrusion on the powers of the president, but again, Congress overrode the veto.[17] Despite his conviction that the law was an unconstitutional violation of separation of powers, Johnson grudgingly obeyed it for the time being. Yet the clash between the president and Congress over the Tenure of Office Act would soon boil over, leading to the first presidential impeachment trial in American history.

## Johnson and the Reconstruction Acts

Fearing that Johnson was right about the political effect of a stalemate over the issue of reuniting the North and the South, Republicans passed a Reconstruction Act ("An act to provide for the more efficient government of the Rebel States") over another veto.[18] The Reconstruction Act of 1867 and subsequent legislation declared the governments established in the South by President Johnson to be provisional, subordinated them to military commanders, and created a new process for restoring states to the Union. Southerners were required to elect new delegates to constitutional conventions, to ratify the resulting documents by a majority vote of those registered, and to elect new state officers. This time, both black and white men would be entitled to vote, while those disqualified from holding office under the proposed Fourteenth Amendment would be barred from the polls. The resulting constitution could not impose racial discriminations in the right to vote and had to be consistent with the Fourteenth Amendment. No state would be restored to representation in Congress until it ratified that amendment. The military commanders appointed by the federal government rather than the recalcitrant civil authorities in the South were to superintend the process. In sum, Congress was taking Reconstruction out of the hands of the president (who had constructed a plan that allowed former Confederate leaders to return to power and continue their discriminatory practices) and was creating its own Reconstruction plan to put loyal men in charge and protect the rights of African Americans.

Johnson bitterly denounced the Reconstruction Acts as unconstitutional. Although he begrudgingly complied at first, after Congress adjourned Johnson did all he could to sustain the authority of the state governments he had fostered and to constrain the actions of the military commanders. He also suspended Secretary of War Edwin M. Stanton, who favored obeying the law, replacing Stanton with the respected commanding general of the army, Ulysses S. Grant. Then, over Grant's objections, Johnson replaced the commanders who were most diligent in carrying out their responsibilities with others more sympathetic to state and local officials.[19]

Although a few white leaders urged their fellow citizens to cooperate in the Republican Reconstruction program, Johnson's dogged opposition led most white Southerners to follow his lead.[20] They encouraged all whites to register but then to abstain from voting in the ratification elections, making it almost impossible to secure a majority for ratification in any but the states where African Americans constituted the majority of voters.[21] Under these circumstances, a growing number of Republicans began to call for the president's impeachment and removal from office.

*Impeachment*

Radicals moved to impeach President Andrew Johnson as early as the spring of 1867, but more cautious leaders referred the matter to the House Judiciary Committee, which began hearings that extended over the summer and into the fall. As the consequences of Johnson's obstruction became more apparent, the support for impeachment grew and the committee recommended that the House bring impeachment articles before the Senate. Advocates of impeachment pointed to the way Johnson had misused his presidential powers—first to unilaterally enact a Reconstruction program and then to frustrate the Reconstruction program duly enacted by Congress. His actions constituted the kind of official malfeasance that justified impeachment, they insisted. But other Republicans retorted that the president could be impeached only if he had actually violated a law. In December 1867, the House defeated this initial impeachment resolution, with its advocates failing to win a majority of even their Republican colleagues.[22]

Perhaps to avoid inflaming Republicans before the impeachment vote, President Johnson sent the Senate his reasons for suspending Stanton, seeming to comply with the Tenure of Office Act despite his conviction that the law was unconstitutional. Yet he did not intend to acquiesce if the Senate ordered Stanton's reinstatement. He thought that he had made a deal whereby Grant would refuse to return the office to Stanton, requiring his former secretary of war to file suit to regain it and bringing the constitutionality of the law before the courts. When the Senate did reject his reasons for removing Stanton, however, Johnson's plan misfired. Grant returned the office to Stanton, denying that he, Grant, had ever agreed to do otherwise. Johnson ordered Stanton's removal in defiance of the Tenure of Office Act. And with Johnson now apparently violating the law, House Republicans, without a dissenting voice, voted to impeach him.[23]

Most of the articles of impeachment related to Johnson's effort to remove Stanton from office in violation of the Tenure of Office Act, but the last one, Article XI, alleged that he had violated the Tenure of Office Act as part of a pattern of obstructing the Congress's Reconstruction program. With a two-thirds majority of Republicans in the Senate, most observers expected Johnson to be convicted on the articles and removed from office. Yet Johnson's counsel argued effectively that the Tenure of Office Act was in fact unconstitutional, that Johnson had violated the law only for the purpose of raising a court case to test that question, and that the law, even if constitutional, did not encompass members of the cabinet. One of the president's distinguished lawyers, William M. Evarts, captivated the crowd in the Senate chamber, declaring that this was not just the trial of a chief executive, but that "it is indeed the trial of the Constitution."[24] Alluding to the presence of the House managers who served as prosecutors in the trial, Evarts admonished the senators and Chief Justice Salmon P. Chase, who presided, that all three branches of government were convened together in the Capitol to determine "whether one of them shall be made to bow by virtue of constitutional authority confided to the others."[25]

Johnson made his lawyers' task easier by ceasing to interfere with Reconstruction in the South. The new state constitutions were ratified, as was the Fourteenth Amendment. Nearly all of the Southern states were restored to normal relations in the Union while the impeachment trial went on. With the crisis subsiding, a number of Republican senators worried about the effect of a conviction on the presidency as an institution. Under Article I, Section 3, of the Constitution, a two-thirds majority was necessary to convict the president. In the end, seven Republican senators, the exact number needed to save Johnson, voted against conviction. Thus, Johnson was acquitted by a single vote. Stanton immediately surrendered his office, and Johnson filled it with a general who, though generally conservative, was committed to enforcing Congress's Reconstruction law in good faith.[26]

## Conclusion

After losing the Democratic Party's nomination for president in 1868, Johnson retired to his home state of Tennessee. After several unsuccessful runs for Congress, he was elected to the U.S. Senate and took his seat in 1875, one of only two U.S. presidents to serve in Congress after leaving the White House.[27] He died of a stroke several months later.[28]

Andrew Johnson's fierce commitment to states' rights, a strong presidency, and white supremacy confronted congressional Republicans' equally strong belief that the national government had to have power to protect individual rights, that Congress had primacy in the making of public policy, and that justice required that African Americans be recognized as equal citizens. The confrontation led to a profound constitutional crisis that culminated in the first impeachment of a president and the only impeachment that came close to succeeding. It was resolved only when Johnson ceased using his presidential powers to obstruct the enforcement of congressional Reconstruction legislation. Until the end of his presidency, however, Johnson insisted that he represented the people of the United States at least as fully as Congress did. Most historians consider his stubborn insistence on his own plan for restoring the Union and his dogged opposition to equal rights for the newly freed slaves a permanent blot on his record. But they disagree whether his intransigence justified impeachment, which might have had serious consequences for the future balance of executive and legislative power.

### NOTES

1. Annette Gordon-Reed, *Andrew Johnson* (New York: Henry Holt, 2011); Hans L. Trefousse, *Andrew Johnson: A Biography* (New York: W.W. Norton, 1989).
2. Hans Trefousse, "American President: Andrew Johnson," reprinted in *New York Times*, accessed May 27, 2015, http://topics.nytimes.com/top/reference/timestopics/people/j/andrew_johnson/index.html.

3. For an illuminating analysis of the conflict between Johnson and Congress from the perspective of constitutional jurisprudence, see Bruce Ackerman, *We the People*, vol. 2, *Transformations* (Cambridge, MA: Harvard University Press, 1998), 97–252. For a sweeping account more from the perspective of his opponents, see Garrett Epps, *Democracy Reborn: The Fourteenth Amendment and the Fight for Equal Rights in Post-Civil War America* (New York: Henry Holt, 2006).

4. See Chapter 7, "Andrew Jackson."

5. See Chapter 16, "Abraham Lincoln."

6. Brooks D. Simpson, *The Reconstruction Presidents* (Lawrence: University Press of Kansas, 1998), 69.

7. For Johnson's Reconstruction program, see Paul H. Bergeron, *Andrew Johnson's Civil War and Reconstruction* (Knoxville: University of Tennessee Press, 2011), 74–84; Eric L. Foner, *Reconstruction: America's Unfinished Revolution* (New York: Harper& Row, 1988), 176–227; Albert Castel, *The Presidency of Andrew Johnson* (Lawrence: Regents Free Press of Kansas, 1979), 17–54; Michel J. Perman, *Reunion Without Compromise: The South and Reconstruction, 1865–1868* (Cambridge: Cambridge University Press, 1973), 57–143, 81; Trefousse, *Johnson*, 214–233.

8. Dred Scott v. Sandford, 60 U.S. (19 How.) 393 (1857).

9. Foner, *Reconstruction*, 199–210; Perman, *Reunion Without Compromise*, 78–81; Theodore B. Wilson, *The Black Codes of the South* (Tuscaloosa: University of Alabama Press, 1965).

10. Bergeron, *Andrew Johnson's Civil War and Reconstruction*, 84–93; Hans L. Trefousse, *Impeachment of a President: Andrew Johnson, the Blacks, and Reconstruction* (Knoxville: University of Tennessee Press, 1975), 3–16.

11. Johnson, First Message to Congress, in *A Compilation of the Messages and Papers of the Presidents of the United States*, ed. James D. Richardson, 10 vols. (New York: Bureau of National Literature, 1897), 8:3556.

12. Johnson, "Veto of the Freedman's Bureau Bill," in *A Compilation*, 8:3602.

13. For Congress's initial Reconstruction policy, see Michael Les Benedict, *A Compromise of Principle: Congressional Republicans and Reconstruction, 1863–1869* (New York: W.W. Norton, 1974), 134–187; Foner, *Reconstruction*, 228–261; Eric L. McKitrick, *Andrew Johnson and Reconstruction* (Chicago: University of Chicago Press, 1960), 251–363; Patrick W. Riddleberger, *1866: The Critical Year Revisited* (Carbondale: Southern Illinois University Press, 1979).

14. Johnson, "Veto of the Civil Rights Bill," in *A Compilation*, 8:3611.

15. Kurt T. Lash, "The Origins of the Privileges or Immunities Clause, Part III: Andrew Johnson and the Constitutional Referendum of 1866," *Georgetown Law Journal* 101 (June 2013): 1275–1335; McKitrick, *Andrew Johnson and Reconstruction*, 364–347.

16. Perman, *Reunion Without Compromise*, 229–265.

17. Michael Les Benedict, *The Impeachment and Trial of Andrew Johnson* (New York: W.W. Norton, 1973), 46–52.

18. Benedict, *A Compromise of Principle*, 210–243; Foner, *Reconstruction*, 271–280; McKitrick, *Andrew Johnson and Reconstruction*, 448–485.

19. Castel, *Presidency of Andrew Johnson*, 124–144; Trefousse, *Impeachment of a President*, 67–84.

20. While Johnson did what he could to undermine the enforcement of the Reconstruction Acts, he did not cooperate when lawyers for the Southern state governments petitioned the Supreme Court to enjoin him from enforcing them. The Supreme Court had no authority to order presidential action on any other than a perfunctory ministerial matter, his lawyers insisted. The justices unanimously agreed. Mississippi v. Johnson, 71 U.S. 475 (1867).

21. African Americans and a few native whites and Northern immigrants organized Republican parties to elect convention delegates, ratify the new constitutions, and elect new governments in a tense atmosphere of intimidation and potential violence. If state officials succeeded in defeating the proposed constitutions, they believed, the stalemate over Reconstruction would continue. Michael W. Fitzgerald, *Splendid Failure: Postwar Reconstruction in the American South* (Chicago: Ivan R. Dee, 2007), 2–89; Foner, *Reconstruction*, 281–307, 316–333.

22. Michael Les Benedict, "The Impeachment Investigation of Andrew Johnson, 1867," in *Congress Investigates, 1792–1974*, ed. Arthur M. Schlesinger and Roger Bruns (New York: Chelsea House, 1975), 133–167; Trefousse, *Impeachment of a President*, 48–66.

23. Benedict, *Impeachment and Trial of Andrew Johnson*, 95–112; Trefousse, *Impeachment of a President*, 115–145.

24. *Trial of Andrew Johnson, President of the United States Before the Senate of the United States, on Impeachment by the House of Representatives for Crimes and Misdemeanors* (Washington, DC: U.S. Government Printing Office, 1868), 2:270–271; Sherman Evarts, ed., *Arguments and Speeches of William Maxwell Evarts* (New York: Macmillan, 1919), 1:348–350. See also Ken Gormley, *Archibald Cox: Conscience of a Nation* (Reading, MA: Addison-Wesley, 1997), xv–xxii;

25. Evarts, *William Maxwell Evarts*, 1:348–350.

26. Benedict, *Impeachment and Trial of Andrew Johnson*, 126–180.

27. John Quincy Adams served in the House of Representatives for several terms after retiring from the presidency. See Chapter 6, "John Quincy Adams."

28. Trefousse, "American President: Andrew Johnson."

# 18

# Ulysses S. Grant

### JOHN F. MARSZALEK

*Ulysses S. Grant, a war hero who sought peace after the horrors of Civil War, struggled with a Congress that was divided on the issue of civil rights. He watched his own Supreme Court appointments undermine the new Reconstruction amendments to the Constitution as the Court interpreted them in a narrow, even harsh, fashion. Grant never lost his status as an American hero. Yet he left the presidency frustrated that he had failed to unite a divided nation and had failed to meaningfully protect the rights of black citizens.*

# Introduction

H is tomb sits upon high ground in upper Manhattan, one of the most famous and largest mausoleums in the world. President Ulysses S. Grant and his beloved wife, Julia, lie there side by side. Along with Abraham Lincoln, he was one of the heroes of the Civil War, which preserved the American Union and ended slavery. His election to the presidency in 1868 seemed almost preordained, as Grant was, even more than Lincoln, the most revered American of his time. Both Northerners and Southerners hoped he would bring the nation back together after the horror of war, the Lincoln assassination, and the harsh political and constitutional conflict between President Andrew Johnson and Congress. Grant seemed to be the right man at the right time and place. When he said "Let us have peace," the nation hoped he could indeed make it happen.

The future president was born Hiram Ulysses Grant on April 27, 1822, in Point Pleasant, Ohio, the son of Jesse R. and Hannah Simpson Grant.[1] His father was a businessman (a tanner), a newspaper writer, and a member of the Whig Party. His mother, Hannah Simpson, came from Pennsylvania from a family of staunch Democrats.[2]

The young Hiram Ulysses hated the thought of entering his father's tannery trade. He loved farming, and he spent many contented hours plowing and chopping wood and attending to the horses needed for such heavy labor. When he reached the age for advanced education, his father told him that he was going to be attending the U.S. Military Academy: He could gain an education in engineering, and the tuition would be free.

The young Grant had no desire to be a soldier, but the thought of travel all the way to the Hudson River in New York to enter the military academy was enticing. Yet, on the journey, he had misgivings. "A military life had no charms for me," he recalled.[3] When he arrived, the military not only changed his way of life, but also changed his name. Because the appointing congressman had mistakenly written the nomination for "Ulysses S. Grant" instead of the correct Hiram Ulysses Grant, the military academy insisted that Ulysses S. was his correct name. He now became known as U. S. Grant to his fellow cadets.

Graduating in the middle of his class, but renowned as the best horseman at West Point, Grant fought a stint in the Mexican-American War;

married Julia Dent; led a regiment across the isthmus of Panama; then returned to his family outside St. Louis, building a log cabin he called "Hardscrabble," where he struggled to make a living at farming. After becoming seriously ill and failing as a farmer, he moved his family to Galena, Illinois, to work in his father's tannery.

When the Civil War began, however, everything changed. A Democrat, Grant opposed slavery, years earlier working alongside the slave that his father-in-law had given to him. Rather than selling the slave to earn a profit, he had gone to the government offices in St. Louis and let the man go free. Now, Grant aligned himself with the Union cause. Because Grant was a West Point graduate, the citizens chose him to serve as a leader and to organize their military response to secession. Grant recruited a company and then took it to Springfield, the state capital. Impressed, the Illinois governor ultimately named him a colonel and put him in charge of Illinois's Twenty-First Regiment, an obstreperous unit that he soon brought under discipline. From this point on, Grant's advancement seemed meteoric. He captured key river sites, including Paducah, Kentucky, and then Forts Henry and Donelson. At Fort Donelson, he refused to accept anything less than unconditional surrender from an old West Point classmate, Confederate General Simon Bolivar Buckner. Ulysses S. Grant now became known as "Unconditional Surrender Grant."

After a near disaster at Shiloh, which he turned into a victory the following day, Grant went on to capture Vicksburg and the Mississippi River, gained President Abraham Lincoln's nod as commanding general, and then out-battled Robert E. Lee in Virginia in 1864–1865. No matter the obstacle, he continued pushing forward.

His generous peace terms to Lee and the defeated Confederates gave him a new reputation, that of a healer. When Lincoln was tragically assassinated in April 1865 at the conclusion of the Civil War, Grant became the living symbol of the federal victory and the preservation of the Union.

As postwar commanding general, Grant found himself in the middle of a bitter conflict between President Andrew Johnson and Congress over the direction of Reconstruction in the South. After Lincoln's assassination, Secretary of War Edwin M. Stanton refused to give up his office at the demand of the new president, and Johnson tried to remove Stanton (an action that led to the impeachment proceedings against Johnson in Congress). Grant, the war hero, distanced himself from this political disagreement and thus emerged as a leading candidate for the presidency in 1868.

He defeated Horatio Seymour, the controversial Democratic governor of New York, and became the nation's eighteenth president, the youngest man, up to that time, to hold this office.

## Presidency

The Grant presidency encompassed two terms, during which he had to deal with the physical, social, economic, racial, sectional, and political rubble from the Civil War. Because the murder of Abraham Lincoln and the disastrous presidency of Andrew Johnson had prevented a thorough approach to the problems of that day, Grant faced daunting issues. The role of the former slaves now free in the United States and the role of the former Confederate states in the reconstructed Union were the primary problems to be solved.

Grant's response to his party's nomination to the presidency was "Let us have peace." He wanted to put an end to the conflict spawned by Reconstruction, but he wanted to do it carefully, so that former slave states would accept blacks as full voting citizens when the states settled back into the Union. Inherent racism in both the South and the North made this change a most difficult task for Grant. White Southerners were intransigently opposed to allowing blacks into full political and economic life. Many Northerners shared these white-supremacy beliefs and wanted to make sure that blacks would remain where they were and not move north. Democrats swiftly came under the control of the entrenched, wealthy Southern landowners. Republicans split over how reunion should occur. Many demanded that the South pay a price for inciting the war. Grant found himself presiding over a splintered nation.

Moreover, Grant was almost alone among major American leaders of that day in supporting fair treatment for the American Indian. In this quest, he faced enormous opposition. Similarly, he was unsuccessful in annexing the island of Santo Domingo (the Dominican Republic), which he hoped to add to the United States as a naval base and to provide a haven for recently freed Southern blacks, whom he believed would be safer there than at home. Grant met opposition in Congress. In addition, faced with charges that his administration was plagued by widespread political patronage, nepotism, and corruption, Grant in 1871 asked for and secured from Congress an appropriation to establish a Civil Service Commission and begin reforming how federal positions were filled. Unfortunately, his efforts were thwarted when the appropriation for the commission's continuation was not forthcoming.[4]

If all these problems were not enough, Grant also had to deal with the Panic of 1873, a financial downturn that brought economic life in the United States to a place of crisis. It was a difficult time for the nation and for the president. The old issues of secession and the tariff were overshadowed by modern problems of the economy and race relations. Grant struggled to hold the nation together.

### Civil Rights Legislation

The Civil War had decided the issue of secession, making clear that the separation would not be tolerated. The Supreme Court validated this position in *Texas v. White* in 1869, holding that "the Constitution, in all its provisions, looks to an indestructible Union."[5] By this definition, the states had never left the Union.

Yet, it was more complicated than that. The dominant Republicans did not believe that the Civil War had fundamentally changed the Constitution's definition of the relationship between the national government and the individual states. "Let us go back to the original condition of things," declared Republican Senator Lyman Trumbull. In other words, once the war was over and the states restored into the Union, Republicans wanted to return to the status quo antebellum conditions. Under this view, later adopted by the U.S. Supreme Court, the states alone had the power to pass laws to protect the former slaves and to ensure their rights as citizens. The federal government had no power over the states in this domain. Of course, this view would sound the death knell for newly freed black citizens, when it came to any meaningful enjoyment of rights, particularly in the Southern states.[6]

The political and social battle over Reconstruction had reached an intense pitch, even before Grant had become president in March 1869. Congress had passed, and the states had ratified, the Thirteenth and the Fourteenth Amendments, freeing the slaves and insuring their citizenship. To provide protection for voting rights, Congress next passed the Fifteenth Amendment, ratified a year after Grant took office. Grant was so pleased with this victory that, contrary to custom, he sent Congress a proclamation: "The adoption of the 15th Amendment to the Constitution completes the greatest civil change, and constitutes the most important event that has occurred, since the nation came into life."[7] Like many other Americans, Grant believed that the fundamental problem of Reconstruction had now been solved.

But the struggle over the proper role of the freed slaves persisted. The Southern states refused to countenance any equality for its former slaves, and the Northern states (along with many Republicans) believed that protecting civil rights was a state function, not a federal one. During his eight years in office, Grant sought doggedly to change these attitudes.

A month into his term, Grant signed a bill providing equal rights for blacks in the nation's capital. Later, he hosted Louisiana's black lieutenant governor, Oscar J. Dunn, at the White House; the president also spoke to a delegation from the National Labor Convention, a mostly black organization. In 1870, Grant issued his proclamation enthusiastically announcing the ratification of the Fifteenth Amendment. Two years later, he discussed possible civil rights legislation with blacks and told visiting black Methodists and a delegation of blacks from Philadelphia that his desire was for all black people to have the rights of citizenship. On September 2, 1874, writing to his secretary of war, William W. Belknap, President Grant reacted strongly to the racial violence in the South: "The recent atrocities . . . show a disregard for law, civil rights, and personal protection that ought not to be tolerated in any civilized government."[8]

Indeed, Grant supported the passage of a variety of laws designed to bolster the Fourteenth and Fifteenth Amendments to ensure civil rights to black citizens. (These included the 1870 Enforcement Acts, prohibiting anyone from using violence to keep blacks from the polls, and the 1871 Ku Klux Klan Act, designed to quash violence by the Klan.) Grant also intervened in numerous Southern states, such as July 22, 1870, when he ordered troops to North Carolina against the Klan there. In October 1871, he suspended habeas corpus in several areas of South Carolina.[9] On March 1, 1875, Grant signed the Civil Rights Act, protecting the rights of blacks to use public facilities and to serve on juries.

The president's resolve notwithstanding, the Supreme Court would have to determine the constitutional meaning of the amendments and any legislation passed as a result. Thus, the makeup and philosophy of the Court was crucial.

## Supreme Court Appointments

When Grant was inaugurated in early March 1869, the Court had already undergone recent change in the midst of the Reconstruction battle between Congress and President Andrew Johnson. To prevent the embattled President Johnson from appointing like-minded justices to the Court, on July 23, 1866, Congress had shrunk the Court from ten justices to seven. It did not force any justice off the bench to meet that lower number.[10] Thus, there were eight justices on the bench when Grant became president. At that time, the Court was heavy in age and experience, and all the justices came from Northern states. Several of them had been on the bench during major antebellum and Civil War cases. Justice Robert C. Grier, for example, had participated in the infamous *Dred Scott* decision. Thus, Grant needed to appoint justices who would support his plan to ensure equality to the newly freed black people.

On April 10, 1869, Congress gave Grant the opportunity to put his mark on the Court, allowing him to add a ninth justice immediately.[11] More vacancies swiftly followed. By the middle of Grant's second term, therefore, the Supreme Court consisted of as many Grant nominees as those of Abraham Lincoln's Court.[12] Each man appointed four justices. On the surface, the future of civil rights began to look promising. To Grant's dismay, however, his judicial appointees and those of the other president famous for supporting newly freed slaves ended up rendering decisions that took the nation in the opposite direction. Indeed, this period came to be known as the Dreadful Decade because of the Supreme Court's gruff uninterest in civil rights issues.[13]

Among the first of the decisions handed down while Grant occupied the White House was the ruling in the *Slaughterhouse Cases*.[14] This decision involved a Louisiana law that granted a single company a twenty-five-year monopoly over the slaughter and processing of animals in New Orleans and the surrounding area, presumably for health and safety reasons—to prevent health risks to those living near the unsanitary slaughterhouses. A group of Louisiana butchers challenged the law, arguing that it stripped them of their "privileges or immunities" to carry out their trade without governmental interference. Writing for the five-to-four majority, Lincoln appointee Samuel Freeman Miller rejected the butchers' argument and took a limited view of the "privileges or immunities" language of the Fourteenth Amendment. He drew a sharp (somewhat artificial) distinction between the rights of U.S. citizenship and those of state citizenship, concluding that only the former were privileges protected by the Fourteenth Amendment. Because the rights of national citizenship consisted of a narrow, relatively obscure subset of rights—such as the right to sue in federal court, the right to travel to the national capital, and so forth—the Court's decision in the *Slaughterhouse Cases* virtually destroyed any hope that the "privileges or immunities" clause might be used to protect basic civil rights that formed the foundation of American democracy.[15] Enforcement with respect to these rights, the Court concluded, remained within the province of the states, under their police powers.

The *Slaughterhouse Cases* dealt only peripherally with the issue of race.[16] The decision, however, slammed the door shut on a key potential use of the Fourteenth Amendment and constituted a major setback to newly freed blacks and their supporters until *Plessy v. Ferguson*, in 1896.[17]

The Court also quickly undercut the Fourteenth Amendment as it applied to female citizens. By an eight-to-one vote, with Salmon P. Chase dissenting, the Court ruled in *Bradwell v. Illinois* that the "privileges or immunities" clause of the Fourteenth Amendment did not protect the right of Myra Bradwell to become an attorney.[18] Grant's appointee Joseph P. Bradley went so far as to write: "The paramount destiny and mission of women are to fulfill the noble and benign offices of wife and mother."[19] Next, in the case of *Minor v. Happersett*, the Court interpreted the language and intent of the Fifteenth Amendment to conclude that it was constitutionally acceptable for a state to deprive a woman citizen of the right to vote.[20] The Fifteenth Amendment, the Court held, did not force states to allow *all* citizens to vote.[21] These findings suggested, of course, that the Fifteenth Amendment might not provide federal protection to black voters, either.[22]

In *U.S. v. Cruikshank*, in 1875, the Court went even further.[23] Chief Justice Morrison R. Waite, another Grant appointee, wrote for the majority, ruling that the Ku Klux Klan Act was invalid. Waite explicitly wrote that the Fourteenth and Fifteenth Amendments reached only *state* (or governmental) action, not individual acts.[24] Dealing with private atrocities committed by the Klan belonged to the jurisdiction of the states, not the federal government. Thus, the Court ruled that those arrested, indicted, and tried by federal authorities for the murder of black citizens in Colfax, Louisiana, had to be set free. As one biographer of Grant later put it, "when the

Supreme Court overturned those convictions in *Cruikshank*, it doomed the Grant administration's legal efforts to protect the freedmen."[25]

The Supreme Court thus put the Reconstruction Amendments into a straitjacket. There was a lack of will to maintain soldiers in the Deep South to protect blacks and whites from the KKK and other white supremacists; President Grant had the support of neither the political system nor the people. The Supreme Court, during the Dreadful Decade, reflected the attitude of the age, both popular and constitutional. Thus, it regularly limited President Grant's power as head of the federal government. Indeed, it took another hundred years for the nation to rejoin the fight against blatant racial injustice begun in the post–Civil War United States.

Grant certainly felt increasingly frustrated. As he stated in his eighth and final annual message to Congress on December 5, 1876: "I leave comparisons to history, claiming only that I have acted in every instance, from a conscientious desire to do what was right, constitutional, within the law, and for the very best interests of the whole people. Failures have been errors of judgment, not of intent."[26]

## Conclusion

After taking a tour around the world and refurbishing his public image, Grant flirted with the idea of breaking tradition dating back to George Washington and running for a nonconsecutive third term in 1880. He was supported primarily by Stalwart Republicans. At the convention in Chicago, Grant initially led the Republican nominees, but fell short of a majority. After the twenty-sixth ballot, Representative James A. Garfield of Ohio won the nomination as a compromise candidate, and Grant fully supported Garfield's election.[27] Beset by financial problems and failed business ventures, Grant set about writing an autobiography, *The Personal Memoirs of Ulysses S. Grant*, to provide financial support for his family, some $500,000. (The book was produced by Mark Twain's publishing company.) Grant completed the outstanding two-volume work just days before his death, on July 23, 1885.[28]

Over a million and a half citizens poured into the streets to see Grant's funeral procession in New York City. To the end, he remained an American war hero. Yet, as president, he never realized his goal of healing a war-torn nation. Indeed, Grant failed in his repeated attempts to bring the former Confederate states back into the Union; he never forged a new, united nation, where the former slaves were treated as full citizens. The Supreme Court of his time reflected the unwillingness of both Congress and the people to meaningfully address white supremacy and made it impossible for him to succeed. As a result, black citizens suffered the consequences of the Court's harsh interpretation of the Constitution.

Ulysses S. Grant, however, can be remembered as a president who understood that the new Reconstruction Amendments to the Constitution—and legislation designed to enforce them—would have to take hold if the nation was to ever overcome the horrors of Civil War. Although at one time in the twentieth century Grant was considered among the two worst presidents, by the twenty-first century, he was ranked in the middle and rising. Americans were beginning to realize the validity of his belief in black-white equality.

NOTES

1. Recent years have seen the publication of a spate of Grant biographies that have demolished the long-held critical view of the man and his presidency. The generally accepted standard biography is Jean Edward Smith, *Grant* (New York: Simon & Schuster, 2001). William S. McFeely, *Grant: A Biography* (New York: W.W. Norton, 1981) won both the Pulitzer Prize for Biography and the Francis Parkman Prize of the Society of American Historians. Brooks D. Simpson, *Let Us Have Peace: Ulysses S. Grant and the Politics of War and Reconstruction 1861–1868* (Chapel Hill: University of North Carolina Press, 1991), is a perceptive evaluation of Grant as a politician. Joan Waugh, *U. S. Grant: American Hero, American Myth* (Chapel Hill: University of North Carolina Press, 2009), while not a biography, provides excellent insight into Grant, his life and career, and the historical and public attitude toward him. Ulysses S. Grant, *Personal Memoirs of U. S. Grant*, 2 vols. (New York: Charles L. Webster & Co., 1885–1886; reprint New York; Library of America, 1990), is widely considered a classic of American literature. *The Papers of Ulysses S. Grant*, 32 vols. (Carbondale: Southern Illinois University Press, 1967–2012), is equally important. John Y. Simon was the longtime editor of these volumes. When he died in 2008, John F. Marszalek took his place and, under the leadership of Ulysses S. Grant Association President Frank J. Williams, the papers, notes, and memorabilia moved to Mississippi State University.
2. It was later said that Grant's mother never visited her son in the White House, because she did not approve of the Republican Party.
3. Grant, *Personal Memoirs*, 31.
4. Leonard D. White, *The Republican Era, 1869–1901: A Study in Administrative History* (New York: Macmillan, 1958), 283–301.

5. Texas v. White, 74 U.S. (7 Wall.) 700 (1869); Harold M. Hyman and William M. Wiecek, *Equal Justice Under Law, Constitutional Development 1835–1875* (New York: Harper and Row, 1982), 461.

6. Michael Les Benedict, "Preserving the Constitution: The Conservative Bias of Radical Reconstruction," *Journal of American History* 61 (1974):65; Jonathan Lurie, review of *Preserving the Constitution: Essays on Politics and The Constitution in the Reconstruction Era*, by Michael Les Benedict, in *American Journal of Legal History* 51 (2006):375.

7. Ulysses S. Grant to Congress, March 30, 1870, in *The Papers of Ulysses S. Grant*, 20:131.

8. See chronology in the digitized edition of *The Papers of Ulysses S. Grant*, available at Mississippi State University, University Libraries, Digital Collection, "Papers of Ulysses S. Grant," accessed May 27, 2015, http://usgrantlibrary.org; Grant to William W. Belknap, September 2, 1874, in *The Papers of Ulysses S. Grant*, 25:187.

9. *The Papers of Ulysses S. Grant*. See also Charles Fairman, *Reconstruction and Reunion 1864–1888, History of the Supreme Court of the United States*, vol. 7, part 2 (New York: Macmillan, 1987).

10. Smith, *Grant*, 506.

11. Ibid., 506–508, 558–562.

12. These included William Strong of Pennsylvania; Joseph P. Bradley of New Jersey; Ward Hunt of New York, an important New York politician who had served on the New York Court of Appeals; and Morrison R. Waite, the son of a former chief justice in Connecticut, who had moved to Ohio and became a nationally prominent attorney in Toledo.

13. Ken Gormley, "Private Conspiracies and the Constitution: A Modern Vision of 42 U.S.C. Section 1985(3)," *Texas Law Rev* 64 (1985): 541.

14. Slaughterhouse Cases, 83 U.S. (16 Wall.) 36 (1873).

15. Ibid., 79–80.

16. The Court briefly addressed the butchers' argument that the law also deprived them of "equal protection of the laws" under the Fourteenth Amendment. It concluded that this provision was clearly designed to deal with discrimination against "newly emancipated negroes," and permitted Congress to address that issue in proper situations. Ibid., 80. However, the law in question did not raise this issue; thus, the Court declined to opine on the scope of the equal-protection language, other than to say it did not apply here.

17. Justice Stephen J. Field dissented, joined by three other justices, arguing that the Fourteenth Amendment's Due Process Clause "inhibit(s) any legislation which confers special and exclusive privileges like these under consideration." *Slaughterhouse Cases*, 83 U.S. at 93; see also Gormley, "Private Conspiracies," 541–543; Kermit L. Hall, ed., *Oxford Guide to the United States Supreme Court* (New York: Oxford University Press, 2002), 286–289; Alfred H. Kelly, Winfred A. Harbison, and Herman Belz, *The American Constitution*, 6th ed. (New York: W.W. Norton, 1983), 365.

18. Bradwell v. Illinois, 83 U.S. (16 Wall.) 130, 142 (1873).

19. Ibid., 141.

20. Minor v. Happersett, 88 U.S. (21 Wall.) 162, 178 (1874).

21. Ibid., 177.

22. For more information on women and the Fifteenth Amendment, see Waugh, *U. S. Grant: American Hero*, 330, n. 96. In U.S. v. Reese, 92 U.S. 214 (1876), the Court ruled that key sections of the Enforcement Act of 1870 were unconstitutional because the Fifteenth Amendment did not insure the right to vote in state and local elections.

23. U.S. v. Cruikshank, 92 U.S. 542 (1876).

24. Ibid., 554.

25. Smith, *Grant*, 562.

26. Ulysses S. Grant, Draft Annual Message to Congress, December 5, 1876, in *The Papers of Ulysses S. Grant*, 28:63.

27. H. W. Brands, *The Man Who Saved the Union: Ulysses S. Grant in War and Peace* (New York: Doubleday, 2012), 600–609.

28. Grant, *Personal Memoirs*.

# PART V

# The Gilded Age

# 19

# Rutherford B. Hayes

MICHAEL A. ROSS

*President Rutherford B. Hayes, the first Gilded Age president, began his career as an antislavery Union soldier. Yet the Compromise of 1877, which led to his prevailing in the wake of the hotly contested Hayes-Tilden election, caused Hayes to abandon Reconstruction and turn his attention to economic priorities such as using federal troops to subdue railroad strikes. By the end of his single term, Hayes—dubbed "His Fraudulency"—had largely permitted the dismantling of civil rights advances achieved during Reconstruction. He thus paved the way, albeit unintentionally, for an era of white supremacy and Jim Crow laws in the South.*

## Introduction

When Rutherford B. Hayes is called the first Gilded Age president, it is usually not meant as a compliment. Instead, Hayes is regularly depicted as the president who steered the Republican Party away from its commitment to guarding the rights of African Americans in the South and toward support for unfettered corporate industrialism. He was the president who ended Radical Reconstruction and then used some of the federal troops that had been protecting the freedmen to put down the Great Railroad Strike of 1877. The Republicans under Hayes, one historian has written, "with scarcely a shrug . . . abandoned the freed people of the South to their fate" and thereby "free[d] themselves to pursue a policy of economic development unencumbered by moral baggage." It is no coincidence, another scholar has maintained, that "the same administration which withdrew the last federal troops from the South, within a few months sent them against strikers in the North." In today's textbooks, Hayes is usually portrayed as the Republican candidate who gained the presidency by agreeing to let Southern black people "fend for themselves."[1]

If he were alive today, Hayes would almost certainly be appalled by these characterizations. Born in Ohio and raised by a single mother (his father died before he was born), Hayes was a self-made man who attended Harvard Law School, practiced criminal defense law in Cincinnati, and became an antislavery Republican in the 1850s.[2] He was a decorated Union veteran who viewed the war as "a glorious struggle against slavery." After Appomattox, Hayes expressed genuine concern for African Americans in the South. As a member of Congress from Ohio, he supported the Civil Rights Act of 1866 and military Reconstruction, voted to impeach the "pigheaded" Andrew Johnson, and admired Representative Thaddeus Stevens of Pennsylvania, who led the Radical Republicans and pushed to end discrimination against black people. As governor of Ohio, Hayes lobbied for ratification of the Fourteenth and Fifteenth Amendments and for equal access to free public education. He also battled corruption in a corrupt era, running for president as a reformer committed to curtailing executive and congressional patronage. And although he counted railroad magnates like Tom Scott among his friends and supporters, Hayes was no laissez-faire ideologue or robber baron lap dog. He favored eight-hour-day laws and regulations to rein in railroads' discriminatory rates, speed-limit violations, and bond-issuance abuses.[3]

## Presidency

### The Disputed Hayes–Tilden Election

Unfortunately for Hayes's legacy, his presidency began amid a constitutional crisis that permanently damaged his political and moral credibility. In the presidential election of 1876, Hayes's Democratic opponent Samuel Tilden won the popular vote and led in the Electoral College, 184 to 166. However, 19 votes remained uncertain after the counting of the ballots. Returns from three Republican-controlled states in the South—Louisiana, Florida, and South Carolina—were in dispute, and one of Oregon's votes was also being challenged. In the three Southern states, the election had been plagued by violence and chicanery. White thugs had stuffed or stolen ballot boxes, intimidated black voters, and printed Democratic ballots with the Republican symbol to trick illiterate voters. Republican-controlled state returning boards, empowered to throw out votes from districts where fraud and violence skewed the results, invalidated returns from key counties and parishes. The result was a Hayes victory in all three states. Democrats cried foul and threatened rebellion if Tilden's alleged victory was stolen from him. In all four states, Republican and Democratic electors met, voted, and forwarded conflicting returns to Washington. Determining who had won legitimately in those states was crucial, for if all four states came in for Hayes, he would win by one electoral vote.[4]

The Constitution provided little guidance on how to proceed. The Twelfth Amendment, added in 1804, required that the votes of the Electoral College be "directed to the President of the Senate," who "shall, in the Presence of the Senate and House of Representatives, open all the Certificates, and the Votes shall be counted." Yet it did not delineate what to do about contested electoral votes. Republicans argued that the president of the Senate (a Republican) should decide which votes were legitimate. Democrats demanded that the House of Representatives (which they controlled) should have a say. The debate quickly degenerated into a fierce partisan battle. As passions flared, some Southern Democrats threatened a second Civil War if Tilden were not declared the winner. "Tilden or Blood!" they shouted. As calls for a new Southern uprising increased, the outgoing president, Ulysses S. Grant, stationed troops throughout the capital.[5]

In an effort to end this constitutional crisis, Congress appointed an electoral commission in January 1877. The group consisted of ten congressmen and four Supreme Court justices—all fourteen members evenly divided by political affiliation—to resolve the disputed Hayes-Tilden election. The four justices had the added task of picking a fifteenth, potentially tie-breaking member of the commission from among their fellow justices. They chose Joseph Bradley, a Grant appointee, whom many considered the Court's most open-minded member. Bradley's selection gave Republicans a bare majority on the commission, and much to the Democrats' dismay, he remained loyal to his party. As the commission began its work, Bradley sometimes voted with the Democrats on procedural matters, but his critical votes favored Hayes. In three 8-to-7 votes, the commission chose to accept (without evidentiary hearings) the results that the Republican governors and secretaries of state in Florida, Louisiana, and South Carolina had certified. The members of the commission voted strictly along partisan lines. Hayes was thus declared the winner with only days to spare before the inauguration.[6]

Outraged House Democrats threatened to obstruct, with motions to adjourn and other filibuster measures, the congressional vote needed to certify the commission-sanctioned electoral tally. If the March 5 inauguration day arrived and Hayes had not officially gained the presidency, they strategized, it would be another major blow to the public's perception of his legitimacy. Some Democrats planned to assert that under Article II, Section 1, of the Constitution, the House could unilaterally elect Tilden since neither candidate would have received a majority of electoral votes by the prescribed deadline of March 4. Republicans in turn intended to insist that under the Twelfth Amendment, the president of the Senate had sole authority to count votes and resolve disputes. Rumors swirled that President Grant, embracing the Republican position, would use the military to ensure Hayes's inauguration.[7]

To avoid those unsavory possibilities and end the crisis, four Southern Democrats met with five Ohio Republicans who had close ties to Hayes in an effort to find a compromise. Backroom negotiations between Hayes's lieutenants and key Southerners had been ongoing; now they met with the inauguration less than a week away to finalize the terms of a deal, dubbed the Compromise of 1877. While the exact pledges of Hayes's emissaries at the famous meeting at Washington's Wormley House Hotel on February 26 are unknown, Hayes was clearly willing, in return for the presidency, to allow "local self-government" in the South. He would pursue a policy of noninterference in Southern affairs, order federal troops to stop protecting the remaining Republican governments in Louisiana and South Carolina, and allow the Democrats to take control of those statehouses. Southerners, in turn, made Janus-faced promises to protect the civil and political equality of African Americans after federal troops left the South.[8]

## Abandoning Reconstruction

Some Republicans, particularly those in the South, felt betrayed. Hayes had run for the presidency pledging strong support for the Reconstruction amendments. He had vowed to "sacred[ly]" uphold the Constitution—"the parts that are new no less than the parts that are old." He had figuratively "waved the bloody shirt," warning against the dangers of letting the former rebels reclaim power. During the election crisis, Hayes had assured Frederick Douglass and other black leaders that he would not sacrifice their rights to gain the support of white Democrats. When Hayes, six weeks after taking office, ordered federal troops in the South to stand down, Republican critics decried him as a turncoat who was trying to "Johnsonize" the party. In response, Hayes offered only limp political excuses. He argued that the military intervention he had once supported in the South had exacerbated racial tensions and it was time "to put aside the bayonet." A policy of conciliation, Hayes predicted, would help attract moderate white Southerners into the Republican Party and allow the wounds of the Civil War to heal. Those moderate whites would then help ensure the protection of their black neighbors' civil and political rights, Hayes argued. In a speech to a biracial audience in the South, the new president assured African Americans that their "rights and interests would be safer if this great mass of intelligent white men were let alone by the general government."

President Hayes was wrong, of course. White Southerners neither enforced nor obeyed the Reconstruction amendments. Moderate whites failed to join the Republican Party. And Democrats in Florida, Louisiana, and South Carolina relentlessly pursued a white supremacist agenda.[9]

Some historians suggest that in agreeing to end Reconstruction, Hayes did not lose anything that was not already lost. By 1876, Reconstruction was arguably already doomed. "Redeemers" had restored white

Democratic rule in all but three Southern states. In the others, Republican regimes were barely hanging on, controlling only small areas around their statehouses. To save them would require more troops, but Democrats controlled the House of Representatives and vowed to block appropriations for the army until the remaining twenty-eight hundred federal soldiers went home. Northern support for intervention in the South had also waned amid an ongoing economic depression. So the question, Hayes's defenders maintained, was not whether to withdraw most of the troops, but when. His critics, however, suggested that Hayes all too quickly abandoned his commitment to his own oft-stated principles. As one scholar has written, "1877 marked a decisive retreat from the idea, born during the Civil War, of a powerful national state protecting the fundamental rights of American citizens."[10]

### Breaking Railroad Strikes

Hayes' conciliatory "let alone" policy for the South in matters pertaining to African Americans' rights stood in stark contrast to his aggressive assertion of federal power in other areas. Only a few months after Hayes ordered the troops in the South to stand down, he used federal soldiers to help end the Great Railroad Strike of 1877. When Hayes took office that year, the nation was still suffering from the longest economic depression in its history. More than a quarter of the working population was unemployed. That spring, the nation's four largest railroads colluded in lowering their employees' wages by 10 percent, the second major wage cut since the depression began. On July 16, workers on the Baltimore & Ohio Railroad in West Virginia walked off their jobs in protest. The strike quickly spread to fourteen rail centers in seven states. Railroads east of the Mississippi came to a standstill. In some locales, miners and steelworkers staged sympathy strikes. In St. Louis, the nation's first-ever general strike halted commerce.[11]

When state governors ordered their police and state militia to prevent strikers from blocking railroad routes, violence erupted. In Pittsburgh, local militiamen refused to fire on striking laborers, but troops called in from Philadelphia killed twenty workers who had seized the railroad switches. The strikers retaliated by torching one hundred locomotives and two thousand railroad cars. Much of the nation blamed railroads and railroad speculators for having caused the depression and sympathized with the strikers. But members of the urban elite and upper middle classes feared that the strikes were a prelude to revolution, and they called for President Hayes to act. One nervous governor after another formally requested Hayes to send federal troops. Hayes had filled his cabinet with corporate attorneys and men with close ties to the railroads. They also urged him to take forceful action.[12]

Hayes did not oppose strikes; forcing men to work, he argued, violated the Thirteenth Amendment. Nor did he believe the warnings that the strikes were a precursor to a communistic revolution. The strikers, he recognized, were angry with corporations and were not revolting against the concept of private property. But Hayes also deplored violence and worried about mounting food and coal shortages in the cities. Some advisers suggested that the president suspend habeas corpus or take the position that federal authority over interstate commerce and the mails gave the government the constitutional power to use troops to reopen railroad routes. Because that approach was linked to legislative powers under Article I and Congress was out of session, however, Hayes instead relied on Article IV, Section 4, of the Constitution, along with a federal statute, both of which empowered the president to respond to state requests for assistance in suppressing domestic violence and insurrections.[13]

Some historians claim Hayes acted with admirable caution and only after considerable deliberation about the scope of executive power. Hayes had required governors to certify that the violence in their states had risen to the level of a "domestic insurrection," adhering to the language of the federal statute.[14] He refused, for example, to act on requests from the governors in California, Michigan, and Wisconsin, who reported only "lawlessness," "threatening conditions," or "labor insurrection." But Hayes's critics say his legalistic response was all form and no substance, because he failed to verify the governors' claims. In West Virginia, for example, Governor Henry Mathews claimed that the strikers who had blocked trains were "rioters" even though there had been no bloodshed or damage to property. Hayes nevertheless sent three hundred troops from Fort McHenry. The soldiers arrived on July 19 with rifles and Gatling guns and proceeded to act as strikebreakers by "opening railroad lines, protecting non-striking workers, and preventing union meetings."[15]

Hayes viewed himself as a friend of workers and wrote in his diary that "the R.R. strikers, as a rule are good men, sober, intelligent, and industrious." But his critics suggested that if he was really a friend of labor, he could have refused to send troops unless the railroad owners rescinded their wage cuts and agreed to negotiations. In the end, Hayes would be remembered for sending troops out against strikers and siding with the forces of concentrated capital. Subsequent presidents and federal court judges would follow his lead.[16]

Although it is unclear whether Hayes recognized the symbolic power of the decisions he made early in his term, President Ulysses Grant, only a few months out of office, certainly saw the irony in what Hayes had done. Grant noted that during his own administration, the entire Democratic Party and "reform" Republicans had thought it "horrible" to use federal troops "to protect the lives of negroes." Now, however, there was no "hesitation about exhausting the whole power of the government to suppress a strike on the slightest intimation that danger threatens."[17]

## Moonshiners

Throughout the remainder of his term, Hayes continued to demonstrate an uneven commitment to "local self-government" in the states. Although he had ended Reconstruction, he did not hesitate to use force in the South when revenues, rather than African Americans' rights, were at stake. The Civil War had led the federal government to institute a far-reaching system of taxes on whiskey, tobacco, and other items, and the taxes continued in force after the war ended. In the Southern mountains, many residents who had once resisted Confederate draft agents and efforts to ban illegal distilling, now battled the federal officials who first appeared during Reconstruction demanding that moonshiners pay a whiskey tax. Initially, federal troops aided the revenue collectors, but the collapse of Reconstruction emboldened the resistance to federal power. Moonshiners became local folk heroes for "running the blockade" of revenue officers, and state authorities often turned a blind eye when tax resisters beat, wounded, or killed federal revenue officials.[18]

When state and local prosecutors, judges, and law enforcement officers sided with the moonshiners and arrested and tried federal revenue officials for murder, carrying concealed weapons, trespassing, and other offenses, Hayes administration lawyers turned to the Reconstruction-era statute that allowed removal of cases involving federal officials to federal court.[19] During a raid on an illegal still in Tennessee in 1878, revenue collector James Davis shot and killed a moonshiner who had fired at him first.

Tennessee authorities charged Davis with murder and refused to cooperate when the Hayes administration requested to remove the case to federal court. State officials claimed that the relevant statute (Section 643 of the Revised Statutes of the United States) that allowed for removal of criminal cases against federal officers for acts committed in the line of duty was an unconstitutional infringement on state sovereignty. In 1879, in *Tennessee v. Davis*, the U.S. Supreme Court sided with the Hayes administration and issued a powerful endorsement of federal law under the Supremacy Clause of the Constitution (Article VI, Clause 2). If states could arrest federal officials and bring them to trial in a state court for alleged offenses committed while acting in their official capacities, and if the federal government could not "interfere at once for their protection," Justice William Strong wrote for the majority, then "the operations of the general government may at any time be arrested at the will of one of the states. No such element of weakness is to be found in the constitution."[20]

Backed by the Supreme Court's opinion, President Hayes authorized a full-scale offensive against Southern moonshiners during the 1879–1880 distilling season. Forbidden by the Posse Comitatus Act of 1879 from using soldiers to help federal officers carry out arrests, Hayes turned to heavily armed civilian posses, which swept through counties in the Southern mountains destroying stills and arresting "blockaders." Although these efforts turned many former mountain unionists against the federal government, the raids proved to be effective in breaking the back of organized resistance. Federal authority prevailed. While there was widespread sympathy for the moonshiners, the white South could not muster for illegal distillers the same level of massive resistance it had mounted against Reconstruction. As one historian has noted, "White supremacy carried a profound psychological and emotional weight that moonshine never acquired."[21]

### Polygamy

Hayes also abandoned his commitment to "local self-government" when it came to the Mormons and their practice of polygamy in the Utah Territory. Hayes believed that the Mormons, who made up 95 percent of the population of Utah, were a threat to sacred American institutions. A religious liberal and proponent of the separation of church and state, Hayes had long opposed efforts by the Roman Catholic Church to have public funds diverted for parochial schools. In the case of Utah, Hayes believed that

Mormon leaders had turned the territorial government into an appendage of the church and that their insistence on strict obedience to church
doctrines undermined fundamental civil rights. Polygamy, in particular,
angered Hayes as he believed it enslaved Mormon women. Congress had
made polygamy illegal in the territories in 1862, but Mormons continued
to insist that that law violated their First Amendment rights and that principles of federalism and popular sovereignty should apply to Utah. Even
after President Buchanan's use of military troops in 1857–1858 to exert control over Utah, the territory's residents repeatedly nullified the law banning
polygamy by refusing to convict accused bigamists.[22]

Hayes pushed Congress and territorial officials to strike aggressively at
polygamy. Mormons had hoped the collapse of Reconstruction would lead
to more autonomy, but Hayes felt emboldened by the Supreme Court's
1879 decision—*Reynolds v. United States*—in which a unanimous court
compared polygamy to human sacrifice and found that the practice did
not enjoy First Amendment protection.[23]

In 1880, Hayes fired Utah's incumbent territorial governor, who he
thought was too close to the Mormons, and replaced him with Eli Huston Murray, a Civil War general from Kentucky who staunchly opposed
polygamy and believed that one could not be both a Mormon and a loyal
American. Murray pledged to team with federal prosecutors to drive Mormon leaders out of political office or into the penitentiary. Hayes also
called for federal legislation that would ban polygamists from voting, holding office, or sitting on juries. Shortly after Hayes left the White House,
his campaign bore fruit when Congress passed the Edmunds Act of 1882,
which prohibited anyone who believed in polygamy from serving on grand
and petit juries, and added a new offense of "unlawful cohabitation" that
allowed prosecution of even "the appearance of polygamy." Thanks, in part,
to Hayes, there would be no "local self-government" in Utah.[24]

## Conclusion

In the end, Hayes's presidency never really recovered from the constitutional controversy that engulfed his election. In January 1877, Democratic
editors gave him a nickname, "His Fraudulency," and the nickname stuck.
Many Republicans never trusted him after the Compromise of 1877. And
his decision to use troops previously stationed in the South against strikers in the North permanently scarred his historical reputation. When

Democrats gained control of both houses of Congress in the 1878 elections, Hayes knew he had blundered. He acknowledged that the elections in the South that year had been plagued "by frauds, by intimidation, and by violence of the most atrocious character." Already a lame duck because of his promise to run for only a single term, he now faced a congressional majority that repeatedly passed legislation limiting federal power to prosecute perpetrators of election violence and fraud. To his credit, Hayes vetoed those bills, as well as one that would have blocked federal troops from protecting polling places during national elections unless requested by state officials. But too much damage had already been done. Hayes's conciliatory policy of "local self-government" had cleared a path for a near-total dismantling of Reconstruction policies. "I am reluctantly forced to admit that the experiment was a failure," Hayes conceded in an interview after the 1878 election. He was all too right.[25]

Hayes returned to Ohio after his term ended in 1881 and lived almost twelve more years, before his death in early 1893. President-elect Grover Cleveland and future President William McKinley (then governor of Ohio) led the snowy funeral procession for Hayes.[26] They laid to rest a man who had begun his career as a foe of slavery but who ultimately helped usher in a period of total white supremacy in the South and the birth of Jim Crow laws.

NOTES

1. William Wiecek, *The Lost World of Classical Legal Thought: Law and Ideology in America, 1886–1937* (New York: Oxford University Press, 2001), 77; Eric Foner, *Politics and Ideology in the Age of the Civil War* (New York: Oxford, 1981), 126. See also Howard Gillman, *The Constitution Besieged: The Rise and Demise of Lochner-Era Police Powers Jurisprudence* (Durham, NC: Duke University Press, 1992), 84; C. Vann Woodward, *Reunion and Reaction: The Compromise of 1877 and the End of Reconstruction* (Boston: Little, Brown, 1951). For critical views of Hayes in college textbooks, see Jacqueline Jones et. al., *Created Equal: A History of the United States*, 3rd ed. (New York: Pearson Longman, 2009), 488; James Oakes et. al., *Of the People: A History of the United States* (New York: Oxford University Press, 2010), 567. Hayes did not actually withdraw all the federal troops from the South. A few remained after 1877, but with orders not to intervene in Southern political affairs. Clarence C. Clendenen, "President Hayes' 'Withdrawal' of the Troops: An Enduring Myth," *South Carolina Historical Magazine* 70 (October 1969): 240–250.
2. Ari Hoogenboom, *Rutherford B. Hayes: Warrior and President* (Lawrence: University Press of Kansas, 1995), 7–99.
3. Ibid., 48, 57, 112, 116, 204, 205, 207, 233, 237, 256, 265, 327.

4. James A. Rawley, "Rutherford B. Hayes: 19th President, 1877–1881," in *To the Best of My Ability": The American Presidents*, ed. James M. McPherson (New York: DK Publishing, 2000), 140–144; Michael A. Ross, *Justice of Shattered Dreams: Samuel Freeman Miller and the Supreme Court During the Civil War Era* (Baton Rouge: Louisiana State University Press, 2003), 227–229. One electoral vote in Oregon was also disputed, but for complicated reasons. Hayes carried the state, but one Republican elector on the ballot was also was a federal officeholder, in violation of Article II, Section 1, of the Constitution's prohibition against the appointment of "a Person holding an office of Trust or Profit under the United States" as an elector. The elector was disqualified, but Oregon's Democratic governor replaced him with a Tilden supporter. Hoogenboom, *Rutherford B. Hayes*, 277–279.

5. For "Tilden or Blood!" see James Grant, *Mr. Speaker!: The Life and Times of Thomas B. Reed, the Man Who Broke the Filibuster* (New York: Simon and Schuster, 2011), 52. See also Hoogenboom, *Rutherford B. Hayes*, 279–280, 291; Ross, *Justice of Shattered Dreams*, 227; Eric Foner, *Reconstruction: America's Unfinished Revolution* (New York: Harper & Row, 1988), 575–587.

6. Hoogenboom, *Rutherford B. Hayes*, 286–287; Ross, *Justice of Shattered Dreams*, 228–229; C. Vann Woodward, *Reunion and Reaction: The Compromise of 1877 and the End of Reconstruction* (Boston: Little, Brown, 1951). The commission also voted to award all three of Oregon's electoral votes to Hayes.

7. Foner, *Reconstruction*, 580; Paul Leland Haworth, *The Hayes-Tilden Disputed Election of 1876* (Indianapolis: Bobbs-Merrill Company, 1906), 208; Michael Holt, *By One Vote: The Disputed Election of 1876* (Lawrence: University Press of Kansas, 2008), 238–243.

8. Foner, *Reconstruction*, 580; Holt, *By One Vote*, 240; Brooks D. Simpson, *The Reconstruction Presidents* (Lawrence: University Press of Kansas, 1998), 207–208.

9. For "put aside the bayonet," see Philip Dray, *There Is Power in a Union: The Epic Story of Labor in America* (New York: Doubleday, 2010), 109. See also Hoogenboom, *Rutherford B. Hayes*, 2, 112, 193, 204, 256, 266, 270, 273, 275, 288, 289, 307; Simpson, *The Reconstruction Presidents*, 199–201, 211–212, 214, 224–225; Foner, *Reconstruction*, 558.

10. For the argument that Hayes had no choice but to remove the troops, see Hoogenboom, *Rutherford B. Hayes*, 2, 270–271, 304–307, 317; Hoogenboom, "Rutherford B. Hayes: Real & Substantial Greatness," *Hayes Historical Journal* 7 (1988): 32–33. See also Eric Foner, *Reconstruction*, 558, 567, 580–581, 582; Charles Lane, *The Day Freedom Died: The Colfax Massacre, the Supreme Court, and the Betrayal of Reconstruction* (New York: Henry Holt, 2008), 247–253; Simpson, *The Reconstruction Presidents*, 204–205.

11. Gerald Eggert, *Railroad Labor Disputes: The Beginnings of Federal Strike Policy* (Ann Arbor: University of Michigan Press, 1967), 3, 24–25; Foner, *Reconstruction*, 558; Hoogenboom, *Rutherford B. Hayes*, 326–327; Rawley, "Rutherford B. Hayes," 142.

12. Eggert, *Railroad Labor Disputes*, 27–29; Hoogenboom, *Rutherford B. Hayes*, 331–333.

13. Hoogenboom, *Rutherford B. Hayes*, 327–329.

14. The statute was Section 5297 of the Revised Statutes of the United States.

15. Eggert, *Railroad Labor Disputes*, 19–27, 31, 41–45; Foner, *Reconstruction*, 583, 584; Hoogenboom, *Rutherford B. Hayes*, 327–329. In the 1880s and 1890s, both the commerce clause

and the obstruction of the mails became a basis for federal intervention after federal judges began to use them as authority to enjoin railroad strikes.

16. Eggert, *Railroad Labor Disputes*, 19, 34, 51; Hoogenboom, *Rutherford B. Hayes*, 334.

17. Foner, *Reconstruction*, 586.

18. Wilbur R. Miller, *Revenuers and Moonshiners: Enforcing Federal Liquor Law in the Mountain South, 1865–1900* (Chapel Hill: University of North Carolina, 1991), 1–15, 16, 17–42, 40–44, 52–104.

19. In 1866, Congress passed Section 643 of the Revised Statutes of the United States, which declared that "when any civil suit or criminal prosecution is commenced in any court of a state against any officer appointed under or acting by authority of any revenue law of the United States now or hereafter enacted, or against any person acting under or by authority of any such officer, on account of any act done under color of his office or of any such law or on account of any right, title, or authority claimed by such officer or other person under any such law, . . . the said suit or prosecution may, at any time before the trial or final hearing thereof, be removed for trial into the circuit court next to be holden in the district where the same is pending, upon the petition of such defendant to said circuit court."

20. In their dissent, Justices Nathan Clifford and Stephen J. Field argued that "large concessions were made by the states to the United States, but they never ceded to the national government their police powers or the power to define and punish offences against their authority, as admitted by all courts and all commentators upon the constitution." Tennessee v. Davis, 100 U.S. 257, 302 (1879). Hoogenboom, *Rutherford B. Hayes*, 373–374; Miller, *Revenuers and Moonshiners*, 103–110; William Wiecek, "The Reconstruction of Federal Judicial Power, 1863–1875," *American Journal of Legal History* 13 (October 1969): 333–359.

21. Miller, *Revenuers and Moonshiners*, 16 ("blockaders"), 43–44, 59 ("White supremacy").

22. Hoogenboom, *Rutherford B. Hayes*, 101, 257 (quotation).

23. Sarah Barringer Gordon, *The Mormon Question: Polygamy and Constitutional Conflict in Nineteenth-Century America* (Chapel Hill: University of North Carolina Press, 2002), 4–5, 48–51, 120–150; Hoogenboom, *Rutherford B. Hayes*, 383, 421, 422.

24. Gordon, *The Mormon Question*, 149–154; Hoogenboom, *Rutherford B. Hayes*, 422; Biography of Eli Huston Murray, www.arlingtoncemetary.net/ehmurray.htm.

25. Leslie H. Fishel Jr., "Rutherford B. Hayes," in *Popular Images of the American Presidency*, ed. William C. Sprague (Westport, CT: Greenwood Press, 1988), 105; Pamela Brandwein, *Rethinking the Judicial Settlement of Reconstruction* (New York: Cambridge University Press, 2011), 140–141; Stanley Hirshson, *Farewell to the Bloody Shirt: Northern Republicans and the Southern Negro, 1877–1893* (Bloomington: Indiana University Press, 1962), 46–62; Hoogenboom, *Rutherford B. Hayes*, 374, 375–376, 392–400; Hoogenboom, "Rutherford B. Hayes: Real & Substantial Greatness," 29–36; Rawley, "Rutherford B. Hayes," 143; Simpson, *The Reconstruction Presidents*, 218, 220–224, 228.

26. Hoogenboom, *Rutherford B. Hayes*, 530–533.

# 20

# James A. Garfield

### THOMAS C. SUTTON

*James Garfield, a powerful figure in the Reconstruction-era Congress, took office in 1881 with a goal of uniting the Republican Party, which was split between the Stalwarts (who strongly favored political patronage) and the so-called Half-Breeds (who believed patronage bred corruption). Garfield sought to shake off Congress's persistent challenges to the president's constitutional power to appoint and simultaneously favored broad reforms to the system of federal appointments. Ironically, he was assassinated by a mentally disturbed, disgruntled office-seeker and died barely six months after he took the oath of office. In death, Garfield accomplished reforms that had eluded him during his brief presidency.*

## Introduction

James Abram Garfield was in many ways an unintended president, a position that resulted from the deadlocked Republican National Convention of 1880. A man with perhaps the potential to be a great leader, he served the second-shortest term of any president, dying within six months of his inauguration. President Garfield was shot by Charles Guiteau, a delusional office-seeker, at the Washington, D.C., train station on July 2, 1881. Had Garfield been treated properly by doctors, he might have survived the shooting. Medical deficiencies and professional pride resulted in his slow, agonizing decline and death on September 19, 1881.[1] Garfield's life story, personal character, and rise to political prominence suggest that he may well have been a successful president, at least by the standards of the Gilded Age. During his brief tenure in office, he helped shore up the president's power in the realm of executive appointments and dramatically altered the nation's view of political patronage in the executive and legislative branches, ushering in massive civil service reforms. Yet these changes were brought about as much by Garfield's tragic death as by his actions while he was in office.

Garfield was born on November 19, 1831, to Abram and Eliza Ballou Garfield as the youngest of their four children. He is considered the last of the log-cabin presidents, having been born in a cabin on his family farm in Orange Township, Ohio. Garfield worked on the canals in Cleveland and as a carpenter before studying at the Geauga Seminary, at the Western Reserve Eclectic Institute (later renamed Hiram College), and at Williams College in Massachusetts. After serving briefly as a preacher and president of the Eclectic Institute, Garfield studied law at the firm of Williamson and Riddle, was elected the youngest member of the Ohio Senate, and was admitted to the Ohio Bar in 1861.[2]

As with many aspiring politicians of his time, Garfield volunteered to be a Union soldier at the outset of the Civil War, serving as a lieutenant colonel of the Forty-Second Regiment Ohio Volunteer Infantry and rising to the rank of major general.[3] Beset by various illnesses, Garfield received a medical furlough in 1862 and thereafter decided to run for the Republican nomination to serve in Congress for the Ohio Nineteenth District. He spent four months in Washington before his election to Congress as a guest and protégé of Secretary of the Treasury Salmon P. Chase, learning the arcane details of public finance and becoming a firm supporter of the Radical Republicans during the war. He was elected to Congress by a two-to-one margin and continued military service as the chief of staff to Major General William S. Rosecrans. President Lincoln prevailed upon Garfield to take his seat in Congress, however, needing his support in Washington. Garfield agreed and resigned his military commission to return to Congress in December 1863.[4]

While in Congress, Garfield also practiced law periodically. As one author noted, "he started at the top, with his very first legal argument made before the U.S. Supreme."[5] The case was *Ex parte Milligan*, argued in April 1866.[6] During the Civil War, a group of Indiana "Copperheads" who sympathized with the Confederacy were arrested and tried before a military court, rather than a civil court where full due-process guarantees applied. Milligan and his coconspirators were convicted and ordered to be hanged. When the Civil War ended, however, a team of distinguished lawyers, including Garfield, took up the cause. They contended that the military tribunal was without jurisdiction to try civilians as long as the civil courts were in operation. Garfield argued eloquently "that a republic can wield the vast enginery of war without breaking down the safeguards of liberty; can suppress insurrection, and put down rebellion, however formidable, without destroying the bulwarks of law."[7] The Supreme Court agreed, giving Garfield and his team a landmark victory. At the time, however, the decision was not viewed favorably by most of Garfield's Radical Republican colleagues.

Yet Garfield had strongly supported Lincoln's agenda in Congress. He favored passage of the Thirteenth Amendment ending slavery and, after Lincoln's assassination, nonetheless became a leading figure among Radical Republicans in Congress.[8] Garfield favored an aggressive approach to Reconstruction and eventually became Republican minority leader in the House. His future struggles regarding patronage appointments were foreshadowed during this time in Congress, when the Stalwarts (the Republican Party faction that followed Senator Roscoe Conkling of New York) clashed with the later-dubbed Half-Breeds (including Garfield and President Hayes's secretary of treasury John Sherman), who favored varying degrees of civil service reform.[9]

Garfield served as a member of the Ohio delegation at the Republican National Convention in Chicago in April 1880.[10] To his own surprise, after a protracted balloting deadlock, Garfield emerged as a compromise candidate. By the thirty-sixth ballot, he had received a unanimous nomination. The motion was made by none other than Senator Roscoe Conkling of New York—the leader of the Stalwart faction that strongly favored political patronage as a means of wielding and protecting power.[11]

Along with his vice presidential running mate, Chester A. Arthur of New York (a Conkling protégé who was a beneficiary of patronage), Garfield won the general election by a comfortable margin of 255 electoral votes to 155 for Democratic nominee Major General Winfield Scott Hancock, carrying most of the South, Ohio, Indiana, New York, and Maine.[12]

## Presidency

### A Brief Administration

After taking office on March 4, 1881, President Garfield was faced with the contentious task of forming his administration. Factions of the Republican Party sought accommodation in the new administration. Office seekers filled the White House daily, wanting the ear of the president and his staff to plead their cases for appointments. The barrage wearied and frustrated Garfield, who wanted to focus on addressing important issues of the day: "My day is frittered away by the personal seeking of people," he wrote, "when it ought to be given to the great problems which concern the whole country."[13]

Garfield sought diversity in geography and among the factions of the Republican Party in his appointments. Robert Todd Lincoln of Illinois, Abraham Lincoln's only son to live to reach adulthood, was appointed secretary of war.[14] Senator Conkling of New York—who made his career dealing in political patronage—pressed for appointment of Levi Morton to be treasury secretary and was angered when Garfield appointed William Windom of Minnesota.

Garfield further riled Conkling when he challenged the long-standing custom of "senatorial courtesy" by ignoring Conkling's wishes concerning the filling of a vacant federal position within Conkling's state.[15] Despite fierce opposition from Conkling, Garfield rejected the senator's choice and appointed William H. Robertson as the collector for the Port of New York, a coveted position. Senator Conkling and his colleague, newly elected New York senator, Thomas Platt, threatened to resign their seats in protest. When Garfield refused to change the appointment, both stepped down. To the senators' surprise, the press and the public expressed their enthusiastic support for this outcome and lauded Garfield for his steely resolve.[16] Garfield's decision marked a new level of autonomy in the presidential power of executive appointment as set forth in Article II, Section 2, Clause 2, of the Constitution:

> He shall nominate, and by and with the Advice and Consent of the Senate, shall Appoint Ambassadors, other public Ministers and Consuls, Judges of the Supreme Court, and all other Officers of the United States, whose Appointments are not herein otherwise provided for, and which shall be established by Law: but the Congress may by Law vest the Appointment of such inferior Officers, as they think proper, in the President alone, in the Courts of Law, or in the Heads of Departments.

Thus, the battle to achieve independence from congressional influence over presidential appointments—a battle begun in the Hayes administration—continued in the first weeks of Garfield's presidency. Garfield's actions began to erode the practices of patronage and congressional appeasement and to revitalize the president's constitutional power to appoint.[17]

The president's resolve was again tested when he was forced to launch an investigation into the ongoing allegations of corruption in the Post Office. The so-called Star Route Frauds, the awarding of inflated contracts to choice postal routes, dated back to the Grant administration in 1872. The involvement of prominent Republican leaders such as Stephen Dorsey, who served as secretary of the Republican National Committee, did not dissuade Garfield from continuing the effort to reform the Post Office and to root out corruption.[18]

Ironically, however, historical evidence suggests that Garfield's view toward civil service reform was "ambiguous, pragmatic and complex."[19] While he generally favored competitive examinations and supported fixed terms of office for certain low-level government workers—so that they could not be terminated for political reasons—his vision of reform was relatively modest. Garfield favored rehabilitating the patronage system in part for pragmatic reasons: Office seekers were forever swarming around elected officials in Washington like "vultures (hungering) for a wounded bison."[20] Civil service reform would help correct that problem. Yet Garfield never would have imagined that he would become a martyr for that cause.

## Assassination and Succession

The struggle over patronage took an ugly turn in the person of Charles Guiteau, a failed lawyer involved in the periphery of Republican politics. Guiteau began his career in law in Chicago in 1868, working mostly as a bill collector.[21] He moved to New York after the 1871 Chicago fire and was soon divorced and bankrupt. After supporting Horace Greeley for president in 1872 and Hayes in 1876, Guiteau campaigned as a Stalwart for Garfield in 1880 after initially supporting Ulysses S. Grant. When Guiteau delivered a speech titled "Garfield vs. Hancock" to a small group of black voters in New York City, his speaking style and content were so poor that he was told to never again speak on the campaign.[22] This admonition did not deter Guiteau, who believed he had played an important role in Garfield's election and deserved a choice appointment in the administration.

Guiteau visited the White House, as did many other office seekers in the opening weeks of the new presidency. He sought out newly appointed Secretary of State Blaine to ask to be considered for the position of consul to Vienna. When that effort failed, he continued to press for an appointment, this time as consul to Paris. On May 14, 1881, Secretary Blaine directed Guiteau to stay out of the White House and the State Department. Guiteau saw Blaine as an obstacle to his success. Moreover, considering himself a voice for the Stalwarts, he was angered by the resignation of Roscoe Conkling from the Senate. Guiteau therefore began devising a plot to assassinate Garfield, believing that this action would return the Stalwarts to leadership of the Republicans and unite the party under Vice President Arthur. In his delusion, Guiteau believed he would be hailed as a hero for his action.[23]

Guiteau purchased a large-caliber handgun with an ivory handle (so that it would be prized as a future museum exhibit) and practiced with the weapon, having never handled firearms. He first planned to assassinate Garfield at the president's Sunday church service, seeing this location as a fitting symbol of divine guidance of his actions.[24] The plan never materialized. Guiteau instead tracked Garfield's movements and plotted an attack at the Baltimore and Potomac Railroad station in Washington on Sunday morning, July 2. Garfield had planned to travel to a summer retreat in New England; the president appeared in plenty of time for his train. Guiteau approached Garfield from behind and, at a distance of six feet, shot Garfield twice, first grazing his back, then firing a bullet that lodged in his lower back near the spinal cord. Garfield was assisted by James Blaine, Robert Todd Lincoln, and Garfield's sons, Harry and James, who got him immediate medical attention. Guiteau was arrested; a letter written to explain his actions was found in his pocket that stated that "the President's death was a sad necessity, but it will unite the Republican Party and save the Republic."[25]

Reaction was swift, with most Americans in shock at the shooting. Vice President Arthur was with Conkling in Manhattan when they received the news. Initial reports were that the president was still alive, but in grave condition. Immediate suspicions arose, particularly in Ohio, that the shooting was orchestrated so that Arthur would become president and be nothing more than a puppet of Conkling. Former President Hayes exclaimed: "Arthur for President! Conkling the power behind the throne, superior to the throne!"[26] After several cables from Blaine, Arthur finally came to Washington from New York. He was refused permission to see the president (doctors severely limited visitors), but he did meet with the cabinet. Meanwhile, rumors of a Conkling connection to the shooting continued to circulate, as Conkling maneuvered surrogates to speak on his behalf to the media.

By mid-July, Garfield's condition had stabilized, with doctors believing that his liver was the only organ damaged by the bullet, which still had not been found in his body. His condition changed as an infection appeared at the wound site, and doctors focused on efforts to remove the bullet, which only worsened his condition (basic sanitary and antiseptic practices, not yet fully developed, probably contributed to the deterioration of Garfield's condition).[27] He continued to decline through August, suffering high fevers, unable to eat, dropping from 210 to 130 pounds. Garfield expired late in the evening of September 19, dead from the prolonged effects of infection probably caused by efforts to remove the bullet.[28]

In New York, Vice President Arthur was informed by cable of Garfield's death. He took the oath of office administered by New York Supreme Court Judge John R. Brady at 2:15 a.m. on September 20 in his parlor, after sending a telegram of condolence to Garfield's widow, Lucretia. The new president also mailed a proclamation calling for a special session of the Senate to be convened that day to choose a president pro tempore, so that the line of succession would be ensured in case of his own death.[29] In his sudden succession to the presidency, Arthur was mindful of the constitutional requirement of the continuity of the executive office. Article II, Section 1, Clause 6, provided: "In Case of the Removal of the President from Office, or of his Death, Resignation, or Inability to discharge the Powers and Duties of the said Office, the Same shall devolve on the Vice President."

The office of the presidency inevitably changes its occupants. Within hours of President Garfield's death, Vice President Chester A. Arthur had taken the oath of office and was greeted with general public support, despite earlier questions concerning his fitness for office and his potential susceptibility to influence by the Conkling machine. The *New York Times* editorialized: "No man ever assumed the Presidency of the United States under more trying circumstances; no President has needed more the generous appreciation, the indulgent forbearance of his fellow citizens. . . . He is a much better and broader man than the majority of those with whom his recent political career has been identified."[30]

## Conclusion

The presidency had only three prior occupants who took office when their predecessors died, with outcomes that presaged the Arthur presidency. John Tyler and Millard Fillmore were one-term presidents who failed to win the Whig Party renomination and were then succeeded by Democrats. Andrew Johnson barely survived impeachment and was denied a second term, being replaced by Ulysses S. Grant. In similar fashion, Chester Arthur—who succeeded James Garfield—was not renominated in 1884 (he was already ill with Bright's disease); his party lost the White House to Democrat Grover Cleveland, ending twenty-four years of continuous Republican presidencies.

In one of the great ironies of history, Garfield's general desire to reform the practice of patronage ultimately found a solution in his death at the hands of a frustrated and mentally unbalanced office-seeker. Garfield's death shored up the president's independent appointment power under the Constitution and laid the groundwork for major overhauls of a political spoils system in which members of Congress and presidents had used their respective powers to appoint a slew of lower-level federal employees. In Garfield's memory, civil service reform moved quickly under the administration of his vice president and successor, Chester A. Arthur, with the passage of the Pendleton Act in 1883. Republican factionalism had led to Garfield's nomination, and the battles over patronage had featured prominently during his brief tenure and ultimately precipitated his untimely death and formed a foundational element of his legacy.

NOTES

1. Ira Rutkow, *James A. Garfield*, The American Presidents, ed. Arthur M. Schlesinger Jr. (New York: Henry Holt and Company, 2006), analyzes the circumstances of Garfield's medical treatment after the assassination attempt by Charles Guiteau and concludes that inadequate treatment and physician vanity may have been the primary causes of Garfield's death.

2. Benson J. Lossing, *A Biography of James A. Garfield* (New York: Henry S. Goodspeed & Co., 1882) is one of several laudatory biographies published in the wake of Garfield's death.

3. Rutkow, *James A. Garfield*, 15.

4. Richard O. Bates, *The Gentleman from Ohio: An Introduction to Garfield* (Durham: Moore Publishing, 1973).

5. Allan Peskin, "James A. Garfield: Supreme Court Counsel," in *America's Lawyer-Presidents*, ed. Norman Gross (Evanston, IL: Northwestern University Press, 2004), 165, 167.

6. Ex parte Milligan, 71 U.S. (4 Wall.) 2 (1866).

7. Peskin, "James A. Garfield," 169.

8. Garfield became involved in public finance issues, developing plans to reduce the national debt, which had dramatically increased from less than $30 million before the Civil War to $2.8 billion in 1864. Garfield introduced a bill in 1868 to stabilize currency value and reduce the corrosive effects of inflation by increasing requirements for hard currency backing of greenbacks. Later, after being named to the Rules Committee and as chair of the Committee on Banking and Currency, he opposed the income tax and favored tax cuts and reduced spending to balance the federal budget and reduce national debt.

9. For a critique of this rigid differentiation between the Stalwarts and Half-Breeds, see Allan Peskin, "Who Were the Stalwarts? Who Were Their Rivals? Republican Factions in the Gilded Age," *Political Science Quarterly* 99, no.4 (winter, 1984–1985): 703–716. For a lively discussion of Garfield's views on civil service reform, see Allan Peskin, "Unwilling Martyr," *Hayes Historical Journal* 4, no. 3 (1984): 29–37.

10. Presidential nominees included Senator James Blaine of Maine, John Sherman of Ohio, and former president Ulysses S. Grant.

11. Bates, *The Gentleman from Ohio*, 233–260.

12. Ibid., 289.

13. Kenneth D. Ackerman, *Dark Horse: The Surprise Election and Political Murder of President James A. Garfield* (New York: Carroll & Graf Publishers, 2003), 354.

14. Bates, *The Gentleman from Ohio*, 290–311.

15. Sidney M. Milkis and Michael Nelson, *The American Presidency: Origins and Development, 1776–2011*, 6th ed. (Washington, DC: CQ Press, 2012), 200.

16. Justus D. Doenecke, *The Presidencies of James A. Garfield and Chester A. Arthur* (Lawrence: Regents Press of Kansas, 1981), 37–54.

17. Mitchel A. Sollenberger, "The Law: The President 'Shall Nominate': Exclusive of Shared Constitutional Power?" *Presidential Studies Quarterly* 36, no.4 (December 2006): 714–731.

18. Garfield's ability to resist the pressure of Senator Conkling and his willingness to face an inherited scandal with resolve show his success in initial tests of the character of his leadership as president. Dennis F. Thompson, "Constitutional Character: Virtues and Vices in Presidential Leadership," *Presidential Studies Quarterly* 40, no. 1 (March 2010): 23–37.

19. Peskin, "Unwilling Martyr," 30.

20. Ibid., 34.

21. Bates, *The Gentleman from Ohio*, 334–335.

22. The speech was originally written to support Grant for president; Guiteau simply substituted Garfield's name in the speech, which was filled with clichés and exaggerations. Douglas O. Linder, "The Trial of Charles Guiteau: An Account," University of Missouri-Kansas City School of Law, 2007, http://law2.umkc.edu/faculty/projects/ftrials/guiteau/guiteauaccount.html.

23. Bates, *The Gentleman from Ohio*, 339–340.

24. Ackerman, *Dark Horse*, 356.

25. Ibid., 374.

26. Ibid., 395.

27. For a complete account of the events surrounding Garfield's death, including the grave mistakes made by his doctors, see Candice Millard, *Destiny of the Republic: A Tale of Madness, Medicine, and the Murder of a President* (New York: Random House, 2011).

28. Rutkow, *James A. Garfield*, 130–137. See also Millard, *Destiny of the Republic*, 267–269.

29. Ackerman, *Dark Horse*, 429.

30. Ibid., 430.

# 21

# Chester A. Arthur

THOMAS C. SUTTON

*Chester A. Arthur, who had profited from a plum patronage position during the presidency of Ulysses S. Grant, found himself thrust into a difficult role when his predecessor, James Garfield, died of a gunshot wound. With Garfield's death, the controversy over political patronage bubbled to a head. President Arthur became the unlikely defender of the Pendleton Act, which accomplished sweeping civil service reform and sharpened the respective roles of the president and Congress when it came to federal appointments. Ultimately, however, the act caused Arthur to lose his political base and swept him out of office.*

# Introduction

Chester Alan Arthur was born October 5, 1829, in the farming community of Fairfield, Vermont. His father, William, had settled in Vermont after emigrating from his native Ulster, Northern Ireland, to Canada. To support his large family, William Arthur moved around frequently in the New York area, abandoning plans for a legal career to become a Baptist minister.[1]

From his father, Arthur inherited strong abolitionist views. He enrolled in Union College in New York in 1845 and studied the classics, earning part of his tuition teaching in schools around the area. Thereafter, he moved to New York City in 1854 to study law and to work in the firm of Culver and Parker. At that time, one case handled by the firm involved the Lemmons, a Virginia couple traveling with eight slaves through New York City. A local freed black discovered the slaves and applied to Judge Elijah Paine of the Superior Court for a writ of habeas corpus to free them. To the horror of Southerners and fellow slave owners, Judge Paine issued the writ. The Lemmons then appeared with counsel claiming that the slaves were in transit, did not reside in New York, and therefore were still property under the Fugitive Slave Act. Culver and Parker represented the slaves as special counsel to the state. Arthur probably played a minor role during this historic case just before the Civil War. The legal battle continued for five years, ending in a pronouncement by the state's highest court upholding the freedom of the slaves, in a controversial ruling in 1860 dubbed *The Lemmon Slave Case*.[2] The case presaged Arthur's own views sympathetic to the plight of black slaves seeking freedom.

Arthur soon became more politically active, joining the new Republican Party in 1854. Two years later, he campaigned for the Republican presidential candidate John C. Fremont, who opposed the expansion of slavery. As Arthur's legal practice and party involvement grew, he met and married Ellen Lewis Herndon in 1858. After the outbreak of the Civil War, Arthur was commissioned as engineer in chief of the New York Militia, and he became quartermaster of New York City.

After the war, Arthur's wealth and stature grew, partly due to his status as a protégé of a rising powerhouse in New York politics, Senator Roscoe Conkling. In 1871, Arthur was offered the post of collector of the New

York Custom House by President Grant in the wake of alleged corruption in that office. This choice position controlled over a thousand patronage positions and collected the largest single source of federal revenue.[3]

After the election of President Rutherford B. Hayes in 1876, however, the Hayes administration unearthed problems of overstaffing and salary kickbacks under Arthur's watch. When President Hayes suspended Arthur from his position, Arthur returned to his law practice in New York.[4]

Yet Arthur continued to be involved in Republican politics and emerged as the vice presidential nominee in 1880, when James Garfield won the surprise nomination for president on the thirty-sixth ballot.[5] Arthur's emergence on the national stage coincided with the recent death of his beloved wife, Ellen Herndon Arthur, who died in January 1880 from pneumonia. Arthur grieved for his wife through his tenure as vice president and president, leaving her room in their New York brownstone untouched from the day she died.[6]

Despite the controversy over his removal as head of the New York Custom House, Arthur received the number two spot on the ticket in exchange for support of Garfield's nomination by Conkling, who was the leader of the Stalwart faction of the Republican Party.[7]

As vice president, Arthur had to contend with conflict between President Garfield and Arthur's political patron, Senator Conkling. The senator's support for Garfield faded quickly when the president refused to appoint office seekers suggested by Conkling. After Garfield ignored these suggestions for an appointment to the New York Custom House, Conkling resigned from the Senate in protest. In loyalty to Conkling, Arthur had no further contact with Garfield, preferring to stay in New York whenever possible and only coming to Washington to preside over the Senate.[8]

## Presidency

Vice President Arthur's minimalist approach to the position was suddenly shaken on July 2, 1881, with news that President Garfield had been shot and critically wounded while waiting for a train in Washington, D.C. Charles Guiteau, a pestering office-seeker who considered himself the savior of the Stalwarts, shot President Garfield in the back at close range.[9] Initial rumors suggested that the shooting was the work of a conspiracy of the Conkling faction, casting a dark shadow over Vice President Arthur as the possible beneficiary of the crime.[10] However, this view was not widely shared; most believed the underlying cause of the shooting to be the corrupting influence of the spoils system. According to an editorial in the *National Republican*, "this desperate deed of the assassin Guiteau was mainly, if not entirely, the promptings of a disappointed office-seeker. There is but little doubt that if Guiteau had not come here for the purpose of getting an office and had failed to do so he would not have attempted to shoot the President."[11]

Yet there were still many who feared that if Garfield did not survive, Arthur as president would be a pawn of Conkling.[12] Arthur immediately traveled to Washington after word of the shooting and met with the cabinet members to assure them of his support and grief over the president's condition.[13] It was clear to most who knew Arthur that the last thing he wanted was to move into the White House.[14]

Arthur found himself taking the oath of office as president in New York at 2:15 a.m., less than two hours after receiving a telegram notifying him of Garfield's death. His first official act as president was to call a special session of the Senate to elect a president pro tempore, to ensure that a successor to the presidency would be in place. His brief inaugural address in Washington inspired guarded optimism among critics and continued to soften the suspicions that had followed Garfield's shooting in early July.[15]

President Arthur focused on maintaining stability rather than on launching his own ambitious program. This effort was successful, at least partly because of his somewhat leisurely approach to the office. He appeared in the presidential office about ten o'clock each morning, receiving visitors, enjoying a long lunch at noon, and then continuing with visits and office work until finishing at five o'clock. Critics said he was indolent; Arthur complained about the stress of living where he worked and not being able to escape. He was bothered by the constant stream of callers and office seekers and was particularly perturbed by the press. Arthur met with the cabinet twice each week and made three weekly public appearances. Despite his disdain for this duty, Arthur was publicly very popular.[16]

### Executive Power and Appointments

President Arthur enjoyed sympathy in the wake of President Garfield's assassination and was considered a bright and able administrator from his days as a military quartermaster and as head of the New York Custom

House. He initially kept the Garfield cabinet in place as a sign of unity and continuity. Arthur then began to carefully make his own appointments, preferring to select those he knew and trusted, most of whom were pro-patronage Stalwarts. Those who suspected that Arthur would resume the patronage practice of filling Treasury and Post Office positions with supporters, however, were surprised at the small turnover in these positions; only sixteen staff were removed and replaced in the Treasury Department by 1882. Also, President Arthur resisted calls by Stalwarts to replace William H. Robertson—Senator Conkling's archrival—as head of the New York Custom House.[17]

## Legislative Leadership

With a slim majority of supporters in the House and Senate, President Arthur did not challenge the priorities of Congress. He sought to cut taxes to reduce the Treasury surplus and advocated a plan for presidential succession as well as a reform of the process for counting electoral votes to prevent another situation like the disputed 1876 Hayes-Tilden election. Arthur also endorsed the regulation of interstate commerce to prevent the pricing collusion practiced by railroad companies.

Although President Arthur was not shy about exercising his constitutional power of the veto, he did so with mixed success. He vetoed a law banning Chinese immigration for a period of twenty years, considering this approach too severe and favoring restrictions but not an outright ban on Chinese immigrants. Among other things, Arthur was concerned that this law violated an 1880 treaty with China. When the ban was shortened to ten years, it passed with veto-proof majorities in both chambers and Arthur signed it into law as the Chinese Exclusion Law on May 6, 1882.[18] In this instance, President Arthur successfully flexed his constitutional muscles.[19]

The signature achievement during the Arthur administration, however, was the passage of the Pendleton Civil Service Reform Act during the lame-duck Forty-Seventh Congress in January 1883. Public calls for civil service reform had grown loud in the wake of President Garfield's assassination, which was seen as the culmination of decades of the corrupting influence of patronage. The bill was introduced by Senator George Hunt Pendleton, a Democrat from Ohio, and called for the creation of a five-member civil service examination board with authority to supervise government activities and remove office holders. Additional legislation added competitive exams as part of employment qualification and promotion on the basis of merit and competition. The law also banned soliciting campaign contributions from federal employees and protected them from punitive action for political reasons.

Although debate over political patronage rarely identified the constitutional underpinnings of this practice, it amounted to a complex mishmash of presidential and congressional powers. When presidents like James Garfield were doling out low-level federal positions to office seekers who flooded the White House in the mid-1800s, the executives were primarily relying on their powers under Article II, Section 2, Clause 2, of the U.S. Constitution. This provision gave the chief executive the power to appoint principal officers with the advice and consent of the Senate, "and all other Officers of the United States, whose Appointments are not herein otherwise provided for, and which shall be established by Law." However, the provision also gave the legislators some measure of control: "The Congress May by Law vest the Appointment of such inferior Officers, as they think proper, in the President alone, in the Courts of law, or in the Heads of Departments."[20]

Thus, under the latter portion of this constitutional provision, Congress maintained the power to create "inferior Officers" and to determine whether the president, the courts, or department heads would make those appointments. (Congress also maintained the power under Article I, Section 1, to wield all legislative powers, including, the document implied, the power to create federal agencies and offices.) Therefore, even when it came to lower-level executive branch appointments and removal, the president and Congress shared the powers to hire appointees, a delicate balance that would seesaw toward one branch or the other at various times throughout history.[21] The significance of the Pendleton Act, however, was that it would circumscribe—via legislation—how such lower-level executive branch officials were to be hired and removed. Thus, the act would create sweeping civil service reform that would limit the president and individual members of Congress who might wish to dole out jobs indiscriminately.[22]

The immediate political environment favored passage of the Pendleton Act. Democrats held a wide majority in the House, while the GOP clung to a four-seat majority in the Senate. The Republican Party was viewed on the national level as a regular beneficiary of patronage, despite a number of weak reform efforts extending back to the Hayes administration. The bill passed by margins of 155 to 47 in the House and 39 to 5 in the Senate and was signed into law by President Arthur on January 16, 1883.[23]

## The Supreme Court: Continued Limiting of Civil Rights

During his administration, Arthur made two U.S. Supreme Court appointments that were both considered good choices: Horace Gray of the Massachusetts Supreme Judicial Court and Samuel Blatchford, who had served for fifteen years on the federal district court in New York. Former Senator Conkling refused Arthur's offer of a Supreme Court appointment, choosing instead to complete his career in corporate law.[24]

Dozens of decisions were issued by the U.S. Supreme Court during the Arthur administration. Three stand out as significant cases, each in the area of civil rights and liberties. In *U.S. v. Harris*, also referred to as the *Ku Klux Case*, the Supreme Court continued down the path it had begun during the Grant administration, declaring it unconstitutional for the federal government to penalize local crimes that should, instead, be handled by the states.[25] At issue was a situation in which four African Americans were removed from a Tennessee jail by Sheriff Harris and were then beaten by nineteen men; one of the African American victims died in the attack. Attorneys for the victims sued under the Force Act of 1871, by which the federal government could intervene to supervise local elections if the voting rights of African Americans were being violated. The act, signed into law by President Grant, was aimed at protecting African Americans from the violence of the Ku Klux Klan, which had been conducting lynchings and beatings to intimidate African Americans and to prevent them from voting and exercising rights protected under the Fourteenth and Fifteenth Amendments. The Supreme Court invalidated Section 2 of the act as unconstitutional, ruling that the Fourteenth Amendment reached only state action, not private conduct. Thus, the Court concluded that Congress lacked power to pass a federal law criminalizing the atrocities of the Klan.

A similarly famous (or infamous) decision of the Supreme Court handed down during the Arthur administration came in the form of the *Civil Rights Cases* of 1883.[26] Several cases had been brought to the court under the Civil Rights Act of 1875, which sought to ban racial discrimination in public places including public accommodations. President Arthur's solicitor general, Samuel F. Phillips, argued that such discrimination violated the Thirteenth Amendment by imposing a form of servitude on

African Americans and violated the Fourteenth Amendment guarantee of equal protection. The Supreme Court declared the Civil Rights Act unconstitutional, however, stating that discrimination was not a form of slavery and that Congress could neither legislate integration nor require private businesses to serve African Americans if they did not wish to do so. The Court again made clear that the Fourteenth Amendment only applied to state action and not to "every act of discrimination" carried out by private individuals or establishments.[27]

The lone dissent in the case was Justice John Marshall Harlan, who argued that the majority's interpretation violated the spirit of the newly adopted Fourteenth Amendment. (Justice Harlan continued to be a lone voice against such restrictive decisions through the *Plessey v. Ferguson* case; his opinions were cited three-quarters of a century later by plaintiffs in *Brown v. Board of Education*, the case that overturned segregation in public schools.)[28]

Unfortunately, there is no record of Arthur's views regarding these controversial decisions. He burned all of his personal papers in 1886, two days before his death. One can speculate, however, that Arthur's strong support for African American civil rights, marked by his strong abolitionist upbringing and his work in New York as a young attorney, was indicative of his private views about the Supreme Court's rulings in the *Civil Rights Cases* and *U.S. v. Harris*. Yet Arthur also remained deferential to both Congress and the Court and did not publicly criticize the Court's decisions, as was typical of presidents in the Gilded Age.

A third civil rights case, equally unhelpful to Congress's efforts to curb rampant discrimination, held that Native Americans were not citizens of the United States subject to the protections of the Fourteenth and Fifteenth Amendments.[29] In *Elk v. Wilkins*, the Supreme Court reached the harsh conclusion that the voluntary surrendering of tribal allegiance by Native Americans was not a sufficient ground for considering them citizens and granting them voting rights. John Elk was a Native American who lived outside the Chinook Indian Reservation in Nebraska. He applied to vote, claiming that he had surrendered his claims as a Native American on the reservation and therefore was a U.S. citizen entitled to the right to vote.[30] The Court concluded that the Fourteenth Amendment permitted Native Americans to become citizens through naturalization, a process that was pursued by several but not all tribes after enactment of the amendment. However, simply because a member of an American

Indian tribe was born in the United States did not make him a citizen even if (as here) he had severed his relation with that tribe. The Supreme Court ruled that Elk needed to apply for naturalization if he wished to vote, in accordance with the Fourteenth Amendment, and he could be blocked from voting until he did so.

This ruling was not the only indignity visited on Native Americans. During this period, reformers sought to "mainstream" Native Americans by providing them with residential schools, by ending the reservation system, and by instituting private land ownership. Native schools funded by the federal government were opened in Pennsylvania, Virginia, and Oregon. President Arthur supported these efforts, which included a "severalty" law that would gradually apportion land to individual tribal members while extending federal protection for a period of twenty to twenty-five years. Yet the effort to protect Native American reservations while opening land for white settlement proved to be a continued source of suffering for Native Americans. Through the experiment in private land ownership, approximately eleven thousand land patents were issued to Native Americans by 1885; most Natives, however, lost their land. Although the Arthur administration tried to restrict white settlement of Indian Territory, the effort largely failed, as pressure to open these lands to ranching and farming meant further restriction of Native Americans to reservations.[31]

In the end, despite his natural empathy for the plight of former slaves and Native Americans, President Arthur did little to stop the march of the factions within the United States that continued to oppress them.

## Conclusion

Arthur was diagnosed in 1882 with Bright's disease, a fatal kidney ailment that causes nausea, depression, and fatigue. By March 1883, he had pushed back the start of his workday until noon. The disease continued to plague him throughout his term.[32] When President Arthur, largely because of his illness, did not seek the Republican presidential nomination in 1884, the party faced the challenge of whom to nominate. Although James Blaine emerged as the Republican nominee, Liberal Republicans defected to support Democrat Grover Cleveland, helping him win the White House for the Democrats for the first time since 1856.

Arthur returned to his home in New York after the end of his presidency in 1885. By April 1886, he was confined to his bed by the progress of

Bright's disease. He died of a ruptured artery in the brain on November 18, 1886.[33]

President Chester A. Arthur has earned a place in history as a forgotten president, in part due to his conscious effort to restore stability to the country after the assassination of President Garfield. Although he was undoubtedly troubled by the continuing abuse of the civil rights of African Americans and Native Americans, he accomplished little to halt such mistreatment. Rather, Arthur did his best to avoid rocking the boat, partly by remaining deferential to the Supreme Court and Congress, as was characteristic of presidents of the Gilded Age. President Arthur will be remembered for the passage of the Pendleton Act during his administration—a bill that ushered in the era of professionalization of the federal workforce. Although he restored respect to the office of the president, he was consigned—by his own inaction and conservative approach to fulfilling the duties of office—to relative obscurity in the history of the American presidency.

NOTES

1. George F. Howe, *Chester A. Arthur: A Quarter Century of Machine Politics* (1934; repr., Norwalk, CT: Easton Press, 1987), 4.

2. Lemmon v. People, 20 N.Y. 562 (1860). Arthur confronted the pre–Civil War tensions that separated the North and the South over slavery in other settings, as well. Early in his practice, Arthur served as an attorney for Lizzie Jennings, a black woman forcibly removed from a streetcar. Arthur sued the company for personal injury on behalf of Jennings, winning a judgment of $500 and forcing the company to adopt a policy to protect black riders. Howe, *Chester A. Arthur*, 13–15.

3. As collector, Arthur's annual salary of $12,000 increased to $50,000 from "moieties," making him the highest-paid public official in the U.S. (In contrast, the president's annual salary was $25,000). Reformers succeeded in ending moieties with passage of the Anti-Moiety Act of 1874, which resulted in an 80 percent drop in Arthur's compensation.

4. Thomas C. Reeves, *Gentleman Boss: The Life of Chester Alan Arthur* (1975; repr., Newtown, CT: American Political Biography Press, 1991), 134–136. Hayes initially attempted to replace Arthur with Edwin Merritt, but the appointment was blocked by Senator Conkling, as chair of the Commerce Committee. Hayes resorted to a recess appointment on July 2, 1878.

5. Benson J. Lossing, *A Biography of James A. Garfield* (New York: Henry S. Goodspeed & Co., 1882).

6. "First Lady Biography: Ellen Arthur," National First Ladies Library, Canton, OH, accessed January 24, 2015, www.firstladies.org/biographies/firstladies.aspx?biography=22.

7. Senator Conkling—who generally favored the patronage system—believed that the deal would also ease the pressure to reform patronage abuse in New York, after the efforts at reform by the Hayes administration. Thomas C. Reeves, "Chester A. Arthur and the Campaign of 1880," *Political Science Quarterly* 84, no.4 (winter 1969): 629. For a discussion on the Stalwarts (who generally supported patronage) and the so-called Half-Breeds (who favored varying degrees of civil service reform), see Allan Peskin, "Who Were the Stalwarts? Who Were Their Rivals? Republican Factions in the Gilded Age," *Political Science Quarterly* 99, no.4 (1984–1985): 703–716.

8. Justus D. Doenecke, *The Presidencies of James A. Garfield and Chester A. Arthur* (Lawrence: Regents Press of Kansas, 1981), 37–53.

9. Reeves, *Gentleman Boss*, 237.

10. According to the arresting officer, Guiteau stated, "I did it and will go to jail for it. I am a Stalwart, and Arthur will be president."

11. Reeves, *Gentleman Boss*, 240–241.

12. An editorial in the *New York Times* described Arthur's "self-interest as a politician" and declared: "While his succession to the Presidency of the United States depends simply on the issue of a strong man's struggle with death, Gen. Arthur is about the last man who would be considered eligible to that position, did the choice depend on the voice either of a majority of his own party or a majority of the people of the United States." Ibid., 241.

13. Friends described his demeanor as similar to the heartbreak of his wife's death a few years earlier.

14. Reeves, *Gentleman Boss*, 242.

15. Ibid., 249–250.

16. Zachary Karabell, *Chester Alan Arthur* (New York: Holt, Henry and Co., 2004), 93–94.

17. Doenecke, *Garfield and Arthur*, 75–76.

18. Reeves, *Gentleman Boss*, 279.

19. Ibid., 279–280.

20. U.S. Const. art. II, § 2, cl. 2.

21. For an excellent discussion of the overlapping powers of the president and Congress when it comes to appointment and removal, see Jerry L. Marshaw, "Federal Administration and Administrative Law in the Gilded Age," *Yale Law Journal* 119 (2010): 1383–1394.

22. President Andrew Jackson was famous for rewarding political loyalists through a vast spoils system, "rotating" political appointees out of office and replacing them with employees of his own choosing. Sidney M. Milkis and Michael Nelson, *The American Presidency: Origins and Development, 1776–2011*, 6th ed. (Washington, DC: CQ Press, 2012), 138. (For instance, Jackson removed hundreds of postmasters from their positions.) President Ulysses S. Grant successfully pressed Congress to establish the first Civil Service Commission in 1871 and appointed that commission's first members to address rampant corruption. However, Congress—which relied heavily on political patronage—funded the commission for only two years; as a result, it lapsed. Leonard D. White, *The Republican Era, 1869–1901: A Study in Administrative History* (New York:

MacMillan, 1958), 283–284. The Pendleton Act renewed funding for the Civil Service Commission. In this and other ways, the act reduced patronage and eliminated much of the president's direct role in appointing low-level officer-seekers. President Arthur appointed members to a permanent commission, which then administered the civil service system, including personnel matters. Melvin I. Urofsky, *The American Presidents* (New York: Garland Publishing, 2000), 231.

23. Doenecke, *Garfield and Arthur*, 96–103. Initially the law only applied to federal custom houses, the postal service, and employees in offices in the District of Columbia, totaling about 14,000 of the 131,000 federal workforce. President Arthur appointed Dorman Eaton, a longtime civil service reform advocate, as chair of the new Civil Service Commission, along with Leroy Thoman, a Democratic judge from Ohio, and John M. Gregory, president of what later became the University of Illinois. For a general reference, see Ari Arthur Hoogenboom, *Outlawing the Spoils: A History of the Civil Service Reform Movement, 1865–1883* (Urbana: University of Illinois Press, 1961).

24. Ibid., 76.

25. United States v. Harris, 106 U.S. 629 (1883).

26. Civil Rights Cases, 109 U.S. 3 (1883).

27. Kevin B. Witherspoon, "Civil Rights Cases," in *Historical Dictionary of the Gilded Age*, ed. Leonard Schlup and James G. Ryan (Armonk, NY: M.E. Sharpe, 2003), 92.

28. Jeffrey Rosen, *The Supreme Court: The Personalities and Rivalries That Defined America* (New York: Henry Holt and Company, 2006), 93–97.

29. Elk v. Wilkins, 112 U.S. 94 (1884).

30. Nebraska law declared that all males over the age of twenty-one and who had lived in the state for at least six consecutive months were eligible to register to vote. Native Americans had been treated as foreign nations under the U.S. Constitution, exempted from most federal and state laws, including those relating to taxation. Instead, they had been governed by treaties between tribes and the federal government. Practically speaking, Native Americans had become wards of the federal Bureau of Indian Affairs by this time.

31. Doenecke, *Garfield and Arthur*, 85–92.

32. Gregory J. Dehler, *Chester Alan Arthur: The Life of a Gilded Age Politician and President* (New York: Nova History Publications, 2007), 89–90.

33. Karabell, *Chester Alan Arthur*, 130–140.

# 22

# Grover Cleveland

*First Term: 1884–1888*

DONALD GRIER STEPHENSON JR.

*Grover Cleveland, the only president to serve two nonconsecutive terms, stood up to Congress in asserting his constitutional prerogative to remove certain federal appointees without the Senate's approval, forcing the repeal of the Tenure of Office Act, which had plagued his predecessors. President Cleveland also used his veto power with gusto, shaping an image of the presidency as an office suited for a man of action. Although Cleveland lost his reelection bid in 1888, he would return to the White House four years later, again prepared to flex his muscles as chief executive.*

## Introduction

By virtually all accounts, President Grover Cleveland was openly conscientious, honest, principled, purposeful, determined, energetic, and even courageous, in an age when corruption and sloth were sometimes countenanced in high places.[1] In those same accounts, however, Cleveland often appears as unimaginative and the antithesis of a reformer and intellectual, reflecting instead a conservative, property-oriented outlook on public affairs—an outlook shared at that time by many Republicans and Democrats alike. Indeed, this solitary Democratic president between James Buchanan's election in 1856 and Woodrow Wilson's victory in 1914 was seen as so intensely conservative that Wilson supposedly once jested that he, not Cleveland, was the first Democrat since 1860 to take up residence in the White House.[2] But to say that Cleveland was conservative is not to say that he believed in an altogether passive presidency or that he was unwilling to make abundant use of the available tools of his office.

Electorally, Cleveland is unique among American presidents in at least three ways. Having been defeated for reelection, he later regained the nation's highest office. For this reason he is counted twice—as both the twenty-second and twenty-fourth president. Additionally, he received the most popular votes in three elections, including the one he lost when opponent Benjamin Harrison garnered the necessary electoral vote majority to beat him in 1888. Finally, Cleveland retains the distinction of having won an election by one of the smallest popular-vote margins: by about 0.3 percent out of nearly ten million votes cast in 1884.

Politically, Cleveland's bifurcated terms fell during an era of heightened polarization of, and intense competition between, political parties, in which a new class of party bosses at the state and local levels often sought material advantage for both themselves and their subordinates. In national politics, although Republicans usually won the presidency, Democrats were usually serious contenders, frequently within reach of victory, particularly with respect to control of Congress.[3]

In this polarized setting, Cleveland seemed overall to ascribe to what some political historians have called the Whig theory of the presidency that was largely dominant in the years between Abraham Lincoln and Theodore Roosevelt. By this approach, chief executives were not expected

to attempt to shape congressional policy but generally to confine themselves instead to an administrative role.[4] "The office of the President is
essentially executive in nature," Cleveland insisted. "It don't look as though
Congress was very well prepared to do anything," he wrote in 1885. "If a
botch is made at the other end of the Avenue, I don't intend to do anything."[5] Yet Cleveland's dual administrations reflect a few distinctive
exceptions to this overall posture, especially concerning the veto power.

Good fortune surely plays at least some role in every successful politician's rise to elected office, and Stephen Grover Cleveland seems to have
possessed it in abundance. He was a textbook example of the right person
being at the right place at the right time. In early 1881, he was practicing
as an attorney in Buffalo, New York. Four years later, he was president of
the United States. Yet in Cleveland's case, good luck was supplemented by
possession of a combination of personal qualities that were in demand at
the time.

Cleveland's character building began on March 18, 1837, in Caldwell,
New Jersey, when he arrived as the fifth of nine children of Anne and
Richard Cleveland. When Grover was four, the Clevelands moved to Fayetteville, New York, east of Syracuse. When his father died twelve years
later, the family's financial situation led "Grove" to New York City, where
he taught for a year at the New York Institute of the Blind. Finding the
work both personally and financially unrewarding, he ventured west in
1855, but only as far as Buffalo, where a wealthy uncle found him a clerkship in a law firm. In the nineteenth century before the proliferation of
law schools, one became a lawyer by first "reading law" under another's
guidance—typically for several years—in a law office where the novice
would learn by asking, by observing, and by doing. Then the novice would
have to pass an examination administered by a panel of local attorneys
who, if satisfied, would admit the neophyte to the bar. Through such a
process, Cleveland entered the legal profession in 1859.

As the Civil War engulfed the nation in 1861, Cleveland believed that
the Union should be preserved, but apparently feeling a stronger obligation to help support his mother and sisters, he did not enlist. Instead,
he avoided military service through the legally, if not altogether publicly
acceptable, route of hiring a substitute. Accordingly, for $500, Cleveland
secured a recently arrived Polish immigrant to enroll in his place. Thus,
practically from the outset, he parted from many of his generation who
viewed military duty as a key asset to career advancement, validly leaving

himself open to charges, later hurled by opponents, that he was a "slacker." During the war years, Cleveland served as assistant district attorney in Erie County. There he earned the reputation not only as a hardworking lawyer but also as one who presented arguments to judge and jury from memory, a practice he carried to Washington, where he departed from his predecessors by delivering his two inaugural addresses without notes.

Cleveland's first serious foray into politics came in 1870, when he was elected to a three-year term as sheriff of Erie County, a position he held with integrity, not so much as flinching when on one occasion he pulled the lever to complete the hanging of two convicted murderers. By 1881, Cleveland successfully ran for mayor against a corrupt Republican administration. Even brief service in city hall was sufficient time for him to establish a statewide reputation as the "veto mayor," proving himself a dedicated watchdog of the public purse. By this time, the mayor had also acquired considerable girth, weighing in at about 250 pounds.

The miles separating Buffalo from Tammany Hall Democrats and William M. ("Boss") Tweed in New York City allowed the "Buxom Buffalonian" (others called him "Uncle Jumbo") to stand out as an appealing upright urban reformer in the good-government mold. He thus was elected governor in 1882, handily beating the machine-tainted Republican, Charles J. Folger. As governor, Cleveland vetoed social reform legislation, including wage and hours regulations, reflecting the pro-business wing of the Democratic Party (known as the Bourbon Democrats). Ironically, his plain disregard of public opinion seemed to enhance his reputation and elevate his public standing in many quarters. Yet in refusing patronage entreaties from Tammany Hall, he managed to split his party statewide and thus made his own political future within New York problematic.

Cleveland managed to cement alliances with non-Tammany Democrats in the Empire State and with others who found him an especially attractive prospect for the presidency in 1884. The Republicans had nominated James Blaine of Maine, who, though talented and experienced politically, had been stained by scandal. Cleveland had a scandal of his own: It turned out that he had engaged in an affair with a widow named Maria Halpin. Although the future president had doubts that he was the father of her child, he did accept financial responsibility. As a result, "Ma, Ma, Where's My Pa?" forever secured a place in the nomenclature of American electoral chants. Ultimately, the election turned on New York's thirty-six electors. Cleveland won those electors by the slimmest possible margins: Of the

1,167,003 popular votes cast for president in that state, Cleveland's margin over Blaine was just 1,047.

## Presidency

Socially, the new bachelor president had preferred the company of "rowdy masculine friends" to that of women.[6] He did not marry until age forty-nine, in 1886, a year after his election as the nation's chief executive. His bride, only the second person to wed a sitting president and the first woman to be married in a ceremony at the White House, was twenty-one-year-old Frances Folsom, daughter of a Buffalo lawyer and a close Cleveland friend.[7] President Cleveland's wedding attracted inordinate attention; indiscreet journalists followed the president and his bride on their honeymoon, hidden amid the trees to catch a glimpse of the couple. This experience prompted Cleveland to launch an assault on "yellow journalism," issuing one of the first calls for a right of privacy in American life.[8] The couple's union later produced a little girl, who by one account became the namesake of the Baby Ruth candy bar.[9]

### Presidential Removal Power; Repeal of the Tenure of Office Act

Although the Supreme Court later insisted, without formally holding, that the Tenure of Office Act of 1867 was unconstitutional, President Cleveland deserves credit for effectively forcing its repeal.[10] The statute had haunted his predecessors—including Andrew Johnson, who had been impeached ostensibly for failing to adhere to its command. Pursuant to this controversial legislation, the president not only had to seek the Senate's constitutionally mandated advice and consent for an appointment—as all presidents had done—but also had to gain the Senate's concurrence on a removal.

In July 1885, President Cleveland suspended George M. Dushkin, a Republican, who was U.S. attorney for the Southern District of Alabama, replacing Dushkin with a recess appointee named John D. Burnett, a Democrat. When the Republican-controlled Senate reconvened in December, the Judiciary Committee asked Attorney General Augustus Garland to turn over all documentation relating both to Dushkin's removal and to Burnett's nomination. Garland complied with materials on Burnett but explained that the president had barred the attorney general from releasing supporting materials on Dushkin. As a result, the Senate censured Garland and, by extension, the president, for noncompliance. This constituted a significant step, as Congress employed a censure power nowhere specifically listed in the Constitution, in an effort to force compliance by the executive branch of a congressional inquiry and to add potency to the advice and consent provision. As one of Cleveland's biographers has explained, "what began as an exchange of messages between a Senate committee and the head of an executive department had escalated into a major national debate over whether a President could or could not remove federal officers without congressional interference."[11] Cleveland seemed intent on staying the course to protect what he regarded as the constitutional prerogatives of "the people's office."[12] Congress eventually capitulated. A bill to repeal the Tenure of Office Act was introduced in July 1886 and passed the Senate in December (with four Republicans joining Democrats to create a majority). Soon, it gained approval in the Democrat-controlled House. Cleveland's signature formalized the repeal in March 1887.[13]

### Veto Power

Grover Cleveland established a deserved reputation as a determined naysayer, wielding a total of 170 regular and pocket vetoes in his first term, followed by 414 such vetoes in the later term, most often taking aim at private bills trying to emerge as law from Congress. Perhaps his most notable target was the Dependent Pension Bill of 1887, which would have extended pensions even to the impecunious parents of men who had died while in their country's service. Cleveland's large tally of vetoes surpasses those of all his presidential predecessors combined and those of each of his successors, save Franklin Roosevelt.[14]

Institutionally, this enthusiastic resort to executive vetoes—whatever the short-term effect on Cleveland's years in the White House—may have had a broader effect on the presidency itself by helping to shape longer-term perceptions and expectations of the office.[15] Ironically, the future President Wilson, although later distancing himself in policy from his Democratic predecessor, wrote an essay in 1897 in which he characterized Cleveland as "the sort of President the makers of the Constitution had vaguely in mind: more man than partisan: with an independent executive will of his own." Cleveland, it seemed, had been president in "ordinary times but after an extraordinary fashion: not because he wished to form or revolutionize or save the government but because he came fresh to his tasks without the common party training, a direct, fearless, somewhat unsophisticated man of action" who "has refreshed our notion of an American chief magistrate."[16]

## Conclusion

During his first term as president, Cleveland faced significant issues involving currency and the protective tariff. To reduce an embarrassingly high surplus and thereby avoid economic calamity, wise policy dictated reducing the tariff. Congress, however, did not agree, and Cleveland's position became the central focus of the presidential election of 1888, when Republicans nominated arch-protectionist Benjamin Harrison. The Indiana senator, grandson of former President William Henry Harrison, convincingly equated a high tariff with high wages and a lowered tariff with hard times—a view that appealed to the electorate in the industrial swing states of the North. Harrison's consequent appeal in the North allowed him to win the Electoral College vote despite falling short on the nationwide popular vote, thus narrowly defeating Cleveland in the election.

After this loss, Cleveland was determined to enjoy his freedom from the burdens of public office. He was exhausted after four years of rancorous partisan battles in Washington and viewed his defeat as an opportunity to become a "respectable private citizen again." Soon, he landed at a New York City Law firm—Bangs, Stetson, Tracy, and MacVeigh—and began to practice law at his own pace. During the summer, he would exit the city and spend time with friends and family at his home in coastal Massachusetts. Yet, Cleveland did not fade quietly away into the history books. His strong political convictions and enduring popularity with the electorate left the door open for a political comeback. Indeed, as Grover Cleveland left the White House in the spring of 1889, his wife Frances presciently informed the staff that they would return in four years' time—a comment that opened the door to new constitutional challenges.[17]

### NOTES

1. Allan Nevins, *Grover Cleveland: A Study in Courage*, 2 vols. (New York: Dodd, Mead & Company, 1948). Nevins's biography, originally printed in 1932, did much to open

Cleveland's life to a generation that would not have remembered him, as did Allan Nevins, ed., *Letters of Grover Cleveland, 1850–1908* (Boston: Houghton Mifflin, 1933).

2. Henry J. Abraham, *Justices and Presidents: A Political History of Appointments to the Supreme Court*, 3rd ed. (New York: Oxford University Press, 1992), 140.

3. In fourteen postwar congressional elections between 1868 and 1894, inclusive, Democrats controlled both the House and the Senate as a result of two (1878 and 1892) and held a majority in the House as a result of six (1874, 1876, 1882, 1884, 1886, and 1890).

4. Michael J. Korzi, "Our Chief Magistrate and His Powers: A Reconsideration of William Howard Taft's Whig Theory of the Presidency," *Presidential Studies Quarterly* 33, no. 2 (2003): 305.

5. John A. Garraty, "Grover Cleveland," in *The Presidents: A Reference History*, 3rd ed., ed. Henry F. Graff (New York: Scribner, 2002), 281.

6. H. Wayne Morgan, *From Hayes to McKinley: National Party Politics, 1877–1896* (Syracuse, NY: Syracuse University Press, 1969), 193.

7. Oscar Folsom had been killed in an accident in 1875, whereupon Cleveland became executor of his estate and informal guardian of eleven-year-old Frances, who called the future president "Uncle Cleve."

8. Ken Gormley, "One Hundred Years of Privacy," *Wisconsin Law Review* 1992:1335, 1352. President Cleveland attacked the intrusive techniques of these "new journalists," accusing them of "silly, mean, and cowardly lies that every day are found in the columns of certain newspapers which violate every instinct of American manliness, and in ghoulish glee desecrate every sacred relation of private life." Ibid., 1352, n. 84.

9. According to one account, the Baby Ruth candy bar was named for Grover and Frances's first child: daughter, Ruth, who was born in 1891 and who died of diphtheria in 1904. When the Curtiss Company of Chicago manufactured its candy bar in 1921, the company bestowed on the confection the name journalists had given the president's daughter. Henry F. Graff, *Grover Cleveland* (New York: Times Books, 2002), 100.

10. For the Supreme Court's view of the act, see Myers v. United States, 272 U.S. 52, 176 (1926). In his opinion for the Court, Chief Justice Taft quoted from President Cleveland's statement on the subject in 1886: "I believe the power to remove or suspend such officials is vested in the President alone by the Constitution, which, in express terms, provides that 'the executive power shall be vested in a President of the United States of America,' and that 'he shall take care that the laws be faithfully executed.'" Ibid., 169. For a discussion of Myers, see Chapter 30, "Calvin Coolidge." For Cleveland's role in its repeal, see Alfred H. Kelly, Winfred A. Harbison, and Herman Belz, *The American Constitution: Its Origins and Development*, 7th ed. (New York: W.W. Norton, 1991), 2:365.

11. Alyn Brodsky, *Grover Cleveland: A Study in Character* (New York: Truman Talley Books, 2000), 136.

12. Grover Cleveland, *Presidential Problems* (New York: Century Co., 1904), 10. Cleveland explained that by "people's office," he meant "that it is especially the office related to the people as individuals, in no general, local, or other combination, but standing on the firm footing of manhood and American citizenship. . . . [U]nder the constitutional mandate . . . every citizen, in the day or in the night, at home or abroad, is constantly

within the protection and restraint of the Executive power—none so lowly as to be beneath its scrupulous care, and none so great and powerful as to be beyond its restraining force." Ibid., 10–11.

13. For additional material on Cleveland's struggle with the Senate, see Louis Fisher, "Grover Cleveland Against the Senate," *Congressional Studies* 7, no.1 (1989): 11–25.

14. Data drawn from U.S. Senate, "Summary of Bills Vetoed, 1789–Present," table, accessed November 10, 2012, www.senate.gov/reference/Legislation/Vetoes/vetoCounts.htm.

15. The "chief change" in the veto under Cleveland "was not in the nature of its use but in it frequency, which had the effect of producing a public which was accustomed to, and indeed expected and applauded, the 'courage' of a president standing out against the political satraps inhabiting the halls of Congress. By the time of Teddy Roosevelt the policy of the veto was so customary that all he could really do that was new was to dramatize it or to use it as a threat." Loren P. Beth, *The Development of the American Constitution, 1877–1917* (New York: Harper & Row, 1971), 13.

16. Woodrow Wilson, "Mr. Cleveland as President," *Atlantic Monthly* 79, no. 473 (March 1897): 289.

17. Nevins, *Grover Cleveland*, 448, 450–463.

# 23

# Benjamin Harrison

ALLAN B. SPETTER

*Benjamin Harrison, the "Centennial President," failed to achieve many of his goals (for instance, he was unable to secure passage of federal legislation to ensure public school education and voting rights for African Americans in the South). Yet he successfully pressed Congress to pass the Sherman Anti-Trust Act to deal with the growing threat posed by corporate trusts and monopolies. Using his presidential power to protect a Supreme Court justice who had received threats of physical harm, Harrison also expanded the president's power under the Constitution's Take Care Clause and began a practice that continues today. Ironically, the Supreme Court that Harrison helped shape subsequently thwarted many of his principal initiatives during his single term.*

## Introduction

Benjamin Harrison remains one of the least known of the nation's presidents over the past 125 years. Harrison served only one term between the two separate terms of Grover Cleveland, and it is as though Harrison has been lost among the presidents of the Gilded Age of the late nineteenth century—those presidents who served between Abraham Lincoln and Theodore Roosevelt and who have been viewed as inept, powerless, or both. Yet Harrison deserves recognition for what his administration accomplished or tried to accomplish, particularly concerning the Constitution.

Benjamin Harrison was born in Ohio on August 20, 1833, the great-grandson of another Benjamin Harrison, who signed the Declaration of Independence. The only grandson of a president (William Henry Harrison) to become president as well, Benjamin Harrison graduated from Miami University in Oxford, Ohio, in 1852 and moved to Indianapolis in 1854. He built a successful legal career and rose through the ranks of the newly formed Republican Party.

Harrison joined the Union forces in the Civil War in 1862 as a colonel and commanding officer of the Seventieth Indiana Regiment. Under the command of General William Tecumseh Sherman in Georgia in 1864, Harrison participated in the campaign to capture Atlanta and ended his military career as a brevet brigadier general. He returned to Indiana, where he encountered almost unlimited political opportunity.

Harrison had three assets for an aspiring politician in the late nineteenth century: name recognition, an outstanding Civil War record, and the fact that his home state of Indiana was a swing state in presidential elections. The Republican-controlled legislature elected Harrison to the U.S. Senate early in 1881. Though he failed to win a second term in 1887, Indiana Republicans, realizing the potential of a candidate from their state, began to work for Harrison's nomination for president.

Harrison turned out to be the second choice of enough delegates at the Republican National Convention of 1888; he won the nomination on the eighth ballot. Harrison then defeated incumbent President Grover Cleveland in the Electoral College, 233 to 168, though Cleveland, boosted by large margins in the states of what had become a "Solid South" under Democratic control, led the popular vote by about 100,000.[1]

## Presidency

Benjamin Harrison, the "Centennial President," took office one hundred years after George Washington first occupied the presidency in 1789. The United States had experienced unimaginable change, but except for the long struggle over slavery culminating in the Civil War, in the 1890s the nation may have faced challenges equal to or even greater than any other over the past hundred years. When photojournalist Jacob Riis produced the classic *How the Other Half Lives* in 1890, many Americans became aware of the miserable living conditions of the working class in the tenements of New York City.[2] Both farmers and workers began protesting against the unprecedented wealth that seemed to be concentrated in the hands of a privileged few.

During Harrison's one term in office, as corporations continued to grow and to strengthen their hold on the economy, the nation would be forced to confront dramatic signals that both farmers and workers had become much more militant and demanded change. Farmers in the South struggled with low prices for cotton; farmers in the West faced the same low prices for corn and wheat and a lingering drought. By the beginning of the 1890s, many farmers turned their backs on the Democrats and the Republicans and formed a third party, the People's Party, better known as the Populists.

The Populist platform in the 1892 presidential election sent shock waves across the nation. The new party demanded the free and unlimited coinage of silver in an attempt to increase crop prices (one of its signature issues); called for government ownership of communication and transportation (i.e., the nation's telegraph and telephone systems and the railroads); and pressed for a graduated income tax.

If the Populist platform did not seem enough of a threat to the established order, the nation witnessed incredible violence when strikers clashed with Pinkerton guards at Andrew Carnegie's steel mill in Homestead, Pennsylvania, in July 1892. The confrontation left many dead and wounded. These developments may have indicated the beginning of an upheaval when the nation's economy plunged into the Depression of 1893 and did not even begin to improve until 1897.[3]

In his First Annual Message of December 3, 1889, President Harrison called on Congress to expand the role of the federal government in three areas—all, he believed, within the implied power granted by the Constitution. First, he professed to voice a national consensus for action when he asked Congress to consider "how far the restraint of those combinations of capital commonly called 'trusts' is a matter of Federal jurisdiction."

Harrison also pointed out that Congress had used land grants to provide federal aid to education. He emphasized that there had never been a question about the power of Congress to do so. Therefore, he thought there should be no disagreement about the power of Congress to provide money as a direct federal aid to education. Such aid seemed "necessary and proper," as stipulated in Article I, Section 8, of the Constitution.

Finally, Harrison asserted that Congress had to act to protect the civil rights of African Americans, including the voting rights of African American men in the South: "When and under what conditions is the black man to have a free ballot? When is he in fact to have those full civil rights which have so long been his in law?" Harrison emphasized that because the Constitution gave Congress the power to control the election of members of the House of Representatives, it was Congress's duty to address this problem head-on.[4]

Harrison has properly been recognized for adding "important new dimensions" to the presidency, rejecting the view that the Constitution prohibited the president from interfering in the legislative process.[5] For the first time in fifteen years, Republicans had control of the White House and both houses of Congress. Harrison played an active role, as the Fifty-First Congress produced more important legislation than any other Congress in almost a half century, from 1866 to 1913. The Fifty-First Congress passed four major pieces of legislation in 1890: the Dependent Pension Act for veterans of the Union Army, the McKinley Tariff, the Sherman Anti-Trust Act, and the Sherman Silver Purchase Act, an attempt to inflate prices and wages. This Congress also admitted six new states to the Union in 1889–1890: Idaho, Montana, North Dakota, South Dakota, Washington, and Wyoming.

## The Sherman Anti-Trust Act

When John D. Rockefeller's Standard Oil formed what became known as a *trust* in 1879, it marked a turning point in the development of corporations that became virtual monopolies. A trust was a business arrangement in which several competing companies in an industry combined to form a jointly managed enterprise. Under this arrangement, the shareholders of the companies transferred their stock to a single body of trustees in exchange for a certificate entitling them to a specified share of the earnings. By placing management decisions in one set of trustees, the trusts operated like monopolies, fixing prices and controlling output.[6] Entire industries, such as oil, steel, sugar, whiskey, and tobacco, were brought under the control of the very few, and competitors found it impossible to enter or survive in the marketplace.[7] The industrialists, or so-called robber barons, who formed the trusts and accumulated vast sums of wealth in the process were seen by ordinary Americans as becoming filthy rich at the public's expense and were deeply resented for it.[8] Through the 1880s, the federal government felt increasing pressure to begin to regulate the trusts and their monopolistic practices. With the creation of the Interstate Commerce Commission, an attempt to regulate the nation's railroads, in 1887, the federal government took its first step to inject itself into the economy.

Having fought to defend the Union and the Constitution, Harrison believed in the power of the executive branch as delegated or implied by the Constitution. The Interstate Commerce Commission of 1887 had been created under Article I, Section 8 of the Constitution, which delegated to Congress the power to regulate commerce; Harrison believed that the same clause implied the power to move against the growing threat of monopolies. The Harrison administration, working with Congress, produced the Sherman Anti-Trust Act of 1890.

That landmark piece of legislation faced no real opposition in either house of Congress. The Senate passed the bill with only one opposing vote. The House of Representatives followed with a unanimous vote. Harrison signed the law on July 2. The law stated "every contract, combination in the form of trust or otherwise, or conspiracy, in restraint of trade or commerce, among the several states, or with foreign nations, is hereby declared to be illegal."[9]

Many members of both the House and the Senate may have voted for the Sherman Anti-Trust Act to satisfy public opinion and may not have expected that the law would be vigorously enforced or enforced at all. As it turned out, in the 1890s the Sherman Anti-Trust Act would be used against labor unions, which the courts declared to be "illegal combinations." Finally, in 1911, the Sherman Anti-Trust Act would be used to break up Standard Oil. Nearly 125 years later, the law remains a powerful force in restraining unfair business monopolies in the United States.

### The Blair Education Bill

Harrison was not successful in all of his legislative efforts, however. Henry W. Blair, Republican senator from New Hampshire, first offered a bill to provide federal financial aid to education at the end of 1881. Primarily concerned with the terrible plight of former slaves in the Southern states, the Blair Education Bill was designed to tackle illiteracy. Blair's bill passed the Senate, under Republican control, three times, but the House of Representatives, under Democratic control, refused to consider the bill each time. Trying once more, Blair knew that he had the support of President Harrison, who had voted for the bill while in the Senate.

The bill sought to provide some $77 million in federal aid for public education. The aid received by each state would be based on the state's illiteracy rate for all those over ten years of age, as had been determined by the Census of 1880. According to that census, nearly 75 percent of all illiterate people lived in the South. African Americans made up almost 70 percent of this illiterate population, meaning that African Americans in the South stood to benefit most from the bill. Blair and Harrison believed that the General Welfare Clause in Article I, Section 8, of the Constitution permitted federal aid to education, to assist the former slaves.

Unfortunately for Harrison, Blair, and others who supported the bill, opposition to the legislation grew through the 1880s. Some Republicans had doubts. Who would determine the curriculum to be offered in schools subsidized by the government? Could the South be trusted to use the aid as intended?

Other significant opposition to the bill emerged. Reflecting the anti-Catholicism still prevalent in the late nineteenth century, Blair had proposed a constitutional amendment to prohibit federal aid to parochial schools. Now many within the Catholic Church, specifically the Jesuits, called for defeat of the bill.[10] In March 1890, the proposed legislation failed by a narrow vote in the Senate.

### The Lodge Elections Bill

Harrison favored a moderate approach that would protect the right to vote in federal elections (primarily for African Americans) to select members of the House of Representatives. He stated his position firmly in his First Annual Message in 1889: "A partial and qualified supervision of these elections is now provided for by law, and in my opinion this law may be so strengthened and extended as to secure on the whole better results than can be attained by a law taking all the processes of such election under Federal control."[11]

Henry Cabot Lodge introduced what became known as the Lodge Elections Bill in the House of Representatives in March 1890. The original version would have provided, in response to a petition from voters in a congressional district, complete federal control of the election process. Lodge then met with President Harrison and, two months later, presented a version of the bill that Harrison could support.

The bill created a federal supervisor of elections for cities of twenty thousand or more in population. Supervisors would also be established for congressional districts and counties in response to petitions. For the next seventy-five years, until passage of the Voting Rights Act in 1965, the bill represented the most serious attempt to protect the right to vote for African Americans in the South. A three-man board of canvassers, appointed by a federal circuit court judge, would check the vote totals and certify the results in each congressional district. In essence, the bill would eliminate state control of election results. The South felt threatened by these provisions, and, under Democrat attack as a "force bill," the legislation was defeated in the Senate.[12]

### Protecting the Supreme Court and the Judges

On February 4, 1890, the nation marked the hundredth anniversary of the Supreme Court with a celebration at the Metropolitan Opera House in New York City. Around this same time, Harrison would end up demonstrating his strong support for the judicial branch of the federal government, in an unusual way.[13]

On August 14, 1889, David Terry, once chief justice of the California Supreme Court, assaulted Stephen Field, a justice of the Supreme Court of the United States. (Field had also been chief justice in California.)

Terry had sworn revenge against Field, who, while serving as a circuit court judge, ruled against Terry's wife in a sensational lawsuit in California, sentencing the couple to prison for contempt of court.

Terry, who stood six feet three and weighed 250 pounds, had already shot and killed two men, including a member of the U.S. Senate. Harrison and U.S. Attorney General William Henry Harrison Miller had taken the unprecedented step of assigning a deputy U.S. marshal to act as bodyguard for Field. When Terry attacked the seventy-two-year-old Field in a train bound for San Francisco, Deputy Marshal David Neagle ordered Terry to stop before the officer fired two shots, killing Terry.

Field and Neagle were charged with murder. Field was released quickly, but Neagle's fate seemed uncertain, as California authorities seemed bent on prosecuting him. Neagle sought federal habeas corpus relief, asserting that he was merely carrying out the nation's laws. In the meantime, Harrison made his position clear in his First Annual Message: "I recommend that more definite provision be made by law not only for the protection of Federal officers, but for a full trial of such cases in the United States courts."

In April 1890, the Supreme Court upheld Harrison's decision to provide protection for Field and held that Neagle was acting pursuant to federal law. By a six-to-two vote, with Field abstaining in the case of *Cunningham v. Neagle* (or *In re Neagle*), the majority declared: "We cannot doubt the power of the president to take measures for the protection of a judge of one of the courts of the United States." The majority cited the Take Care Clause contained in Article II, Section 3, of the Constitution three times: the president "shall take care that the laws be faithfully executed."[14] Thus, Harrison's power as chief executive to protect other federal officials from physical harm was established in a dramatic way.

## Conclusion

After Democrats gained control of the House of Representatives in 1890, with 235 seats to only 88 for the Republicans, Harrison accomplished little over the next two years. He would seek a second term without enthusiasm, having lost his wife to tuberculosis late in the campaign in October 1892.

One million Americans voted for the Populists in the presidential election of 1892, but former President Grover Cleveland, a Democrat, achieved a solid victory, leading Harrison by almost four hundred thousand votes.

The Democrats won control of both houses of Congress, with the Depression of 1893 looming.

Harrison returned to Indianapolis and remained active through the 1890s, delivering a series of lectures at Stanford University and serving as chief counsel for Venezuela in its boundary dispute with British Guiana. In a move that alienated perhaps every member of his family, Harrison married the much younger niece of his first wife in 1896 and became a father again in 1897. Harrison died in March 1901.[15]

Notwithstanding Harrison's relative obscurity, his presidency cannot be viewed as a failure. The Sherman Anti-Trust Act, which Harrison strongly supported to curb abuses by monopolies, remains an integral part of the American legal system over a century later.

Additionally, Harrison never wavered in his commitment to the Fifteenth Amendment, added to the Constitution in 1870, giving African American men the right to vote. He made a more serious effort than any president in the succeeding seventy-five years to protect voting rights for African Americans in the South and to provide public school education for former slaves.[16]

Additionally, Supreme Court Justice Stephen J. Field survived an assault, or perhaps an attempted murder, because of unprecedented police protection provided by Harrison. (The protection of Supreme Court justices and federal judges by the executive branch, through the U.S. Marshal's office, continues today.)

Yet, his most lasting legacy, in a final touch of irony, would involve his four appointments to the Supreme Court: Justices David Brewer, Henry Brown, George Shiras Jr., and Howell E. Jackson. In the midst of the Depression of 1893, which was punctuated by unrest among farmers and continuing labor violence, the judiciary emerged "as the principal bulwark of conservative defense." The Supreme Court that Harrison helped build would assist in undoing some of his major legislative initiatives. It would lead the way with "the near emasculation of the Sherman Anti-Trust Act"—declaring that manufacture of a product should not be covered under the law and rejecting the income tax passed by Congress in 1894 as unconstitutional.[17]

Thus, President Benjamin Harrison aspired to achieve great things during a difficult period of American history. He remains largely forgotten not because he suffered from lack of vision or noble ideas, but because his efforts were overpowered by Congress, by recalcitrant Southern states, and by an uncooperative Supreme Court that he had helped shape.

NOTES

1. For Harrison's life through the Civil War, see Harry J. Sievers, *Benjamin Harrison, Hoosier Warrior: Through the Civil War Years, 1833–1865* (New York: University Publishers, 1952, 1960). For Harrison's life from the Civil War to the presidency, see Harry J. Sievers, *Benjamin Harrison, Hoosier Statesman: From the Civil War to the White House, 1865–1888* (New York: University Publishers, 1959). See also Charles W. Calhoun, *Benjamin Harrison* (New York: Henry Holt, 2005).

2. See, for instance, Jacob A. Riis, *How the Other Half Lives: Studies Among the Tenements of New York*, ed. David Leviatin (Boston and New York: St. Martin's Press, 1996).

3. Robert W. Cherny, *American Politics in the Gilded Age, 1868–1900* (Wheeling, IL: Harlan Davidson, 1997), 140; H. Wayne Morgan, *From Hayes to McKinley: National Party Politics, 1877–1896* (Syracuse, NY: Syracuse University Press, 1969), 423; R. Hal Williams, *Years of Decision: American Politics in the 1890s* (New York: John Wiley and Sons, 1978), 64–65.

4. James D. Richardson, *A Compilation of the Messages and Papers of the Presidents, 1789–1897* (Washington, DC: Government Printing Office, 1898), 9:43, 54–56.

5. Williams, *Years of Decision*, 36.

6. Michael J. Gerhardt, *The Forgotten Presidents: Their Untold Constitutional Legacy* (New York: Oxford University Press, 2013), 146.

7. Wayne D. Collins, "Trusts and the Origins of Antitrust Legislation," *Fordham Law Review* 81 (April 2013): 2315–2319.

8. Sean Dennis Cashman, *America in the Gilded Age* (New York: New York University Press, 1993), 36–44.

9. 15 U.S.C. §§ 1, 2. Homer E. Socolofsky and Allan B. Spetter, *The Presidency of Benjamin Harrison* (Lawrence: University Press of Kansas, 1987), 52–55; Cherny, *American Politics in the Gilded Age*, 91. Vigorous prosecution of trusts, however, did not follow until the early twentieth century. Even if President Theodore Roosevelt wanted to get serious about "busting" the trusts, the federal government would have to figure out which trusts could be prosecuted after a Supreme Court ruling in 1895 in a case involving the sugar trust, *United States v. E.C. Knight Co.*, limiting the scope of the Sherman Anti-Trust Act.

10. Gordon B. McKinney, *Henry W. Blair's Campaign to Reform America: From the Civil War to the U.S. Senate* (Lexington: University Press of Kentucky, 2013), 88–89, 92–95, 97, 113, 117, 119–121, 123; Stanley P. Hirshson, *Farewell to the Bloody Shirt: Northern Republicans and the Southern Negro, 1877–1893* (Bloomington: Indiana University Press, 1962), 192–193, 199.

11. Richardson, *Papers of the Presidents*, 9:56.

12. Calhoun, *Benjamin Harrison*, 90–91; Cherny, *American Politics in the Gilded Age*, 92; Hirshson, *Farewell to the Bloody Shirt*, 204–205, 226, 233; Morgan, *From Hayes to McKinley*, 340; Socolofsky and Spetter, *The Presidency of Benjamin Harrison*, 62–65; Williams, *Years of Decision*, 30–31, 58.

13. Arnold M. Paul, *Conservative Crisis and the Rule of Law: Attitudes of Bar and Bench, 1887–1895* (Ithaca, NY: Cornell University Press, 1960), 61.

14. Harry J. Sievers, *Benjamin Harrison, Hoosier President: The White House and After* (Indianapolis: Bobbs-Merrill Company, 1968), 93–101; Socolofsky and Spetter, *Presidency of Benjamin Harrison*, 186–187; Richardson, *Papers of the Presidents*, 9:42; Cunningham v. Neagle, 135 U.S. 1 (1890).

15. Calhoun, *Benjamin Harrison*, 149; Cherny, *American Politics in the Gilded Age*, 108, 141; Morgan, *From Hayes to McKinley*, 436–437; Sievers, *Hoosier President*, 242, 248, 255–257, 264; Williams, *Years of Decision*, 50, 66, 68.

16. George Sinkler, *The Racial Attitudes of American Presidents from Abraham Lincoln to Theodore Roosevelt* (Garden City, NY: Doubleday, 1971), 252, 261–262, 284; McKinney, *Henry W. Blair's Campaign to Reform America*, 90.

17. Paul, *Conservative Crisis and the Rule of Law*, 2–3, 182, 209, 211, 219. See United States v. E.C. Knight Co., 156 U.S. 1 (1895); Pollock v. Farmers' Loan and Trust Co., 158 U.S. 601 (1895).

24

# Grover Cleveland

*Second Term: 1892–1896*

DONALD GRIER STEPHENSON JR.

*Grover Cleveland's second term, after a four-year hiatus in private life, was marked by a willingness (once again) to take bold action. When socialist union leader Eugene Debs led a railroad strike that threatened to cripple rail transportation and the postal service, President Cleveland and his attorney general used the Sherman Anti-Trust Act to obtain an injunction and to successfully prosecute Debs, creating a new weapon in the arsenal of executive powers. Cleveland demonstrated that, as the unitary head of the executive branch, the president enjoyed power as a symbolic leader. This power was as potent as his formal powers under the Constitution, thus helping to shape the modern presidency.*

## Introduction

G rover Cleveland, the only president to win nonconsecutive terms in the White House, retreated to New York City after his defeat in the election of 1888, waiting for his opportunity to return to public life. That opportunity arose when the Harrison administration both raised the tariff to record levels and instituted a heavy purchase of silver, policies that Cleveland viewed as risky. Seizing the moment, Cleveland spoke out with an open letter to reformers. The "silver letter" sharply criticized the runaway coinage of silver and thrust him back into the political spotlight. Although initially viewed as political suicide, the "silver letter" turned out to be a masterstroke. As Cleveland mobilized his forces, economic troubles in 1892 preceding what would be a major depression in 1893 further paved the way for his return to the White House. Cleveland snatched the Democratic nomination before going on to trounce Harrison in the general election.[1] As he did in his earlier campaigns, Cleveland relied on the slogan "Public Office Is a Public Trust," words that, along with the phrase "Tariff Reform," were embossed on small medals supporting his election.[2]

After a campaign in which Cleveland again trumpeted not only tariff reform but also firm reliance on gold to ensure a sound currency, the stage was set for his second term. He had only marginal success with Congress on the first issue, but scored a major victory on the second. At the same time, Cleveland faced new issues that tested his strength as chief executive.

## Presidency

### The Pullman Strike, the Debs Case, and Executive Power

Amid the so-called Panic of 1893, shortly after Cleveland's return to the White House, unemployment averaged 18.4 percent overall and reached as high as 50 percent in construction and some manufacturing sectors.[3] In this climate of hard times and attendant labor unrest, workers in May 1894 struck the Pullman Palace Car Company in Illinois. They did so after that maker and operator of railroad sleeping cars cut wages as much as 40 percent without also reducing stock dividends, executive salaries, or rents in company-owned housing.

To bolster the strikers' insistence on arbitration, the American Railway Union, headed by the Socialist union leader Eugene V. Debs, called a sympathetic strike (or secondary boycott), directing its 150,000 members to refrain from handling any train in the United States with Pullman equipment in its complement of railroad cars.[4] The effects were widespread, crippling rail transportation and the postal system in many parts of the United States.

At this time, the federal courts were subjecting the activities of labor unions to the prohibitions of the Sherman Anti-Trust Act and enjoining strikes and boycotts deemed socially or economically harmful as unlawful restraints of trade.[5] Accordingly, on July 2, Cleveland's attorney general, Richard Olney, invoked the act and secured a provisional federal injunction, directing the union and its officials, including Debs, to refrain from interfering with the mail trains and named railroads engaged in interstate commerce. The injunction specifically barred Debs (and the others) from issuing further directives or assisting subordinates to continue the boycott.[6] Attempts to protect the rail yards in Chicago provoked a riot. Twenty people were killed, trains were derailed, and some two thousand rail cars were destroyed.

To restore order President Cleveland, with some doubts about his own constitutional authority to act in this situation—particularly over the objection of Illinois prolabor governor John Peter Altgeld—dispatched some two thousand U.S. Army troops from four states and deputized an additional five thousand marshals. The appearance of troops, however, exacerbated the situation, and mayhem continued. President Cleveland nevertheless forged ahead. With the president's unyielding support, federal officers arrested Debs and four union leaders for violating the terms of the injunction. They were tried and found guilty of criminal contempt and sentenced to terms of imprisonment. Debs, represented by famed American lawyer Clarence Darrow, filed an appeal and a writ of habeas corpus with the Supreme Court (as did the others).

In May 1895, the U.S. Supreme Court unanimously affirmed Debs's conviction, in *In re Debs*, an important decision that expanded the president's power to uphold the laws and address matters concerning the public welfare.[7] Justice Brewer's opinion had to surmount a high hurdle: There was no obvious federal constitutional or statutory basis for holding Debs accountable for the turmoil arising out of a labor dispute.[8] Yet the Court justified this extraordinary action because the government found itself in "the throes of rebellion and revolution."[9] The Court concluded that the use of force by the executive branch was constitutional when "obstructions arise to the freedom of interstate commerce or the transportation of the mails." Moreover, the "entire strength of the nation may be used to enforce in any part of the land the full and free exercise of all national powers and the security of all rights entrusted by the Constitution to its care."[10] Thus, the attorney general could properly ask for the injunction not simply because the American Railway Union and its officials were interfering with interstate commerce and the movement of the mails, but also because their actions also endangered the national economic union. As a result, the government could invoke its power "to keep the peace" and to ensure the "general welfare" of the public. Moreover, it was proper for the executive branch to appeal to the courts to enforce the laws by issuing an injunction.[11]

Cleveland's action in standing firm on the Pullman Strike had far-reaching effects.[12] For nearly thirty years, the injunction in the Pullman Strike was the model for others, the first effective example of what soon came to be called "government by injunction." This form of executive-branch intervention quickly became both a tool to cope with social and economic problems and a symbol of "the propertied classes' fear of social revolution."[13] Although the constitutional basis for permitting this forceful use of executive power was viewed as attenuated by some, its successful use by President Cleveland was pathbreaking. The *Debs* case, and Eugene Debs's conviction, took the wind out of the sails of the labor movement, at least for a time.

### The Supreme Court, Federal Income Taxes, and Segregation

During his years in office, Cleveland made four appointments to the Supreme Court, two in the earlier term and two in the later.[14] Significantly, the four appointments included the naming of a chief justice, Melville W. Fuller, making Cleveland only the fifth president after 1789 to be afforded that distinction.[15]

Constitutionally, the second Cleveland presidency in particular coincided with several landmark decisions by the Supreme Court, apart from the *Debs* case, demarcating powers of both national and state governments. One—*Pollock v. Farmers' Loan & Trust*—declared the federal income tax unconstitutional, precipitating the later ratification of the Sixteenth

Amendment in 1913.[16] At least since his days as New York's governor, Cleveland had favored a tax on incomes as the fairest method of taxation.[17] Thus, he was undoubtedly displeased with the High Court's five-to-four decision. Yet his only public comment in the wake of the 1895 ruling was to insist that no special session of Congress would be needed to cover the likely revenue shortfall of about $50 million that the tax had been designed to address.[18]

In *U.S. v. E.C. Knight Co.*, one of the first major prosecutions brought under the Sherman Anti-Trust Act, the U.S. Supreme Court substantially weakened the federal government's ability to combat monopolies and trusts. In a decision authored by Chief Justice Fuller, the Court ruled (eight to one) that the manufacturing of a product within the boundaries of a state (in this case, sugar refining) was a local activity and thus beyond the scope of the act and Congress's Article I power to regulate interstate commerce.[19]

Another, more infamous case—*Plessy v. Ferguson*—sanctioned the racist public policy of "separate but equal" that prevailed until its abandonment by the High Court midway through the next century.[20] With respect to *Plessy*, Cleveland probably approved of the Court's decision, given his own disposition toward African Americans. Although not hostile toward blacks by the standards of the Gilded Age, Cleveland was not interested in reform. During his time as governor of New York, he had publicly stated that he did not favor integrated schools, owing to his belief that blacks would benefit from segregation. Likewise, in remarks delivered long after his second term had ended, Cleveland, who admired Booker T. Washington, plainly asserted, as did many Americans, that blacks were inferior to whites because of natural "deficiencies" such as "ignorance" and "laziness" that were a by-product of race.[21]

## Conclusion

Nearing the end of his second term in 1896, Cleveland declined entreaties to seek reelection from some Democrats in his wing of what was now a badly fractured party. Instead, he retired to Princeton, New Jersey, with his wife and three children (two more would be born after the conclusion of Cleveland's presidency), hoping to spend time with his young family. Cleveland soon became a member of Princeton University's Board of Trustees, where he battled with Princeton's President Woodrow Wilson on the issue of where to locate the graduate residence facility.[22] After Cleveland's death in Princeton in 1908, the two-time president was memorialized in 1913 by the construction of a Gothic tower at the entrance of Princeton's Graduate College that today bears his name.[23]

By twenty-first-century expectations, Cleveland was not a strong president. Yet, when his later term ended, he left the presidency larger than he had found it and so contributed to its expansion under his successors. Indeed, the secretive arrangements made to carry out necessary surgery for President Cleveland demonstrate how symbolically important the presidency had become by the 1890s. To remove a serious, cigar-induced malignancy from Cleveland's mouth, doctors performed the surgery surreptitiously at sea aboard the yacht *Oneida*, which was owned by a wealthy banker friend of Cleveland's. At that time, with the nation fully in the grip of the Panic of 1893, fear that the president might be seriously ill and thus incapable of governing in midsummer might have turned what was already an economic calamity into a national crisis. Even the cabinet was not informed of the president's surgery in advance.[24] Thus, Cleveland's tenure in the White House marked the beginning of a new sort of presidency in which the chief executive's power as a symbolic leader—the unitary head of the executive branch—began to overshadow the president's formal powers under the Constitution.

### NOTES

1. Allan Nevins, *Grover Cleveland: A Study in Courage*, 2 vols. (New York, Dodd, Mead & Company, 1948) 491, 506–407.
2. William Safire, *Safire's Political Dictionary* (New York: Oxford University Press, 2008), 586.
3. Paul Kens, *Judicial Power and Reform Politics: The Anatomy of Lochner v. New York* (Lawrence: University Press of Kansas, 1990), 36; Robert Higgs, *Crisis and Leviathan: Critical Episodes in the Growth of American Government* (New York: Oxford University Press, 1987), 84–85.
4. Debs later polled nearly one million votes in two presidential elections (1908 and 1912) as a third-party candidate. His more than nine hundred thousand votes in 1908 amounted to nearly 6 percent of the votes cast.
5. H.A. Artists & Associates, Inc. v. Actors' Equity Ass'n, 451 U.S. 704, 713 (1981) (citation and internal quotations omitted).
6. United States v. Debs, 64 F. 724 (C.C.N.D. Ill. 1894).
7. In re Debs, 158 U.S. 564 (1895).

8. The Court was being called upon to uphold a federal court's injunction against "forc-ible obstructions," which seemed only another way of referring to maintaining order, quintessentially a function of state and local governments.

9. *In re Debs*, 158 U.S. at 597.

10. Ibid., 582–583.

11. Ibid., 579, 584–586. Although the Court in *Debs* did not cite a specific provision of the Constitution to support the president's power in this regard, it flowed from the Con-gress's power in Article I of the Constitution over interstate commerce and the instrumentalities thereof, such as the interstate railroads. In *Debs*, the Commerce Clause and federal legislation enacted thereunder were held to empower the president as chief executive to keep the channels of interstate commerce free from blockage.

12. Cleveland wrote a lengthy essay on his and the government's actions during the Pull-man strike. Grover Cleveland, *Presidential Problems* (New York: Century, 1904), 79–117.

13. Alfred H. Kelly, Winfred A. Harbison, and Herman Belz, *The American Constitution: Its Origins and Development*, 7th ed. (New York: W.W. Norton, 1991), 2:400.

14. The first-term appointees were L. Q. C. Lamar (1888–1893) and Melville W. Fuller (1888–1910). Lamar had been Cleveland's secretary of the interior. His appointment to the Court was particularly noteworthy in that it was the first appointment of a true Southerner since Franklin Pierce named John Campbell in 1853. Lamar was also the first Supreme Court nominee whose résumé included active service in the Confederate Army. The second-term appointees were Edward Douglass White (1894–1910) and Rufus W. Peckham (1896–1909). White would be elevated to Chief Justice by President Taft in 1910.

15. Melville W. Fuller was appointed in 1888 and served until 1910.

16. Pollock v. Farmers' Loan & Trust Co., 158 U.S. 601 1895) (rehearing).

17. Henry F. Graff, *Grover Cleveland* (New York: Times Books, 2002), 32. Apparently Cleveland's only reservation about the 1894 income tax provision had been that the doubts expressed about its constitutionality might impede the tariff bill's progress.

18. "No Extra Session of Congress," *New York Times*, May 21, 1895, 1.

19. United States v. E.C. Knight, Co., 156 U.S. 1 (1895). Cleveland did not object to passage of the Sherman Anti-Trust Act (during Harrison's presidency), but he did have his doubts about its constitutionality. Nonetheless, it was Cleveland's attorney general, Richard Olney, who brought the case against the American Sugar Refining Company, which controlled about 98 percent of all the sugar refining in the country. Melvin I. Urofsky, ed., *The American Presidents: Critical Essays* (New York: Garland Publishing, 2000), 243. Moreover, in his 1896 annual message, Cleveland denounced the trusts as "creatures of special privilege and enemies of the nation's social and economic health" and urged Congress to enact new antitrust legislation. Robert E. Welsh Jr., *The Presi-dencies of Grover Cleveland* (Lawrence: University of Kansas Press, 1988), 152. Still, Chief Justice Fuller's restrictive view of the congressional commerce power only echoed Cleveland appointee L. Q. C. Lamar's admonition from Kidd v. Pearson, 128 U.S. 1 (1888): "No distinction is more popular to the common mind . . . than that between manufactures and commerce. . . . If it be held that [commerce] includes the regulation

of all such manufactures as are intended to be the subject of commercial transactions in the future, . . . Congress would be invested, to the exclusion of the States, with the power to regulate, not only manufacture, but also agriculture, horticulture, stock raising, domestic fisheries, mining—in short, every branch of human industry." Ibid., 20–21.

20. Plessy v. Ferguson, 163 U.S. 537 (1896); Brown v. Board of Education, 347 U.S. 483 (1954).

21. For Cleveland's admiration of Washington, see Alyn Brodsky, "Cleveland and the Blacks," appendix 1 in *Grover Cleveland: A Study in Character* (New York: Truman Talley Books, 2000), 450–453. For Cleveland's statements on the inferiority of blacks, see Richard E. Welch Jr., *The Presidencies of Grover Cleveland* (Lawrence: University Press of Kansas, 1988), 67–69.

22. Willard Thorp, Minor Myers Jr., and Jeremiah Finch, *The Princeton Graduate School: A History* (Princeton, NJ: Princeton University Press, 1978), 108–109.

23. A magnificent carillon with sixty-seven bells was installed in the 173-foot Cleveland Tower in 1927.

24. The public did not learn of the surgery until one of the surgeons, W. W. Keen, wrote an article about it a quarter century later for the September 22, 1917, issue of *The Saturday Evening Post*.

# 25

# William McKinley

THOMAS C. SUTTON

*President William McKinley initially tried at all costs to avoid war with Spain over a rebellion in Cuba. Refusal by Spain of his offer to arbitrate an end to the conflict triggered U.S. military action, which resulted in a swift American victory. This led to U.S. acquisition of Spanish territories in Puerto Rico, the Philippines, and Guam, acquisitions that (along with the annexation of Hawaii) established McKinley as an imperialist president. To maintain his maximum freedom of action, he favored giving limited citizenship to the residents of the territories, without extending to them all of the rights and privileges contained in the U.S. Constitution. On the domestic front, McKinley spoke out against the increasingly powerful corporate trusts, yet accomplished little to restrain them. He was assassinated by an anarchist less than a year after winning a second term.*

## Introduction

William McKinley was born January 29, 1843, in Niles, Ohio. His parents, William and Nancy McKinley, had nine children, of whom William Jr. was the seventh. His father was a farmer who also worked in a local iron furnace and was an inventor.[1] The family was of Scotch-Irish heritage; originally Presbyterian, the McKinleys became committed Methodists after moving from Pennsylvania before William Jr.'s birth. Their conversion and commitment to Methodism, born out of the revivalism of the early nineteenth century, had a profound effect on William. According to Aaron Morton, the pastor of McKinley's church in 1867, McKinley's faith was a central element throughout his life: a commitment to belief in the "loving kindness of God . . . and source of his inner serenity."[2] His faith included a strong commitment to the abolition of slavery.

William attended a seminary school after the family moved to Poland, Ohio, in 1852. After spending a year at Allegheny College in 1860, he returned home because of poor health and financial constraints.[3] In June 1861, McKinley enlisted in what became Company E of the Twenty-Third Regiment of the Ohio Volunteer Infantry, serving in the battle of Antietam, the first major battle of the Civil War to take place on Union soil.[4] The commander of the Twenty-Third Regiment, Rutherford B. Hayes, recommended McKinley for promotion to second lieutenant.[5] He ultimately became brevet major under General George Cook.

At the end of the Civil War, McKinley decided to return to civilian life and spent a term at Albany Law School in New York, followed by a year reading law with Mahoning County Judge Charles Glidden.[6] McKinley combined law practice with politics, campaigning for Rutherford B. Hayes in his gubernatorial election in 1867, making a strong positive impression as a stump speaker advocating support for Reconstruction and African American suffrage. He also became a strong proponent of sound money policy, an issue that remained a central focus of McKinley's work throughout his political life. He was elected to Congress in 1876, representing the Seventeenth District in northeast Ohio, a seat that had been held by Republicans since 1863.[7]

McKinley's personal life during this period was marked by tragedy. He married Ida Saxton in 1871, a beautiful young woman from a prominent

Canton, Ohio, banking and newspaper family, but their two children (both girls) died at young ages.[8]

Nonetheless, McKinley's political career soared. He became a rising leader of the Republican caucus in the House during the 1880s. He continued to advocate for African American rights by speaking out against Jim Crow in the South and the limits on congressional efforts to stop segregation by decisions of the U.S. Supreme Court (such as the *Civil Rights Cases* of 1883). He also supported the Pendleton Act of 1883, joining many Ohio reformers in the effort to end patronage, in part to honor the memory of their slain colleague, James Garfield.[9]

As chair of the Ways and Means Committee, McKinley managed in 1890 to push through a major tariff bill that would reimburse U.S. importers for tariffs paid on raw materials if these were used for manufacturing goods designated for export—a measure designed to protect U.S. manufacturing interests.[10] McKinley narrowly lost his House seat by 303 votes in 1890, but swiftly rebounded by winning the race for Ohio governor in 1892.

The Panic of 1893, the worst recession in U.S. history up to that point, shook public confidence in the policies of President Grover Cleveland, particularly concerning free trade and his refusal to adopt silver as part of the national currency. Voters turned to the Republican Party, which gained a two-to-one majority in the House and held a narrow majority in the Senate. Noting McKinley's success and potential for the 1896 presidential race, his friend and political mentor, Mark Hanna, stepped away from his corporate activity and began to lay the groundwork to get McKinley nominated, starting with a national speaking tour in support of the Republican ticket.[11]

Together, Hanna and McKinley developed what has become legendary as the first modern presidential campaign. The two men believed that the country's economic health and growth depended on the strength of the growing corporate sector and that corporate leaders needed to contribute heavily to political campaigns. McKinley's support for corporate interests was rooted in his belief that they held the power to provide good paying jobs for workers. This was the first organized effort to bring corporate leaders directly into a political campaign by actively soliciting funds. Hanna formed McKinley for President clubs in towns and cities across the East and Midwest, building grassroots support for his nomination. The night his nomination was secured, McKinley spoke to a stream of well-wishers from his front porch in Canton; the crowds totaled over fifty thousand by the end of that evening.[12]

The ensuing campaign of 1896 pitted McKinley against the populist William Jennings Bryan, who had won the Democratic nomination on a platform supporting free silver.[13] McKinley ran on a gold-standard platform, partly to allay concerns of industrial supporters.[14] McKinley's signature phrase, "Good money never made times hard," became a campaign slogan emblazoned on campaign buttons, banners, umbrellas, and canes.[15] He attracted urban, labor, and immigrant support with convincing arguments that the gold standard would increase export demand for American goods, producing more jobs for workers. When the campaign of 1896 barreled to a conclusion, McKinley won with a comfortable margin.[16]

## Presidency

McKinley's cabinet reflected his focus on rewarding loyal supporters and seeking sectional balance.[17] While many of the appointees had ties with industrialists such as Andrew Carnegie and John D. Rockefeller, industrialists did not necessarily control his presidential appointments.[18] One significant appointment designed to assuage the New England faction was Theodore Roosevelt as assistant secretary of the navy (Roosevelt had strong support from his college classmate, Massachusetts Senator Henry Cabot Lodge). McKinley took a risk with this appointment, knowing that Roosevelt advocated for war with Spain and expansion of U.S. territorial claims, which McKinley firmly opposed.

### The Spanish-American War

The Spanish-American War soon tested McKinley's abilities as both head of state and commander in chief. New communications technologies ushered in a new era of executive involvement not possible during previous wars. Finally, the war marked the arrival of the United States as an imperial power and created unique constitutional issues regarding foreign territories.

The 1898 conflict had its roots in a rebellion against the Spanish control of Cuba led by José Marti and Máximo Gómez during the period of 1868 to 1878. In 1895, Gómez focused his efforts at disrupting the island's economy, destroying commercial facilities and burning sugarcane fields. The

Spanish military, led by Captain-General Valeriano Weyler (dubbed the "Butcher of Havana" in the American press), responded by forcing rural populations in Cuba to move to resettlement camps (*reconcentrados*) to minimize infiltration by insurgents. Although President McKinley offered to mediate the conflict, he faced strong criticism in the press for refusing to send troops to support the Cuban rebellion against Spain. McKinley's efforts to pressure Spain to ease the suffering in the camps and to initiate steps toward granting Cuba independence were largely ignored. The president's goal was to avoid war and to achieve an accommodation between the nationalists and Spain through diplomacy.[19]

However, in January 1898, President McKinley took a step that would ultimately lead to war. Exercising his power as commander in chief, he offered to send the USS *Maine* warship to Havana in exchange for a Spanish warship visiting a U.S. harbor as a gesture of friendship. This initiative was swiftly criticized in a private letter by Dupuy de Lome, the Spanish ambassador to the United States. He called McKinley "weak and catering to the rabble, and besides, a low politician."[20] The letter was leaked to the press on February 9; de Lome was recalled to Spain, which issued an apology and accepted the warship exchange. On February 15, just days after the ship's arrival, the USS *Maine* exploded and sank to the bottom of Havana harbor, killing 266 U.S. sailors. The American press, in particular the newspapers published by William Randolph Hearst and Joseph Pulitzer, blamed Spain for the explosion and pressed for the United States to invade Cuba.[21] U.S. investigators confirmed that the ship had hit mines planted in the harbor by Spain. McKinley's efforts to convince Spain to grant Cuba independence had clearly failed.

Increasing tensions after the sinking of the *Maine* led to the evacuation of American citizens from Cuba. President McKinley offered to act as arbitrator between the rebels and Spain, which had also rejected an offer of mediation by Pope Leo XIII. On April 19, Congress issued a joint resolution that demanded both Spanish withdrawal from Cuba and Cuban independence. In response, Spain broke off diplomatic relations with the United States, which then instituted a naval blockade of Cuba. Spain declared war on the U.S. on April 23, and the U.S. reciprocated two days later.

The Spanish-American War escalated rapidly, resulting in a swift U.S. defeat of Spain.[22] The Treaty of Paris, which formally ended the war, was signed on December 10. The treaty granted independence to Cuba (with conditions provided under the Platt Amendment of 1901), while Puerto Rico, the Philippines, and Guam became U.S. possessions, despite a movement in the Philippines for independence.[23]

McKinley strongly favored annexation of the Philippines, believing that the Filipinos were not ready for self-governance and self-defense. There was also concern for protecting trade routes to Asia and a fear that if the U.S. did not annex the islands, a European power would do so. Opponents of annexation included author Samuel Clemens (Mark Twain), who believed that taking over these islands was undemocratic, and he equated the U.S. with imperialist European powers. Others opposed the move because they did not wish to see additional U.S. military expenditures in protecting far-flung territories. Opponents to annexation were close to defeating Senate ratification of the Treaty of Paris, which included purchase of the Philippines for $20 million from Spain. An armed revolt in the Philippines against U.S. occupation that began just before the ratification vote tipped the balance in McKinley's favor. The Treaty of Paris was ratified by a one-vote margin. The U.S. continued to battle the Filipino insurgency led by Emilio Aguinaldo for three years until his defeat in 1902.[24]

The Spanish-American War was a watershed event in American history, not only because it marked a new chapter in the rise of the American Empire, but also because of McKinley's creative exercise of presidential authority. For the first time in American history, the president was able to conduct a foreign war remotely from the White House. This was made possible by the advent of the telephone and the telegraph, which enabled McKinley to speak directly with his commanders in the field in real time and coordinate their movements. Likewise, after the war was won, McKinley participated in the peace process with similar vigor and did not hesitate to administer the conquered territories as commander in chief.[25]

## The New Territories under the Constitution

Acquisition of the territories of the Philippines, Puerto Rico, and Guam was not the only area of U.S. expansion beyond its continental borders. The growing presence of American commercial interests in Hawaii led to U.S. interference in the islands' local governance. This interference included the eventual deposing of Queen Liliuokalani and culminated in the annexation of Hawaii by the U.S. in July 1898. President McKinley supported this annexation as a way to ensure access to Hawaii's sugar plantations and to use the Hawaiian Islands as a means of entry into Asian markets and as a military base.[26]

One of the unique issues that inevitably surfaced during the McKinley administration concerned the extent to which the U.S. Constitution applied, or did not apply, to the new territories acquired during the war. A set of court challenges known as the *Insular Cases* made its way to the Supreme Court, testing to what extent the Constitution applied to these new territories.[27] Three of the defining cases in this group—*DeLima v. Bidwell*, *Downes v. Bidwell*, and *Dooley v. United States*—challenged tariffs levied under the Dingley Act and the Foraker Act, passed, respectively, in 1898 and 1900, as applied to Puerto Rico.[28] These cases carried broad implications for all the territories acquired during the war with Spain. The issue was whether Puerto Rico enjoyed the same status as a fully incorporated state, in which case the tariff would be unconstitutional because, according to the Uniformity Clause of Article I, Section 8, Clause 1, "all duties, imposts, and excises [must] be uniform throughout the United States."[29]

Both Congress and the McKinley administration favored the application of these tariffs and did not view Puerto Rico as equal to the states. Ultimately, the Supreme Court agreed and, relying on Article IV, Section 3, of the Constitution (dealing with admitting new states to the union), held that Congress had unrestricted authority to determine the legal status of the territories. The Court stated that because Congress had not incorporated Puerto Rico into the Union as a state, the island was a "possession" of the United States rather than a part of the nation.[30] Drawing on practical considerations to justify its approach, the Court opined in *Downes*:

A false step at this time might be fatal to the development of what Chief Justice Marshall called the American empire. Choice in some cases, the natural gravitation of small bodies towards large ones in others, the result of a successful war in still others, may bring about conditions which would render the annexation of distant possessions desirable. If those possessions are inhabited by alien races, differing from us in religion, customs, laws, methods of taxation, and modes of thought, the administration of government and justice, according to Anglo-Saxon principles, may for a time be impossible.[31]

This statement echoed the imperialist sentiment of the McKinley administration. Two years prior, in a speech to Methodist Church officials, McKinley stated that the people inhabiting the territories were "unfit for self government" and that it was the duty of the United States to "educate . . . and uplift and Christianize and civilize them."[32] Thus, the residents of the territories technically became U.S. citizens, but did not enjoy all of the privileges and rights contained in the Constitution, such as the right to vote. Accordingly, on McKinley's watch, the United States became an imperial power and subscribed to many of the paternalistic, racist pretenses that prevailed in America at the turn of the twentieth century.

### McKinley Fails to Confront the Trusts

Issues surrounding the new territories were not the only important matters decided by the Court during this period. McKinley's presidency also coincided with a heightened public outcry against the monopolistic abuses of trusts. Concern over the power of trusts to set prices and control competition had led to passage of the Sherman Anti-Trust Act in 1890, during Benjamin Harrison's presidency. This famous law was designed to control monopolies and prevent big business from eliminating competition in the marketplace. The bloodshed of the Homestead Steel Strike in 1892 only reinforced the notion that industrialists like Andrew Carnegie, Henry Clay Frick, and others were using their wealth to maintain a lock on government and that corporate monopolies had to be held in check by federal legislation.

In 1895, the Supreme Court decided the case of *United States v. E.C. Knight* (popularly known as the *Sugar Trust* Case), which involved the first major challenge to the Sherman Anti-Trust Act.[33] Here, the Court struck a blow to the antitrust movement while sharply curtailing Congress's power under the Commerce Clause. The *E.C. Knight* decision concerned the American Sugar Refining Company, which had gained control of E.C. Knight and other companies, giving it a 98 percent monopoly in the sugar refining business in the United States. Yet the Court, in an opinion by Chief Justice Melville Fuller, concluded that this combination of capital related solely to the *manufacture* of goods and did not implicate interstate commerce. Thus, the Court declared, in a rigid holding that would restrict legislative authority under the Commerce Clause for decades, Congress had injected itself into a purely local matter properly left to the states and thus had exceeded its powers under the Commerce Clause.

When McKinley took office just after the *E. C. Knight* decision had been handed down, Congress appeared powerless to combat the trusts.[34] Indeed, McKinley seemed to have viewed trust building as an inevitable by-product of capitalism; he seriously doubted whether any action against the trusts was legally feasible. Nevertheless, during the presidential campaign of 1900, McKinley had invoked the populist rhetoric of the day and spoke out as an opponent of trusts: "Combinations of capital organized into trusts to control the conditions of trade among our citizens, to stifle competition, limit production, and determine the prices of products used and consumed by the people, are justly provoking public discussion, and should early claim the attention of the Congress."[35] Growing public concern about the power of trusts may have led McKinley to act on these sentiments had his second term in office not been cut short. Nevertheless, during his one term in office, McKinley did little to combat the trusts and was therefore criticized, fairly, for his passive approach to the problem.[36]

### A Short-Lived Reelection

President McKinley began 1900 with strong prospects for a rematch against William Jennings Bryan against the backdrop of a resurgent economy and increasingly complex foreign involvement. The United States joined Germany, Great Britain, France, Japan, and Russia in sending troops to quell the Boxer Rebellion in China in 1899–1900. This action was significant both because the United States was included in a coalition of the world's most powerful nations and because McKinley dispatched U.S. forces without consulting Congress.[37]

On the domestic front, the economy had recovered from the lingering effects of the Panic of 1893, although a potential political problem for McKinley lay in the growing public concern over the power of the trusts and the perception that the president was being controlled by corporate interests through his long political partnership with industrialist Mark Hanna. McKinley faced no opposition in the renomination. Despite Hanna's strong objection, McKinley accepted the selection of Theodore Roosevelt as his running mate (Vice President Garret Hobart had died unexpectedly in November 1899). Party leaders believed that TR would add some luster to the ticket. Roosevelt had returned from leading the Rough Riders in the 1898 Spanish-American War to great public acclaim and had won the governorship of New York later that year. An effective public speaker and vigorous campaigner, TR had the backing of East Coast political leaders, especially Massachusetts Senator Henry Cabot Lodge. McKinley saw TR as a positive addition to the ticket, despite their very different temperaments.[38]

The McKinley-Roosevelt ticket ran on a platform of protectionism and reform, pledging to rein in abusive trusts, raise the age limit for child labor, provide workers insurance, build the Panama Canal, and return the U.S. to the gold standard. Their Democratic opponents, William Jennings Bryan and Adlai Stevenson (the latter of whom had been vice president during Grover Cleveland's second term), opposed the trusts in favor of free trade, opposed the U.S. suppression of the Filipino rebellion, and supported a silver-based currency. McKinley won with more electoral votes and a larger margin than in 1896. The election results are often described as a realignment of American politics in favor of the GOP—a situation that lasted, except for the Wilson presidency, until 1932.[39]

## Conclusion

McKinley's triumphant reelection was tragically cut short by his assassination, less than eight months into his second term, at the Buffalo World's Fair. While greeting attendees at a reception on the afternoon of September 6, 1901, McKinley was shot twice by Leon Czolgosz, an anarchist from Cleveland, the son of Polish immigrants. Czolgosz was self-declared disciple of Emma Goldman, a Russian-born anarchist, and he held McKinley responsible for the poor conditions of labor. McKinley survived the shooting and appeared to be improving, but six days later, he relapsed and died the next day, September 14.[40] Vice President Theodore Roosevelt was hiking in the Adirondacks when McKinley took a turn for the worse; Roosevelt received the news from a park ranger running toward him clutching a telegram.[41] The vice president raced back to Buffalo, and after McKinley's death, took the oath of office, pledging to maintain "absolutely unbroken the policy of President McKinley for the peace, prosperity and the honor of our beloved country."[42]

An imperialist president who gathered power relating to foreign territories, McKinley never lived to address the growing issue of abuses by corporations on American soil. He left that problem, along with challenging independence movements in Puerto Rico, Cuba, and the Philippines, to his successors.

NOTES

1. Margaret Leech, *In the Days of McKinley* (Newtown, CT: American Political Biography Press, 1959).
2. Ibid., 17.
3. Deborah R. Marinski, *William McKinley: A Modern Man* (New York: Nova Science Publishers, 2011), 1–7.
4. Ibid., 8–15.
5. Kevin Phillips, *William McKinley* (New York: Times Books, 2003), 21–22.
6. Marinski, *William McKinley*, 10–12.
7. Charles S. Bullock III, *Redistricting: The Most Political Activity in America* (New York: Rowman and Littlefield, 2010), 107–138.
8. Their first child, Katie, died of typhoid fever. The trauma severely affected Ida, who suffered convulsions and became an epileptic plagued by seizures for the rest of her life. Leech, *In the Days of McKinley*, 18–33.
9. Marinski, *William McKinley*, 41–62.
10. Ibid., 59.
11. Daniel P. Klinghard, "Grover Cleveland, William McKinley, and the Emergence of the President as Party Leader," *Presidential Studies Quarterly* 35, no. 4 (2005): 753.
12. Marinski, *William McKinley*, 81–83.
13. McKinley had solid support in the Middle West: Ohio, Indiana, Michigan, Illinois, Wisconsin, Minnesota, and Iowa.
14. William Jennings Bryan's "Cross of Gold" speech denounced the lack of access to currency by farmers because of the gold standard and advocated for adding silver to currency valuation. The gold standard meant that the value of currency was measured in gold reserves held by the U.S. government. Adding silver as a standard for valuation would make access to currency and credit easier, as more currency would be available in the market. This step would also lead to inflation of currency valuations, which was opposed by business interests supporting the McKinley campaign. A. Craig Baird, *American Public Address* (New York: McGraw Hill, 1956), 194–200.
15. Bryan's rough populism and ignorance of economic issues led many Democratic-leaning papers, such as *The Nation*, to support McKinley.
16. Phillips, *William McKinley*, 66–85.
17. Richard F. Hamilton, *President McKinley, War and Empire*, vol. 1, *President McKinley and the Coming of War, 1898* (New Brunswick, NJ: Transaction Publishers, 2006), 66–98, notes that these appointments assumed that competence necessary for public administration was proven through prior experience in business or politics, or both.
18. Ibid., 66–98.
19. Justin Rex, "The President's War Agenda: A Rhetorical View," *Presidential Studies Quarterly* 41, no. 1 (2010): 98–100.

20. Elizabeth V. Burt, *The Progressive Era: Primary Documents on Events from 1890 to 1914* (Westport, CT: Greenwood Press, 2004), 104.

21. Hearst and Pulitzer competed to increase circulation through sensational stories, a practice that came to be known as "yellow journalism," after the yellow ink that was used in some political cartoons. Hearst supported U.S. involvement to help the Cuban rebels and used his papers, especially the *New York Journal*, to promote the cause. The competition for readers through lurid, sensationalist reporting is often credited with having pushed President McKinley into the war with Spain. However, this practice was largely in the competition of papers in New York City and probably was not a major influence on national public opinion. W. Joseph Campbell, *Yellow Journalism: Puncturing the Myths, Defining the Legacies* (Westport, CT: Praeger Press, 2003), 97–140.

22. McKinley's call for 125,000 volunteers was quickly filled, including the Rough Rider regiment organized by Theodore Roosevelt after the future president resigned his post as assistant secretary of the navy. The Spanish fleet in Manila harbor was destroyed by U.S. forces led by Admiral John Dewey on May 1, 1898. With Spain's Pacific fleet decimated, the United States could focus on the fight in the Caribbean. Accordingly, Spain's Caribbean fleet was destroyed two months later on July 3. By the end of July, U.S. troops had defeated Spanish ground forces in Cuba and the nearby island of Puerto Rico. The Philippines were next taken on August 3, and an armistice with Spain was signed on August 12.

23. Congressional opponents to the annexation of Cuba attached the Teller Amendment, requiring Cuban independence, to the 1898 resolution authorizing military action in Cuba. The Platt Amendment (attached to a 1901 military appropriations bill) required that the Cuban government not allow other nations to infringe on its independence or use the country as a military base. The amendment also required Cuba to allow the U.S. to intervene if necessary to protect Cuba and U.S. interests and to allow the U.S. to lease land for military bases (leading to the establishment of the perpetual lease for the U.S. military base at Guantanamo Bay). The Platt Amendment requirements ended through mutual agreement in 1934. U.S. State Department, Office of the Historian, "Milestones: 1899–1813; The United States, Cuba, and the Platt Amendment, 1901," accessed May 27, 2015, https://history.state.gov/milestones/1899–1913/platt.

24. Burt, *The Progressive Era*, 110–125.

25. Steven G. Calabresi and Christopher S. Yoo, *The Unitary Executive: Presidential Power from Washington to Bush* (New Haven, CT: Yale University Press, 2008), 236–237.

26. Marinski, *William McKinley*, 105–106.

27. The term *Insular Cases* is generally considered to include DeLima v. Bidwell, 182 U.S. 1 (1901), Downes v. Bidwell, 182 U.S. 244 (1901), Dooley v. United States, 182 U.S. 222 (1901), Goetze v. United States, 182 U.S. 221 (1901), Armstrong v. United States, 182 U.S. 243 (1901), and Huus v. New York & Porto Rico Steamship Co., 182 U.S. 392 (1901).

28. Thomas. C. Sutton, "'Insular Cases," in *Historical Dictionary of the Gilded Age*, ed. Leonard Schlup and James G. Ryan (Armonk, NY: M.E. Sharpe, 2003), 250.

29. *Downes*, 182 U.S. at 249 (quoting U.S. Const. art. I, § 8).

30. *Dooley v. United States* also challenged the Foraker Act concerning application of the export clause in Article I, Section 9, of the Constitution, which provided that "no Tax

or Duty shall be laid on any articles exported from any State." The question was, again, whether Puerto Rico had the same constitutional status as that of a state. If so, the Foraker Act would be unconstitutional. The case was decided five to four, with Justice Brown again writing for the majority that Puerto Rico was not the equivalent of a state and therefore was not subject to the limitation of Article I, Section 9. Thus, Congress could levy a tariff on this territory. Erik M. Jensen, *The Export Clause*, 6 Fla. Tax Rev. 1 (2003).

31. *Downes* at 286–287.
32. Daniel Schirmer and Stephen Rosskamm Shalom, eds., *The Philippines Reader: A History of Colonialism, Neocolonialism, Dictatorship, and Resistance* (Brooklyn, NY: South End Press, 1987), 22–23.
33. United States v. E.C. Knight Co., 156 U.S. 1 (1895).
34. The Court handed down a similar ruling in 1899 in United States v. Addyston Pipe and Steel Co., 175 U.S. 211 (1899).
35. Lewis L. Gould, *The Presidency of William McKinley* (Lawrence: University Press of Kansas, 1980), 162–164.
36. See also Quentin R. Skrabec Jr., *William McKinley: Apostle of Protectionism* (New York: Algora Publishing, 2008), 166–167, 247–248.
37. Calabresi and Yoo, *The Unitary Executive*, 237.
38. New York Republican leader Tom Platt supported Roosevelt for the national ticket to get Roosevelt out of New York politics.
39. Skrabec, *William McKinley: Apostle of Protectionism*, 168–173.
40. Ibid., 176–177. A detailed examination of the life of Leon Czolgosz in the context of the McKinley presidency is provided in Scott Miller, *The President and the Assassin* (New York: Random House, 2011).
41. Miller, *The President and the Assassin*, 318.
42. Ibid., 332.

# PART VI

# The Progressive Era

# 26

# Theodore Roosevelt

WILLIAM D. BADER

*President Teddy Roosevelt was a colorful leader who had been a boxer as a young man and took a free-swinging, pugilistic approach to the presidency. A dedicated Progressive, he pushed through important initiatives like the Panama Canal plan by dint of sheer willpower and devoted much of his career seeking to whittle down the Supreme Court (and his own appointee Oliver Wendell Holmes), which he believed was using its judicial powers to undermine his Progressive agenda. Roosevelt went out fighting on these issues—yet he never achieved many of his Progressive goals (including neutering the federal courts) that had energized him while he was in office.*

# Introduction

P resident Theodore Roosevelt regarded the Constitution as a stubborn obstacle to overcome in the fight for his Progressive political agenda. In this respect, he was the forerunner of his distant cousin Franklin D. Roosevelt and other "imperial presidents."

Theodore "Teddy" Roosevelt Jr. was born on October 27, 1858, into an old and aristocratic New York family.[1] His father, Theodore Roosevelt Sr., was independently wealthy and spent most of his time pursuing good works in New York City.[2]

Young Roosevelt was deeply influenced by his father.[3] A special bond was created between the two because of the boy's severe asthma. When Teddy had breathing difficulties at night, his father would take him for long and soothing coach rides through the streets of New York City.[4] After the sickly child turned twelve, his father built him a gymnasium, arranged for boxing lessons, and gave him the advice that inspired young Roosevelt to pursue a rugged life style: "You have the mind but not the body. You must make your body."[5]

Teddy loved books, particularly volumes of natural science and history. In pursuit of the former interest, he always kept a large menagerie in his room.[6]

Young Theodore Roosevelt entered Harvard College with the ambition of becoming a scientist. When he learned that science then involved lab work, rather than field work in a natural environment, he gave up on that dream.[7] Nevertheless, he thrived in Harvard's liberal arts milieu and graduated Phi Beta Kappa in June 1880.[8]

After Harvard College, Theodore Roosevelt enrolled in Columbia University School of Law, where he spent less than two years.[9] His attitude toward the law, which later characterized his presidency, became manifest at this time. He was impatient with technical legal concepts and legal reasoning and concluded that the law, through lawyers and judges, protected the privileged classes while impeding true justice for the remainder of society. Louis Auchincloss, a man of letters and the law, later wrote revealingly: "Even in his brief time at law school he [Roosevelt] had been repelled by the doctrine of caveat emptor, which flew in the teeth of what to him was the revered code of a gentleman's honor. How could any man calling himself that invoke a law to protect himself from some poor bloke to whom he had sold shoddy goods?"[10]

After quitting law school, Roosevelt immediately embarked on a career in politics.[11] Impatient and feisty, Roosevelt viewed the political arena as one where he could effect dramatic results quickly without the burden (as he saw it) of legal formalities. Roosevelt's political perspective was that of a Progressive. James W. Ely Jr. has described the essence of the Progressive philosophy to which Roosevelt subscribed as follows:

> Their primary concern . . . was the imbalance of power associated with the new economic order. They accepted private property and market ordering as the basis for the economy but attempted to mitigate the abuses and harshness of industrialization. To achieve such goals Progressives insisted on more active involvement by the state and federal governments in the economy to control corporate enterprise and to improve conditions in the industrial workplace. . . . [Progressives] challenged the prevailing con-stitutional norms that stressed limited government and entrepreneurial liberty.[12]

Roosevelt rose impressively in politics while instituting Progressive reforms, making the political branches of government bigger and more powerful at the expense of constitutionalized economic liberty in particu-lar and the judiciary in general.[13] In 1881, he was elected to the New York State Assembly as its youngest member. Then, in an amazing twenty-year span, he served in a remarkable number of influential positions: U.S. Civil Service commissioner (1889–1895); president of the New York City Board of Police Commissioners (1895–1897); assistant secretary of the navy under President McKinley (1897–1898); war hero during the Spanish-American War (leading a courageous charge on San Juan Hill while he was com-mander of the First U.S. Volunteer Cavalry, also known as the Rough Riders); governor of New York (1898–1900); vice president of the United States (1900–1901); and, upon the assassination of McKinley in September 1901, president of the United States.[14]

## Presidency

After his unexpected swearing-in as president in 1901 and his own victory for a full term in the White House from 1904 to 1908, Roosevelt worked feverishly to increase the power of the presidency. His success is evidenced by a legacy of powerful chief executives since his time, up through the modern era.

## Conservation

Roosevelt is widely considered the first president to advance the conservation movement, firmly believing that it was the federal government's obligation to preserve and carefully manage the nation's resources. Deeply committed to this Progressive cause, he used his presidential powers to create national forests, national parks, and wildlife refuges, and he formed the U.S. Forestry Service, appointing Gifford Pinchot, a forester and committed conservationist, as its first chief. In 1906, Roosevelt signed into law the Antiquities Act, which gave the president the authority to designate and set aside public areas as national monuments by executive order and eventually led to the creation of the National Park Service in 1916.[15]

## The Removal Power

In the Supreme Court case of *Shurtleff v. United States*, decided in 1903, the Roosevelt administration took the opportunity to argue strongly for broad presidential power of removal. The administration maintained that the president could remove an executive branch official for any reason from an office to which the president had appointed the person, even though an act of Congress specified that this official could be removed only for "inefficiency, neglect of duty, or malfeasance in office."[16] This issue had haunted presidents since Andrew Johnson had been impeached for ignoring the Tenure of Office Act and for removing Secretary of War Edwin M. Stanton without permission of Congress. In *Shurtleff*, an individual in 1890 had been appointed by the president, with the advice and consent of the Senate, to the office of "general appraiser of merchandise." He was thereafter removed by Roosevelt's predecessor, President McKinley, in 1899. Shurtleff's office did not have a fixed term of years. No specific grounds were given for the removal. Now, Roosevelt and his administration strongly endorsed the power of the president to make such decisions in removing executive officers—particularly those without fixed terms—even without the approval of Congress. The opinion of the Supreme Court obligingly construed the statute broadly with a presumption in favor of a constitutionally strong president. Justice Rufus Peckham wrote:

> In making removal from office it must be assumed that the President acts with reference to his constitutional duty to take care that the laws are faithfully executed, and we think it would be a mistaken view to hold that the mere specification in the statute of some causes for removal thereby excluded the right of the President to remove for any other reason which he, acting with a due sense of his official responsibility, should think sufficient.[17]

Thus, Roosevelt helped to shore up an important, previously disputed power of the president to remove executive branch appointees, paving the way for future chief executives to assert even broader authority in this domain.[18]

## Foreign Policy

Roosevelt also believed in a positive and expansive constitutional role for the chief executive in foreign policy matters.[19] His interventions in Colombia to incite a Panamanian revolution represented the high point of this philosophy.

Roosevelt determined that a Latin American canal route was essential to U.S. national security because it would permit U.S. naval vessels to move strategically from the Atlantic to the Pacific (or vice versa) in three weeks instead of three months.[20] However, his attempts to negotiate with Colombia to permit such a canal were proceeding slowly, hampered by poor communications.[21] He therefore helped Panama to revolt and to declare its independence from Colombia. The exact methods he used in this affair remain murky.[22]

On November 3, 1903, Roosevelt recognized an independent Panama and paid it to cede a Panama Canal Zone to the United States. The Roosevelt Corollary to the Monroe Doctrine, introduced in 1904 and approved by the Senate in 1907, codified such presidential interventions in the domestic affairs of sovereign states in Latin America and the Caribbean.[23] Thus, Roosevelt interpreted his powers broadly in the area of foreign affairs, laid the foundation for the Panama Canal through his tenacious efforts, and helped create an image of the United States as a world power.

## Upholding the Sherman Anti-Trust Act

Another test of the president's power came a year after the United States secured control of the Panama Canal Zone. The Northern Securities Co., a holding company, was established to purchase and control the stock of the competing Northern Pacific Railway Company and the Great Northern Railway Co. President Roosevelt placed a high priority on putting teeth into the weakly drafted Sherman Anti-Trust Act by prosecuting the Northern Securities Co. for behaving in an anticompetitive fashion.[24]

In *Northern Securities Co. v. United States*, the Supreme Court agreed with the Roosevelt administration. In a plurality opinion authored by Justice John Marshall Harlan, the Court ended up increasing the power of the federal government, including the "imperial presidency," at the expense of states' rights and individual economic liberties. Holding broadly for the U.S. government, Justice Harlan declared that maintaining competition was the intent of the Sherman Anti-Trust Act and that the federal government could prosecute the purchasers (i.e., the Northern Securities Co.) of stock shares of the competing railroads. Thus, the Court for the first time held that the Sherman Anti-Trust Act, broadly construed in this fashion, was within Congress's constitutional power under the Commerce Clause.[25]

There were two dissenting opinions. One of these was authored by Theodore Roosevelt's first Supreme Court appointee, Justice Oliver Wendell Holmes, who minced no words in arguing that the statute did not extend to the purchase of the railroad stock in this case.[26] Holmes took aim at the majority opinion (and indirectly at the Roosevelt administration's position): "If such a remote result of the exercise of an ordinary incident of property and personal freedom is enough to make that exercise unlawful, there is hardly any transaction concerning commerce between the states that may not be made a crime by the finding of a jury or a court."[27]

President Roosevelt had appointed Holmes to the Supreme Court in 1902. As with his other two Supreme Court appointees, William R. Day (1903) and William H. Moody (1906), Roosevelt had been persuaded that Holmes would use his seat primarily to further the administration's Progressive agenda. Roosevelt's Square Deal domestic program involved protecting the public from detrimental business practices by permitting vigorous government regulation of big business.[28] To accomplish this goal, TR needed the help of the Supreme Court, including his appointee Holmes. Although the president was satisfied with Justices Day and Moody, he regarded Holmes as a colossal mistake. After Holmes issued his *Northern Securities* dissent, an angry President Roosevelt railed against the justice: "I could carve a better judge out of a banana." Holmes, dismissive of the president, told friends: "What the boys like about Roosevelt is that he doesn't give a damn about the law!"[29]

Roosevelt had made a disastrous, but common, error in evaluating Holmes as a potential Supreme Court justice: The president had viewed him through political, rather than lawyerly, eyes. President Roosevelt had been impressed by the Progressive nature of the legislation Holmes had upheld as a member of the Supreme Judicial Court of Massachusetts.[30] Yet it had never occurred to the president that Holmes loathed the Progressive agenda.[31] Rather, Holmes was a scrupulous legal methodologist, a practitioner of judicial restraint who upheld legislation when he believed it was constitutionally defensible, regardless of which political team supported it.

### The Lochner Decision

*Lochner v. New York*, the soon-to-be vilified decision handed down in 1905, was another huge setback for politicians with a Progressive agenda. It made Theodore Roosevelt even angrier at the Supreme Court and the judiciary generally (though his appointees, Holmes and Day, dissented). In *Lochner*, Justice Rufus Peckham held for the majority that a New York statute prohibiting bakery employees from working more than ten hours per day or sixty hours per week was unconstitutional. In doing so, Justice Peckham found that this Progressive exercise of state police power violated an implied liberty of contract guaranteed under a substantive reading of the Due Process Clause of the Fourteenth Amendment.[32]

President Roosevelt and his fellow Progressives became furious that this abstract concept of "substantive due process"—which appeared nowhere in the words of the Constitution—had been used to block a public health measure and threatened to disrupt their reform agenda consisting of laws they believed were in the public interest. Indeed, "Lochnerism" was swiftly, but controversially, equated with conservative activist judges who legislated from the bench to protect entrenched economic interests.[33]

President Roosevelt, the committed Progressive and the statist reformer, became even more impatient and angry with the judiciary, an unelected branch of government that was standing in the way of what he strongly believed was best for the country. Justice Holmes's lack of dependability and the property-protecting majority on the "*Lochner* Court" eventually became unbearable to Roosevelt.[34]

Remarkably, President Roosevelt went so far as to question and criticize the very basis of Article III, the judicial article of the Constitution. He questioned the judiciary as an institution and began a campaign to redefine it completely. As president, he "tucked . . . criticisms of the Court into lengthy Presidential messages" so he would not offend too many "Republican Old Guardsmen." Yet criticize he did.[35]

Nonetheless, TR did not remain in the White House long enough to make good on his goal of whittling down the judicial branch, though he never stopped trying. In 1908, after having reluctantly decided to leave office to keep an old pledge that he would only run for one additional term after filling McKinley's unexpired term, Roosevelt groomed William Howard Taft as his successor and worked diligently and successfully to get him elected.

## Post-Presidency

After going on a lengthy safari to Africa with his son Kermit, TR slowly turned on the Taft administration and his old protégé. He also turned up his criticisms of the judiciary. Roosevelt began to publicly campaign against Article III, in effect, with an eye toward the next presidential election. He defended his radical legal positions against conservative criticism by claiming that his appointee, Justice William H. Moody, had directly influenced his thinking.[36] In an essay in *The Outlook*, TR advocated a rather extreme plan to permit popular elections to nullify unpopular judicial precedents. In a 1912 speech, he urged: "When a judge decides a constitutional question, when he decides what the people as a whole can and cannot do, the people should have the right to recall that decision if they think that it is wrong."[37] Roosevelt further advocated popular elections to remove judges, including federal judges appointed for life under Article III of the Constitution, if they impeded the will of the public at any particular time.[38]

His successor and now rival, President William Howard Taft, who later served as chief justice of the United States, put it well in response, summing up Roosevelt's disregard for the Constitution in stinging words: "One who so lightly regards constitutional principles, and especially the independence of the judiciary, one who is naturally so impatient of legal restraints, and due legal procedure, and who has so misunderstood what liberty regulated by law is, could not be safely endorsed with successive presidential terms."[39]

Indeed, Roosevelt's disagreements with Taft over the judiciary, his general frustrations with Taft's cautiously Progressive record, and his substantial ego caused Roosevelt to decide to challenge the sitting president for the 1912 Republican nomination.

The Republican Convention in June was a bitterly contentious event. Roosevelt had trounced Taft in the newly created popular primaries, proving that he still had public support. However, at the convention—which was dominated by party leaders—Roosevelt and his Progressive Republicans lost to Taft's "Old Guard" by a solid margin of 550 to 450.[40] As a result, Roosevelt and his supporters angrily left the convention, alleging dirty tactics. They formed the new Progressive Party (otherwise known as the Bull Moose Party) and nominated Roosevelt for president at their August convention.[41]

During the general election campaign, the cantankerous Roosevelt was shot in the chest at a Milwaukee event, but refused medical assistance until he had completed his 1½-hour speech. Despite such heroic efforts, Roosevelt only managed to split the Republican vote with Taft and to come in second to the Democrat Woodrow Wilson.[42]

## Conclusion

Once again a private citizen, Teddy Roosevelt sought out new challenges. In 1913, he led a scientific expedition to the Brazilian jungle. There he mapped an unexplored river located in the roughest terrain, the River of Doubt. He also contracted malaria and dysentery and suffered with an infected leg. True to form, Roosevelt persevered and was carried out at mission's end weighing fifty-seven pounds less than when he started. He never fully regained his robust health.[43]

In August 1914, when war broke out in Europe, Roosevelt expressed disdain for President Wilson's neutral stance in the conflict.[44] In 1917, after the continued belligerence of Germany left the reluctant Wilson no alternative but to ask Congress to declare war, Roosevelt immediately asked Wilson's permission to lead a brigade against the Germans. Wilson refused, most likely because he did not wish to make his old rival a hero.[45]

Roosevelt was heartbroken when three of his four sons were wounded in the World War I effort in Europe and when the fourth, Quentin, was killed.[46] Depressed and seriously ill, Theodore Roosevelt passed away in his sleep on January 6, 1919. Son Archie wired his surviving brothers: "The old lion is dead."[47]

Joseph "Uncle Joe" Cannon, Speaker of the U.S. House of Representatives during TR's presidency, had summed up Teddy Roosevelt's constitutional legacy by declaring: "Roosevelt's all right, but he's got no more use for the Constitution than a tomcat has for a marriage license."[48] Teddy Roosevelt was impatient with legal requirements and constitutional impediments to his Progressive agenda. He charged forward and won victories on the domestic and foreign affairs fronts through a free-swinging, pugilistic view of the presidency. Yet his dominance over the American political scene was cut short, in part because—like most fighters—he eventually lost his edge to a new generation of political contenders.

## NOTES

1. Aida D. Donald, *Lion in the White House: A Life of Theodore Roosevelt* (New York: Basic Books, 2008), 2.
2. Louis Auchincloss, *Theodore Roosevelt* (New York: Henry Holt and Company, 2002), 9.
3. Donald, *Lion in the White House*, 3.
4. H. W. Brands, *T.R.: The Last Romantic* (New York: Basic Books, 1997), 10–11.
5. Donald, *Lion in the White House*, 15–16.
6. Ibid., 12–13.
7. Ibid., 25.
8. Ibid., 33.
9. Ibid., 34–35.
10. Auchincloss, *Theodore Roosevelt*, 54.
11. Ibid., 15.
12. James W. Ely Jr., *The Fuller Court: Justices, Rulings, and Legacy* (Santa Barbara, CA: ABC-CLIO, 2003), 10.
13. Donald, *Lion in the White House*, 40–43.
14. John Allen Gable, ed., *The Man in the Arena: Speeches and Essays by Theodore Roosevelt* (Oyster Bay, NY: Theodore Roosevelt Association, 1987), 4.
15. U.S. National Park Service, "Theodore Roosevelt: The Father of Conservation," accessed August 23, 2014, www.nps.gov/aboutus/history.htm.
16. Shurtleff v. United States, 189 U.S. 311, 313–314 (1903).
17. Ibid., 317.
18. See Myers v. United States, 272 U.S. 52 (1926), discussed in Chapter 30, "Calvin Coolidge."
19. Donald, *Lion in the White House*, 163.

20. Ibid.,160.

21. See generally David McCullough, *The Path Between the Seas: The Creation of the Panama Canal, 1870–1914* (New York: Simon & Schuster, 1977).

22. Ibid., 160–161.

23. Ibid., 158–159.

24. Northern Securities Co. v. United States, 193 U.S. 197 (1904).

25. Ibid., 342, 359–360. Roosevelt won another victory in Swift & Co. v. United States, 196 U.S. 375 (1905), in which the Supreme Court upheld the ability of Congress to regulate and dismantle the Beef Trust (a conspiracy by six leading meatpackers to fix prices), pursuant to its Commerce Clause powers.

26. *Northern Securities*, 193 U. S. 197 at 403–404. The other dissent was by Justice Edward Douglass White. Holmes and White concurred in each other's opinions, and Chief Justice Melville Fuller and Justice Rufus Peckham also concurred in both dissents.

27. Ibid., 403.

28. Paul M. Rego, *American Ideal: Theodore Roosevelt's Search for American Individualism* (Lanham, MD: Lexington Books, 2008), 97.

29. Auchincloss, *Theodore Roosevelt*, 53.

30. Donald, *Lion in the White House*, 167.

31. Auchincloss, *Theodore Roosevelt*, 54.

32. Lochner v. New York, 198 U.S. 45, 64–65 (1905).

33. David E. Bernstein, *Rehabilitating Lochner: Defending Individual Rights Against Progressive Reform* (Chicago: University of Chicago Press, 2011), 23. More recently, however, legal scholars like James W. Ely Jr. and David E. Bernstein have reevaluated the standard account of *Lochner*. They conclude essentially that *Lochner* was a vindication of individual rights against statist dictates. Bernstein argues persuasively that the hours legislation at issue in *Lochner* was, in reality, championed by the bakery union to shut down small nonunion establishments employing immigrant workers. Ibid.; Ely, *The Fuller Court*, 110–111. Ironically, it was Theodore Roosevelt's distant cousin, President Franklin D. Roosevelt, who orchestrated the dismantling of the *Lochner* decision to push through his New Deal agenda. After FDR proposed the "Court Packing Plan" that would add additional justices to the Supreme Court as a transparent means of shifting the balance in favor of New Deal legislation, the Court altered its position and overruled the *Lochner* line of cases. West Coast Hotel Co. v. Parrish, 300 U.S. 379 (1937); Robert G. McClosky, *The American Supreme Court* (Chicago: University of Chicago Press, 1960), 161–169, 174–179.

34. John Milton Cooper Jr., *The Warrior and the Priest: Woodrow Wilson and Theodore Roosevelt* (Cambridge, MA: Harvard University Press, 1983), 150.

35. Ibid.

36. Ibid.

37. Talmage Boston, "Theodore Roosevelt and the Law," *Texas Bar Journal* 74 (2011): 512.

38. Ibid.

39. Ibid.

40. Donald, *Lion in the White House*, 249–250.

41. Ibid., 250–251.

42. Ibid., 252–254.

43. See generally Candice Millard, *Theodore Roosevelt's Darkest Journey: The River of Doubt* (New York: Anchor Books, 2005).

44. Donald, *Lion in the White House*, 257.

45. Millard, *The River of Doubt*, 342.

46. Ibid., 342–343.

47. Brands, *T.R.: The Last Romantic*, 811.

48. Donald, *Lion in the White House*, 207.

# 27

# William Howard Taft

FRANCINE SANDERS ROMERO

*William Howard Taft adopted a conservative view of presidential power in stark contrast to the feisty and (in Taft's view) dangerous activism of his predecessor, Theodore Roosevelt. A stickler for strict adherence to the Constitution, Taft helped steer through the Sixteenth Amendment to permit a variety of federal income taxes, so that Congress would not cut corners in adopting Progressive-era reforms. He also initially vetoed the bill granting statehood to New Mexico and Arizona, believing that the latter's proposed state constitution contained unconstitutional defects. Although Taft lasted only one term, he became the first and only former president to thereafter serve on the Supreme Court, building as chief justice a sterling legacy that eclipsed his record as president.*

## Introduction

William Howard Taft's path to the U.S. presidency in 1909, in retrospect, appears logical and measured. Born in 1857, and raised in Cincinnati, he came from lawyerly stock. Both his grandfather and father were attorneys, his father serving in President Grant's cabinet and as ambassador to Austria and Russia. After working steadily to obtain his undergraduate degree at Yale and while earning a law degree at Cincinnati Law School, Taft launched a career of increasing stature and visibility in the fields of law and government. With only one slightly out-of-the-ordinary job as a reporter during his law school years, he rose from his first appointed position as assistant prosecutor of Hamilton County, Ohio, in 1880 to a state judgeship in 1887 and then to solicitor general of the United States in 1890. From there, higher-profile appointments followed. Taft became a judge on the federal bench in 1892, dean of his alma mater law school in 1896, and head of the Governing Commission of the Philippines in 1901. After turning down a U.S. Supreme Court appointment from President Theodore Roosevelt in 1902, Taft accepted the position as secretary of war, which he held from 1904 to 1908. In that closing year, Taft won the presidency, defeating Democratic nominee William Jennings Bryan.

Taft's well-documented, conservative approach to governance was undoubtedly a product of an educational and professional background almost fully dominated by the practice and implementation of law. Yet Taft's philosophy of power has been too readily underestimated as the mere passive counterpart to Teddy Roosevelt's activism, which focused on increasing the scope and strength of presidential authority. Although the restrained executive may not draw the same level of excitement as the pacesetter president, the former role—embodied by President Taft—perhaps accurately reflects the importance of the rule of law and deliberate approach to policy making evident in the nation's founding documents. Taft firmly believed that the president may legitimately act only if a law or the Constitution specifically grants such authority in clear terms. In sharp contrast, Roosevelt held that an executive who governed by such a restrained view was either "high-minded and wrong-headed or merely infirm of purpose."[1]

Roosevelt believed that the will of the people could only be carried out through an energetic commitment to action. Taft's rejection of Roosevelt's approach was largely fostered by his deeply held respect for the rule of law. Yet there was more to his different perspective than that. As Taft explained in a speech delivered several years after leaving office, not only did he consider Roosevelt's approach illegal, but he also found its implications potentially dangerous. Taft was not particularly concerned with the possibility of an unpopular president's pushing the limits of authority, since the lack of public support would impel Congress to counter the executive's moves. Rather, it was the well-liked and admired president—Taft believed—who was to be most feared. He explained that a president became dangerous "when his popularity is such that he can be sure of the support of the electorate and therefore of Congress, and when the majority in the legislative halls respond with alacrity and sycophancy to his will."[2] This sort of situation could undermine the infrastructure of democracy to which the checks and balances of governmental authority are crucial. The primary constitutional challenge for Taft as president was to continue, and even expand, the Progressive reforms that the public had come to expect, while remaining true to that view of the law and Constitution.

## Presidency

### Ongoing Battle against Trusts

Continuing, and even expanding upon, one of Roosevelt's signature causes, President Taft continued to battle trusts and corporate monopolies that he thought distorted bedrock principles of the free market. Two cases in particular, *Standard Oil Company v. U.S.* and *U.S. v. American Tobacco Company*, were decided well into Taft's administration and were significant in upholding the 1890 Sherman Anti-Trust Act. These decisions found that Standard Oil and American Tobacco, two giants that had cornered their respective markets, were guilty of illegal and monopolies.[3]

Nonetheless, the business community held on to a strong sentiment that the government simply had no legal authority to disrupt commerce in this way. On this point, President Taft was not to be swayed.[4] An opinion he had written when he served on the Circuit Court of Appeals for the Sixth Circuit had already made his sentiment on this matter clear: "If this extends federal jurisdiction into fields not before occupied by the general government, it is not because such jurisdiction is not within the limits allowed by the Constitution of the United States."[5] While control of monopolies might have been seen, legitimately, as a key part of Roosevelt's reform agenda, Taft considered it not so much politically but legally justified. For Taft, Congress had every right to enact this piece of legislation and the courts had an obligation to uphold it, thus adding a layer of formality and severity to this question that had been absent in Roosevelt's much more flexible approach.

Taft's position, however, did not always prevail in the High Court, and the most notable example helped spur a lasting rift between Taft and Theodore Roosevelt. A major antitrust suit filed by the Taft administration against U.S. Steel in 1911 suggested that Roosevelt had been wrong in agreeing with the corporation's 1907 argument that its acquisition of the Tennessee Coal, Iron and Railroad Company was not a Sherman Act violation. In turn, an incensed Roosevelt wrote an editorial in the *Outlook*, sharply questioning the wisdom of the suit. When the case was finally decided a decade later in 1921, the U.S. Supreme Court rejected the Taft administration's argument, finding no evidence of a monopoly and no public interest in corporate dissolution, thereby vindicating Roosevelt's position.[6] Thus, as Taft continued to wage his war on increasingly powerful trusts and corporations, he made some enemies in the process.

## The Progressive Agenda: Conservation

The broad narrative of Taft's challenges in accommodating various popular reforms was fairly consistent. The primary question was generally whether a specific policy or proposed governmental action was justified by the law and the Constitution. If not, either it was rejected out of hand or, Taft believed, a legal or constitutional amendment had to be considered.

Part of the Progressive cause related to conservation of natural resources. Teddy Roosevelt had tried to ram through conservationist reforms by executive order under the theory that "the President is the steward of the public welfare," a tactic that had rankled Congress.[7] Taft took a different approach. In 1909, he wrote to California Congressman William Kent, a noted conservationist, describing the approach: "We have a government of limited power under the Constitution, and we have got to work out our problems on the basis of law."[8] Taft therefore asked Congress for legislation that would allow him to "withdraw" certain public lands for conservation—an approach that gained Congress's approval.[9] Yet some conservationists complained that Taft's deferential approach neutered the executive branch and left too much to the legislature.[10]

## Income Tax

Taft had come to believe that new sources of government revenue were crucial to the economic health of the nation and to deal with growing federal deficits. Import duties alone, Taft believed, would not provide the necessary amounts. Although there was general disagreement about whether the Constitution prohibited such a federal income tax, the U.S. Supreme Court had ruled in *Pollock v. Farmers' Loan and Trust Company* (1895) that such a tax was unconstitutional.[11] Specifically, *Pollock* held invalid a national tax on personal income flowing from real estate investments, rents, and stocks and bonds. The government had argued that Congress had the power to enact the Income Tax Act of 1894, pursuant to Congress's broadly stated power in Article I, Section 8, of the Constitution to "lay and collect Taxes, Duties, Imports and Excises, to pay the Debts and provide for the common Defence and general Welfare of the United States."[12] Yet the Court rejected that argument. While acknowledging that Congress's power to tax was extensive, the Court pointed to other constitutional provisions that limited the federal government's power to impose "direct taxes."[13] Article I, Section 2, Clause 3, instructs: "Representatives and direct Taxes shall be apportioned among the several States . . . according to their respective numbers." Article I, Section 9, further states: "No Capitation, or other direct, tax shall be laid unless in Proportion to the Census."[14] Finding that the income tax was a "direct" tax within the meaning of Article I, Section 2, and that Congress failed to allocate the tax burden among the states on the basis of population, the Court concluded that the tax ran afoul of the Constitution's apportionment requirement.[15]

For President Taft, the only appropriate course of action after the *Pollock* decision was to initiate the constitutional amendment process set forth in Article V, rather than simply to hope that the Court might change its mind. In his 1909 address to Congress on the matter, Taft recommended this strategy not simply because it seemed more efficient and sure, but because of the implications of the alternative to governmental legitimacy: "For the Congress to assume that the Court will reverse itself, and to enact legislation on such an assumption, will not strengthen popular confidence in the stability of judicial construction of the Constitution."[16]

On July 12, 1909, Congress passed a resolution proposing the Sixteenth Amendment to the Constitution, permitting the legislature to levy a federal income tax. The language of the resolution was specifically approved by Taft in advance.[17] Three years later, the Sixteenth Amendment was ratified by the states. Thus, Taft accomplished a major policy victory by adhering to the constitutional processes and guiding through an amendment that gave Congress great latitude to adopt a wide array of federal income taxes.

## Admitting New States

Another proposed reform, however, met with Taft's unyielding resistance. In 1911, Taft vetoed the act granting statehood to both New Mexico and Arizona.[18] He focused on a provision in the latter's state constitution that allowed for judicial recall, a practice that he considered antithetical to basic democratic principles.[19] Although some Progressives championed an array of measures putatively designed to bring more accountability to the judicial branch at all levels of government, President Taft viewed the judicial-recall provision as "injurious to the cause of free government."

Here, Taft could not simply point to a constitutional provision that Arizona had violated. He admitted as much in his veto message: "A mere difference of opinion as to the wisdom of details in a state constitution ought not to lead me to set up my opinion against that of the people of the territory." Yet Taft went on to ground his objection on a more abstract premise of a free versus tyrannical government. He said that the measure would lead to an unrestrained majority rule—allowing an iron fist to govern the judicial branch, which was meant to remain independent of external political pressure—with no built-in structure to defend minority rights.[20]

After the offensive recall provision was removed, Taft signed separate bills in 1912 making New Mexico the forty-seventh state and Arizona the forty-eighth. Arizona citizens, however, later placed the judicial-recall provision back into their state constitution, getting the last word.

## Post-Presidency

Taft's limited fluency in the art of politics became apparent in the election of 1912, when he lost the presidency to Democrat Woodrow Wilson, while also battling Theodore Roosevelt's third-party candidacy—representing the new Bull Moose Party—which Roosevelt had established after failing to wrest the Republican nomination from Taft. After winning the Republican nomination in June, President Taft declared relief that "a most serious menace to our republican institutions has been averted" and that "whatever may happen in November, a great victory for the Republican Party and the people of the United States has already been won."[21] Once it became a three-way race, Taft was much more concerned about the consequences of losing to Roosevelt than to Wilson, since Taft's views had now moved so far from those of his predecessor. Yet in November, Taft's traditionalist approach relegated him to a third-place finish in both electoral and popular votes, behind the victor Wilson and the second-place Roosevelt.

Upon leaving office, Taft accepted a law professorship at Yale, which he referred to as "a dignified retirement," where he hoped to impart his restrained philosophy of law to students.[22] His teaching career ended, however, when he was appointed chief justice of the United States by President Warren G. Harding in 1921. In this position, so well suited to his overall approach to conservative governance, Taft shone as chief justice, earning a broad regard that had often eluded him as president.

As chief justice, Taft sought to build consensus on the Supreme Court, but wrote relatively few majority decisions, preferring to assign those to one of the associate justices. The majority opinions he did write often picked up the thread of his circumscribed but robust view of executive power.[23] In one of Taft's most sweeping interpretations of presidential power, perhaps inspired by his own time in the White House, he wrote the landmark decision in *Myers v. U.S.*[24] This case involved a postmaster who had been removed by President Wilson in contravention of a federal statute that provided that such officials could only be removed with the "advice and consent" of the Senate. Taft concluded that the president had exclusive power under the "vesting clause" of Article II, Section 1, to remove executive branch officials—even though the appointment of officials like the postmaster could only take place with the advice and consent of the Senate. With this decision, Chief Justice Taft endorsed a surprisingly expansive view of the un-enumerated powers of the president—a view largely at odds with his strict interpretation of presidential power under the Constitution, as espoused during his time as chief executive. Thus, *Myers* seems to provide a window into Taft's constitutional philosophy relating to the presidency, as much as any actions that he took while serving in the White House.

In one of his few dissenting opinions, in the 1923 case of *Adkins v. Children's Hospital*, Taft displayed the narrower yet definitely Progressive tendencies evidenced during his presidency.[25] In keeping with his belief that the U.S. Constitution did allow for vigorous government action in some areas, he respectfully but sharply disagreed with the majority's decision to strike down the District of Columbia's minimum-wage law for women and children. Rather, Taft supported the Progressive law as an appropriate use of the police power to protect these less powerful workers. In doing so, he rejected the notion that the law violated an implied right to contract that flowed from the Due Process Clause of the Fourteenth Amendment.[26]

Taft's leadership as chief justice extended to his active support of new legislation that would give the justices greater discretion over which cases to hear.[27] He also led the push for a new U.S. Supreme Court building, which was ultimately approved in 1929 and completed in 1935, to replace the Court's cramped quarters within the Capitol Building.

Taft continued to work on this project until he resigned his post on February 3, 1930. He died about a month later, on March 8, from cardio-vascular disease. He was seventy-two.

## Conclusion

As a model of the American president who saw his role as constitutional and legal trustee, William Howard Taft has few rivals. Taft often employed this model to put the brakes on what could be described (at least during this era) as the runaway train of the Theodore Roosevelt presidency. For some, this was a comforting return to traditionalism. For others, it was a disappointing step back from the dynamism of his predecessor. Yet most agreed that this respect for the rule of law was the very essence of the man. Moreover, Taft carried out his charge to execute the laws and the Constitution with enthusiasm and vigor, as was evident in the careful attention he gave to his rare opportunity to appoint six U.S. Supreme Court justices.[28]

While Taft earned his reputation for a conservative approach to governance, he was not one to oppose change in all cases. This was illustrated by his important support for the Sixteenth Amendment (1913), which authorized a federal income tax, and his reluctant endorsement of the Seventeenth Amendment (1913), which provided for the direct election of U.S. senators and eliminated the practice by which senators were selected by state legislatures. (The prior method was criticized for encouraging corruption; hence, Taft finally gave his lukewarm support to this populist reform.)[29]

Yet there were limits to Taft's willingness to support change, in cases where he felt that public passions were overtaking the importance of careful consideration of the need for change. This caution informed his veto of both the New Mexico and Arizona statehood bill, because of Arizona's judicial-recall provision and, in one of his final notable acts as president in 1913, a bill requiring a literacy test for immigrants. The latter veto was a significant stand at a time when public and legislative opinion was moving toward support for more severe restrictions on newcomers.

Commentators tend to cast the Taft presidency as a failure because of the lost opportunities to actively pursue new policy initiatives. As seen from that framework, the criticism may be apt. Still, it is helpful to keep in mind the actions, evolutions, and even the principled refusals to act that mark his administration. Though a paradigm of conservatism, Taft's presidency was far from an archetype of paralysis.

## NOTES

1. Theodore Roosevelt, *An Autobiography* (New York: Charles Scribner's Sons, 1913), 362–365.

2. William Howard Taft, "Lecture on Presidential Power," *The Annals of America* (Chicago: Encyclopedia Britannica, 1968), 95.

3. United States v. American Tobacco Co., 221 U.S. 106 (1911); Standard Oil Co. v. United States, 221 U.S. 1 (1911).

4. For a detailed review of this episode, see Henry F. Pringle, *The Life and Times of William Howard Taft* (Hamden, CT: Archon Books, 1964), chap. 34.

5. United States v. Addyston Pipe and Steel Co., 85 F. 271, 301 (1898).

6. United States v. United States Steel Corp., 251 U.S. 417 (1920); see also Paolo E. Coletta, *The Presidency of William Howard Taft* (Lawrence: University Press of Kansas, 1973), 157–160.

7. Sidney M. Milkis and Michael Nelson, *The American Presidency: Origins and Development, 1776–2011*, 6th ed. (Washington, DC: CQ Press, 2012), 236–237; Michael J. Gerhardt, *The Forgotten Presidents: Their Untold Constitutional Legacy* (New York: Oxford University Press, 2013), 175–176.

8. Milkis and Nelson, *The American Presidency*, 237.

9. Ibid. See also United States v. Midwest Oil Co., 236 U.S. 456 (1915), validating President Taft's withdrawal of three million acres of oil-rich public land in California and Wyoming in 1909, before passage of the aforementioned legislation, to protect it from private extraction. The Supreme Court found that the chief executive could withdraw public lands for the good of the nation, particularly given Congress's tacit approval of this practice at that time.

10. Milkis and Nelson, *The American Presidency*, 237. Reviews of the Taft record on conservation remain mixed. See Lewis J. Gould, *The William Howard Taft Presidency* (Lawrence: University Press of Kansas, 2009), for a reasonable argument that this is an area where Taft fell short. For a somewhat alternate take, see Francine Sanders Romero,

*Presidents from Theodore Roosevelt Through Coolidge, 1901–1929* (Westport, CT: Greenwood Press, 2002).

11. Pollock v. Farmers' Loan and Trust Co., 158 U.S. 601 (1895).

12. U.S. Const. art. I., § 8.

13. *Pollock*, 158 U.S. at 640. See Erik M. Jensen, "The Apportionment of 'Direct Taxes: Are Consumption Taxes Constitutional?" *Columbia Law Review* 97 (1997): 2341.

14. U.S. Const. art. I, § 2, cl. 3, § 9. In addition to requiring the apportionment of direct taxes, the Constitution requires that so-called indirect taxes, that is, "all duties, imposts and excises," be "uniform throughout the United States." U.S. Const. art. I, § 8. See Head Money Cases, 112 U.S. 580, 594 (1884). The difference between a direct tax and an indirect tax is often murky. Direct taxes are imposed on a person's "general ownership of property." Bromley v. McCaughn, 280 U.S. 124, 136 (1929). However, excise taxes are laid "upon a particular use or enjoyment of property or the shifting from one to another of any power or privilege incidental to the ownership or enjoyment of property." Fernandez v. Wiener, 326 U.S. 340, 352 (1945).

15. *Pollock*, 158 U.S. at 637. A national income tax was first proposed by President James Madison's secretary of the treasury to help pay for the War of 1812. Congress, however, took no action on the proposal. Until the Civil War erupted, the revenue the federal government received from customs duties and sales of land was more than sufficient to finance the activities of the national government. Shelton D. Pollack, "The First National Income Tax, 1861–1872," *Tax Lawyer* 67 (2014): 312. When the expenses for the Civil War consistently exceeded federal receipts, the federal government was compelled to find additional revenue. Congress responded with the passage of an unapportioned income tax in the Revenue Act of 1861. Under that act, a flat tax of 3 percent was imposed on annual income above $800. This later turned into a graduated income tax in 1862. Ibid. In *Springer v. United States*, 102 U.S. 586, 602 (1880), the Supreme Court rejected a challenge to the constitutionality of the Civil War income tax (which had since expired in 1872), emphasizing that only capitation and land taxes were direct taxes that must be apportioned.

In *Pollock*, however, the Court departed from precedent and concluded that direct taxes were not restricted to capitation and real estate. Rather, direct taxes also encompassed levies on personal property, including stocks and bonds. *Pollock*, 158 U.S. at 618. Moreover, according to the Court, since a tax on the yield from both real and personal property was essentially no different from a tax on the property itself, it too was direct. Ibid. Thus, while *Pollock* permitted Congress to levy an income tax on earned incomes, it precluded one of the aims of the Progressive movement—to reach the accumulated wealth of the capitalists of the Gilded Age. Bruce Ackerman, "Taxation and the Constitution," *Columbia Law Review* 99, no. 1 (1999): 28. The Sixteenth Amendment was therefore adopted in 1913, to give the federal government a wide berth to enact income taxes "from whatever source derived" without apportioning them. Francis R. Jones, "Pollock v. Farmers' Loan and Trust Company," *Harvard Law Review* 9 (1895): 198–211.

16. "William Howard Taft on the Income Tax, June 16, 1909," in *William Howard Taft 1857–1930*, ed. Gilbert J. Black (Dobbs Ferry, NY: Oceana Publications, 1970), 32.

17. Gerhardt, *The Forgotten Presidents*, 188.

18. Everything Taft wrote in his veto message references only the Arizona provision. The two states were tied together on this because one bill granted statehood to both states, so it was impossible to untangle them. While New Mexico had some progressive provisions as well, they were apparently nothing analogous to Arizona's recall provision.

19. In addition to their initial election, county and state judges were subject to a recall election, which would be triggered by a public petition process.

20. William Howard Taft, "Veto of New Mexico-Arizona Enabling Act," in *Congressional Record*, 62nd Congress, 1st session, 1911, vol. 47, 3964–3966.

21. William Howard Taft, letter to the editor, *New York Times*, June 23, 1912. See also Romero, *Presidents from Theodore Roosevelt Through Coolidge*, 87–92.

22. Pringle, *Life and Times of William Howard Taft*, 850.

23. See *Hampton v. U.S.* in 1928, establishing the "intelligible principle" standard for legislative delegations of power to the executive branch.

24. Myers v. United States, 272 U.S. 52 (1926).

25. Adkins v. Children's Hospital, 261 U.S. 525 (1923).

26. Ibid., 563. (Taft, CJ. dissenting).

27. Jonathan Sternberg, "Deciding Not to Decide: The Judiciary Act of 1925 and the Discretionary Court," *Journal of Supreme Court History* 33 (March 2008): 1–16.

28. Taft's appointees were Charles Evan Hughes, Edward Douglass White (as chief justice), and Horace Harmon Lurton, all appointed in 1910; Willis Van Devanter and Joseph Rucker Lamar, both appointed in 1911; and Mahlon Pitney, appointed in 1912. Gould, *The William Howard Taft Presidency*, 128.

29. Gerhardt, *The Forgotten Presidents*, 188–189.

# PART VII

# World War I and the Great Depression

# 28

# Woodrow Wilson

SALADIN M. AMBAR

*President Woodrow Wilson ushered in a new brand of domestic and international politics for the United States. A champion of Progressive policies, including the right of women to vote, Wilson believed in a muscular chief executive, especially in times of war and crisis. He led the United States into World War I, at times bypassing Congress. He also acquiesced in the government's suppression of citizens' speech that the government perceived to be subversive. His presidency helped cement the nation's place as a world leader, yet it also had the contradictory result of a period of harsh restrictions on First Amendment freedoms.*

Introduction

When Woodrow Wilson was elected America's twenty-eighth president in 1912, he was, perhaps since John Quincy Adams, the office holder who was best educated on the basic provisions and arguments concerning the American Constitution. Owing to his roles as a political scientist and former president of Princeton University, Wilson's understanding of the founding period was rooted in years of academic training and writing. Coupled with his practical political experience as governor of New Jersey, Wilson's unique set of skills made him, arguably, among the most prepared executive leaders to ever take the reins of the presidency. Yet, despite Wilson's formal training in politics and his unique perspective on constitutional questions, he found himself at odds with the basic institutions and principles characteristic of the American polity. He was the man most singularly responsible for leading the United States into World War I—a watershed conflict that forever changed the role of the United States and its presidential office. As a result, Wilson's tenure as president provoked new questions about the president's constitutional authority in wartime, while resurrecting the earliest debates about the protection of American civil liberties.

Wilson's path to the presidency was as paradoxical as the man himself. Born in Staunton, Virginia, in 1856, Thomas Woodrow Wilson grew up in the South amid the turmoil of the Civil War and Reconstruction. His father, the Ohio-born Reverend Joseph Ruggles Wilson, led the small town's Presbyterian church, and his mother, Janet Woodrow—English by birth—belonged to a prominent family with high status in Presbyterian circles. When young Wilson was two, his family moved to Augusta, Georgia, where the future president witnessed "the captured former Confederate president, Jefferson Davis, being transported to prison."[1] Wilson came of age in Georgia, struggling early in school, experiencing the phenomenon of racial difference for the first time, and being introduced to the world of religious training and politics by his father.

## Academic Leadership

At Princeton—then still known as the College of New Jersey—Wilson indulged his interest in British political institutions while serving as editor of the *Princetonian*. In 1885, he married Ellen Louise Axson and became a highly sought-after professor of political science at Bryn Mawr College and Wesleyan University. He ultimately became a professor of jurisprudence and politics at Princeton before becoming president of his alma mater in 1902.[2] His dynamic and deeply embattled time as president of Princeton University helped prepare him for the world of New Jersey politics as governor and ultimately revealed the strengths and weaknesses of his executive leadership style in Washington.[3]

While Wilson's most comprehensive prospectus on the presidency, *Constitutional Government in the United States*, was written in 1908, his earliest insights on the office were drawn from the executive leadership of Grover Cleveland. In 1897, in an essay for the *Atlantic Monthly*, Wilson wrote that he saw in Cleveland the "sort of President the makers of the Constitution had vaguely in mind: more man than partisan; with an independent executive will of his own."[4] Cleveland's record as mayor of Buffalo, governor of New York, and twice-elected president of the United States offered to Wilson and future Democratic Party stalwarts the closest example of a successful national party leader seen among Democrats since the age of Jackson. Cleveland's veto record, his use of executive privilege, and his "intrusion" into the legislative domain of Congress drew Wilson's attention and early admiration. "The President stands at the centre of legislation," argued Wilson, "as well as of administration in executing his great office."[5]

Given America's expanding role in world affairs, Wilson developed a particularly muscular view of the president's unique position as foreign policy leader of the United States. As Wilson himself stated in 1916, "in times of peace when domestic problems are uppermost Congress comes to the front, but when foreign affairs intrude the people look to the president. His foreign affairs policy must then be his own."[6]

While the rising tide of historic violence brought the arrival of World War I in Europe—a circumstance that clearly spoke to Wilson's advocacy of presidential leadership and America's place in the world—Wilson's most relevant practical political experience with executive power, before the presidency, was honed while he served as the governor of New Jersey.

## Governor Wilson's Progressive Agenda

When Woodrow Wilson campaigned for the governorship of New Jersey in 1910, he did so in the growing tradition of state-level Progressives who sought to enact reforms through the office of governor. Robert M. La Follette of Wisconsin was among the most influential of this group of state executives who, through greater concessions to executive power in state constitutions around the country, came to reflect the growing popular disenchantment with legislatures. As John Milton Cooper Jr. noted in his biography of Wilson, "the accomplishments of this academic-turned-governor were part of a bigger picture" of the rising power of dynamic state executives."[7]

Wilson slowly but surely moved into this camp. Delivering the keynote address at the 1910 Governors' Conference, Wilson put his finger on the source of this newfound executive power. The "real power" of these governors, he argued, "is their ability to convince the people. If they can carry an opinion through the constituencies, they can carry it through the legislatures."[8] Employing impressive rhetorical skills and innovations such as formal press conferences, Wilson developed his emphasis on leadership of public opinion while he was governor—and ultimately practiced the same technique as president. Wilson exercised gubernatorial authority as few New Jersey governors had done before him—and in doing so, rejected state party bosses. Wilson put it best himself while campaigning for the governorship of New Jersey in October 1910: "If you elect me I will be an unconstitutional Governor. . . . I will talk to the people as well as the Legislature and I will use all moral force with that body to bring about what the people demand."[9]

Ironically, Wilson won the presidency in 1912 having defeated another former governor and president, Theodore Roosevelt, while also besting the sitting president, William Howard Taft. The race was perhaps the last full reflection of the diversity of the American electorate, with the Socialist Eugene Debs finishing a distant fourth, despite a striking nine hundred thousand–plus votes. In what has been called "the decisive battle of the Progressive era," Wilson campaigned as a stalwart Progressive, cutting into Roosevelt's Republican (and now Bull Moose) hold on left-leaning politics.[10] Wilson thus became the first Democrat to win the White House since Grover Cleveland's reelection in 1892.

# Presidency

Wilson's domestic agenda was sizable from the start—it included plans to create a Federal Reserve System and Federal Trade Commission, while implementing tough antitrust policies (such as the Clayton Act). Wilson also tragically supported his administration's segregation of federal departments, much to the dismay of the National Association for the Advancement of Colored People (NAACP) and early supporters of desegregation in the nation's capital.[11] On the foreign policy front, Wilson faced the increasingly difficult task of maintaining neutrality and keeping the United States out of battle as the carnage of World War I spread. Inside the White House, the twenty-eighth president faced his own challenges. His wife, Ellen, died in 1914 and left him widowed; Wilson remarried the following year.[12] In 1916, he won reelection by an extremely narrow margin against the former Republican governor of New York, Charles Evans Hughes, as Germany marched forward.

## *The Constitutional Dilemmas of Wilson's Foreign Policy*

When Germany initiated unrestricted warfare against all shipping to Great Britain and its Allies in early 1917, Woodrow Wilson was faced with what he would describe as the "fearful" prospect of leading "this great peaceful people into war."[13] As president, Wilson understood that the constitutional authority to take this step had to be his, and his alone. In deciding to arm American vessels—a posture of "armed neutrality"—Wilson recognized the belligerent nature of that move and the constitutional questions it invited. In seeking congressional approval to arm the ships, Wilson declared: "No doubt I already possess that authority without any special warrant of law, by the plain implication of my constitutional duties and powers."[14] When a bipartisan group of Democratic and Republican senators filibustered against the move to arm the vessels—even in the aftermath of the release of the Zimmerman telegram that revealed a proposed alliance between Germany and Mexico to further threaten the United States—Wilson acted on his own, without congressional approval.[15] As one scholar of constitutional law, Louis Fisher, has put it, "it was Wilson then, who made the crucial policy decision to move from neutrality to armed neutrality and finally to a state of war with Germany."[16]

Wilson's unilateral action and its attendant developments forever altered America's role in the world. And while it did not put an end to Congress's role in making war, it was a decisive step in the direction of curtailing the legislative branch's authority to do so. When Wilson famously uttered in his message to Congress that, in seeking a declaration of war, "the world must be made safe for democracy," he forever stamped not only his country's imprimatur upon that vision, but also—in the public's perception—the seal of the president of the United States as well.[17]

Indeed, Wilson's own cabinet remained largely in the dark about his decision on war, compelling Colonel Edward M. House, Wilson's closest aide and confidante, to confess that the lack of conference with his policy team was "humiliating."[18]

Wilson's decision to effectively end neutrality was reminiscent of the first great foreign policy debate in America's history—the question of whether President George Washington's Proclamation of Neutrality in 1793, during the time of the great sea battles between Great Britain and France, was constitutional.[19] Ultimately, Wilson's muscular foreign policy would win the day. By 1936, the U.S. Supreme Court would all but validate Wilson and other future presidential claims of exclusive authority when it came to foreign affairs. In *U.S. v. Curtiss-Wright Export Corporation*, the Court would acknowledge "the very delicate, plenary and exclusive power of the President as the sole organ of the federal government in the field of international relations—a power which does not require as a basis for its exercise an act of Congress."[20] Indeed, by the end of the twentieth century, Wilson's gesture of seeking support from Congress to make war would become de rigueur, if not less eloquent. "I didn't have to get permission from some old goat in the United States Congress," President George H. W. Bush would later remark, "to kick Saddam Hussein out of Kuwait."[21]

Yet despite President Wilson's willingness to bypass Congress in matters of foreign affairs, congressional opposition to Wilson's postwar agenda derailed his most ambitious initiative: the League of Nations. After the war, Wilson laid out his famous Fourteen Points for Peace. At the heart of this plan was an attempt to create an intergovernmental organization capable of guarding against the outbreak of another world war. In Wilson's view, the minimal amount of sovereignty that the United States would lose by entering the League of Nations was a small price to pay for the geopolitical stability that would be gained. Yet Congress, led by prominent Senator Henry Cabot Lodge of Massachusetts, was hostile toward the idea of pooled sovereignty. The legislature exercised its Article II treaty power in refusing to allow the United States to become a member of the league.[22] Wilson tried desperately to muster popular support for his cause by going on a nationwide speaking tour, but his failing health, coupled with his unwillingness to compromise with his opponents, doomed any hope of reconciliation with the Senate.[23] Thus, while many nations would join the league, the absence of the United States as a member dealt that organization a blow from which it would not recover.

## Restrictions against "Subversive" Speech

Wilson's domestic actions and initiatives during the war were no less significant in their constitutional implications than those in the realm of foreign affairs. As Cooper has pointed out, Wilson began a program to restrict public speech against the war, the day after his speech seeking a declaration of war from Congress.[24] Wilson also initiated a campaign to censor or imprison dissenters, including the jailing of conscientious objectors, using the newly enacted Espionage Act of 1917 and related amendments to do so. Moreover, Wilson tolerated "violence against and repression of ethnic minorities and radicals," with German Americans enduring the worst of such anti-immigrant repression during the war.[25]

Despite the protestations of men such as Senator Lodge, who deemed part of the Espionage Act of 1917 too extreme, Wilson's restrictive domestic policies during the war would come in many ways to define the focus of the war effort at home.[26] "To attempt to deny the press all legitimate criticism either of Congress or the Executive is going very dangerously too far," complained Senator Lodge to little avail.[27] Wilson's own vehemence in linking support for the war with love of one's country made questioning the war effort for those who professed to support and defend American democracy fraught with danger. "Instruction in patriotism has always been a duty in American schools," President Wilson wrote in his remarks to be delivered at the University of Georgia in July 1918. "It is now more than ever a duty to teach a burning, uncompromising patriotism which will admit of no divided allegiance but demands all that the heart and energy of the citizen can give."[28]

In a sense, the Espionage Act of 1917 and its legislative offspring, the Alien Act of 1918, ushered in the beginnings of what Americans would ultimately come to know as the "national security state" that developed after World War II.[29] Both acts were strongly supported by Wilson. And both would lead to the arrest of some fifteen hundred people, rendering the John Adams's Alien and Sedition Acts of 1798 tame by comparison.[30] Among other things, the Espionage Act made it a crime for an individual to "promote the success of (the country's) enemies" or to "cause or attempt to cause insubordination, disloyalty, mutiny, or refusal of duty in the military or naval forces of the United States" or to "obstruct the recruiting or enlistment of service of the United States."[31] The Sedition Act of 1918, amended to make the Espionage Act "more drastic," resulted in what constitutional scholar Geoffrey R. Stone has called "the most repressive legislation in American history." It added a host of prohibitions against publishing, writing, or uttering anything deemed counterproductive to the American war effort or bringing the image of the U.S. government or armed forces into disrepute.[32] The scope of these laws, combined, was historic in cutting back the basic protections afforded Americans in the Bill of Rights.

The Supreme Court countenanced this restrictive view of the free speech rights after a man named Charles T. Schenck was arrested for violating the Espionage Act for disseminating antiwar leaflets. Schenck was sentenced to six months in prison. Justice Oliver Wendell Holmes upheld the conviction in *Schenck v. United States* on the premise that "the most stringent protection of free speech would not protect a man in falsely shouting fire in a theatre and causing a panic."[33] Holmes himself would later retreat some from his position.[34] Yet by 1919, J. Edgar Hoover and the Bureau of Investigation were ordering the detention and possible deportation of alleged anarchists such as Mollie Steimer.[35] The Supreme Court, using language in the *Schenck* decision, allowed the government to suppress speech that the government concluded created a "clear and present danger" of subverting the United States, with wide latitude for the government to decide what speech fell into that category.[36]

### The Pardon Power

On the domestic front, President Wilson left his mark in other realms. The important Supreme Court decision of *Burdick v. U.S.* (1915) flowed from a clash between the press and the Wilson administration relating to the president's pardon power. *New York Tribune* editor George Burdick had been subpoenaed to appear before a federal grand jury but refused to reveal—on Fifth Amendment grounds—the government sources who had improperly leaked information to his newspaper regarding alleged customs fraud. After Burdick's initial refusal, he was directed to report again to the grand jury. When he arrived, Burdick was handed a pardon signed by President Wilson. It granted Burdick "a full and unconditional pardon for all offenses against the United States which he . . . has committed or may have committed."[37] The pardon was designed to eliminate Burdick's invoking of the Fifth Amendment and his argument that he might incriminate himself by providing testimony about the individuals who had leaked information to his paper. Despite receiving this preemptive presidential pardon, Burdick still refused to answer questions. He was held in contempt, was ordered to pay a fine, and was threatened with jail time if he failed to comply.

In hearing the case, the U.S. Supreme Court focused on whether Burdick had to accept the pardon before it became effective. The Court determined that a pardon carried with it "an imputation of guilt." Moreover, acceptance of the pardon was a "confession of [guilt]."[38] Thus, the Court determined that Burdick could not be forced to testify, despite the president's attempted use of a pardon to extract testimony from him. Although the *Burdick* case was merely a footnote during the Wilson presidency, the decision would eventually set the stage for legal posturing over the pardon of President Richard Nixon almost sixty years later.

## The Right of Women to Vote

The framers did not expressly grant the right to vote in the Constitution.[39] At the nation's founding, the parameters of the franchise were determined by the states, and women were universally denied the vote. Women began to clamor for suffrage in an organized fashion in 1848, holding a women's rights convention in Seneca Falls, New York.[40] In 1874, during the Grant administration, the U.S. Supreme Court, in *Minor v. Happersett*, made it clear that women could not to look to the Constitution for the right to vote, declaring that a Missouri statute that gave only men the vote did not infringe on women's federal citizenship rights.[41] Some women campaigned to change state constitutions, while others decided to press for a federal solution. By the time that Wilson ran for office in 1912, the voting rights of women and a constitutional amendment to enfranchise them had blossomed into a national debate. Wilson's support for women's suffrage, however, was muted at best, and his responses when asked about the issue (at least initially) were evasive.[42]

As the nation's effort in World War I required women to tend farms, work in factories, transport freight, and otherwise fulfill roles traditionally occupied by men, however, women saw the war as an opportunity to argue that they, like men, were patriots and entitled to vote. In addition, as women listened to their president proclaim that it was America's responsibility to make the world "safe for democracy," they began to assert in increasing numbers that it was intolerable that full participation in the democratic process was denied them at home.[43] The more militant among the suffragists picketed outside the White House, demanding that President Wilson pay more than mere lip service to the cause. The demonstrations, at first peaceful, turned violent, and several women were arrested and incarcerated. In response, they protested with hunger strikes. Wilson was appalled when he learned that many of these women were force-fed while in jail. He reconsidered his position and ultimately gave the women's suffrage movement his full support.[44]

In a speech before the Congress, in 1918, Wilson publically endorsed the right to vote for women and the necessity of a constitutional amendment to secure it. He posed a question to the Congress: "We have made partners of the women in this war. . . . Shall we admit them only to a partnership of suffering and sacrifice and toil and not to a partnership of privilege and right?"[45]

On June 4, 1919, the amendment finally received the votes necessary in Congress to be sent to the states for ratification. It would take another year, but ultimately, on August 18, 1920, the amendment was ratified by the essential number of states, and the Nineteenth Amendment was added to the Constitution, declaring: "The right of citizens of the United States to vote shall not be denied or abridged by the United States of by any State on account of sex."[46] Recognizing the profound significance of the Nineteenth Amendment's ratification, Wilson stated: "I deem it one of the greatest honors of my life that this great event, so stoutly fought for, for so many years, should have occurred during the period of my administration."[47]

### End of the Presidency

During his two terms in the White House, Woodrow Wilson appointed three members of the Supreme Court, including Justice Louis Brandeis, the first Jewish justice to serve on the Court.[48] While Wilson continued to build a legacy as a strong president, his second term was marked by unexpected challenges, as millions of soldiers returned home from the war, and the nation faced labor strikes and violent race riots. President Wilson himself suffered a serious stroke in October 1919, in the midst of his fight with Congress over the League of Nations. The stroke left him partially paralyzed and blind in one eye. For much of the rest of his time in the White House, he was kept out of the public eye and watched over by his second wife, Edith.[49]

## Conclusion

In 1924, having left office three years earlier, Wilson died after a second massive stroke. He was buried in the Washington, D.C., National Cathedral, the only president to be interred in the nation's capital.[50]

By placing the United States on an early war footing without congressional authorization, Woodrow Wilson acted in accordance with a handful of his presidential predecessors, including Abraham Lincoln in the early days of the Civil War and Theodore Roosevelt and his theory of the stewardship presidency. But Wilson was undoubtedly also doing something quite different, as World War I involved unprecedented commitments from the United States in both human and physical capital. His presidency helped make the United Nations a world leader. Although he failed in his quest to push the country into joining the League of Nations, the later evolution of the United Nations largely vindicated Wilson and gave him the appearance of a visionary. Yet Wilson also set the nation on a contradictory path, in permitting the curtailment of free expression and other civil liberties on America's own soil, thus setting a dubious example for other nations committed to freedom. Indeed, his tolerance of such conduct made future abuses in the United States during periods of wartime fear and insecurity even more likely.

President Wilson's unitary approach to orchestrating the nation's entrance into the war certainly helped cement the emergence of America as a presidential republic. However, his commitment to "make the world safe for democracy" remains an ambiguous and often impractical, if not dangerous, call for the nation to assume duties it is unwise or unable to deliver. Such ambiguity is perhaps befitting of a president whose understanding of America's founding and its Constitution was based on a notion that government is made to adapt to changing times—with the chief executive leading the way—as opposed to the more restrained notion of governmental power so esteemed by the founders.

NOTES

1. John Milton Cooper Jr., *Woodrow Wilson: A Biography* (New York: Alfred A. Knopf, 2009), 18.

2. Ibid., 14–25, contrasts the incongruities of Wilson's often-stereotyped upbringing with the more complex realities of a childhood marked by genuine distinctiveness.

3. W. Barksdale Maynard, *Woodrow Wilson: Princeton to the Presidency* (New Haven, CT: Yale University Press, 2008).

4. Woodrow Wilson, "Mr. Cleveland as President," *Atlantic Monthly* 79, no. 478 (March 1897).

5. Ibid., 294.

6. Woodrow Wilson, interview with Ray Stannard Baker, cited in Daniel D. Stid, *The President as Statesman: Woodrow Wilson and the Constitution* (Lawrence: University Press of Kansas, 1998), 124.

7. Cooper, *Woodrow Wilson*, 135.

8. "Proceedings of the Third Meeting of the Governors of the States of the Union Held at Frankfort and Louisville, KY," November 29–December 1, 1910, Woodrow Wilson Papers Project, Box 81, Princeton University Library, Department of Rare Books and Special Collections, Seeley G. Mudd Manuscript Library, Princeton, NJ.

9. "Dr. Wilson Says He Is Owned by No One," *New York Times*, October 4, 1910. Wilson wrote that few other public officials were battle-tested for the presidency: "The best men prepared, no doubt, are those who have been governors of states." Woodrow Wilson, *Constitutional Government in the United States* (New York: Columbia University Press, 1908), 64.

10. Sidney M. Milkis, *Theodore Roosevelt, the Progressive Party, and the Transformation of American Democracy* (Lawrence: University of Kansas Press, 2009), 1.

11. Cooper, *Woodrow Wilson*, 205–206.

12. Wilson's second wife, Edith Galt, was a direct descendant of Pocahontas, the legendary Native American figure from the Tidewater area of Virginia. Ibid., 281–282, 306.

13. Ibid., 386.

14. Stid, *The President as Statesman*, 125.

15. The Zimmerman telegram proposed an alliance between Germany and Mexico; through this alliance, the territory won by the United States from Mexico in the Mexican-American War would be restored. The published document generated increased public support for war. Arthur S. Link, *Woodrow Wilson: Revolution, War, and Peace* (Arlington Heights, IL: Harlan Davidson, 1979), 70.

16. Louis Fisher, *Presidential War Power* (Lawrence: University of Kansas, 2004), 68–69.

17. Cooper, *Woodrow Wilson*, 386–387.

18. Ibid., 127.

19. See Chapter 1, "George Washington."

20. United States v. Curtiss-Wright Export Corp., 299 U.S. 304, 319 (1936). As Arthur M. Schlesinger Jr., *The Imperial Presidency* (New York: Mariner Books, 2004), 102, 443, has noted, "the constitutional defense of unilateral presidential war-making continues to rest on the Supreme Court's *Curtiss-Wright* decision." In 2015, however, the U.S. Supreme Court jettisoned the sole-organ doctrine articulated in the *Curtiss-Wright* case. See Zivotofsky v. Kerry, 135 S.Ct. 2076, 2090 (2015).

21. Fisher, *Presidential War Power*, 172.

22. U.S. Const. art. II, §2. One of the primary reservations of those who opposed the League of Nations was the belief that membership would infringe on Congress's constitutional power to declare war. Cooper, *Woodrow Wilson*, 509.

23. Ibid., 558–560.

24. Ibid., 391.

25. Ibid., 397–399; see also Daniel J. Tichenor, *Dividing Lines: The Politics of Immigration Control in America* (Princeton, NJ: Princeton University Press, 2002), 139.

26. Paul L. Murphy, *World War I and the Origin of Civil Liberties in the United States* (New York: W.W. Norton, 1979), 25.

27. Ibid., 76.

28. Ray Stannard Baker, *Woodrow Wilson: Life and Letters, Armistice: March 1–November 11, 1918* (New York: Charles Scribner's Sons, 1946), 240.

29. Kate Doyle, "The End of Secrecy: U.S. National Security and the Imperative for Openness," *World Policy Journal* 16, no. 1 (spring 1999): 37–39.

30. The first Alien and Sedition Acts brought ten convictions compared with the one thousand of the Wilson years. William E. Leuchtenburg, *The Perils of Prosperity, 1914–1932* (Chicago: University of Chicago Press, 1993), 42.

31. Geoffrey R. Stone, *Perilous Times: Free Speech in Wartime* (New York: W.W. Norton, 2004), 151–152.

32. Ibid., 184–186.

33. Schenck v. United States, 249 U.S. 47 (1919); Michael R. Levinson, "Clear and Present Danger During World War I," *Litigation* 35, no. 4 (summer 2009): 48–49.

34. Christopher M. Finan, *From the Palmer Raids to the Patriot Act: A History of the Fight for Free Speech in America* (Boston: Beacon Press, 2007), 5.

35. Stone, *Perilous Times*, 233.

36. For cases after *Schenck* discussing the clear and present danger test, see Abrams v. United States, 250 U.S. 616, 624–631 (1919) (Holmes, J., dissenting); Gitlow v. New York, 268 U.S. 652, 672–673 (Holmes, J., dissenting); and Dennis v. United States, 341 U.S. 494 (1951).

37. Burdick v. United States, 236 U.S. 79, 86 (1915).

38. Ibid., 94.

39. The founding fathers did not include the phrase "right to vote" in the Constitution. The absence of the phrase reflects, in part, the unwillingness of the slave states at the time of the Constitution's drafting to cede any authority over the franchise to the federal government. Akhil Reed Amar, *America's Unwritten Constitution: The Precedents and Principles We Live By* (New York: Basic Books, 2012), 183–184.

40. American Civil Liberties Union, *Voting Rights Act Timeline*, American Civil Liberties Union, March 4, 2005, www.aclu.org/files/assets/voting_rights_act_ timeline20111222.pdf.

41. Minor v. Happersett, 88 U.S. 162 (1874).
42. Christine A. Lunardi and Thomas J. Knock, "Woodrow Wilson and Woman Suffrage: A New Look," *Political Science Quarterly* 95 (winter 1980–1981): 656–658.
43. Ibid., 663–664.
44. Global Women's Leadership Initiative, "Woodrow Wilson and the Women's Suffrage Movement: A Reflection," Woodrow Wilson International Center for Scholars, Wilson Center, Washington, DC, June 4, 2013.
45. Woodrow Wilson, Address to Senate (September 30, 1918), *Supplement to the Messages of the Presidents: Covering the Second Term of Woodrow Wilson, March 4, 1917 to March 4, 1921* (Washington, DC: Bureau of National Literature, 1921).
46. U.S. Const. amend. XIX.
47. Global Women's Leadership Initiative, "Woodrow Wilson and the Women's Suffrage Movement: A Reflection," Woodrow Wilson International Center for Scholars, Wilson Center, Washington, DC, June 4, 2013.
48. The other appointments were Justice James McReynolds and Justice John Clarke.
49. Cooper, *Woodrow Wilson*, 532–533, 536.
50. Ibid., 598.

# 29

# Warren G. Harding

JAMES D. ROBENALT

*President Warren G. Harding faced a wrecked economy in the after-math of World War I and a period of intense fear and suspicion of foreign threats. Despite a Supreme Court that continued to countenance the sup-pression of citizens' speech under the First Amendment, Harding bucked his advisers and commuted the sentence of Socialist activist Eugene V. Debs, eventually freeing numerous other political prisoners to repair the nation's commitment to the Bill of Rights after the horrors of war had receded. Although his administration was later tainted by the Tea-pot Dome scandal, Harding's personal role in the misadventure remains unclear. His legacy was more positive than negative: Harding's use of the presidential pardon practice helped undo the damage done by a war-frenzied Congress, paved the way for a "return to normalcy," and helped restore core freedoms under the Constitution.*

## Introduction

War leaves in its aftermath economic misery and social turmoil. Opportunistic greed overruns the public good. Markets jump and jitter. Hysteria runs rampant. This is the precisely the world that Warren Harding confronted on his fifty-fifth birthday, November 2, 1920, which was also the day he was elected the twenty-ninth president of the United States.

Warren Harding came from a common Ohio background. His father was a Civil War soldier (he once met Lincoln in the White House along with a group of fellow Ohio soldiers) and became a country doctor, traveling on horseback between patients and otherwise farming to support the family.[1] Warren, the oldest of the family's eight children, grew up with different interests: He became fascinated with government and politics. Harding's career as a newspaper editor in small-town Marion, Ohio, kept him in touch with local, state, and national politics. He served in the Ohio Senate and then served one term as lieutenant governor of Ohio before winning a seat in the U.S. Senate in 1914 (the first direct election of a senator in Ohio after the passage of the Seventeenth Amendment).[2]

As World War I drew to a close, the economy was in a near state of collapse. Agricultural prices began to fall precipitously in May 1920, followed by wholesale price drops. The country experienced one of its worst periods of deflation. Food pricing dropped by 37 percent, while clothing prices fell by nearly 42 percent. Farmers were particularly hard hit.[3] Incomes declined drastically, with no bottom seemingly in sight. Unemployment, on the other hand, grew rapidly.

In addition to economic turmoil, tensions had been building in the country since the war ended in 1918. During the searing summer of 1919, anarchists had bombed the homes and offices of public officials. Race riots had broken out with deadly ferocity in cities like St. Louis and Chicago. By the summer of 1920, economic conditions had so rapidly soured that across the land, there was a palpable dread that labor unrest would turn to revolution—fueled by the success of the recent and brutal Bolshevik revolution in Russia.

Campaigning on a platform of a "return to normalcy," including a vibrant economy, Harding not only won the presidential election of 1920, but also took the contest by one of the greatest popular vote margins in all American history, defeating his Democratic opponent, James Cox of Ohio, by a margin of 60.3 to 34.1 percent. This was the first presidential election to be held since ratification of the Nineteenth Amendment and, thus, the first in which women were eligible to vote in all forty-eight states.

## Presidency

### The Constitution under Assault

A sense of fear and suspicion pervaded the nation when Harding took office. After the United States had joined the war, in April 1917, a massive secret volunteer police force had grown up and then quickly exploded in size across the country, run by everyday businessmen in virtually every city and town in the nation. Known as the American Protective League (APL), more than 250,000 men were essentially deputized by the attorney general of the United States to act as a vigilante spy-catching machine. Armed with badges and titles like "Chief," "Captain," and "Lieutenant," these men had blatantly violated the civil liberties of their neighbors with unlawful searches of mail, break-ins, wiretaps, secret arrests, and, at times, murder.[4] Their badges proclaimed that the APL men worked as an "auxiliary to the Department of Justice." Created as a web to ensnare pro-German spies and saboteurs, the APL morphed into an antilabor bulwark, hunting down leaders and members of the Industrial Workers of the World (IWW, or the "Wobblies") and other labor and socialist organizations.[5]

The assault on free speech had been aggressive. As a part of America's declaration of war, President Wilson had issued extensive regulations relating to "alien enemies," restricting their movements and speech. But the most noxious of the war measures that emerged—the Espionage Act of 1917 and its amendment passed in 1918, referred to as the Sedition Act—applied not just to aliens but also to every citizen of the United States. The Espionage Act of 1917 was directed at traditional spying and espionage activities, making it a crime to intentionally interfere with the operation or success of the military or naval forces of the United States or to aid the enemy. This included acts to willfully obstruct recruiting or enlistment services of the United States. A controversial attempt to include a press censorship provision in the Espionage Act failed to pass in the Senate by a one-vote margin. Warren Harding, a newspaperman by trade and profession, had been one of the senators who voted against the press censorship provision.[6]

But the Sedition Act amendment to the Espionage Act in 1918 was a frontal attack on speech. It prohibited the use of "disloyal, profane, scurrilous, or abusive language about the form of government of the United States, or the flag of the United States, or the uniform of its army or navy," or any language that might bring "the form of Government of the United States, or the Constitution, into contempt, scorn, contumely, or disrepute."[7] Twenty-six senators, including Harding, voted against the bill.[8] It nevertheless became law on May 16, 1918.

One of the most famous arrestees under the Espionage and Sedition Act was Eugene V. Debs. This Indiana man was known as a legend in the labor movement since his days as an organizer in the 1894 Pullman strike. Debs would run for president five times as the candidate of the Socialist Party of America. In 1912, Debs had garnered nearly one million votes (in an election where the winner, Woodrow Wilson, received six million votes). On June 16, 1918, exactly one month to the day after the sedition amendment to the Espionage Act became law, Debs spoke in a public park in Canton, Ohio, to an audience of around one thousand listeners, mostly Ohio Socialists, at a party picnic. Debs's address lauded the IWW and Socialism and attacked corporate leaders who he believed were abusing workers in the name of a war-induced patriotism. Debs began his speech by briefly commending three local Socialist leaders who sat in a nearby jail after being convicted of providing aid to a draft dodger.

During his lengthy speech, Debs never explicitly advocated resistance to the draft or to the war effort. Indeed, the speech Debs delivered in Canton was so innocuous that even the top leadership within the Department of Justice in Washington, after looking at stenographers' notes of the speech, concluded that the local U.S. attorney in Cleveland should decline to initiate prosecution. Nevertheless, the U.S. attorney had pressed the matter with a federal grand jury, and Debs was indicted and then arrested in Cleveland on ten violations of the Espionage Act, as amended in 1918. Debs's trial and sentencing took place in September 1918, less than two months before the war's abrupt end. He was sentenced to ten years in prison, a term that he began serving five months after the Armistice and the exhaustion of all of his appeals. Unmoved by pleas for leniency, a healthy and later stroke-disabled Woodrow Wilson denied every request to pardon Debs, even one recommended by his own attorney general, A.

Mitchell Palmer, who was not known as an especially warm friend of civil rights.[9]

Debs's case made its way to the U.S. Supreme Court in the winter of 1919, but the Court had done little to limit the use of the Espionage Act to suppress free speech. Justice Oliver Wendell Holmes interpreted the First Amendment to permit such incursions on free speech in *Schenck v. United States*, which was decided in 1919 and which ushered in the restrictive "clear and present danger" test for limiting speech deemed subversive.[10] In light of *Schenck*, Debs did not stand a chance in his own case. In *Debs v. United States*, Holmes again upheld the Espionage and Sedition Acts and affirmed Debs's conviction. The problem Holmes faced, however, was that Debs had not expressly advocated or counseled against the draft; nor had he urged active resistance to any war measure. In fact, Debs had begun his speech in Canton with his own self-admonition that he had to be careful in his speech.[11] Yet Holmes inferred intent on the part of Debs to violate the Espionage Act's proscriptions. The justice concluded that "if a part of the manifest intent of the more general utterances was to encourage those present to obstruct the recruiting service," the speech was not protected.[12] Debs's criminal conviction was therefore upheld.

Holmes was roundly criticized by his closest friends and confidants for these two opinions. Almost instantly, he regretted what he had done.[13] Eight months after *Schenck* and *Debs*, Holmes revisited the Espionage Act, this time voting to overturn a conviction in *Abrams v. United States*.[14] But the damage had been done. As one distinguished historian has written: "Holmes' opinion in the *Abrams* case may have helped to redeem his reputation, but the fact remained that the nation's highest tribunal had overwhelmingly endorsed the most aggressive wartime assault on (freedom of speech)."[15]

Debs remained in his prison cell (a man of always fragile health), and President Wilson would not hear of a pardon. Debs again became the candidate for the Socialist Party of America for president in the 1920 election, even though he was imprisoned in Atlanta. "Convict No. 9653" won 913,000 write-in votes, more than what he had accumulated in 1912.

Candidate Warren Harding was troubled by what had happened in Debs's case. Even before the November presidential election, he began to actively consider amnesty for Debs and other political prisoners should he win the election, depending on the merits of each case. Careful politician that he was, he held his counsel on Debs throughout the campaign, making no commitments other than to keep an open mind. But behind the scenes, he set matters in motion to effect Debs's eventual release. Before addressing the amnesty question, though, the new president would have to attend to a reeling economy and then find a way to formally end the war with Germany and the other Central Powers.

And though he did not know for sure, newly elected President Harding also had an inkling that he might have the occasion, sooner rather than later, to make some significant appointments to the Supreme Court, including perhaps the next chief justice.

## Shaping the Supreme Court

Former President William Howard Taft had a unique understanding of appointments to the Supreme Court. During his one term as president (1909–1913), Taft had the extraordinary fortune to fill six seats on the Supreme Court (in this distinction, he stood behind only George Washington, who had appointed the entire first Court). As a former state judge and federal judge on the Sixth Circuit Court of Appeals, Taft also had an uncommon grasp of the judiciary. He openly coveted a spot on the Court, especially the job of chief justice, even before moving to the White House. Harding's election as president at the end of 1920 provided a ripe opportunity.

Taft and Harding were friends and political allies. Harding delivered Taft's nominating speech at the raucous 1912 Republican Convention in Chicago, a famous affair that ended with Theodore Roosevelt's disastrous bolt to the Progressive Party and the establishment of the Bull Moose Party. Woodrow Wilson's election to the presidency was made possible only because of this devastating schism within the Republican Party. Harding, for one, remained a party loyalist and maintained great respect for his fellow Ohioan Taft.[16]

Following Harding's victory in the fall of 1920, Taft showed up at the home of the president-elect for an appointment and, after breakfast, was shown into the humble library on the first floor of the home in Marion, Ohio. The two men discussed matters of presidential protocol and succession planning. Harding surprised Taft by asking, directly, if Taft would consider an appointment to the Supreme Court. Taft acknowledged that a position on the Court "was and always had been the ambition of my life." He quickly added, though, that because of his previous position as president, and having appointed so many members of the current Court, he could not "accept any position but the Chief Justiceship."[17]

"I don't feel at all confident it will work out as I would like it," Taft wrote his wife the next day, "but it is more favorable to my hope and life ambition than I thought possible."[18]

### *Turning the Page on War and the Suppression of Dissent*

After his inauguration on March 4, 1921, Warren Harding was besieged by farmer and Socialist groups, the American Civil Liberties Union, and delegations of prominent citizens seeking amnesty for political prisoners, especially Debs. Symbolically, the president agreed to meet with members of the Political Amnesty Committee on April 13, 1921, the second anniversary of the date that Debs reported to prison. This group pointed out that amnesty had been widely granted in Europe and that it was ironic that America lagged behind these Old World countries. They further argued that there was an American tradition of general amnesty for political prisoners: Jefferson's pardon for those convicted under the Alien and Sedition Acts of 1798 and a general amnesty for political prisoners proclaimed by Lincoln at the close of the Civil War.[19] In public, Harding was cordial but said he could contemplate no decision on amnesty "before a technical peace with the Central Powers was brought about."[20]

Though Harding made no open commitment, there were favorable signs that he had already started the process for the release of Debs. Two weeks before his inauguration in March 1921, Harding instructed the man who would be his attorney general, Harry Daugherty, to make inquiry into Debs's case. Within the first weeks of the administration, Daugherty sent a request to the warden of the Atlanta prison, directing him to send Debs by train, unguarded and in civilian clothes, to Washington, D.C., to meet with Daugherty. Debs slipped unnoticed into Union Station in Washington on March 24, a cold and wet day, and met with Daugherty for much of the afternoon before returning to Atlanta. "He left me with the conviction that I have never met a man of more appealing personality than Eugene V. Debs," Daugherty wrote of the interview.[21] While Daugherty cautioned Debs not to discuss their meeting, the attorney general made sure the newspapers knew of the interview and of the president's approval of Debs traveling on his own personal recognizance. "The action of the Government in granting permission to Debs to come to Washington without guard of any sort is said to be unprecedented in the Federal prison annals," the *New York Times* reported.[22]

The newsmen at Daugherty's press conference the day of Debs's visit could not help but note the unusual presence of former President Taft in the attorney general's office. Taft had called on Daugherty just before the newspapermen were ushered into Daugherty's office for what they thought was going to be an ordinary weekly conference, and he remained as Daugherty discussed his meeting with Debs. "He appeared extremely interested in the Debs case and the questions asked about it," one witness reported.[23]

Meanwhile, President Harding began to take steps to right the economy and to liquidate the war. He called a special joint session of Congress in April; his agenda included lowering taxes and the creation of a national budget for the first time to get spending under control. The economy eventually stabilized.[24]

How to end the war was another question. The issue had bedeviled the Wilson administration, as the proposed Treaty of Versailles had gone down in defeat in Congress. Harding had to deal with an emboldened and aggressive Senate, which needed to ratify any treaty of peace. As a former member of the Senate, Harding knew how to navigate through the conflicting egos and institutional obstacles. After much wrangling, the Senate ratified the necessary peace treaties and Harding signed a proclamation on November 14, 1921, retroactively declaring an end to the war as of July 2, 1921.[25] "When the ratifications for the German peace treaty were exchanged in November 1921," Harding's biographer later wrote, "the last barrier to Debs's release was removed."[26]

Despite strenuous objections from his own wife and many within the administration, including Herbert Hoover, who served as his secretary of commerce, President Harding instructed Daugherty to draw up the commutation papers for Debs and twenty-three other political prisoners. Pursuant to the pardon power in Article II, Section 2—granting the "Power to grant reprieves and pardons for Offenses against the United States"— the president has the authority to "commute" the sentence or shorten the period of incarceration.[27] President Harding wanted Debs to be at home with his wife for Christmas and changed Daugherty's proposed December 31 release date to December 24. Significantly, Harding refused to base amnesty on the condition of the prisoner's signing a loyalty oath. "It is my judgment that this sort of pledge would be of little avail," he wrote

Daugherty. "It would have the savor of bargaining for amnesty and I doubt if that would meet with any marked degree of approval."[28]

Debs learned of the commutation on Christmas Eve. He left the Atlanta prison that day as nearly twenty-three hundred prisoners cheered him wildly. "Debs raised his hat in one hand and his cane in the other and waved back at them," one newspaper recorded.[29] Harding asked that Debs meet him on the way home, so on December 26, Debs met with Harding in the White House. Again, Taft was on the scene. By now, he was serving as chief justice of the United States, having been confirmed on June 30, 1921, the same day that President Harding sent his nomination to the Senate.[30] The new chief justice met with Harding just before Debs arrived at the White House.[31]

Over the next two years, Harding continued to free political prisoners. While he did not agree to general amnesty and believed it his constitutional obligation to review each case on its merits, by the end of his presidency, "he had virtually emptied the nation's jails of all wartime prisoners."[32]

### Teapot Dome Scandal

Any account of President Harding's time in office is incomplete without a mention of the Teapot Dome scandal. While the affair was of limited historical importance—especially when compared with Harding's significant achievements—the term Teapot Dome has become synonymous with the Harding presidency. The evidence, however, strongly suggests that Harding had little or nothing to do with the scandal. Indeed, it has never been authoritatively established that he knew anything about the affair before he died.

The roots of Teapot Dome can be found in the Wilson administration. With a growing, worldwide navy in need of fuel, oil reserves that were being discovered in the American West were of particular interest to the Department of the Navy. These same resources, though, were coveted by private oilmen, who wished to exploit the oil fields—including the stupendous find in Wyoming called the Teapot Dome—to service the ever-expanding domestic market demand created in part by the postwar explosion of automobile ownership.

Albert Fall, Harding's secretary of the interior, was in debt and misused his office to enrich himself. During 1921 and 1922, Fall orchestrated the transfer of the Teapot Dome oil field in Wyoming and another field in California from the navy to his Department of the Interior.[33] President Harding, unaware of any improper motive, issued an executive order making this transfer.[34] Without engaging in any competitive bidding process, Secretary Fall then leased the oil production rights at Teapot Dome to Harry F. Sinclair, owner of Mammoth Oil Company.[35] Fall also leased the production rights at the California fields to Edward L. Doheny, an oil tycoon who headed Pan American Petroleum Company.[36] As part of the deal, Fall obtained "loans" from Sinclair and Doheny totaling over $404,000—a fortune at that time.[37]

Senator Thomas J. Walsh, Democrat from Montana, launched a sensational congressional investigation.[38] Questions about the independence of Attorney General Dougherty led to the appointment of two special counsels, Owen J. Roberts and Atlee Pomerene, who were appointed by President Calvin Coolidge and charged with unearthing the facts.[39] (The Teapot Dome investigation became the forerunner to modern special prosecutor investigations during the Nixon and Clinton presidencies.) This investigation ultimately proved that Fall became rich from the bribes and had funneled money into a cattle ranch and other business ventures.[40] With public trust in government badly damaged, the case ultimately went to the Supreme Court, which invalidated the oil leases, returning the property to the U.S. Navy.[41] Fall was fined $100,000 and sentenced to a year in prison, making him the first former U.S. cabinet officer to be incarcerated for misconduct in office.[42] The Teapot Dome incident came to be synonymous with government corruption.

As discussed above, it was never demonstrated that Harding was complicit in the scheme; nor is there any credible evidence that Harding benefitted in any way from Fall's activities.[43] It was neither the first time nor the last that a president was let down by a cabinet member whom he trusted.[44] As President Harding remarked to William Allen White, a prominent newspaper editor from Kansas, "I have no trouble with my enemies. I can take care of my enemies all right. But my damn friends, my God-damn friends . . . they're the ones who keep me walking the floor nights!"[45] Ultimately, the Teapot Dome scandal and other allegations that his administration was corrupt took their toll on President Harding's reputation.[46]

## Conclusion

After a physically exhausting tour of Alaska—designed to encourage settlement of that remote territory—President Harding grew sick from complications of advanced heart disease. Physically worn down by the rigorous travel through the West and into Alaska, and anxious about the growing concern of alleged scandals in his administration, Harding died in San Francisco on August 2, 1923. He was succeeded by his vice president, Calvin Coolidge.

Harding left his mark as the twenty-ninth president, though he did not live to see the end of his term. In Taft, he had installed a creditable and administratively accomplished chief justice, even though several of Harding's other appointments were less impressive.[47] Chief Justice Taft oversaw a major restructuring of the federal judiciary; he also advocated in favor of a separate building for the Supreme Court, which was completed years later in 1935.[48]

Unquestionably, however, President Harding's pardon of Eugene Debs and other political prisoners was one of his most important and underappreciated legacies. Specifically, his act was a singular contribution to the development of the pardon practice under Article II, Section 2, of the Constitution. These commutations served as a check on potential abuse by *both* coequal branches of government. Harding's strategic use of the presidential pardon helped undo the damage done by a war-frenzied Congress in enacting the Espionage and Sedition Acts, which had been compounded by the failure of the Supreme Court to defend the First Amendment of the Constitution. It was an impressive demonstration of constitutional authority by a president.[49]

Seen in this context, Harding's call for a "return to normalcy" hardly seems as trite as it is often portrayed in historical texts. His ending the abuses of the Sedition Act and the American Protective League did more than simply effect a nonviolent transition back to prewar conditions. The action also clearly showed that President Warren Harding understood the critical need for the executive to use constitutional power to counterbalance pernicious legislation or unwise court rulings that might threaten core freedoms under the U.S. Constitution.

## NOTES

1. Harding's mother was also a medical care provider, generally referred to as a midwife but performing duties of a doctor at the time.
2. John W. Dean, *Warren G. Harding* (New York: Times Books, 2004), 5–30.
3. Robert K. Murray, *The Harding Era: Warren G. Harding and His Administration* (Minneapolis: University of Minnesota Press, 1969), 81–89; James Grant, *The Forgotten Depression, 1921: The Crash That Cured Itself* (New York: Simon & Schuster, 2014), 5–9, 71.
4. David M. Kennedy, *Over Here: The First World War and American Society* (New York: Oxford University Press, 1980; 25th anniv. ed. 2004), 165. In conjunction with the overworked and overmatched Bureau of Investigation, they also conducted raids to apprehend suspected draft dodgers, so-called slacker raids, rounding up nearly fifty thousand men of draft age, for example, over one long weekend in September 1918 from the streets of New York and northern New Jersey.
5. Joan M. Jensen, *The Price of Vigilance* (Chicago: Rand McNally, 1968). The running joke was that IWW stood for "I Won't Work." The theory was that the members of these organizations were not only unlawfully speaking out against the war and conscription but also disrupting and interfering with the industrial mobilization that was needed to power the war.
6. James D. Robenalt, *The Harding Affair: Love and Espionage During the Great War* (New York: Palgrave, 2009), 254.
7. Kennedy, *Over Here*, 79–80.
8. "Senate Accepts Sedition Bill," *New York Times*, May 5, 1918. (The vote was forty-eight to twenty-six in favor of the adoption of the conference report on the Sedition bill.)
9. Nick Salvatore, *Eugene V. Debs, Citizen and Socialist*, 2nd ed. (Urbana: University of Illinois Press, 2007), 291–301. Palmer's name became infamous in American history for the so-called Palmer Raids, the harassment and deportation of thousands of radical leftists and suspected anarchists carried out by, among others, a very eager and young J. Edgar Hoover. Kenneth D. Ackerman, *Young J. Edgar: Hoover, the Red Scare and the Assault on Civil Liberties* (New York: Carroll & Graf Publishers, 2007).
10. Schenck v. United States, 249 U.S. 47 (1919).
11. Referring to the men in the local workhouse he had just visited and mocking Wilson's vaunted "war to make the world safe for democracy," Debs said: "I have just returned from a visit from yonder (pointing to the workhouse) where three of our most loyal comrades are paying the penalty for their devotion to the cause of the working class. They have come to realize, as many of us have, that it is extremely dangerous to exercise the constitutional right of free speech in a country fighting to make democracy safe for the world. I realize in speaking to you this afternoon that there are certain limitations placed upon the right of free speech. I must be extremely careful, prudent, as to what I say, and even more careful and prudent as to how I say it. I may not be able to say all I think, but I am not going to say anything I do not think. And I would rather a thousand times be a free soul in jail than a sycophant or coward on the streets. They may put those boys in jail and the rest of us in jail, but they cannot put the Socialist

movement in jail. . . . They are simply paying the penalty that all men have paid in all the ages of history for standing erect and seeking to pave the way for better conditions for mankind." Eugene V. Debs, speech in Canton, Ohio, June 16, 1918, stenographer transcript attached to the indictment of the Grand Jury, Case No. 4057, U.S. District Court, Northern District of Ohio. The docket papers for the case were provided to the author by U.S. District Court Judge Lesley B. Wells, who sits in the same courtroom where the Debs trial took place in 1918.

12. Debs v. United States, 249 U.S. 211, 212–213 (1919). Debs's expression of such ideas and praise for some who had been jailed for resisting the war were enough for Holmes to find that Debs's speech, taken as a whole, was "so expressed that *its natural and intended effect* would be to obstruct recruiting."

13. Ackerman, *Young J. Edgar*, 150–152.

14. Abrams v. United States, 250 U.S. 616 (1919).

15. Kennedy, *Over Here*, 86.

16. Robenalt, *The Harding Affair*, 63.

17. Taft would tell his politically savvy spouse, Helen Herron "Nellie" Taft, about the meeting, writing her a fourteen-page missive on the day after Christmas. William Howard Taft to Helen Herron Taft, December 26, 1920, Harding Papers, Ohio Historical Society, Columbus, Ohio.

18. Ibid.

19. "Harding to Receive Amnesty Committee," *New York Times*, April 1, 1921.

20. "Harding Refuses Amnesty Grant Now," *New York Times*, April 13, 1921. Among the visitors was Norman Thomas, a rising Socialist who had once worked as a paperboy at the *Marion Star* when Harding was the editor.

21. Harry M. Daugherty, *The Inside Story of the Harding Tragedy* (New York: The Churchill Co., 1932), 120.

22. "Debs, Minus Guard, Visits Washington to Plead His Cause," *New York Times*, March 25, 1921.

23. Ibid.

24. Murray, *The Harding Era*, 125–128, 170–198; Grant, *The Forgotten Depression*, 135–141.

25. "War with Germany Ended July 2, 1921," *New York Times*, November 15, 1921; Murray, *The Harding Era*, 129–140. Peace treaties were signed by the end of the summer, and the Senate then approved them.

26. Murray, *The Harding Era*, 167.

27. U.S. Const. art. II, § 2, cl. 1; Schick v. Reed, 419 U.S. 256, 260 (1974).

28. Murray, *The Harding Era*, 167–168.

29. "Debs Is Released, Prisoners Joining Crowd in Ovation," *New York Times*, December 26, 1921.

30. After the death of Chief Justice Edward White in May 1921, Taft had been swiftly nominated by Harding. He was confirmed by the Senate on June 30, the same day the Senate received his nomination from the president. "Ex-President Taft Succeeds White as Chief Justice," *New York Times*, July 1, 1921.

31. "Debs Sees Harding; Not Asked, He Says, to Alter His Views," *New York Times*, December 27, 1921.

32. Murray, *The Harding Era*, 168–169.

33. Dean, *Warren G. Harding* 155–156.

34. David H. Stratton, *Tempest over Teapot Dome: The Story of Albert B. Fall* (Norman: University of Oklahoma Press, 1998), 237–238.

35. Laton McCartney, *The Teapot Dome Scandal: How Big Oil Bought the Harding White House and Tried to Steal the Country* (New York: Random House, 2008), 106–108.

36. Ibid., 96–97.

37. Stratton, *Tempest over Teapot Dome*, 5, 266–269.

38. Burl Noggle, *Teapot Dome: Oil and Politics in the 1920's* (Baton Rouge: Louisiana State University Press, 1962), 46–47.

39. Ibid., 108–115; Dean, *Warren G. Harding*, 158.

40. Stratton, *Tempest over Teapot Dome*, 266–270; Noggle, *Teapot Dome*, 68–95.

41. Pan-American Petroleum & Transport Co. v. United States, 273 U.S. 456 (1927) (invalidating the leases in Elk Hills, CA); Mammoth Oil Co. v. United States, 275 U.S. 13 (1927) (invalidating the leases in Teapot Dome, WY).

42. McCartney, *Teapot Dome Scandal*, 312–313.

43. Dean, *Warren G. Harding*, 159.

44. Robert H. Ferrell, *The Strange Deaths of President Harding* (Columbia, MO: University of Missouri Press, 1996), 106–114.

45. Francis Russell, *The Shadow of Blooming Grove: Warren G. Harding in His Times* (New York: McGraw-Hill, 1968), 560.

46. McCartney, *The Teapot Dome Scandal*, 137–138.

47. Harding would have the opportunity to appoint three other justices to the Supreme Court before his unexpected death in the summer of 1923: former Senator George Sutherland, Pierce Butler, and Edward T. Sanford. Butler and Sutherland were part of the notorious "Four Horsemen" who fiercely opposed President Franklin D. Roosevelt's New Deal programs. See Chapter 32, "Franklin D. Roosevelt." See also Christopher Tomlins, ed., *The United States Supreme Court: The Pursuit of Justice* (Boston: Houghton Mifflin, 2005), 246–248). Nonetheless, while these justices' records toward labor were quite hostile (see, e.g., Atkins v. Children's Hospital, 261 U.S. 525 [1923]), the Taft Court was generally in step with a large segment of public opinion at the time.

48. Jeffrey B. Morris, "What Heaven Must Be Like: William Howard Taft as Chief Justice, 1921–1930," *Journal of Supreme Court History*, 1983 Yearbook (Washington, DC: Supreme Court Historical Society, 1983), 80–101.

49. Harding's actions with respect to those imprisoned under the Espionage and Sedition Acts were arguably unique among presidential pardons. Pardons and commutations can serve the ends of clemency in an individual case or a broader goal of national healing and reconciliation (President Ford's pardon of Richard M. Nixon, for example). But the Debs commutation seemed to do more. Harding used it as a tool to support a core freedom—free speech under the First Amendment. At a time of war in particular, this sort of farsightedness took both political daring and uncommon wisdom.

# 30

# Calvin Coolidge

JOHN W. JOHNSON AND DALE E. P. YURS

*Calvin Coolidge inherited a presidency tainted by the Teapot Dome scandal and sought to bring stability to the White House to restore public trust. He won a victory in asserting his pardon power to commute the jail sentence of an Illinois man imprisoned for violating the unpopular Prohibition laws, and he appointed Justice Harlan Fiske Stone—a forward-thinking justice—to the Supreme Court. Although some critics attribute the arrival of the Great Depression to Coolidge's laissez-faire approach to governance, he left office with his public support and integrity intact.*

## Introduction

The reputation of John Calvin Coolidge, the nation's thirtieth president, as a preternaturally quiet man with a wry sense of humor is well known.[1] Yet the man who bore the sobriquet "Silent Cal" holds an important place that is frequently overlooked in American history. Coolidge's administration was perhaps the most trouble-free of any twentieth-century chief executive, and it would be hard to identify an American president who left office with greater popularity than that enjoyed by Coolidge. Thus, to paraphrase one biographer, it is important to delve beneath the witticisms and blather to properly understand—and appreciate—Coolidge's strengths and weaknesses.

Coolidge was born on July 4, 1872, in the Vermont hamlet of Plymouth Notch. His father was a storekeeper and a part-time Vermont legislator. Hardly wealthy, the Coolidge family managed to send young Calvin to Amherst College in nearby Massachusetts. After graduation, Coolidge was apprentice to a Bay State lawyer and was admitted to the bar in 1895. He followed his father's example and plunged into politics, completing a remarkable two-decade ascent from the Northampton, Massachusetts, city council to the state governor's mansion. Governor Coolidge attracted national attention by breaking a Boston police strike in the midst of the 1919 Red Scare. This episode helped secure him a place as the vice presidential nominee on the Republicans' "return to normalcy" ticket headed by Warren Harding in 1920.

## Presidency

At 2:30 a.m. on August 3, 1923, Vice President Coolidge was awakened from a sound sleep and informed that President Harding had died the previous afternoon of a heart attack. Reportedly, Coolidge knelt in prayer, took the presidential oath of office administered by his father, a notary public, and returned to bed to complete his interrupted night sleep.

Ironically, this very conventional president was fated to hold office during the so-called Roaring Twenties, a decade known for its modernity and break from tradition. In historical accounts as well as in popular mythology, the 1920s are remembered for jazz music, the flapper styles of urban women, the rise of major spectator sports, and sleek automobiles. Another dimension of the 1920s was Prohibition, the legal ban on the manufacture, sale, and transportation of alcoholic beverages. Accomplished by the Eighteenth Amendment to the Constitution and by federal statute, Prohibition reigned from 1920 to 1933. Although many Americans flagrantly violated the ban, President Coolidge followed the law and served no alcohol in the White House. In addition, the president added his voice and leadership to the efforts of federal agencies that attempted, with little success, to enforce this "noble experiment."

Among Coolidge's first decisions as president was to retain most of Harding's stalwartly Republican cabinet—notably Charles Evans Hughes as secretary of state, Andrew Mellon as secretary of treasury, and Herbert Hoover as head of the Commerce Department. Although his conservative orientation was virtually identical to that of the man he replaced, Coolidge was less garrulous and more remote than Harding. His dealings with Congress were polite but cool. When congressmen joined the president for breakfast in the White House, Coolidge typically consumed his hearty meal in silence. He kept to a relaxed schedule, tending to business only a few hours a day and taking afternoon naps and long vacations. During his first term, Coolidge proposed massive spending cuts and submitted the smallest budget since the years prior to World War I. His distaste for government spending even led him to veto veterans' benefit bills.[2] Indeed, in later years, Coolidge would become a symbol for Americans who believed that the scope of the federal government should be sharply limited.[3]

Coolidge allowed Republican Party bosses to run the election campaign of 1924 in which he sought his own term. The principal reason for Coolidge's absence on the campaign trail was the profound grief that he and Mrs. Coolidge experienced as they mourned the death of their son, Calvin Jr., after he developed an infection from a blister (produced by playing tennis on the White House courts). Young Calvin died a week later, at age sixteen.[4] In many ways, President Coolidge would never be the same. Nonetheless, that November, in a subdued campaign against a weak Democratic nominee (John W. Davis) and a strident Progressive candidate (Robert M. LaFollette), Coolidge took 54 percent of the popular vote and won a landslide victory in the Electoral College.[5]

Coolidge began his own term with characteristic caution. In matters of foreign affairs, he avoided the volatile issue of membership in the League of Nations, while pushing for "outlawing of war" as an instrument of national policy in the Kellogg-Briand Pact of 1928. With Andrew Mellon as his long-serving and faithful secretary of the treasury, the Coolidge administration's support for unfettered business activity continued unabated. Low taxes, minimal regulation of commercial activity, and a blind eye toward stock speculation were hallmarks of the Coolidge years. Coolidge later mused that "four-fifths of all our troubles . . . would disappear if we would only sit down and keep still." The looming hard times, apparently, were a problem that the thirtieth president believed could be avoided by inertia. For that inaction, Coolidge justifiably bears a share of the blame for the Great Depression that began just a few months after he left office.

Historians have paid much more attention to constitutional issues in the administrations of Woodrow Wilson, the chief executive during World War I, and Franklin D. Roosevelt, who would later lead the United States through the Great Depression and World War II, than the man who calmly resided in the White House during the 1920s.[6] Yet some important constitutional dimensions of the Coolidge years deserve discussion in their own right.

## Executive and Legislative Powers

Some of the most notable constitutional decisions of the U.S. Supreme Court during the Coolidge presidency shored up powers of the chief executive in a fashion that would have a lasting impact on future occupants of the White House. One such case concerned the president's right to grant pardons under Article II of the U.S. Constitution. The Constitution extends the power to grant pardons to the chief executive in rather cryptic language: "The President . . . shall have Power to grant Reprieves and Pardons for Offenses against the United States, except in Cases of Impeachment."[7] In *Ex Parte Grossman*, a man who owned a small business was convicted of violating the National Prohibition Act, otherwise known as the Volstead Act.[8] Philip Grossman allegedly caused a nuisance by selling alcoholic beverages at his place of business. An order restraining him from continuing to sell liquor was issued, yet Grossman violated that order. He was arrested, found guilty of contempt in an Illinois federal district court, sentenced to a year's imprisonment in the Chicago House of Correction, and ordered to pay a fine of $1,000. Shortly after Grossman began his term of imprisonment, President Coolidge issued the bootlegger a pardon, commuting his prison sentence and requiring only that he pay his fine. Grossman complied with this agreement and was released from custody.

Yet the district court in *Grossman* maintained that contempt of court was not a pardonable offense against the United States under Article II of the U.S. Constitution. In a move that directly challenged the presidential order, the district court had Grossman rearrested in 1924 and ordered him to return to federal prison to serve out the remaining months of his original sentence.[9] The Supreme Court, in a unanimous opinion authored by Chief Justice William Howard Taft, overturned the order. Surveying precedents in England and America, the Court, in *Ex Parte Grossman*, found that criminal contempt had been consistently understood to fall within the scope of executive pardoning power. Pointedly, the Court noted that on twenty-seven prior occasions, American presidents had exercised their right to pardon individuals convicted of contempt of court.[10]

Moreover, Chief Justice Taft explicitly rejected the lower court's argument that the constitutional principle of separation of powers between the executive and the judiciary would be weakened by a contrary ruling. The chief justice concluded the opinion: "Nowhere is there a more earnest will to maintain the independence of federal courts . . . afforded by the Constitution than in this Court. But the qualified independence which they fortunately enjoy is not likely to be permanently strengthened by ignoring precedent and practice and minimizing the importance of the coordinating checks and balances of the Constitution."[11] In this decision, President Coolidge won a significant victory against a federal court that sought to hamstring him and prevent him from exercising his broad pardon powers.

Another major case dealt with the power of presidents to remove certain executive officials without congressional approval. In *Myers v. U.S.*, decided in 1926, Chief Justice Taft examined history from the Constitutional Convention. He concluded that the framers' silence on the matter of removing such officials (when *appointment* required the "advice and consent" of the Senate) implied that this power rested squarely with the president. His rationale was the Vesting Clause of Article II, Section 1, which vested the executive power in the president of the United States.[12] Back in 1920, President Wilson had removed a postmaster in Portland, Oregon, in contravention of an act of Congress stating that postmasters could be "appointed and removed" by the president only "with the advice and consent of the Senate." Six years later, the Court now concluded that this federal law violated the separation of powers between the executive and legislative branches and was unconstitutional. The power to remove, the Court indicated, was implicit in the power to appoint. (The Court, in dicta, further declared that the controversial Tenure of Office Act, which had likewise sought to restrict the president in removing appointees and had led to the impeachment of President Andrew Johnson when he sought to remove his secretary of war, was likewise unconstitutional. By that time, the Tenure of Office Act had long since been repealed by Congress.)[13]

Perhaps the most important case handed down during the Coolidge presidency, however, was *McGrain v. Daugherty*.[14] This decision marked an important boundary line between congressional and executive branch power, representing the culmination of the Teapot Dome oil leasing scandal that had all but paralyzed the Harding administration in the early 1920s. Mally S. Daugherty, brother of former Attorney General Harry M. Daugherty (who had served as attorney general under both Presidents Harding and Coolidge until he was forced to resign under the cloud of this scandal), had been president of an Ohio bank. He was subpoenaed to appear before a congressional committee and instructed to bring with him certain bank records that might bear on his brother's alleged illegal acts involving Teapot Dome—notably, the former attorney general's intentional failure to prosecute violators of federal antitrust laws because of his own complicity. The banker refused to honor the subpoenas, arguing that Congress did not have a sufficiently clear constitutional basis for issuing these commands to deliver over documents. Daugherty was duly arrested by the Senate's sergeant at arms for contempt, in light of his failure to comply with congressional subpoenas.

A unanimous Supreme Court (including Coolidge's sole appointee, Justice Harlan Fiske Stone) ruled that the federal district court had acted improperly in releasing Daugherty from his obligation to respond to congressional subpoenas, and it upheld Daughtery's contempt conviction.[15] Daugherty's claim that the Senate did not have the power to compel him to appear and bring with him certain documents had no validity, Justice Willis Van Devanter wrote, because "the power of inquiry—with process to enforce it—is an essential and appropriate auxiliary to the legislative function."[16] Thus, *McGrain v. Daugherty* made clear that Congress had power to carry out its own investigations, issue subpoenas, and exact testimony, separate from those functions carried out by the executive and judicial branches.

The key constitutional question resolved in *McGrain* was whether a legislative purpose could be presumed simply because a subpoena for testimony and documents had been issued. Justice Van Devanter acknowledged that it would have been ideal if there had been "an express avowal" of legislative purpose by Congress. Yet the Court concluded that the object of the Senate's inquiry—that is, relating to the Teapot Dome scandal—"was such that the presumption should be indulged that . . . [a legislative purpose] was the real object."[17] The Court in *McGrain* thus set the bar low for permitting Congress to compel testimony and produce documents, even without an express articulation of a legislative purpose. In future years, this decision would be cited regularly to justify far-reaching and often controversial congressional investigations—including those that took place during the McCarthy era of the 1950s, as well as investigations of presidents during the Watergate scandal of the 1970s and again during the investigation of President Bill Clinton in the 1990s.

Although former Attorney General Daugherty was ultimately cleared by the two special prosecutors in the Teapot Dome affair, his assistant attorney general, Jess Smith, committed suicide, and the scandal seriously damaged public trust in government. *McGrain v. Daugherty* helped bring closure to the scandal, which had carried over from the Harding to the Coolidge presidency. It also clearly demonstrated that Congress had a weapon that it could use, directly and indirectly, in investigating the executive branch.

### The Supreme Court's Docket

Coolidge benefited by having a brilliant judicial administrator and legal visionary, William Howard Taft (appointed by President Harding in 1921), serve as chief justice of the United States throughout the entirety of his presidency.[18] From virtually the moment he took the reins of the Court, Chief Justice Taft had championed a proposal to grant the U.S. Supreme Court unprecedented control over its docket of cases, a modification first proposed by Chief Justice John Marshall a century earlier.[19] This restructuring was finally realized during the Coolidge presidency, with the enactment of the Judiciary Act of 1925, generally known as "the Judges' Bill."[20] Before the passage of this law, cases reached the High Court via several routes, primarily through "writs of error." This cumbersome process, created by the Judiciary Act of 1789, forced the Court to hear time-consuming but often trivial appeals from lower federal courts and state supreme courts.[21]

After the Judiciary Act of 1925 was enacted into law, petitioning for a writ of certiorari became the principal route by which a federal or state case could reach the Supreme Court. If, in the estimation of four of the nine justices, the case presented "an important question of federal law" or a "split" in the federal circuit courts of appeal or among the highest state courts, the high court could elect to grant certiorari.[22]

With the certiorari process established by the Judges' Bill, the Supreme Court was finally able to control its own docket. It eliminated from the Supreme Court's calendar cases the justices deemed of minimal importance, and it allowed the chief justice and his colleagues to reach down into the vast state and federal pool of appealable cases and select the most important controversies for resolution by the nation's highest court. Thus, the passage of the Judges' Bill in 1925 was a victory for Chief Justice Taft and, indirectly, for President Coolidge.

President Coolidge's imprint on the Supreme Court was not limited to the innovations of Chief Justice Taft. It was also linked to the contributions of his sole nomination to the Court—his Amherst College friend, Harlan Fiske Stone.[23] Throughout the 1920s, Stone became the quiet partner in a famous triumvirate—along with Oliver Wendell Holmes and Louis D. Brandeis—frequently dissenting from decisions of the Taft Court that gave short shrift to civil liberties.[24] Years later, Justice Stone would write one of the most famous footnotes in U.S. constitutional law, authoring the Court's opinion in *U.S. v. Carolene Products* (1938), and laying the foundation for modern "strict scrutiny" under the federal Due Process and Equal Protection Clauses of the Fourteenth Amendment.[25] Although Coolidge himself was no advocate of extending constitutional freedoms to individuals exhibiting less-than-mainstream ideas or behaviors, the opinions of his sole appointee nonetheless helped shape the jurisprudence of the Court for the rest of the twentieth century.

## Conclusion

Coolidge would not live to see many of these famous cases. While on summer vacation in 1927, he announced that he would not seek another term, content to have served five years in the White House. He retired with his wife to his hometown of Northampton, Massachusetts, where he enjoyed the outdoors and completed his autobiography.[26] Coolidge died of heart failure shortly after lunch on January 5, 1933.[27]

Not long after Coolidge's presidency, the specter of the Great Depression had begun to creep over the United States, with a stock market crash and economic contraction causing critics to question whether some of these disastrous events might be attributable, in hindsight, to Coolidge's policies while he was in office. Yet Calvin Coolidge managed to leave office in 1929 with substantial public support, largely because he had brought calmness to the White House following the scandals that overtook the Harding administration.[28] Alfred E. Smith, the unsuccessful Democratic nominee for president in 1928, offered an apt valedictory for the nation's thirtieth president: Coolidge, he submitted, was "distinguished for character more than for heroic achievement. . . . His great task was to restore the dignity and prestige of the Presidency when it had reached the lowest ebb in our history . . . in a time of extravagance and waste."[29] In helping accomplish that goal, "Silent Cal" left behind an honorable legacy as chief executive.

## NOTES

1. General background on Calvin Coolidge and his administration is drawn primarily from Robert H. Ferrell, *The Presidency of Calvin Coolidge* (Lawrence: University Press of Kansas, 1998). See also John W. Johnson, "John Calvin Coolidge," in *The American Presidents*, ed. Melvin I. Urofsky (New York: Garland Publishing, 2000), 313–322. One example of Coolidge's humor: A young Calvin Coolidge journeyed to Burlington, Vermont, in 1905 to ask his future father-in-law for Grace Anna Goodhue's hand in marriage. Mr. Goodhue inquired of the bold suiter, "Does Grace know yet?" Coolidge replied: "No, but she will soon." "Coolidge Humor," *Calvin Coolidge: 30th President*, accessed December 30, 2011, www.calvincoolidge.us/humor.html.

2. In addition to the conventional veto power, Coolidge also relied on what became known as the pocket veto. In 1925, Congress sent him a bill that would have allowed American Indians in Washington State to sue for damages from the loss of their tribal lands. Coolidge neither signed nor vetoed the bill; instead, he waited for the legislative session to end ten days later. This practice had been used by many past presidents and was upheld by the Supreme Court in this instance. The Pocket Veto Case, 279 U.S. 655 (1929).

3. Robert Sobel, *Coolidge: An American Enigma* (Washington, DC: Regnery, 1998), 12–13; David Greenberg, *Calvin Coolidge: The American Presidents Series* (New York: Times Books, 2006), 49–53.

4. Russel Fowler, "Calvin Coolidge: Country Lawyer," in *America's Lawyer Presidents*, ed. Normal Gross (Evanston, IL: Northwestern University Press, 2004), 246.

5. Donald R. McCoy, *Calvin Coolidge: The Quiet President* (New York: Macmillan, 1967), 262.

6. Melvin I. Urofsky and Paul Finkelman, *A March of Liberty: A Constitutional History of the United States*, 2nd ed., vol. 2 (New York: Oxford University Press, 2011).

7. U.S. Const. art. II, § 2.

8. Ex Parte Grossman, 267 U.S. 87 (1925); Volstead Act, 41 Stat. 305 (1919).

9. *Ex Parte Grossman*, 267 U.S. at 107–108.

10. Ibid., 108–119.

11. Ibid., 119–122.

12. Myers v. United States, 272 U.S. 52 (1926).

13. Ibid., 165–176.

14. McGrain v. Daugherty, 273 U.S. 135 (1927).

15. Ibid., 150–154.

16. Ibid., 174; Akhil Reed Amar, *America's Unwritten Constitution: The Precedents and Principles We Live By* (New York: Basic Books, 2012), 335–340.

17. *McGrain v. Daugherty*, 178.

18. On Taft as chief justice, see Robert C. Post, "William Howard Taft," in *The Supreme Court Justices: A Biographical Dictionary*, ed. Melvin I. Urofsky (New York: Garland Publishing, 1994), 457–463.

19. Taft and a committee of justices—Associate Justices Willis Van Devanter, William Day, James McReynolds, and George Sutherland—prepared a draft bill and worked tirelessly for the passage of the Judges' Bill. Merlo J. Pusey, "The 'Judges' Bill' After a Half Century," *Supreme Court Historical Society Yearbook* (1976): 56–57. Taft went so far as to personally introduce the bill to the House Judiciary Committee in 1922. Jonathan Sternberg, "Deciding Not to Decide: The Judiciary Act of 1925," *Journal of Supreme Court History* 33, no. 1 (2008): 9.

20. Judiciary Act of 1925, 43 Stat. 936 (1925). See Pusey, "The 'Judges' Bill,'" 55.

21. Judiciary Act of 1789, 1 Stat. 73 (1789); Sternberg, "Deciding Not to Decide," 4.

22. H. W. Perry Jr., *Deciding to Decide: Agenda Setting in the United States Supreme Court* (Cambridge, MA: Harvard University Press, 1991), 33–34. See also William H. Rehnquist, *The Supreme Court*, rev. and updated (New York: Vintage Books, 2001), 12.

23. Alpheus T. Mason, *Harlan Fiske Stone: Pillar of the Law* (New York: Viking Press, 1956). See also John W. Johnson, "Harlan Fiske Stone," in *The Supreme Court Justices: A Biographical Dictionary*, ed. Melvin I. Urofsky (New York: Garland Publishing, 1994), 423–434.

24. For one example, see Olmstead v. United States., 277 U.S. 438 (1928). The case involved the conviction of Roy "Big Boy" Olmstead for liquor smuggling. Police obtained a conviction by using hundreds of pages of transcribed phone conversations obtained by wiretapping. Although there was no physical intrusion into Olmstead's place of business or any taking of tangible evidence, his lawyers asserted that there had been an "unreasonable search and seizure" under the Fourth Amendment. The Supreme Court, led by Chief Justice Taft, concluded that this novel technology of wiretapping was an effective tool to aid law enforcement, and it did not constitute a search or seizure. Justices Holmes, Brandeis and Stone dissented.

25. United States v. Carolene Products Co., 304 U.S. 144, 152 n. 4 (1938).

26. Calvin Coolidge, *The Autobiography of Calvin Coolidge* (New York: Cosmopolitan Book Corp., 1929).

27. Claude M. Fuess, *Calvin Coolidge: The Man From Vermont* (Boston: Little, Brown and Co., 1940), 445, 464.

28. Fowler, "Calvin Coolidge: Country Lawyer," 250–251.

29. Frank Freidel, *The Presidents of the United States of America* (Collingdale, PA: Diane Publishing, 1998), 65.

# 31

# Herbert Hoover

JOHN Q. BARRETT

*Herbert Clark Hoover, first an international businessman, a global hero during World War I, and then a cabinet officer under Presidents Harding and Coolidge, was elected president in 1928. The next year, as President Hoover embarked on his progressive agenda for the country, the Roaring Twenties ended, crashingly, in the Great Depression. Hoover responded inadequately, constrained more by his own beliefs in volunteerism than by constitutional limits on his powers. His failure to relieve public suffering overshadowed his presidential accomplishments, including innovative government programs and three Supreme Court appointments.*

## Introduction

F̲ew reputations have risen and fallen like that of Herbert Hoover. By the end of World War I, he was a world hero whom many Americans could not wait to elect president, if only he would run. In 1928, he sought the office (as a Republican), and they did elect him. Less than a year later, the stock market crashed and the Great Depression began. During the rest of Hoover's presidential term, the American public, which had viewed him as a managerial superman, came to conclude that he was not solving and could not solve this calamity. In 1932, the voters rejected him resoundingly. For much of the rest of Hoover's long life, he was a political pariah. And in the years since his death, most have regarded Hoover as among the most failed of failed presidents. Underneath that defining reality, however, his life story, his pre-presidential accomplishments, his views on U.S. constitutional government, and his productivity into old age make his a life worth studying.

Hoover, a descendant of Swiss immigrants, was born on August 10, 1874, in West Branch, Iowa, a Quaker settlement. Nicknamed "Bertie," he was the middle of three children. His father Jesse, a blacksmith who became a businessman and a local politician, died when Herbert was six, leaving the family impoverished. His mother Hulda(h), a Society of Friends minister, raised her children in the strictness of her faith and often put this ministry ahead of their care. When she died soon after her husband, her orphaned children were parceled out to relatives. Herbert moved to an uncle, and six years of hard labor, in Oregon. Some believe that his childhood scarred his personality for life, producing the stiffness, the shyness, and the lack of political skills that, in the crisis of the Great Depression, doomed his presidency.[1]

Hoover's boyhood made him hardworking, self-reliant, and a Westerner. In 1891, he was admitted to Stanford University's first class. He studied geology, became a campus leader, and met Lou Henry, the student whom he later married. After graduating in 1895 (ironically, a time of economic depression), he worked in gold mines and eventually found work as a mining engineer. That position took him to London and eventually to Australia, where his employer struck gold and Hoover became a hard-driving mine manager. He next worked in China, supervising vast mining operations, and in many other spots across Asia. In 1908, he started his own global mining and engineering firm, achieving business renown and great personal wealth.[2] These experiences shaped Hoover's economic and social outlook. He believed that individual effort, corporate power, business self-regulation, and citizen volunteerism were the proper paths—and for an American, the constitutional paths—to progress.[3]

When World War I began in August 1914, Hoover worked initially in London to provide financial aid and evacuation to two hundred thousand American travelers in Europe. Next, he headed the Commission for Relief in Belgium, administering food aid to civilians who, cut off from supplies by the war and blockades, otherwise would have starved. Through this work, which lasted through 1916, Hoover saved millions and became a global emblem of selflessness, talent, and administrative genius.[4]

In 1917, after the U.S. joined the war, President Wilson recruited Hoover to serve as U.S. food administrator. Exercising vast powers—sometimes without any statutory authorization—Hoover encouraged, directed, and enforced food rationing to free up supplies for U.S troops fighting in Europe. After the war, Hoover assisted President Wilson at the Paris Peace Conference and then became U.S. relief administrator in Europe. By 1920, his popularity was so great that the Democratic Party and the Republican Party each wanted Hoover to run as its presidential candidate.[5]

Hoover declined to run for president in 1920. Instead, he supported the Republican nominee, Senator Warren G. Harding, who, after his inauguration, appointed Hoover as secretary of commerce. In that position, which he held through Harding's presidency (1921–1923) and most of Calvin Coolidge's (1923–1929), Hoover exercised considerable power and stayed in the public eye. He promoted government regulation of new industries, including aviation and radio, and led government policy regarding business and industry during a time of great economic advances.

When President Coolidge decided not to seek reelection in 1928, Hoover, running for elective office for the first time in his life, finally sought the presidency. Nominated by the Republicans, he campaigned to lead America's "final triumph over poverty." His life story, including business successes and world achievements, was his platform. Benefitting from his reputation, from general prosperity, and probably from public prejudice against the Catholicism of his opponent (Governor Alfred E. Smith of New York), Hoover carried forty out of forty-eight states (with 58 percent of the popular vote), winning 444 electoral votes and the White House.[6]

## Presidency

After taking office in March 1929, President Hoover sought immediately and energetically to complete America's rise to greatness. Through legislation and executive actions, he addressed some of the "uncompleted tasks in government," including greater protections for labor, tax reform, patronage reform, and natural resource conservation. Exercising his constitutional power under Article II, Section 3, he called Congress into a special session on April 15, 1929—the twenty-second special session in U.S. history—to combat distress in the farm economy.[7] By the time the session ended on November 22, 1929, Hoover had obtained a farm bill providing new support for agricultural cooperatives.[8] In its regular session, which began a week later, Congress passed and the president signed one item that had not been finished in the special session: greater tariff protection for industry. That law, the protectionist Hawley-Smoot tariff law of 1930, probably hampered trade during the Great Depression.

President Hoover also focused on crime and law enforcement. In spring 1929, he established a commission, headed by former U.S. Attorney General George W. Wickersham (who had served under President Taft), to identify causes of crime, especially violations of laws enforcing the Eighteenth Amendment prohibition of alcohol, and to make policy recommendations. The Wickersham Commission—officially called the National Commission on Law Observance & Enforcement—investigated public behavior under Prohibition laws and studied police practices in the states. The commission's reports documented the widespread non-enforcement of Prohibition (which Hoover supported, as a candidate in 1928 and throughout his presidency) and abusive police interrogation practices.[9] Although the commission called for more vigorous enforcement of Prohibition, its reports created widespread knowledge of Prohibition's failure, contributing to the ratification of the Twenty-First Amendment in December 1933, repealing the Eighteenth and returning to the states the constitutional power to become "wet." By documenting police abuses, the Wickersham Commission also contributed to expanded judicial interpretations of Fourteenth Amendment limits on such conduct.[10]

Herbert Hoover revered the U.S. and its Constitution. He was not a lawyer, however, so his constitutional knowledge and understanding were not formed by legal education, law practice, or much legal theory. As he described it in a Constitution Day speech early in his post-presidency, he saw the Constitution as a "working plan" with three core characteristics. The Constitution, he said, (1) preserves "a great Federation of States"; (2) places the States under a system of representative national government; and (3) through the Bill of Rights, protects "the vital principles of the American system of liberty"—and, he added with a trace of self-congratulation, "it does not require a lawyer to interpret those provisions."[11]

## Response to the Great Depression

In October 1929, on Black Tuesday, the U.S. stock market crashed. Hoover, believing that the resulting downturn was an American recession, sought voluntary responses from business and labor. He also called for more public works and other spending by states and cities, rather than by the federal government. U.S. banks began to fail; by 1930, over a thousand banks had suspended operations. Foreclosures rose precipitously, with over a million families losing their homes and farms. In 1931, the Committee for Unemployment Relief issued a report stating that between four and five million Americans had been thrown into unemployment. A believer in the power of the free market and individual initiative, Hoover opposed direct federal relief for suffering Americans. The public perceived this as presidential hard-heartedness—by 1932, camps of homeless people in cities across the nation were known as Hoovervilles—and that view was compounded by the army's forceful response in 1932 to World War I veterans who marched on Washington seeking benefits. To Hoover, his resistance to the federal "dole" reflected the proper, limited, constitutional role of the federal government.

## Supreme Court Decisions and Appointments

In 1932, a Washington, D.C., newspaper headline reported "Docket of Supreme Court Has No Cases of National Import."[12] Although that was an exaggeration, the Hoover years did not feature Supreme Court decisions as important as those in earlier and later eras. President Hoover did, however, win Court decisions that clarified the breadth of the president's powers to veto and sign bills into law and to make executive branch appointments. He also appointed notable Supreme Court justices and, indeed, played a small ceremonial role in building the "marble temple" that is the Court's home today.

In *The Pocket Veto Case*, the new attorney general, William DeWitt Mitchell, who had served as solicitor general under President Coolidge, argued on behalf of the United States on the Hoover administration's eighth day. That May, the Supreme Court decided unanimously that under Article I, Section 7, of the Constitution, the president's power to "pocket-veto" legislation by not signing it after a Congress's adjournment applied not only to the adjournment at the end of a two-year Congress, but also to an adjournment at the end of Congress's first regular session.[13] In other words, the pocket veto could be used during an adjournment midway through a Congress's two-year lifespan.[14]

Three years later, the Hoover administration won another Supreme Court case that clarified a related dimension of a president's constitutional powers in the legislative process. *Edwards v. United States* was a test case designed to make the Supreme Court answer a question that had loomed unresolved over every president.[15] The Court held, again unanimously, that the Constitution did not limit the president's "ten Days (Sundays excepted)" for signing a bill into law to the period before a Congress's final adjournment. A president had all of that time—"ten Days (Sundays excepted)"—to sign a bill into law or veto it, even if the period extended beyond the final adjournment of Congress. This decision spared President Hoover and his successors from the pressured work, which he and each of his predecessors had engaged in, of sitting in the Capitol building as a Congress was about to adjourn, hurriedly reviewing and then signing or vetoing the many bills that the House and Senate typically would pass in those final hours.

Finally, the Supreme Court also ruled in President Hoover's favor in a case concerning the constitutional process by which presidents appoint executive branch officials. In late 1930, Hoover nominated George Otis Smith, longtime director of the U.S. Geological Survey, to head the newly created Federal Power Commission. The Senate confirmed Smith's nomination and so notified the president, who then signed Smith's commission and had it delivered to Smith. The new commission head then took his oath of office and began work. Under Smith's leadership, the Federal Power Commission promptly dismissed its accountant and its solicitor. Outraged, the Senate invoked its rules defining procedures for handling presidential nominations and asked President Hoover to return the Senate resolution consenting to Smith's appointment. Hoover refused, declaring that Smith was duly appointed and that returning the Senate's consent would give the legislative body an unconstitutional power to encroach on completed presidential appointments. The Senate, employing outside counsel, then began a high-profile test case.[16] In *United States v. Smith*, the Supreme Court held unanimously in favor of the president's authority. According to Senate rules, the Court said, when the Senate notified the president of its confirmation of a nomination, the president was empowered to make a final appointment. The appointment had to occur (as it had in Smith's case) before the Senate notified the president that it was recalling the nomination and reconsidering its vote to confirm.[17]

In addition to winning these decisions clarifying presidential powers, President Hoover, fulfilling one of his important constitutional responsibilities, made three extremely significant appointments to the Supreme Court.[18] In early 1930, following the resignation of Chief Justice (and former president) Taft, Hoover appointed the next chief justice, Charles Evans Hughes.[19] Hughes was a former associate justice, the 1916 Republican presidential candidate (and near winner), and secretary of state from 1921 to 1925. As Hoover's former cabinet colleague and the president's trusted friend, Hughes served on the Court until 1941. He led the Supreme Court during a decade of significant transition. The Hughes Court, first actively hostile to New Deal laws under President Franklin Roosevelt, became a Court of restraint and deference toward the political branches; Hughes became one of the greatest chief justices in history.

Associate Justice Edward T. Sanford died less than one month after Chief Justice Hughes received his commission. To fill the vacancy, President Hoover first nominated John J. Parker of the U.S. Court of Appeals for the Fourth Circuit, but the nominee was rejected by the Senate.[20] Hoover then nominated Philadelphia lawyer Owen J. Roberts, who in 1924 had served as a Teapot Dome special prosecutor, to fill the vacancy. The Senate confirmed Justice Roberts, who served on the Court until he resigned in 1945. Justice Roberts ended up playing a key role as the swing vote in the "Switch in Time that Saved Nine" during the Roosevelt administration, saving FDR's New Deal program (see Chapter 32, "Franklin D. Roosevelt"). He also led the Roberts Commissions, which investigated the Japanese attack on Pearl Harbor and other matters during World War II, leaving an important mark on the country.

In early 1932, following the resignation of Associate Justice Oliver Wendell Holmes Jr., President Hoover made his final appointment to the Court. Responding to the overwhelming consensus of the legal profession, he selected Benjamin N. Cardozo, then chief judge of the New York Court of Appeals. Justice Cardozo served only six years, but on the Supreme Court, he completed one of the greatest judicial careers in U.S. history.[21]

Hoover's contributions to the Supreme Court also included a ceremonial connection to its edifice. On October 13, 1932, flanked by the justices and many other officials, the president—using a trowel made from mahogany and silver taken from articles once used in the old Supreme Court chamber—placed the first dab of mortar beneath the "A.D. 1932" cornerstone of what would become the Supreme Court building in Washington.[22] When it was completed in 1935, the Court had, for the first time, its own home.

## Post-Presidency

The Great Depression caused the U.S. economy to spiral downward, culminating in one of the worst economic disasters in the nation's history. With it, citizens' morale and confidence in the government sank, along with the public's approval of President Hoover. In November 1932, New York Governor Franklin D. Roosevelt carried forty-two of forty-eight states (with 57 percent of the popular vote), winning 472 electoral votes to President Hoover's 59. Once the world's hero, Hoover had become a rejected leader and a political pariah.

Yet Hoover, age fifty-eight when he left office, never retired or accepted his defeat. Over the next three decades, he worked to attack his critics, to rehabilitate his reputation, to write extensively, and to perform meaningful national and international service. In his first years out of office, Hoover tended to be a combative, partisan critic of FDR and the New Deal.[23] Indeed, Hoover worked aggressively but unsuccessfully behind the scenes to secure the Republican nomination to run against Roosevelt in 1936 and especially in 1940.[24] His messages focused on liberty, freedom, and what he viewed as unconstitutional excesses in national government.

After FDR's time, and as a memories of the Depression became more distant, however, Hoover came to be viewed as an elder statesman. After years of exile from the White House, he was welcomed back by President Harry Truman and they became friends.[25]

In 1946, in something of a reprise of Hoover's World War I–era activities, Truman sent Hoover on a 35,000-mile trip to thirty-eight countries on five continents, to survey post–World War II conditions, including food shortages and the plight of refugees.[26] Under Truman and again under President Dwight D. Eisenhower, Hoover twice headed commissions that recommended reorganizations of the federal government, which had vastly expanded since his presidency.

## Conclusion

On October 20, 1964, President Hoover, age ninety and then the longest-surviving former president in U.S. history, died in his apartment in New York's Waldorf Astoria Hotel. His remains are buried in West Branch, Iowa, near the site of his birth and what is today his presidential library and museum.[27] Another towering tribute to Hoover's memory can be found at Stanford University, in the form of the Hoover Institution on War, Revolution and Peace.[28] This leading academic research center developed from the archive of war-related material that Hoover first collected in Paris in 1919. Herbert Hoover probably formed his constitutional views by self-projection. He, an American from very humble beginnings, rose and flourished in business because of individual freedom and effort. He then functioned in important and historic roles—including as president of the United States—by considering, exercising, and addressing the chief executive's constitutional place, powers, and limits for almost fifty years. He viewed the U.S. Constitution as empowering individuals and government officials to take the steps he regarded as necessary and wise, and as limiting those who would seek to do otherwise.

## NOTES

1. See generally William E. Leuchtenburg, *Herbert Hoover* (New York: Times Books, Henry Holt & Co., 2009). This chapter relies significantly on this scholarly and elegant book.
2. See generally George H. Nash, *The Life of Herbert Hoover*, vol. 1, *The Engineer, 1874–1914*, vol. 1 (New York: W.W. Norton, 1983).
3. Joan Hoff, "Hoover, Herbert Clark" in *American National Biography* 11 (1999): 151–155. See, for example, Herbert Hoover, *American Individualism* (Garden City, NY: Doubleday, 1922).
4. See generally George H. Nash, *The Life of Herbert Hoover*, vol. 2, *The Humanitarian, 1914–1917* (New York: W.W. Norton, 1988).
5. See generally George H. Nash, *The Life of Herbert Hoover*, vol. 3, *Master of Emergencies, 1917–1918* (New York: W.W. Norton, 1996).

6. Allan J. Lichtman, *Prejudice and the Old Politics: The Presidential Election of 1928* (Chapel Hill: University of North Carolina Press, 1979), cited in Daniel Okrent, *Last Call: The Rise & Fall of Prohibition* (New York: Scribner, 2011), 308.

7. U.S. Const. art. II, § 3. In 1929, the Seventieth Congress, which had been elected in 1926 and had become a lame duck following the 1928 election, adjourned on March 3, the day before President Hoover's inauguration. As a result, absent the calling of a special session, the new Seventy-First Congress would not have met until the first Monday in December, almost nine months later. U.S. Const. art. I, § 4, cl. 2. The Twentieth Amendment, which the states ratified unanimously during Hoover's presidency but which did not take effect until after he had left office, changed Congress's ordinary meeting date to January 3. The amendment also changed the presidential inauguration date from March 4 to January 20. As a result, after a presidential election, the new Congress meets shortly before the new president is inaugurated. U.S. Const., amend. XX, § 2 (effective October 15, 1933); "Next Extra Session of Congress Is 22d," *Washington Post*, February 24, 1929, M14.

8. In the special session, Congress also passed President Hoover's recommended bill providing for a comprehensive 1930 federal census and then automatic reapportionment of House districts using the population data collected. Congress rejected, however, his request to postpone the effective date of new national origin-based immigration quotas.

9. Okrent, *Last Call*, 304–305, 315–316. Hoover emphasized "respect for all law." Noting that the Constitution provides for no presidential role in its amendment, he also believed that a president's duty is to enforce that Constitution as it is and to take no positions on its possible amendment.

10. See, for example, Ashcraft v. Tennessee, 322 U.S. 143, 150 n. 5 (1944) (reversing a defendant's criminal conviction because it was based on his confession after thirty-six hours of unconstitutionally coercive police detention and sleep deprivation, and quoting Wickersham Commission findings about secret, illegal "third degree" practices conducted by police in their stations' upstairs and back rooms); Miranda v. Arizona, 384 U.S. 436, 445 (1966) ("From extensive factual studies undertaken in the early 1930's, including the famous Wickersham Report to Congress by a Presidential Commission, it is clear that police violence and the 'third degree' flourished at that time"). See also Stein v. New York, 346 U.S. 156, 201–202 (1953) (Frankfurter, J., dissenting) ("By its change of direction the Court affords new inducement to police and prosecutors to employ the third degree, whose use the Wickersham Commission found 'widespread' more than thirty years ago and . . . unsparingly condemned").

11. Herbert Hoover, "Meaning of Constitution & Bill of Rights," speech, San Diego, CA, September 17, 1935, www.constitution.org/cmt/hh/constitution_day_speech_1935.html.

12. *Washington Post*, September 25, 1932, 11.

13. U.S. Const., art. I, § 7, cl. 2, provides: "Every Bill which shall have passed the House of Representatives and the Senate, shall, before it become a Law, be presented to the President of the United States; If he approve he shall sign it, but if not he shall return it, with his Objections to that House in which it shall have originated, who shall enter the Objections at large on their Journal, and proceed to reconsider it. If after such

Reconsideration two thirds of that House shall agree to pass the Bill, it shall be sent, together with the Objections, to the other House, by which it shall likewise be reconsidered, and if approved by two thirds of that House, it shall become a Law. But in all such Cases the Votes of both Houses shall be determined by yeas and Nays, and the Names of the Persons voting for and against the Bill shall be entered on the Journal of each House respectively. If any Bill shall not be returned by the President within ten Days (Sundays excepted) after it shall have been presented to him, the same shall be a Law, in like Manner as if he had signed it, unless the Congress by their Adjournment prevent its Return, in which Case it shall not be a Law."

14. The Pocket Veto Case (The Okanogan, Methow, San Poelis, Nespelem, Colville, and Lake Indian Tribes or Bands of the State of Washington v. United States), 279 U.S. 655 (1929).

15. Edwards v. United States, 286 U.S. 482 (1932).

16. The Senate's lawyers were former presidential nominee John W. Davis and former Michigan governor Alexander J. Groesbeck. Smith was represented by former U.S. senator George Wharton Pepper. The United States, which took cooperative administrative steps that allowed the Senate to bring the case on the merits was amicus curiae on Smith's side of the dispute; the U.S. lawyers were Attorney General Mitchell, Solicitor General Thomas D. Thacher, and Department of Justice attorney (and future Harvard Law School dean and, decades later, solicitor general) Erwin N. Griswold.

17. United States v. Smith, 286 U.S. 6 (1932). In *Smith*, Justice Brandeis's opinion for the Court tracked the legal opinion on this issue that the attorney general had provided earlier to President Hoover. William D. Mitchell, *Legality of Appointment of Certain Members of the Federal Power Commission*, 36 Official Opinions of the Attorneys General 382–388 (January 10, 1931).

18. U.S. Const., art. II, § 2, cl. 2 (the President "shall nominate . . . Judges of the supreme Court"). See generally Henry J. Abraham, *Justices, Presidents & Senators*, 5th ed. (Lanham, MD: Rowman & Littlefield, 2008), 155–162.

19. Merlo J. Pusey, *Charles Evans Hughes*, vol. 2 (New York: Macmillan, 1951), 650–652. A competing account of this event is Frederick Bernays Wiener, "Justice Hughes' Appointment: The Cotton Story Re-Examined," *Supreme Court Historical Society* (1981): 78–91. A possible harmonization is James M. Buchanan, "A Note on the 'Joe Cotton Story,'" *Supreme Court Historical Society* (1981): 92–93.

20. The NAACP, outraged by Parker statements that were hostile to black people voting, and labor unions, and outraged by Parker decisions upholding antilabor injunctions, organized and lobbied successfully to defeat his nomination. Judge Parker continued to serve in the Fourth Circuit until his death in 1958. He was mentioned prominently as a leading candidate, but was not selected, for Supreme Court appointment by Presidents Roosevelt, Truman, and Eisenhower. Judge Parker did, by appointment of President Truman, serve as the U.S. alternate member of the International Military Tribunal in Nuremberg during 1945 and 1946.

21. Andrew L. Kaufman, *Cardozo* (Cambridge, MA: Harvard University Press, 1998), 455–456, 461–465; Andrew L. Kaufman, "Cardozo's Appointment to the Supreme Court," *Cardozo Law Review* 1 (1979): 23.

22. "Corner Stone of New Home of Supreme Court of the United States Is Laid," *American Bar Association Journal* 18 (1932): 729 (reporting the use of the trowel by President Hoover, Chief Justice Hughes, and ABA President Guy A. Thompson, and that it was "made of silver and mahogany from old articles long used in the Court's Chamber").

23. See, for example, Herbert Hoover, *The Challenge to Liberty* (New York: Charles Scribner's Sons, 1934).

24. George H. Nash, editor's introduction to *The Crusade Years, 1933–1955: Herbert Hoover's Lost Memoir of the New Deal Era and Its Aftermath* (Stanford, CA: Hoover Institution Press, 2013), xxiii.

25. Nancy Gibbs and Michael Duffy, *The Presidents Club: Inside the World's Most Exclusive Fraternity* (New York: Simon & Shuster, 2012). An online archive is "Hoover & Truman: A Presidential Friendship," a joint project of the Herbert Hoover Presidential Library and the Harry S. Truman Presidential Library, accessed May 27, 2015, www.trumanlibrary.org/hoover/book.htm.

26. Eugene Lyons, *Herbert Hoover: A Biography* (Garden City, NY: Doubleday, 1964), 385–390.

27. The Herbert Hoover Presidential Library and Museum, in West Branch, IA, is a federal government facility administered by the National Archives and Records Administration. The website is www.hoover.archives.gov.

28. See the website of the Hoover Institution, Stanford, CA, and Washington, DC, at www.hoover.org.

# PART VIII

# The New Deal and World War II

# 32

# Franklin Delano Roosevelt

WILLIAM D. PEDERSON

*Franklin Delano Roosevelt, the only president elected to four terms, expanded presidential powers in a fashion unparalleled in American history. He launched the New Deal; fought off constitutional attacks of his bold legislation by proposing to pack the Supreme Court; greatly expanded the president's powers in foreign affairs; sent Japanese Americans to relocation camps after the bombing at Pearl Harbor; and seized an airplane manufacturing plant as part of his "emergency" powers. While FDR guided America out of the Great Depression and navigated a dangerous world war, he demonstrated that even great leaders can become blinded by success and unchecked power, particularly during times of war and hysteria.*

# Introduction

Scholars often rank Franklin D. Roosevelt as the greatest president of the twentieth century and second only to Abraham Lincoln (and, in some rankings, George Washington) among all the presidents of the United States.[1] Just as Lincoln, the Great Emancipator, successfully dealt with the twin domestic issues of secession and slavery, FDR successfully dealt with the twin international issues of the Great Depression and then World War II. Elected to an unprecedented four terms (1933–1945), the active and flexible president forever changed the institution of the presidency and transformed the nation into the world's most successful constitutional democracy.

Born on January 30, 1882, in Hyde Park, New York, Franklin was the second son of James Roosevelt and his much younger and strong-willed second wife, Sara Delano. Both parents were wealthy and socially prominent. Raised as an only child despite having a much older brother (James, nearly thirty years his senior) from his father's first marriage, Franklin had a secure childhood except perhaps for his aging father's health. The boy's overly protective upbringing sometimes left him a social outsider. His slightly older schoolmates disliked him once he entered Groton Academy, a Massachusetts prep school, in 1896; he was isolated from classmates who were more socially advanced. In 1900, Franklin began Harvard and was rejected from the Porcellian Club. The rejection was a major social disappointment he never forgot. After his father died, in 1902, his mother rented an apartment near the campus to stay closer to Franklin; he graduated from Harvard in 1904.

In virtually every aspect of his political life, FDR used his distant fifth cousin Theodore Roosevelt as a role model. This contributed to FDR's unusual self-confidence while he faced enormous personal and political challenges. The links between the two Roosevelts were striking.[2] The Democratic Hyde Park FDR married into the Republican Oyster Bay clan through Eleanor Roosevelt, TR's niece, whom Franklin wed in 1905. In fact, TR gave her away at their wedding. From that point on, FDR closely followed TR's political script. TR had begun law school without finishing it; FDR entered law school at Columbia, but dropped out after he was admitted to the bar in New York, expecting that he would go into politics. Both TR and FDR began their political careers in the New York legislature, each man becoming assistant secretary of the navy, governor of New York, and a vice presidential candidate.

Yet FDR's rise to political prominence in the United States—becoming a highly successful governor of New York (1929–1932)—was especially remarkable given the physical disability that he was forced to overcome. In 1921, he had been diagnosed with infantile paralysis, or polio, which left him paralyzed from the waist down. Only thirty-nine years old, he might have forsaken any aspirations of political office. Yet FDR pursued a grueling rehabilitation program, including periodic trips to a resort in Warm Springs, Georgia, where the waters rich in mineral content were believed to have special healing powers.[3]

FDR's heroic efforts in dealing with his polio mirrored his cousin Teddy's determination to transform himself from a proverbial ninety-nine-pound weakling into a man who proved himself through blood sports and warfare. Moreover, FDR's greater capacity to empathize with others went beyond TR's sense of noblesse oblige. FDR's wife, Eleanor, aided his understanding of how others lived.[4] His efforts to walk again would set a model for himself and the nation when it sought to get back on its economic feet during the Great Depression.

## Presidency

As the governor of the most populous state in the nation, FDR had a towering bully pulpit from which to assail Herbert Hoover's failed policies. He won the presidential election of 1932 with 57 percent of the vote and carried all states but six, realigning the electoral map in favor of the Democrats in a fashion that would last for two decades.[5]

Moving into the White House, President Roosevelt projected steely resolve and confidence. He rarely appeared in public in a wheelchair or using the metal braces he needed to walk.[6] Rather, he overcame his disability through sheer willpower and seemed to relish the challenges of high office.

FDR had the advantage of learning from the successes and mistakes of both TR and Woodrow Wilson, each of whom had viewed Abraham Lincoln as a political hero. FDR effortlessly took Lincoln from the Republican Party and adapted him to the Democratic Party, using an approach he formed after taking courses at Harvard from William James, the great

American philosopher of pragmatism. FDR adapted that pragmatic approach to the political world.[7] He largely borrowed TR's 1912 presidential platform to deal with the Great Depression and revised Wilson's League of Nations into a more realistic United Nations for the postwar world. For the most part, FDR avoided the more serious blunders of TR and Wilson despite adopting their Lincoln-like approach to presidential power.

## The New Deal as an Ad Hoc Experiment

Franklin Roosevelt and his advisers (the so-called Brains Trust) came up with a series of ad hoc legislative proposals to deal with the Great Depression. The public wanted immediate action after his election in 1932, and the new Congress was ready to respond favorably to his proposals during his first hundred days in office. FDR's New Deal grew into a large economic, social, and political program to cope with the Great Depression of the 1930s and involved regulation of the private sector through new federal agencies. Regardless of whether several measures conflicted with FDR's initial desire to balance the budget and to launch bold new programs, the cooperation between Congress and the presidency reached a new peak. As a result, the first hundred days of FDR's long tenure in the White House became a benchmark against which to judge subsequent presidents' legislative agendas. It also gave hope to the American people that the government was on its side and at least trying to help. If Lincoln was the Great Emancipator, then FDR became the Great Improviser. Though Herbert Hoover had been active, he had appeared quite rigid to the public. FDR was less constrained by ideological and constitutional rigidity—he was by nature pragmatic. Though his extreme critics saw him as a dictator, FDR's socialization in democratic values prevented him from traveling down that route as a leader.

Moreover, FDR was armed with TR's stewardship theory of presidential power and used this to steer the ship of state safely to shore during turbulent times. As long as the Constitution did not explicitly forbid it, he believed, the chief executive could act. It was an activist approach to presidential power first expressed by Alexander Hamilton in *Federalist Paper* No. 70: "Energy in the executive is a leading character in the definition of good government."[8] FDR understood that democracy was on trial in a totalitarian age. Rather than give in to extremism on the right or the left,

FDR creatively helped enact some of the most important legislation in the history of the nation. He did this in cooperation with Congress, which at times pushed him further than he had originally intended. In doing so, however, he also created a looming set of constitutional issues that would take decades to sort out.

The first in the trio of touchstone bills during the FDR years was the Social Security Act of 1935, which effectively established a "welfare state" in the United States.[9] The legislation grew out of the efforts of Frances Perkins, FDR's secretary of labor and the first female cabinet secretary in American history.[10] Perkins chaired a committee that endorsed the state of Wisconsin's experiment to provide a safety net in the form of unemployment compensation benefits for its citizens. The most well-known part of the Social Security Act became the social insurance system. Secretary Perkins's primary ally in the U.S. Senate was Robert F. Wagner (1877–1953), who became a chief legislative architect of the New Deal.[11] By the mid-1930s, FDR's New Deal was well under way.

Much more controversial was the creation of the National Labor Relations Act (NLRA), or the Wagner Act, sometimes described as "Labor's Magna Carta."[12] The NLRA made collective bargaining part of the New Deal's economic recovery policies, recognizing for the first time in American history the right of employees to organize. The legislation created a National Labor Relations Board (NLRB) to implement these provisions and was sponsored by the same Senator Wagner who was pushing the New Deal.

The final piece of landmark social legislation during the FDR years came in the form of the G.I. Bill of Rights (Servicemen's Readjustment Act of 1944).[13] FDR asked for this legislation in 1943, but some conservative Southern Democrats objected to its unemployment benefits because the assistance would include minorities. Nonetheless, a majority in Congress backed the proposal and FDR finally signed the legislation in June 1944. It built on the pioneering efforts of the Land Grant College Act, which Lincoln had signed in 1862. The new legislation provided a host of benefits for returning World War II veterans, including job training, hiring priority, higher education, and low-interest loans for homes, farms, and small businesses. It transformed the scope of higher education for veterans and kicked off a housing boom, as soldiers returned home, thus creating an expanding middle class.

## *"The President Needs Help": The Brownlow Committee*

FDR understood that American democracy was being tested and scrutinized. Though a pragmatist, he was also a visionary who appreciated that change was necessary. The New Deal was an essential part of that. However, by the end of his first term (1932–1936), FDR recognized that both the New Deal and the possibility of war abroad required the chief executive to have more administrative latitude. Rather than go to a leftist extreme like Joseph Stalin abroad or Governor Huey Long of Louisiana at home, or become a right-wing militarist extreme like Benito Mussolini or Adolf Hitler abroad, or possibly like General Douglas MacArthur at home, FDR favored a modest enlargement of executive powers.

For that reason, FDR recruited Louis Brownlow in March 1936 to chair the Committee on Administrative Management (the Brownlow Committee) to improve the managerial role of the president.[14] Brownlow gave the final committee report to FDR in early January 1937. The report's title was remarkably plainspoken: "The President Needs Help." It recommended managerial power for the president commensurate with his role as the chief executive of the largest bureaucracy in the world.[15]

In February 1937, Congress began hearings on the report. The initial reaction seemed favorable, mostly because of the overwhelming Democratic majorities in each chamber after the landslide reelection of FDR in 1936. Unfortunately, FDR had failed to consult any member of Congress in advance for suggestions regarding his proposal to strengthen the presidency and had insisted on total secrecy while the Brownlow Committee prepared its findings. Worse, his timing was unfortunate, since he had also hatched a secret plan to handle an activist conservative bloc on the Supreme Court—a bloc that he believed was declaring too many pieces of New Deal legislation unconstitutional. The two secret plans collided on Capitol Hill. It proved to be a costly personal and political blunder.

When Brownlow suffered a heart attack at the end of May, the proposal's most able defender was lost. Critics described the bill as a call for executive dictatorship. Dwarfed by FDR's much more aggressive Supreme Court–packing plan (described below), the Brownlow Committee bill suffered a narrow defeat in April 1938, after the Court-packing plan had fallen the previous summer. Yet time and a world war would eventually work in FDR's favor. Congress approved most of what FDR wanted from the Brownlow Committee's recommendations the next year in the

Reorganization Act of 1939, after the threat of war focused congressional minds on the need for decisive executive action.

The upshot of the Brownlow Committee work was a dramatic retooling of the office of the presidency, giving it expansive new powers to manage the sprawling world of nascent administrative agencies and to shape domestic policies. It led to the creation of the Executive Office of the President, a vigorous new White House staff of loyal presidential aides, and the development of an *administrative presidency*, in which domestic policy could be implemented swiftly through executive orders.[16]

Critics believed that FDR was running amok and "the balance and separation of powers established by the Constitution was being destroyed by a power-seeking presidency gathering into itself the power that should be exercised by Congress and the states."[17] Yet FDR declared to the nation in one of his famous fireside chats: "The only thing that has been happening has been to designate the President as the agency to carry out certain of the purposes of Congress. This was constitutional and in keeping with past American traditions."[18] Without a doubt, FDR won the battle. As one scholar would later write, this expansion of executive branch authority was an "epoch making event in the history of American institutions" and constituted "perhaps the most important single step in the institutionalization of the presidency."[19]

### The Court-Packing Plan

Even as the Supreme Court started to back the president in foreign affairs, as World War II threatened the nation, the so-called Four Horsemen— Justices George Sutherland, James C. McReynolds, Willis Van Devanter, and Pierce Butler, a group named after the biblical Four Horsemen of the Apocalypse—were intent on blocking the New Deal. In primarily five-to-four votes, the activist conservative justices declared several major pieces of New Deal legislation unconstitutional, including the National Industrial Recovery Act (in *Schechter Poultry Corp. v. U.S.*), the Agricultural Adjustment Act of 1933 (in *U.S. v. Butler*), and the Bituminous Coal Conservation Act (in *Carter v. Carter Coal Co.*).[20] By the end of 1936, seven major opinions of the highest Court had struck down New Deal legislation.

The situation was aggravated by the fact that FDR had not had an opportunity to nominate even a single justice to the Supreme Court during his first term. After FDR and Homer S. Cummings, his first attorney general, concluded that a constitutional amendment to address the Court's composition would take too long, Cummings secretly drafted a bill, which came to be known as the Court-packing plan, to deal with the situation.[21] The plan was designed to add a new justice to the Court for each justice over the age of seventy, to overpower the obstinate bloc standing in the way of FDR's New Deal legislation. The president concealed the plan's underlying intent by including provisions to allow for forty-four new judges on the lower federal benches and up to six additional justices on the High Court. The plan applied to everyone with ten years of judicial service who failed to retire within six months after reaching the age of seventy. Other than FDR, Cummings, and two top aides, only Solicitor General Stanley F. Reed and Assistant Attorney General Robert H. Jackson knew of the plan.

Successful Court enlargement schemes had been hatched seven times, from the era of John Adams to the Grant administration. An irony of this effort to assure a younger judiciary was that the most recent attempt had been proposed and abandoned by Woodrow Wilson's former attorney general, James McReynolds, now one of the sitting Four Horsemen.[22] Now, FDR confronted McReynolds and the three other conservative activists on the Court. A frustrated FDR accused them of trying to turn the nation back to its "horse-and-buggy days."

FDR stunned Congress on February 5, 1937, when he introduced the Court-packing plan. A bitter five-month battle ensued. Congressional Republicans, newspaper editors, and the organized bar vociferously opposed the plan. By contrast, it initially attracted considerable Democratic support. Senator Hugo L. Black and Congressman Fred Vinson, along with Reed and Jackson, helped FDR prepare his March 9, 1937, fireside chat to the American public justifying the proposal.[23] Ultimately, the president was counting on the popular leadership of Senate Majority Leader Joseph T. Robinson (D-AR), to carry the fight. The Senate knew that Robinson had been tapped to become the first Court nominee under the scheme.[24]

Soon, the bill unraveled. FDR had not expected the intervention of Chief Justice Hughes, one of the great secretaries of state, governors, and justices of the twentieth century.[25] Though TR had once referred to his fellow New York progressive as "an iceberg with a beard," both TR and FDR underestimated the serious talent of their rival. Unbeknownst to FDR, Hughes had engineered a swing vote to support the New Deal in judicial conference in December 1936. The new five-to-four votes would tilt the majority of the Court in favor of New Deal legislation. Hughes first took the unprecedented step of sending a letter to the Senate Judiciary Committee refuting the charge that the present members of the Court could not keep up with its docket. Then on May 18, conservative activist Justice Van Devanter announced his retirement from the Court, on the same day that the Senate Judiciary Committee voted ten to one against the bill. Finally, FDR's point man in the Senate, Joseph Robinson, suffered a fatal heart attack on July 14. Suddenly, a group of freshmen Democratic senators announced their opposition to the bill, and others felt Robinson's death freed them from their pledge of support. The game was now over.

Though FDR lost the Court-packing battle, he ironically was on his way to winning his judicial war. In *West Coast Hotel Co. v. Parrish*, decided on March 29, 1937, by a five-to-four vote, Chief Justice Hughes and Justice Owen J. Roberts led the Court in the so-called "switch in time that saved nine."[26] The Court in this case upheld a Washington State law regulating a minimum wage law for women. The year before, the Court had struck down a similar law in New York, thwarting a piece of state legislation that mirrored FDR's New Deal.[27] Hughes now made clear that the U.S. Constitution did not include an implied "freedom of contract" as the Four Horsemen had maintained, sounding the death knell of the controversial *Lochner* decision.[28] Justice Roberts provided the critical fifth vote, switching sides to give a victory to New Deal forces and to protect the integrity of the Court.

Again, in *NLRB v. J & L Steel*, decided in 1937, the Court upheld a major piece of New Deal legislation—the National Labor Relations Act—by giving Congress enormous deference in exercising its power under the Commerce Clause.[29] Justice Roberts and Chief Justice Hughes again departed from their prior positions and sided with FDR's legislation. Likewise, in 1942, in *Wickard v. Filburn*, the Court upheld the Agricultural Adjustment Act of 1938, which authorized Congress to regulate the production of wheat, even including wheat grown solely for home consumption, in order to stabilize prices.[30] Embracing an expansive interpretation of the Commerce Clause, the Court unanimously held that Congress was empowered to regulate *intrastate* activities that, when aggregated, would have a substantial effect on interstate commerce. FDR's "judicial revolution" was under way.

In hindsight, the Court-packing plan was an unnecessary distraction and a costly blunder by FDR. He would have suffered less political damage if he had withdrawn the bill. Unfortunately, the controversy post-poned for more than two years the Brownlow plan to strengthen and reor-ganize the executive branch. In the meantime, the Supreme Court clipped Roosevelt's wings in *Humphrey's Executor v. U.S.*, concluding that FDR lacked the power to terminate a Federal Trade Commission member who he thought did not share his New Deal philosophy.[31] President Hoover had appointed, and the Senate had confirmed, Humphrey for a seven-year term. However, the function of this federal agency created by Congress, said the Court, was not executive in nature, but quasi-legislative and quasi-judicial.[32] Thus, the Court seized on this opportunity to limit the presi-dent's removal power, a decision that FDR "resented" greatly.[33]

Worse, the decision undermined the New Deal by contributing to the emergence of the "conservative coalition" of Republicans and South-ern Democrats. The ultimate irony is that FDR went on to name eight new justices—more than any other president since George Washington had nominated. Thus, he got his wish despite the collapse of the Court-packing plan.

## Foreign Affairs

Even while the Supreme Court's most conservative activist justices had been declaring parts of the New Deal unconstitutional, the same justices were granting the president sweeping power in foreign affairs.[34] The Curtiss-Wright Export Corporation and two other companies had been convicted of selling aircraft machine guns to Bolivia during the Gran Chaco War between Bolivia and Paraguay, in violation of FDR's procla-mation against such sales. The companies had been charged with violating a joint congressional resolution that had empowered the president to for-bid the sale of articles of war to nations engaged in armed conflict. The companies now challenged their convictions, arguing that the president's proclamation constituted an improper delegation of congressional power.

Justice George Sutherland wrote the seven-to-one decision in *U.S. v. Curtiss-Wright Export Corp.* on December 21, 1936, in which the majority distinguished between permissible delegations of congressional power in domestic affairs and those in foreign affairs.[35] The Court recognized that in addition to wielding the enumerated and applied powers, the president could exercise inherent powers in the realm of foreign affairs under Arti-cle II. Indeed, the Court endorsed sweeping presidential powers when it came to foreign affairs. Justice Sutherland declared that the president was "the sole organ of the federal government in international relations." The granting of power was so expansive that observers joked that even when a president exercised dubious actions abroad, he would be safe in proclaiming as he paced the White House halls at night: "Curtiss-Wright, Curtiss-Wright, I must be right!"

## An Unprecedented Third Term

Roosevelt parted with the two-term tradition set by President George Washington when he ran for and won reelection in 1940.[36] Initially, Roosevelt had intended to return to Hyde Park after the conclusion of his second term, having signed a contract to become a contributing editor of *Collier's* magazine.[37] He had confided to Secretary of State Henry Morganthau that he had no desire to run for a third term unless "things get very, very much worse in Europe."[38]

As the situation in Europe deteriorated and moved closer to war, Roosevelt "saw himself more as commander in chief than president and recognized the necessity to prepare for war," particularly in the face of Congress's isolationist tendencies.[39] At the 1940 Democratic National Convention in Chicago, Roosevelt sent a cryptic message to the convention through Senator Alben Barkley: FDR encouraged the delegates to vote for any candidate.[40] Despite the ambiguous message, Roosevelt overwhelmingly received the Democratic nomination and went on to win the general election (again decisively) against Republican Wendell Willkie.

## Japanese American "Relocation"

FDR's penchant for action was not only encouraged by his electoral landslides and by the Supreme Court's support in the realm of foreign affairs, but also further spurred forward by America's being drawn into World War II. The sneak attack by the Japanese on December 7, 1941, at Pearl Harbor was completely unexpected. Much of the American naval fleet was destroyed. Suddenly, Dr. New Deal became Dr. Win-the-War. Denied the chance to serve in World War I—unlike TR, who became a hero in the Spanish-American War—FDR followed TR's pattern of overreaction. Fearing that an invasion might be immediate, FDR collaborated with state and local officials on the West Coast, as well as the two other branches of the federal government and the public, in violating the rights of Japanese Americans on the West Coast. In this setting, Roosevelt succumbed to the fear that he had warned the public against at the beginning of his presidency.

On February 19, 1942, FDR, as commander in chief, issued Executive Order 9066, which empowered military commanders to issue curfews and establish temporary "assembly centers" for Japanese American citizens on the West Coast, while permanent "relocation camps" were being built further inland. Military advisers feared an attack on America's mainland—an attack assisted by spies and saboteurs of Japanese descent. Within a half year, some 112,000 persons of Japanese descent (more than two-thirds of whom were American citizens) were effectively imprisoned.[41]

Gordon Hirabayashi, a twenty-four-year-old American-born student at the University of Washington and a devout Quaker, resisted the curfew order by refusing to register for evacuation. He was found guilty and sentenced to three months in jail. On June 21, 1943, Chief Justice Harlan Fiske Stone, in a nine-to-one decision, upheld the government's curfew order in *Hirabayashi v. U.S.*, but left the evacuation issue undecided; Congress had just unanimously passed legislation in 1942 ratifying FDR's executive order.[42]

Two years later, the Supreme Court had a second chance to revisit this troublesome issue. Fred T. Korematsu had sought unsuccessfully to evade the harsh evacuation order. On May 30, 1942, he was apprehended, convicted, paroled, and sent to a relocation camp to join the rest of his family. On December 18, 1944, Justice Hugo L. Black, FDR's first appointee to the High Court, wrote the now-infamous decision in the *Korematsu* case. In a narrow six-to-three ruling that avoided considering the constitutionality of the order requiring detention in assembly and relocation centers, Justice Black justified the executive order as a proper exercise of a president's war powers. The Court's majority was unwilling to disregard the advice of the military and Congress during wartime.[43] It would be decades before Japanese Americans received a measure of justice.[44]

*Seizing North American Aviation*

In other ways, FDR exercised his powers to the fullest, setting new precedents that were unparalleled in the history of American presidents. On May 27, 1941, several months before the Japanese bombing of Pearl Harbor in December and before the United States officially declared war, FDR proclaimed an "unlimited national emergency." This presidential proclamation required that the nation enter military readiness to counter the Axis powers' objective to overthrow the world's existing democratic order.[45] A few weeks later, FDR was confronted with a strike at the North American Aviation Company's military airplane production plant in California. At the time, Congress had not set forth how the federal government would respond to threats to industries vital to the nation's security and defense. Invoking his emergency powers and citing the importance of aircraft production (including bombers) to defend the U.S. and its allies, FDR issued a directive on June 6, 1941, that strikers at the North American Aviation plant had to return to their jobs or face consequences.[46] When workers tried to cross the picket line at the plant, violence broke out. Responding swiftly, FDR issued Executive Order 8773 on June 9, citing his power under the Constitution "as President and Commander in Chief of the armed forces of the United States," and directing that "the Secretary of War shall immediately take charge of the plant and remain in charge and operate the plant until normal production shall be resumed." FDR declared: "Our country is in danger and the men and women who are now making airplanes play an indispensable part in its defense."[47] Upon issuance of the executive order and the arrival of federal troops, the striking workers at the plant yielded.

FDR's attorney general, Robert H. Jackson (later a Supreme Court justice), opined on the constitutional basis for the order: "There can be no doubt that the duty constitutionally and inherently rested upon the President to exert his civil and military, as well as his moral authority, to keep the defense efforts of the United States a going concern."[48]

FDR thus prevailed in this bold move, injecting himself into a labor dispute and seizing private property to maintain production of defense-related airplanes. In this way, the presidential power that FDR established during wartime seemed unparalleled and almost unbounded.[49]

## Conclusion

Time takes its toll—even on political giants. In 1944, Roosevelt ran for a fourth term out of a sense of duty: "Reluctantly, but as a good soldier, I will accept and serve in this office, if I am ordered to do so by the Commander in Chief of us all—the sovereign people of the United States."[50] Stress from the war and ill health soon began to show. Still willing to listen to others, he accepted the relatively unknown Senator Harry Truman of Missouri as a running mate in 1944; together, they won the Electoral College vote by a landslide. However, FDR retained a mild streak of stubbornness that kept him from adequately preparing his vice president if unforeseen events would require the untested Truman to step into the presidency. In April 1945, FDR left the White House for a vacation at his beloved "Little White House" retreat in Warm Springs, Georgia, where he had sought relief from his polio for decades. On April 12, a clear spring day, FDR complained of a terrible head pain shortly after noon and collapsed unconscious. Within two hours, the president was pronounced dead of a massive cerebral hemorrhage.

Viewing this period with the benefit of historical hindsight, FDR's presidency established a benchmark for democratic leadership in the United States and abroad, on many fronts. He proved worthy of Mount Rushmore for his unprecedented four presidential electoral victories, for addressing the Great Depression, and for confronting World War II, while transforming the office of the presidency and altering the direction of American domestic and foreign policy. FDR pushed his constitutional authority to its outermost limits, both at home and abroad, and created a nimble, powerful presidency that has few parallels in American history. Rather than suffering from Winston Churchill's inability to pry himself loose of an empire or Joseph Stalin's fixation on power alone, FDR remained active and flexible while adhering to the democratic constraints that circumscribed his high office.

FDR's leadership becomes even more impressive when measured against the leadership of other world leaders from the same era. He was elected in 1932, during an age when communist and fascist regimes could conceive and implement executive decisions rapidly without constitutional checks. At this time, totalitarian governments were romanticized by some observers, even in the United States, and portrayed as the wave of the future. In contrast, FDR remained yoked to a system of government that at times seemed slow and inefficient. Yet the New Deal and the Allied war effort disproved both his own critics and those of the American democratic system. Likewise, FDR's conception of a United Nations as an international organization in which both the major powers and the rest of the world could work together toward progress proved to be visionary.

Though FDR left behind a stellar record in handling the twin crises of the Great Depression and World War II, his occasional blunders should serve as a warning that even pragmatic, active, and flexible democratic leaders may be blinded by success and power. Indeed, FDR's most egregious missteps during the dark days of World War II—memorialized in decisions like *Korematsu*—suggest that he failed to learn from the excesses of previous administrations during wartime, especially those of his predecessors Theodore Roosevelt and Woodrow Wilson. Thus, FDR's mixed legacy should serve as a stark reminder that wartime hysteria itself poses a grave danger to all citizens and leaders in a constitutional democracy.

## NOTES

1. Robert K. Murray and Tim H. Blessing, *Greatness in the White House: Rating the Presidents* (University Park, PA: Pennsylvania State University Press, 1994); Robert W. Merry, *Where They Stand: The American Presidents in the Eyes of the Voters and Historians* (New York: Simon & Schuster, 2012), 5–13.
2. Ronald D. Rietveld, "Franklin D. Roosevelt's Abraham Lincoln," in *Franklin D. Roosevelt and Abraham Lincoln: Competing Perspectives*, William D. Pederson and Frank J. Williams (Armonk, NY: M.E. Sharpe, 2003), 10–60.
3. Jean Edward Smith, *FDR* (New York: Random House, 2007), 188–192, 215–216.
4. From the beginning of their relationship, Eleanor widened Franklin's eyes to the condition of others and promoted the political values they shared regarding human rights. Though earlier in her life she had opposed women's suffrage and was mildly anti-Semitic and patronizing toward African Americans, she came to identify with the Bonus Marchers, labor, women, and minorities. Becoming unconventional, she vastly expanded the role for the First Lady, from holding press conferences for female reporters to becoming the first presidential spouse to testify before a congressional committee, the first to briefly hold a federal government job (assistant director of the Office of Civilian Defense), and the first to write a newspaper column. She later was appointed as a delegate to the UN General Assembly by President Harry S. Truman after FDR's death. Norman W. Provizer, "Eleanor Roosevelt Biographies," in *A Companion to Franklin D. Roosevelt*, ed. W. D. Pederson (Oxford, UK: Wiley-Blackwell, 2011), 15–33; Maurine H. Beasley, Holly C. Shulman, and Henry R. Beasley, eds., "Eleanor Roosevelt Encyclopedia" (Westport, CT: Greenwood Press, 2001); William D. Pederson, *The FDR Years* (New York: Facts on File, 2006).
5. Smith, *FDR*, 287.
6. FDR's image was also maintained through the understanding he had with the press that he would not be photographed in his wheelchair. Robert E. Gilbert, "Disability, Illness, and the Presidency: The Case of Franklin D. Roosevelt," *Politics and Life Sciences* 7 (1988): 36.

7. Hubert D. Humphreys, "History of an Idea Whose Time Had Come: Franklin Roosevelt's CCC," in *The New Deal and Public Policy*, ed. B. Daynes, W. Pederson, and M. Riccards (New York: St. Martin's Press, 1998), 51–53.

8. Alexander Hamilton, James Madison, and John Jay, *Selected Federalist Papers* (Mineola, NY: Dover Publications, 2001), 162.

9. Dennis W. Johnson, *The Laws That Shaped America* (New York: Routledge, 2009) 175–201.

10. Pederson, *The FDR Years*, 210–211.

11. By the late 1990s, one in seven Americans received social security benefits. Ibid., 265.

12. Johnson, *The Laws That Shaped America*, 140–174. Senator Wagner's principal aide, Leon Keyserling, drafted the legislation. Pederson, *The FDR Years*, 142–q43.

13. Johnson, *The Laws That Shaped America*, 202–228.

14. Pederson, *The FDR Years*, 32–34.

15. William D. Pederson, "Brownlow Committee," in *A Historical Guide to the U.S. Government*, ed. George T. Kurian (New York: Oxford University Press, 1998), 76–81.

16. Sidney M. Milkis and Michael Nelson, *The American Presidency: Origins and Development, 1776–1990* (Washington, DC: CQ Press, 1990), 296–298.

17. Melvin I. Urofsky, *The American Presidents* (New York: Garland Publishing, 2000), 343.

18. Ibid.

19. Luther Gulick, quoted in Clinton Rossiter, *The American Presidency*, 2d ed. (New York: Harcourt, Brace & World, 1960), 129, cited in Milkis and Nelson, *The American Presidency*, 298.

20. Schechter Poultry Corp. v. United States, 295 U.S. 495 (1935); United States v. Butler, 297 U.S. 1 (1936); Carter v. Carter Coal Co., 298 U.S. 238 (1936).

21. Pederson, *The FDR Years*, 60–61.

22. McReynolds had been Woodrow Wilson's first attorney general until his Court appointment, which was designed to rid the racist and disruptive attorney general from Wilson's cabinet. Ibid., 182–183.

23. Ibid., 366–372.

24. Ibid., 224–225.

25. Ibid., 124–126.

26. West Coast Hotel Co. v. Parrish, 300 U.S. 379 (1937).

27. Morehead v. New York ex rel. Tipaldo, 298 U.S. 587 (1936).

28. Lochner v. New York, 198 U.S. 45 (1905).

29. NLRB v. Jones & Laughlin Steel Corp., 301 U.S. 1 (1937). The case dealt with an unfair labor practices claim against a steel company for discriminating against its workers through coercion and intimidation intended to prevent the workers from organizing a union. The claim was brought under FDR's National Labor Relations Act, and the Court, in finding for the workers, upheld the act under the Commerce Clause and thus provided a major boost to FDR's efforts by validating a crucial piece of his New Deal program.

30. Wickard v. Filburn, 317 U.S. 111 (1942).

31. Humphrey's Executor v. United States, 295 U.S. 602 (1935).

32. The Court distinguished this situation from that in Myers v. United States, 272 U.S. 52 (1926) (see Chapter 28, "Woodrow Wilson"), in which the Court held that President

Wilson had the power to remove a postmaster. The function of a postmaster, the Court stated, was purely executive. In contrast, the Federal Trade Commission was an administrative body created by Congress and performed quasi-legislative and quasi-judicial functions, to wit, creating and interpreting regulations. Here, Congress had provided that the removal of commissioners—who were appointed by the president for fixed terms—was limited to instances of "inefficiency, neglect of duty, or malfeasance in office." Since President Roosevelt failed to establish any of those grounds for removal, he lacked the authority to terminate Humphrey, even though Humphrey had been a presidential appointee. Ibid., 626–631. This decision made clear that not all presidential appointees can be removed at the whim of the chief executive, particularly if they are not performing functions relating to the executive office.

33. Robert H. Jackson, *That Man: An Insider's Portrait of Franklin D. Roosevelt*, ed. John Q. Barret (New York: Oxford University Press, 2003), 18–19.

34. For the Court's domestic decisions, see Railroad Retirement Bd. v. Alton Railroad Co., 295 U.S. 330 (1935); *Schechter Poultry Corp.*, 295 U.S. at 495; Louisville Joint Stock Land Bank v. Radford, 295 U.S. 555 (1935); *United States v. Butler*, 297 U.S. at 1; *Humphrey's Executor*, 295 U.S. at 602; *Carter Coal Co.*, 298 U.S. at 258; and *Tipaldo*, 258 U.S. at 379. The Court's tendency to grant the president more power in foreign affairs was also illustrated in the case Ex parte Quirin, 317 U.S. 1 (1942), where the Court upheld the jurisdiction of a military tribunal in the trial of several German prisoners of war accused of sabotage and who were being held inside the United States. The case would later be cited by President George W. Bush's administration as precedent for its use of military tribunals in the war on terror.

35. United States v. Curtiss-Wright Export Corp., 299 U.S. 304 (1936). James McReynolds dissented, Harlan Stone did not participate. In 2015, the U.S. Supreme Court jettisoned the sole-organ doctrine articulated in the *Curtiss-Wright* case. See Zivotofsky v. Kerry, 135 S.Ct. 2076, 2090 (2015).

36. The two-term tradition was an unwritten rule until 1951, when the Twenty-Second Amendment, which sets a two-term limit for election to the office of the presidency, was ratified.

37. Smith, *FDR*, 441.

38. Ibid., 442.

39. Ibid., 456.

40. Ibid., 460.

41. FDR's policy was largely driven by General John DeWitt, the overall army commander on the West Coast. The general's statements evidenced a racist bias against and deep mistrust of Japanese Americans. Thomas W. Woo, "Presumed Disloyal: Executive Power, Judicial Deference, and the Construction of Race Before and After September 11," *Columbia Human Rights Law Review* 34 (fall 2002): 22, n. 91.

42. Hirabayashi v. United States, 320 U.S. 81 (1943).

43. Korematsu v. United States, 323 U.S. 214 (1944). In the Civil Liberties Act of 1988, Congress offered a formal apology to people of Japanese descent who were evacuated and relocated in internment camps. In addition, immediately following the war, Congress appropriated a total of $37 million in reparations to those who suffered under the

internment policies; in the 1980s, Congress provided each surviving person who was confined with an additional $20,000. Smith, *FDR*, 552.

44. Peter Irons, *The Courage of their Convictions: Sixteen Americans Who Fought Their Way to the Supreme Court* (New York: Penguin, 1990), 37–62; Richard Goldstein, "Gordon Hirabayashi," *New York Times*, January 4, 2012, A16.

45. "U.S. Ready to Seize Plane Plant," *Los Angeles Times*, June 7, 1941, 1; 6 Fed. Reg. 2777 (1941).

46. Executive Order 8773 on the Seizure of the North American Aviation Company Plant at Inglewood, California, 6 Fed. Reg. 2777 (1941).

47. Ibid.

48. Jackson, *Insider's Portrait of Franklin D. Roosevelt*, 216 n. 26, 220 n. 1.

49. Relying on the president's constitutional powers and his seizure of the North American Aviation Company as precedent, FDR seized several additional plants in war-related companies (shipbuilding, aeronautics, machinery, cable, explosives, and bearings) when interruptions in production were looming. Patricia L. Bellia, "The Story of the Steel Seizure Case" (Legal Studies Paper 08-20, Notre Dame Law School, South Bend, IN, 2008), 4–7. See also Arthur H. Garrison, "National Security and Presidential Power: Judicial Deference and Establishing Constitutional Boundaries in World War Two and the Korean War," *Cumberland Law Review* 39 (2009): 667–668. Further, in response to persistent labor unrest in the bituminous coal industry, FDR seized the nation's coal mines in 1943. Youngstown Sheet and Tube Co. v. Sawyer, 343 U.S. 579, 696 & n. 67 *(1952)* (Vinson, J. dissenting). This particular seizure led to passage of the War Labor Disputes Act, which, until its termination at the end of the war in 1946, provided the president with a statutory basis for seizures. Pub. L. No. 78–89, 57 Stat. 163, 164 (1943). Citing the War Labor Disputes Act and the powers of the commander in chief, FDR issued an Executive Order in 1944, seizing the property of the Montgomery Ward & Company, a retail and mail order business, for refusing to comply with a War Labor Board order to recognize a union and institute the terms of a collective bargaining agreement. Bellia, "Steel Seizure Case," 6.

50. Smith, *FDR*, 617.

# 33

# Harry S. Truman

JAMES N. GIGLIO

*Harry S. Truman, a farmer and soldier from Missouri and a latecomer to politics, was thrust unexpectedly into the presidency when President Roosevelt died in office with World War II raging in Europe. Truman was a plain-speaking, decisive, and sometimes impulsive leader who dropped the atomic bomb to end the war; waged war against North Korea to stop the spread of communism; and tried to seize America's steel mills to support troops abroad. This last action led the Supreme Court to issue a stinging rebuke of the president in the landmark Steel Seizure Case. Although Truman left office after the 1952 elections a frustrated and unpopular president, many scholars today give him high marks for his strong leadership and integrity at a difficult time in American history.*

# Introduction

Harry S. Truman assumed the presidency on April 12, 1945, when a war-weary President Franklin D. Roosevelt suddenly succumbed to a cerebral hemorrhage at Warm Springs, Georgia. While the nation mourned the loss of one of its greatest presidents, a relatively unknown vice president took the oath of office. The next day, the stunned Truman remarked to reporters, "Boys, if you ever pray, pray for me now. I don't know whether you fellows ever had a load of hay fall on you, but when they told me yesterday what had happened, I felt like the moon, stars, and all the planets had fallen on me."[1] He had ample reason to feel that way. World War II still raged on, and the Allied powers, especially the Soviet Union, differed over how postwar security could best be assured. Those unresolved conflicts would soon lead to the Cold War. Domestic problems at home, meanwhile, would also demand decisive action by the chief executive.

Who exactly was this new president? He was born in Lamar, Missouri, on May 8, 1884. Of humble origins, he was one of two twentieth-century presidents to lack a college education, although he completed fourteen courses at the Kansas City School of Law. Harry Truman sprang from a nineteenth-century Jeffersonian-Jacksonian tradition that embodied Victorian virtues, rural provincialism, and an optimistic belief in progress and economic opportunity. Years of farming and distinguished military service in World War I further defined him, as did various small business ventures, including a failed haberdashery in the early 1920s. On June 28, 1919, Harry Truman married Virginia "Bess" Wallace, whom he had known since childhood. They moved into a home at 219 North Delaware Street in Independence, Missouri: a home they would maintain until Truman's death over fifty year later.

In many ways, Truman embodied small-town America. He entered politics as a member of the Boss Tom Pendergast machine, serving as presiding judge of Jackson County (including Kansas City) and then receiving the backing of Pendergast to win election to the U.S. Senate, beginning in 1935. Although never engaging in any dishonest behavior, his association with the corrupt Pendergast machine later hurt him, as did his unimpressive appearance and his shortcomings as a public speaker. Yet Truman managed to overcome his limitations by being an effective senator and a loyal New Dealer. In 1944, with President Roosevelt ailing and Democratic Party leaders worrying that Vice President Henry Wallace was too left-leaning and unduly prolabor, Wallace was bumped from the ticket. While some Democrats (including FDR himself) seemed inclined to pick U.S. Supreme Court Justice William O. Douglas for the vice presidential slot, party leaders pushed for the relatively obscure senator from Missouri, and FDR accepted the selection. After the Roosevelt-Truman ticket won by a landslide electoral margin of 432–99 against Governor Thomas Dewey of New York and Governor John Bricker of Ohio, Truman was sworn in as vice president on January 20, 1945.[2]

Roosevelt rarely consulted with his vice president. Largely, the president treated Truman as an afterthought right up until his death, eighty-two days after the inauguration.[3]

## Presidency

After President Truman's historic decision to drop the atomic bomb on Hiroshima and Nagasaki in August 1945—actions that led to the surrender of the Japanese and the end of World War II—the new president turned his attention to other threats.[4] Truman's greatest challenge as president was an emerging Cold War that led Western nations to believe that the Soviet Union was seeking to communize Europe, if not the world. The fear of communist expansion permeated American foreign policy, leading to the creation of the Truman Doctrine (designed to stop Soviet expansion), the Marshall Plan (designed to give economic aid to rebuild Europe), and the North Atlantic Treaty Organization (a peacetime military alliance). Communism was viewed as an evil ideology that also threatened American institutions at home. Thus, the Truman years marked a period when national security considerations dominated, often at the expense of civil liberties. To Truman, the times called for strong executive action in the face of the Red Menace, leading to several constitutional conflicts. The postwar years under Truman also saw the passage of the National Security Act of 1947 and the establishment of new executive branch entities, most notably, the National Security Council and the Central Intelligence Agency, which reflected the increasing emphasis on national security embodied in the foreign policy of the United States.[5]

During his years in the Senate, Truman had felt comfortable in supporting the expansion of presidential powers, including the president's controversial Court-packing plan, to uphold the constitutionality of New Deal legislation.[6] Yet Truman's constitutional conception of a strong presidency was best expressed after he left office. In 1959, he delivered a series of lectures on presidential power at Columbia University, six years after the end of his presidency. During those talks, Truman asserted: "Whenever the country is in an emergency . . . nobody can meet it but the President of the United States. He never goes outside of the Constitution. Sometimes he stretches it a little. You take Jefferson: when he purchased Louisiana, he stretched the Constitution until it cracked, but if he hadn't bought Louisiana, think where we we'd have been." Truman insisted that "the real strength of the Constitution . . . is what it implies and not the words exactly as they are set down in the document."[7] When a perceptive Columbia student asked who determines the existence of an emergency that would determine what a president could do, Truman responded that the president makes that decision, and it was up to Congress to agree to it by passing legal authorization, appropriations, or whatever else was needed to formulate action.[8]

In his memoir, *Mr. Citizen* (1960), Truman explained that presidents were granted inherent powers beyond those enumerated in Article II of the Constitution. These powers could not be transmitted to a successor, because they "only go to the man who can take and use them." The failure to use such power, he later wrote, produced "failure" or "chaos." In Truman's mind, there were eight great presidents, all of whom were strong presidents: George Washington, Thomas Jefferson, Andrew Jackson, Abraham Lincoln, Grover Cleveland, Theodore Roosevelt, Woodrow Wilson, and Franklin Roosevelt.[9]

President Truman used his presidential powers to the fullest. During his uphill battle to secure his own term in the White House in the presidential campaign of 1948 against, again, Governor Dewey, Truman called the "Do Nothing" Congress into special session, pursuant to his powers under Article II, Section 3, challenging it to pass legislation implementing elements of the Republican Party platform.[10] When Truman won a last-minute upset victory over Dewey, he entered his own term feeling strong and determined to carry out his agenda.

## Korea

Perhaps Truman's greatest exercise of presidential power involved Korea, a country bordered on the north by Manchurian China and separated from Japan on the east by the Sea of Japan. After forty years of Japanese control in 1945, the Korean peninsula was liberated by the United States, which was entering from the south, and the Soviets, from the north. During World War II, although the two powers decided that Korea would be independent, they failed to agree on the nature of its government. Thus, Korea became a victim of the Cold War. By 1948, the Soviet Union, occupying the peninsula north of the thirty-eighth parallel, established a communist government headed by Kim Il Sung. In South Korea, meanwhile, the United States sponsored elections, which enabled the autocratic Syngman Rhee to become president.[11]

When North Korea attacked South Korea on June 25, 1950, Truman officials wrongly assumed that the Soviet Union had engineered the invasion. Most likely, the Soviet Union played only a secondary role in Kim Il Sung's initiative. Joseph Stalin, the cautious, Machiavellian Soviet dictator, had advised the North Koreans that if the invasion went badly, they could not rely on the Soviets for ground support. Nonetheless, if the North Koreans succeeded, Truman believed, the Soviets would have extended their aggression in Asia, then swallowed up the Near East and Europe. He consequently invoked the "lessons" of the immediate past in declaring that the United Nations must not fail, as the League of Nations had failed in response to the Japanese invasion of Manchuria in 1931.[12]

The United States reacted strongly to the North Korean attack. The next day, an American resolution in the UN Security Council branded the North Koreans as aggressors. On June 27, Truman ordered air and naval units into action without consulting Congress. That same day, the U.S.-led United Nations recommended that member nations provide military assistance to South Korea. Sixteen nations eventually contributed to the UN "police action," with the United States providing most of the force and suffering 142,000 casualties.

The American military commitment that ultimately exceeded 300,000 troops came with hardly any questioning from Congress, except for Republican senators Robert Taft of Ohio and Kenneth Wherry of Nebraska, both of whom favored a declaration-of-war vote. They believed that such a declaration was a congressional prerogative that outweighed the president's constitutional authority as commander in chief. Truman was worried about a possible partisan debate in Congress over the fall of China and other alleged Far Eastern policy failures. He agreed with Secretary Acheson that the United States had to circumvent the constitutionally prescribed role of Congress in declaring war, in order to show the world that the United States could respond quickly to communist aggression. Therefore, he relied solely on his own authority as commander in chief.[13]

As a result, Truman's actions almost certainly violated the UN Participation Act of 1945, which restricted the president's authority in the context of U.S. military participation through the United Nations. The act specifically stated that "nothing herein contained shall be construed as an authorization to the president by the Congress to make available to the Security Council . . . armed forces, facilities and assistance provided for in such special agreement or agreements."[14] Thus, without congressional authorization, Truman probably had no authority to commit troops to Korea on behalf of the United Nations. Senator Taft thus asserted that the president had "simply usurped authority, in violation of the laws and the Constitution" when he sent troops to Korea. The administration responded that Truman had employed the "traditional power of the president to use the forces of the United States without consulting Congress."[15]

Without a congressional resolution to justify U.S. military action in Korea, public and congressional support began to wane as the war progressed. Support dropped even more dramatically after the Truman administration changed its war objectives from containment of communism north of the thirty-eighth parallel to liberation of Korea from communist rule. Under the direction of General Douglas MacArthur, UN supreme commander, the U.S-directed operations had racked up military successes, particularly after MacArthur's brilliant amphibious landing in September at Inchon, 150 miles behind North Korean lines. Because of these actions, the North Korean army was in retreat. The administration's decision to cross the thirty-eighth parallel with UN endorsement, however, ultimately brought MacArthur's forces to the Yalu River bordering China. Soon China, asserting that this action threatened its national security, intervened and drove back the UN troops, both forcing them to retreat south of the thirty-eighth parallel and forcing the Truman administration to return to its containment policy.

Truman's policy "retreat" caused MacArthur, who wanted to expand the war against China, to publicly challenge Truman's authority as commander in chief. In addition to causing confusion abroad and embarrassing Truman, MacArthur's insubordination challenged the constitutional authority of the president, a matter that Truman, for good reason, did not take lightly. Yet when Truman responded by firing MacArthur, public opinion turned even more sharply against his administration.[16] Like MacArthur, a frustrated public, convinced of American military superiority, failed to understand why the United States had not already prevailed. When negotiations, begun in the summer of 1951, failed to produce a settlement, frustration and criticism escalated. Thus, Korea became the issue on which Democrats were most vulnerable in the 1952 presidential contest. It also exposed the constitutional land mines that faced an activist wartime president.

## Steel Seizure Case

That same year, Truman found himself involved in another constitutional fracas when he sought to use the inherent powers of commander in chief to resolve a conflict between the steel industry and the United Steelworkers of America, who pushed for a thirty-five-cent hourly pay raise as part of a new contract agreement. When management refused to negotiate, the union announced that it would go on strike as soon as the contract expired on December 31, 1951. Nine days before that deadline, Truman referred the matter to the Wage Stabilization Board, which recommended an hourly raise of twenty-six cents. The union accepted this compromise, but the steel companies rejected it unless it was accompanied by a steel price increase of $12 a ton. Facing this deadlock, organized labor agreed to postpone the strike until April 8 while discussions continued.

Throughout this ordeal, Truman sided more with the Steelworkers union, partly because of his longtime antipathy toward big corporations such as U.S. Steel and because organized labor represented a major part of the Democratic Party's constituency. More than this, he considered the wage increase proposed by the Wage Stabilization Board "fair and reasonable." Additionally, he believed that management's proposal would lead to inflation and raise the cost of the war because the government was the steel industry's biggest customer. Truman could have invoked the Taft-Hartley Act of 1947, which would have enjoined a strike for eighty days. That alone might have pressured management and labor to forge an agreement. But the strike had already been delayed for some ninety days. Truman thought it was unfair to ask steelworkers to continue working for another eighty days without a pay increase. Thus, he again turned to his general executive prerogative as commander in chief. Deeming it an emergency wartime situation in which steel production was essential, Truman seized control of the steel mills on April 8, a few hours before the scheduled strike. Secretary of Commerce Charles Sawyer now assumed control of the industry, with wages and prices remaining the same.[17]

When asked by a newspaper reporter what authority he had to take over the steel mills, President Truman replied bluntly: "Tell 'em to read the Constitution. The president has the power to keep the country from going to hell."[18]

Government takeover of the steel mills invited a constitutional crisis, albeit one that Truman thought he could win. After all, both Lincoln and Franklin D. Roosevelt had stretched presidential powers in times of crises and war. Not only had FDR seized the North American Aviation plant just before Pearl Harbor, but he had also taken control of several additional war-related industrial concerns and the nation's coal mines without statutory authority to avert interruptions in production.[19] If the matter reached the Supreme Court, Truman believed that he could surely count on a favorable outcome since either he or Franklin Roosevelt had appointed all nine justices. Moreover, one of those justices, Robert H. Jackson, had been FDR's attorney general who had issued a strong statement defending FDR's ability to seize North American Aviation. The current chief justice, Fred Vinson, reportedly had sent Truman a confidential statement communicating his view that seizing the mills was constitutional and that the court would support him.[20] Truman believed he had the matter locked down.

Following the steel industry's suit to regain its property, the case reached the Supreme Court as *Youngstown Sheet and Tube Co. v. Sawyer*.[21] On June 2, the Court rendered its opinion on a six-to-three vote: It declared that the president's steel seizure constituted an unconstitutional usurpation of legislative power. Justice Hugo Black, who wrote the Court's majority opinion, contended that no presidential powers as commander in chief authorized Truman's actions, for the Constitution limited his role in lawmaking "to the recommending of laws he thinks wise and the vetoing of laws he thinks bad." Justice Felix Frankfurter and Justice Harold Burton, concurring, emphasized that in seizing the plants, the president had ignored the "clear will of Congress" that had been expressed in the Taft-Hartley Act. While Frankfurter did not reject the notion of executive prerogative in certain circumstances, he argued that plant seizures during World War I and World War II were distinguishable. Frankfurter noted that of FDR's twelve seizures before Congress passed the War Labor Disputes Act of 1943, three had been sanctioned by prior legislation and six others after Congress had formally declared a state of war, thus transferring additional power to the president. Justice William O. Douglas, meanwhile, was also troubled by the "legislative nature of the action taken by the President," since it was up to Congress—not the executive branch—to regulate domestic labor disputes and to regulate private property on American soil (and to pay "just compensation" under the Fifth Amendment if it was seized).

Justice Jackson, who had served as solicitor general and attorney general under President Roosevelt and had confronted myriad presidential-power issues during World War II, wrote a concurrence that would become the most important statement regarding the scope of presidential power, to this day.[22] At oral argument, Jackson bristled at the notion that Truman's seizure of the steel plants could be analogized to FDR's seizure of North American Aviation. For Jackson, who had lived through these events as FDR's attorney general, this was a preposterous comparison—the aviation company had a direct contract with the government, which meant that the communist-led strike in 1941, as America was facing the likelihood of war, was essentially an action against the government.[23]

Jackson went on to articulate a test that would obliterate the Truman administration's argument. He laid out three categories of presidential power that created a spectrum within America's constitutional system. In the first category, when the president acted pursuant to express or implied authorization of Congress, the executive's powers were strongest. Here, the president was acting according to whatever powers he possessed (inherently) in the Constitution, *plus* whatever power Congress was allowed to delegate him. In the second category, when the president acted where Congress had neither granted nor denied authority, he was in a middle ground. He had to rely on his own powers in the Constitution, but there was a "zone of twilight" in which he and Congress could comfortably coexist. In the third category, where the president acted in a manner incompatible with the express or implied will of Congress, his power was at the lowest ebb. He could only rely on his own powers, minus the Constitution's powers given to Congress. As one scholar has observed, "here, the 'equilibrium' of the government's system of separation of powers is at stake. Thus, the courts must be leery when they venture into this third zone of danger."[24]

In this case, Justice Jackson concluded, President Truman was in the third, weakest category. The Constitution did not specifically or even implicitly authorize him to seize private property on U.S. soil. Nor had Congress given him that power. In fact, when Congress debated the Taft-Hartley Act in 1947, it specifically rejected an amendment that would have allowed the president to seize businesses in times of emergency. The president's powers were thus at their low point here.

Truman's own appointee and former attorney general, Justice Tom Clark, embraced the theory of an expanded executive prerogative "in times of grave and imperative national emergency." Even so, he concluded that the president's violation of strike-settlement procedures contained in Taft-Hartley meant that the present seizure was unconstitutional.[25]

Only Chief Justice Vinson, Truman's close friend and poker-playing partner, wrote a dissenting opinion joined by Justices Stanley Reed and Sherman Minton.[26] Vinson argued that "those who suggest that this is a case involving extraordinary powers should be mindful that these are extraordinary times." He advocated a broad view of Article II of the Constitution: that the president "shall take care that the laws be faithfully executed." Numerous precedents existed, Vinson insisted. For example, there were President Lincoln's actions during the Civil War and Grover Cleveland's deployment of the army to protect the mails and interstate commerce during the Pullman Strike of 1894. Additionally, Woodrow Wilson had created wartime agencies during World War I and Franklin Roosevelt had seized the North American Aviation plant before Pearl Harbor—both presidents had accomplished these actions without statutory authority.

Yet the Court as a whole emphatically rejected the president's position. As a result, Truman suffered a humiliating—and unexpected—defeat. As one Truman adviser later reported, "there was blue smoke around the White House for a couple of days."[27]

No member of the Supreme Court disappointed Truman more than his appointee Tom Clark. Truman would later tell author Merle Miller that appointing that "damn fool [Clark] from Texas" to the Court was the biggest mistake he made as president.[28] Meanwhile, the steel strike that followed the Court's decision lingered on for seven weeks. Ultimately, a settlement was achieved that provided workers with a $0.21 hourly increase and a steel price increase of $5.20 per ton—not far from the terms that Truman had proposed.[29]

## Conclusion

In November 1952, the Democratic Party suffered a crushing defeat in the elections, as Dwight D. Eisenhower captured the presidency. Even though Adlai Stevenson had replaced Truman as the Democratic presidential candidate, the failures of the Truman presidency remained the major theme of the Republican campaign. Although the *Steel Seizure Case* itself received little attention, no issue dominated the debates more than Truman's failures in Korea, even though constitutional questions relating to the U.S. entrance into that war remained unresolved.

On leaving the White House, Harry and Bess Truman returned to Independence, Missouri, and their home on North Delaware Street. Truman spent much of his time planning and overseeing construction of his presidential library and museum in Independence, frequently appearing to greet visitors and to give tours after its opening in 1957. Truman died of heart failure in December 1972, at age eighty-eight. He was buried in the courtyard of the Harry S. Truman Presidential Library, where Bess was buried ten years later.[30]

Despite the negative attention that some scholars have given to Truman's overreaching of presidential authority, most of them have conceded that the times required strong presidential action. Without a doubt, Truman's actions in seizing the steel mills during the Korean War served to whittle down the constitutional power of American presidents—particularly on the domestic front—in a fashion that would haunt future occupants of the White House. And Truman's actions in Korea would play into the debate and passage of the War Powers Act two decades later, during the presidency of Richard M. Nixon. Yet most historians have concluded that Truman acted out of a sincere belief that he needed to take firm steps to protect troops abroad. Indeed, neither Korea nor the *Steel Seizure Case* has diminished Truman's reputation as a plain-speaking, decisive leader during a difficult time in American history. In various recent scholarly polls, Truman ranks as one of the nation's best presidents, somewhere just below Lincoln, Washington, and Franklin Roosevelt.[31]

### NOTES

1. Robert J. Donovan, *Conflict and Crisis: The Presidency of Harry S. Truman, 1945–1948* (New York: W.W. Norton, 1977), 17. Three major Truman biographies emerged during the 1990s, and all of them treated Truman favorably but not without occasional

criticism: David McCullough, *Truman* (New York: Simon & Schuster, 1992); Alonzo L. Hamby, *Man of the People: A Life of Harry S. Truman* (New York: Oxford University Press, 1995); and Robert H. Ferrell, *Harry S. Truman: A Life* (Columbia: University of Missouri Press, 1994).

2. Jean Edward Smith, *FDR* (New York: Random House, 2008), 627–628.

3. Hamby, *Man of the People*, 288–289.

4. *Encyclopedia Britannica Online*, "The decision to use the atomic bomb," http://www.britannica.com/EBchecked/topic/712569/Trumans-decision-to-use-the-bomb.

5. Kate Doyle, "The End of Secrecy: U.S. National Security and the Imperative for Openness," *World Policy Journal* 16, no. 1 (Spring 1999): 37–39.

6. Hamby, *Man of the People*, 215. Hamby also contended that early in his life, Truman's "great exemplar" was Andrew Jackson, known for his expansive view of presidential power. Alonzo L. Hamby to James N. Giglio, e-mail, November 28, 2011.

7. Harry Truman, *Truman Speaks* (New York: Columbia University Press, 1960), 53–54.

8. Ibid., 55.

9. Harry S. Truman, *Mr. Citizen* (New York: Bernard Geis Associates, 1960), 222–224.

10. The Constitution states that the president "may, on extraordinary Occasions, convene both Houses, or either of them." U.S. Const. art. II, § 3.

11. James N. Giglio, "Cooperation to Conflict: The United States, Russia and the Emergence of Bipolarism, 1945 to 1952" in *Conflict and Change: America 1939 to Present*, ed. William W. MacDonald, Walter Sutton, John M. Carroll, and Frank W. Abbott (St. Louis: River City Publishers, 1983), 22–23; Hamby, *Man of the People*, 536.

12. The North Korean Kim, an ardent nationalist, most likely initiated a war of unification independently of the USSR as he had threatened to do. Giglio, "Cooperation to Conflict," 22. Years later, Nikita Khrushchev, no defender of Stalin, insisted that "the war wasn't Stalin's idea, but Kim Il Sung's. Kim was the initiator." Ibid.

13. Hamby, *Man of the People*, 538–539.

14. For the UN Participation Act of 1945, see "A Decade of American Foreign Policy 1941–1949, United Nations Participation Act, December 20, 1945," Avalon Project, Lillian Goldman Law Library, Yale Law School, http://avalon.law.yale.edu/20th_century/decad031.asp; Thomas F. Eagleton, *War and Presidential Power: A Chronicle of Congressional Surrender* (New York: Liveright, 1974), 67–68. When the author e-mailed Alonzo L. Hamby about the UN Participation Act of 1945 and its amendments of 1949, he responded: "I wasn't even aware of its existence and can't ever recall ever seeing any mention of it, either at the time or by later historians." Indeed, no major Truman historian has written about it, despite its existence.

15. Eagleton, *War and Presidential Power*, 71.

16. For detailed coverage of MacArthur's dismissal, see McCullough, *Truman*, 833–856, and Hamby, *Man of the People*, 554–564.

17. The background for the case comes primarily from McCullough, *Truman*, 896–899.

18. Ibid., 897.

19. Patricia L. Bellia, "The Story of the Steel Seizure Case," Notre Dame Law School, (Legal Studies Paper No.08–20, Notre Dame Law School, South Bend, IN, 2008). See

also Youngstown Sheet and Tube Co. v. Sawyer, 343 U.S. 579, 696 & n. 66 & Appendix II (1952) (Vinson, J. dissenting).

20. McCullough, *Truman*, 901; Ferrell, *Truman: A Life*, 372, 373–374. If this indeed were true, it would have represented a gross violation of judicial ethics and separation of powers.

21. Youngstown Sheet & Tube Co. v. Sawyer, 343 U.S. 579 (1952).

22. Ken Gormley, foreword, *President Truman and the Steel Seizure Case: A Symposium*, *Duquesne Law Review* 41 (2003): 674.

23. Robert H. Jackson, *That Man: An Insider's Portrait of Franklin D. Roosevelt*, ed. John Q. Barrett (New York: Oxford University Press, 2003), 21–22:216 n. 26, 220 n. 1.

24. Ibid., 674–675.

25. Alfred H. Kelly and Winfred A. Harbison, *The American Constitution: Its Origins and Development* (New York: W.W. Norton, 1976), 811–812.

26. Ken Gormley, *Archibald Cox: Conscience of a Nation* (Reading, MA: Addison-Wesley, 1997), 675.

27. Kelly, *The American Constitution*, 813–814; Gormley, *Conscience of a Nation*, 675 (quoting Truman adviser Ken Hechler).

28. Merle Miller, *Plain Speaking: An Oral Biography of Harry S. Truman* (New York: Berkley Books, 1980), 242.

29. McCullough, *Truman*, 901–902; Ferrell disagreed that the strike imposed any major impact on production or appreciable harm to national security. Ferrell, *Truman: A Life*, 373.

30. Hamby, *Man of the People*, 634.

31. See, for example, the *Chicago Sun Times* Survey on the American Presidency, October 2000, in which fifty historians who had published on the American presidency participated. Truman ranked as the fifth best president. The C-SPAN 2009 poll also ranked Truman at number five.

# PART IX

# The Civil Rights Era

# 34

# Dwight D. Eisenhower

RICHARD V. DAMMS

*Dwight D. Eisenhower earned public acclaim during World War II as supreme commander of Allied forces in Europe. The first Republican since Herbert Hoover to occupy the White House, "Ike" planned to hold the line against further expansion of federal powers. He worked assiduously to avoid being dragged into the school desegregation issue, believing in a "gradualist" approach to eliminating racial discrimination. Eisenhower helped steer the Supreme Court toward a middle-ground "with all deliberate speed" approach in Brown v. Board of Education II and hoped to allow states and local communities to work out the desegregation issue themselves. When the governor of Arkansas refused to allow black children to attend public school in Little Rock, however, Eisenhower was forced to send in National Guard troops to restore order. In the end, Eisenhower's commitment to "gradualism," albeit well-intentioned, allowed those dedicated to preserving segregation to advance their agenda, ushering in the period of violence and civil rights protests that would plague the nation in the 1960s.*

## Introduction

Dwight David Eisenhower, the last American president to be born in the nineteenth century, capitalized on his tremendous personal popularity and image as a war hero to secure election to the White House in 1952. Eisenhower's impeccable national security credentials made him the overwhelmingly popular choice for president, considering the volatile global environment. The U.S. was mired in an increasingly dangerous Cold War (as evidenced by the Soviet Union's then-recent acquisition of nuclear weapons and the establishment of the communist People's Republic of China). There was mounting anxiety at home over the dangers of communist subversion, and an unresolved "hot war" on the Korean peninsula. Internationally, Eisenhower accepted the general wisdom of former President Harry S. Truman's global policy of containing the Sino-Soviet bloc, but he also wished to maximize the American technological advantage in nuclear weapons. Domestically, although he resisted calls from some Republican Party leaders to roll back the previous two decades of Democratic social welfare and economic reforms, he believed that it was necessary to "hold the line" against any further expansion of federal powers and responsibilities.[1] Ironically, Eisenhower would find himself drawn into an issue—the racial integration of public schools—about which he was personally ambivalent but which would significantly extend the scope of federal involvement in people's daily lives.

Dwight D. Eisenhower was born in 1890 in Denison, Texas, the third of seven sons to parents of Pennsylvania Dutch (German) stock who belonged to the Mennonite River Brethren. He was raised in Abilene, Kansas, where his father worked at a creamery. Eisenhower's upbringing in small-town Kansas instilled in him values of hard work, thrift, education, modesty, and faith. After high school, Eisenhower won a place at the U.S. Military Academy at West Point, where he graduated in the top half of the class of 1915; however, he was frustrated as he spent World War I stateside training recruits in the new art of tank warfare. In 1916, he married Mamie Doud while stationed in Texas and later served at a base in Panama. In the interwar years, Eisenhower's leadership potential caught the eye of military leaders like Douglas MacArthur and others, who advanced his career and groomed him for high command. At the outbreak of World War II, Army Chief of Staff George C. Marshall quickly summoned Eisenhower to Washington and assigned him ever-increasing levels of responsibility, which culminated in his elevation to supreme commander. Eisenhower masterminded D-day (the Allied invasion of Normandy in 1944) and proved adept at the diplomacy of coalition warfare.

After he received the unconditional surrender of German forces, speculation immediately began about a possible political career for "Ike." He initially resisted approaches from both political parties, finding partisan politics distasteful. Nonetheless, after retiring from the army in 1948 to accept the presidency of Columbia University, Eisenhower learned that he shared many of the concerns of Republican internationalist business leaders with whom he increasingly associated. After serving as the first military commander of the newly established North Atlantic Treaty Organization (NATO), Ike became drawn into politics. To stave off the prospect of an isolationist Republican winning the presidency, Eisenhower allowed his moderate Republican friends to convince him to enter the presidential race in 1952.[2] Along with his running mate, Senator Richard M. Nixon of California, Ike easily rolled over his opponent, Illinois Governor Adlai Stevenson, becoming the nation's thirty-fourth president. In 1956, despite suffering a heart attack a year earlier, President Eisenhower was reelected, defeating Stevenson even more handily.

## Presidency

Like most conservatives, President Eisenhower took seriously the view that the framers of the Constitution had deliberately sought to avoid an overcentralization of power by specifying that powers not explicitly assigned to the federal government should be reserved to the states or to the people themselves. Under the guise of responding to national emergencies at home and abroad, Ike believed, New Dealers in the federal government had abused the powers of national taxation to impoverish the states and enhance the central government's role over citizens' lives, thereby undermining the principle of federalism. Wherever possible, Eisenhower preferred that state and local authorities, not the national government, take responsibility for addressing citizens' needs. He argued that these governmental bodies would be more attuned to local circumstances and would be more fiscally responsible given their limited resources.[3]

Unlike some fellow conservatives, however, Eisenhower was reluctant to press for amending the Constitution to accomplish contemporary political ends. When Republican Senator John W. Bricker of Ohio proposed an amendment to limit the power of the executive branch and expand the role of Congress in treaty making, Eisenhower strongly resisted. The president considered the amendment—driven partly by fears that U.S. membership in international organizations like the United Nations might result in a proliferation of "treaty law"—an unwise infringement on the foreign policy prerogatives of the president. He also warned that such an amendment would hamstring U.S. foreign relations with friends and allies at a time of increasingly complex and dangerous international affairs. Employing what one scholar later dubbed his "hidden-hand" managerial style, Eisenhower worked with fellow Republicans and sympathetic Democrats to water down and, eventually, to narrowly defeat the proposed Bricker amendment in the Senate.[4]

## McCarthyism and the "Red Scare"

Eisenhower's presidency coincided with rampant investigations of alleged Communists and their sympathizers, in hearings spearheaded by the House Committee on Un-American Activities and Senator Joseph McCarthy (R-WI). Initially, responding to his party's support of these investigations fueled by the Cold War and fear of Soviet spies and subversives, Ike had declared during the 1952 campaign: "Any kind of Communistic, subversive, or pinkish influence will be uprooted from responsible places in our government."[5] Years later, however, Eisenhower would describe McCarthyism as an assault on "personal liberties and constitutional process."[6]

McCarthy, who headed the Permanent Committee on Investigations, steamed forward with widely covered hearings, some of which questioned whether the State Department and the executive branch more broadly had been infiltrated by Communists. In May 1954, McCarthy called for "all employees of the executive departments to ignore Eisenhower's order of confidentiality, and instead to come forward to the congressional investigators with evidence of subversion and infiltration."[7]

President Eisenhower urged "mutual respect" among the branches of government, but increasingly viewed McCarthy as an extremist. The Red Scare hearings reached near-hysterical proportions, culminating in televised hearings of alleged communist subversion of the U.S. Army. Ultimately, McCarthy was publicly "condemned" by the Senate on December 2, 1954, for conduct that "tended to bring the Senate into dishonor and disrepute."[8] At a dinner in late December, when asked what he intended to do about Senator McCarthy, Ike responded: "Nothing. I think I'll just let the son of a bitch kill himself."[9]

One upshot of the era of McCarthyism is that it undoubtedly contributed to the Supreme Court's decision in *Yates v. U.S.* (1957), which finally rendered impotent the harsh "clear and present danger" test established during the World War I era.[10] That constitutional test had allowed the government to suppress First Amendment rights in a heavy-handed fashion in the name of curtailing "subversive" speech (see Chapter 28, "Woodrow Wilson"). In the *Yates* case, the Court overturned conspiracy convictions, under the Smith Act, of fourteen low-level members of the Communist Party USA in California. Justice John Harlan wrote that in interpreting the Smith Act, "we should not assume that Congress chose to disregard a constitutional danger zone so clearly marked." The Congress did not (and could not) prohibit "advocacy of forcible overthrow of the government as an abstract doctrine." Merely belonging to the Communist Party and espousing its views could not justify criminal prosecution, consistent with the guaranty of free speech under the First Amendment. Under the Smith Act, "it is only the advocacy of forcible action that is proscribed" the Court wrote, and not "the advocacy of abstract doctrine[.]"[11]

The *Yates* decision amounted to the end of the repressive "clear and present danger" test.[12] In large part, *Yates* reflected the sense of national shame that followed the extreme behavior of the McCarthy era. Senator McCarthy died in May 1957, just one month before the *Yates* decision was handed down. Although Eisenhower was faulted by critics for not taking a stronger public stance against McCarthy's abuses, the president's low-key approach of refusing to cooperate with him, one scholar argued, "defused the McCarthy crisis by providing McCarthy with the rope with which to hang himself.[13]

## The Brown Case

By the time Eisenhower entered the White House, the most pressing moral issue facing the nation was the African American struggle for full civil and political rights. Born and raised in a racially segregated society and professionalized in a similarly segregated military establishment, Eisenhower largely accepted the racial status quo. Although he periodically stated his support for the principle of equality for all American citizens, his concept of federalism led him to take the position that the administration should only take decisive action to eliminate racial discrimination in areas where the federal government had undisputed authority. Thus, Eisenhower completed the desegregation of the armed forces and military facilities initiated by his predecessor, President Truman, and brought his influence and power to bear in integrating public accommodations in the nation's capital, where racial discrimination against nonwhite foreigners had become an international embarrassment. Nevertheless, he was reluctant to use federal power to compel the individual states to abandon their segregationist practices. His reluctance derived largely from his belief that enacting national laws and handing down court rulings could not alter deep-seated prejudices. Rather, he believed, attitudes could only be changed over time by education and exposure to people of different races. As a result, Eisenhower consistently advocated a "gradualist" approach to desegregation and preached patience to African American leaders, advice that was not well received given the failure of the nation to live up to the promises of the Fourteenth and Fifteenth Amendments for almost a century.

Eisenhower initially hoped that his administration could sidestep involvement in the five public school desegregation cases pending before the Supreme Court, collectively known as *Brown v. Board of Education of Topeka, Kansas*, which challenged the constitutionality of racially segregated schools. Yet he was thwarted when invited by the Court to submit an amicus curiae (friend of the court) brief, after the Court reargument of the case in 1953.

Eisenhower's attorney general, Herbert Brownell, a strong supporter of civil rights, submitted a brief arguing that segregated public schools violated the Equal Protection Clause of the Fourteenth Amendment and urging a gradual transition to integrated schools. In correspondence with Southern friends like Governor James E. Byrnes of South Carolina, Eisenhower distanced himself from the brief and insisted that Brownell's submission represented the attorney general's "own convictions and understanding" of the matter.[14]

Ironically, Eisenhower's most important contribution to the eventual ruling came indirectly when he appointed Governor Earl Warren of California as chief justice following Fred Vinson's sudden death in September 1953. Although critics claimed that this appointment derived from the governor's support of Eisenhower during the 1952 Republican Convention, Eisenhower insisted that politics played no role in his thinking. Rather, he considered Warren "a statesman . . . a man of national stature . . . of unimpeachable integrity, of middle-of-the-road views," qualities that would enable him to build consensus on the Court.[15] On May 17, 1954, the Warren Court handed down its landmark decision in *Brown v. Board of Education*, ruling unanimously that "separate educational facilities are inherently unequal." Segregated public education, declared the Court, violated the Fourteenth Amendment's provision mandating equal protection of the laws for all citizens.[16] Acknowledging the variety of local conditions, however, the Court decided to postpone issuing a definitive ruling on appropriate measures of relief, pending a new round of briefs and arguments.

Eisenhower had serious reservations about the *Brown* decision. Indeed, some of his aides later claimed that he considered it a mistake. Yet the president refused to be drawn into public comment on the merits of the case or the wisdom of the Court's action, remarking simply that the decision was now the law of the land and that he would fulfill his constitutional responsibilities to uphold the law. Some observers, without a doubt, took Eisenhower's public remarks as an indication of his dissatisfaction with the ruling. However, his stance also reflected his deeply held convictions about the separation of powers and the inappropriateness of a president rendering a personal judgment on a judicial matter. Privately, Eisenhower worried that some states would simply close down their publicly funded school systems and devise methods by which to divert state resources to support "private" all-white institutions. (Indeed, this happened in several states, most notably Virginia.) Such a development would effectively destroy the public school system in the South, he believed, to the detriment of both African Americans and poor whites. President Eisenhower also feared that any attempt by federal authorities to force integration on the states would generate a segregationist backlash that could set back the cause of racial equality for years.[17]

Unlike the first *Brown* ruling, Eisenhower played a much more active role in addressing the question of implementation in *Brown v. Board of Education II*. In speeches, press conferences, and correspondence with friends and associates, he championed his preference for gradualism as the wisest approach. White Southerners needed time, he argued, to adjust to the new reality that racial segregation long sanctioned by the doctrine of "separate but equal" was now unconstitutional. As he somewhat warily told a meeting of the National Association for the Advancement of Colored People (NAACP), there had to be "patience without compromise of principle" and "continued social progress, calmly but persistently made." Although not stated in public, his personal preference was for desegregation to begin in graduate and professional schools, then colleges, and finally public schools, working downward one grade at a time. He understood that this approach would not satisfy African American leaders. Nonetheless, he argued that it was the most effective way to achieve "an orderly integration process." Complete integration, he believed, would require a long period of education and adjustment to overcome deeply ingrained assumptions and prejudices.[18]

Eisenhower directly participated in the drafting of the Justice Department's brief on implementation in *Brown II*. In fact, he personally inserted wording that shifted the tone of the document away from immediate integration toward a more deliberate process that would allow white Southerners time to accommodate to the changed legal environment. For example, Solicitor General Simon E. Sobeloff's original draft had called for the vindication of the plaintiffs' constitutional rights to be "as prompt as possible." After meeting with President Eisenhower at the White House, Sobeloff amended the language to read "as prompt as feasible." Indeed, "feasible" replaced "possible" throughout the brief, a subtle but significant shift in meaning that opened the door to a variety of justifications for delaying immediate integration. Similarly, the White House conference removed entirely a passage that had noted how rapid desegregation of the armed forces had managed to reduce prejudice among service personnel and had implied that swift desegregation in the public schools would have a similar effect on community attitudes. Finally, Eisenhower inserted a passage suggesting that just as the original *Brown* ruling had taken into consideration the psychological and emotional harm that segregation caused black children, the Court should similarly consider the psychological and emotional health of white Southerners when they were faced with the changes required in their educational systems. Through these interventions, Eisenhower clearly intended to present the strongest possible case for gradualism.[19] The day before the brief was filed, Eisenhower called a press conference to reiterate his hope that the Court would "take into consideration these great emotional strains" and devise "some form of decentralized process" to achieve desegregated schools.[20]

On May 31, 1955, the Warren Court delivered its second unanimous *Brown* ruling (*Brown II*), which closely followed the Justice Department's brief and Eisenhower's preferences. After reiterating that racial discrimination in public education was unconstitutional, the Court ordered that school desegregation should proceed "with all deliberate speed," language that offered an opportunity for opponents of immediate integration to gain room to maneuver.[21] The Court placed the onus for devising acceptable school desegregation plans on the local school districts and remanded the cases back to the district courts for further fact finding and deliberation. The Court also suggested that the districts would have the opportunity to convince the courts of the necessity of delay in implementing desegregation, in the interest of the public good. Reasons for delay might include administrative issues, the condition of physical facilities, the adequacy of school transportation systems, personnel matters, and necessary revisions of local laws and regulations. Significantly, the Court omitted the Justice Department's proposal for school districts to submit desegregation plans within ninety days or face the prospect of court-ordered desegregation the following school term, a major victory for opponents of immediate integration.[22]

For Eisenhower, the *Brown II* ruling represented a perfectly reasonable solution to the thorny issue of school desegregation. Moreover, it generally adhered to his philosophy of federalism, leaving local communities to work out the exact formula for reforming their school systems after the High Court had settled the fundamental constitutional issues. In Ike's mind, the whole affair represented a triumph for his "middle-of-the-road concept of moderation with a degree of firmness." With this ruling behind him, he hoped that contentious racial issues would no longer burden his administration.[23]

Indeed, after *Brown II*, Attorney General Brownell convinced Eisenhower to support a package of civil rights measures designed to protect African American voting rights. Eisenhower considered the vote-protection package the most effective way to achieve racial equality while avoiding further federal intervention in local affairs.[24] Although the Democratic-controlled Congress watered down the legislation and weakened the voting rights protections, in 1957 the administration secured passage of the first civil rights act since 1875—this one primarily aimed at ensuring equality in voting rights.[25]

## The Little Rock Crisis

Ike undoubtedly hoped that the school desegregation cases and the enact-ment of civil rights legislation would mark the end of a difficult chapter in his presidency. Yet his failure to issue a strong endorsement of *Brown*, and his overly solicitous concern for the welfare of white Southerners, created the impression that the administration was lukewarm, at best, when it came to the issue of protecting civil rights.[26] White Citizens' Councils sprang up to resist school desegregation by legal and extralegal means, and angry mobs persuaded the University of Alabama to expel its first African American student. Meanwhile, over a hundred Southern congressmen and senators signed the "Southern Manifesto," denounc-ing the Supreme Court's "unwarranted decision" in the *Brown* case and promising to use "all lawful means" to reverse it and "prevent the use of force" to implement it.[27]

The most direct challenge to the Supreme Court's ruling came in Little Rock, Arkansas, where Governor Orval E. Faubus—perhaps encouraged by the president's perceived weak support for school desegregation—saw an opportunity to mobilize segregationist voters for his upcoming reelec-tion campaign. In Little Rock, the local school board had developed a plan for the gradual integration of schools. Segregationists thereupon challenged the plan in state court, with Faubus testifying that integration might provoke violence. He succeeded in obtaining a restraining order. When the U.S. District Court in Arkansas enjoined the plaintiffs from using the state courts to block the integration plan sanctioned by the fed-eral court, Faubus remained defiant and absolved himself from any further responsibility for maintaining law and order in the matter. When angry white mobs assembled at the school on September 23 and 24 to harass the black students and obstruct integration, the mayor of Little Rock desper-ately appealed to the president for assistance.[28]

President Eisenhower was reluctant to employ military force against the governor. Yet Faubus's continued open defiance of a federal court forced the president's hand. Attorney General Brownell advised Eisenhower that state authorities had a constitutional responsibility to enforce federal laws and suppress violent efforts to obstruct them. Brownwell explained: "When State officers refuse or fail to discharge their duty in this respect, it becomes the responsibility of the national government, through the Chief Executive, to dispel any such forcible resistance to Federal Law."[29]

Given the mob violence, the inability of local law enforcement to handle the situation, and the governor's refusal to fulfill his legal responsibilities, Brownell assured Eisenhower that he had the necessary constitutional and legal authority to act. The president could mobilize the National Guard and use whatever additional forces might be necessary "to suppress the domestic violence, obstruction, and resistance of law" in Little Rock.[30]

Armed with these legal opinions, Eisenhower federalized the Arkansas National Guard and dispatched elements of the 101st Airborne Division to Little Rock to restore order and ensure that the desegregation of Central High School proceeded in compliance with federal court orders. Significantly, when addressing the nation at the height of the crisis, Eisenhower justified his actions as necessary to uphold the law while still avoiding an endorsement of the *Brown* ruling: "Personal opinions about the decision have no bearing on the matter of enforcement."[31]

Eisenhower's use of federal troops secured only a short-term victory. In February 1958, the Little Rock school board, citing continued public dissatisfaction with school desegregation and the possibility of further disruption, petitioned the U.S. District Court to allow the withdrawal of the African American students currently enrolled at Central High School at the end of the school year and the postponement of the desegregation plan for 2½ years. In June, a federal judge granted that petition, citing conditions of "chaos, bedlam and turmoil" that undermined the educational mission. Lawyers for the affected children, in conjunction with the U.S. Justice Department, appealed to the U.S. Court of Appeals for the Eighth Circuit. In August, the appeals court overturned the lower court's decision but granted a stay pending an appeal to the Supreme Court. Two days later, still hoping to avert the use of federal troops, President Eisenhower reiterated his determination to enforce the law. Governor Faubus remained equally resolute. Meanwhile, the Arkansas state legislature enacted new laws empowering the governor to close any school desegregated by federal court order and to transfer state aid from such schools to private, all-white institutions (a similar maneuver had been used in Virginia).[32]

Ultimately, in *Cooper v. Aaron*, the U.S. Supreme Court declared that the constitutional rights of the black schoolchildren to attend public schools, as outlined in the *Brown* ruling, could "neither be nullified openly and directly by state legislators or state executives or judicial officers, nor nullified indirectly by them through evasive schemes for segregation whether attempted 'ingeniously or ingenuously.'" Under Article VI of the

Constitution, the Supremacy Clause, *Brown* was now the "supreme law of the land" and the states were required to enforce it. State officials who continued to resist the decision, the Court declared, violated their "solemn oath" to uphold the Constitution.[33]

Faubus and the segregationists again had the last word. The governor closed Little Rock's four high schools for the 1958–1959 school year, a decision overwhelmingly ratified by a special election. In 1959, the Arkansas legislature enacted a Pupil Placement Law, whereby local school boards could claim to comply with federal mandates requiring desegregation by assigning a limited number of African American children to formerly all-white public schools. Thus, when Little Rock's public schools reopened in 1959, little more than token integration had occurred.[34]

Following the *Cooper v. Aaron* decision and subsequent school closings by state officials in Arkansas and Virginia, Eisenhower reiterated the duty of all Americans to comply with the rulings of the Supreme Court.[35] He condemned the school closings, particularly the "disastrous" effects that they would have on the affected schoolchildren, but he recognized that for the moment, the federal government had no power to compel the states to reopen the schools. Eisenhower was encouraged, however, by progress made in several states, including parts of Arkansas, and "the shrinking perimeter of the area where prejudices of this kind run so deep," with only Virginia, Alabama, Mississippi, South Carolina, and Georgia continuing to offer "total resistance" to desegregation.

Ultimately, Eisenhower retained his faith in federalism and the ability of local communities to find workable solutions to school desegregation. The school closings, he mused, might even have a salutary effect if students began to pressure parents, school boards, and local leaders to reopen the schools, if only to resume the extracurricular activities that were so important to the children and their communities.[36]

## Conclusion

In 1947, because of the ordeal caused by FDR's death during his fourth term in office, Congress had passed the Twenty-Second Amendment, limiting a president to two elected terms in office.[37] That provision was ratified in 1951, making Dwight D. Eisenhower the first president bound by this new constitutional limitation.[38] Running for a third term was not an option.

Ike actively campaigned for his vice president, Richard Nixon, and was deeply troubled that Democratic candidate, John F. Kennedy of Massachusetts, adopted a platform that advocated greater federal activism and an escalation of Cold War military programs. When Nixon lost, Eisenhower used his farewell address to deliver one final warning against excessive defense spending that might undermine the nation's economic health and constitutional freedoms. While a sound defense was imperative, he cautioned that "in the councils of government, we must guard against the influence, whether sought or unsought, by the military-industrial complex. The potential for the disastrous rise of misplaced power exists and will persist."[39]

After the election, Ike and Mamie moved back to their working farm near Gettysburg, Pennsylvania. He died of congestive heart failure in Walter Reed Army Hospital in Washington, on March 28, 1969. The former president was buried on the grounds of the Eisenhower Presidential Library in Abilene, Kansas.

Richard M. Nixon, now president in his own right at the time of Eisenhower's death, would pay tribute to his former commander in chief as "the world's most admired and respected man, truly the first citizen of the world."[40]

Looking back on Eisenhower's time in office, scholars have criticized Eisenhower for his failure to bring to bear his considerable personal prestige and the full weight of the executive branch of the government on the side of African American civil rights as a moral imperative. Some have condemned Eisenhower's actions in this area as little more than tokenism, intended to convey the impression of change partly to serve Cold War purposes.[41] But Eisenhower was not the only prominent white leader of the day who failed to come to grips with the rising demands and changing societal role of African Americans.

Although Chief Justice Earl Warren would later assert in his memoirs that Eisenhower was too accommodating to segregationists, Ike's five nominees to the Supreme Court and numerous appointments to the federal bench would seem to belie such a suggestion.[42] Eisenhower's greatest fault, perhaps, was that he overestimated the common sense and goodwill of the American people when it came to developing workable solutions to school desegregation at the local level. He was correct that deep-seated prejudices could not be eliminated overnight. Yet his consistent counsel for gradualism and local initiative played into the hands of those seeking to prevent school desegregation altogether. In the end, Eisenhower himself was probably surprised that by the time of his death in 1969, some fifteen years after the original *Brown* decision had made school desegregation the law of the land, school integration had still not been fully achieved in the United States.

NOTES

1. For elaboration on these themes, see Richard V. Damms, *The Eisenhower Presidency, 1953–1961* (London: Longman, 2002), 7–26, 56–79; Steven Wagner, *Eisenhower Republicanism: Pursuing the Middle Way* (DeKalb: Northern Illinois University Press, 2006); and Charles C. Alexander, *Holding the Line: The Eisenhower Era* (Bloomington: Indiana University Press, 1975).

2. Eisenhower's pre-presidential career is thoroughly documented in Stephen E. Ambrose, *Eisenhower: Soldier, General of the Army, President-Elect, 1890–1952* (New York: Simon & Schuster, 1983).

3. Dwight D. Eisenhower to William E. Robinson, February 12, 1952, in *The Papers of Dwight David Eisenhower*, ed. Louis Galambos and Daun Van Ee, vol. 13, *NATO and the 1952 Campaign* (Baltimore, MD: Johns Hopkins University Press, 1989), 984–992.

4. For a full discussion of the Bricker Amendment, see Duane A. Tananbaum, *The Bricker Amendment Controversy: A Test of Eisenhower's Political Leadership* (Ithaca, NY: Cornell University Press, 1988). On the "hidden hand" concept, see Fred I. Greenstein, *The Hidden-Hand Presidency: Eisenhower as Leader* (New York: Basic Books, 1982).

5. Geoffrey Perret, *Eisenhower* (New York: Random House, 1999), 491.

6. Dwight D. Eisenhower, *The White House Years: Mandate for Change, 1953–1956* (Garden City, NY: Doubleday, 1963), 320.

7. Martin J. Medhurst, ed., *Eisenhower's War of Words: Rhetoric and Leadership* (East Lansing: Michigan State University Press, 1994), 78.

8. Perret, *Eisenhower*, 504; Ronald E. Powaski, *The Cold War: The United States and the Soviet Union, 1917–1991* (New York: Oxford University Press, 1998), 100.

9. Ibid.

10. Yates v. United States, 354 U.S. 298 (1957).

11. Ibid., 329. Yates essentially abandoned the Court's earlier decision in Dennis v. United States, 341 U.S. 494 (1951), which had permitted criminal prosecutions of high-ranking communists, including Eugene Debs, under the Smith Act, on the basis of mere advocacy of the violent overthrow of government. For an excellent discussion of the evaluation of Supreme Court decisions during this period, see Marc Rohr, "Communists and the First Amendment: The Shaping of Freedom of Advocacy in the Cold War Era," *San Diego Law Review* 28 (1991): 1, 66–69.

12. This restrictive test was later replaced by a test much more protective of free speech rights in Brandenburg v. United States, 395 U.S. 444 (1969).

13. Peter G. Boyle, *Eisenhower: Profiles in Power* (Harlow, UK: Pearson Longman, 2005), 23–24.

14. Dwight D. Eisenhower to James F. Byrnes, December 1, 1953, in *Papers of Dwight David Eisenhower*, 15:712–714 .

15. Dwight D. Eisenhower to Edgar Eisenhower, October 1, 1953; Dwight D. Eisenhower to Milton Eisenhower, October 9, 1953, in *Papers of Dwight David Eisenhower*, 14:551 and 576, respectively.

16. Brown v. Board of Education, 347 U.S. 483 (1954).

17. Robert H. Ferrell, *The Diary of James C. Hagerty: Eisenhower in Mid-Course, 1954–1955* (Bloomington: Indiana University Press, 1983), 54; Michael S. Mayer, "With Much Deliberation and Some Speed: Eisenhower and the Brown Decision," *Journal of Southern History* 52 (February 1986): 59–60.

18. Dwight D. Eisenhower, *The White House Years*, vol. 1, *Mandate for Change, 1953–1956* (Garden City, NY: Doubleday, 1963), 151.

19. Mayer, "With Much Deliberation," 68–69.

20. President's News Conference, November 23, 1954, *Public Papers of the Presidents of the United States: Dwight D. Eisenhower, 1954* (Washington, DC: Government Printing Office, 1960), 1060 (hereafter cited as *Public Papers: Eisenhower*).

21. A gradualist approach to desegregation was also preferred by several members of the Court. Justice Felix Frankfurter proposed the phrase "with all deliberate speed" and repeatedly urged Chief Justice Warren to include the phrase in the Court's opinion. Gordon B. Davidson et al., "Supreme Court Law Clerks' Recollections of Brown v. Board of Education II," *St. John's Law Review* 79, no. 4 (2005): 835–837.

22. Brown v. Board of Education, 349 U.S. 294 (1955).

23. Robert F. Burk, *The Eisenhower Administration and Black Civil Rights* (Knoxville: University of Tennessee Press, 1984), 150.

24. Under the proposed legislation, a Civil Rights Division would be established in the Department of Justice, the attorney general would be given the authority to intervene in local voter discrimination suits and seek injunctive relief, and a bipartisan Civil Rights Commission would be established to investigate allegations of discrimination and make recommendations, supposedly removing civil rights issues from party politics.

25. Civil Rights Act of 1957, Public Law 85–315, *United States Statutes at Large* 71 (1957).

26. During the debate over the 1957 Civil Rights Act, for example, Eisenhower went so far as to attempt to reassure white Southerners that he could not imagine "any set of circumstances" under which he would send federal troops "into any area to enforce the orders of a federal court." What Eisenhower meant was that he could not conceive of a situation where law-abiding Americans or state and local officials charged with maintaining public order would openly defy the law of the land. Yet in some quarters, his words were taken to mean that he would not enforce the *Brown* rulings. *Public Papers: Eisenhower, 1957, 547.*

27. The Southern Manifesto, 102 Cong. Rec., pt. 4, 4459–60 (March 12, 1956), 84th Congress, 2d Sess.

28. Herbert Brownell with John P. Burke, *Advising Ike: The Memoirs of Attorney General Herbert Brownell* (Lawrence: University Press of Kansas, 1993), 206–210 365–368.

29. Ibid., 375.

30. Ibid., 376. He was referring to Sections 332 and 333 of Title 10 of the United States Code.

31. *Public Papers: Eisenhower*, 1957, 689–694; *President's Power to Use Federal Troops to Suppress Resistance to Enforcement of Federal Court Orders*, Little Rock Arkansas, 41 Op. Att'y Gen. 313.

32. David A. Nichols, *A Matter of Justice: Eisenhower and the Beginning of the Civil Rights Revolution* (New York: Simon & Schuster, 2007), 222–225.

33. Cooper v. Aaron, 358 U.S. 1, 18 (1958).

34. Elizabeth Jacoway, *Turn Away Thy Son: Little Rock, the Crisis That Shocked the Nation* (New York: Free Press, 2007), 326–330, 352.

35. *Public Papers: Eisenhower*, 1958, 722; Nichols, *Matter of Justice*, 232.

36. Dwight D. Eisenhower to Ralph McGill, October 3, 1958, in *Papers of Dwight David Eisenhower*, 19:1134.

37. "No person shall be elected to the office of the President more than twice, and no person who has held the office of President, or acted as President, for more than two years of a term to which some other person was elected President shall be elected to the office of the President more than once. But this article shall not apply to any person holding the office of President when this article was proposed by the Congress, and shall not prevent any person who may be holding the office of President, or acting as President, during the term within which this article becomes operative from holding the office of President or acting as President during the remainder of such term." U.S. Const. amend. XXII.

38. By its terms, the amendment created an exception for the then incumbent, President Truman.

39. *Public Papers: Eisenhower*, 1961, 1035–1040.

40. Richard Nixon, "Eulogy Delivered at the Capitol During the State Funeral of General Eisenhower," March 30, 1969, *The American Presidency Project*, ed. Gerhard Peters and John T. Woolley, www.presidency.ucsb.edu/ws/?pid=1987.

41. For a critical handling of Eisenhower and civil rights, see Burk, *Eisenhower Administration and Black Civil Rights*; more favorable assessments are provided by Mayer, "With Much Deliberation and Some Speed"; and, more recently, Nichols, *A Matter of Justice*. For a study explicitly linking domestic civil rights with Cold War considerations, see Mary J. Dudziak, *Cold War Civil Rights: Race and the Image of American Democracy* (Princeton, NJ: Princeton University Press, 2000).

42. Earl Warren, *The Memoirs of Chief Justice Earl Warren* (Lanham, MD: Madison Books, 2001), 291. Despite pressure from Southerners in Congress for judicial nominees sympathetic to their concerns, Eisenhower's four appointments to the Supreme Court following Warren and the *Brown* ruling were: John Marshall Harlan II of New York, grandson of the sole dissenting justice in the 1896 *Plessy v. Ferguson* case sanctioning "separate but equal"; William Joseph Brennan, a liberal Democrat and Catholic from New Jersey; Charles E. Whittaker, an experienced but undistinguished jurist from Kansas; and Potter Stewart, a Yale-educated lawyer and navy veteran who told the Senate Judiciary Committee during the nomination process that he would not overturn the *Brown* decision. Nichols, *A Matter of Justice*, 75–90, argues persuasively that Eisenhower erected a "judiciary to enforce *Brown*," a view seconded by Michael A. Kahn, "Shattering the Myth About President Eisenhower's Supreme Court Appointments," *Presidential Studies Quarterly* 22 (winter 1992): 47–56.

# 35

# John F. Kennedy

BARBARA A. PERRY

*President John F. Kennedy, the first Catholic elected as the nation's chief executive, tried to dodge politically sensitive issues, maintaining a cautious, moderate approach. Yet, try as he might, JFK was unable to maintain such a position toward civil rights. After riots by segregationists and the murder of innocent blacks in the Deep South, President Kennedy abandoned his cautious posture and advocated sweeping civil rights reform. An assassin's bullet cut his life and presidency short, changing the national mood and laying the foundation for the greatest civil rights revolution since the Civil War. Thus, JFK may have accomplished in death what had eluded him during his crisis-filled presidency.*

# Introduction

John F. Kennedy's presidency constituted little more than a thousand days in office. Yet two issues that arrived with him at the White House's threshold on January 20, 1961, race and religion, would draw him into constitutional debates that remained on the public agenda well into the twenty-first century.

Kennedy's life story illuminates how the issues of religion and race informed the constitutional issues he faced during his presidency. Born into the parochial world of Boston's Irish-Catholic middle class on May 29, 1917, young Jack felt the tug of his parents' divergent approaches to Roman Catholicism. The devout product of a Prussian convent education, his mother, Rose, wanted her sons to attend religious schools. Their father, Joseph P. Kennedy, having experienced the sting of religious discrimination more acutely, decreed that his four male offspring (as opposed to their five sisters) should attend non-Catholic prep schools and then follow in his footsteps to Harvard, where they could rub elbows with the WASP power elite. In fact, as business drew him increasingly to Wall Street, Joe moved his family from Boston to a posh New York City suburb, where they could thrive beyond Back Bay Brahmin prejudices.[1]

Making millions in the stock market and movie business, Joe Kennedy became a major donor to and campaigner for New York governor, Franklin Roosevelt, in the 1932 presidential race. Meanwhile, Jack and his older brother, Joe Jr., attended Choate, an elite Connecticut prep school, where Joe excelled in studies and sports and Jack played the class clown. The same dynamic repeated itself at Harvard until Joe graduated and left Jack to thrive outside his older brother's shadow.[2]

By this time, 1938, Joe Sr. had been appointed by President Roosevelt to serve as U.S. ambassador to the Court of St. James's, and the photogenic Kennedy clan became the toast of prewar London. During his final year at Harvard, Jack produced a senior honors thesis on Britain's lack of preparation to fight the Axis powers and, with his father's assistance, published this work as a book titled *Why England Slept*.[3]

Ambassador Kennedy resigned his position in early 1941 and returned to the States to rejoin his family, who had evacuated London after Hitler's invasion of Poland and Britain's declaration of war in September

1939. Though the former ambassador feared for his sons' lives, Joe Jr. and Jack both enlisted in the navy. In August 1943, Lieutenant (junior grade) John F. Kennedy was skippering a PT boat off the Solomon Islands during a nighttime patrol when a Japanese destroyer collided with JFK's vessel, slicing it in half. Two sailors in Jack's crew were killed instantly. The eleven remaining men clung to the PT boat's wreckage, until JFK, despite an injured back, led them on a perilous swim to nearby islands, as he towed a badly burned sailor. After a week hiding from the Japanese, the crew was rescued by friendly native islanders and an Australian coast watcher. One year later, Joe Jr. perished when his navy plane exploded over England.[4]

Suffering from war injuries, malaria, and undiagnosed Addison's disease, JFK contemplated his future. Ultimately, the decorated veteran decided to assume Joe Jr.'s mantle as the family's designated political aspirant. In 1946, an untested John F. Kennedy won a seat representing Massachusetts's Eleventh Congressional District, following his maternal grandfather and namesake (John F. Fitzgerald) to the House of Representatives.[5]

In 1952, Kennedy won a long-shot victory over incumbent U.S. Senator Henry Cabot Lodge Jr., relying on his father's financial assets and his mother's acumen at hosting festive teas for female voters. Still hobbled by back pain, Jack often campaigned on crutches, attracting woman voters who hoped either to mother or to marry him, depending on their age. Jacqueline Bouvier, a beautiful Newport socialite, finally captured his attention and married him in 1953. Reelected to the Senate by a landslide in 1958, Kennedy began to plan a national presidential campaign for two years later.[6]

Al Smith, the first Catholic major party candidate for president, had been trounced by Herbert Hoover in 1928. Since that time, no Catholic had headed a presidential ticket. Proving his electability during the 1960 Democratic primaries, especially by defeating Senator Hubert Humphrey of Minnesota in heavily Protestant West Virginia and eventually winning his party's nomination, JFK decided to address anti-Catholic bias directly in a September 1960 speech to the Greater Houston Ministerial Association.[7] Borrowing from Jeffersonian theory, Kennedy declared to the Protestant ministers: "I believe in an America where the separation of church and state is absolute. . . . I believe in a president whose religious views are his own private affair."[8] Poignantly observing that no one had asked his brother's religion before he died for his country in World War

II, JFK continued: "This is the kind of America for which our forefathers died—when they fled here to escape religious test oaths that denied office to members of less favored churches—when they fought for the Constitution, the Bill of Rights, [and] the Virginia Statute of Religious Freedom."[9] Only by manifesting strict public secularism, while following his Catholic faith in private, did Kennedy believe he could overcome the religious barrier to capturing the White House.[10] In a competitive race against Vice President Richard M. Nixon, Kennedy's poised performance in the first-ever televised debates helped turn the tide in his favor. Winning the popular vote by only 0.1 percent, JFK secured 83 percent of the Catholic vote and nearly one-third of the Protestant ballots. His large margin with Catholics and the respectable number of Protestant votes helped make the difference and gave him a comfortable Electoral College margin.[11]

## Presidency

The Kennedy presidency was filled with dramatic constitutional issues, both on the domestic front and in foreign affairs. They set the stage for the cascading controversies that would confront the nation over the next few decades.

### The Cuban Missile Crisis

In foreign affairs, the Cuban missile crisis, which many regard as the moment the Cold War came closest to nuclear conflict, stands as the Kennedy presidency's defining event. In October 1962, President Kennedy survived a chilling standoff with the Soviet Union when U.S. aerial reconnaissance discovered that the Soviets were secretly deploying long-range nuclear missiles in Cuba. Over an agonizing thirteen days, Kennedy quietly consulted with a small group of his closest advisers and weighed his options. Using his commander-in-chief powers, JFK ordered a naval "quarantine" around Cuba.[12] At the same time, as the "constitutional representative" of the United States in international affairs, JFK conducted back-channel negotiations with his Soviet counterpart, Premier Nikita Khrushchev, hoping to find a diplomatic solution to the confrontation.[13] Kennedy averted a nuclear conflagration when the two sides struck a deal. Khrushchev agreed to dismantle the offensive missiles in Cuba and return them to the Soviet Union in exchange for Kennedy's promise that the

United States would refrain from invading Cuba and would eventually withdraw American ballistic nuclear missiles based in Turkey and targeting the Soviet Union.

## Religious Issues

At home, Kennedy's Catholicism raised constitutional questions about the links between religion and education. Would President Kennedy support federal aid to parochial schools? What about organized prayer in public schools? During JFK's second year in the White House, the U.S. Supreme Court issued a landmark ruling on whether New York Regents could draft a nondenominational prayer and mandate its daily recitation in public schools. *Engel v. Vitale* (1962), a six-to-one decision written by Hugo Black, the Baptist justice from Alabama, drew a sharp line between church and state.[14] Justice Black wrote: "It is no part of the business of government to compose official prayers for any group of the American people to recite as part of a religious program carried on by the government."[15] New York's mandated prayer, the Court concluded, "established the religious beliefs embodied" therein and thus violated the First Amendment's Establishment Clause.[16]

The Court's decision provoked a storm of protest, particularly in Southern states, and Congress introduced an amendment to overturn it. Within days, Kennedy held a regularly scheduled press conference. The first questioner asked the president to comment on *Engel* and the proposed amendment to the Constitution "to sanction prayer or religious exercise in the schools."[17] JFK replied: "It is important for us if we are going to maintain our constitutional principle that we support the Supreme Court decisions even when we may not agree with them."[18] Additionally, Kennedy told the press and television viewers: "We have in this case a very easy remedy and that is to pray ourselves."[19]

The issue of prayer in public schools was followed immediately by a question from the press on President Kennedy's position toward federal funding of higher education, specifically whether he supported government aid to private, church-related colleges and universities. Kennedy drew a bright-line distinction between the constitutional status of secondary schools and higher education. Attendance at high schools, President Kennedy emphasized, was "compulsory," and public schooling was central "in the traditional and constitutional life of our country." Therefore,

Kennedy adhered to his separationist view that *religious* primary and secondary schools should receive no government funding. Because higher education was not compulsory, however, he believed that Congress could provide funding to private (presumably even church-related) colleges and universities "in the same fashion" as public institutions of higher learning.[20]

Despite JFK's careful adherence to secular funding policies for primary and secondary schools (ironically prompting Catholic opposition), his education bill stalled in the House of Representatives. Southern Democrats, fearful that the bill might link funding to school desegregation, joined Catholic legislators to stymie the proposal.[21] Thus, President Kennedy met mixed success in negotiating the choppy waters surrounding the relationship between religion and government, an issue that had dogged him since he had first decided to run for president.

### Reapportionment: "One Person, One Vote"

One of the most nettlesome constitutional issues tackled by the Kennedy administration on the domestic front involved reapportionment—the redrawing of district lines for state and federal legislative seats throughout the United States. Since the early twentieth century, when much of the country became industrialized, many legislative districts had become demonstrably unbalanced as population shifted from rural to urban. The president and his attorney general, Robert (Bobby) Kennedy, understood that urban areas were prime Democratic territory. Moreover, for reasons of fairness, they concluded that each citizen's vote should carry roughly the same weight at the ballot box.[22]

In March 1962, the Kennedy Justice Department won a major victory when the Supreme Court handed down its historic decision in *Baker v. Carr*, holding that state legislative maps across the country were subject to constitutional review under the Fourteenth Amendment's Equal Protection Clause.[23] *Baker* opened the door to challenge state legislative maps as unconstitutional. With the president's support, Solicitor General Archibald Cox filed briefs in an Alabama case, in which legislative districts had not been redrafted since 1900 and had become clearly unequal in population.

After a full-court press by the Kennedy administration, the Supreme Court would ultimately hand down its landmark voting decision in

*Reynolds v. Sims*, embracing the "one-person, one-vote" principle under the Fourteenth Amendment, outlawing legislative districts that did not give each citizen's vote the same weight in electing representatives.[24] Indirectly, this decision also signaled a victory for African American voters. Southern states had used their refusal to reapportion as a means to maintain power in rural white areas, rather than in urban centers, heavily populated by blacks. Ultimately, after putting its toe in the water in the redistricting cases, the Kennedy administration was forced to wade directly into a host of civil rights issues that had now bubbled to the surface as demands for equality swept the nation.

## Civil Rights: Race in the Kennedy Presidency

Jack Kennedy came late to the modern civil rights movement. Personal experience and politics contributed to his tardiness. He spent the first ten years of his life in Boston, which in the 1920s was only about 3 percent black.[25] Although his family had always employed servants, they were usually drawn from shanty Irish. Choate, Harvard, London aristocracy, and the U.S. Navy officer corps had not exposed young Jack to the plight of Negroes. As a senator, JFK had tried to find a midpoint between the Northern pro-civil-rights Democrats and Southern segregationist Democrats as they debated the 1957 Civil Rights Act.[26] His votes reflected a purely pragmatic (some might say opportunistic) mix of conservatism and liberalism.[27] During the 1960 presidential campaign, JFK and his brother Bobby understood that Southern Baptists and Protestants viewed his Catholic faith as one strike against the candidate. They did not want to add another strike by taking an activist stand on civil rights.

Both the Democratic and the Republican Parties' 1960 presidential platforms called for an end to discrimination based on race, color, national origin, or religion in employment, education, transportation, housing, and voting. Grandly titled "The Rights of Man," the Democratic platform added the administration of justice to the areas of proposed nondiscrimination. An end to racial discrimination became a signature element of his New Frontier theme in Kennedy's acceptance speech at the Democratic convention.[28] Yet JFK rarely referred to his party's civil rights plank on the campaign trail. During his first two years in office, he refused to send any sweeping civil rights proposals to Congress for fear that the Southern Democrats would not only defeat them but also stall his other

New Frontier policies. Somewhat timidly, he did use executive action for addressing equal opportunity in federal service and in contracts let by the federal government.[29]

The last thing the Kennedy administration wanted was provocation of Southern segregationists. Thus, the so-called Freedom Riders, young black and white activists who boarded Greyhound busses in the North and headed south to challenge Jim Crow laws in public transportation, vexed the Kennedys during the first year of JFK's presidency. Attorney General Kennedy initially called on Freedom Riders organizers to rein in their participants to avoid violent clashes with police and people in the erstwhile Confederacy. The protesters, hoping to desegregate bus travel as a form of interstate commerce, refused to relent. To protect his brother from direct involvement, Bobby Kennedy deployed U.S. marshals in a failed effort to keep the peace. Throughout this time, the Kennedy administration refused to follow civil rights leaders' plea to label their cause a moral one.[30]

Soon, trouble erupted in connection with efforts to desegregate the flagship universities of Mississippi and Alabama. When James Meredith, a slave's grandson, applied to Ole Miss in 1961, the segregated institution rejected the twenty-eight-year-old air force veteran. The NAACP's Legal Defense and Educational Fund brought suit in federal court. The Kennedy Justice Department, taking a bold step, filed amicus briefs supporting Meredith's claim. The case swiftly moved to the U.S. Supreme Court.[31]

Worried about his chances for reelection in 1964, JFK tried to thread the needle of performing his constitutional duty while not provoking violence or the wrath of Mississippi governor, Ross Barnett. In a recorded phone call, Kennedy explained his predicament to the intractable governor: "Listen, I didn't put him in the university, but on the other hand, under the Constitution . . . I have to carry out the orders. . . . Now, I'd like to get your help in doing that."[32]

Barnett's help was anything but forthcoming. He defiantly pledged to protect Mississippi's "sovereignty" and held demagogic rallies designed to vow allegiance to Mississippi's "customs," whipping town and gown into a frenzy. Court-sanctioned attempts to lead Meredith onto campus were met by thousands of angry protesters. Finally, President Kennedy concluded he had no alternative to dispatching U.S. troops to Ole Miss, but not before two journalists were shot to death and scores of injuries resulted from the vigilantism. As troops began to calm the campus, Meredith finally registered, flanked by U.S. Justice Department officials, becoming the first African American to enroll at Ole Miss under a federal court order.[33]

The summer of 1963 proved just as volatile as the previous fall. Now the flashpoint became Birmingham, Alabama, where the Reverend Martin Luther King Jr. had decided to bring his civil disobedience campaign to bear on the city's entrenched segregationist power structure. As black civil rights advocates took to the streets, Bull Connor, the inaptly titled commissioner of public safety, turned police dogs and water hoses on the peaceful protesters, many of whom were young students. The vicious attacks on nonviolent protesters, most of them African Americans, who were simply exercising their First Amendment right to assemble, flashed around the world in news photos and videos. President Kennedy was personally horrified by Connor's response; he also knew that such images damaged the U.S. reputation abroad.[34] How could he convince Third World countries, many of which had black and brown populations, to side with the "Free World" in the Cold War when the U.S. was denying the benefits of full citizenship to American Negroes, nearly a century after the adoption of the Fourteenth Amendment had presumably guaranteed equal protection of the laws for all citizens?

Once again, a Southern university campus became a battlefield for the clash between state-sponsored segregation and the U.S. Constitution's requirement of equal protection of the laws in state institutions. Vivian Malone and James Hood, two unsuccessful black applicants at the University of Alabama, received in the summer of 1963 a U.S. District Court ruling ordering the university to admit them. Governor George Wallace chose a symbolic act of standing in the entrance of a university building to block the students' path. President Kennedy, rather than mustering regular army troops, as he had in Oxford, Mississippi, federalized the Alabama National Guard and threatened to send them to the Tuscaloosa campus to enforce the federal order. With that, Wallace finally yielded to Malone and Hood, accompanied by Deputy Attorney General Nicholas Katzenbach, and the University of Alabama became the nation's last racially segregated state university.[35]

Although JFK had tried to sidestep danger and follow a policy of political incrementalism, he finally decided that he had to take a moral stand on civil rights. The Alabama race riots pushed JFK over the brink. On June 11, 1963, the president decided to deliver a televised speech so hastily prepared by Ted Sorensen, the adviser who served as his "intellectual blood bank," that it still lacked a conclusion as the broadcast began. Its most memorable declaration would echo into the twenty-first century: "We are confronted with primarily a moral issue. It is as old as the scriptures and it is as clear as the American Constitution."[36]

Abandoning his passivity, by which he had tried to mollify the Southern caucus in Congress, President Kennedy now announced that he would send to Capitol Hill proposed legislation to, among other things, ban segregation in hotels, restaurants, theaters, stores, and other private businesses. Because these were not state-related institutions, post–Civil War precedent suggested that the Fourteenth Amendment's Equal Protection Clause did not apply. President Kennedy and his brother, the attorney general, wanted to challenge that precedent directly under the Fourteenth Amendment. Yet Kennedy's solicitor general, Archibald Cox, pressed the argument that Congress could enact this new civil rights law under its authority to regulate interstate commerce pursuant to the Commerce Clause, an approach with a likelier chance of succeeding before the contemporary U.S. Supreme Court.[37]

Despite Kennedy's new sense of urgency, he was too late to stem the tide of protest by those who were growing impatient with Congress's inaction. On August 28, 1963, some two hundred thousand marchers (black and white) converged on the nation's capital for the March on Washington for Jobs and Freedom, culminating in Rev. Martin Luther King's historic clarion call for color blindness. Fearing violence, the Kennedy administration amassed unprecedented law enforcement and military presence in and around Washington. Relieved that no violent outbreaks occurred and genuinely impressed with King's soaring oratory, JFK welcomed the civil rights leader and his compatriots to the Oval Office to exchange views on that sweltering August day.[38]

The Kennedy administration continued to step deliberately through the civil rights minefield. In May 1963, the Kennedy Justice Department had won a group of sit-in cases involving blacks who had been arrested for attempting to eat at "white" lunch counters in various Southern states.[39] Solicitor General Cox had also won a case in which black children had been barred from Glen Echo Amusement Park in Maryland.[40] In each instance, Kennedy's solicitor general had been extraordinarily cautious. He had argued (and won) the cases on the narrowest possible grounds, waiting for Congress to pass civil rights legislation so that the Supreme Court would have a more solid basis for its decisions in order to address racial discrimination directly.

## Conclusion

As President Kennedy looked toward his 1964 reelection campaign, he continued to worry about how his support of the civil rights cause would affect his electoral chances in the South. A rift among conservative and liberal Texas Democrats drew him to the Lone Star State for fence-mending and fund-raising in November 1963. Riding through the streets of downtown Dallas on November 22 in an open limousine, the forty-six-year-old president was stalked by an assassin who positioned himself with a high-powered rifle on the sixth floor of the Texas School Book Depository along the presidential motorcade route. In a split second that shocked the world, President Kennedy suffered a fatal gunshot wound to the head. When Attorney General Robert Kennedy informed his sister-in-law Jackie that the accused assassin, Lee Harvey Oswald, was an avowed Marxist, she responded bitterly, "[Jack] didn't even have the satisfaction of being killed for civil rights. [I]t had to be some silly little Communist."[41]

Ironically, the new president, Vice President Lyndon Johnson, infused the chief executive's martyrdom with meaning, using it to inspire the civil rights bill's passage.[42]

JFK had been cautious—some would say to a fault—in addressing the festering civil rights issues that he had inherited when he took office. Yet Kennedy acted with political courage in confronting the violent segregationists in Oxford, Mississippi, and Tuscaloosa, Alabama, using the full might of the executive branch to break the back of the Southern resistance. He also became the first twentieth-century president—after he finally reached a point of moral outrage—to demand civil rights legislation that would end legally sanctioned discrimination that had weakened the nation's constitutional fabric.

It had taken twelve months of crisis, and President Kennedy's own tragic assassination, for his moral declaration of constitutional clarity in opposing racial discrimination to illuminate a clear path for the advancement of American civil rights. After JFK's death, the next sequence of historic events, in dismantling the pernicious remnants of Jim Crow, would occur under the administration of a new president, Lyndon B. Johnson.

## NOTES

1. Barbara A. Perry, *Rose Kennedy: The Life and Times of a Political Matriarch* (New York: W.W. Norton, 2013).

2. Robert Dallek, *An Unfinished Life: John F. Kennedy, 1917–1963* (New York: Back Bay Books, 2003), 35–61.

3. Ibid., 53–66; John F. Kennedy, *Why England Slept* (New York: Wilfred Funk, 1940).

4. Perry, *Rose Kennedy*. The definitive biography of Joe Kennedy is David Nasaw, *The Patriarch: The Remarkable Life and Turbulent Times of Joseph P. Kennedy* (New York: Penguin Press, 2012).

5. Dallek, *An Unfinished Life*, 122–133.

6. Perry, *Rose Kennedy*; Barbara A. Perry, *Jacqueline Kennedy: First Lady of the New Frontier* (Lawrence: University Press of Kansas, 2004), 33–47.

7. Theodore C. Sorensen, *Kennedy* (New York: Harper and Row, 1965), 122–151.

8. Theodore C. Sorensen, *"Let the Word Go Forth": The Speeches, Statements, and Writings of John F. Kennedy* (New York: Delacorte Press, 1988), 131.

9. Ibid., 132.

10. Barbara A. Perry, "Catholics and the Supreme Court: From the 'Catholic Seat' to the New Majority," in *Catholics and Politics: The Dynamic Tension Between Faith and Power*, ed. Kristin E. Heyer, Mark J. Rozell, and Michael A. Genovese (Washington, DC: Georgetown University Press, 2008), 156.

11. James N. Giglio, *The Presidency of John F. Kennedy* (Lawrence: University Press of Kansas, 1991), 18.

12. The use of the term "quarantine" was used to indicate that the United States had taken a measure of self-defense since the quarantine only applied to stopping the shipment to Cuba of materials necessary to effectuate the threat of a nuclear war and to distinguish the action from a blockade, which the Office of Legal Counsel had concluded could be regarded by Cuba and the Soviet Union as an act of war. Arthur H. Garrison, "The History of Executive Branch Legal Opinions on the Power of the President as Commander-in-Chief from Washington to Obama," *Cumberland Law Review* 43 (2013): 420 and n. 164.

13. On "constitutional representative," see United States v. Curtiss-Wright Export Corp., 299 U.S. 304, 319–20 (1936).

14. Barbara A. Perry, "Jefferson's Legacy to the Supreme Court: Freedom of Religion," *Journal of Supreme Court History* 31, no. 2 (2006): 196.

15. Engel v. Vitale, 370 U.S. 421, 425 (1962).

16. Ibid., 430.

17. Harold W. Chase and Allen H. Lerman, eds., *Kennedy and the Press: The News Conferences* (New York: Thomas Y. Crowell, 1965), 274.

18. Ibid.

19. Ibid.

20. Ibid., 274–275 (emphasis added).

21. Giglio, *The Presidency of John F. Kennedy*, 101; Lawrence J. McAndrews, "Beyond Appearances: Kennedy, Congress, Religion, and Federal Aid to Education," *Presidential Studies Quarterly* 21, no. 3 (summer 1991): 545–557.

22. Ken Gormley, *Archibald Cox: Conscience of a Nation* (Reading, MA: Addison Wesley, 1997), 163–177. JFK had published an article for the *New York Times Magazine* during his Senate tenure, decrying the evils of malapportionment. John F. Kennedy, "The Shame of the States," *New York Times Magazine*, May 18, 1958, 18.

23. Baker v. Carr, 369 U.S. 186 (1962).

24. Reynolds v. Sims, 377 U.S. 533 (1964).

25. Lorraine Elena Roses, "After Abolition: Where's Black Boston?" *Boston Black History*, accessed April 30, 2013, http://academics.wellesley.edu/AmerStudies/BostonBlackHistory/history/where.html.

26. Nick Bryant, *The Bystander: John F. Kennedy and the Struggle for Black Equality* (New York: Basic Books, 2006), 66.

27. Giglio, *The Presidency of John F. Kennedy*, 13.

28. Barbara A. Perry, *The Michigan Affirmative Action Cases* (Lawrence: University Press of Kansas, 2007), 3.

29. Ibid., 6.

30. Dallek, *An Unfinished Life*, 283–288; Arthur M. Schlesinger Jr., *Robert Kennedy and His Times* (New York: Ballantine Books, 1978), 317.

31. As the justice assigned to deal with emergency issues in his home circuit, the Fifth, Alabamian Justice Hugo Black ordered Ole Miss to admit the plaintiff for the 1962 fall term, and the U.S. District Court drew up the necessary judicial order. Bryant, *The Bystander*, 331–333; Jonathan Rosenberg and Zachary Karabell, eds., *Kennedy, Johnson, and the Quest for Justice: The Civil Rights Tapes* (New York: W.W. Norton, 2003), 32–33.

32. Timothy Naftali and Philip Zelikow, *The Presidential Recordings, John F. Kennedy: The Great Crises*, vol. 2 (New York: W.W. Norton, 2001), 233.

33. Bryant, *The Bystander*, 332–350.

34. Perry, *The Michigan Affirmative Action Cases*, 9.

35. Bryant, *The Bystander*, 417–420.

36. Ibid., 422–423; Peniel E. Joseph, "Kennedy's Finest Moment," *New York Times*, June 11, 2013.

37. Perry, *The Michigan Affirmative Action Cases*, 10–13. Interestingly, both JFK and Robert Kennedy preferred premising the law on the Fourteenth Amendment and attacking private discrimination under the Equal Protection Clause, even though prior precedent from the Reconstruction era (the Civil Rights Cases, 109 U.S. 3 [1883]) directly held that the Fourteenth Amendment could not form the predicate for congressional legislation of this sort because there was no state action. Bobby Kennedy preferred the Fourteenth Amendment because he believed it was the most direct path to address civil rights injustices, despite past precedent. President Kennedy worried about using the Commerce Clause as a political matter, because FDR had utilized that provision so heavily to enact his New Deal Legislation that JFK feared Republicans would rebel against it. Yet for Archibald Cox, a former labor lawyer who knew the Commerce Clause precedent well, this avenue would be "as easy as ducks rolling of a log" for the Supreme Court, as a basis for upholding the proposed new civil rights legislation. Gormley, *Archibald Cox*, 189.

38. Richard Reeves, *President Kennedy: Profile of Power* (New York: Simon & Schuster, 1993), 584–585.

39. Peterson v. Greenville, 373 U.S. 244 (1963).

40. Griffin v. Maryland, 378 U.S. 130 (1964).

41. William Manchester, *The Death of a President* (New York: Harper and Row, 1967), 465–466.

42. Lyndon Baines Johnson, Address to Joint Session of Congress, November 27, 1963, Rector and Visitors of the University of Virginia, 2013, http://millercenter.org/president/speeches/detail/ 3381.

# 36

# Lyndon B. Johnson

JOHN L. BULLION

*President Lyndon B. Johnson, who was sworn in aboard Air Force One hours after JFK's assassination in Dallas, used his ample skills in cajoling and arm-twisting to push through the most significant civil rights legislation in American history, in the form of the Civil Rights Act of 1964 and the Voting Rights Act of 1965, after Kennedy's death. A towering Texan, LBJ also believed in using political muscle to overpower the intransigent courts and legal precedent that stood in his way. He thus managed to use the Commerce Clause cases of the New Deal era to advance his Great Society agenda. Yet when LBJ left office after a single full term, he was bitter, frustrated, and exhausted, having been engulfed by public controversy over the Vietnam War. Nonetheless, Lyndon Johnson left in place one of the greatest constitutional and legislative achievements in the nation's history.*

## Introduction

"When I was young," Lyndon Johnson recalled in 1965, "poverty was so common that it didn't have a name." Economic distinctions between the comparatively better-off in Johnson City, Texas, and those struggling to pay the mortgage were slight by the standards of the outside world. Some accepted the wearing routines of farming, ranching, and day labor as their fate; others seized on education as the way to change their lives. "Education," LBJ observed later, "was something you had to fight for."[1]

From the beginning of his life on August 28, 1908, Lyndon seemed to be marked for great things. His father, Sam Ealy Johnson, announced that a U.S. senator had just been born, proof of a father's pride and Sam's expectation that his progeny would do better than he, a failed rancher, an unsuccessful land speculator, and a dedicated but minor state legislator, had done. Significantly affected by the teaching of the Christian Church about the duties the strong had to the weak, Lyndon taught for several years in Texas.[2] However, once Congressman Richard Kleberg put him in charge of his office in Washington, D.C., in 1931, Johnson gladly left teaching behind.[3] That job in the Capitol gave Johnson another chance at the profession he had set his sights on in 1924 after graduating from high school: the law. At first, Johnson served as a clerk for a distant cousin who had a lucrative practice in San Bernardino, California. However, when the relative began chasing women and drinking, Johnson feared he might face prosecution if the clients discovered they were being counseled by a teen-ager who was unlicensed to practice law. Unable to pay for law school, Lyndon returned to Texas and took a job on a road crew. Hard labor drove him to enroll at Southwest Texas State Normal College, where he earned a degree in education.[4]

Johnson took one more stab at becoming a lawyer. In 1934, he took night classes at the Georgetown University School of Law. He found these to be tedious and pointless. One friend remembered that Johnson had no trouble mastering specific rules of law, but stubbornly resisted instruction in the historical context or jurisprudential reasoning behind them. After two months, Johnson dropped out.[5] Thus, LBJ began to develop an attitude toward the law that was extremely pragmatic: It was something that had to be manipulated into place by those skillful enough to master this sublime art.[6]

## The Political Arena

Johnson's first campaign for office was in the special election to fill the vacancy in the Texas Tenth Congressional District in 1937. In this contest, he distinguished himself from seven other candidates by supporting Franklin Roosevelt's controversial Court-packing plan.[7] If elderly doctrinaire conservatives on the bench were thwarting policies he deemed essential to the nation's recovery from the Depression and to his own political rise, LBJ felt, why not cancel out their votes by adding younger, liberal justices who would support the FDR agenda? To Johnson, the federal bench was clearly an intensely political institution. To see judges as anything but politicians with unique opportunities to affect the nation's life for decades, he concluded, was an exercise in naïveté. Indeed, when the Supreme Court buckled to FDR's threat, this suggested to Johnson that the Court could be manipulated, massaged, and even manhandled, just as the law itself could be.[8] Johnson's position on the New Deal and the Supreme Court helped him win the special election for Congress by three thousand votes on April 8, 1937. Also crucial to his success was his prodigious capacity for campaigning and his extraordinary ability to win votes in rural precincts.

Johnson next won a hotly contested U.S. Senate race in 1948, prevailing in the Democratic primary by only eighty-seven votes in a runoff election and earning himself the nickname "Landslide Lyndon." In the Senate, Johnson rose rapidly, ultimately becoming the most powerful majority leader in the institution's history. Chief among his many accomplishments was helping to enact the Civil Rights Act of 1957, the first piece of civil rights legislation since Reconstruction. He also became a figure in national politics and a legitimate candidate for the presidency. He foundered in the 1960 campaign, overpowered by the personal and televised charisma of Senator John F. Kennedy of Massachusetts. Reasoning that Lyndon could help him win Texas and hang on to most of the South, Kennedy selected LBJ as his running mate over strenuous opposition from Northern liberals, including his brother and campaign manager, Robert F. (Bobby) Kennedy. Lyndon fulfilled JFK's hopes. In the closest presidential election of the twentieth century, the ticket prevailed.

## Vice Presidency and JFK's Death

LBJ was profoundly unhappy as vice president. He had minimal influence over policy, enjoyed no input on congressional relations, and was subject to rude behavior from many in the administration, particularly Attorney General Bobby Kennedy. Thus, Johnson mostly observed from the sidelines as the president and his attorney general wrestled with racial issues.[9]

Throughout Johnson's years on Capitol Hill, he had remained sure that the federal government could help all Americans fulfill their basic needs, including "a roof over their heads, food on their tables, milk for their babies, a good job at good wages, a doctor when they need him, an education for their kids . . . and a nice funeral when they die."[10] Dating back to 1937, the same year Johnson was elected to Congress, Supreme Court decisions on the Commerce Clause had opened the door to far-reaching legislative experiments.[11] Johnson saw great potential in these openings, but as vice president, he had no power to devise a plan.[12]

Vice President Johnson had no role in the Kennedy administration's decision to base the constitutionality of its proposed civil rights bill on the Commerce Clause. In fact, he had not been asked to participate in drafting legislation or planning the campaign to secure the law's passage. As LBJ remarked to one of JFK's advisers, he learned about the bill by reading the *New York Times*. Indeed, he had to insist on a fifteen-minute meeting with the president to ensure that his concerns would be heard. LBJ believed that the president and his advisers had badly erred in their handling of the bill. By introducing it *before* the federal budget and tax cut legislation, he believed, the Kennedy administration had handed Southern senators a potent piece of ammunition in their inevitable filibuster. As time passed, LBJ predicted, the administration would feel compelled to withdraw the proposed civil rights bill or water it down to end the filibuster and take up other vital legislation.[13]

LBJ was right. By November 20, 1963, JFK had no budget, no tax reduction, no wheat deal with the Soviets, and nothing else of significance. Moreover, he had buckled under to political pressure and agreed to eliminate key provisions of his administration's proposed civil rights package.[14] Most discouraging of all for Johnson, JFK had left the White House for his Texas trip in November 1963, aware that these significant concessions had not brought any sort of civil rights legislation closer to passage during the 1963–1964 session of Congress.[15]

## Presidency

### *The Civil Rights Act*

When President Johnson spoke to a joint session of Congress on November 27, five days after JFK's tragic assassination in Dallas, his tone was resolute and sober: "No memorial oration or eulogy could more eloquently honor President Kennedy's memory than the earliest possible passage of the civil rights bill for which he fought so long."[16] In fact, JFK's commitment had been grudging (at least for the first two years of his presidency), much more the result of political imperatives than of moral or policy principles.[17] Johnson privately noted to a friend that Kennedy's "'cause' was by no means clear." He added that his job was "to take the dead man's program and turn it into a martyr's cause. That way Kennedy would live forever and so would I."[18]

LBJ's cause and his commitment to it were completely different from JFK's. "I want that bill!" he told black leaders. Not part of it, either. He wanted the entire original version of the civil rights bill. When a Southern senator asked if LBJ would agree to weakening amendments, another senator who knew LBJ intimately replied, "No. The way that fellow operates, he'll get the whole bill, every last bit of it."[19]

Getting the whole bill meant relying squarely on the Commerce Clause of the Constitution to guarantee that the law would survive the Supreme Court's scrutiny. Johnson was bullish on his chances. Aside from his confidence that the justices would apply the sweeping Commerce Clause cases spawned by the New Deal era, there were compelling political reasons to stick with this choice. Kennedy's attorney general, who happened to be the slain leader's brother, had already tussled with Archibald Cox, JFK's solicitor general, over this issue. Cox had succeeded in persuading Robert Kennedy that the Commerce Clause was a much stronger basis for sustaining the Civil Rights Act than the Equal Protection Clause of the Fourteenth Amendment.[20] LBJ could not afford to cross any of these players; he needed their support.[21]

Yet Johnson had his own reasons for favoring the Commerce Clause as the constitutional lynchpin. He was gauging the reaction of the white South. The Fourteenth Amendment was widely regarded in the Southland as part of the Radical Reconstruction imposed by brute force on the defeated and devastated Confederacy. The timing of the civil rights movement—the Civil War Centennial—rubbed salt on old wounds. Invoking the Fourteenth Amendment might inspire bitter resentment and spark actual violence in the South. Indeed, LBJ feared that a divided Supreme Court vote could encourage massive popular resistance. On the other hand, the Commerce Clause was much more likely to win unanimous Court approval. Additionally, it would give LBJ the opportunity to preach that this law would benefit *all* Southerners by expanding commercial activity and growing the region's economy. Johnson never failed to emphasize the moral rightness of civil rights when he spoke to the white South. But he also never failed to remind Southerners that this would help to fill their wallets, too.[22]

The full story of the passage of the Civil Rights Act of 1964 displays Lyndon Johnson at the peak of his powers as a brilliant legislative strategist—the master of the congressional and national stages.[23] As he himself had vowed on the bleak morning of November 23, 1963, the day after Kennedy was killed: "I'm going to get that bill passed by Congress, and I'm gonna do it before the next year is done."[24] Indeed, as predicted, he got the whole bill. Johnson's emotional appeal, combined with his unmatched ability to twist legislators' arms on Capitol Hill, ultimately won the day. After a relatively easy journey through the House of Representatives and a lengthy Senate filibuster mounted by Southern senators, the bill passed. Surrounded by the legislation's supporters, including a still grief-stricken Robert Kennedy, LBJ signed the bill into law on July 2, 1964, at a televised White House East Room ceremony.

LBJ next wanted to swiftly get Supreme Court approval, to seal the deal. So Johnson sprang into action as soon as the legislation was passed. Business interests in the South wanted to challenge the law's constitutionality as soon as possible, so they would know whether they had to obey it in toto or in part. They initiated several test cases and moved them with lightning speed to the Supreme Court.

On October 5, 1964, the Court heard arguments on *Heart of Atlanta Motel v. United States* and *Katzenbach vs. McClung*.[25] Two months later, in unanimous decisions written by Justice Tom Clark, a Texan, the Court affirmed the constitutionality of the public accommodations sections of the new civil rights bill—a key piece of the landmark legislation. *Heart of Atlanta Motel* was an ideal test case from the government's perspective: the motel in question was located in downtown Atlanta—it was easily accessible from two interstate and two major state highways, and its registration records showed that 75 percent of its lodgers were interstate travelers. Applying the expansive New Deal–era definition of what commerce Congress could regulate, the Court found for the United States, as articulated in cases like *Wickard v. Filburn*, in which the Court had permitted Congress to regulate locally grown wheat because of its "substantial economic effect" on interstate commerce.[26] Now, Justice Clark applied that rule generously and expanded its reach to permit Congress's sweeping civil rights legislation aimed at banning discrimination in privately owned hotels and accommodations.

*McClung*, in contrast, was more complicated. From the standpoint of Birmingham business leaders and other opponents of the new law, the case was a golden chance to limit the impact of the Civil Rights Act. Ollie McClung's barbecue restaurant was miles away from downtown Birmingham and remote from federal and state highways. It was located in a black section of the city, and its reputation depended on word of mouth. Testimony and records showed the clientele was exclusively local, with whites served at tables and blacks restricted to takeout service. McClung did concede that the pork he cooked and served came from outside Alabama, but he argued that this did not change the purely local nature of his enterprise. A panel of three federal appeals judges in Birmingham agreed with him, ruling that the 1964 civil rights legislation did not (and could not) apply to McClung's place, because the restaurant neither involved nor had a "substantial effect" on interstate commerce. Yet the Supreme Court unanimously ruled in the government's favor, again upholding the Civil Rights Act under the Commerce Clause. In its opinion, the Court emphasized the harmful effect that any restaurant's segregation would have on interstate travel by blacks and the resultant loss of income that all restaurants would suffer because of such discrimination. Thus, the Johnson administration's gamble that the Court would use *Wickard*'s sweep to extend Washington's regulations even to neighborhood rib joints ended up paying off.[27]

### The Voting Rights Act

Second on President Johnson's agenda was a meaningful voting rights act. In February 1963, the Kennedy administration had proposed sweeping voting rights legislation, yet it had remained stalled in Congress.[28] After the passage of the public accommodations law in 1964, LBJ now declared: "I'm going to get a bill through that's gonna make sure everybody's got a right to vote. You give people a vote, and they damn sure have power to change their lives for the better."[29] The order of these two acts was not coincidental. The moment the constitutionality of public accommodations was established, even conservative judges would find it hard to resist the momentum in favor of black citizens' rights. Once the white South began abiding by the Civil Rights Act of 1964, LBJ figured, there would be less need for unanimous decisions in support of civil rights. Already, some justices seemed prepared to apply the Fourteenth Amendment directly to combat race discrimination.[30] Johnson met with Nicholas Katzenbach, the acting attorney general, on December 14, 1964, and with the Reverend Martin Luther King Jr. on January 15, 1965. These conversations revealed the president's perfect confidence that the government could draft a voting rights bill that the Supreme Court would approve.[31]

Without question, Johnson was also heartened by how speedily the Twenty-Fourth Amendment outlawing the poll tax in federal elections had been ratified.[32] It was a clear sign that the politics of voting rights reform was falling into place.[33]

The overall purpose of the Voting Rights Act was summed up in its first article: "No voting qualification or prerequisite to voting, or standard practice or procedure, shall be imposed or applied by any state or political subdivision to deny or abridge the right of any citizen of the United States to vote on account of race or color."[34] What struck Johnson more forcefully than this formulation was how transparently fair it was, so fair in fact that it would convince white citizens of its essential justice. He told Reverend King: "Where a man has got to memorize Longfellow, or he has got to quote from the First Ten Amendments . . . [and] some people don't have to do that, but when a Negro comes in, he has got to do it . . . [if that became known] then pretty soon the fellow who didn't do anything but drive a tractor would say, 'well, that's not right—that is not fair.'"[35] LBJ was sure the Supreme Court would have the same reaction as the guy on the tractor. He was correct. Indeed, even before the Court rendered its judgment in *South Carolina v. Katzenbach*, upholding the historic Voting Rights Act under the enforcement provision of the Fifteenth Amendment, LBJ felt fully justified in declaring, as he signed the act, that it was "a triumph for freedom as huge as any victory that has ever been won on any battlefield."[36]

With the passage of the Voting Rights Act of 1965, followed by the Court's sustaining the law's constitutionality, and finally its speedy success in enabling the registration of black voters, Johnson capped his greatest triumphs as president. They also proved to be his most successful and enduring victories. His political skills on Capitol Hill, on the stump in the South, and in intense, private lobbying sessions were crucial to that success. Important, as well, was LBJ's understanding that the constitutional moment was right as a moral issue. Judicial extension of the Commerce Clause provided the constitutional grounds for the Civil Rights Act of 1964; growing judicial sympathy for desegregation *now* rather than with "all deliberate speed" set the stage for federal intervention in voter registration in the South. And Lyndon Johnson, in accomplishing this great victory, credited in eloquent words the bravery of African Americans who made it possible.[37]

## Vietnam

Across the globe in Indochina, the U.S. involvement in the conflict between North Vietnam and South Vietnam escalated dramatically during the Johnson presidency. In the early 1960s, the Kennedy administration had enhanced U.S. military presence in Indochina as part of the U.S. effort to contain communism in that region of the world. The war between North Vietnam (supported by China, the Soviet Union, and other communist governments) and South Vietnam (supported by the U.S. and other anticommunist forces) had turned into a raging conflagration by the time LBJ was running for his own term as chief executive in 1964. Ultimately, the protests and domestic discontent sparked by the Vietnam conflict would severely damage the Johnson presidency. One of the pivotal contributing events was LBJ's controversial use of military force in the Gulf of Tonkin incident in the summer of 1964; the incident would later be criticized as an improper use of presidential power and an effort to mislead the American public to drag the country further into an unpopular war.

Following a "graduated escalation" policy, Johnson's military advisers had pressed hard to neutralize North Vietnam, convinced that this small communist-led nation would shrink from engaging in warfare with a superpower like the United States.[38] When the USS *Maddox* steamed into North Vietnam coastal waters as part of its patrol of that area, North Vietnamese boats fired torpedoes on August 2 and damaged the American destroyer. Two days later, as the *Maddox* and another U.S. destroyer continued their patrols in the gulf, they received word of an "imminent" attack; in response, the U.S. destroyers fired torpedoes and dropped depth charges to ward off the perceived enemy. Calling the action an unprovoked attack, President Johnson carried out "retaliatory" air strikes on the North Vietnamese. Simultaneously, he pressed Congress for broad authority to ramp up military action in Southeast Asia. Congress responded with the swift passage of the Gulf of Tonkin Resolution on August 7, "to prevent any further aggressions" by the North Vietnamese.[39] This muscular use of presidential power based on the ambiguous circumstances surrounding the Gulf of Tonkin incident (critics later questioned whether the U.S. destroyers had actually been attacked by the North Vietnamese on August 4) led to the growing escalation of the war in Southeast Asia. It also fueled accusations that the Johnson administration had obscured and withheld information about the U.S. actions in the Gulf of Tonkin incident, essentially picking a fight with the North Vietnamese to justify LBJ's unpopular military agenda.[40]

## Growing Problems

On the domestic front as well, President Johnson faced increased challenges. Using his presidential power of appointment in Article II, Section 2, to advance his policy agenda, LBJ scored a political victory in 1967 by nominating the first African American to the Supreme Court: Thurgood Marshall, who had argued *Brown v. Board of Education* in the High Court and was himself the great-grandson of slaves. Marshall was confirmed by the Senate and served as a justice on the Supreme Court for twenty-four years. Determined to prevent conservative justices from causing "a dissipation of the forward legislative momentum we had achieved during the previous eight years," LBJ in 1968 nominated Justice Abe Fortas to succeed Earl Warren as chief and federal judge Homer Thornberry, a reliable liberal, to occupy Fortas's vacated seat. However, Republicans and conservative Democrats in the Senate quickly squashed the plan, filibustering until Johnson was forced to withdraw his nominations.[41]

The Fortas fiasco was one of a seemingly endless string of misfortunes and disappointments for LBJ during his last full year in the White House. A growing number of Americans had tired of the reforming spirit and legislative experiments of the Great Society, grumbling about their expense. Alleged favoritism to the poor and minorities helped fuel a white backlash and a Republican comeback. Voters became obsessed with what they perceived as rising crime rates; many explained the rise by pointing to Washington's so-called coddling of "delinquents." Looming above all else, however, was the seemingly endless escalation of the war in Vietnam, ever more costly in lives and money and increasingly politically controversial. Demonstrations in the streets and insurgent Democrats on the primary trail drove Johnson to declare on March 31, 1968, that he would not seek reelection. When he tried to renege on that pledge during the tumultuous Democratic Convention in Chicago in late August, he discovered he could count on the support of only a handful of delegates. Lyndon Johnson left office a bitter, frustrated, exhausted man.

## Conclusion

After the heady experience of leading a transformative administration, LBJ returned to ranching in Johnson City, Texas, fearing that he was leaving behind no enduring legacy. On January 22, 1973, roughly four years after leaving the White House, he died of a heart attack at his ranch, unhappy and largely alone.[42]

LBJ's own final assessment of his years in power was too harsh, however. That he presided over the genesis of two of the nation's most significant pieces of civil rights legislation, shepherded them through Congress, convinced white Southerners of the laws' benefits to all the South's people, and anticipated and defeated possible constitutional challenges to the legislation are towering testimonies to Lyndon Johnson's wisdom and skill. His administration's civil rights legislation fundamentally changed American political and social behavior. Historians might say of LBJ what was said of architect Sir Christopher Wren on his tomb in St. Paul's Cathedral, London, a magnificent structure that Wren had designed: "*Si monumentum requiris, circumspice.*" "If you are searching for a monument (of this person), look around you."

NOTES

1. Lyndon Johnson's press conference of July 28, 1965, quoted in Nick Kotz, *Judgment Days: Lyndon Baines Johnson, Martin Luther King, Jr., and the Laws That Changed America* (Boston: Houghton Mifflin, 2005), 349. Emmette Redford, quoted in Robert A. Caro, *The Years of Lyndon Johnson*, vol. 1, *The Path to Power* (New York: Knopf, 1982), 119. Caro's ongoing multivolume study *The Years of Lyndon Johnson* is the most comprehensive treatment of LBJ's life from 1908 to 1964. The best one-volume survey is

Randall B. Woods, *LBJ: Architect of American Ambition* (Cambridge, MA: Harvard University Press, 2006). For a shorter biographical study, see John L. Bullion, *Lyndon B. Johnson and the Transformation of American Politics* (New York: Pearson, 2008).

2. Bullion, *Transformation*, 13. See also Woods, *LBJ*, 41.
3. Johnson's teaching career is extensively covered in Caro, *Path to Power*, 166–173, 202–214.
4. The fullest account of LBJ's tenure in Tom Martin's law office is ibid., 123–129.
5. Ibid., 338.
6. This attitude strongly characterized his relationship with one of his principal personal attorneys, the prominent Dallas tax attorney J. W. Bullion. For examples, see John L. Bullion, *In the Boat with LBJ* (Plano, TX: Taylor Trade Publishing, 2001), 66–68, 97–102.
7. The Court-packing plan was FDR's attempt to add judges to the Supreme Court by way of congressional statute to gain constitutional approval for his New Deal programs, which the old conservative wing of the Court had been consistently obstructing. The legislation intended to pack the Court ultimately failed, partly because of public outcry against it. See Chapter 32, "Franklin D. Roosevelt."
8. For a lucid description of the Court's movement away from the doctrines of dual federalism and direct and indirect restrictions on Congress's power to regulate interstate commerce, see Richard C. Cortner, *Civil Rights and Public Accommodations: The Heart of Atlanta Motel and McClung Cases* (Lawrence: University of Kansas Press, 2001), 22–24.
9. For a brief summary of these years in the Senate and as vice president, see Bullion, *Transformation*, 37–68.
10. Ibid., 10.
11. NLRB v. Jones & Laughlin Steel Corp. (1937), 301 U.S. 1 (1937); United States v. Darby, 312 U.S. 100 (1941); and Wickard v. Filburn, 317 U.S. 111 (1942).
12. President John F. Kennedy's administration saw clearly, long before the cases unfolded, the dangers inherent in grounding civil rights legislation on the Equal Protection Clause of the Fourteenth Amendment. For a fuller discussion of the debate within the Kennedy Justice Department—in which Attorney General Robert Kennedy favored attacking race discrimination squarely under the Fourteenth Amendment, and Solicitor General Archibald Cox argued that this was far too risky—see Ken Gormley, *Archibald Cox: Conscience of a Nation* (Reading, MA: Addison-Wesley, 1997), 155–160, 177–178. As a practical matter, giving the Department of Justice the power to initiate suits when African Americans alleged they were being denied equal protection under federal law would potentially inundate the department and the courts. Robert Dallek, *An Unfinished Life: John F. Kennedy, 1917–1963* (New York: Little, Brown & Company, 2003), 382; Richard Reeves, *President Kennedy: Profile of Power* (New York: Simon & Schuster, 1993), 500.
13. Caro, *The Passage of Power*, 258–261.
14. The Kennedy administration agreed to eliminate retail stores and personal services from the public accommodations section of the civil rights bill. It had also done away with the Fair Employment Practices Commission, whittled away the Equal

Employment Opportunity Commission's enforcement powers over both the private sector and federally assisted projects and programs, and dropped the extension of voting rights provisions to state and local elections.

15. Dallek, *Unfinished Life*, 648–649.

16. Quoted in Kotz, *Judgment Days*, 33.

17. Kennedy conceivably shrugged off some deletions from the public accommodations section by saying to himself what he had told Birmingham city officials: Integration would be relatively uneventful because few blacks could afford hotels, motels, and other amenities. Dallek, *Unfinished Life*, 647.

18. Bullion, *Transformation*, 69–70.

19. Ibid., 78.

20. Although Robert Kennedy originally favored basing the Civil Rights Act of 1964 on the Equal Protection Clause of the Fourteenth Amendment, because he believed it was the morally correct position, he eventually yielded to the advice of his solicitor general, who was revered as a Supreme Court advocate. Archibald Cox believed that premising the legislation on the Fourteenth Amendment would require the Court to overrule the *Civil Rights Cases* from the Reconstruction era, a daunting proposition. On the other hand, Cox—a seasoned labor lawyer—was intimately familiar with the old Commerce Clause cases from the New Deal era. He believed these would give the Court all of the latitude it needed in upholding Congress's passage of the Civil Rights Act of 1964. For Cox, it was as easy as "ducks rolling off a log." Gormley, *Conscience of a Nation*, 155–165, 188–190.

21. Ibid., 69, 71. See also Caro, *Passage of Power*, 409–413.

22. For a discussion of Johnson's appeals to the white South, see Bullion, *Transformation*, 83–86.

23. A full description of LBJ's virtuoso performance may be found in Caro, *Passage of Power*, 484–499, 558–570.

24. Bullion, *Transformation*, 70.

25. Heart of Atlanta Motel, Inc. v. United States, 379 U.S. 241 (1964); Katzenbach v. McClung, 379 U.S. 294 (1964).

26. Wickard v. Filburn, 317 U.S. 111 (1942), upheld the regulations of the Agricultural Adjustment Act of 1938, which made federal price supports for corn, cotton, and wheat mandatory, to maintain market supplies during low production periods. When applied to Roscoe Filburn's farm in Ohio, these formulas permitted him to plant only 11.1 acres in wheat. Since this still-small amount of wheat would not be in interstate or intrastate commerce, he claimed that growing it was permissible to feed his own livestock. The agency fined him on the grounds that violating allotments would encourage enough other farmers to do the same and, by reducing the amount of crops sent to market, depress further their market price. The Court found for the agency. "Though [Filburn's wheat crop] might not be regarded as commerce, it may still, whatever its nature, be reached by Congress if it exerts a substantial economic effect on interstate commerce, and this irrespective of whether such effect might at some earlier time have been defined as 'direct' or 'indirect.'" Ibid., 125; Cortner, *Civil Rights*, 23. In later cases, the Supreme Court "repeatedly affirmed that the modern scope of congressional power

under the Commerce and Necessary and Proper Clause included the power not only to regulate interstate commerce itself but also local activities that substantially affected, burdened, or obstructed interstate commerce." Ibid., 24.

27. Cortner, *Civil Rights*, 28–194, is the definitive account of the genesis, progress, argument, and disposition of *Heart of Atlanta Motel* and *McClung*. Probably Chief Justice Warren chose Clark to write the opinions because Clark was from Texas and his political and judicial leanings were conservative. Thus the Texan was a geographical and ideological signal to white Southerners not to expect any divisions on public accommodations from these justices.

28. Ken Gormley, *Conscience of a Nation*, 178–179.

29. Bullion, *Transformation*, 70.

30. In their concurring opinions in *Heart of Atlanta Motel* and *McClung*, Justices Arthur Goldberg and William O. Douglas had expressed disappointment that their brethren had shrunk back from declaring the act constitutional directly under the Fourteenth Amendment. Cortner, *Civil Rights*, 180.

31. Kotz, *Judgment Days*, 245–246, 250–252.

32. Lyndon Johnson, "Remarks upon Witnessing the Certification of the 24th Amendment to the Constitution," February 4, 1964, *The American Presidency Project*, ed. Gerhard Peters and John T. Wooley, www.presidency.ucsb.edu/ws/?pid=26056. Sent by Congress to the states on August 27, 1962, it had received the necessary thirty-eighth approval by January 23, 1964. Particularly encouraging was the decision of the Georgia legislature to become the thirty-eighth state to ratify that amendment. LBJ took the unprecedented step of being present at the certification of ratification. After congratulating South Dakota and Georgia for racing to complete the process, he observed "now there can be no one too poor to vote. There is no longer a tax on his rights."

33. Among other things, the new law permitted the attorney general to suspend literacy tests and other qualifications in any county or state where less than 50 percent of citizens over the age of twenty-one had voted or had been registered as of November 1, 1964. These political units were designated "covered jurisdictions." The steps such jurisdictions took to correct past discrimination were closely monitored. Moreover, these jurisdictions could not change any voting procedure during the next five years without "preclearance" from either the attorney general or the Federal District Court for the District of Columbia. Both the attorney general and private citizens were empowered to file suits in federal courts to enforce these provisions. Gormley, *Archibald Cox*, 190–191.

34. Description of the Voting Rights Act of 1965 in Earl A. Pollock, *The Supreme Court and American Democracy: Case Studies in Judicial Review and Public Policy* (Westport, CT: Greenwood Press, 2009), 313.

35. Kotz, *Judgment Days*, 334. LBJ's prediction was borne out by the spectacular increase in black voting in the South during the two years after the act's passage. Bullion, *Transformation*, 123–125.

36. The Court sustained the constitutionality of the Voting Rights Act of 1965 in South Carolina v. Katzenbach, 383 U.S. 301 (1966), by a vote of eight to one, and in Katzenbach v. Morgan, 384 U.S. 641 (1966), by a vote of seven to two. The Fifteenth

Amendment, Section 1, provides: "The right of citizens of the United States to vote shall not be denied or abridged by the United States or by any state on account of race, color, or previous condition of servitude." Section 2 provides: "The Congress shall have power to enforce this article by appropriate legislation." For LBJ quote, see Bullion, *Transformation*, 123. By the close of 1966, state and local poll taxes had been ruled unconstitutional by the Supreme Court in Harper vs. Virginia Board of Elections, 363 U.S. 663 (1966), by a vote of six to three. Kotz, *Judgment Days*, 329–331.

37. See, for example, Woods, *LBJ*, 583–584.
38. Edward J. Marolda, "Grand Delusion: U.S. Strategy and the Tonkin Gulf Incident," *Naval History* 28 (August 2014): 24–31.
39. Lyndon B. Johnson, "Report on the Gulf of Tonkin Incident," Miller Center at the University of Virginia, August 4, 1964, http://milllercenter.org/president/speeches/speech-3998.
40. Pat Paterson, "The Truth About Tonkin," *Naval History* 22 (February 2008): 52–59.
41. Bullion, *Transformation*, 210–211, 222–223.
42. Ibid., 185–234. For the concerns of J. W. Bullion, Johnson's friend and tax attorney, about the former president's psychological condition, see Bullion, *In the Boat with LBJ*, 305–306.

# PART X

# The Watergate Era and Reform

# 37

# Richard M. Nixon

STANLEY KUTLER

*President Richard M. Nixon, the first president to resign from office in disgrace, sought to exert so much power in office that he eventually became tangled up in the Watergate scandal and its cover-up. These incidents ultimately led to the appointment of a special prosecutor and a burgeoning criminal investigation of his own conduct. Nixon's secret White House taping system provided the smoking gun that would lead to the unraveling of his administration. The Supreme Court's landmark decision in U.S. v. Nixon made clear that no person, not even the president, was above the law. With the drumbeat for impeachment growing louder, Nixon resigned. Flying away in a helicopter, he left the White House before Congress had the opportunity to impeach him.*

## Introduction

The Succession Clause of the U.S. Constitution, Article II, Section 1, provides for the death or resignation of the president or the executive's inability to discharge the powers and duties of the office of president. Richard Nixon, the man who liked to claim numerous firsts, uniquely is the first and thus far the only president to resign—and in disgrace. His final official act involved the Constitution, undoubtedly with a choice he preferred not to make.

Impeachment is the only constitutional means to bridge the separation of powers and bring the head of state to accountability. Of the nation's presidents thus far, only Andrew Johnson (1868) and William J. Clinton (1998) were impeached, although both ultimately escaped conviction in their Senate trials. Both trials failed because they were perceived at the time as partisan challenges, although many modern historians support the validity of the case against Johnson. In any event, no member of either president's own political party voted to impeach or convict him.

In President Nixon's case, it will never be known if he would have been impeached and removed from office. On August 9, 1974, Nixon short-circuited the process when he tendered his unprecedented resignation.

Richard Nixon was born in Yorba Linda, California, on January 9, 1913, in a house his father built, as Richard Nixon described it, likely from a Sears kit. His mother, a devout Quaker, no doubt instilled a clear set of moral values in her son. His father, on the other hand, was a "thumper" (to use a Nixon term), an argumentative, unhappy man who instilled another set of characteristics in his son.

Nixon went to public school in Whittier, California, and attended the Quaker Whittier College, stating that he could not afford to go to an Eastern school. After graduation, he attended Duke University's new law school from 1934 to 1937, compiling an excellent record. He asserted that his law school Supreme Court heroes were Justices Louis D. Brandeis and Benjamin N. Cardozo, both of whom were Jewish—somewhat ironic considering that Nixon later instructed his aides not to submit Jewish lawyers and judges as potential Supreme Court nominees when he was president.

After failing to secure a position within the FBI or a New York law firm—his first choices for employment—Nixon reluctantly returned to

California to practice law. Shortly afterward, he met Thelma Pat Ryan, whom he married in 1940. To appease his Quaker mother, he did not join the military after the outbreak of World War II, but instead went to work in the Office of Price Administration in Washington. Eventually, he secured a naval commission and served in the South Pacific. To his later regret, he saw no combat, unlike his later political rival, John F. Kennedy.

After the war, Nixon returned to Southern California, where he gained political prominence through his 1946 victory against a rather strong Democratic incumbent member of the House of Representatives. During his four years in the House, his national reputation grew because of his role supporting the House Committee on un-American Activities, the controversial committee that investigated alleged disloyalty and subversive activities of the citizens and entities suspected of having communist ties. After two terms, Nixon coasted to victory in a 1950 campaign for the U.S. Senate. Good fortune and his own careful positioning brought him the nomination as Dwight D. Eisenhower's running mate in 1952. In that campaign, Nixon delivered his famous "Checkers" speech in which he deflected charges of receiving illegal campaign funds while indulging in an almost unprecedented revelation of his personal finances and life. During this speech, Nixon invoked the name of a "little cocker spaniel dog" named Checkers, which had been given to him as a gift for his daughter, Tricia, and declared, "Regardless of what they say about it, we're going to keep it." The speech became a model for future politicians; more importantly, it established Nixon's reputation as a fighter and endeared him to rank-and-file Republicans.

The Republican Party inevitably nominated Nixon for the presidency in 1960, but he lost an extremely close contest to John F. Kennedy, by 120,000 popular votes. Nixon's contention that Chicago mayor, Richard Daley, stole the election held little weight, for without Illinois, Nixon still lacked the necessary electoral votes. Bitter and depressed, Nixon tried to stage a comeback when he ran for governor of California in 1962, but he suffered another humiliating defeat. Claiming that his political life was over, Nixon moved to New York City to practice law. From the very beginning, however, he carefully worked with several law partners to prepare the way for his return to what he called the "Great Game."

Nixon wisely stayed out of contention in 1964, although his vigorous support of the party's nominee, Barry Goldwater, certainly enhanced his own standing within the party. Nixon won the Republican nomination four years later, and in another close race, he defeated Hubert Humphrey by a slim 0.7 percent margin in the popular vote, although he easily won the Electoral College. Nixon, following his own dictum to "run right in the primaries; later govern from the center," had won the Republican Party's support at its 1968 convention. Yet, he left a significant portion of the party distrustful and disenchanted with him from the outset until the end of his presidency.

## Presidency

Richard Nixon was undoubtedly well schooled in constitutional meaning; he was also no stranger to strong assertions of executive power. Throughout his presidency, he faced a Congress controlled by the opposition party, yet he had strong support among Southern conservative Democrats. Nixon relished the politics of confrontation; *battle* and *fight* were two words that summed up the essence of his political career. Along the way, he more often than not successfully invoked his view of executive power. In the end, however, Nixon had to succumb to a national consensus that he had abused his powers and had obstructed justice, a crushing end to an otherwise powerful presidency.

### *Impoundment*

Presidential impoundment of duly authorized congressional appropriations is not an unusual or new thing in American governance. In June 1803, President Thomas Jefferson matter-of-factly told Congress that he would not spend a $50,000 appropriation for Mississippi River gunboats, because "the favorable and peaceful turn of affairs . . . rendered an immediate execution of the law unnecessary." However, Richard M. Nixon transformed an occasional practice into a test of wills with Congress by defining impoundment as part of his constitutional responsibility. In a January 1973 press conference, Nixon announced "the Constitutional right for the President of the United States to impound funds, and that is not to spend money when the spending of money would mean . . . increasing prices or increasing taxes for all the people, that right is absolutely clear."

Nixon's rhetoric declared a constitutional right that had no direct grounding in constitutional language. After World War II, every president exercised impoundment, to a certain degree, to control defense spending and ease the burgeoning, luxuriant demands of war and defense industries. Lyndon Johnson in 1966 made a rare presidential public statement that he would not spend $5.3 billion in appropriated funds for various domestic programs, largely to restrain inflationary pressures created by the Vietnam War. LBJ's attorney general offered a formal opinion justifying impoundment on the grounds that "an appropriation act itself does not constitute a mandate to spend." From FDR to JFK, however, attorneys general repudiated the notion that a president could unilaterally decide to ignore Congress's will to expend funds for the purpose appropriated. These voices included that of William Rehnquist, Nixon's assistant attorney general, who contended that the president was "not at liberty to impound in the case of domestic affairs."

Congressional inertia on impoundment during the Nixon years, however, resulted in benign acquiescence. In October 1972, Congress overrode Nixon's veto of amendments to the Clean Water Act. The measure was enormously popular, for at that time, environmental issues commanded significant bipartisan support. Both houses of Congress decisively canceled Nixon's veto. Nixon relished the confrontation and escalated it to new levels. Usually, if Congress overrode a veto, this action signaled an end of the matter. But Nixon took what had been a stylized, often benign disagreement to a shrill public confrontation. In his veto message, Nixon announced he would refuse to spend the money, even if Congress overrode his veto. He gave free rein to his speechwriters and ended up stating, with poetic flair, that the "solution to pollution is not the dilution of the dollar."

Nixon's challenge presented a new wrinkle to what had been an accepted practice in the politics of defense spending. In this case, a mandated constitutional process had run its prescribed course. Congress had passed a bill, the president had vetoed it, and Congress had overridden the veto. The bill was law, even without a presidential signature. Nixon, however, did not plan on "faithfully executing" it—and he correctly counted on accommodating congressional inaction.

The 1974 impeachment inquiry, formed in response to the infamous Watergate scandal (later discussed in this chapter), also briefly considered whether Nixon's impoundment activities offered grounds for impeachment. The committee's staff conceded that his position could be rationally defended, but they failed to acknowledge Congress's complicity, for it had traditionally acquiesced in the uses of impoundment. Still, this consideration of Nixon's impoundment practices as possible grounds for impeachment further demonstrated the fury that Nixon aroused.[1] Indeed, Congress went so far as to enact the Impoundment Control Act of 1974— the domestic policy version of the War Powers Act passed the same year earlier—to curtail what it perceived to be abuses by the Nixon administration in this regard.[2]

In the end, however, Nixon had the last word as he successfully imposed his position. His willingness to defy the will of Congress and to impound funds, invoking the Constitution to do so, elevated that practice to a new level.[3]

## The Vietnam War: Overview

Richard Nixon inherited the war in Vietnam. Nonetheless, he certainly was an active proponent of intervention there, dating back to his vice presidential years, when he advocated using atomic weapons in the jungle at Dien Bien Phu in 1954, hoping to prevent a native Vietnamese victory over the French colonial power. President Eisenhower, with his immense popularity and political capital, resisted such counsel. But late in Eisenhower's presidency, he offered a virtual blank check in support of the South Vietnam government.

President Kennedy reinforced Eisenhower's commitment with muscular policies, including economic aid, military weaponry, military "advisers" and other civilian personnel, and, finally, combat troops. Presidents Johnson and Nixon enlarged the military role in Vietnam, and with catastrophic results. More than one-half million troops eventually were committed, and more bombs were dropped than in all of World War II. Despite Nixon's protestations that he "would not be the first American president to lose a war," he had to agree to a cease-fire and troop withdrawals in early 1973, largely on the same terms he could have brokered four years earlier, and with little appearance of anything remotely resembling "victory."

## The Pentagon Papers Case

During his presidency, Nixon waged and lost several key political battles, which prevented him from conducting the war in Southeast Asia in a manner entirely of his choosing. In the summer of 1971, the *New York Times* and *Washington Post* began publication of the "Pentagon Papers," which contained embarrassing classified material, showing that the Kennedy,

Johnson, and (by implication) Nixon administrations had misled Congress and the public about the nation's war effort.[4] In response, Nixon took legal action against the two newspapers, seeking to enjoin the publication of the documents. The historic case, *New York Times Co. v. United States*, reached the Supreme Court quickly.[5] The Court, however, rebuffed Nixon's attempt to restrain publication of the sensitive material, concluding that the First Amendment freedom of press protected the newspapers from such prior restraint.[6] This decision further embarrassed the administration and intensified the public outcry against the war in Southeast Asia.

### The War Powers Resolution

After 1972, Nixon confronted an increasingly active Congress, which was determined to force him to end American participation in the Vietnam War. Until that point, Nixon's Vietnam policy had been unfettered by any congressional opposition. Additionally, his historic trip to China in 1972 made Nixon an unquestioned powerhouse in the field of foreign affairs. But his own growing unpopularity and declining public support for the Vietnam War emboldened Congress to forcefully challenge his power. Not since 1919, when Congress had thwarted President Woodrow Wilson's efforts to take the United States into the League of Nations, had a president faced a Congress so determined to assert its constitutional authority and powers to gain a measure of participation in foreign and military policy. Nixon greatly admired Wilson and, like the earlier president, chose to battle his congressional adversaries rather than seek a meaningful compromise.[7]

As nationwide protests against the war escalated, Congress stipulated a cutoff of the Cambodian bombing, effective in August 1973. The lawmakers took even bolder action when they passed the War Powers Resolution in November 1973. The resolution (frequently referred to as the War Powers Act) obligated the president to notify Congress of armed action within forty-eight hours of its onset and further required him to withdraw military forces within sixty days unless Congress provided an extension. In Nixon's view, the resolution offered to the North Vietnamese a clear signal of American military strategy; in his version of history, it directly enabled the enemy to overrun all of South Vietnam in April 1975. Nixon complained that the new law made it difficult for presidents to act "swiftly and secretly." Nixon blamed Congress, the media, and the peace movement for this "potentially fatal" limitation on the president's power.[8]

Although Nixon vetoed the War Powers Resolution, Congress swiftly overrode his veto. For Nixon, his defeat was humiliating, particularly for such a vigorous advocate of unlimited presidential power in foreign affairs. But in the long run, the resolution has had relatively marginal consequences. During the decades after its passage, Congress has regularly deferred to presidents because of its own passivity and reluctance to challenge executive assertions on the need for military intervention.

Indeed, most presidents since the passage of the War Powers Resolution have honored it, primarily, in the breach.[9] As it has turned out, Congress used the law most forcefully toward Richard Nixon, in seeking to curb his authority to commit troops during the Vietnam conflict. Congress's actions were partly prompted by the surging public opposition to the war. But the lawmakers were also reacting to Nixon's seeming defiance of Congress and (eventually) his growing state of paralysis and distraction caused by the worsening Watergate scandal.

### The Twenty-Sixth Amendment

One outgrowth of the Vietnam War was the strong campaign to allow eighteen-year-olds to vote. During World War II, the age for drafting soldiers had been lowered from twenty-one to eighteen. As more American youth put their lives at risk and were shipped overseas to fight in Indochina, the refrain "Old enough to fight, old enough to vote!" grew louder.[10] Initially, Congress passed a voting rights bill seeking to lower the voting age in all federal, state, and local elections. President Nixon reluctantly signed the bill, stating that he favored the measure but that he believed a constitutional amendment was necessary to make this fundamental change. The Supreme Court in *Oregon v. Mitchell*, decided in 1970, essentially agreed with Nixon.[11] In a badly splintered vote, a majority of the justices concluded that Congress only had the power to lower the voting age in federal elections, not in state and local elections.

The following year, Congress approved a proposed constitutional amendment, and, with lightning speed, three-fourths of the states ratified the Twenty-Sixth Amendment in the spring of 1971. This new provision stated: "The right of citizens of the United States, who are eighteen years of age or older, to vote shall not be denied or abridged by the United States or by any State on account of age." In signing the new constitutional amendment into law, President Nixon offered these reasons at a

White House ceremony: "The reason I believe that your generation, the 11 million new voters, will do so much for America at home is that you will infuse into this nation some idealism, some courage, some stamina, some high moral purpose, that this country always needs."[12] Of course, President Nixon was aware—as protests swept across the country—that the youth of America overwhelmingly opposed his policies in Vietnam and were unlikely to support him in his bid for reelection in 1972. Nixon thus supported this change as politically necessary, but understood that he would have to take other steps to accomplish the landslide reelection victory that he so desperately desired.

## *Nixon's Supreme Court and* Roe v. Wade

On the presidential campaign trail in 1968, Nixon had railed against the judicial activism of the Supreme Court under Chief Justice Earl Warren and vowed to populate the federal bench with "strict constructionists" who followed a "properly conservative" course, seeing themselves as "caretakers" of the Constitution and duty-bound to interpret the law, and not as "super-legislators with a free hand to impose their social and political viewpoints on the American people."[13] Nixon nominated Chief Justice Warren Burger and three associate justices—Harry A. Blackmun, Lewis F. Powell Jr., and William H. Rehnquist—to the Supreme Court during his tenure as chief executive.

While Burger and Rehnquist, in particular, would help reshape the Court in a more conservative fashion, no appointee ended up angering conservatives more than Harry Blackmun. He was a lifelong Republican and was expected to adhere to conservative principles. Yet, it was Blackmun who authored *Roe v. Wade*, the 1973 landmark Supreme Court decision that legalized abortion.[14] In *Roe*, the Court found that the concept of liberty encompassed in the Fourteenth Amendment implicitly included a fundamental right of privacy, which protected a woman's right to terminate a pregnancy.[15] An outcry erupted over the ruling—which invalidated abortion statutes in all but four of fifty states—with conservatives accusing Blackmun of having usurped legislative prerogatives and having created constitutional rights out of whole cloth.[16]

When the Court announced its controversial *Roe* decision on January 22, 1973, Nixon made no public comment. In private discussions with his aides, however, Nixon expressed concern that this new access to abortion after *Roe* would encourage "permissiveness"; at the same time, he concurred that there was a need for abortion in certain circumstances, like interracial pregnancies or in cases of rape.[17] Nixon was, in other words, ambivalent on this hot-button issue that generated so much controversy. By the time the *Roe* decision was handed down in early 1973, however, President Nixon had other things occupying his mind.

## Watergate

Nixon won a landslide reelection victory in 1972. Yet in the process, five burglars—who turned out to have ties with the White House—were caught breaking into the Democratic National Committee headquarters in the Watergate hotel complex in Washington, D.C. As the Watergate affair exploded in the media, President Nixon's innermost circle was caught up in the scandal. Former attorney general turned campaign manager John Mitchell and Attorney General Richard Kleindienst resigned. White House Counsel John Dean was fired by Nixon, while Chief of Staff H. R. Haldeman and Chief Domestic Advisor John Ehrlichman were forced out in the face of criminal prosecution for participating in a cover-up.[18]

Soon, Nixon himself was engulfed in the scandal. After the existence of a White House taping system was made public by former White House aide Alexander Butterfield in July 1973, the Watergate affair settled into a yearlong struggle for access to those tapes.[19] Again, Alexis de Tocqueville's 1837 observation that "scarcely any question arises in the United States that is not resolved, sooner or later, into a judicial question" proved prophetic. Nixon was determined to retain control of the tapes, while his adversaries well understood that the tapes potentially offered irrefutable corroboration of testimony against the president. Watergate Special Prosecutor Archibald Cox, who had been appointed to get to the bottom of the Watergate affair, subpoenaed nine critical tape recordings to determine whether Nixon had been complicit in the Watergate cover-up.

In the meantime, Nixon's vice president, Spiro T. Agnew, faced serious charges of his own for accepting bribes as governor of Maryland and as vice president. Agnew finally pleaded nolo contendere to a single charge of income tax fraud and resigned on October 10, 1973. With his administration under siege, Nixon appointed House Minority Leader Gerald R. Ford to serve as his vice president, undoubtedly aware that congressional impeachment proceedings could be looming on the horizon.

When U.S. District Judge John J. Sirica ordered Nixon to turn over tapes subpoenaed by Special Prosecutor Cox, Nixon refused. The president then took a bold gamble: On October 20, 1973, Nixon fired Cox in the infamous Saturday Night Massacre. His attorney general, Elliot Richardson, resigned rather than carry out the order to fire Cox, as did Richardson's deputy, William Ruckelshaus. Nixon's solicitor general, Robert Bork, finally carried out the order. Although Nixon appeared ready to shut down the special prosecutor's office and to return the Watergate investigation to his own loyal appointees in the Justice Department, this plan failed. The president's firing of Cox unleashed a firestorm of public protest; led to the hiring of a new special prosecutor, Leon Jaworski, who subpoenaed even more White House tapes; and produced a deepening constitutional crisis for the nation and for Richard M. Nixon.[20]

On April 30, 1974, Nixon announced he would not release tapes and instead released edited transcripts of requested tapes. He also repeated he had "nothing to hide in this matter." This attempt to win public support failed completely. As the conflict wound its way through the courts, it reached the Supreme Court in the spring of 1974. James St. Clair, the president's counsel, urged the Court to deny the justiciability of the case as a "political question" and to leave Nixon's fate to impeachment proceedings in the House. The new Special Prosecutor Jaworski, however, urged the Court to act. He invoked John Marshall's iconic phrase in *Marbury v. Madison* (1803): "It is emphatically the province and duty of the judiciary to say what the law is."

In his appearance for Nixon, Counsel St. Clair argued that the president should be held to a constitutional standard different from anyone else's. He could be impeached, St. Clair conceded, but he could not be indicted while in office, or in any way suffer a diminution of his powers. St. Clair specifically had to defend the president's right to protect his control of his tapes. The lawyer first argued that separation of powers prevented a federal court from issuing a subpoena to the chief executive—from compelling him to turn over private, internal communications related to his executive duties. St. Clair also contended that the preservation of candor in the president's conversations constituted an overriding public interest; such materials, he maintained, required confidentiality (for national security and other purposes) and could be released only at presidential discretion. Nixon appointee Justice Lewis Powell asked what possible public interest could exist in preserving the secrecy of a criminal conspiracy. St.

Clair only begged the question: "The answer, sir, is that a criminal conspiracy is criminal only after it's proven to be criminal." Whatever St. Clair's goals, the president's counsel found himself in the uncomfortable position of defending a client who acted as if he were above the law.

Meanwhile, pessimism had enveloped Nixon for several weeks. He knew he would not be able to defy the Supreme Court, yet he hoped to devise a plan to delete some material in the damning tapes. The so-called smoking-gun tape—recorded on June 23, 1972—in which Nixon and Haldeman discussed using the CIA (Central Intelligence Agency) to quash the FBI investigation of the Watergate burglary, "worried" him for he knew it could not be "excerpted properly," as he confided in his diary. On July 23, 1974, Nixon spoke to both Chief of Staff Alexander Haig and his press secretary about the possibility of resigning. That night he stayed up late, reviewing a draft speech on economic matters, but his troubles never left his side. At midnight that evening, he wrote in his diary: "Lowest point in the presidency, and Supreme Court still to come."[21]

Chief Justice Warren Burger, Nixon's own appointee, secretly had his clerks preparing him for the possibility of presiding over an impeachment trial. On July 24, 1973, the Court announced a unanimous decision in *U.S. v. Nixon*, directing the president to surrender the tapes specified in the prosecutor's subpoenas.[22] In this landmark ruling, the Court made clear that no person, not even the president, was above the law. While Chief Justice Burger acknowledged that a limited executive privilege existed to protect the confidentiality of presidential communications and so forth, such a privilege was not absolute. Here, "the generalized assertion of [executive] privilege," the Court wrote, "must yield to the demonstrated, specific need for evidence in a pending criminal trial."[23] The president's limited interest in confidentiality could be protected in this case by requiring that U.S. District Judge John J. Sirica review the material first, *in camera*, to ensure that the president's national security concerns could be addressed. The Court thus issued a final, decisive stamp of legitimacy on challenges to the president's authority and credibility and rejected Nixon's limitless claims to "executive privilege."

Nixon was in his home in San Clemente, California, when the Court's ruling was announced. Haig called the president with the news and added that his lawyers had vetted the opinion. "Unanimous?" Nixon asked. "Unanimous," Haig replied, "there's no air in it at all." "Not at all?" The president persisted. "It's as tight as a drum," Haig said.

*U.S. v. Nixon* thus delivered the final blow to Nixon's presidency: President Nixon was required to surrender his tapes. Accordingly, Nixon turned over the subpoenaed tapes on August 5, including the fateful June 23 smoking-gun conversation showing that he participated in a cover-up. This material, along with a mysterious 18½-minute gap in one of the key tapes, which the experts concluded had been caused by erasures, proved to be damning. Within hours, most of the remaining Republican members of the impeachment inquiry in the House of Representatives urged Nixon to resign.

As soon as the tapes became public, Congressman Charles Wiggins (R-CA), probably Nixon's most articulate defender in the House committee's deliberations, announced that he would support the first impeachment article, sadly noting that the "magnificent public career of Richard Nixon must be terminated involuntarily." The next day, the president met with leading congressional Republicans, led by Senator Barry Goldwater (R-AZ), who never directly advised Nixon to resign, but who left no doubt as to his lack of congressional support. On August 8, 1974, the thirty-seventh president addressed the nation from the Oval Office and announced he would resign the next day at noon.

On September 8, 1974, Nixon's vice president and successor, President Gerald R. Ford, stunned the world when he announced a full and unconditional pardon of Nixon for any crimes he may have committed related to the Watergate scandal or during his time as president, thus foreclosing criminal prosecution and closing the door on a troublesome chapter of American history.[24]

## Conclusion

After his resignation, Nixon, who had been a dominant figure in the public political stage for nearly three decades, tried to rebound. He left his California home and moved to New York City, carefully plotting his return to public life. He published his memoirs and made trips abroad, largely as a self-described informal U.S. ambassador, seeking to regain his status as a respected world figure. Nixon spent the last twenty years of his life waging a relentless campaign for history and tenaciously defended his right to control his tapes and papers. That, of course, ended with his death in 1994, when many of Nixon's remaining presidential materials became available, including the invaluable tapes he had created.[25] Ironically, these materials offered neither exoneration nor an easy explanation for his behavior as president.

After Nixon's resignation, the country found consolation in declaring that the "system had worked." Indeed, it largely had, yet Watergate vitally affected subsequent political developments, many of which left the nation wondering whether the governmental system that it sought to repair after Watergate might still be broken. Without a doubt, President Nixon accomplished great foreign policy victories, most notably in his historic visit to the People's Republic of China and in his normalizing of U.S. relations with China. He fought consistently to strengthen presidential power in relation to Congress, but had his wings clipped with the passage of the Impoundment Control Act and the War Powers Act, each of which created a check on future presidents. Nixon's battle over the White House tapes also established that the papers, tapes, and other documents of future presidents could be subpoenaed by the courts and that executive privilege was sharply limited, particularly where it collided with the judicial branch's need to obtain evidence in an ongoing criminal case. In the end, Watergate and the constitutional crisis it spawned remain Richard Nixon's indelible legacy to the nation's constitutional history.

Thus, Richard M. Nixon was a brilliant politician who squandered the public trust and left behind a damaged record.

## NOTES

1. See generally, Stanley Kutler, *The Wars of Watergate: The Last Crisis of Richard Nixon*, Watergate 40th anniversary ed. (New York: W.W. Norton, 2012), 133–137.

2. The Congressional Budget and Impoundment Control Act of 1974, Pub. L. 93–344 (1974) essentially put an end to the practice of presidential impoundment. The current version of the statute is available at 2 U.S.C. §§ 681–688, 691, 691a to 691f.

3. Three decades later, President George W. Bush employed a similar tactic by announcing his determination not to comply with certain congressional directives at bill-signing ceremonies. Bush received widespread criticism, but to no effect. Indeed, Barack Obama, his successor, who criticized Bush for his signing statements that sought to ignore Congress's directives on a host of subjects, did not hesitate to do so himself.

4. The Pentagon Papers were the result of a classified government study regarding the conduct of the Vietnam War; the study was authorized in 1967 by former Defense Secretary Robert McNamara. A former national security analyst, Daniel Ellsberg, leaked the documents to the *New York Times* and *Washington Post* in June 1971. The information contained in the papers was primarily embarrassing to the Kennedy and Johnson administrations, but also put Nixon in a difficult position. Although he was

not directly implicated in the Pentagon Papers, the publication of such sensitive material during his presidency reflected poorly on him. Indeed, Nixon came to believe that the leak was part of a broader conspiracy against him, prompting him to authorize illegal countermeasures. For more discussion and excerpts of Nixon's conversations with his aides regarding the Pentagon Papers, see Stanley Kutler, *Abuse of Power: The New Nixon Tapes* (New York: Free Press, 1997), 1–42.

5. New York Times Co. v. United States, 403 U.S. 713 (1971). The Court concluded that prior restraint of speech and the press by the government is generally contrary to the First Amendment.

6. As the Court noted in its opinion: "Any system of prior restraints of expression comes to this Court bearing a heavy presumption against its constitutional validity." Ibid., 714. This is because, traditionally, the Court has sought to protect the rights of the press under the First Amendment, and therefore it has typically rejected attempts by the government to restrain freedom of press in advance of publication.

7. Kutler, *Wars of Watergate*, 155–160.

8. The passage of this potent piece of legislation was clearly linked to Nixon's increasingly desperate political position. The House passed the bill one day after Nixon claimed executive privilege for his Oval Office tapes. On the heels of Nixon's pronouncement that he would not "wallow in Watergate," the Senate quickly followed suit and overwhelmingly approved the measure. Between the first House vote on October 12 and the vote to override Nixon's veto, thirty-three members switched their votes. After the Saturday Night Massacre, resulting in the firing of Watergate Special Prosecutor Archibald Cox, the chairman of the House Foreign Affairs Committee declared that the "time was ripe" for action.

9. See, for example, John Robert Greene, *The Limits of Power: The Nixon and Ford Administration* (Bloomington: Indiana University Press, 1992), 207; Duane Tananbaum, "Gerald Ford and the War Powers Resolution," in *Gerald R. Ford and the Politics of Post-Watergate America*, vol. 2, ed. Bernard J. Firestone and Alexej Ugrinsky (Westport, CT: Greenwood Press, 1993), 534. See also Chapter 39, "Jimmy Carter."

10. Kelly Sarabyn, "The Twenty-Sixth Amendment: Resolving the Federal Circuit Split Over College Students' First Amendment Rights," *Texas Journal on Civil Liberties & Civil Rights* 14 (2008) 27, 55–65; Kenneth J. Guido Jr., "Student Voting and Residency Qualifications: The Aftermath of the Twenty-Sixth Amendment," *New York University Law Review* 47 (1972): 32, 38–44.

11. Oregon v. Mitchell, 400 U.S. 112 (1970).

12. Richard Nixon, "Remarks at a Ceremony Marking the Certification of the 26th Amendment to the Constitution," July 5, 1971, *The American Presidency Project*, ed. Gerhard Peters and John T. Wooley, http://www.presidency.ucsb.edu/ws/index.php?pid=3068.

13. Campaign speech, November 2, 1968, quoted in *Congressional Quarterly*, Weekly Report, May 23, 1969, 798.

14. Roe v. Wade, 410 U.S. 113 (1973).

15. Ibid., 152–153.

16. Henry J. Abraham, *Justices, Presidents, and Senators: A History of the U.S. Supreme Court Appointments from Washington to Clinton* (Lanham, MD: Rowman & Littlefield Publishers, 1999), 260.

17. Charlie Savage, "On Nixon Tapes, Ambivalence over Abortion, Not Watergate," *New York Times*, June 23, 2008.

18. See generally Ken Gormley, *Archibald Cox: Conscience of a Nation* (Reading, MA: Addison-Wesley, 1997), 229–268.

19. For a detailed account concerning the discovery of the taping system and its aftermath, see Kutler, *Wars of Watergate*, 383–414.

20. Gormley, *Archibald Cox*, 318–358.

21. Kutler, *Wars of Watergate*, 513.

22. United States v. Nixon, 418 U.S. 683 (1974).

23. Ibid., 713.

24. For a thorough discussion of Nixon's pardon and its ramifications, see Kutler, *Wars of Watergate*, 553–573.

25. A Nixon legacy was the Presidential Records Act of 1978, which mandated, starting January 20, 1981, that the legal ownership of the official records of the presidents and vice presidents resides with the public. Before this act, ownership rested with the previous presidents and vice presidents. The act also established procedures by which presidents and vice presidents were to manage their records.

# 38

# Gerald R. Ford

JEFFREY CROUCH

*President Gerald R. Ford, a member of Congress on the verge of retire-
ment, was selected by President Nixon to serve as vice president when
Spiro T. Agnew abruptly resigned after being charged with accepting
bribes. Within months, Ford would become president when Nixon himself was forced to resign in the wake of the Watergate scandal. An honest,
square-jawed, straight-shooting Midwesterner, Ford pardoned Nixon,
believing a pardon was the best thing for the country. The Nixon pardon—as well as Ford's standing up to Congress on other issues—quickly
ended Ford's honeymoon and wrecked his chances for election in 1976. Yet
Ford's steady handling of the presidency during the unstable aftermath of
Watergate ended up setting the nation on a safer course.*

# Introduction

G erald R. Ford never planned to become the thirty-eighth president of the United States. He recited the oath of office having never run on a national ticket for the presidency or vice presidency; nor had he ever served in the Senate or as a state governor. He had aspired to be Speaker of the House, but because Republicans were not the majority party during most of Ford's time in the legislature, he had to settle for the role of minority leader.

After serving twenty-five years in the House of Representatives representing Michigan's Fifth District, Ford found himself sitting in the Oval Office after a series of unlikely events that had elevated him to the presidency. Ford assumed the office on August 9, 1974, a little over a week after investigators discovered the smoking-gun tape that proved President Nixon's knowledge of the Watergate cover-up and led to his resignation. On becoming president, Ford famously announced: "Our long national nightmare is over."[1]

It is tempting to view the 895-day Ford term as a placeholder or an accidental presidency and to consider Ford's legacy simply as that of a healer who brought the country back together after the Watergate scandal, one of the greatest challenges to the rule of law the country ever faced. A closer look, however, reveals that Ford made another major contribution: holding the line for presidential power against Congress. Coming to office on the heels of Nixon's "imperial presidency," Ford struggled to preserve executive power and to prevent the presidency from becoming "imperiled."[2]

Gerald Rudolph Ford began life on July 14, 1913, as Leslie Lynch King Jr. in Omaha, Nebraska. Dorothy, his mother, and Leslie Lynch King Sr., his biological father, divorced shortly after the future president's birth. Dorothy and her son moved to Grand Rapids, Michigan, where she met and married a small-business owner, Gerald Ford Sr., after whom her son was renamed. Growing up, Ford had three half-brothers and led a normal family life, earning money by helping out in his stepfather's paint and varnish store. He was a gifted football player who starred in high school and later at the University of Michigan. In 1941, he graduated from Yale Law School, where he had helped put himself through school by coaching football.[3]

Embarking on a career in politics, Ford served Michigan's Fifth District in Congress for twenty-five years, from 1949 to 1973, and won at least 60 percent of the vote each election. Following President John F. Kennedy's assassination, Ford was asked by President Lyndon B. Johnson to serve on the Warren Commission, which was charged with investigating the late president's assassination to bring closure to this tragedy for a grieving nation. He was selected minority leader by House Republicans in 1965. In that capacity, in 1970, Ford led the charge to impeach the ultraliberal Supreme Court Justice William O. Douglas; that effort failed.

On October 10, 1973, Vice President Spiro Agnew resigned amid a cloud of scandal—having been accused of accepting bribes while serving as governor of Maryland and vice president. This left the seat vacant for President Nixon to fill via the newly adopted Twenty-Fifth Amendment, added to the Constitution in 1967 after the death of John F. Kennedy. The amendment provided for the orderly succession of the presidency and vice presidency in the case of a vacancy.[4] Although Nixon initially wanted former treasury secretary John Connally to replace Agnew, he instead selected Ford—a popular congressional leader—because Ford would be a more palatable choice to the House and Senate members who would vote on the confirmation.[5] On December 6, 1973, as the Watergate crisis worsened, Ford was sworn in, becoming the first individual to be appointed to office pursuant to the Twenty-Fifth Amendment.

Ford had been vice president for only about eight months when he learned of the smoking-gun tape containing evidence of Nixon's guilt in the Watergate cover-up—evidence that would almost certainly lead to the president's impeachment. Abruptly, on August 8, Nixon chose to resign the following day at noon, leaving Ford to become president of the United States.

## Presidency

Gerald Ford had the misfortune to become the first president of the post-Watergate era. He took over with virtually no time to plan a transition and initially even avoided naming a chief of staff because of the sense of distrust Nixon's tainted chief of staff, H. R. Haldeman, had inflicted on the position. Ford also confronted a difficult decision regarding former president Nixon's legal fate. The new president faced a Congress dominated by Democrats who, desiring to make their influence felt, were eager to rein in the chief executive. As Nixon's handpicked successor and without any electoral mandate of his own, Ford faced the risk that a mistake in any of these areas could be blown out of proportion by his political opponents, the press, and the public, all of whom were sensitive to the slightest hint of executive dishonesty in the post-Nixon years. Few presidents have taken office under such difficult circumstances as did Gerald Ford.[6] Nonetheless, Ford did not shrink from a fight, invoking his executive powers on several occasions to exercise fully the powers of the presidency, with varying degrees of effectiveness.

Almost immediately, Ford had to decide whether to rely on former Nixon staffers, his own people, or some combination thereof. He chose the last option. President Ford initially tried to serve as his own chief of staff in a "spokes of the wheel" arrangement by which several staffers had unlimited access to the president (and his time). Yet he soon discarded the concept. He designated Donald Rumsfeld as "staff coordinator" because Haldeman had sullied the title of chief of staff. Ford also swiftly nominated former New York governor Nelson Rockefeller to serve as his vice president pursuant to the new Twenty-Fifth Amendment (the same provision by which Ford had been named vice president a year earlier). In an environment where the president had virtually no time to put a transition into place, the new administration had trouble "hitting the ground running."[7]

Still, the American public saw Ford as a trustworthy, honorable person and viewed his family favorably. This tranquility lasted roughly thirty days, when Ford suddenly decided to offer pardons to Nixon and Vietnam draft dodgers and thereby brought an abrupt halt to his cordial relationship with the American public. Ford's relationship with his former colleagues in Congress also changed, as they no longer welcomed the president back to the legislature with open arms.[8]

### The Nixon Pardon

Serious constitutional issues had arisen while Nixon was in office as to whether a sitting president could be indicted; scholars were split on this question. Nixon's solicitor general, Robert Bork, filed a government brief during the Agnew affair, stating that a sitting president—as unitary head of the executive branch—could not be indicted or criminally prosecuted until he left office.[9] The only alternative while a president was in office,

Bork opined, was the constitutionally prescribed impeachment process. The question had nagged at the Watergate Special Prosecution Force as long as Nixon had remained in office. Now that he had resigned, however, there was no question that citizen Nixon could be indicted and subjected to criminal prosecution for Watergate crimes.

Still, this new state of affairs presented its own perils. The new Watergate special prosecutor, Leon Jaworski, issued a confidential memo stating that it would be unwise to proceed with a grand jury indictment of Nixon, because the Supreme Court would most likely not uphold this as constitutional.[10] Jaworski also fretted that even with Nixon out of office, it might be impossible to give the former president a fair trial (at least for a year or so) given the unprecedented amount of publicity surrounding the Watergate saga. In a conversation with Nixon's attorney, Herbert Miller, Jaworski signaled that he would be likely to approve of a pardon for Richard Nixon.[11]

President Ford did not take Nixon's criminal conduct lightly. Yet he feared that if Nixon was criminally prosecuted, the country might be dragged through years of turmoil. Ford also worried about getting anything accomplished as president, if this cloud hung over the nation.

After church services on September 8, 1974, President Ford shocked the world by announcing that he was issuing a full and complete pardon to Richard Nixon for "all offenses against the United States" that the former president might have committed while in office. With the stroke of a pen, the new president reopened the wounds of Watergate and did serious damage to his image. Unfortunately, Ford had not attempted to prepare the press or the American people for the Nixon pardon—indeed, his public statements shortly before the final decision had conveyed the impression that a decision on Nixon would wait until after the matter had run its course in the legal system. To make matters worse, the pardon did not specify Nixon's crimes, and Nixon merely issued a lukewarm statement acknowledging that he understood how people might believe he mishandled Watergate—he offered no forthright apology. Ford's press secretary, Jerald terHorst, a man greatly admired by the Washington press corps because he had been one of them for decades, resigned in frustration shortly after the announcement.[12]

The question immediately arose whether President Ford had the legal power to pardon Nixon. The clause of the Constitution in question, Article II, Section 2, Clause 1, provided: "The president . . . shall have Power to grant Reprieves and Pardons for Offenses against the United States, except in Cases of Impeachment." Several constitutional scholars offered strong objections to the Nixon pardon. First, they argued that the Constitution's framers favored strict limits as to when the clemency power could be used before conviction and that the Nixon case—involving allegations of official misconduct—did not qualify. They also contended that the "except in Cases of Impeachment" clause demonstrated the framers' intent to prevent the clemency power from being used to benefit someone in Nixon's position. One private citizen even sued President Ford, arguing that the pardon was constitutionally invalid because Nixon had not yet been indicted. A federal court in *Murphy v. Ford* favorably cited *Ex parte Garland* (1867), and concluded that a pardon could be extended to an offender "*at any time after*" the crime occurred "*either before legal proceedings are taken or during their pendency.*" Thus, the federal district court sustained the pardon.[13]

For the rest of his life, Ford would remain perplexed that the media and the American public did not fully understand his reasons for pardoning Nixon. For Ford, this step was necessary to heal the nation after the ordeal of Watergate and to allow the country to move on. Indeed, Ford later revealed that he relied heavily on a 1915 decision of the Supreme Court, *Burdick v. U.S.*, which made clear that this sort of presidential pardon "carries an imputation of guilt; acceptance, a confession of it"[14] (See Chapter 27, "Woodrow Wilson.") As part of the pardon negotiations, Ford went so far as to dispatch a young legal adviser, Benton Becker, to Nixon's home in California to advise the former president that his acceptance of the pardon would amount to a public admission of guilt. Thus, by obtaining Nixon's agreement to take the pardon, Ford believed that "he had extracted the 'confession' [from Nixon] that the country so desperately wanted." Ford even alluded to Nixon's guilt in a September 16, 1974, press conference. Unfortunately for Ford, the media and most American citizens never came to appreciate his reasoning.[15]

Notably, the pardon negotiations were also used to address the issue of who owned President Nixon's White House records and tapes. The Ford White House was worried that Nixon's controversial records and tapes—which (among other things) constituted key evidence in the upcoming trials of the Watergate codefendants—would be shipped to California and then destroyed. Although the public did not appreciate the wisdom of the negotiations, the pardon was part of a package by which Nixon agreed to allow the government to maintain custody of his personal papers and the controversial White House tapes. The plan thus froze all the documentation in place until Congress could pass the Presidential Recordings and Materials Preservation Act of 1974, thus preserving an important piece of American history. This agreement further laid the foundation for the Presidential Records Act of 1978, which preserved the papers and communications of future presidents.

Yet the public remained suspicious and angry. Many citizens and commentators believed that Ford might have agreed to an unsavory deal with Nixon: a pardon in exchange for Nixon's resignation. In the weeks after the pardon, Ford's popularity plunged from 71 to 49 percent. On Capitol Hill, members strongly condemned his action. Ford acknowledged that he might have been offered a deal by General Alexander Haig, Nixon's former chief of staff, on August 1, 1974, but insisted that it "never became a deal because I never accepted." His decision to pardon Nixon a month later, Ford insisted, was designed to allow the country to move beyond Watergate. In Ford's mind, the pardon was also necessary to give his administration a chance to govern. He argued that he was forced to spend one-quarter of his time dealing with Nixon-related issues—a major distraction—so the pardon was "the only way to clear the deck." Ford had started his presidency on a high note. Now, with his presidential image in tatters, he needed to start winning back the public.[16]

He was not able to do so quickly enough, however, to save his presidency. Popular culture had already decided that Ford was much like the out-of-touch klutz portrayed by *Saturday Night Live* comedian Chevy Chase. People laughed at the jokes that Ford had played too much football without wearing his helmet and that he was "so dumb he can't fart and chew gum at the same time." The press, ignoring Ford's lifetime of academic and scholarly achievement, portrayed him as an "intellectual lightweight." The Nixon pardon unquestionably played a major role in these assessments. Ironically, it was perhaps the most consequential decision of Ford's presidency. Unfortunately for the president, it also dragged down his administration. In time, however, a large segment of the American public came to view the pardon as both well-intentioned and correct. Public opinion shifted over the years to recognize the pardon as the right decision made under very difficult circumstances, and many scholars reached the same conclusion.[17] In 2001, the John F. Kennedy Library awarded Ford its Profile in Courage award, recognizing his bravery in taking this action.[18]

## Congress's Attempts to Limit Presidential Power

Republicans faced the electorate in the 1974 midterm elections and paid a heavy price for Watergate. Democrats claimed 49 new seats in the House of Representatives and eventually 4 Senate spots as well, giving them a 147-member majority in the House and a 23-member majority in the Senate. In light of Congress's lack of agreement with the president and its desire to tangle over federal priorities, President Ford looked for a way to assume control over the legislative agenda and thus to appear in command. As a result, he began to rely on the president's constitutional veto power to strike down spending proposals generated by Congress, albeit with mixed results. Ford, perhaps more than any of his predecessors or successors, wielded the veto power in an effort to drive legislative decision making. He exercised his veto sixty-six times and was overridden a dozen times. The veto both allowed Ford to show his commitment to the Republican philosophy before the 1976 election and helped him fulfill one of his main domestic goals: restraining federal spending levels.[19] In this fashion, Ford tried to handle a Congress dominated by Democrats who had attempted to rein in the "imperial presidency" of his predecessor by passing the War Powers Resolution and the Impoundment Control Act. To compound Ford's problems, members of both chambers were also spoiling for a confrontation over intelligence oversight after revelations from a *New York Times* reporter that the executive branch had been engaged in domestic spying.

Ford recognized that the stakes were high; he later noted: "I was absolutely dedicated to doing whatever I could to restore the rightful prerogatives of the presidency under the constitutional system."[20] In doing so, Ford chose his battles carefully. He at least gave lip service to the War Powers Resolution—although his professed commitment to that congressional edict would soon be tested in the context of an overseas rescue operation that would require him to assert his powers as commander in chief.

## War Powers

In response to what it viewed as reckless executive behavior overseas, Congress had enacted the War Powers Resolution (also known as the War Powers Act) in 1973 to force the president to consult on war-related decisions. President Ford was the first commander in chief bound by the resolution, and despite some ambivalence on the issue earlier in his career, he was not a fan of the legislation while president. Indeed, Ford not only believed that the War Powers Resolution was unconstitutional, but also thought that it damaged the relationship between the commander in chief and the legislature and complicated the president's efforts to maintain relations with foreign nations.[21]

In May 1975, Ford acknowledged an obligation under the new law to inform Congress when he sent Marines to Cambodia to retrieve the kidnapped crew of the American vessel *Mayaguez*—although he did not notify Congress until the mission had ended. The *Mayaguez* was a merchant freighter vessel heading from Hong Kong to Thailand; its crew was attacked and captured by the Khmer Rouge, a communist-led group that had gained power. A rescue mission, carried out with mixed results, cost forty-one American military operatives their lives, but all of the *Mayaguez* sailors were returned home safely. Ford's approval rating shot up from 39 to 51 percent. The *Mayaguez* incident allowed the new president to save some face after having to preside over the fall of Cambodia and South Vietnam to Communist forces. It also allowed Ford to bring to a close a frustrating period in American foreign policy.[22] At the same time, the *Mayaguez* incident showed that Ford was prepared to sidestep what he viewed as rigid, unacceptable aspects of the War Powers Resolution Act, while complying with the spirit of the law to avoid provoking Congress.

## Intelligence Oversight and Executive Privilege

Congress was eager to confront President Ford over allegations, contained in a December 1974 story by *New York Times* reporter Seymour Hersh, that the CIA had undertaken a secret operation dubbed Operation CHAOS to monitor American citizens (particularly political dissidents) during the Johnson and Nixon years. Despite Ford's efforts to take control of the situation by establishing a commission led by Vice President Rockefeller, the Senate and House instead appointed their own committees to investigate the charges. The Senate select committee, headed by Senator Frank Church (D-IA), was largely successful in detecting and proposing solutions to abuses. President Ford's Executive Order 11905 addressed these issues by establishing stronger oversight mechanisms and outlawing government-sanctioned assassinations. The president was able to argue against and undermine the House committee led by Representative Otis Pike (D-NY), however, by contending that congressional investigators were putting American security and intelligence personnel at risk. Ford also skillfully used the media to convey that the death of a CIA agent was a consequence of the legislature meddling with intelligence matters. In the end, President Ford's Executive Order 11905 largely calmed the critics, and his successful undermining of the Pike Committee showed that despite criticism from Congress and the press, the president was not completely helpless—indeed, in this case, he "shrewdly outmaneuvered the congressional investigators."[23]

Ford also relied on executive privilege, in one instance, to resist congressional oversight on intelligence operations.[24] Thus, he ordered Secretary of State Henry Kissinger to cite executive privilege in refusing to turn over documents on clandestine foreign operations to the Pike Committee. Even though Ford backed down, once Congress threatened to vote on a contempt citation for Kissinger, his willingness to invoke executive privilege led to a compromise by which Pike Committee staff members received a briefing on the contents of the materials in question, but did not receive the papers themselves. Ford's use of executive privilege in this and other cases revealed political savvy for which he is rarely credited. It also demonstrated that Ford tried to preserve his presidential power even while he took pains not to appear Nixonesque.[25]

Ford, like his predecessor, also attempted to claim executive privilege to avoid judicial process, albeit under vastly different circumstances than those that had propelled Nixon to invoke this doctrine. On September 5, 1975, a follower of serial killer Charles Manson named Lynette "Squeaky" Fromme attempted to assassinate Ford as he greeted citizens in Sacramento, California. At her subsequent criminal trial, Fromme subpoenaed Ford himself to appear as a defense witness to rebut the charge that she intended to kill him. Although the president resisted, the trial court ordered him to provide a video deposition. This ruling echoed the Supreme Court's then-recent holding in *United States v. Nixon*, which had stated that the president could not evade judicial process and disrupt the criminal justice system simply because of his high office.[26]

## Conclusion

In part because of his controversial pardon of Richard M. Nixon and the nation's desire to put the painful memories of Watergate behind it, Governor Jimmy Carter of Georgia defeated President Ford when Ford ran for his own term in the White House during the hard-fought presidential election of 1976. Despite speculation that Ford might run for the presidency or vice presidency again in 1980, he retreated into private life at his home in Rancho Mirage, California, with his wife, Betty. He published a memoir, *A Time to Heal*, in 1979 and lived for another quarter century. Ford passed away on December 26, 2006, at the age of ninety-three, having regained widespread respect as an elder statesman and an honorable public servant.[27]

Although his contributions are often understated, Gerald Ford's constitutional legacy is significant. His greatest assertions of presidential power were the pardon of Richard Nixon and his mission to rescue the crew of the *Mayaguez*. The pardon reopened the wounds of Watergate and probably contributed to Ford's failed bid for the presidency in 1976. Yet it eventually became his most memorable act and came to be seen as an act of courage that helped to heal the nation. Though Ford took over the presidency during one of the most intense constitutional crises in American history, he righted the ship of state through his strength of character and leadership. The *Mayaguez* incident, too, was significant on many levels—it illustrates primarily that Ford was the first president to confront the restraints of the War Powers Resolution and demonstrate that he would defend his role as commander in chief and not yield entirely to Congress's directive.

In a vacuum, these decisions do not make Ford's use of executive power particularly impressive. However, Ford assumed office engulfed in a toxic political situation not of his own making. In an atmosphere that viewed any assertion of presidential power with great suspicion, Ford's dogged ability to hold the line for the chief executive's constitutional authority is noteworthy. If a different person had inherited the broken office left behind by Richard M. Nixon, a severely weakened chief executive might have emerged from the ruins of the Watergate scandal. Thus, the modern presidency might look quite different today had Gerald R. Ford not worked so diligently—and walked such a tightrope—to heal the nation while defending executive power from congressional encroachments after the trauma of the Nixon presidency.[28]

## NOTES

1. Gerald R. Ford, "Remarks on Taking the Oath of Office," *Public Papers of the Presidents of the United States: Gerald R. Ford* (hereafter cited as *Public Papers: Ford*) (Washington, DC: Government Printing Office, August 9, 1974), 2:2.

2. John Robert Greene, *The Presidency of Gerald R. Ford* (Lawrence: University Press of Kansas, 1995), xii, 190–193, disputes the view that "healing" is the only lasting legacy of the Ford administration and notes that Ford fought to preserve executive power. See also Gerald R. Ford, interview with Cokie Roberts, October 15, 2004, *Morning Edition*, National Public Radio. Arthur M. Schlesinger Jr.'s popular book *The Imperial Presidency* (Boston: Houghton Mifflin, 1973) explained how presidents up to and including Nixon had accumulated power at the expense of Congress until a backlash emboldened the legislature to fight back.

3. Greene, *The Presidency of Gerald R. Ford*, 1–2. See also Gerald R. Ford, *A Time to Heal: The Autobiography of Gerald R. Ford* (New York: Harper & Row, 1979), 42–56.

4. John D. Feerick, "The Twenty-fifth Amendment: An Explanation and Defense," *Wake Forest Law Review* 30 (1995): 481.

5. John Robert Greene, *The Limits of Power: The Nixon and Ford Administration* (Bloomington: Indiana University Press, 1992), 186–187; Greene, *The Presidency of Gerald R. Ford*, 3, 6–8, 11, 12.

6. Greene, *The Limits of Power*, 235.

7. Ibid., 194–195; A. James Reichley, *Conservatives in an Age of Change: The Nixon and Ford Administrations* (Washington, DC: Brookings Institution, 1981), 303; James Pfiffner, *The Strategic Presidency: Hitting the Ground Running* (Lawrence: University Press of Kansas, 1996). Donald Rumsfeld was George W. Bush's secretary of defense from 2001 to 2006.

8. Greene, *The Presidency of Gerald R. Ford*, 31–32, 35, 55.

9. Ken Gormley, "Impeachment and the Independent Counsel: A Dysfunctional Union," *Stanford Law Review* 51 (1999): 315.

10. Ibid.

11. President Ford's Pardon of Richard M. Nixon, forum, Duquesne University, Pittsburgh, November 12, 1999, C-SPAN Video Library, www.C-SPAN video.org/program/FordsP; Adam Clymer, "At First, Nixon Spurned Idea of a Pardon, Lawyer Says," *New York Times*, November 13, 1999, www.nytimes.com/1999/11/13/us/at-first-nixon-spurned-idea-of-a-pardon-lawyer-says.html.

12. Gerald R. Ford, "Proclamation 4311, Granting Pardon to Richard Nixon," *Public Papers: Ford*, September 8, 1974, 2:103–104. See also Jeffrey Crouch, *The Presidential Pardon Power* (Lawrence: University Press of Kansas, 2009), chap. 4. At the same time as the pardon dilemma, Ford was trying to figure out how to handle the ownership and possession of Nixon's presidential papers. Crouch, *The Presidential Pardon Power*, 167–168, n. 3.

13. Murphy v. Ford, 390 F. Supp. 1372, 1374, (1975) (emphasis added). Plaintiff Murphy, a private citizen, asked for a declaratory judgment that the Nixon pardon was invalid, but was rebuffed. The court noted that the Nixon pardon was "within the letter and the spirit of the Presidential Pardoning Power granted by the Constitution [and] was a prudent public policy judgment" by President Ford. Ibid. See also Ex Parte Garland, 71 U.S. 333, 380 (1867); U.S. Const., art. II, § 2, cl. 1; Edwin Brown Firmage and R. Collin Mangrum, "Removal of the President: Resignation and the Procedural Law of Impeachment," *Duke Law Journal* 6 (1974): 1095, 1099–1102; Mark J. Rozell, "President

Ford's Pardon of Richard M. Nixon: Constitutional and Political Considerations," *Presidential Studies Quarterly* 24 (1994): 123–124, 128.

14. Burdick v. United States, 236 U.S. 79, 94–95 (1915). For President Ford's account of the role of *Burdick* in his decision making, see Gerald R. Ford, *A Time to Heal: The Autobiography of Gerald R. Ford* (New York: Harper & Row, 1979), 157–180. Of course, some pardons (e.g., those based on later-discovered evidence that establishes the innocence of a convicted individual) do not constitute an admission of guilt. Gurleski v. United States, 405 F.2d 253 (5th Cir. 1968). However, pardons exercised in the best interests of the country—such as the pardons issued by President George Washington to rebels involved in the Whiskey Rebellion, by Andrew Johnson to high-ranking members of the Confederacy at the conclusion of the Civil War, and the pardons or amnesty granted by Jimmy Carter to "draft dodgers" who had fled to Canada during the Vietnam War era—fell within the *Burdick* principle. President Ford's pardon of Richard M. Nixon likewise fell into that category. The modern U.S. Department of Justice instructions relating to the awarding of pardons states in part that "a presidential pardon is ordinarily a sign of forgiveness and is granted in recognition of the applicant's acceptance of responsibility for the crime and established good conduct for a significant period of time after conviction or release from confinement. A pardon is not a sign of vindication and does not connote or establish innocence. . . . [W]hen considering the merits of a pardon petition, pardon officials take into account the petitioner's acceptance of responsibility, remorse, and atonement for the offense." U.S. Department of Justice, "Pardon Information and Instructions," accessed August 23, 2014, U.S. Department of Justice, www.justice.gov/pardon/pardon_instructions.htm.

15. Ford, *A Time to Heal*, 163–164; Ken Gormley, *Archibald Cox: Conscience of a Nation* (Reading, MA: Addison-Wesley, 1997), 388–390; President Ford's Pardon of Richard M. Nixon, forum; Gerald R. Ford, "The President's News Conference of September 16, 1974," *Public Papers: Ford*, September 16, 1974, 2:147–148; Clymer, "At First, Nixon Spurned Idea."

16. "Support for Ford Declines Sharply," *New York Times*, September 12, 1974; Crouch, *The Presidential Pardon Power*, 66, 67, 75, 81–83, 168; Bob Woodward, "Closing the Chapter on Watergate Wasn't Done Lightly," *Washington Post*, December 28, 2006; Ford, interview with Cokie Roberts; Mark J. Rozell, *The Press and the Ford Presidency* (Ann Arbor: University of Michigan Press, 1992), 178.

17. Ken Gormley and David Shribman, "The Nixon Pardon at 40: Ford Looks Better than Ever," *Wall Street Journal*, September 5, 2014; President Ford Pardon of Richard Nixon, forum, Gerald R. Ford Presidential Museum, Grand Rapids, MI, October 20, 2014, www.c-span.org/video/?321682-1/president-ford-pardon-richard-nixon.

18. Greene, *The Presidency of Gerald R. Ford*, 6; Harold Jackson, "Gerald Ford," obituary, *Guardian*, December 27, 2006, www.guardian.co.uk/world/2006/dec/27/guardianobituaries.usa; Rozell, *The Press and the Ford Presidency*, 3; Crouch, *The Presidential Pardon Power*, 135.

19. Howard J. Silver, "Presidential Power and the Post-Watergate Presidency," *Presidential Studies Quarterly* 8 (1978): 210; John W. Sloan, "The Ford Presidency: A Conservative Approach to Economic Management," *Presidential Studies Quarterly* 14 (1984): 532; Reichley, *Conservatives in an Age of Change*, 325.

20. Kathryn Olmsted, "Reclaiming Executive Power: The Ford Administration's Response to the Intelligence Investigations," *Presidential Studies Quarterly* 26 (1996): 726.

21. U.S. Const. art. I, § 8 and art. II, § 2; 87 Stat. 555 (1973); Duane Tananbaum, "Gerald Ford and the War Powers Resolution," in *Gerald R. Ford and the Politics of Post-Watergate America*, vol. 2, ed. Bernard J. Firestone and Alexej Ugrinsky (Westport, CT: Greenwood Press, 1993), 534; Gerald R. Ford, "Congress, the Presidency and National Security Policy," *Presidential Studies Quarterly* 16 (1986): 201.

22. Ford's military response to the *Mayaguez* incident has been called into question in recent years. Although then viewed as an effective display of military might, the operation was plagued by the same command and intelligence failures emblematic of the Vietnam era. For a complete account, see Ralph Wetterhahn, *The Last Battle: The Mayaguez Incident and the End of the Vietnam War* (New York: Carroll & Graff, 2001); Louis Fisher, *Presidential War Power* (Lawrence: University Press of Kansas, 1995), 136–137; Tananbaum, "Gerald Ford and the War Powers Resolution," 532; Greene, *The Limits of Power*, 217, 219.

23. Ford Executive Order 11905, at *American Presidency Project*, ed. John Woolley and Gerhard Peters, accessed June 18, 2014, www.presidency.ucsb.edu/ws/?pid=59348. Frank J. Smist Jr., "Seeking a Piece of the Action: Congress and Its Intelligence Investigation of 1975–1976," in *Gerald R. Ford and the Politics of Post-Watergate America*, vol. 2, ed. Bernard J. Firestone and Alexej Ugrinsky (Westport, CT: Greenwood Press, 1993), 463–464, 473, 485; Olmsted, "Reclaiming Executive Power," 725, 729, 730–731.

24. See generally Mark J. Rozell, *Executive Privilege: Presidential Power, Secrecy, and Accountability* (Lawrence: University Press of Kansas, 2010).

25. Mark J. Rozell, "Executive Privilege in the Ford Administration: Prudence in the Exercise of Presidential Power," *Presidential Studies Quarterly* 28 (1998): 293–294; Philip Shabecoff, "The House-Kissinger Battle over Contempt: A Compromise on Presidential Power and Confidentiality," *New York Times*, December 15, 1975; "Contempt Action Dropped: Kissinger Citation Dropped," *Washington Post*, December 11, 1975.

26. Douglas Brinkley, *Gerald R. Ford* (New York: Times Books, 2007), 120–121. Seventeen days after the first attempt on Ford's life, a second female assassin opened fire, narrowly missing the president. United States v. Fromme, 405 F.Supp 578 (1975); United States v. Nixon, 418 U.S. 683 (1974); Clinton v. Jones, 520 U.S. 681 (1997). Presidents Jefferson and Monroe have also been subpoenaed to testify. For a detailed account, see Ronald D. Rotunda, "Presidents and Ex-Presidents as Witnesses: A Brief Historical Footnote," *University of Illinois Law Forum* 1 (1975). Likewise, the Supreme Court would later cite *United States v. Nixon* in *Clinton v. Jones* as precedent for requiring a sitting president to provide testimony by court order.

27. "Timeline of President Ford's Life and Career," Gerald R. Ford Presidential Library and Museum, Grand Rapids, MI, accessed June 18, 2014, www.fordlibrarymuseum.gov/grf/timeline.asp#post.

28. Rozell, "Executive Privilege in the Ford Administration," 286; Scott Shane, "Recent Flexing of Presidential Powers Had Personal Roots in Ford White House," *New York Times*, December 30, 2006.

# 39

# Jimmy Carter

SCOTT KAUFMAN

*President Jimmy Carter, a peanut farmer from Georgia, won over an American electorate distrustful of government because of the Vietnam War and Watergate. He prevailed in 1976 with a pledge of honesty and openness. Carter, who viewed himself as an enlightened trustee of the American people, championed the cause of affirmative action for minorities when much of the country still resisted this concept. Crippled politically by his botched handling of the Iran hostage crisis, Carter became a oneterm president viewed as a weak leader. Yet his post-presidential activism in favor of international human rights—earning him a Nobel Peace Prize—transformed Carter into one of the most successful former presidents in U.S. history.*

## Introduction

Jimmy Carter entered the presidency at a time of transition. Diplomatically, the so-called Cold War consensus, which had emphasized a communist conspiracy driven by the Soviet Union to achieve world dominion, was breaking down. Demographically, the Sun Belt had gained influence as Americans moved from the North and East to the South and West. Politically, the liberalism that had been ascendant from the New Deal of the 1930s through the Great Society of the 1960s was being challenged by an increasingly influential fiscal and social conservatism. Finally, the Vietnam War and Watergate scandals had moved Americans to seek honest leadership in Washington and had pushed Congress to rein in the power of the executive branch. Jimmy Carter had taken advantage of these changes to win the 1976 presidential election.

Born in Plains, Georgia, on October 1, 1924, James Earl Carter Jr. was the oldest of four children born to James Earl Sr. and Lillian Carter. His father was a businessman and a peanut farmer, while Lillian worked as a registered nurse. Though the Carters were financially comfortable, they were not rich. Indeed, it was not until Jimmy was eleven years old that the Carter home became equipped with electricity and indoor plumbing.

As a fiscally conservative businessman, James Sr. had opposed the New Deal and clung to the prevailing Southern sentiment on race relations. Lillian was more prepared than her husband to push for equality by offering health services to local African Americans free of charge. Though Jimmy came to share his father's fiscal leanings, he shared his mother's progressive views regarding minorities. That many of the children with whom Jimmy played as a child were black, including his closest friend, reflected his open-mindedness toward minorities.[1]

As a child, Carter had wanted to join the U.S. Navy. He was admitted to the U.S. Naval Academy in 1943, earning the rank of lieutenant and working on a program designed to create nuclear-powered submarines. Graduating in 1946, he married Rosalynn Smith, a close friend of his sister's. Carter had intended to make the armed forces his career, but news that his father was dying of cancer convinced him to resign from the service and return to Plains to take over the family's peanut warehouse business. Active in the community and financially successful, he developed a reputation as a leader in Plains.

Carter began his political career in 1955, when he won a seat on the Sumter County Board of Education, serving as the board's chairman from 1960 to 1962. While not yet a proponent of integration of schools, he was offended by the treatment of African American students and the condition of all-black schools. He ended his service on the board to run as a Democrat for the Georgia state senate. During the next four years, he developed a reputation as a hard worker who opposed the influence of special interests in government and sought to do more for the poor and minorities.[2]

Depressed after a failed run for governor in 1966, Carter found solace in religion and declared himself a born-again Christian. In 1970, after aligning himself with a pro-segregationist platform that appealed to white voters, Carter won the keys to the governor's mansion. He then shocked his fellow Georgians when he announced in his inaugural address that he would lead the state toward racial equality and social justice. In short order, he added over 1,800 African Americans to the state payroll, bringing the total number of black state employees to 6,684.[3]

The most important objective for Governor Carter, however, was to reorganize Georgia's government to make it more efficient and cost-effective. In this effort, he made errors he would repeat as president. Viewing himself as an enlightened trustee, he angered state legislators by insisting on his own righteousness and by not playing the game of give-and-take common in politics.[4] As his wife later put it, "Jimmy was never really a politician. . . . My definition of a politician is you let the people guide you. Jimmy is more of a leader who wants people to follow him."[5]

By 1974, Carter had attracted a national audience, primarily because of his progressive stance on race. That same year, he announced his decision to campaign for the U.S. presidency. Promising an American electorate distrustful of government because of Vietnam and Watergate that he would be honest and open, and presenting himself as a moderate alternative to his competitors, Carter won his party's nomination.[6] In a close election, he defeated the Republican nominee and incumbent president, Gerald R. Ford.

## Presidency

### *Affirmative Action*

Carter was asked many times whether it was difficult for him to simultane-ously uphold his deeply held religious beliefs and his duties as president under the Constitution. "There is probably not a great incompatibility between our patriotic ideals for America and Judeo-Christian values," he later wrote. "Justice, equal opportunity, human rights, freedom, democracy, truth—those are the kinds of things that were spelled out by Thomas Jef-ferson and others in the founding days of our country."[7] Advancing the cause of civil rights fell within these categories. Thus, Carter was a strong proponent of the Equal Rights Amendment, which would have expressly guaranteed equal rights of all Americans regardless of gender. Without a constitutional requirement to do so, he signed a House resolution that granted a three-year extension for its ratification by the states.[8]

Yet the push for civil rights also caused a serious problem for the presi-dent when the Supreme Court in 1977 decided to hear the most important civil rights case in a generation. At issue was affirmative action, a policy dating back to the administration of Lyndon B. Johnson. Though Johnson had denied that the Civil Rights Act of 1964 was designed to give prefer-ential treatment to African Americans, a year later he announced support of what later would become known as the policy of *affirmative action*. It was not enough, LBJ had asserted in a June 1965 speech, to say to a person who had been treated as a second-class citizen that he or she was now able "to compete with the others." Instead, he declared, African Americans had to be given support to make sure they could take advantage of the new opportunities available to them. By implication, a form of quotas was needed to guarantee a level playing field for blacks and other minorities.[9]

To many whites, it was one thing to bar discrimination; it was another to suggest that special treatment should be given only to minorities, which would amount to reverse discrimination. By the early 1970s, scathing articles had begun appearing in newspapers and magazines charging that universities had given African Americans preferential treatment in admis-sions, equating such favoritism to the racism that the civil rights move-ment had fought to eliminate. In late 1971, Sidney Hook wrote a *New York Times* article titled "Discrimination Against the Qualified?" and Brewster

Denny, in the journal *Science*, decried the perceived problem in the piece titled "The Decline of Merit."[10]

President Carter's record as governor of Georgia suggested that he would be a proponent of affirmative action, and his record as president bore that out. In May 1977, Carter signed the Public Works Employment Act, which required that at least 10 percent of funds offered by the Department of Commerce for public works projects at the state or local level be awarded to companies owned by minorities. Two months later, he ordered all agencies within the executive branch to improve adherence to affirmative action requirements. By the end of his term in office, Carter had appointed more African Americans to federal judgeships than had any previous president. Quotas were another matter, however. This president was skeptical of quotas and said as much during the 1976 campaign.[11] How Carter planned to stand on affirmative action and quotas became even more important when the Supreme Court announced that it would hear arguments in *University of California Board of Regents v. Bakke*, a blockbuster case involving a direct challenge to affirmative action in the setting of higher education.

The origins of the *Bakke* case traced their way back to 1968, when the University of California opened a medical school at its branch in Davis. Racial tension and rioting throughout the country had convinced the Association of American Medical Colleges to urge medical schools to fight discrimination by admitting more minorities. In 1969, the Davis school thus set up a task force, which was largely composed of minority faculty and students, whose job it was to increase the medical program's diversity. Davis also began setting aside 16 percent of its slots for minority students.[12]

Four years later, Allan Bakke (who was white) applied for admission. Bakke was a former U.S. Marine who had served a tour of duty in Vietnam and, after leaving the armed forces, received a master's degree in engineering. In 1972, Bakke applied to two medical schools but was denied admission. He tried again the following year and submitted applications to eleven medical schools, including that at the University of California at Davis. Despite high scores academically and on the Medical College Examination Test (MCAT), he again received only rejection letters. Aware of Davis's special admissions program for minorities, he threatened to sue but was encouraged by a member of the university's admissions committee to apply again the following year. After doing so and receiving another denial letter, he brought suit against the University of California's Board of Regents.[13]

Bakke's attorneys took note that their client had MCAT scores far higher than those of "affirmative action" students and comparable to or higher than those of many successful applicants. They charged that the University of California, which received federal monies, had violated both Title VI of the Civil Rights Act and the Equal Protection Clause of the Fourteenth Amendment by giving preferential treatment to nonwhite students. The university defended the special admissions program as necessary both to overcome years of discrimination against minorities and to improve medical services in predominantly nonwhite communities. The California Supreme Court, in a six-to-one ruling, had declared the special admissions program illegal under the Fourteenth Amendment. However, the U.S. Supreme Court stayed the order and agreed to hear the case.[14]

*Bakke* posed political problems for President Carter. The case was the most significant one involving civil rights since the *Brown v. Board of Education* decision in 1954 had declared school segregation illegal. Nearly sixty amicus briefs, some of them from Democratic constituencies, were filed with the Supreme Court, taking strong positions on both sides of the issue. The National Association for the Advancement of Colored Peoples (NAACP) defended the quota for minorities. Briefs submitted by the Anti-Defamation League, the American Jewish Committee, and the American Jewish Congress, however, urged the High Court to ban the use of racial quotas. The Congressional Black Caucus asked the White House to submit a brief endorsing the special admissions program, while Jewish organizations urged the president to remain silent.[15]

Any brief submitted by the executive branch to the Supreme Court has to be originated by the Office of the Solicitor General in the Department of Justice. Such a brief can have an enormous impact on the decision of the Court; a litigant who has the support of the Justice Department has a success rate of approximately 85 percent, or 65 to 70 percent higher than an individual or entity that does not.[16] The Carter administration knew that if it proceeded to file a brief, any position it took was certain to upset some constituents and, potentially, to cost the president and the Democratic Party votes in the upcoming elections.

The White House nonetheless decided it should submit a brief defending affirmative action. The job fell upon Attorney General Griffin Bell, Solicitor General Wade McCree Jr., and the assistant attorney general of the department's Civil Rights Division, Drew Days III.[17] McCree was the second African American to hold his post, and Days (also African American) was a Yale-trained lawyer who had litigated cases for the NAACP Legal Defense Fund.[18] Both McCree and Days pressed to give minorities greater influence in government.

In August, Attorney General Bell took his draft brief to the White House to update the president on the Justice Department's proposed position. He told Carter that the document would declare that the administration supported affirmative action programs but opposed quotas, meaning that Bakke had to be admitted to the Davis program. Carter's top aides were split on the issue. Vice President Walter Mondale and others feared that opposing quotas would anger African Americans, including members of the Congressional Black Caucus. Carter demanded alterations that would make a stronger case for affirmative action. However, the president did not see quotas as the correct way to comply with affirmative action mandates: "I hate to endorse the proposition of quotas for minority groups, for women or for anyone else, that contravene the concept of merit selection," he said at a July news conference.[19]

Over the next month, the Justice Department reworked the brief, reflecting the president's position. The brief took a stronger stand in support of affirmative action, yet it also declared opposition to quotas without detailing why.[20]

In June 1978, the Supreme Court issued its splintered, five-to-four decision invalidating the UC Davis program but permitting affirmative action under certain circumstances. Justice Lewis Powell Jr. announced that he and his colleagues "speak today with a notable lack of unanimity." Four justices took the position that the Constitution permitted the use of race to help groups that had faced discrimination "as long as there was an important public purpose in doing so." The four in dissent argued that Title VI of the Civil Rights Act of 1964 made it illegal for any program receiving federal funding to discriminate in any fashion; thus, the dissenters believed the California program was per se invalid and there was no need to reach the Constitutional issue. The deciding vote came from Justice Powell. He found nothing in the Constitution that permitted the use of racial quotas. However, he wrote that encouraging *educational diversity* constituted a "compelling government interest" that justified programs such as that created at Harvard and many other universities that gave a "plus" for racial diversity in the admissions process. The net result of the *Bakke* decision was that the UC Davis plan was illegal because it resembled a quota; Alan Bakke thus had to be admitted. At the same time, the practical result of the ruling was that affirmative action programs in most institutions of higher education throughout the United States were constitutional, as long as they followed the Harvard model and simply treated race as a "plus" factor necessary to achieve a diverse student body.[21]

## Terminating Treaty with Taiwan

In the international realm, President Carter took risks that produced mixed results, as he tested the boundaries of presidential authority in foreign affairs. One pivotal decision occurred in late 1978, when Carter announced that the United States would continue to normalize relations with China—a process that had begun under President Nixon—by recognizing the People's Republic of China (PRC) as the sole legal government of China.[22] As part of that announcement, President Carter also declared that he was using his executive authority to terminate a 1954 U.S. mutual defense treaty with Taiwan, or the Republic of China (ROC)—a treaty initiated by President Harry Truman and consummated with the consent of the Senate.

Sixteen U.S. senators, led by Barry Goldwater (R-AZ), filed suit in federal court, claiming that Carter's unilateral termination of the 1954 Sino-American treaty—without the consent of Congress—exceeded the president's power under Article II of the Constitution. Since congressional advice and consent was required before this treaty was adopted, the argument went, President Carter could not unilaterally terminate the treaty without the vote of two-thirds of the Senate or the approval of both houses of Congress.[23] Ultimately, the U.S. Supreme Court chose not to wade into this thicket, concluding that the matter of the president's ability to invoke treaty power—as it intersected with Congress's constitutional role of providing advice and consent—constituted a nonjusticiable "political question" that the Court should not address.[24] As Justice William H. Rehnquist noted, concurring in the judgment in *Goldwater v. Carter*, this matter "involves the authority of the President in the conduct of our country's foreign relations." Justice Rehnquist added: "While the Constitution is express as to the manner in which the Senate shall participate in the ratification of a Treaty, it is silent as to that body's participation in the abrogation of a Treaty."[25] Thus, a majority of the Court determined that the wisest course was to have this unanswered question resolved in the political arena rather than in the courts. In the process, Carter won a modest victory in the realm of foreign affairs—leaving the ultimate question of the president's power to terminate treaties for another day. Yet he managed to provoke the ire of certain members of Congress, a result that would repeat itself in short order.

### The Iran Hostage Crisis

The unpopular war in Vietnam and the corrosive Watergate scandal had already convinced Capitol Hill that the executive branch had too much power, requiring Congress to take steps to rein it in. The War Powers Resolution of 1973 reflected this effort.[26] President Ford's formal report to Congress, when he ordered U.S. troops to rescue the crew of the American ship *Mayaguez*, which had been seized by Cambodia in 1975, was not submitted until after the rescue operation was completed, leaving a question mark as to whether he had actually followed the requirements of the resolution. Now, in 1980, President Carter decided to use the armed forces to try to rescue Americans being held hostage in Iran, in a botched effort that generated enormous controversy. He did not follow the mandates of the statute, fueling a debate as to whether he had flatly violated the law.

The circumstances leading to Carter's secret use of military force were tense and dramatic. Iran and its leader, the shah Mohammed Reza Pahlavi, had been allies of the United States for decades. Nonetheless, the shah had grown unpopular; increasingly large and violent protests had forced him to flee in early 1979. The shah moved from country to country seeking a place to live in exile. When Carter learned that Pahlavi was suffering from cancer, he allowed the deposed leader to come to the United States for treatment. The new Iranian government demanded that the president send Pahlavi home so he could be put on trial. Carter, believing the Iranians would kill the shah, refused. Infuriated, in November 1979, a group of Iranian militants stormed the U.S. embassy in Tehran and took dozens of Americans hostage. Months of fruitless negotiations followed. Frustrated by this impasse, Carter authorized a U.S. Special Forces team to embark on a secret mission to free the captured Americans. The rescue mission, which took place in April 1980, was an abject failure. Not only were the hostages not freed, but eight servicemen died when a U.S. helicopter crashed into a C-130 tanker aircraft.[27]

President Carter sent a message to Congress after the failed mission, declaring that he was required neither to consult with lawmakers nor to invoke the War Powers Act. First, he cited his constitutional role as commander in chief of the armed forces. Additionally, Carter called the mission "humanitarian," rather than one aimed at Iran or Iranians. Whether he had violated the law would quickly become a matter of intense debate in Washington. White House Counsel Lloyd Cutler asserted that Carter "had an 'inherent constitutional power to conduct this kind of rescue operation.'" That included the right to proceed with the operation without consulting Congress if the president believed such consultation could endanger the mission. Many lawmakers agreed. However, Senators Frank Church (D-ID) and Jacob Javits (R-NY) suggested that Carter had acted illegally.[28] In the end, the War Powers Act question was never resolved.[29] Moreover, the failed rescue mission in Tehran became a blot on Carter's record—a blot that lasted for the duration of his presidency.

### The Controversial Claims Tribunal

In negotiating the agreement to free the hostages, Carter was again accused of going beyond his constitutional authority by freezing all asset claims by Americans against the Iranian government and creating a claims tribunal to allocate and disperse the funds. When the American hostages had been seized in 1979, Carter had imposed several sanctions on Tehran, including an embargo of Iranian oil imports. He also had declared a national emergency, had frozen all Iranian assets held in the United States, and had suspended all judicial proceedings related to Iranian interests. The Carter administration justified the latter measures by invoking the International Emergency Economic Powers Act, which granted the president broad authority with regard to foreign assets in times of national peril.[30] By Election Day 1980, however, neither these measures nor ongoing negotiations with Iranian officials had secured the hostages' release, and the poor state of the U.S. economy made matters worse for the incumbent. A frustrated American electorate overwhelmingly voted for Carter's Republican opponent, Ronald Reagan.

On January 20, 1981, just hours after Reagan's inauguration, the hostages were released pursuant to an executive agreement that had been in the works for months between Carter's administration and Iran's government. Under this agreement, American courts were obligated to terminate all legal proceedings related to claims against Iran. The claims were then to be dispatched to an Iranian-U.S. Claim Tribunal for binding arbitration. After Carter left office, Reagan issued an executive order "ratifying" Carter's agreement.[31]

Litigation soon erupted over these events, with geopolitical implications. In *Dames & Moore v. Regan*, an opinion delivered by Justice Rehnquist, the Supreme Court upheld Carter's action.[32] The Court reasoned that the president, who already possessed significant constitutional power in the realm of foreign affairs, gained additional authority from the relevant act of Congress. Moreover, the Court noted that since the passage of the International Emergency Economic Powers Act, Capitol Hill had never objected to presidential nullification of claims concerning foreign assets.[33] Therefore, both Carter and Reagan, who were authorized by the act to freeze and to transfer foreign assets, were also permitted to nullify rights to such property in light of practical considerations that could not have been anticipated.

Although the Court's decision in *Dames & Moore* came after Carter had officially left office, it was nonetheless a modest victory for the beleaguered former president. Indeed, it vindicated one aspect of Carter's otherwise flawed handling of the hostage crisis. The decision perhaps reflected the Court's desire to allow the country to put the hostage crisis behind it and allow a new, popular president (Reagan) to move forward with his own foreign policy agenda. In the long term, however, it was even more significant. The decision represented a legal stamp of approval for the president's sweeping use of economic measures as a bargaining chip in foreign negotiations.

## Conclusion

Carter's last two years in office were a rocky time for him politically. Having signed the Ethics in Government Act into law in 1978 to end the period of public distrust after Watergate, the president was himself the subject of a special counsel investigation into alleged financial irregularities involving his family's peanut warehouse in Georgia. Although the investigation found no wrongdoing, it reinforced his image as a hobbled chief executive.[34] Crippled politically by the Iran hostage crisis and the perception that he was a weak leader, Carter was strongly challenged in the 1980 Democratic primary by Senator Edward M. Kennedy of Massachusetts.

Carter ultimately prevailed but then lost to Reagan in a landslide, becoming the first elected president since Herbert Hoover (in 1932), to lose his bid for reelection.

Returning to Georgia, Carter became a champion for human rights, founded the Carter Center in Atlanta, and seemed to grow in stature after leaving office. In 2002, he won the Nobel Peace Prize for his work in resolving international conflicts and advancing human rights around the globe.

Although Carter never had the opportunity to name a justice to the Supreme Court, he appointed more women and minorities to lower courts than any of his predecessors had.[35] Indeed, two of his later appointments to the federal appeals courts, Ruth Bader Ginsburg and Stephen Breyer, went on to earn seats on the U.S. Supreme Court.

Most lasting, however, was Carter's legacy of post-presidential activism. For a chief executive to remain politically involved after leaving the White House is nothing new.[36] However, no president went further than Carter did in this respect. For these efforts, he received both sharp criticism and high praise. His denunciation of Israel's policy toward the Palestinians produced angry responses at home and abroad. Yet Carter also sought to end poverty and illness, and to promote democracy through his work with Habitat for Humanity and the Carter Center. While Jimmy Carter's record as a president has gone down in history as mediocre, he has been recognized as one of the best (if not one of the most controversial) *former* presidents of the United States.

## NOTES

1. Burton I. Kaufman and Scott Kaufman, *The Presidency of James Earl Carter, Jr.*, 2nd ed., rev. (Lawrence: University Press of Kansas, 2006), 2–3.
2. Ibid., 8–9; E. Stanly Godbold Jr., *Jimmy and Rosalynn Carter: The Georgia Years, 1924–1974* (New York: Oxford University Press, 2010), 86–87, 106, 109.
3. Kaufman and Kaufman, *Presidency of James Earl Carter, Jr.*, 9–10, 11.
4. Unwilling to play the political game of give-and-take as governor of Georgia, Carter did not change his ways as president. As House Speaker Tip O'Neill (D-MA) once remarked: "When it came to the politics of Washington, D.C., [Carter] never really understood how the system worked. . . . [H]e didn't want to learn about it, either." Thomas O'Neill, with William Novak, *Man of the House: The Life and Political Memoirs of Speaker Tip O'Neill* (New York: Random House, 1987), 297.
5. Ibid.,10–11; Godbold, *Jimmy and Rosalynn Carter*, 199; "True Believer," *People*, June 12, 2000, 155.

6. When running for president, Carter promised that unconditional pardons would be granted to anyone who evaded the draft during the Vietnam War. He kept that promise on January 21, 1977. Andrew Glass, "Carter Pardons Draft Dodgers, Jan. 21, 1977," *Politico*, January 21, 2008.

7. Jimmy Carter, *Living Faith* (New York: Three Rivers Press, 2001), 125–126.

8. Jimmy Carter, "Equal Rights Amendment Remarks on Signing H.J. Res. 638," October 20, 1978, *The American Presidency Project*, ed. Gerhard Peters and John T. Woolley, www.presidency.ucsb.edu/ws/index.php?pid=30010&st=equal+rights+amendment&st1=. The Equal Rights Amendment was first written in Seneca Falls by Alice Paul and was introduced in Congress in 1923. The amendment was introduced in each subsequent session of Congress before passing the House and Senate in 1972. Congress had established a seven-year deadline for thirty-eight states to ratify the amendment, per the Constitution. Only thirty-five states ratified the amendment at the time of the 1979 deadline. The amendment was introduced in Congress again in 1982, and has been reintroduced in each subsequent session of Congress, but has never been ratified.

9. *Public Papers of the Presidents of the United States: Lyndon Johnson* (Washington, DC: Government Printing Office, 1996), 1:635–640; Randall B. Woods, *LBJ: Architect of American Ambition* (Cambridge, MA: Harvard University Press, 2006), 589.

10. Jerome Karabel, *The Chosen: The Hidden History of Admission and Exclusion at Harvard, Yale, and Princeton* (Boston: Houghton Mifflin, 2005), 486, 658 n. 15.

11. Hugh Davis Graham, "The Civil Rights Act and the American Regulatory State," in *Legacies of the 1964 Civil Rights Act*, ed. Bernard Grofman (Charlottesville: University of Virginia Press, 2000), 53; Kaufman and Kaufman, *Presidency of James Earl Carter, Jr.*, 133; Carter, *Living Faith*, 125.

12. Joel Dreyfuss and Charles Lawrence III, *The Bakke Case: The Politics of Inequality* (New York: Harcourt Brace Jovanovich, 1979), 18–19.

13. Ibid., 13–15, 16, 20–21; Howard Ball, *The Bakke Case: Race, Education, and Affirmative Action* (Lawrence: University Press of Kansas, 2000), 46, 49.

14. Timothy J. O'Neill, *Bakke and the Politics of Equality: Friends and Foes in the Classroom of Litigation* (Middletown, CT: Wesleyan University Press, 1985), 30; Ball, *Bakke Case*, 58–61.

15. Ball, *Bakke Case*, 77; Kaufman and Kaufman, *Presidency of James Earl Carter, Jr.*, 88; Dreyfuss and Lawrence, *Bakke Case*, 103–137.

16. Ball, *Bakke Case*, 71–72.

17. Bell had served on the Court of Appeals for the Fifth Circuit before having joined the Carter administration. In that role, his record on civil rights had been mixed. Burton I. Kaufman, *Presidential Profiles: The Carter Years* (New York: Facts on File, 2006), 41–42; Ball, *Bakke Case*, 72.

18. The first African American solicitor general was Thurgood Marshall, who now sat on the Supreme Court.

19. Kaufman and Kaufman, *Presidency of James Earl Carter, Jr.*, 88; Ball, *Bakke Case*, 71, 72, 74, 75; *Public Papers of the Presidents of the United States: Jimmy Carter* (Washington, DC: Government Printing Office, July 28, 1978), 2:1372.

20. Ball, *Bakke Case*, 75–76.

21. For a discussion of the Court's oral argument and decision in *Bakke*, see Ken Gormley, *Archibald Cox: Conscience of a Nation* (Reading, MA: Addison-Wesley, 1997), 401–406. Kermit L. Hall and John J. Patrick, *The Pursuit of Justice: Supreme Court Decisions That Shaped America* (New York: Oxford University Press, 2006), 207–208. Since 1980, the Supreme Court has continued to come to grips with affirmative action. Most notably, in the 2003 case *Grutter v. Bollinger*, the High Court in a five-to-four vote upheld the University of Michigan Law School's use of affirmative action in its admissions policy on the grounds that the practice did not involve an illegal use of quotas; while in *Gratz v. Bollinger*, the Court in a six-to-three decision struck down the University of Michigan's undergraduate admissions policy, which used a points scale to increase the likelihood of minorities receiving entry. In 2013, the Court declined to modify its affirmative action doctrine in Fisher v. Univ. of Tex. at Austin, 133 S. Ct. 2411 (2013).

22. L. Peter Schultz, "*Goldwater v. Carter*: The Separation of Powers and the Problem of Executive Prerogative," *Presidential Studies Quarterly* 12 (winter 1982): 34–41.

23. Goldwater v. Carter, 481 F. Supp. 949 (D.D.C. 1979).

24. Goldwater v. Carter, 444 U.S. 996 (1979).

25. Ibid., 1002–1003 (Rehnquist, J., concurring in judgment).

26. Designed to avoid another Vietnam-style war, the War Powers Resolution required the president to consult with Congress within two days of having U.S. troops engage in military action. Unless the commander in chief had the lawmakers' approval, he was required to cease all military action within sixty days. John Robert Greene, *The Presidency of Gerald R. Ford* (Lawrence: University Press of Kansas, 1995), 148, 150.

27. This mission called for six helicopters and several C-130 transport planes. Upon arriving at their staging ground in Iran, one of the helicopters developed engine trouble, and the commander of the operation decided to abort. As the aircraft prepared to leave, a helicopter crashed into a C-130, causing a fire that killed the eight servicemen.

28. *Congressional Quarterly Almanac* 36 (1981): 49–50E; James N. Giglio, *Call Me Tom: The Life of Thomas F. Eagleton* (Columbia: University of Missouri Press, 2011), 143; Martin Tolchin, "Some in Congress Criticize Mission Because of a Lack of Consultation," *New York Times*, April 26, 1980, 11; *Congressional Record* 126, pt. 7 (1980): 9150–9151, 9191, 9275.

29. As of 2012, presidents had submitted 134 reports to Congress to comply with the War Powers Act. However, chief executives have continued to engage in military action without invoking the law. These actions include Ronald Reagan's decision to send troops to Lebanon in 1982 and Grenada in 1983, and George H. W. Bush's overthrow of the government of Manuel Noriega in Panama in 1989. Though there has been discussion within Washington about amending the resolution, no such amendment has yet taken place. Richard F. Grimmett, "War Powers Resolution: Presidential Compliance," February 1, 2012, www.fas.org/sgp/crs/natsec/RL33532.pdf.

30. Hossein Alikhani, *Sanctioning Iran: The Anatomy of a Failed Policy* (London: I.B. Tauris & Co., 2000), 67–69. A copy of the statute is available at 50 U.S.C.A. § 1701. Carter's Executive Order 12170 is available at 44 Fed. Reg. 65729.

31. David Patrick Houghton, *U.S. Foreign Policy and the Iran Hostage Crisis* (New York: Cambridge University Press, 2001), 141–143; Pierre Salinger, *America Held Hostage: The*

*Secret Negotiations* (Garden City, NY: Doubleday & Company, 1981), 294–295; Dames & Moore v. Regan, 453 U.S. 654, 662–66 (1981). Pursuant to the claims settlement agreement, any American citizen or company with a claim against Iran lost the ability to litigate its dispute in the nation's courts. One such company, the engineering firm Dames & Moore, initiated a federal lawsuit against the Iranian government and several of its banks in 1979, alleging that the company was owed a substantial sum of money for consulting work it had performed. At the time, the district court issued an order of attachment to secure funds should an eventual judgment be entered in favor of Dames & Moore. Thereafter, the hostage release agreement was brokered by Carter and carried out by Reagan in January 1981, leaving Dames & Moore unable to obtain a judgment in American courts. In response, the company sued the Treasury Department, alleging that the government lacked the constitutional authority to freeze assets in this fashion.

32. In reaching this decision, the Court adopted the rationale of Justice Robert Jackson's concurring opinion in Youngstown Sheet and Tube Co. v. Sawyer, 343 U.S. 579 (1952). Specifically, the Court found that Carter's authority was at a peak when he was acting under the International Emergency Economic Powers Act because Congress had expressly endorsed his ability to act by passing the law.

33. *Dames & Moore*, 453 U.S. at 672–673, 678–683.

34. "Carter Family Peanut Warehouse White House Statement on Findings of a Special Investigation," October 16, 1979, *The American Presidency Project*, ed. Gerhardt Peters and John Woolley, www.presidency.ucsb.edu/ws/?pid=31540. This investigation took place prior to the enactment of the independent counsel law.

35. Henry J. Abraham, *Justices, Presidents, and Senators: A History of U.S. Supreme Court Appointments from Washington Bush II*, 5th ed. (Lanham, MD: Rowman and Littlefield, 2008), 263–264.

36. On this score, see Burton I. Kaufman, *The Post-Presidency from Washington to Clinton* (Lawrence: University Press of Kansas, 2012).

# PART XI

# New Conservatives, New Democrats, and Polarization

# 40

# Ronald Reagan

KENNETH W. STARR

*President Reagan was a popular and transformative chief executive who chipped away at what he considered a runaway federal bureaucracy to bring a more conservative vision to all three branches of American government. While the Iran-Contra affair during Reagan's second term galvanized critics, he still managed to win major victories to curb what he perceived to be overreaching by Congress. He exercised executive power with vigor and assuredness, and he systematically reshaped the federal judicial branch to take on a more conservative, originalist complexion. Thus, the "Reagan Revolution"—built largely on the dual constitutional principles of separation of powers and federalism—continued to reconfigure the landscape of American government long after Reagan left office.*

## Introduction

The year was 1911. The world was a perilous place. Woodrow Wilson would soon take the oath of office. Meanwhile, in the latter years of his short-lived presidency, William Howard Taft was wistfully looking ahead to life teaching at Yale Law School. In this same year, Ronald Wilson Reagan was born in America's heartland on February 6 to John Edward and Nelle Wilson Reagan. Growing up, as his family moved from one small town in Illinois to another, the future president was involved in sports and drama and worked for a few years as a lifeguard.

In 1928, student-athlete Ronald Reagan enrolled at Eureka College in central Illinois. He graduated in 1932 with a degree in economics and sociology. Reagan then worked as a radio sports announcer before landing his first acting contract in 1937 with Warner Brothers Studio in California. During the next few decades, he acted in many movies, most notably *Knute Rockne, All American.* In that film, the now-flourishing Hollywood actor starred as legendary Notre Dame footballer George "The Gipper" Gipp. Then, the war came. Reagan served in the Army Air Corps film unit during World War II, making films to support the war effort. After the war, he rose to the presidency of the Screen Actors Guild, seeking to curb communist influence in Hollywood. After a failed marriage to actress Jane Wyman, Reagan married Nancy Davis, a film star in her own right.[1]

In 1954, Reagan began a new professional chapter as "an ambassador of goodwill" for General Electric, a position that foreshadowed his career in politics. In this highly public role, Reagan traveled across the country giving pro-business, anti-big-government speeches. Reagan also became more politically active and vocal. In 1964, he delivered "A Time for Choosing," a breakout political address on television in support of Republican Barry Goldwater's ill-fated presidential campaign. By this time, Reagan had completed his transformation from New Deal Democrat to small-government, pro-business Republican. In 1962, he formally joined the Republican Party. Reagan famously stated: "I didn't leave the Democratic party. The party left me."[2]

In 1966, Reagan was elected to the governorship of California, an office he held until 1974. He was popular in the Golden State. Over the next few years, Reagan trumpeted his brand of conservatism across the country through op-eds and radio broadcasts. After narrowly losing the Republican presidential nomination in 1976 to then President Gerald R. Ford, Reagan readily secured the nod in 1980. Along with his vice presidential running mate, George H. W. Bush, Reagan sounded a conservative theme of states' rights, lower taxes, a leaner federal bureaucracy, and a stronger national defense program. Reagan defeated the Democratic incumbent, President Jimmy Carter, by an Electoral College landslide, carrying forty-four states and winning 489 electoral votes to Carter's 49. On January 20, 1981, Reagan was sworn in by Chief Justice Warren Burger as the nation's fortieth president, becoming the oldest individual—at age sixty-nine—to be elected to that high office.

## Presidency

President Ronald Reagan took the presidential oath in 1981 armed with a clear vision of what constituted America's proper constitutional order—a vision his administration vigorously sought to implement. This constitutional vision consisted of two pivotal elements: separation of powers, which governed the ordering and operation of the federal government, and federalism, which guided the federal government's relationship with the several states.

According to William French Smith, Reagan's first attorney general, separation of powers served as "the ultimate guarantee of a working republic."[3] The Reagan administration understood separation of powers in Madisonian terms: no one branch of the federal government should be allowed to aggregate to itself undue power through which that branch might ultimately infringe on individual liberty. The arrogation of legislative, executive, and judicial authority within a single branch constituted "the very definition of tyranny."[4]

For President Reagan, the other priority was restoring the proper balance between the federal government and the states. In 1981, Reagan described federalism as "one of the underlying principles of our Constitution," and one to which his administration was "committed heart and soul." He explained: "The Founding Fathers saw the federal system as constructed something like a masonry wall: The States are the bricks, the National Government is the mortar. For the structure to stand plumb with the Constitution, there must be a proper mix of that brick and mortar."[5]

Reagan began by openly rejecting the FDR vision of a very powerful central government. He believed that the federal government, over time, had inappropriately conferred to Washington, D.C., many of the states' powers and responsibilities. Echoing the late (and iconic) Justice Louis Brandeis, Reagan referred to states as "dynamic laboratories of change in a creative society."[6] He wanted, therefore, to return power and responsibility to the states.

Thus, President Reagan immediately set out to accomplish his twin goals. He sought to rebalance the powers among the three branches of government and to limit (in certain respects) both Congress and the judiciary after years of what he considered overreaching. He also took steps to return spheres of power to the states—ushering in an era of new federalism—believing that the federal government had grown too amorphous and that states were better suited to represent the will of the citizenry. "I believe in people doing as much for themselves at the community level and at the private level," Reagan said in an August 1980 speech.[7] Reagan concentrated on states' rights partly with federal block grants as a means of giving states more power and flexibility with respect to receiving federal funding.[8] In addition, Reagan eventually issued an executive order that explicitly stated that the "presumption of sovereignty should rest with the individual States" and that any ambiguities should be resolved in favor of the states without national regulation.[9] Thus, he began to implement his new constitutional vision by revamping the relationship between the national government and the states, as well as between the executive, legislative, and judicial branches of the federal government.

### Attacking the "Legislative Veto"

Shortly after his election, Reagan was afforded an opportunity to deliver a major blow to what he viewed as congressional encroachment on the powers of the executive branch in the watershed case of *INS v. Chadha*. Jagdish Chadha, an Indian man born in Kenya but bearing a British passport, came to the United States in 1966 to attend Bowling Green State University. Upon graduation, Chadha found he had nowhere to go. His application for Kenyan citizenship was lost in bureaucratic limbo; to make matters worse, the nationalist Kenyan government was unsympathetic to Asians. Great Britain—inundated with Asian immigrants fleeing Kenya and Uganda— told Chadha to look elsewhere for residency. Chadha therefore determined to remain and work in the United States. When the Immigration and Naturalization Service (INS) discovered that Chadha had remained stateside after the expiration of his student visa, the agency ordered him deported.[10]

Yet the Immigration and Nationality Act permitted the executive branch, in the person of the attorney general, to suspend deportation orders of aliens having good moral character and who had been in the United States for seven years, if deportation would cause hardship. Thus, on June 25, 1974, an immigration judge (appointed by the attorney general) suspended Chadha's deportation order, as long as "Congress takes no action adverse to the order."[11]

The Immigration and Nationality Act, Section 244(c)(2), specifically required the attorney general to submit a list of suspensions of deportation orders to Congress for approval. Under the statute, either House was then empowered to overturn the suspension.[12] This override provision was, in effect, a legislative veto. Congress could "veto" what the executive branch was otherwise authorized to do. Such legislative vetoes were found in numerous laws. They were intended primarily as a legislative check on executive power. Presidents of both parties had long denounced these measures as unconstitutional.[13] Reagan's Department of Justice closely examined the concept of legislative veto and again concluded that it violated the constitutional principle of separation of powers.[14] Accordingly, the Reagan administration consistently opposed the device in the courts.[15]

Unfortunately for Chadha, Congress invoked its veto power to overturn the suspension of his deportation order. Again, Chadha was ordered deported. He appealed that decision, and the case slowly wended its way to the Supreme Court.[16] As Chadha's fate hung in limbo, the Supreme Court finally declared that the legislative veto—as exercised here—was unconstitutional. Chief Justice Warren E. Burger, writing for the majority, declared that the legislative veto, as a legislative act, had to adhere to the Constitution's carefully crafted requirements for enacting legislation. Because the particular veto in question required only the resolution of *one* house of Congress, it violated the bicameralism requirement of the Constitution that mandated that pieces of legislation be approved by both the House and Senate.[17] It also violated the Presentment Clause contained in Article I, Section 7, requiring bills to be presented to the president for his approval.[18] These requirements, Chief Justice Burger emphasized, "are integral parts of the constitutional design for the separation of powers."[19]

Later, in 1984, Chief Justice Burger listed *Chadha* as one of the fifty most important Supreme Court cases ever decided.[20] By rolling back this congressional assertion of power, the Supreme Court had, in Attorney General Smith's words, "helped reduce friction between the branches" by keeping each branch of government within its proper constitutional domain.[21] While legislative and committee vetoes continued to a certain extent because the legislative and executive branches found this practice to be mutually convenient, *Chadha* nonetheless represented a significant confirmation of the Reagan administration philosophy.[22]

## Challenging the Balanced Budget Law

In 1985, in response to the skyrocketing federal deficit (which had reached $211.9 billion at the end of the 1985 fiscal year), Congress passed the Balanced Budget and Emergency Deficit Control Act, otherwise known as the Gramm-Rudman-Hollings Act. The statute provided that if Congress and the president failed to make prescribed reductions in federal spending (to meet deficit-reduction goals), automatic cuts or "sequestration" would take place.

Section 251 of Gramm-Rudman-Hollings directed the comptroller general, as head of the Government Accounting Office, to instruct the president which cuts to make. President Reagan believed the statute was "an important step toward putting our fiscal house in order." Yet, Reagan signed the bill with reservations. By empowering the comptroller general—who functioned as an appendage of Congress—to decide which cuts the chief executive had to make, the statute seemed to confer executive authority on a legislative official. In President Reagan's view, this violated basic separation of powers principles.[23]

In *Bowsher v. Synar*, decided the following year, the Supreme Court agreed. Delivering the opinion of the Court, Chief Justice Burger wrote that because the comptroller general could be removed by Congress, he was, at bottom, a congressional agent.[24] Further, by instructing the president which budgetary cuts to make in the event of sequestration, the comptroller general was enforcing the law (an executive function). This therefore violated separation of powers and the Presentment Clause, Chief Justice Burger wrote, relying on *Chadha*: "The Framers recognized that, in the long term, structural protections against abuse of power were critical to preserving liberty."[25] The Court ruled, therefore, that this odd statutory mechanism for implementing budget cuts was constitutionally invalid.

### Executive Power: The PATCO Strike and Signing Statements

In addition to resisting congressional encroachment, President Reagan was determined to take affirmative steps to maintain the strength and independence of the executive branch. At the heart of a strong executive, he believed, was the vigorous power of enforcement—namely, the execution of the laws. He also believed that executive branch prerogatives in the legislative process had to be exerted and protected.

In early 1981, the nation's largest group of air traffic controllers—the Professional Air Traffic Controllers Organization (PATCO)—began negotiating the renewal of its contract with the Federal Aviation Administration (FAA). Negotiations did not go well. By the summer, PATCO and the FAA were on the verge of an impasse. Although it was illegal for federal employees to strike, PATCO had long prepared to do exactly that.[26] Indeed, the union went so far as to prepare its members for arrest and imprisonment. By March, 84 percent of the air traffic controllers represented by the union expressed their willingness to strike.[27] The FAA likewise prepared for the worst, ensuring that the agency could manage air traffic even without PATCO's members.[28] Finally, deep into the night on August 2, negotiations failed. Early the next morning, PATCO went on strike.

For President Reagan, the issue before him was clear: The air traffic controllers had violated a federal law prohibiting federal employees from striking, as well as a solemn oath not to strike.[29] Under the Take Care Clause in Article II, Section 3, it was the president's constitutional duty, he believed, to faithfully execute the law. Reagan's response was therefore unequivocal. In a press conference held on the first morning of the strike, he asserted: "I must tell those who fail to report for duty this morning they are in violation of the law, and if they do not report for work within 48 hours, they have forfeited their jobs and will be terminated."[30] Two days later, no fewer than eleven thousand air traffic controllers lost their jobs.[31]

Employing the bully pulpit, President Reagan maintained that he was the best friend organized labor ever had in the White House—indeed, he noted that as a member in good standing of the Screen Actors Guild, he was probably the only lifetime member of the AFL-CIO to hold the nation's highest office.[32] Yet, for Ronald Reagan as president, the law clearly stated that federal employees could not strike. For Reagan, the air traffic controllers had not been fired: "What they did was terminate their own employment by quitting."[33] Speaking afterward about the PATCO strike, Reagan opined: "Our freedom is secure because we're a nation governed by laws, not by men. We have the means to change the laws if they become unjust or onerous. We cannot, as citizens, pick and choose the laws we will or will not obey."[34]

In December 1981, in a *New York Times* poll, 48 percent of respondents said that President Reagan's firm handling of the PATCO strike was the thing they liked most about his job performance. In an NBC/AP poll, Reagan garnered a healthy 64 percent approval rating for his handling of the strike.[35] As scholar David Morgan observed at the time, "the [PATCO] story demonstrates many truths about American government and politics, but none more clearly than the effectiveness of the presidency when law and popular support are with it."[36] As the nation's chief executive, President Reagan fervently believed that it was his constitutional duty to enforce the law. By discharging this foundational duty, Reagan carried out his constitutional vision of a strong, independent executive.

President Reagan's commitment to maintain the constitutional prerogatives of the executive branch was also reflected in his use of the signing statement, the official pronouncement a president may issue upon signing a bill into law. Although signing statements originated in the Monroe administration, it was President Reagan who first put them to systematic use, wielding them as a presidential tool to assert executive authority in relation to Congress.[37] Reagan repeatedly issued signing statements to explain his understanding of statutory language, in anticipation of future judicial review, and occasionally to express his concerns regarding a statute's constitutionality.[38] In fact, the Reagan administration broke new and somewhat controversial ground when the attorney general at the time, Edwin Meese, advanced the significance of a presidential signing statement as a piece of legislative history. He arranged with the West Publishing Company to include the statements in the "Legislative History" section of the *United States Code Congressional and Administrative News*, a practice that continues to this day.[39]

## The Independent-Counsel Law and Iran-Contra

In 1978, in response to President Richard Nixon's wildly controversial firing of Special Prosecutor Archibald Cox during the so-called Saturday Night Massacre—Congress passed the Ethics in Government Act. Title VI of that far-reaching statute created the position of special prosecutor (later to be called independent counsel), an attorney to be appointed temporarily to investigate and prosecute wrongdoing by certain high-level executive branch officials, including the president. The special prosecutor was to be appointed upon a formal request made by the attorney general to a special panel of federal judges who were designated by the chief justice.[40] President Reagan's Justice Department harbored "serious reservations concerning the constitutionality of the act." After all, the Constitution vested the execution of the law—including the processes of investigation and prosecution—solely in the executive branch. Yet the special prosecutor was neither appointed by the president (contrary to the Appointments Clause) nor removable by the chief executive (or, more specifically, by the attorney general) except under extraordinary circumstances. For this reason, Attorney General Smith concluded, "the act appears fundamentally to contradict the principle of separation of powers erected by the Constitution."[41]

Despite the Reagan administration's steadfast opposition, Congress renewed the statute in 1982—when the position was renamed independent counsel—and again in 1987. By this time, President Reagan had won a second term, demolishing Jimmy Carter's former vice president, Walter Mondale, in the 1984 election, sweeping forty-nine of fifty states, and racking up 525 electoral votes—more than any other presidential candidate in U.S. history had won.[42] Yet now President Reagan and his administration were embroiled in a thorny scandal—the Iran-Contra affair—that had set into motion an independent-counsel investigation.

This episode flowed from the Reagan administration's secret arms sales to Iran (which was subject to an arms embargo), to fund the anticommunist Contra rebels in Nicaragua, when such aid had been forbidden by Congress.[43] The scandal resulted in the criminal indictment of Secretary of Defense Caspar Weinberger, although he was later pardoned by President George H. W. Bush before he could be tried. Oliver North, who facilitated the transfer of funds to the Contras, was convicted for his role in the operation, but his conviction was vacated because he had previously given congressional testimony after being granted immunity.

Ultimately, investigators found no direct evidence to indicate that President Reagan had knowledge of the operation; however, he was faulted with failing to provide proper oversight of his top aides. In a March 4, 1987, address to the nation from the Oval Office—after a special Commission headed by former Senator John Tower (R-TX) issued its report on the Iran-Contra matter—Reagan admitted that his administration had made mistakes on his watch. He stated that the plan had "deteriorated" from a well-intentioned "geopolitical strategy of reaching out to Iran" and turned into "trading arms for hostages." President Reagan acknowledged: "It was a mistake."[44]

Throughout the second half of President Reagan's second term, Independent Counsel Lawrence Walsh steamed forward with his Iran-Contra investigation, which turned into a major distraction for the Reagan White House. Critics charged that top-level White House officials had directly violated an act of Congress in diverting funds to the Contras and that the president himself had failed to fulfill his constitutional duty to "take care that the laws be faithfully executed."[45] The Reagan administration bristled at these allegations, asserting that the investigation was politically motivated and that the chief executive had wide latitude in the realm of foreign affairs. As the Iran-Contra probe expanded in scope, the president's supporters grew even more opposed to the independent-counsel law, which they believed had unleashed an unchecked prosecutor with a political agenda to harm the Reagan White House.

It was therefore a double blow to the Reagan administration when the Supreme Court overwhelmingly (seven to one) upheld the independent-counsel statute in the watershed case of *Morrison v. Olson*. Delivering the opinion of the Court, Chief Justice William H. Rehnquist roundly rejected the administration's constitutional arguments set forth in their amici briefs, broadly concluding: "The Act does not violate separation of powers principles by impermissibly interfering with the functions of the Executive Branch."[46]

The *Morrison* decision was, as described in the *New York Times*, "a stunning rebuff to the Reagan Administration."[47] It would take over a decade, and a controversial independent-counsel investigation during another presidency, before Congress itself would conclude that the independent-counsel law was fundamentally flawed. At that point, Congress allowed the law to expire, thus vindicating the Reagan administration's position.[48] Meanwhile, the thorny Iran-Contra investigation remained a major distraction during Reagan's second term.

## *Reshaping the Federal Judiciary*

Judicial restraint was at the heart of Ronald Reagan's view of the judiciary. As he saw it, "courts had sometimes gone too far in interfering with the constitutional prerogatives of other branches of government" turning into a form of "judicial activism."[49] The separation-of-powers principle, properly understood, required that judges refrain from making or enforcing the law; their task was limited to *interpreting* it. President Reagan and his administration believed it was their duty to restore and to protect this classical model.

Because the federal judiciary vitally shaped the constitutional order, the Reagan administration took judicial appointments "very seriously."[50] Thus, in Attorney General Smith's words, they "thoroughly reviewed and revamped" the process of selecting judicial appointees, creating the Office of Legal Policy within the Justice Department to oversee the process.

Because of this systematic approach, few presidents have had a greater impact on the federal judiciary and the Supreme Court than Reagan did. During his first year in office, fulfilling a campaign promise to appoint a highly qualified woman to the High Court, Reagan appointed Sandra Day O'Connor, a state appeals judge in Arizona, to replace the retiring Justice Potter Stewart.[51] Justice O'Connor thus became the first female on the Supreme Court in American history. In 1986, when Chief Justice Warren Burger stepped down, Reagan elevated the Court's most conservative jurist, William H. Rehnquist, to serve as chief justice. The president then appointed an equally conservative jurist and a founder of the Federalist Society—Judge Antonin Scalia—to fill Rehnquist's seat. All of these justices were generally committed to Reagan's philosophy of federalism and states' rights.

To complete his overhaul of the Court, in 1987, Reagan sought to appoint the intellectual leader of the conservative legal movement, U.S. Court of Appeals Judge Robert Bork, to replace Justice Lewis Powell.[52] Democrats in the Senate, led by Senator Edward M. Kennedy of Massachusetts, launched a sustained attack on the Bork nomination, branding Bork an extremist and pointing to his role in carrying out President Nixon's order to fire Watergate Special Prosecutor Archibald Cox during the Saturday Night Massacre. Bork lost the nomination by a vote of fifty-eight to forty-two, largely along party lines. Next, Reagan nominated Judge Douglas Ginsburg, who withdrew after admitting that he had years earlier experimented with marijuana.[53] Finally, seeking a less controversial choice, Reagan appointed federal appeals judge Anthony Kennedy of California, a more moderate conservative, who was swiftly confirmed.

Even as President Reagan reshaped the Supreme Court, his administration took unprecedented steps to retool the judicial branch in other ways. Besides appointing young, conservative jurists to the federal bench, the Reagan administration developed tools to encourage federal judges to hew to the text and original intent of the framers of the Constitution.[54]

Reagan's strategy, despite some setbacks, seemed to work. Indeed, his appointments to the Supreme Court came to form the core of what commentators later dubbed "the Federalism Five": Associate Justices Sandra Day O'Connor, Antonin Scalia, and Anthony Kennedy and Chief Justice Rehnquist (along with Clarence Thomas, appointed by President George H. W. Bush).[55] Reagan well understood the bedrock importance of these nominations. "It takes leadership from the Supreme Court," he said, "to help shape the attitudes of the courts in our land and to make sure that principles of law are based on the Constitution."[56] In 2003, scholar Dawn E. Johnsen studied the Rehnquist Court decisions and made this observation: "Since 1995, the Rehnquist Court has begun adopting theories of congressional power and federalism strikingly similar to those developed in the reports of the Reagan Justice Department."[57] Thus, through his Supreme Court and other judicial appointees, Reagan made notable strides towards implementing his federalism vision.[58]

## Conclusion

President Reagan retired to his home in the Bel Air community of Los Angeles; he also spent time horseback riding and relaxing at his ranch near Santa Barbara. Later, in 1994, Reagan revealed in a handwritten letter to the nation that he was suffering from Alzheimer's disease. His wife, Nancy, continued to care for him at home, where he died on June 5, 2004, at the age of ninety-three. In Washington, throngs of mourners—including dignitaries and thousands of ordinary citizens—flocked to the nation's capital to pay their final respects.

President Ronald Reagan and his administration had entered office with a clear vision of the proper constitutional order, one that turned on the dual principles of separation of powers and federalism. The president and his administration proactively and consistently worked to realize this vision in each branch of the federal government and in the federal government's relationship with the states. Despite the damage done to his second term by the Iran-Contra scandal and the resulting investigation, President Reagan's popularity continued to soar. The "Reagan Revolution," which sought to realign the federal government to reflect a more conservative view of the federal government's role in American life, took root. As a result, the Reagan constitutional legacy has continued to grow, rather than to diminish, in the years since the fortieth president's death.

## NOTES

1. Reagan and Wyman had two children, Maureen and Michael, the latter of whom was adopted. Reagan and Nancy Davis had two children of their own, Patricia and Ronald Prescott.

2. Dana Milbank, "The New Party of Reagan," *Washington Post*, July 19, 2011, www.washingtonpost.com/opinions/the-new-party-of-reagan/2011/07/19/gIQAuckfOI_story.html.

3. William French Smith, *Challenge, Change, and Achievement: The Department of Justice 1981–1985* (Washington, DC: U.S. Department of Justice, 1985), 13.

4. According to Madison, the true safeguard of American liberty lay not in "parchment barriers," but in the supremacy of each branch within its own proper sphere—and its foundational ability to repel encroachments by the other branches. Office of Legal Policy, *The Constitution in the Year 2000: Choices Ahead in the Constitutional Interpretation* (Washington, DC: U.S. Department of Justice, 1988), 169.

5. Ronald Reagan, "Remarks at the Annual Convention of the National Conference of State Legislatures in Atlanta, Georgia July 30, 1981," *The Public Papers of President Ronald W. Reagan*, Ronald Reagan Presidential Library, Simi Valley, CA (hereafter cited as *Public Papers of Reagan*), www.reagan.utexas.edu/archives/speeches/1981/73081d.htm.

6. Ronald Reagan, "Address Before a Joint Session of the Congress on the State of the Union January 25, 1983," *Public Papers of Reagan*, www.reagan.utexas.edu/archives/speeches/1983/12583c.htm.

7. Ronald Reagan, speech at Neshoba County (Mississippi) Fair, 1980, transcript, *Neshoba Democrat*, November 15, 2007, http://neshobademocrat.com/main.asp?SectionID=2&SubSectionID=297&ArticleID=15599&TM=60417.67.

8. These block grants were designed to be a means to provide the states with a "fairly broad purpose and [with] few conditions attached." Andrew Busch, *Ronald Reagan and the Politics of Freedom* (Lanham, MD: Rowman & Littlefield Publishers, 2001), 37.

9. Executive Order 12612, October 26, 1987: Federalism, Federal Register, vol. 52. no. 210.

10. Barbara Hinkson Craig, *Chadha: The Story of an Epic Constitutional Struggle* (New York: Oxford University Press, 1988), 7–9.

11. Quoted in ibid., 19.

12. Ibid., 19–20. These vetoes were relatively rare. Of the 5,701 suspensions between 1952 and 1981, Congress vetoed only 229.

13. Ibid., 53.

14. Specifically, the Reagan Justice Department concluded that the veto device violated the Constitution's requirement of bicameralism as well as the Presentment Clause. Further, the legislative veto conferred on Congress an unconstitutional check on the executive branch.

15. Craig, *Chadha*, 150–172; William French Smith, *Law & Justice in the Reagan Administration: Memoirs of an Attorney General* (Stanford, CA: Hoover Institution Press, 1991), 281–321.

16. Craig, *Chadha*, 90.

17. Congress is a *bicameral* body, consisting of two chambers: the House of Representatives and the Senate. While the House of Representatives was intended to reflect the popular will of the people, the framers envisioned the Senate as a stabilizing force that would be less susceptible to the whims of the masses.

18. The Presentment Clause outlines the process by which a congressional bill becomes a law of the United States. After passage in the House and the Senate, a bill must be presented to the president for signature. The president then has the option to sign the bill into law or to veto it. A presidential veto has the effect of nullifying the bill, but Congress can override the veto through a two-thirds vote, first in the chamber where the bill originated, and then in the other chamber. U.S. Const. art. I, § 7, cl. 2, 3.

19. INS v. Chadha, 462 U.S. 919 (1983).

20. Craig, *Chadha*, 232.

21. Smith, *Challenge, Change, and Achievement*, 13. *Chadha*, however, did not completely kill the legislative veto. Congress continued to include the vetoes in legislation during Reagan's presidency. Reagan signed some into law and vetoed others. Martin Tolchin, "In Spite of the Court, the Legislative Veto Lives On," *New York Times*, December 21, 1983. Writing in 2009, Ellis says that since *Chadha*, presidents have signed into law more than five hundred legislative vetoes. Richard Ellis, *Judging Executive Power: Sixteen Supreme Court Cases That Have Shaped the American Presidency* (Lanham, MD: Rowman & Littlefield, 2009), 71–72.

22. Louis Fisher, "The Legislative Veto: Invalidated, It Survives," *Law and Contemporary Problems* 56, no. 4 (1993): 288–291.

23. Ronald Reagan, "Statement on Signing the Bill Increasing the Public Debt Limit and Enacting the Balanced Budget and Emergency Deficit Control Act of 1985 December 12, 1985," *Public Papers of Reagan*, www.reagan.utexas.edu/archives/speeches/1985/121285a.htm; Kate Stith, "Rewriting the Fiscal Constitution: The Case of Gramm-Rudman-Hollings," *California Law Review* 76, no. 3 (1988): 595–599.

24. Bowsher v. Synar, 478 U.S. 714 (1986). As in *Chadha*, Reagan's Department of Justice was the nominal defendant but agreed with the plaintiffs that the statutory provision under consideration was unconstitutional.

25. Ibid., 730. Justices Stevens and Marshall concurred, concluding that the comptroller general was essentially making legislative decisions in balancing the budget; if this was the case, he should have to go through the same two-step lawmaking process—with the House and Senate enacting legislation to implement the budget measures—and then having the bill presented to the president. In their view, therefore, the act violated

the principle of bicameralism and the Presentment Clause. Ibid., 754. Either under the majority view, or the concurring view, the balanced budget law violated separation of powers principles.

26. Art Shostak, "An Unhappy Anniversary: The Patco Strike in Retrospective," *New Labor Forum* 15, no. 3 (2006): 76. Shostak, who was sympathetic to PATCO and who worked as its pollster, stated the organization prepared for a strike for two years.

27. Ibid., 78; Joseph A. McCartin, *Collision Course: Ronald Reagan, the Air Traffic Controllers, and the Strike That Changed America* (New York: Oxford University Press, 2011), 278–279, notes that 84 percent may be an inflated number, as strike supporters were more likely to return the survey than those who were opposed to striking.

28. McCartin, *Collision Course*, 281–282. The FAA readied replacement employees, for example, and prepared its Kansas City training center for an influx of trainees.

29. The Civil Service Reform Act stated: "An individual may not accept or hold a position in the Government of the United States or the government of the District of Columbia if he . . . participates in a strike, or asserts the right to strike, against the Government of the United States or the government of the District of Columbia." The oath the air traffic controllers swore stated: "I am not participating in any strike against the Government of the United States or any agency thereof, and I will not so participate while an employee of the Government of the United States or any agency thereof."

30. Ronald Reagan, "Remarks and a Question-and-Answer Session with Reporters on the Air Traffic Controllers Strike August 3, 1981," *Public Papers of Reagan*, www.reagan. utexas.edu/archives/speeches/1981/80381a.htm.

31. Arthur B. Shostak and David Skocik, *The Air Controllers' Controversy: Lessons from the PATCO Strike* (New York: Human Sciences Press, 1986), 16.

32. Ironically, during the 1980 presidential campaign, then Governor Reagan wrote to the president of PATCO, Robert E. Poli, assuring him that he would "take whatever steps are necessary" to improve the situation of air traffic controllers, pledging to "work very closely with you to bring about a spirit of cooperation." Three days later, PATCO endorsed Governor Reagan for president—one of only a handful of major unions to do so. Ibid., 79–80, 91. David Morgan noted, however, that Reagan did not promise to allow PATCO to strike. David Morgan, "Terminal Flight: The Air Traffic Controllers' Strike of 1981," *Journal of American Studies* 18, no. 2 (1984): 165, n. 1.

33. Ronald Reagan, "Remarks on Signing the Economic Recovery Tax Act of 1981 and the Omnibus Budget Reconciliation Act of 1981, and a Question-and-Answer Session with Reporters August 13, 1981," *Public Papers of Reagan*, www.reagan.utexas.edu/archives/speeches/1981/81381a.htm.

34. Ronald Reagan, "Remarks in Chicago, Illinois, at the Annual Convention and Centennial Observance of the United Brotherhood of Carpenters and Joiners September 3, 1981," *Public Papers of Reagan*, www.reagan.utexas.edu/archives/speeches/1981/90381a. htm. In the end, Reagan decided to allow the PATCO members who struck to apply for federal employment again after three years; however, they could not return to work for the FAA.

35. Morgan, "Air Traffic Controllers' Strike," 181, 172.

36. Ibid., 182.

37. Curtis A. Bradley and Eric A. Posner, "Presidential Signing Statements and Executive Power," *Constitutional Commentary* 23 (2006): 307, 312–313.

38. "The President's Role in the Legislative Process," in "Developments in the Law: Presidential Authority," *Harvard Law Review* 125 (June 2012): 2073–2075.

39. American Bar Association, "Report of the Task Force on Presidential Signing Statements and the Separation of Powers Doctrine," 2006, www.americanbar.org/content/dam/aba/migrated/leadership/2006/annual/dailyjournal/20060823144113.authcheckdam.pdf, 10.

40. Ken Gormley, "An Original Model of the Independent Counsel Statute," *Michigan Law Review* 97, no. 3 (1998): 602–604, 608–626, explains that the original purpose of the special prosecutor, as envisioned by Congress in 1973, was twofold: "to prevent the recurrence of a naked exercise of executive power" and "to build into the American system of government a failsafe mechanism that would protect future generations from constitutional meltdowns." The Court handling these matters was referred to as a Special Division of the U.S. Court of Appeals for the District of Columbia Circuit.

41. Smith, *Law & Justice*, 176. These complaints were not new. The constitutionality of the special prosecutor had been hotly debated in Congress during the 1970s. Robert H. Bork, as acting attorney general, said: "The Executive alone has the duty and the power to enforce the laws by prosecutions brought before the courts." Quoted in Gormley, "An Original Model," 611. For a discussion of Myers v. United States, 272 U.S. 52 (1926), which had given the president board power when it came to removing executive branch officials, see Chapter 30, "Calvin Coolidge."

42. See generally Michael Schaller, *Ronald Reagan* (New York: Oxford University Press, 2011).

43. For an overview of the Iran-Contra Affair, see Bob Woodward, *VEIL: The Secret Wars of the CIA 1981–1987* (New York: Simon & Schuster, 1987). For the independent counsel's account of the scandal, see Lawrence E. Walsh, *Firewall: The Iran-Contra Conspiracy and Cover-Up* (New York: W.W. Norton, 1997).

44. Ronald Reagan, "Address to the National on the Iran Arms and Contra Aid Controversy," March 4, 1987, *The American Presidency Project*, ed. Gerhard Peters and John T. Woolley, www.presidency.ucsb.edu/ws/index.php?pid=33938&st=&st1=.

45. U.S. Const. art. II, § 2, cl. 8.

46. Morrison v. Olson, 487 U.S. 654 (1988). Many scholars who commented on *Morrison* affirmed the Court's ruling. Gormley, "An Original Model," 636. For criticism, see Akhil Reed Amar, "Now Playing . . . A Constitutional Nightmare," *Washington Post*, September 20, 1998; Akhil Reed Amar, "Intratextualism," *Harvard Law Review* 112, no. 4 (1999): 747–727.

47. Stuart Taylor Jr., "Supreme Court Vote Upholds Law on Special Prosecutors; 7–1 Ruling Is Rebuff to Reagan; Scalia in Dissent," *New York Times*, June 30, 1988.

48. This author was appointed independent counsel in the Whitewater matter and related investigations during the Clinton presidency. Congress allowed the independent counsel statute to expire in 1999; the author testified in favor of this result because of separation of powers and other problems inherent in the law.

49. Ronald Reagan, "Remarks During a White House Briefing for United States Attorneys October 21, 1985," *Public Papers of Reagan*, www.reagan.utexas.edu/archives/speeches/1985/102185a.htm.

50. Smith, *Law & Justice*, 57–58. Attorney General Smith said: "The main reason we did was our firm belief that judicial activism—the policy of judges substituting their own attitudes and feelings for the laws as passed by the legislatures—had become far too widespread. We believed that the groundswell of conservatism that swept Ronald Reagan into office in 1980 made it an opportune time to urge on the courts a return to fundamental legal principles, thereby diminishing judicial activism." Ibid., 58.

51. Ronald Reagan, "Statement on Senate Confirmation of Sandra Day O'Connor as an Associate Justice of the Supreme Court of the United States September 21, 1981," *Public Papers of Reagan*, www.reagan.utexas.edu/archives/speeches/1981/92181d.htm.

52. Ronald Reagan, "Remarks Announcing the Nomination of Robert H. Bork to Be an Associate Justice of the Supreme Court of the United States July 1, 1987," *Public Papers of Reagan*, www.reagan.utexas.edu/archives/speeches/1987/070187c.htm. In nominating Judge Bork, President Reagan stated: "Judge Bork, widely regarded as the most prominent and intellectually powerful advocate of judicial restraint, shares my view that judges' personal preferences and values should not be part of their constitutional interpretations."

53. Ronald Reagan, "Remarks Announcing the Nomination of Douglas H. Ginsburg to Be an Associate Justice of the United States Supreme Court October 29, 1987," *Public Papers of Reagan*, www.reagan.utexas.edu/archives/speeches/1987/102987g.htm.

54. In 1988, the Office of Legal Policy created by Reagan's Justice Department issued *Guidelines on Constitutional Litigation* "to help ensure that principled and consistent positions are advocated by all Executive Branch litigators." A large portion of *Guidelines* emphasized the limitation on the federal government's power implicit in the enumeration of powers. It also discussed the "Protection of State Sovereignty," declaring that "government attorneys should argue that the Constitution protects the sovereignty of the states and that the federal courts have a duty to enforce the Constitution in this regard." *Guidelines* cited the Tenth Amendment as the constitutional grounds on which states' rights ought to be protected. U.S. Department of Justice, Office of Legal Policy, *Guidelines on Constitutional Litigation* (Washington, DC: U.S. Department of Justice, 1988), 1, 36–55. Although these guidelines were designed for government litigators, the broader goal was to influence the judicial branch itself. Litigators were instructed to include in their briefs a section discussing "the text and original understanding of the relevant constitutional provisions, along with an analysis of how the case would be resolved consistent with that understanding." Ibid., 10. The theory was to this effect: By looking to the text of the Constitution, as interpreted by government litigators, federal judges would begin more clearly to see and implement important principles as originally intended by the founders.

55. On the Federalism Five, see John Q. Barrett, "The 'Federalism Five' as Supreme Court Nominees, 1971–1991," *St. John's Journal of Legal Commentary* 21, no. 2 (2007): 485–496. As Dawn E. Johnsen explained, "almost every Rehnquist Court decision that narrowed congressional power and expanded state sovereignty was decided by the same

five-to-four margin." Dawn E. Johnsen, "Ronald Reagan and the Rehnquist Court on Congressional Power: Presidential Influences on Constitutional Change," *Indiana Law Journal* 78, no. 363 (2003): 17.

56. Ronald Reagan, "Address to the Nation on the Supreme Court Nomination of Robert H. Bork October 14, 1987," *Public Papers of Reagan*, www.reagan.utexas.edu/archives/speeches/1987/101487b.htm.

57. Johnsen, "Ronald Reagan and the Rehnquist Court," 3.

58. Johnsen's argument ought to be tempered with that of Mark Tushnet. While acknowledging the new and substantial strides the Rehnquist Court took toward limiting the federal government, few of the constitutional law changes outlined in U.S. Department of Justice, Office of Legal Policy, *Guidelines*, came to pass. The Supreme Court took a few steps in that direction but quickly stopped. Tushnet stated, in conclusion: "The cases are available for more substantial development in the future, but for now the Court has moved back only inches from where the Warren Court left it. For all practical purposes, the expansive national government that is the constitutional legacy of the New Deal and the Great Society remain[s] with us." Mark Tushnet, "'Meet the New Boss': The New Judicial Center," *North Carolina Law Review* 83 (2005): 1226.

# 41

# George H. W. Bush

LORI COX HAN

*President George H. W. Bush ("Bush 41") was a one-term president who some detractors believed lacked the charisma, vision, and political skill of his predecessor, Ronald Reagan. Consequently, Bush's domestic record was mixed; it was worsened when he broke his "no new taxes" pledge. Yet Bush exercised his constitutional powers in the realm of foreign policy with strength and decisiveness, driving Iraqi dictator Saddam Hussein from Kuwait, in an impressive military victory that used modern technology to redefine warfare. Bush 41 also strongly defended respect for the American flag and patriotism, failing in an effort to amend the Constitution to ban desecrating the flag, but laying the groundwork for a more ardent appeal to patriotism a decade later, when his son George W. Bush became commander in chief.*

# Introduction

The presidency of George H. W. Bush represented a time of both political continuity and transition. Because he had served as Ronald Reagan's vice president for eight years before his own election to the presidency in 1988, the assumption when Bush took the oath of office was that he would continue the Reagan legacy in terms of conservative values and strong leadership. But the American political environment in which Bush needed to govern was changing dramatically by the start of the 1990s. So, too, was the international landscape as the Cold War began to end. Although Bush failed to secure a second term, losing his reelection bid to Bill Clinton in 1992, he is nonetheless remembered as a strong foreign policy steward. Moreover, Bush's willingness to exercise his presidential power so forcefully (particularly in the Persian Gulf War) would lay the foundation for future presidents—including his son and namesake—to take that power a step further.

One of five children born to Prescott and Dorothy Walker Bush, George Herbert Walker Bush arrived in 1924 and would follow his own father's lead at many points during his life. Both attended Yale University, both became successful businessmen early in life, and both would follow up that success with careers in politics and public service. Prescott Bush served as a two-term U.S. senator from Connecticut from 1952 to 1963, a period that began what some refer to as the Bush political dynasty. George H. W. Bush's vast political network, coupled with his success in the private sector and family ties to politics, represents the type of résumé that many presidential hopefuls envy.

At an early age, Bush entered the military and became a decorated World War II veteran. He postponed attending Yale University to enlist in the U.S. Navy in 1942. In 1943, at the age of nineteen, he became the youngest naval aviator at that time. Through 1944, Bush flew fifty-eight combat missions in the Pacific theater as part of the torpedo squadron on the USS *San Jacinto* and survived after his plane was shot down by Japanese anti-aircraft gunners over the Pacific island of Chi Chi Jima. He received the Distinguished Flying Cross, three Air Medals, and the Presidential Unit Citation awarded to the crew of the San Jacinto.

After his military service, Bush married Barbara Pierce in 1945 and began his studies at Yale, where he also played baseball. After graduating from Yale and enjoying professional success in the oil business, in 1966, Bush won a seat in the U.S. House of Representatives from Texas. Although he lost a race for the U.S. Senate in 1970, Bush was U.S. ambassador to the United Nations from 1971 to 1973 and served as Republican National Committee chairman from 1973 to 1974, chief of the Liaison Office to the People's Republic of China from 1974 to 1976, and director of the Central Intelligence Agency from 1976 to 1977. After an unsuccessful bid for the Republican presidential nomination in 1980, Bush became former rival Ronald Reagan's running mate and served as his vice president from 1981 to 1989.[1] Eight years later, Bush would defeat Governor Michael Dukakis of Massachusetts in the 1988 presidential election, winning with an impressive 53 percent of the popular vote, carrying forty states and winning 426 Electoral College votes.

## Presidency

Most observers of the Bush years agree that he was a cautious and prudent president who saw his role as that of a manager and caretaker of the federal government, as opposed to a visionary leader. Bush utilized his vast party and government experience, coupled with his experience in foreign affairs, to handle the job with adeptness.[2] Yet, Bush was challenged from the start to define his own presidency separate from that of his predecessor, the popular and charismatic Ronald Reagan. Right from the outset, Bush had to contend with the long shadow being cast on his presidency by the conservative policy agenda and skilled rhetoric of the Reagan presidency. In truth, the Bush presidency was not merely a redux of the Reagan years. As presidential scholar John Robert Greene has noted, the political environment in which Bush attempted to govern was created, in part, by the "economic instability and cultural anxiety" created by the Reagan years.[3] While Reagan had rolled back government regulations in areas such as environmental policy and supported cutbacks to programs such as Medicaid and Head Start, Bush believed he needed to revive commitments to some of these federal programs.

Bush often appeared to be politically handcuffed to Reagan policies. The conservative base of the Republican Party expected President Bush to continue the Reagan policy agenda, but Bush was not Reagan in terms of vision or political skill. Moreover, Bush was tarred with the Iran-Contra scandal, which lingered into his presidency and periodically flared up as Independent Counsel Lawrence Walsh marched forward with prosecutions against high-level Reagan administration officials.[4] Additionally, Bush faced increased partisanship from a Congress controlled by Democrats, whose own long-standing New Deal coalition had fractured and who were struggling to redefine their own party's agenda. During his four years in office, Bush vetoed forty-four pieces of legislation (fifteen of which were pocket vetoes). Yet Bush seemed comfortable engaging in political compromise. Domestically, this skill was evident when he signed the Omnibus Budget Reconciliation Act of 1990, in which he brokered a deal with both Democrats and Republicans in Congress to raise taxes in order to reduce the federal deficit and debt, a politically complicated maneuver. Although many now credit this move as the first important step that allowed the strong economic growth of the mid to late 1990s, Bush was, at the time, pilloried by Democrats and conservatives within his own party for breaking his "no new taxes" pledge in 1988, in which he had famously proclaimed: "Read my lips: No new taxes."

A president who was more interested in substance than style, Bush was confronted with an increasingly competitive news media that focused on personalized and negative political coverage. This approach left Bush at a disadvantage in seeking to engage in a substantive dialogue on policy issues. By 1989, the twenty-four-hour news cycle had emerged. Unfortunately, as one author has noted, "Bush's public style (or perhaps lack of interest in developing a public style and image) would have been better suited for the news media environment of an earlier time like the 1960s, when the national news cycle was still driven more by words than by images."[5]

## Shaping the Supreme Court

Major constitutional questions working their way through the federal courts during the Bush Presidency included abortion rights, affirmative action, gender discrimination, federalism, and states' rights. Although Bush seemed less interested in following in the footsteps of the Reagan administration when it came to returning the judicial branch and, specifically, the Supreme Court, to a more restrained branch of government that would not engage in the policymaking process, he nonetheless remained committed to leaving his own conservative mark on the courts.[6]

Both of the Bush nominations to the Supreme Court provided the president with an opportunity to replace liberal stalwarts with justices who held stricter and more conservative views of the Constitution. The first such opportunity came in 1990 with the retirement of Associate Justice William Brennan, an Eisenhower nominee who had played a significant role in the expansion of civil rights and civil liberties during the Warren Court era (1954–1969). The Bush White House advanced the name of David Souter of New Hampshire as a "believer in judicial restraint, a tough trial court judge with a great legal mind who will interpret the Constitution not legislate from the bench" because of "his fidelity to the Constitution and the rule of law."[7]

Ironically, Souter's tenure on the Court did not live up to the expectations of the president who had nominated him or Republican Party conservatives who had been assured in 1990 that Souter would be a reliable conservative vote on key issues. Instead, Souter became more often than not a reliable liberal vote during his nineteen years on the Court, joining his more liberal colleagues in high-profile decisions in areas such as upholding abortion rights, banning school prayer, and limiting the scope of the death penalty.[8]

Perhaps no confirmation hearing (at least since Ronald Reagan's failed nomination of Judge Robert Bork) was as controversial as that of Clarence Thomas in 1991. Nominated by Bush to replace the ailing Thurgood Marshall (who had been appointed by Lyndon Johnson in 1967 as the first African American on the Supreme Court), Thomas brought strictly conservative legal views as well as an unexpected burst of controversy to the proceedings. An African American who had served as the head of the Equal Employment Opportunity Commission (EEOC) during the Reagan years, Thomas was a staunch conservative who represented the polar opposite of Thurgood Marshall's liberal, pro-civil-rights views. Thomas had served only a short period on the U.S. Court of Appeals for the District of Columbia before Bush nominated him for the nation's high court. When the president nominated Thomas, Bush had described him as "a fiercely independent thinker with an excellent legal mind who believes passionately in equal opportunity for all Americans" and as a justice who would "approach the cases that come before the Court with a commitment to deciding them fairly, as the facts and the law require."[9]

The confirmation hearings were going smoothly, and on September 27, the Judiciary Committee voted thirteen to one send Thomas's name to the Senate for debate. Unexpectedly, however, accusations of sexual harassment were leaked to the national press and exploded like a bombshell. An Oklahoma University Law School professor named Anita Hill claimed that Thomas had sexually harassed her while he was her supervisor at the EEOC. In the midst of this uproar, Hill and Thomas were called to testify before the Senate Judiciary Committee. Thomas emphatically denied the allegations; nevertheless, the hearings received wall-to-wall coverage on television, creating a soap-opera-like drama. The confirmation hearings also sparked a national debate about sexual harassment in the workplace. In the end, Thomas was confirmed by a narrow vote of fifty-two to forty-eight. Many credited the intense interest in the Thomas confirmation hearings with producing the Year of the Woman in 1992. That year, a record number of women ran for and were elected to public office at the state and federal level as a reaction to the appointment of Thomas.[10] Yet the controversial Thomas confirmation hearings also led to criticism of President Bush, who had touted Thomas as "the best qualified (nominee) at this time," and who seemed insensitive (in the eyes of some critics) to Hill's charges.[11]

## Presidential War Powers and the Persian Gulf War

The buildup to the 1991 Persian Gulf War, although viewed in the international community as a lawful use of military force to repel unlawful aggression, created ample political tension between Congress and President Bush concerning each branch's role with respect to war powers.[12] Indeed, the constitutional debate would foreshadow a similar disagreement that would rekindle itself twelve years later, when the elder Bush's son, President George W. Bush, would seek to reignite hostilities with Iraq.

In August 1990, the threat of instability in the Middle East, coupled with a major disruption in America's oil supply, loomed large. Iraqi leader Saddam Hussein's sizable army had surged into Kuwait, a tiny nation and a U.S. ally situated between Iraq, Saudi Arabia, and the Persian Gulf. President Bush, aware of the risks posed by Iraq's belligerence, reacted aggressively by deploying over 100,000 U.S. troops to Saudi Arabia in what became dubbed Operation Desert Shield. By January 15, 1991, coalition personnel in the region numbered 430,000.[13]

In an effort to drum up strong international support for military action against Iraq, Bush worked closely with the United Nations and secured authorization in November 1990 to "use all necessary means" to remove Iraqi forces from Kuwait.[14] In sharp contrast to these efforts to gain international support, however, Bush did not seek a resolution of support from Congress before initiating the buildup. When pressed by members of Congress who questioned the president's power to unilaterally order such a deployment, Bush defended his conduct by declaring that its purpose was not to wage war—but to defend Saudi Arabia from further Iraqi aggression and to encourage a peaceful resolution to the conflict.[15] Despite these assurances, some members of Congress continued to doubt that the president possessed the authority to conduct offensive military operations against Iraq given the legislature's exclusive constitutional power to declare war. Accordingly, these members of the legislature pressed the courts to enjoin the president from initiating or continuing hostilities. In the resulting case, *Dellums v. Bush*, a district judge held that although individual members of Congress had standing to sue, the action was not ripe for adjudication by the courts, because a majority of Congress had not asserted that its constitutional war-declaration powers had been violated by the president.[16]

Ultimately, President Bush gained congressional approval to use military force for the limited purpose of expelling the forces of Iraqi dictator Saddam Hussein from Kuwait.[17] Meanwhile, Bush's signing statement on January 14 reasserted his view that the president was free to use America's armed forces as he saw fit to defend U.S. interests abroad.[18] Three days later, in the early morning of January 17, U.S. forces led a massive air offensive against Iraq. Operation Desert Storm was a sophisticated military operation that utilized technology to redefine modern warfare. Using Patriot missiles, laser-guided Stealth bombers, and infrared equipment to hit targets in absolute darkness, the U.S. strike obliterated the Iraqi Air Force. Not since President William McKinley had used new technology to enable him to serve as commander in chief remotely from the White House during the Spanish-American War and since President Truman had dropped the atom bomb on Japan had a president deployed new technology so effectively and redefined warfare so dramatically.

Throughout the military buildup, Bush maintained that as commander in chief, he possessed inherent constitutional authority to initiate military action against Iraq, with or without congressional approval. Thus, although

Congress played a role in the decision to go to war, Bush's approach to the conflict illustrated a continued reluctance by the president to meaningfully involve the legislative branch in this war-making process.[19] Perhaps because his operation to obliterate Iraq's military defense was so successful, Bush was able to brush off Congress's involvement and win this test of authority.

## Political Speech and Flag Burning

The presidential campaign of 1988 had produced some of the most negative attacks between the two candidates seen in the modern era.[20] Among the most effective negative attacks launched by the Bush campaign against Michael Dukakis's record as Massachusetts governor had been the charge that Dukakis was unpatriotic. The reason, according the Bush campaign, was that Dukakis had failed to support a Massachusetts bill to make the Pledge of Allegiance mandatory in public schools.[21]

Ironically, while patriotism and allegiance to the flag worked as a positive campaign message for Bush in 1988, one of the more high-profile decisions handed down by the Supreme Court during Bush's first year in office addressed the issue of flag burning. The decision tested Bush's willingness to cross the Supreme Court to defend respect for the flag. In *Texas v. Johnson* (1989), the Court ruled five to four that the burning of an American flag was protected as symbolic speech by the First Amendment's Freedom of Speech Clause. The Court overturned the conviction of Gregory Johnson, who under a Texas state law had been convicted of burning an American flag outside the 1984 Republican National Convention in Dallas. The Court's decision had the effect of invalidating similar laws banning flag burning in forty-eight states. In his majority opinion, Justice William Brennan wrote: "Under the circumstances, Johnson's burning of the flag constituted expressive conduct, permitting him to invoke the First Amendment . . . [and] the government may not prohibit the expression of an idea simply because society finds the idea itself offensive or disagreeable."[22]

Bush did not view the Court's decision favorably; the president had long expressed his devotion to and respect for the American flag and its patriotic symbolism.[23] In response to the Court's decision in *Texas v. Johnson*, Bush immediately sought a constitutional amendment to ban flag burning. While polls showed a large majority of Americans agreed with the president, Democrats in Congress pushed back. Rather than take the dramatic step of seeking to amend the Constitution to achieve their goal, Congress passed H.R. 2978. Also known as the Flag Protection Act of 1989, the bill provided for a prison term of up to one year for anyone who "knowingly mutilates, defaces, physically defiles, burns, maintains on the floor or ground, or tramples upon" a U.S. flag. Although the act was good politics for Congress, Bush knew that it would never withstand the Court's scrutiny in light of the *Texas v. Johnson* ruling. Torn between his own distaste for the Supreme Court's decision and his belief that Congress's solution was constitutionally indefensible, Bush refrained from signing the bill. Instead, he allowed the bill to become law without his signature.[24] Bush then urged Congress, in a written message, to pass a constitutional amendment to directly override the Supreme Court's decision in *Texas v. Johnson*: "Because this bill is intended to achieve our mutual goal of protecting our Nation's greatest symbol, and its constitutionality must ultimately be decided by the courts, I have decided to allow it to become law without my signature. I remain convinced, however, that a constitutional amendment is the only way to ensure that our flag is protected from desecration."[25]

Following passage of the Flag Protection Act of 1989, which took effect on October 30, 1989, hundreds of people took to the steps of the U.S. Capitol Building to burn American flags in protest of the new law, which flew in the face of the Supreme Court's ruling. Numerous protesters engaged in similar demonstrations in Seattle and other cities. Shawn Eichman, who became one of the first to be prosecuted under the new law, after burning a flag on the Capitol steps, saw his conviction overturned when the U.S. District Court for the District of Columbia ruled the Flag Protection Act unconstitutional in February 1990. Next, the U.S. District Court for the Western District of Washington also declared the act unconstitutional. Hoping that the Supreme Court might change course and reverse its ruling in *Texas v. Johnson*, Bush's solicitor general, Kenneth W. Starr, with the support of the White House, appealed both decisions. On June 11, 1990, the Supreme Court upheld its prior ruling in the consolidated case of *United States v. Eichman*, declaring the Flag Protection Act unconstitutional. With the same five-to-four split in the Court that had shaped the decision in *Texas v. Johnson*, Justice Brennan again wrote the majority opinion: "Although Congress cast the Flag Protection Act of 1989 in somewhat broader terms than the Texas statute at issue in *Johnson*, the Act still suffers from the same fundamental flaw: It suppresses expression out of concern for its likely communicative impact."[26]

Despite continued public support after the *Eichman* ruling for a constitutional amendment to ban flag burning in the summer of 1990, neither the House nor the Senate could garner the necessary two-thirds vote to send such a proposed amendment to the states.[27] Thus, President Bush's push for a flag-burning amendment never picked up enough steam. Indeed, Bush's exodus from the White House after a single term probably sealed the fate of that proposed amendment.

## Conclusion

In 1992, Bush became the first Republican president not to win a second term since Herbert Hoover's defeat to Franklin Roosevelt in 1932. Had it not been for a flagging economy in late 1991 to early 1992, as well as the lingering Iran-Contra scandal, Bush may have won a second term in the White House. His strong approval ratings throughout the first three years of his presidency, particularly the high public approval he received during the Gulf War in early 1991 (nearly 90 percent in most national polls), kept many seasoned Democratic politicians from entering the 1992 presidential race. However, with the country still recovering from a recession in early 1992, and many conservatives within the Republican Party unconvinced that Bush was truly a Reagan Republican, Bush's reelection campaign turned into an uphill battle.[28] Independent candidate H. Ross Perot, a wealthy Texas businessman who appealed to swing voters frustrated by "business as usual" in Washington, took away key support from Bush. The three-way race in the fall of 1992 saw an embattled yet charismatic Bill Clinton win the Electoral College while capturing just 43 percent of the popular vote to Bush's 37 percent and Perot's 19 percent.[29]

Bush retired with his wife, Barbara, to their home in Houston, while summering at their beloved family compound in Kennebunkport, Maine. In 2000, Bush's eldest son, George W. Bush, won the presidency, serving two terms, while another son, Jeb, served as governor of Florida for two terms (1999–2007). In 2011, President Barack Obama awarded the senior Bush the Medal of Freedom, the highest civilian honor in the United States.

While George H. W. Bush's one-term presidency was marked by domestic challenges that he failed to conquer because he lacked Ronald

Reagan's vision and political adroitness, he left behind a strong record in the realm of foreign affairs. Bush oversaw the crumbling of the Berlin Wall in 1989, a decisive American military victory in Operation Desert Storm in 1991, and the breakup of the Soviet Union at the end of 1991 to mark the official end of the Cold War. Not only did Bush use his presidential power decisively to deal with the Iraqi buildup in the Middle East, but he defended to the end a devotion to the American flag and a fierce patriotism that would reappear with new vigor, eight years later, when his son George W. Bush became commander in chief.

NOTES

1. For an excellent discussion of Bush's family history and early political career, see Timothy Naftali, *George H. W. Bush* (New York: Times Books, 2007), chaps. 1 and 2; and Herbert S. Parmet, *George Bush: The Life of a Lone Star Yankee* (New York: Scribner, 1997).

2. For example, see Charles Tiefer, *The Semi-Sovereign Presidency: The Bush Administration's Strategy for Governing Without Congress* (Boulder, CO: Westview Press, 1994); Michael Duffy and Dan Goodgame, *Marching in Place: The Status Quo Presidency of George Bush* (New York: Simon & Schuster, 1992); David Mervin, *George Bush and the Guardianship Presidency* (New York: St. Martin's Press, 1996); and Michael Genovese, *The Power of the American Presidency 1789–2000* (New York: Oxford University Press, 2001), 180–185.

3. John Robert Greene, *The Presidency of George Bush* (Lawrence: University Press of Kansas, 2000), 1–2.

4. President Bush ultimately pardoned former Defense Secretary Caspar W. Weinberger and five other officials before Weinberger went to trial, on the eve of Bush's leaving the White House. Walter Pincus, "Bush Pardons Weinberger in Iran-Contra Affair," *Washington Post*, December 25, 1992. After the pardon, critics howled that Bush was complicit in a cover-up. Such criticisms only intensified when it was discovered that Bush had maintained a personal diary containing notes about Iran-Contra—a diary that he had withheld from the Independent Counsel's Office. Lawrence E. Walsh, *Firewall: The Iran-Contra Conspiracy and Cover-Up* (New York: W.W. Norton, 1997), 488–489, 512–516.

5. Lori Cox Han, *A Presidency Upstaged: The Public Leadership of George H. W. Bush* (College Station: Texas A&M University Press, 2011), chap. 3.

6. Jeffrey Toobin, *The Nine: Inside the Secret World of the Supreme Court* (New York: Doubleday, 2008), 20–22.

7. Memo on "White House Discussion Points, Supreme Court Nomination of Judge David Souter," undated, Mary Kate Grant Files, White House Office of Speechwriting, Box 8, George Bush Presidential Library, College Station, Texas.

8. For a discussion on Bush's nomination of Souter, see Henry J. Abraham, *Justices, Presidents, and Senators: A History of U.S. Supreme Court Appointments from Washington to*

*Bush II*, 5th ed. (Lanham, MD: Rowman & Littlefield, 2008), 289–292; and Lori Cox Han and Diane J. Heith, *Presidents and the American Presidency* (New York: Oxford University Press, 2013), 242–243.

9. George Bush, "The President's News Conference in Kennebunkport, Maine," July 1, 1991, *Public Papers of the Presidents: George Bush* (Washington, DC: Government Printing Office, 1992).

10. For a discussion on Bush's nomination of Thomas, see Abraham, *Justices, Presidents, and Senators*, 295–300; David M. O'Brien, *Storm Center: The Supreme Court in American Politics*, 8th ed. (New York: W.W. Norton, 2008), 78–81; and Lori Cox Han, *Women and U.S. Politics: The Spectrum of Political Leadership*, 2nd ed. (Boulder, CO: Lynne Rienner Publishers, 2010), 94–95.

11. George Bush, "The President's News Conference in Kennebunkport, Maine," July 1, 1991, *The American Presidency Project*, ed. online by Gerhard Peters and John T. Woolley, www.presidency.ucsb.edu./ws/index.php?pid=29651&st=&st1=.

12. Louis Henkin, *Foreign Affairs and the US Constitution*, 2nd ed. (New York: Oxford University Press, 1996), 109–110, 253–257.

13. Edward Keynes, "The War Powers Resolution and the Persian Gulf War," in *The Constitution and the Conduct of American Foreign Policy*, ed. David G. Adler (Lawrence: University Press of Kansas, 1996), 241–253.

14. UN SCOR, 45th Sess., 2963rd mtg., UN Doc. S/RES/678 (1990).

15. Henkin, *Foreign Affairs*, 256.

16. Dellums v. Bush, 752 F.Supp 1141 (D.D.C. 1990).

17. Authorization for Use of Military Force Against Iraq Resolution, Pub. L. No. 102–1, 105 Stat. 3 (1991).

18. George Bush, *Statement on Signing the Resolution Authorizing the Use of Military Force Against Iraq*, 27 Wkly. Comp. Pres. Docs. 48 (Jan. 14, 1991). In addition to asserting singular authority over the use of the armed forces, Bush's statement also maintained the executive branch's skepticism about the constitutionality of the War Powers Act.

19. For further analysis and the full text of President Bush's letters to Congress regarding U.S. deployment, UN Security Council Resolution 678, Congress's subsequent authorization of military force, and Bush's signing statement, see Peter M. Shane and Harold H. Bruff, *Separation of Powers Law*, 2nd ed. (Durham, NC: Carolina Academic Press, 2005), 902–910.

20. One of the few issues of substance that the campaigns focused on revolved around the looming national deficit; in this context, Bush made his infamous "Read my lips, no new taxes" pledge at the 1988 Republican National Convention (he would break the promise two years later in a deal with Congress to reduce the national deficit).

21. Other prominent themes included Dukakis as soft on crime and capital punishment (including the infamous Willie Horton ads that criticized the Massachusetts furlough program for convicted felons); Dukakis as soft on defense (including the now-famous ad with footage of Dukakis riding on a tank wearing a large helmet; many found the image to be silly and less than presidential); and Dukakis as ineffective at environmental policy (an ad blamed Dukakis for the sewage in the Boston Harbor).

22. Texas v. Johnson, 491 U.S. 397 (1989).

23. Greene, *The Presidency of George Bush*, 63.

24. Ibid., 63–64; see also Parmet, *Lone Star Yankee*, 400–401.

25. George Bush, "Statement on the Flag Protection Act of 1989," October 26, 1989, *The Public Papers of the Presidents of the United States: George Bush* (Washington, DC: Government Printing Office, 1990).

26. United States v. Eichman, 496 U.S. 310 (1990). As in the *Texas v. Johnson* (1989) case, Justices William Brennan, Thurgood Marshall, Harry Blackmun, Antonin Scalia, and Anthony Kennedy constituted the majority, while Chief Justice William Rehnquist and Justices Byron White, John Paul Stevens, and Sandra Day O'Connor made up the minority (with Stevens writing the dissenting opinion in *U.S. v. Eichman*).

27. The amendment, which simply stated, "The Congress shall have power to prohibit the physical desecration of the flag of the United States," was considered in each successive session of Congress through the 109th Session in 2005, with the House approving the amendment each session between 1995 and 2005. Yet the Senate fell short—several times by just a handful of votes—including a 66–34 defeat (just one vote short) in 2006. While public opinion remains divided on the issue, Congress has not considered the amendment since its close defeat in 2006.

28. Among other things, Bush had to fight off an interparty primary battle from conservative pundit and former Nixon speechwriter Pat Buchanan, who surprised many by winning 23 percent of the vote in the 1992 New Hampshire Republican Primary. For a discussion of Bush's leadership challenges in the aftermath of the Reagan presidency, see Lori Cox Han, *A Presidency Upstaged*.

29. For a thorough analysis of Bush's presidency and the 1992 presidential election, see Greene, *The Presidency of George Bush*.

# 42

# William Jefferson Clinton

KEN GORMLEY

*President William Jefferson Clinton, the first baby boomer to occupy the White House, took office with a group of political foes viewing him as an unworthy president. Clinton was dogged by the Whitewater scandal, the Paula Jones sexual harassment lawsuit, and the Monica Lewinsky revelation. His own decision to sign the controversial independent-counsel statute back into law—which led to the appointment of Independent Counsel Kenneth W. Starr—haunted him throughout his time in office. Indeed, many of the high-profile constitutional issues that emerged during his presidency were linked to those scandals. Yet Clinton proved to be extraordinarily resilient, presiding over an era of economic growth as he battled endless investigations. The second president in American history to be impeached by the House, the tenacious Bill Clinton fought back and was acquitted on all counts in the Senate. A brilliant political figure, notwithstanding his personal shortcomings, which prevented him from accomplishing even more in office, Clinton would eventually become an international symbol of American determination and optimism.*

## Introduction

William "Bill" Jefferson Clinton, the forty-second president of the United States, faced multiple criminal investigations and an impeachment drive during his presidency. Yet he blazed a new trail as a centrist Democrat, and—along with First Lady Hillary Clinton who became a renowned public official in her own right—emerged as one of the most popular chief executives of the twentieth century.

Bill Clinton was born William Jefferson Blythe III in Hope, Arkansas, on August 19, 1946. His father, a traveling salesman, had died in a freak automobile accident three months before the baby was born. His mother, Virginia Cassidy Blythe, widowed at the age of twenty, married a car dealer named Roger Clinton and moved in 1950 to Hot Springs, where young Bill sang in the Baptist church choir and excelled in school.[1]

Bill Clinton attended Georgetown University in the 1960s during the Vietnam War. He was elected president of his class and earned a clerkship on Capitol Hill with Senator J. William Fulbright of Arkansas, catching the bug for politics.[2] While in England on a Rhodes scholarship at Oxford, Clinton received a draft notice, signed up for a graduate ROTC program in Arkansas, yet managed to avoid service. (Detractors would later label him a draft dodger.) In 1970, Bill Clinton returned to the States and enrolled at Yale Law School.[3]

It was here that Clinton met a Wellesley graduate named Hillary Rodham, who was every bit his intellectual equal and shared his love for politics. Immediately after graduation, Clinton returned to Arkansas, where he practiced law briefly and landed a job as a professor at the University of Arkansas School of Law in Fayetteville, where Rodham also taught. The couple was married in a small ceremony in Fayetteville in 1975. Having lost a bid for Congress in 1974, Clinton was elected state attorney general in Arkansas, then won a smashing victory in the race for the governor's mansion in the fall of 1978. At age thirty-two, Clinton was sworn in as the youngest governor in the United States.[4]

The baby-faced Clinton was instantly viewed as a star on the Arkansas political scene. Tall, handsome, brilliant, and possessing a magnetic personality, Clinton shook up the old-boy network in that Southern state. He appointed African Americans to key posts, publicly decrying racial prejudice. This outspokenness was among the factors that contributed to Clinton's defeat in the governor's reelection campaign of 1980.[5] Yet he came roaring back during the election of 1982, returning to the governor's mansion in Little Rock for a span of ten years.

## Presidency

In November 1992, Bill Clinton won a decisive, upset victory over incumbent President George H. W. Bush. Running as a New Democrat who embodied youth and a bold plan to restore economic growth for the "forgotten middle class," Clinton and his vice presidential running mate, Senator Al Gore Jr., of Tennessee, became the first baby boomers to capture the White House. Yet a sizable group of detractors—conservative Republicans, in particular—viewed Clinton as an illegitimate and unworthy president from the moment he moved into the executive mansion.[6]

### Whitewater and Vince Foster's Suicide

Clinton's extraordinary success as governor of Arkansas had been marred by one controversy that now nagged at him as he won national office. The Whitewater scandal had involved a seemingly trivial investment in a land deal in a remote area of northern Arkansas. In the final months of Clinton's stint as Arkansas attorney general in 1978, Bill and Hillary had agreed to become business partners with an eccentric real estate entrepreneur named Jim McDougal. The businessman's grand vision was to build on the White River an elite vacation spot that would be a getaway for political movers and shakers.

The Whitewater project, unbeknownst to the Clintons, had quickly sunk into bankruptcy. Meanwhile, McDougal and his wife, Susan, were charged with savings-and-loan fraud in connection with Madison Guaranty Savings & Loan.[7] Hillary Rodham Clinton, by then the First Lady of Arkansas and a partner at the Rose Law Firm, had done some legal work for McDougal on Madison projects, further entangling the Clintons in the ill-fated McDougal ventures.[8]

Questions about the Whitewater investment had periodically flared up during Clinton's time as governor and again during the presidential campaign, yet they never gained much traction. Indeed, the Clintons noted that they, too, were victims of McDougal's illegal activities. Nevertheless, the spark of the Whitewater scandal was quickly fanned back to life, as Bill and Hillary Clinton moved into the White House.[9]

The first dramatic opportunity for Clinton's political foes to challenge his authority presented itself within six months of his inauguration. In July 1993, Clinton's childhood friend and Assistant White House Counsel, Vince Foster, was found dead in Fort Marcy Park, Virginia, having suffered an apparent self-inflicted gunshot wound. Although multiple investigations confirmed that Foster had committed suicide, probably because of depression, conspiracy theorists pounced on Foster's death. Allegations swirled that the Clintons had somehow been involved in murdering their friend and that incriminating Whitewater documents had been spirited out of Foster's office by the Clintons on the night of his death.[10]

As congressional Republicans demanded the appointment of a special prosecutor to investigate the Whitewater scandal and the mysterious Foster death, President Clinton authorized his attorney general, Janet Reno, to appoint a special prosecutor, hoping to defuse the burgeoning scandal. This was a decision that Clinton would regret for the rest of his presidency.

Republicans generally detested the independent-counsel law, born of the post-Watergate era. Among other things, it had been used to target President Ronald Reagan and Vice President George H. W. Bush in connection with the Iran-Contra investigation. The law had been challenged on constitutional grounds as a violation of separation of powers, yet the Supreme Court upheld it in the 1988 case of *Morrison v. Olson.*[11] Republicans still abhorred the law as an intrusion into executive authority.

The Republican-dominated Congress had allowed the statute to lapse in 1992, but Clinton had campaigned in favor of reauthorizing the law.[12] Now, he was boxed into a corner. Some Republicans saw this as an opportunity for payback. Robert Fiske, a highly respected former U.S. attorney from New York and a registered Republican, was appointed by Attorney General Reno to serve as independent counsel in the Whitewater matter. Republicans in Congress began their own parallel investigation of Whitewater and Vince Foster's death, hoping to find a smoking gun.

## Clinton v. Jones

Just as the Whitewater scandal was reignited, a second bombshell hit the Clinton White House. Paula Corbin Jones—a former purchasing assistant for the Arkansas Industrial Development Commission—filed a federal sexual harassment lawsuit against President Clinton in Arkansas.[13] Jones's complaint alleged that Clinton had invited her to a room during a business conference at the Excelsior Hotel in Little Rock, where he had requested sexual favors from, and exposed himself to, the twenty-four-year-old employee. While Clinton flatly denied the allegations, the Paula Jones lawsuit turned into a second scandal that perpetually dogged the Clinton White House.[14]

The *Jones* case raised the novel constitutional issue of whether a president could be subjected to civil suit while in office, consistent with the separation-of-powers principle. Even if the chief executive was not entitled to blanket immunity from civil suits, the president's lawyers argued, the concept of executive privilege—which protected the office of president from undue interference by other branches of government—certainly permitted the president to delay depositions and trial until he left office.

On May 27, 1997, the Supreme Court handed down its historic decision in *Clinton v. Jones*.[15] The unanimous opinion, authored by Justice John Paul Stevens—a Ford appointee who was viewed as a reliable liberal on the Court—concluded that the Constitution did not give the president immunity from this sort of civil suit while the executive was in office. Moreover, the Court found nothing in the Constitution that required courts to postpone civil proceedings until after a president left office, particularly when the civil suit was unconnected to the president's official duties.[16]

Justice Stevens noted that merely because a case might burden the time and attention of the chief executive, this did not trump the federal court's Article III power to conduct its judicial business. President Truman, for instance, had been forced to devote substantial time and energy to litigating the *Steel Seizure Case* while he was in office. Other presidents, too, had been required to participate in judicial proceedings.[17] Thus, President Clinton could be required to give testimony, under oath, in the *Jones* lawsuit without violating the separation-of-powers principle.[18]

*Clinton v. Jones* constituted a major setback for Bill Clinton.[19] Although the president's lawyers accomplished their primary goal of dragging the matter out beyond the election of 1996, the Paula Jones charges swiftly whipped up anti-Clinton forces and reignited simmering conspiracy theories about Whitewater and Vince Foster's death.[20] In addition, because of legislation and court decisions that had expanded the scope of sexual harassment lawsuits—decisions and laws that Clinton himself had endorsed—the *Jones* case became the framework by which lawyers and political opponents could delve into Clinton's personal life.

## Independent Counsel Kenneth W. Starr

Ironically, it was only because Clinton himself had signed the independent-counsel statute back into law, in 1994, that congressional Republicans who were clamoring for a more aggressive special prosecutor got their wish: A special three-judge panel that oversaw independent-counsel investigations, pursuant to the statute, now removed Robert Fiske, appointing Kenneth W. Starr to take over the Whitewater-related investigations. Starr, a former federal appeals judge and U.S. solicitor general under George H. W. Bush, was highly respected in conservative legal circles. He was also viewed as someone who might conduct a more vigorous investigation of the Clintons' alleged misdeeds.

By the summer of 1996, Starr's team of prosecutors had gained convictions of Jim and Susan McDougal for the savings-and-loan fraud. The team had also convicted sitting Arkansas governor, Jim Guy Tucker, a prominent Democrat, in connection with McDougal's dubious business ventures. Jim McDougal now pointed a finger at the president and First Lady, seeking to implicate them in criminal conduct, in order to strike a plea deal with the Starr prosecutors.[21]

## Domestic Successes

Despite these lingering scandals, by the time he faced reelection in 1996 against Senator Bob Dole (R-KS), Clinton had emerged as a strong and popular chief executive.[22] Dubbed a New Democrat, he seemed able to achieve remarkable compromises. Although Clinton had been forced to abandon his plan to enact sweeping health-care reform—an initiative that had been led by First Lady Hillary Clinton until Republicans in Congress squelched it—he rebounded by compromising on a Republican-sponsored welfare reform bill.[23] Originally pegged by many detractors as a one-term president, Clinton was shoring up the economy, shrinking the deficit that he had inherited, and staring down Republicans in Congress when they shut down the government seeking to gain the upper hand in budget battles.

President Clinton cooperated with Congress to pass the Balanced Budget Act of 1997—fixing constitutional defects that had existed in an earlier version of that law.[24] He then produced the first balanced budget since 1969. Clinton appointed the first female attorney general in the history of the nation: Janet Reno. He also appointed more African Americans (seven) to his cabinet than any prior president, reflecting a deep commitment to racial equality that dated back to his childhood in Arkansas, when federal troops were called in to desegregate Central High School in Little Rock, fifty miles from his home.[25] Clinton's administration also adopted the "Don't ask, don't tell" policy for gays in the military, in 1993, a step presumably designed to soften the harsh treatment of gays who wished to serve in the armed forces.[26]

Clinton repeatedly broke new ground. He successfully pushed through the Line Item Veto Act that was designed to give the president power to strike from Congress's spending bills any items that he deemed unnecessary or extravagant.[27] Many governors had exercised such authority under their state constitutions for a century; every president since Ulysses S. Grant had pressed for such a law, seeking to get the whip hand over Congress in budget matters. In *Clinton v. City of New York*, however, the Line Item Veto Act was ultimately struck down by the Supreme Court as violating the Presentment Clause set forth in Article I, Section 7, of the Constitution.[28] The Court concluded that the law allowed the president to, in effect, amend or repeal duly enacted laws without taking such measures through both Houses of Congress as envisioned by the framers. Nonetheless, Clinton had again displayed his ability to get legislative initiatives enacted as chief executive.

When voters went to the polls in November 1996, Clinton sailed to victory over his rival, Senator Dole, by a wide margin. As the president moved into his second term, it appeared that he was unstoppable. His two appointments to the Supreme Court—Judge Ruth Bader Ginsburg and Judge Stephen Breyer—were considered strong picks who would further Clinton's policy agenda.[29] Moreover, they shared his liberal view that the Constitution was a "living" document that adapted itself over time, rather than remaining static. Clinton seemed to possess enormous potential to advance his administration's policies and to establish himself as one of the greatest presidents of all time—until a new scandal came roaring to life, barely one year into Clinton's second term.

### The Monica Lewinsky Revelation

The Starr investigators by late 1997 seemed to have hit a brick wall. Yet they were convinced the Clintons were hiding evidence. Starr's prosecutors considered indicting the First Lady in connection with her role in the McDougal-related ventures and for allegedly lying about missing White-water billing records that had mysteriously appeared in the White House living quarters. Privately, however, the prosecutors expressed doubts whether they could amass sufficient evidence to succeed in either matter.[30]

Unexpectedly, in January 1998, the Starr prosecutors received a boost to their sagging investigation. A woman named Linda Tripp called Starr's office in a hushed voice and informed them that President Clinton had engaged in a long-standing sexual affair with a young White House intern named Monica Lewinsky. Tripp told the Starr prosecutors that she had secretly recorded Lewinsky admitting to the affair, and that Clinton planned to lie about this relationship in his upcoming *Paula Jones* deposition.[31]

In a week packed with cloak-and-dagger intrigue, FBI agents working with Starr's prosecutors wired Tripp and recorded a damning confession from Lewinsky. Within days, Starr secretly received permission from the three-judge panel overseeing his investigation to expand into the Lewinsky matter. Starr's prosecutors then confronted Lewinsky in a hotel room in an effort to gain cooperation from the former intern. Meanwhile, President Clinton gave testimony in the *Jones* case after taking an oath in the presence of federal Judge Susan Webber Wright, denying that he had engaged in a sexual affair with Lewinsky.[32]

*Impeachment*

As the Starr prosecutors pursued a new, seemingly airtight criminal case against President Clinton for lying under oath in the *Jones* deposition, the Clinton presidency seemed to be teetering on the edge of a dangerous precipice. Although Jim McDougal died in a Texas prison, eliminating one of the Starr team's key witnesses, the team marched forward. Starr's group finally brokered an immunity deal with Lewinsky's attorneys, gaining the former intern's cooperation and obtaining a blue dress that was allegedly stained with the president's semen.

Running out of options, President Clinton finally consented to appear before the Starr grand jury via video hookup in August 1998. Taking his inquisitors off guard, the president admitted to having engaged in an "inappropriate relationship" with Lewinsky, but he declined to address the specifics of that relationship and asserted that he had not technically lied at the *Jones* deposition, because the questions had been imprecisely and unartfully framed.

With key Democrats in Congress prepared to jump ship and abandon the president, and with First Lady Hillary Clinton visibly stunned by her husband's admission of unfaithfulness, the Clinton presidency appeared to be on the verge of collapse. Ironically, the issuance of the controversial Starr Report by the special prosecutor is what helped save President Clinton. Filled with so much sexual detail that it outraged many Americans, the report now caused many congressional Democrats and the First Lady to rally behind the embattled president. The Office of Independent Counsel, which seemed to be accountable to no branch of government, with an inexhaustible budget and the ability to target individuals like a roving "Frankenstein monster," suddenly came under attack.[33] Indignant Democrats charged that extremist Republicans were twisting the meaning of the impeachment clause in Article II, Section 4, of the Constitution and trying to nullify the will of the people by removing the duly elected president. The Constitution, the Democrats charged, was never meant to include lying about one's personal affairs and sex life as one of those "high Crimes and Misdemeanors" that warranted impeachment.

The powerful House Judiciary Committee, headed by Republican Congressman Henry Hyde of Illinois, nonetheless steamed ahead with formal impeachment proceedings against Clinton, calling Starr as its chief witness. As pandemonium erupted in Washington, President Clinton launched a military air strike directed at Iraqi dictator Saddam Hussein on the eve of the impeachment vote, prompting cries of "Wag the Dog!" by skeptical Republicans.[34] Meanwhile, House Speaker-designate Bob Livingston (R-LA) was confronted in the press with a bombshell story that he had engaged in his own unseemly extramarital affairs. Livingston shocked the world by resigning and calling on President Clinton to do the same. The Republican caucus erupted into chaos; angry Republican House members proclaimed that they had a sworn duty to defend the Constitution, and this included protecting the country from a president who had lied under oath and now believed he was above the law.

The Republican-led Congress proceeded to impeach President Clinton on four counts. Article I accused Clinton of lying to the federal grand jury in connection with the Monica Lewinsky matter; Article II charged him with lying under oath in the Paula Jones civil deposition; Article III alleged obstruction of justice and subordination of perjury; and Article

IV alleged a general "misuse and abuse" of Clinton's office as president and chief executive.[35] In a strict party-line vote, the Republican majority succeeded in passing Articles I and III, with two articles failing. Congressional Democrats, in a show of solidarity, assembled on the South Lawn of the White House. Flanked by First Lady Hillary Clinton and Vice President Al Gore, a visibly chastened Bill Clinton stepped to the microphone and begged both political parties in Washington to "rise above the rancor, to overcome the pain and division."[36]

In January 1999, the U.S. Senate geared up for the trial of William Jefferson Clinton, the second president in American history to be impeached by the House of Representatives. Chief Justice William H. Rehnquist, pursuant to Article I, Section 6, of the Constitution, presided over the proceedings. Many observers expected Rehnquist—who had been appointed by President Nixon because of his rock-solid conservative views—to tilt the playing field toward Representative Hyde and the thirteen House managers (all of whom were Republicans and white males). Yet the chief justice remained scrupulously neutral, continuing to work a full schedule in the Supreme Court and eager to bring the unpleasant proceedings to a conclusion.

In a remarkable display of political grit, Clinton delivered a flawless State of the Union address in front of the very members of the House and Senate seeking to remove him. He called on the nation to "put aside our divisions" and usher in a new era of "healing and hopefulness" as the twenty-first century arrived. A large segment of the American public did not view uttering falsehoods about one's personal life to be an impeachable offense that would justify removing Clinton from office. With public sentiment weighing solidly against conviction, Republicans and Democrats in the Senate decided to wrap up the trial quickly, despite protests from the House managers.

The historic impeachment vote took place on Friday, February 12. The Constitution required a vote of two-thirds of the Senate to remove the president. When a roll-call vote was recorded on Article I—dealing with perjury in the grand jury—the tally was forty-five guilty, fifty-five not guilty, with the measure failing by a wide margin. Despite an intense lobbying effort by Senate Majority Leader Trent Lott (R-MS), the Republicans failed to gain even a bare majority on Article II dealing with obstruction of justice, mirroring the American public's distaste for the whole sordid affair.[37] At 12:43 p.m., Chief Justice Rehnquist entered a judgment in favor

of President Clinton, before being escorted out of the Capitol and returning to work at the Supreme Court.[38]

## The Death of the Independent-Counsel Law

With the nation exhausted from the seemingly endless investigation of
the president that had already cost the public approximately $52 million,
Congress allowed the independent-counsel law to expire in the spring
of 1999.[39] All told, there had been twenty separate independent-counsel
investigations (eighteen public and two under seal).[40] These had haunted
every president since President Nixon's misdeeds in Watergate had led
to the law's passage. Ironically, Independent Counsel Kenneth W. Starr
personally appeared in front of the Senate Judiciary Committee and testified against renewing the statute, reiterating many of the criticisms of the
law—dealing with the separation-of-powers nightmares it created—that
had been raised at the law's inception.

Yet, President Clinton did not escape entirely. After the impeachment
proceedings ended, Judge Susan Webber Wright issued an order holding
Clinton in civil contempt for lying under oath in the *Paula Jones* lawsuit.
This was true even though she had dismissed that lawsuit a year earlier
due to lack of proof that Jones had suffered any legal damages. In a stern
thirty-two-page rebuke of the president, Judge Wright reprimanded Clinton for giving "false, misleading and evasive answers that were designed
to obstruct the judicial process."[41] She ordered Clinton to pay $90,000 in
costs and referred the matter to the Arkansas Supreme Court to determine
if Clinton should be disbarred or sanctioned for violating the state's rules
of professional conduct.[42]

Meanwhile, the Office of Independent Counsel continued to weigh
whether to indict Clinton for perjury in the *Paula Jones* deposition and for
obstructing justice, even after he had survived the impeachment proceedings.[43] Within the Justice Department, there was serious debate whether
a sitting president could be indicted while in office—a constitutional issue
that dated back to the Nixon presidency. If the unitary head of the executive branch could be subjected to criminal action, one argument went, this
could potentially cripple that entire branch of government.

In January 2001, just as Clinton was packing up boxes to leave the White
House, with this issue still unsettled, Starr's successor—Independent
Counsel Robert Ray—struck a last-minute deal with President Clinton's

attorney, Washington superlawyer David Kendall. On January 19, 2000—just one day before George W. Bush was sworn in to succeed Clinton as president—Ray announced a final deal: Clinton agreed to have his law license suspended for five years and pay a $25,000 fine. The president also issued an acknowledgment that he "knowingly gave evasive and misleading answers" in the *Paula Jones* deposition.[44] In return, the Office of Independent Counsel agreed not to pursue further criminal action.

With that, the interminable scandals of the Clinton presidency—scandals that had created a heightened new level of polarization in the United States—came to an end.[45]

## Conclusion

After leaving the White House and moving to a new home in New York, President Bill Clinton enjoyed a resurgence in popularity. Establishing the Clinton Presidential Foundation to address HIV/AIDS issues and to assist disadvantaged people throughout the world, Clinton became an international symbol of American determination, resilience, and compassion. Hillary Clinton, too, swiftly rebounded from the trauma of the seemingly endless investigations. She won a U.S. Senate seat in New York; launched a campaign for the presidency in 2008; and, after losing a hard-fought Democratic primary to fellow senator Barack Obama, served as secretary of state during President Obama's first term, becoming the first former First Lady in American history to become a world-renowned public official in her own right. In 2016, she again became a Democratic candidate for president.

Thus, despite the many scandals and constitutional sand traps that faced him during his time in the White House, William Jefferson Clinton earned himself a place in history as a chief executive who presided over a roaring economy and a peaceful time on America's homeland, bounced back after Congress impeached him, and embodied America's spirit of determination and grit. Indeed, Bill Clinton, "the Comeback Kid," ran the political gauntlet and managed to escape largely unscathed. On one hand, the Clinton presidency certainly ushered in a new era of polarization in American government; that polarization remained entrenched for decades. Yet it also illustrated that a president's legacy cannot be dictated solely by adversarial members of Congress or by political foes. Indeed, Clinton's time as chief executive confirms that the bucking bronco of history will gallop where it wishes to gallop. In this case, the House managers who tried to impeach Clinton ended up appearing impolitic and overzealous, rather than as revered defenders of the Constitution. Moreover, the Clinton saga underscores a new phenomenon that would have been likely to surprise the framers: The original notion of an energetic presidency is not at all confined to an individual's time in office. Rather, the later good deeds of a former president—and the independent contributions and successes of a president's spouse—will increasingly come to define an American president's legacy.

NOTES

1. Ken Gormley, *The Death of American Virtue: Clinton vs. Starr* (New York: Crown Publishers, 2010), 16–17; David Maraniss, *First in His Class: The Biography of Bill Clinton* (New York: Simon & Schuster, 1996), 28–29, 41.

2. Gormley, *Death of American Virtue*, 18; Maraniss, *First in His Class*, 69–73, 96–121.

3. Gormley, *Death of American Virtue*, 18.

4. Ibid., 19; Maraniss, *First in His Class*, 355–357.

5. Gormley, *Death of American Virtue*, 23.

6. Nicknamed "Slick Willie" by his detractors in Arkansas, Bill Clinton never shook the perception among his political foes that he was a dangerous liberal from a small, backwater state and was unqualified to govern the nation. This perception persisted even though, ironically, Clinton was a rather moderate Southern Democrat with ample executive experience.

7. In part, Jim McDougal had used bogus loans to pay off Whitewater debts and to engage in a wide array of fraudulent activities.

8. Ibid., 54–65; James Stewart, *Blood Sport* (New York: Simon & Schuster, 1997), 61–62, 94–95; Gene Lyons, *Fools for Scandal: How the Media Invented Whitewater* (New York: Franklin Square Press, 2010), 32; Susan McDougal, *The Woman Who Wouldn't Talk* (New York: Carroll & Graf, 2002), 67, 70, 73, 96; Jim McDougal and Curtis Willkie, *Arkansas Mischief* (New York: Henry Hold & Company, 1998), 171–174, 197–198.

9. Gormley, *Death of American Virtue*, 61–65; Stewart, *Blood Sport*, 183–234.

10. Gormley, *Death of American Virtue*, 81–91; Stewart, *Blood Sport*, 295–311.

11. Morrison v. Olson, 487 U.S. 654 (1988).

12. Gormley, *Death of American Virtue*, 91–95.

13. Paula Corbin, it turned out, had been engaged to Stephen Jones at the time of the incident with Bill Clinton at the Excelsior Hotel.

14. The federal judge in Little Rock assigned to the case, Judge Susan Webber Wright, was a Republican Bush appointee who had once been a student of Bill Clinton's in law school. (He had misplaced her admiralty law exam, causing a brief dust-up.) Judge Wright, while a straight-shooting jurist, was also well aware of Clinton's reputation for womanizing, dating back to Arkansas days. Indeed, Clinton's 1992 presidential campaign was nearly derailed after a former television reporter and lounge singer named

Gennifer Flowers told the media that she had engaged in a twelve-year affair with then-Governor Clinton.

15. Clinton v. Jones, 520 U.S. 681 (1997).

16. The Court distinguished this case from Nixon v. Fitzgerald, 520 U.S. 81 (1982), which held that a president had absolute immunity from civil suit arising out of the execution of his official duties of office. The *Jones* suit involved private conduct, unrelated to the office, that occurred before Clinton became president. Moreover, the Court emphasized that a lengthy and categorical "postponement of the case" would unfairly harm Jones, because it could potentially lead to "the loss of evidence, including the inability of witnesses to recall specific facts, or the possible death of a party." *Jones*, 520 U.S. at 707–708.

17. Precedent was clear that presidents could be subjected to judicial process under the appropriate circumstances. Chief Justice John Marshall, in the treason trial of Aaron Burr, had declared that a subpoena *duces tecum* could be directed to a president. United States v. Burr, 25 F. Cas. 30 (No. 14, 692d) (C.C. Va. 1807). President Monroe had responded to written interrogatories. President Nixon had been required to comply with a subpoena to turn over certain White House tapes in the Watergate affair. U.S. v. Nixon, 418 U.S. 683 (1974). President Ford had complied with a court order to give a deposition in criminal proceedings in the trial of Lynette "Squeaky" Fromme, who had tried to assassinate him. United States v. Fromme, 405 F.Supp. 578 (E.D. Cal. 1975). President Clinton himself had twice given videotaped testimony in court proceedings, including in the ill-fated matter involving Jim McDougal. U.S. v. McDougal, 934 F. Supp. 296 (E.D. Ark. 1996); United States v. Branscum, No. LRP CR 96 49 (E.D. Ark., June 7, 1996).

18. The Court did make one important concession to the president, acknowledging that the "high respect that is owed to the office of the Chief Executive," though not justifying a categorical rule of immunity, "should inform the conduct of the entire proceedings, including the timing and scope of discovery." *Jones*, 520 U.S. at 707. Yet Justice Stevens was quick to add that in more than three hundred years, "only two sitting Presidents have been subjected to suits for their private actions." If the past was any indicator, he concluded, "it seems unlikely that a deluge of such litigation will ever engulf the Presidency." Ibid., 702. The three presidents to have civil complaints filed against them were Theodore Roosevelt and Harry Truman—these complaints were dismissed before they took office—and President John F. Kennedy, who was sued for a minor automobile accident that occurred during the 1960 presidential campaign and who settled the matter out of court. Ibid., 692.

19. Ibid., 702. The only member of the Court who expressed any disagreement with the unanimous opinion was Justice Stephen Breyer, a Clinton appointee. Breyer wrote a concurrence arguing that in private actions for civil damages, the District Court should be empowered to determine if the case "cannot take place without significantly interfering with the President's official duties." *Jones*, 520 U.S. at 724 (Breyer, J., concurring).

20. For a complete discussion of the origin of the Paula Jones lawsuit and its transformation into a scandal that threatened the Clinton presidency, see Jeffrey Toobin, *A Vast*

*Conspiracy: The Real Story of the Sex Scandal That Nearly Brought Down a Presidency* (New York: Touchstone, 2000). For the Whitewater–Vince Foster conspiracy theories, see Gormley, *Death of American Virtue*, 91.

21. Susan McDougal, meanwhile, refused to answer questions in the Starr grand jury and was held in contempt by Judge Susan Webber Wright; McDougal was led away to prison in handcuffs and shackles.

22. Clinton had earned political points in late 1995 during a standoff with the Republican Speaker of the House, Newt Gingrich, when Gingrich threatened to shut down the government rather than yield to Clinton's demands to resolve a budget impasse. Bill Clinton, *My Life* (New York: Knopf, 2004), 680–684. Clinton ultimately prevailed, which gave him the appearance of a strong and steady chief executive.

23. For health-care reform, see John F. Harris, *The Survivor: Bill Clinton in the White House* (New York: Random House, 2005), 110–119; Clinton, *My Life*, 577–578, 601–602. For welfare reform, see Harris, *The Survivor*, 230–239.

24. See discussion of Bowsher v. Synar, 478 U.S. 714 (1986) in Chapter 40, "Ronald Reagan."

25. David Maraniss, *First in His Class*, 16.

26. For a discussion of these and other domestic accomplishments, see Rosanna Perotti, ed., *The Clinton Presidency and the Constitutional System* (College Station: Texas A&M Press, 2012).

27. William J. Clinton, "Statement on Signing the Line Item Veto Act," April 9, 1996, www.presidency.ucsb.edu./ws/index.php?pid=52649&st=&st1=.

28. Clinton v. City of New York, 524 U.S. 417 (1998).

29. Ginsburg had been a leading figure in the gender equality movement, arguing Frontiero v. Richardson, 411 U.S. 677 (1973), an important decision that declared that classifications based on gender triggered a heightened level of scrutiny under the Equal Protection Clause of the Fourteenth Amendment. Breyer, a former Harvard law professor and former chief counsel to the Senate Judiciary Committee, had strong bipartisan support.

30. For an excellent account of the Starr investigation and the clash between the Starr prosecutors and the Clinton White House, see generally Susan Schmidt and Michael Weisskopf, *Truth at Any Cost: Ken Starr and the Unmaking of Bill Clinton* (New York: Harper, 2000).

31. Gormley, *Death of American Virtue*, 286–288.

32. Ibid., 328–392. The Paula Jones lawyers were ostensibly seeking to establish a pattern of sexually inappropriate conduct by Clinton with subordinates, to prove their case of sexual harassment.

33. Ken Gormley, "An Original Model of the Independent Counsel Statute," *Michigan Law Review* 97 (1998): 601, 659.

34. Gormley, *Death of American Virtue*, 3–4. "Wag the Dog" referred to a 1997 film by that name, in which a desperate president, desiring to distract the American public from a scandal involving his sexual dalliances with an underage girl, just days before he stands for reelection, launches a fake war with Albania.

35. Ibid., 3–4, 607–610.

36. Ibid., 610.

37. By a vote of fifty guilty, and fifty not guilty—with Republican Senator Arlen Specter of Pennsylvania casting a Scottish vote of "not proven" to hedge his bets—the second article failed by a wide margin to reach the two-thirds majority.

38. For an excellent discussion of the Clinton impeachment proceedings, see generally Peter Baker, *The Breach: Inside the Impeachment and Trial of William Jefferson Clinton* (New York: Scribner, 2000).

39. The law contained a sunset provision by which it automatically expired after five years unless Congress took affirmative steps to renew it. Gormley, *Death of American Virtue*, 655–666.

40. Ken Gormley, "Impeachment and the Independent Counsel: A Dysfunctional Union," *Stanford Law Review* 51 (1999): 641, n. 166. This number did not include the Watergate investigation headed by Archibald Cox, or the investigation into President Jimmy Carter's peanut warehouse, which had been conducted by special prosecutors appointed by attorneys general, before the statute went into effect.

41. Ibid., 649.

42. The same day that Judge Wright ordered Clinton to pay $90,000, a jury deadlocked on fresh criminal contempt charges filed against Susan McDougal for refusing to testify, and she walked out of federal court in Little Rock a free woman. Ibid., 651–652.

43. Ibid., 657–659. Portions of the *Federalist Papers*, written by the nation's framers, and debates during the Constitutional Convention in 1787, suggested that there were serious problems with indicting a president while the chief executive in office. For instance, a president could be arrested and locked up in jail in a fashion that incapacitated the government, if a political foe was bent on paralyzing the executive branch. The better course, it seemed, was to treat impeachment as the sole method for removing a president from office. Only after a president was removed through this political process, the argument went, could criminal charges be brought. Ken Gormley, "Impeachment and the Independent Counsel: A Dysfunctional Union," *Stanford Law Review* 51 (1999): 315–324. Moreover, in a confidential memo to Attorney General Reno, the Office of Legal Counsel concluded that the issue was seriously "complicated" by the failed impeachment effort in Congress, which raised potential "double jeopardy" issues.

44. Gormley, *Death of American Virtue*, 668.

45. In addition to facing impeachment proceedings, Clinton was sued in federal court by members of Congress. They alleged that the president had violated the War Powers Act by taking military action in Kosovo without congressional authorization. The lawsuit was dismissed for lack of standing. Campbell v. Clinton, 203 F.3d 19 (D.C. Cir. 2000).

# PART XII

# National Security Era: Post-9/11

# 43

# George W. Bush

BENJAMIN A. KLEINERMAN

*George W. Bush ("Bush 43") won office as a result of a highly contested election that was ultimately decided by the Supreme Court, dividing the country anew after the polarizing Clinton impeachment. The son of the forty-first president, George W. Bush sought to build a new, more powerful presidency. When terrorists struck the World Trade Center on 9/11, Bush used the full authority of his office to wage an unprecedented "war on terror." In pushing through the USA Patriot Act, beginning secret NSA wiretaps, defending extraordinary interrogation techniques, and imprisoning "enemy combatants" in military prisons at Guantanamo Bay, Bush and his vice president, Dick Cheney, pushed executive powers to new heights. Ironically, both the nation and the Supreme Court—which seemed prepared to give Bush extraordinary authority to protect the nation after 9/11—concluded that he went too far. Thus, Bush 43 left behind a mixed legacy as a president who did a commendable job fighting a new war on terror, but in the process may have insisted too much on his own controversial understanding of the constitutional presidency.*

## Introduction

Many of George W. Bush's most important constitutional decisions while he was in office were tied to those his administration thought necessary to execute the "war on terror," in the wake of the September 11, 2001, attacks on the World Trade Center in New York. Yet for some high-level Bush advisers, the crises created by the war on terror were seen, simultaneously, as opportunities for the legitimate expansion of presidential power. Dating back to the 1980s, Bush's vice president, Dick Cheney, had written thoughtfully and cogently about the need for a constitutionally independent presidency. Indeed, intellectual leaders of the Republican Party had argued that this independence was constitutionally mandated, largely to give the president more leeway in matters of national security and foreign policy.[1] These views of the presidency also arose from the conviction that a new, powerful chief executive could be harnessed to undo many components of the administrative state created by the past progressive administrations. In the case of President Bush, however, his quest to leave a forceful imprint on the role of the chief executive under the nation's constitutional system sometimes backfired, creating a mixed legacy.

Born July 6, 1946, in New Haven, Connecticut, George W. Bush was the eldest son of George H. W. Bush and his wife, Barbara. The junior Bush attended Yale University as an undergraduate and Harvard Business School. In 1977, he met a librarian named Laura Welch at a backyard barbeque in Texas, marrying her later that year. Bush's father had served as the forty-first president after a distinguished career in politics. However, before the son turned to the family business of politics, he was involved in the oil industry and owned the Texas Rangers baseball team. In 1994, Bush defeated incumbent Ann Richards in the Texas gubernatorial election. Becoming governor of Texas symbolized an important difference between George W. Bush and his father. While the father always gave the appearance of a Yankee blueblood, the son, although he was born in Connecticut and attended Ivy League schools in New England, seemed much more a man of the Southwest.

Bush ran for the presidency in 2000 and won in one of the most controversial elections in American history. A dispute over ballot counting in Florida landed the two main contestants in court against one another. Vice President Al Gore, the Democratic candidate, won the popular vote. But Bush was clinging to a narrow lead in the state of Florida, where his brother Jeb was the governor. A win in Florida would hand Bush a victory in the Electoral College; however, his lead shrunk each day because of an ongoing recount of votes ordered by the Florida Supreme Court. In a rapid series of court moves, Bush's campaign challenged the legality of the recount in an effort to halt it.

The resulting legal battle quickly landed before the U.S. Supreme Court in *Bush v. Gore*.[2] With the election hanging in the balance, a deeply divided Court ended the recount in Florida and, by doing so, delivered the election to George W. Bush.[3] The Court based its decision on the Fourteenth Amendment, holding that the Florida recount could not be conducted in compliance with the requirements of the federal Equal Protection Clause.[4] Not surprisingly, the ruling cast the Court in a negative, partisan light because of the charged political nature of the dispute. Supporters of Vice President Gore asserted that conservative members of the Court had improperly intervened and stolen the election for Bush. Justice Stephen Breyer, dissenting in *Bush v. Gore*, chastised the majority for injecting itself into a political thicket when the Twelfth Amendment "commits to Congress the authority and responsibility to count electoral votes" and to resolve disputed presidential elections.[5] Yet even under these strained political circumstances, power was again transferred peacefully in the United States.

## Presidency

Given how Bush's tenure began, it was perhaps predictable that constitutional problems and controversies would continue to plague his presidency. Presidents typically assert their constitutional authority in the context of attaining their own political goals. By contrast, Bush seemed to go out of his way to assert the constitutional powers of the presidency, in a manner almost divorced from his own political agenda.[6] In fact, Bush's advocacy and behavior as president revealed the establishment of a strong presidency itself as one of his most important political objectives. As former head of the Office of Legal Counsel Jack Goldsmith later wrote, Bush pursued a constitutionally strong presidency with an almost "theological" zeal, which sometimes conflicted with his other political ambitions.

## The Executive Privilege and Presidential Papers

That President Bush planned to aggressively assert the constitutional authority of the presidency was evident within his first year in office.[7] In fact, Bush was so intent on establishing the principle of executive privilege that he chose some very nontraditional cases in which to do so. One involved the question of privilege for former presidents to protect the papers of past administrations. Interestingly, these former presidents had not even asked Bush to protect their papers. The suit came about because Congress had passed laws limiting the duration of executive privilege to a certain period after the president had left office, continuing a battle that had begun during the presidency of Gerald R. Ford over the ownership and control of President Richard M. Nixon's records and tapes. President Bush issued an executive order overriding this legislation and attempting vastly to expand presidential privileges for former presidents.[8] A legal challenge was then brought by the American Historical Association, and a U.S. District Court overturned part of Bush's order, holding that the order conflicted with the scheme developed by Congress to control access to presidential records.[9]

Most observers were surprised that Bush would expend so much political capital protecting the executive privilege of past presidents, many of whom were dead and none of whom had even asked for this protection. In retrospect, this controversy foreshadowed Bush's keen interest in pressing the constitutional foundations of presidential power as a political issue. Bush believed that to allow the privilege of past presidents to be limited statutorily by Congress was to assume that Congress possessed legal superiority over the executive branch. Both for his own sake and for the sake of the constitutional presidency, Bush chose to call this assumption into question.

## Energy Task Force

Almost equally as unusual was Bush's vigorous assertion of executive privilege regarding high-level energy meetings in which Vice President Dick Cheney had participated. Cheney did not claim executive privilege because of the need to protect confidential presidential discussions or advice. Rather, his assertion was based solely on his desire to protect basic information such as names of individuals present at task force meetings, the costs of the meetings, and the subject matter discussed. The energy task force, it was alleged, had been composed of many oil executives and their cohorts who had contributed greatly to Bush's presidential campaign. Fighting to hide these individuals' identities in the name of preserving the sanctity of executive power seemed audacious. Yet the Bush administration waged the battle all the way to the Supreme Court and prevailed.[10]

In *Cheney v. U.S. District Court for Dist. of Columbia*, the Supreme Court distinguished the controversy over the energy task force from that in *U.S. v. Nixon* (in which it ordered President Nixon to turn over the Watergate tapes) by pointing out that the latter was a criminal case and involved an entirely different set of constitutional considerations. The Court in *Cheney* held that in a civil matter, the executive branch could properly obtain a writ of mandamus against a lower court's discovery order if the discovery threatened to unearth sensitive presidential materials. The Court based its ruling on the long-standing principle that "the public interest requires that a coequal branch of Government 'afford Presidential confidentiality the greatest protection consistent with the fair administration of justice.'"[11]

Ironically, although the administration won the court battle, it paid a political price by giving the story much more political traction than it otherwise would have gained, by refusing to disclose the names of those attending the energy task force meetings. Yet the Bush administration believed that Congress had no constitutional or legal right to the documents in question, for any purpose. To compromise that principle, it felt, would be to injure the long-term constitutional independence of the presidency. Thus, President Bush asserted executive privilege with respect to the energy task force issue not so much to protect himself from political harm, but to achieve a broader political objective: constructing a constitutionally powerful presidency.

## 9/11: The Floodgates of Presidential Power Are Opened

The defining moment of the Bush presidency came with the September 11, 2001, attacks on the World Trade Center in New York and on the Pentagon in Washington, D.C. On that crisp September morning, the first plane flew into the World Trade Center in Manhattan just as President Bush was visiting an elementary school in Sarasota, Florida—part of his push for new legislation to reform the national education system that would be called No Child Left Behind. Bush was informed of the incident as he entered the school, but the reason for the crash was not yet clear. As he sat in the classroom listening to the students read aloud, a second plane crashed into another tower. When Bush's chief of staff whispered in the president's ear that America was under attack, Press Secretary Ari Fleischer, aware of the cameras in the classroom, instructed Bush not to immediately react. Bush soon left the classroom and issued a brief statement before being whisked away in Air Force One.

By the time the president reached Barksdale Air Force Base in Louisiana, a third plane had been flown into the Pentagon, and a fourth aircraft, bound for the White House or the Capitol building, had crashed into the ground in Shanksville, Pennsylvania. By the end of the day, both World Trade Center towers had collapsed and nearly three thousand people had lost their lives in the most deadly enemy attack ever to occur on American soil. Soon thereafter, an Islamist militant group named al Qaeda, led by a radical cleric named Osama bin Laden, claimed responsibility.[12]

Although President Bush's initial public responses to the tragedy were somewhat muted, he quickly gathered his composure and made a pair of compelling appearances in the days following the attacks. During an impromptu visit to Ground Zero on September 14, just three days after the twin towers had collapsed, Bush stood atop the wreckage with a weary New York City firefighter at his side. Going off script, as the crowd roared, "USA! USA! USA!" the president grabbed the megaphone and declared: "The people who knocked these buildings down will hear all of us soon." Six days later, Bush appeared before both houses of Congress to lay out his administration's proposed response to the attacks, delivering what many considered the finest speech of his presidency. After pledging to rebuild New York City, Bush issued an ultimatum to al Qaeda and its principal host—the Taliban government in Afghanistan: Hand over the members of al Qaeda who were responsible for the attack, or share in their demise. Bush declared: "I will not yield; I will not rest; I will not relent in waging this struggle for freedom and security for the American people."[13]

Within three days of the 9/11 attacks, with the collaboration of the Bush administration, Congress passed the Authorization for Use of Military Force (AUMF) Resolution, giving the president sweeping power "to use all necessary and appropriate force against those nations, organizations, or persons he determined planned, authorized, committed, or aided the terrorist attacks that occurred on September 11, 2001."[14] A year later, Bush signed into law the Homeland Security Act of 2002, creating the Department of Homeland Security, with a vast arsenal of powers, and authorizing it to prevent terroristic attacks within the country and reduce the vulnerability of the United States to terrorism.[15] In time, Bush evolved from a president focused on domestic policy to become a wartime president; he began bombing the Taliban government in Afghanistan on October 7, 2001. Bush had made an instant decision to treat the 9/11 attacks as an act of war, rather than as an isolated act of criminal conduct. Yet, even after the rapid fall of the Taliban regime, Osama bin Laden was able to flee the country and continued to evade American forces for the duration of Bush's presidency. Likewise, the Taliban regrouped after its initial defeat; the violent insurgency it mounted against the NATO coalition in Afghanistan dragged on well after Bush left the White House.[16]

Part of the Bush administration's failure to prosecute more effectively the war against the Taliban stemmed from its initiation of a second, more controversial conflict. In March 2003, the United States invaded Iraq to depose its dictator Saddam Hussein, who continued to defy UN weapons inspectors, leading many to believe that the dictator possessed deadly weapons of mass destruction (WMD). The White House alluded to a vague connection between al Qaeda and the Iraqi government. Yet evidence that Saddam actually possessed WMD, as well as the existence of a link between his secular regime and the religious extremists of al Qaeda, was scant at best. WMD were never found.[17] Moreover, the fall of Saddam's government spawned a bloody civil war between Iraq's Sunni, Shiite, and Kurdish Muslims. Even after the much-lauded U.S. troop surge ordered by President Bush in early 2007 brought some stability to the country, the situation in Iraq remained volatile throughout Bush's tenure in office.[18]

In ways similar to the outbreak of the Civil War with Abraham Lincoln and the entry of the United States into World War II with Franklin Roosevelt, 9/11 had presented President Bush with enormous opportunities to expand presidential power. Ironically, if Bush had simply allowed the threat of terrorism and the feeling of fear it engendered to speak for itself, the president's power might have grown from within, organically, as it had historically done in times of crises. Because of his administration's insistence on treating the enormous powers of the president as constitutionally vouchsafed to him, however, it engendered much more of a negative reaction from the public, Congress, and the courts.[19]

## The Patriot Act and NSA Wiretaps

In the immediate aftermath of 9/11, Bush had enjoyed unprecedented support in Congress, along with a 90 percent popular approval rating. Taking advantage of this immense political capital, his administration had pushed through a broad antiterrorism surveillance law known as the USA Patriot Act by a ninety-eight-to-one margin in the Senate.[20] The primary purpose of this law was to strengthen America's ability to prevent terrorist attacks by lifting many restrictions on the ability of law enforcement to gather intelligence both inside and outside the United States.[21]

One of the most controversial aspects of the Patriot Act was its sweeping expansion of the government's ability to use wiretaps. Before this time, the government had possessed the ability under the Foreign Intelligence Service Act (FISA) statute to gather up communications of potential terrorists and their allies by obtaining a warrant against the target rather than each device.[22] The Patriot Act now expanded the government's power by requiring even less specificity on the part of law enforcement officials with respect to the target's location and the communication providers in question. Civil libertarians, deeply concerned that the government was running roughshod over the First Amendment free speech and Fourth Amendment privacy rights of Americans in the name of national security, were horrified by the lack of judicial oversight under the Patriot Act. Despite this criticism, both the Patriot Act and FISA were further expanded by Congress after 9/11, creating a powerful weapon in the president's counterterrorism arsenal.[23]

The sense of horror only intensified for critics, when it was revealed that the government was spying on American citizens. After 9/11, the National Security Agency (NSA) had received White House authorization to monitor emails and telephone calls between individuals in the United States and overseas when it was believed that one party had links to terrorist organizations. Traditionally the NSA, much like the CIA, had focused its energies exclusively on foreign spying. Now, although American citizens were targeted, these wiretaps were conducted secretly without obtaining warrants or permission from the courts.[24]

A public outcry ensued when the program's existence was disclosed by the *New York Times* in late 2005. Even worse, the media reported that in March 2004, after a Justice Department review had determined that the program was illegal and should be altered or suspended, Bush's chief of staff, Andy Card, and White House Counsel Alberto Gonzales had gone to the hospital to persuade a seriously ill Attorney General John Ashcroft to reauthorize the wiretap program. Ashcroft's deputy attorney general, James Comey, kept the president's advisers at bay. Finally, in the face of a threat of mass resignations at the Justice Department, President Bush backed down.[25] A public outcry rose up that led to congressional hearings and a national debate on the use of warrantless wiretaps. The Bush administration had believed that the AUMF gave it power to use whatever means were necessary to conduct its war on terror, but Congress and the American public were pushing back. Ultimately, the Bush administration brokered a deal by which Congress amended the FISA statute to give the president more latitude, while revamping the process to give Congress and the judicial branch a direct role in approving these controversial wiretaps. Thus, although Bush was forced to retrench, the NSA wiretap program remained largely intact throughout the Bush years and continued to flourish under the Obama presidency—another testament to the powerful presidency forged by George W. Bush.[26]

## Interrogation and Torture

Among the many controversies in which President Bush found himself embroiled after 9/11, the so-called torture papers and Bush's decisions regarding the use of "extraordinary interrogation techniques" became a lightning rod for criticism. The Bush administration first sought advice from its lawyers (including Attorney General Gonzales) to answer the question "What *can* we do?"[27]

John Yoo, assistant attorney general in the Office of Legal Counsel, and David Addington, who served as legal counsel and later as chief of staff to Vice President Dick Cheney, authored a document that aimed to carve out a large measure of presidential discretion in the conduct of interrogations. In going down this path, these advisers focused on President Bush's commander-in-chief power as overriding all relevant statutory limitations. Specifically, Yoo and Gonzales argued that the Geneva Conventions governing prisoner treatment (which were treaties signed by the United States, making them binding law) did not apply to Taliban and al Qaeda combatants captured in the so-called war on terror—these were not governments but rogue terrorists. Likewise, they asserted that the War Crimes Act, a federal law carrying the death penalty, did not apply to these prisoners. Some in the administration, including Secretary of State Colin Powell, warned about the perils of this approach, citing the risk that *American* prisoners of war might not be afforded the protections of the same treaties if the United States selectively ignored them. Yet these arguments did not win the day. Another memorandum, authored by Jay S. Bybee, an assistant attorney general in the Office of Legal Counsel, argued openly for the use of "enhanced interrogation techniques" to extract information from al Qaeda operatives. Subsequent memoranda suggested that the president was not bound by domestic and international prohibitions of torture in situations where national security was threatened.[28]

In hindsight, the Bush administration's perceived overreaching in this area turned out to be a strategic (if not a legal) blunder.[29] Numerous prisoners captured during the war on terror were detained indefinitely in military facilities such as Guantanamo Bay, Cuba, and CIA "black sites" in other undisclosed locations. To elicit information, some of these detainees were subjected to harsh interrogation techniques, including waterboarding. Even worse, a large-scale torture of prisoners took place at the Abu Ghraib prison, twenty miles west of Baghdad. At that facility, prisoners were subjected to outrageous and dehumanizing treatment, including routine beatings, being stripped naked and piled together, and being subjected to threats of rape. Eventually, photographic evidence of this extreme abuse emerged and was published, resulting in public outrage.[30]

The events at Abu Ghraib were in no way sanctioned by, or even known to, President Bush until after they occurred. Yet they haunted his administration and its prosecution of the war on terror. For one segment of the American public, the crimes committed at Abu Ghraib appeared to be an inevitable extension of the administration's callous approach to human rights, generally, which seemed to be reflected in the torture papers.[31]

The fear engendered by the threat of another terrorist attack had been sufficient to justify, in the public's mind, nearly anything that the president wished to do to prevent and combat this threat. However, suggesting that the president could waterboard, torture, and humiliate suspected terrorists was a tactical decision that ended up backfiring. By issuing legal opinions that sought to justify, in advance, the possibility of lawlessness—and by issuing them as a matter of constitutional right—the administration lost significant credibility.

## Signing Statements

In a related vein, President Bush's signing statements became legendary to some and infamous to others. Bush was perhaps most famous for the signing statement he attached to the Detainee Treatment Act. This bill was signed after considerable negotiation with Senator John McCain (R-AZ) over the issue of its banning of any form of torture. President Bush then attached a signing statement to the bill stating that he would enforce the law in a manner consistent with his commander-in-chief authority. As Professor James Pfiffner, professor of public policy at George Mason University, later noted: "Since his administration previously had asserted that the commander in chief authority could overcome any law, it is reasonable to assume that President Bush felt that his subordinates were entitled to ignore the law and use whatever harsh interrogation procedures he preferred."[32]

President Bush consistently used signing statements to point to aspects of laws he believed could conflict with his constitutional authority, particularly in the realm of national security. Ironically, because Bush called attention to the matter without at the same time explaining that he had combated a serious and concrete threat of terrorism, his ideological commitment to the enlargement of the presidency again seemed to weaken his own position as chief executive.

## The Supreme Court Limits Bush's War Powers

Historically, the Supreme Court has tended to defer to the executive branch during wartime. The Bush administration seemed to depend on this tradition of judicial deference as it conducted its new war on terror and pursued its legal strategy in carrying out that war. Thus, four landmark decisions—*Hamdi, Rasul, Hamdan,* and *Boumediene,* all of which turned out to be major losses for the president—came as a complete surprise to the Bush White House.

In *Hamdi v. Rumsfeld,* Yaser Hamdi—who held both U.S. and Saudi Arabian citizenship—was captured on the battlefield in Afghanistan and taken to Guantanamo Bay. When military officials learned that he was a U.S. citizen, Hamdi was transferred to a navy brig in Virginia (and later, South Carolina), where he challenged the lawfulness of his detention. Although the Supreme Court agreed that Hamdi's detention was permitted under the

AUMF, it also held that Hamdi was entitled to due process of law, pursuant to his status as an American citizen, to challenge his designation as an enemy combatant. The Supreme Court further stung the Bush administration when Justice Sandra Day O'Connor declared: "A state of war is not a blank check when it comes to the rights of the nation's citizens."[33]

*Rasul v. Bush*—released on the same day—announced that the writ of habeas corpus applied to the *noncitizen* enemy combatants being held at Guantanamo Bay. Shafiq Rasul, a British citizen, had been captured on the battlefield during the early stages of the coalition's invasion of Afghanistan. Rasul was designated by the Bush administration as an enemy combatant and detained at Guantanamo, but he petitioned a federal court for a writ of habeas corpus to declare his detention unconstitutional. The administration asserted that the federal courts did not even have jurisdiction over the habeas petition of a noncitizen being held outside the United States. The Court disagreed, concluding that the guaranty of habeas corpus applied to foreign nationals held in Guantanamo. The Court's reasoning was threefold: Rasul was a citizen of a country (Great Britain) not formally at war with the United States, he had denied engaging in any wrongdoing against the United States, and the United States exercised "plenary and exclusive" jurisdiction over the Guantanamo Bay naval base.[34]

*Hamdan v. Rumsfeld* dealt yet another blow to the Bush administration. Salim Ahmed Hamdan, a citizen of Yemen, had allegedly worked as a bodyguard for Osama bin Laden and was captured in Afghanistan. The Bush administration convened its own military commission to try Hamdan.[35] In another firm decision, the Supreme Court held that this military tribunal was not proper, because the procedures used violated American laws of war, including the Geneva Conventions, along with the Uniform Code of Military Justice.[36]

*Boumediene v. Bush* was even more definitive in rejecting Bush policy. Here, the Court declared that Lakhdar Boumediene and all other detainees at Guantanamo were entitled to the constitutional privilege of habeas corpus and that the system established under the Military Commissions Act of 2006 constituted an unconstitutional suspension of habeas corpus in violation of Article I, Section 9, of the Constitution.[37] Significantly, in *Boumediene*, the Court not only rebuked the Bush administration for its failure to stay within its proper constitutional boundaries, but also issued a tacit rebuke to Congress for its failure to do the same. Subsequently,

Boumediene and other detainees were released.[38] Thus, the Supreme Court made clear that the judiciary would constitute a key player in the legal processes of the war on terror and that federal courts would carefully scrutinize the habeas petitions of military detainees held at Guantanamo, no matter what the president or Congress tried to do to box the courts out.

## Conclusion

After a sweeping Democratic victory in the 2006 congressional midterm elections, George W. Bush was a lame-duck president for much of his second term. By the time he left the White House in January 2009, his approval rating had sunk to 22 percent, one of the lowest in American history and a far cry from the height of his popularity during the aftermath of 9/11.[39] Perhaps because of the country's growing skepticism about the war in Afghanistan, combined with domestic problems, including a distressed economy that Democrats blamed on misguided Bush administration policies, Senator Barack Obama won a decisive victory against the Republican standard-bearer, Senator John McCain, with over twice the number of electoral votes. Bush retired quietly to his ranch in Crawford, Texas. He generally avoided politics and remained out of the spotlight, spending his time painting, fishing, and clearing brush at his remote ranch.

While President Bush consistently pursued a legalistic conception of a constitutionally empowered executive, he did not seem to do so for the sake of his own political authority. Indeed, his pursuit of a powerful presidency—particularly in the name of the war on terror—often hindered and undercut his own political agenda. Perhaps Bush's strategy for the enlargement of presidential power followed naturally from the legalistic age in which he occupied the White House. In instances like his reliance on the torture memos to justify sweeping powers, Bush tried to accomplish through legal opinions what presidents like Abraham Lincoln had done through political action.

Ironically, by seeking to politicize the constitutional powers of the presidency to such a large extent, Bush may have done more to weaken his presidency than to strengthen it. Yet in the process, President Obama and later presidents were given a completely new toolbox for the assertion of presidential authority that very much constitutes the legacy of their predecessor, George W. Bush.

NOTES

1. Stephen Skowronek, "The Conservative Insurgency and Presidential Power: A Developmental Perspective on the Unitary Executive," *Harvard Law Review* 122, no. 8 (2009): 2074–2103.

2. Bush v. Gore, 531 U.S. 98 (2000).

3. The Supreme Court, by a vote of seven to two, found that the Florida recount was unconstitutional under the Fourteenth Amendment. The Court's deep division flowed primarily from the fact that its decision seemed to award Bush the election. Nelson Lund, "The Unbearable Rightness of Bush v. Gore," *Cardozo Law Review* 23 (2002): 1243.

4. Bush v. Gore, 531 U.S. at 110.

5. Ibid., 153 (Breyer J., dissenting). Moreover, Justice Breyer pointed out that Congress had passed the elaborate Electoral Count Act after the disputed Hayes-Tilden election to sharpen the rules by which Congress would select the president in case of such disputes. Nevertheless, permitting Congress to resolve the disputed election in this case most likely would not have changed the result—Republicans maintained a clear majority in the House, which selects the president.

6. For the argument that above all things, Bush cared about presidential power, see Jack Goldsmith, *The Terror Presidency: Law and Judgment Inside the Bush Administration* (New York: W.W. Norton, 2007).

7. As Mark Rozell has documented: "President Bush has exercised the privilege in an attempt to reestablish what he perceives as a more correct balance of powers between the legislative and executive branches." Mark J. Rozell, "Executive Privilege Revived: Secrecy and Conflict During the Bush Administration," *Duke Law Journal* 52 (2002): 403–421.

8. Exec. Order No. 13233, 66 FR 56025 (2001).

9. American Historical Ass'n v. National Archives and Records Admin., 516 F.Supp.2d 90, 109–11 (D.D.C. 2007). Later, in 2009, President Barrack Obama would reverse the remainder of Bush's Order. Exec. Order No. 13,489, 74 FR 4669 (2009).

10. The case, Cheney v. U.S. Dist. Court for Dist. of Columbia, 542 U.S. 367 (2004), arose when two groups, Judicial Watch and the Sierra Club, brought suit alleging that the administration had violated federal law by not making required disclosures pertaining to the Energy Task Force. Ultimately, the Bush administration prevailed. The Supreme Court's decision, citing separation of powers principles, rejected the D.C. Circuit's reliance on *U.S. v. Nixon*. *Cheney*, 542 U.S. at 382.

11. *Cheney*, 542 U.S. at 382 (quoting *U.S. v. Nixon*, 418 U.S. at 715).

12. Robert Draper, *Dead Certain* (New York: Free Press, 2007), 134–141.

13. Ibid., 151–153, 156–157. George W. Bush, "Address to a Joint Session of Congress on Thursday Night, September 20, 2001," transcript, CNN.com, http://edition.cnn.com/2001/US/09/20/gen.bush.transcript/.

14. "Authorization for Use of Military Force," P.L. 107–40, 115 Stat. 224 (September 18, 2001).

15. Homeland Security Act of 2002. Pub. L. 107–296. 116 Stat. 2135 (November 25, 2002). President Bush personally proposed to Congress that it enact legislation to create the

Department of Homeland Security. Comparing the challenges from terrorism the country faced after September 11 to the Cold War challenges the county faced at the conclusion of World War II, Bush drew a parallel between his proposal and the reorganization of federal intelligence and military agencies that followed the passage of the National Security Act of 1947 during the Truman administration. Darren W. Stanhouse, "Arbitration and Abdication: Congress. The Presidency, and the Evolution of the Department of Homeland Security," *North Carolina Journal of International Law and Commercial Regulation* 29 (summer 2004): 691, n. 1.

16. For an excellent account of the war in Afghanistan, see Seth G. Jones, *In the Graveyard of Empires* (New York: W.W. Norton, 2010).

17. While WMD were not recovered, American troops did recover chemical weapons predating 1991 from various locations throughout Iraq. C. J. Chivers, "The Secret Casualties of Iraq's Abandoned Chemical Weapons," *New York Times*, October 14, 2014, www.nytimes.com/interactive/2014/10/14/world/middleeast/us-casualties-of-iraq-chemical-weapons.html.

18. Stephen M. Walt, "Top 10 Lessons of the Iraq War," *Foreign Policy*, March 20, 2012. Indeed, the sectarian violence spawned by the U.S. invasion raged on long after the majority of U.S forces departed from Iraq. Tim Arango, "Rising Violence in Iraq Spurs Fears of New Sectarian War," *New York Times*, April 24, 2013.

19. Stephen Knott's important book defending the Bush administration against its critics nonetheless captures a certain truth that many of the scholars in the Pfiffner camp fail to appreciate. Stephen Knott, *Rush to Judgment: George W. Bush, The War on Terror, and His Critics* (Lawrence: University Press of Kansas, 2012). Knott shows although Bush's power grew in the post-9/11 period, that growth in power is not unprecedented in comparison to that of other wartime presidencies. Thus, Knott is critical of scholars who accuse Bush of being lawless and ignoring the Constitution in a manner that is unprecedented among all presidents.

20. Draper, *Dead Certain*, 166.

21. USA Patriot Act of 2001, Pub. L. No. 107–56, 115 Stat. 272 (2001).

22. Foreign Intelligence Service Act of 1978, Pub. L. No. 95–511, 92 Stat. 1783 (1978).

23. Most recently, Bush's successor, Barack Obama, signed a four-year extension of the Patriot Act in 2011. Philip Bridwell and Jamil Jaffer, "Updating the Counterterrorism Tool Kit: A Brief Sampling of Post-9/11 Surveillance Laws and Authorities," in *The Law of Counterterrorism*, ed. Lynne K. Zusman (Chicago: American Bar Association Publishing, 2011), 238–242. In 2013, the U.S. Supreme Court dismissed a lawsuit brought in response to the 2008 expansion of "roving wiretaps" under FISA on procedural grounds. Clapper v. Amnesty Intl. USA, 133 S. Ct. 1138 (2013). The lawsuit challenged the FISA Amendments Act of 2008, 50 U.S.C. §1881(a). The Court held that because wiretaps were secret under the act, there was no way for the victims to prove that they had been targeted and thus had the requisite standing to bring the lawsuit.

24. Dan Eggen and Paul Kane, "Gonzales Hospital Episode Detailed," *Washington Post*, May 16, 2007.

25. Ibid.

26. Shane Harris, "Giving in to the Surveillance States," *New York Times*, August 22, 2012.

27. Philip Zelikow, "Legal Policy for a Twilight War," *Houston Journal of International Law* 30, no. 1 (2007–2008): 89–109. The whole debate about so many of the activities made necessary by the war on terror was framed, in the first place, by that question rather than first asking the question "What *should* we do?" Because the administration was asking lawyers, many of whom had been chosen by the administration for their prior commitment to a powerful presidency, these lawyers answered the "What can we do?" question by articulating the fullest range of presidential discretion possible.

28. "A Guide to the Memos on Torture," *New York Times*, 2005, www.nytimes.com/ref/international/24MEMO-GUIDE.html?_r=0; see also Karen J. Greenberg, Joshua L. Dratel and Jeffrey S. Grossman, eds., *The Enemy Combatant Papers* (New York: Cambridge University Press, 2008).

29. Benjamin A. Kleinerman, *The Discretionary President: The Promise and Peril of Executive Power* (Lawrence: University Press of Kansas, 2009).

30. Seymour M. Hersh, "Torture at Abu Ghraib," *New Yorker*, May 10, 2004.

31. The ACLU maintains a complete collection of papers obtained under the Freedom of Information Act concerning the torture of prisoners in U.S. detention centers. See American Civil Liberties Union, "The Torture Database," accessed May 27, 2015, www.aclu.org/accountability/released.html.

32. James P. Pfiffner, *Power Play* (Washington, DC: Brookings Institution Press, 2008), 213.

33. Hamdi v. Rumsfeld, 542 U.S. 507 (2004).

34. Rasul v. Bush, 542 U.S. 466 (2004). In response to *Rasul*, Congress passed the Detainee Treatment Act of 2005, Pub. L. No. 109–148, 119 Stat. 2739 (2006), which, among other things, amended the federal habeas corpus statute in an attempt to deny federal courts jurisdiction over habeas claims originating from Guantanamo Bay.

35. Supreme Court precedent, dating back to World War II, supported the practice of trying enemy combatants in special military tribunals. Ex Parte Quirin, 317 U.S. 1 (1942). Moreover, the Supreme Court had also upheld the use of military tribunals where the accused enemy combatants had never been detained on American soil. Johnson v. Eisentrager, 339 U.S. 763 (1950).

36. Hamdan v. Rumsfeld, 548 U.S. 557 (2006).

37. Boumediene v. Bush, 553 U.S. 723 (2008). Article I, section 9, of the Constitution states that "the privilege of the Writ of Habeas Corpus shall not be suspended."

38. Lakhdar Boumediene, "My Guantanamo Nightmare," *New York Times*, January 7, 2012.

39. "Bush's Final Approval Rating: 22 Percent," *CBS News Online*, February 11, 2009, www.cbsnews.com/2100-500160_162-4728399.html.

# 44

# Barack Obama

### MICHAEL J. GERHARDT

*President Barack Obama, the first African American chief executive in the history of the United States, inspired millions of people to believe in his message of hope. His administration's signature piece of legislation, the Affordable Care Act, came under persistent attacks as he sought to implement sweeping health-care reform. The Obama administration exercised executive powers aggressively—refusing to deport many undocumented immigrants who had entered the country as children, and refusing to defend the constitutionality of the Defense of Marriage Act (DOMA), becoming the first administration to support same-sex marriage. In the war on terror, President Obama used an elite team of Navy SEALS to kill al Qaeda mastermind Osama bin Laden. Yet, he was criticized for using drones to kill American citizens on foreign soil, for continuing his predecessor's use of NSA data collection to gather intelligence, and for overusing executive orders. President Obama's presidency will doubtless be viewed as transformational; however, some critics will charge that he overreached in exercising his own executive authority, particularly in certain controversial areas that might have been left to Congress.*

## Introduction

As the nation's first African American president, Barack Obama embodied the American dream and symbolized the nation's progress on civil rights since the Civil War, Reconstruction, and the formal abolition of slavery. Yet, some Americans refused to accept, much less abide by, the sight of a black man—particularly a liberal Democrat—in the White House. These skeptics questioned Obama's constitutional legitimacy and judgments throughout his presidency. As the fourth professor of constitutional law to become president, Obama had expertise that many believed would equip him to deal with the constitutional challenges likely to confront him as president.[1] However, his initial election coincided with the rise of the Tea Party, whose members fervently believed that Obama did not represent American values (some asserted that he was born in Kenya and was not even eligible to be president) and that he habitually rejected their view of the Constitution's original meaning.

Barack Hussein Obama was born on August 4, 1961, in Hawaii, the first American president to have been born in the fiftieth state. His father was Kenyan, and his mother was a white woman from Kansas. Less than a month after he was born, Obama's parents separated and divorced. His mother subsequently married a man from Indonesia, where she and Barack lived for several years before he returned to live with his grandparents in Hawaii. Obama moved to Los Angeles to attend Occidental College but transferred two years later to Columbia University, from which he graduated in 1983. After working for nearly three years as a community organizer in Chicago, Obama entered Harvard Law School, where he made history as the first African American to be selected as the president of the prestigious *Harvard Law Review*, earning his law degree in 1991. A year later, he married Michelle Robinson, who had been three years ahead of him at Harvard. Obama turned down opportunities to work with top-notch law firms and judges, instead opting to work as a civil rights attorney in Chicago and as a senior lecturer at the University of Chicago Law School, where he taught constitutional law.

In 1996, Obama won election to the Illinois Senate, where he served for three terms. In 2000, he lost in a bid to unseat a Democratic incumbent in the U.S. House of Representatives. After becoming chair of the Illinois

Senate's Health and Human Services Committee, Obama declared his intent to run for the U.S. Senate. While campaigning, he was selected as the keynote speaker for the 2004 Democratic convention, a performance that allowed him to dazzle a nationwide audience with his oratorical skills. He decisively won the U.S. Senate race.

In February 2007, Obama surprised many pundits by challenging the front-runner for the Democratic presidential nomination: former First Lady and now senator, Hillary Rodham Clinton. During the campaign, in response to controversial statements made by an African American minister whose church Obama had occasionally attended, Obama defused the situation by delivering what would ultimately prove to be a landmark speech on race relations in America and the importance to Americans of putting past racial divisions behind them.[2] In a tight race, Obama won the nomination. With the economy seriously ailing and his Republican opponent, Senator John McCain, lacking the same gift of oratory and message of hope, Obama won the 2008 presidential election with over 52 percent of the popular vote and twice as many votes in the Electoral College as McCain received. On January 20, 2009, Barack Hussein Obama was sworn into office as the nation's forty-fourth president and the first African American to occupy the White House in the nation's history. Almost immediately, he was confronted with major constitutional issues that would test his mettle as chief executive.

## Presidency

### Health-Care Reform

Shortly after his inauguration, President Obama told a joint session of Congress that the centerpiece of his administration would be comprehensive health-care reform, to ensure every American access to health care at an affordable price. With the political parties sharply split over the issue, Obama navigated the legislation through Congress by a narrow vote, signing the Patient Protection and Affordable Care Act (the Affordable Care Act) into law on March 23, 2012.[3]

Lawsuits were filed in multiple federal courts around the country challenging the constitutionality of the controversial legislation, dubbed "Obamacare." Plaintiffs took special aim at the law's *individual mandate* (or minimum-coverage provision), which required virtually all Americans to purchase some minimal level of health-care insurance or pay a penalty. This, said critics, could not be supported as a valid exercise of Congress's power under the Commerce Clause.[4] In addition, they argued that the provision requiring states to expand their Medicaid coverage or forfeit all federal monies they received for health-care services exceeded Congress's authority under the Spending Clause.[5]

On the last day of its term, in June 2012, the Court handed down its ruling in *National Federation of Independent Business v. Sebelius*.[6] To the surprise of most observers, Chief Justice John Roberts, joined by the liberal wing of the Court (Justices Ruth Bader Ginsburg, Stephen Breyer, Sonia Sotomayor, and Elena Kagan), provided the swing vote to uphold Congress's authority to enact the controversial individual mandate provision, relying on Congress's power under the Taxing and Spending Clause rather than under the Commerce Clause.[7]

The chief justice found that Congress did not have the authority under the Commerce Clause to enact the minimum-coverage provision.[8] This provision, said the Roberts, had the effect of *compelling individuals to participate* in an economic activity—namely, the purchase of health insurance—rather than *regulating* an economic activity in which individuals were already engaging.[9] This difference, he concluded, exceeded the powers of Congress under the Commerce Clause.

Yet, Chief Justice Roberts went on to save the individual mandate through a deft maneuver. He characterized the payment mandated from uninsured or underinsured individuals as a tax—rather than as a penalty—for the purposes of the Taxing and Spending Clause.[10] After all, said the chief justice, the funds were to be collected by the IRS and would not be payable by individuals whose income did not require them to file a federal tax return. Although the act itself described the payment as a "penalty," said Roberts, that label was not determinative.[11]

Having upheld the provision that served as the cornerstone of the Affordable Care Act, the Court nonetheless struck down the Medicaid expansion provision.[12] The Court held that the threat of complete withdrawal of Medicaid funding for noncompliant states was an unconstitutionally coercive use of Congress's spending power, in violation of the Tenth Amendment.[13] Yet Chief Justice Roberts also concluded that the Medicaid provision could be stricken from the act, allowing the rest of the law to survive.[14]

President Obama hailed the Supreme Court's decision as a victory (even though he disputed that the penalty was a tax). Even as he weighed in, opponents of the Affordable Care Act—including the Republican presidential nominee Governor Mitt Romney of Massachusetts—vowed to repeal it.[15] Obama won reelection in 2012, but critics continued to charge that the act constituted a reckless expansion of the federal government's power, akin to the unchecked growth of the federal bureaucracy during FDR's New Deal. Opponents filed additional lawsuits challenging the act, including one maintaining that it was improperly introduced in the Senate rather than the House (where all revenue bills should originate). Another suit claimed that the act authorized only states, not the federal government, to establish exchanges for people to obtain health insurance. The fight continued well into Obama's second term. In 2014, the Republican-dominated House accused Obama of abusing his executive powers when the administration delayed the implementation of several Affordable Care Act provisions. The House went so far as to authorize the Speaker of the House to file a lawsuit against Obama, charging that the president had usurped Congress's constitutional role by unilaterally changing the law.[16] In 2015, however, in *King v. Burwell*, Chief Justice Roberts handed the Obama administration a second significant victory, authoring a majority opinion that upheld a central and essential aspect of the Affordable Care Act's tax credit scheme.[17]

## Executive Actions and Same-Sex Marriage

The Obama administration made aggressive use of executive orders and administrative actions to consolidate power and to bypass Congress in areas in which the legislature had failed to take action or to enact Obama's proposed legislative initiatives.[18] In one case, in June 2012, President Obama announced that his administration would no longer deport illegal immigrants who entered the United States as children as long as they met criteria set forth by the administration.[19]

In response to sharp criticism from some members of Congress, the Obama administration declared that it was inherent in the executive branch's enforcement powers to use its discretion in deciding whom to prosecute; this discretion had been recognized by every administration in American history. The administration also pointed to a recent Supreme Court decision that had declared that "the Government of the United States has broad, undoubted power over the subject of immigration and the status of aliens."[20] Nonetheless, critics charged that the White House was running amok, executing power that did not belong to it under the Constitution.

The decision not to enforce federal law in the immigration realm paralleled the president's equally controversial announcement that the federal government would no longer defend the constitutionality of the Defense of Marriage Act (DOMA).[21] This federal law sought to define marriage as the legal union of a man and a woman and aimed to trump state laws permitting same-sex marriage. The administration defended its decision by declaring that it believed the statute was unconstitutional. Every president since Andrew Jackson had argued that, by virtue of his oath of office, the chief executive was not obliged to enforce laws that he regarded as unconstitutional. Because President Obama and his administration had gradually reached the conclusion that DOMA violated the Equal Protection component of the Fifth Amendment Due Process Clause, they felt justified in taking this action.[22]

Many Republican leaders countered that policy disagreements between an administration and Congress were not a legitimate basis for declining to enforce duly enacted laws. Indeed, they suggested that the administration's refusal to enforce DOMA established a dangerous precedent that would allow future presidents and administrations to circumvent any laws they deemed distasteful for any reason.[23]

President Obama, undeterred by these criticisms, used his bully pulpit to actively press for the acceptance of same-sex marriage. In a television interview, Obama referred to a conversation with his two young daughters, stating that "it doesn't make sense to them" that their friends' gay parents were treated differently than other parents.[24] During his second inaugural address, in January 2013, Obama took a bolder step and became the first president to openly proclaim support for gay rights and marriage for same-sex couples. Two months later, the Obama administration urged the Supreme Court to strike down DOMA and a California referendum barring marriage between same-sex couples.

In *United States v. Windsor*, a five-to-four decision authored by Justice Anthony Kennedy, the Court agreed with the Obama administration's position and invalidated the Defense of Marriage Act on Equal Protection grounds.[25] Yet the Court seemed to sidestep a definitive ruling on same-sex marriage by suggesting that marriage and family issues were matters primarily reserved to the states. On the same day, the Court also decided *Hollingsworth v. Perry*, in which it paved the way for dismantling

California's Proposition 8 banning same-sex marriage, by holding that the independent groups backing the law lacked standing to defend it in court.[26] The Obama administration praised both rulings as a crucial first step toward marriage equality in the United States. Ultimately, in *Obergefell v. Hodges*, a landmark opinion authored by Justice Kennedy and lauded by President Obama, the Court ruled that the right to marry is a fundamental right inherent in the liberty of the person under the Fourteenth Amendment and that states may not deny couples of the same sex this right.[27]

Thus, President Obama effectively used executive orders, combined with the power of his presidential bully pulpit, to help create a major legal shift in American law and public policy.

## *Recess Appointment Power*

President Obama also sought to make an aggressive use of presidential authority granted in Article II, Section 2, "to fill up all Vacancies that may happen during the Recess of the Senate." During Obama's first two years in office, when he enjoyed a nearly filibuster-proof Senate with fifty-nine Democratic seats, the Senate approved 87 percent of his judicial and other nominations. However, during the next eighteen months, the Senate approved only 18 percent of his nominations, not acting on many of them. This was the lowest rate of approval for any post–World War II president. Frustrated over the prospect that the Senate would block his nominations to both the National Labor Relations Board (NLRB) and the Consumer Financial Protection Bureau (CFPB) for his entire term, President Obama declared in January 2012 that he was making recess appointments to fill vacancies in those agencies.[28]

Republican members in both the House and the Senate became outraged. House leaders held three hearings, proclaiming that the president's recess appointments were unconstitutional because Congress was not in formal recess when he made those appointments. They argued that as a constitutional matter, a recess could occur only if Congress formally adjourned—however, they contended that the Senate was still meeting every three days in "pro forma" sessions when President Obama made the appointments.[29] The Office of Legal Counsel (OLC) upheld President Obama's decision to make his appointments during the brief period of adjournment between the "pro forma" sessions. According to the OLC, the president's position was consistent with precedent, and in fact, the Department of Justice "has long interpreted the term 'recess' to include intra-session recesses if they are of substantial length."[30] The OLC added that presidents throughout history had made their own judgments as to when Congress was in adjournment; an example was President Coolidge, as recorded in the *Pocket Veto Case* (1929), in which the Supreme Court had upheld his actions.[31]

The Supreme Court eventually granted certiorari in *NLRB v. Canning*, tackling the issue of recess appointments "for the first time in more than 200 years."[32] Justice Breyer, writing for the Court, invalidated the three appointments in question, dealing a blow to President Obama and his administration. Yet the decision, overall, gave enormous latitude to presidents in exercising power to make recess appointments under Article II, Section 2. The Court emphasized that recess appointments were designed as a "subsidiary, not a primary" method of appointing federal officers; the "norm" was for presidents to first obtain Senate approval.[33] Nonetheless, Justice Breyer acknowledged that historical practice was compelling and that "Presidents have made recess appointments since the beginning of the Republic."[34]

In construing the recess appointments provision broadly, the Court concluded that this power applied to both "inter-session" (i.e., between two-year sessions of succeeding Congresses) and "intra-session" (i.e., within a single two-year life of an elected Congress) recesses.[35] The Court furthermore agreed with the Obama administration that the power applied even to vacancies that came into existence *before* the Senate's recess. On a third key point, however, Justice Breyer concluded that President Obama's appointments failed: They had taken place during a three-day period of adjournment between "*pro forma* sessions," when the Senate was still formally doing business. Although it was certainly possible for presidents to make appointments during intrasession breaks, said the Court, the three-day break here was simply insufficient; anything less than ten days was "presumptively too short."[36]

Thus, President Obama's recess appointments that had taken place during a fleeting three-day break between pro forma sessions were struck down. At the same time, Obama won a significant victory for future presidents. While acknowledging that the Senate had the power to decide when it was in session and able to do business, the Court nonetheless refused to disembowel the president's recess appointment power. Indeed, it gave chief executives considerable latitude so that obstreperous Congresses, by refusing to act on nominations indefinitely, could not have a blank check to thwart presidents' constitutional power to make appointments.[37]

## Congress Holds Attorney General in Contempt

Another defining constitutional moment in Obama's presidency involved the decision by the House of Representatives to hold a president's attorney general (Attorney General Eric Holder) in contempt, for the first time in American history. The drama unfolded with a botched effort known as Operation Fast and Furious. This joint undercover operation of the Justice Department and other federal agencies was designed to break up the drug-trafficking activities of Mexican drug cartels. Employing the strategy of gun-walking, federal agents purposely did not seize illegal weapons in the possession of drug smugglers, even though the weapons were within their grasp, instead opting to track these weapons as part of a risky plan to apprehend the kingpins of the Mexican drug gang. The strategy turned deadly as 130 of the weapons were found at crime scenes in the United States, including at the site where a federal Border Patrol agent was killed in December 2010.[38]

Committees of both the House and the Senate investigated the bungled operation. A joint report was released excoriating the Justice Department for its handling of the program.[39] Testifying before the House Oversight Committee in June 2012, Attorney General Holder—the first African American to hold that office—denied any knowledge of the gun-walking strategy in advance.[40] Questioning Holder's truthfulness, House Oversight Committee chair Darrell Issa (R-CA) demanded thirteen hundred additional pages of documents and wrote to Holder on June 13, 2012, warning him that Congress could cite him for contempt if he refused to turn over the items demanded. On June 19, Holder formally asked President Obama to assert executive privilege over the documents in question; the president did so a day later.[41]

On June 28, 2012, the House voted 255 to 67 to hold Attorney General Holder in contempt of Congress, a historic vote that generated heated partisan rhetoric on both sides.[42] Outraged House Democrats engaged in a mass walkout and refused to participate in the voting, which otherwise fell along party lines.[43] As a result, Holder became the first cabinet officer in American history to be held in contempt by Congress.[44] Some Republicans went so far as to urge that the attorney general should be jailed in the Capitol because of his refusal to cooperate.

On September 19, 2012, the Justice Department's inspector general completed his investigation of Operation Fast and Furious and concluded that Holder knew nothing about the matter until after the events in question. The contempt citation went nowhere. While the Supreme Court had previously upheld the inherent authority of Congress to enforce its contempt citations in court, Congress had not exercised this authority since 1935, because enforcement had generally been considered too "cumbersome, time-consuming, and relatively ineffective, especially for a modern Congress with a heavy legislative workload that would be interrupted by a trial at the bar."[45] Thus, the Fast and Furious episode ended in a standoff, with irate House members and the Obama administration both licking their wounds.

## Osama bin Laden and Drones

On May 2, 2011, President Obama ordered an elite team of U.S. Navy SEALs to raid a compound in Abbottabad, Pakistan. Its mission was to kill or capture Osama bin Laden, founder of the al Qaeda terrorist organization that had claimed credit for the September 11 attacks on the World Trade Center in New York and the Pentagon in Washington, D.C. During the harrowing operation that followed, the SEALs deployed in the dead of night from an air base inside Afghanistan. The teams entered Pakistani airspace onboard special stealth Black Hawk helicopters, landed around the compound, and stormed bin Laden's living quarters, where they killed bin Laden and four others.[46] The al Qaeda leader's body was flown back to Afghanistan and positively identified before being taken to the USS *Carl Vinson* and buried at sea.[47] President Obama thus demonstrated that he was prepared to take decisive action against America's enemies, without consulting with Congress in advance.[48]

The Obama administration also adopted an aggressive policy utilizing unmanned aircraft, commonly referred to as drones, to attack al Qaeda operatives in Pakistan, Yemen, and Somalia. These drones, operating remotely from bases in the United States, allowed the CIA and the Pentagon to disrupt al Qaeda's operations without placing American military personnel in harm's way. Midway through Obama's presidency, these "targeted killings" generated enormous controversy.

During Obama's first term alone, the executive branch had conducted approximately three hundred drone strikes in Pakistan, sixty in Yemen, and several more in Somalia.[49] Most of these covert operations targeted foreign nationals believed to be associated with al Qaeda and its branch organizations. However, in 2012, the highly publicized killings of two American citizens in Yemen—Anwar al-Awlaki and his sixteen-year-old son—raised unprecedented new constitutional issues under the Due Process Clause of the Fifth Amendment.[50]

As graphic details of drone killings sanctioned directly by President Obama continued to emerge, the administration came under increased pressure from Congress and the media to clarify its policy, particularly in the targeting of American citizens.[51] Attorney General Holder rejected the charge that the president lacked constitutional authority to order the killing of American terror suspects without involving Congress or the judiciary. He asserted that such operations were based on "imminent" threats posed by certain individuals, the infeasibility of capture, and the applicable law of war principles. Holder asserted that the presence of these circumstances together with a careful decision-making process within the executive branch satisfied the due-process requirement and that judicial oversight was neither appropriate nor necessary.[52] Eventually, President Obama offered similarly nonspecific assurances that the decision-making process had been thorough before targeted killings had taken place.[53]

Criticism erupted on both sides of the political aisle. Liberal Democrats, who had castigated George W. Bush over the use of "enhanced interrogation" techniques (or torture) on detainees during his presidency, now criticized President Obama (who had campaigned against the prior administration's policies) as going even further by ordering Americans to be killed in secret without public accountability. Conservative Republicans, while less troubled by the killings themselves, were quick to accuse liberals and the media of hypocrisy for not attacking Obama's drone program as fervently they had attacked Bush's torture policies. An internal Department of Justice white paper, which attempted to provide legal justification for the targeted killing of Americans, only enraged critics further.[54]

This roiling controversy returned the nation to a question that had lingered throughout much of its history: How much liberty are Americans willing to sacrifice in the name of national security? At times, presidents have gained sweeping authority to carry out armed conflict without the usual checks and balances, particularly during times of heightened danger. In the post-9/11 era, presidents have expanded this power even further in the name of the so-called war on terror. Yet the drone program by which individuals could be targeted and killed through previously unimaginable technology, without prior approval of Congress or the courts, now directly implicated the due-process rights of American citizens. Thus, with particular concern generated by the targeted killings of Anwar al-Awlaki and his teenage son, President Obama was ultimately pressured to bring the drone program out of the shadows and into the view of Congress, the courts, and the public.[55]

## Conclusion

Many historians will surely view President Obama's 2012 reelection by a wide margin of electoral votes as vindicating his constitutional record. Some will call his presidency transformational: the first African American to serve as chief executive after two centuries of strife over the race issue in the United States. Others, however, can be counted on to dismiss Obama as an apostate who was guilty of constitutional overreaching. Even as he entered the final stretch of his presidency, Obama made robust use of executive actions, partly in response to congressional inaction.[56] He took significant steps to ease the threat of deportation with respect to certain illegal immigrants. Obama also took executive action to reinstate diplomatic relations with Cuba and relax import and export restrictions that had been in place for five decades with respect to that communist-led government.[57] He provoked the ire of the Republican-led Senate when he sought to strike a deal on nuclear arms with Iran, causing a group of Republican senators to publicly challenge his authority in his realm of foreign affairs.

In the last stretch of his presidency, Obama began negotiating with Iran with an eye toward reaching an executive agreement relating to nuclear arms. Forty-seven Republican members of the Senate, led by freshman Senator Tom Cotton of Arkansas, criticized the purported deal as a blatant usurpation of congressional authority. They trod on questionable constitutional ground by signing and releasing an open letter to the Islamic leaders of Iran. The letter expounded on the allocation of power between the executive and legislative branches in the realm of international agreements and cautioned Iran that any agreement that was entered without legislative approval could be reversed by the next president. Despite vigorous debate about whether the so-called Cotton Letter unconstitutionally encroached on the president's powers to direct foreign policy, there was little dispute that the letter was without precedent. Moreover, it perhaps reflected a reordering of the tradition of presidential preeminence and congressional nonintervention when it came to the nation's diplomatic negotiations and foreign affairs.[58] In 2016, President Obama again used his executive authority to strengthen background checks and step up enforcement of the nation's gun laws to address the growing problem of gun violence, provoking the ire of some members of Congress. Ultimately, the outcome of issues concerning the scope of executive power will dictate whether future presidents regard President Obama's actions as precedents to follow or as missteps to avoid.

NOTES

1. Woodrow Wilson taught classes on the Constitution at Princeton University, and Bill Clinton's first job after graduating Yale Law School was as a professor of constitutional law at the University of Arkansas Law School. Before becoming president, William Howard Taft was dean and a professor of law at the University of Cincinnati Law School. Taft taught constitutional law at Yale Law School in the years between his leaving the presidency and his appointment as chief justice of the United States.
2. As president, Obama had to confront the racial divisions that persisted in the county. When, for example, an unarmed black teenager was shot to death by a white policeman in Ferguson, Missouri, in August 2014, and rioting and looting continued unabated for several days, Obama felt compelled to send his attorney general, Eric Holder, to meet with the FBI and other officials investigating the incident.
3. On March 21, 2010, the House narrowly passed the Senate's version of the bill, by a vote of 219 to 212, with 34 Democrats and all Republican members voting against it. Although Republicans introduced legislation the next day to repeal the bill, President Obama swiftly signed it into law. Pub. L. No. 111–148, 124 Stat. 119 (2010).
4. Plaintiffs maintained that Congress's Commerce Clause authority only enabled Congress to regulate economic activity affecting interstate commerce; however, the plaintiffs said, the Affordable Care Act improperly attempted to extend to economic *inactivity*, that is, the choice *not* to buy something. Moreover, they asserted that the law could not be justified as a valid exercise of Congress's taxing power. In each circuit, the federal government defended the constitutionality of the law. It noted that at least since 1937, the Supreme Court had upheld every congressional regulation of economic activity, and the purchase of health-care insurance was, at least to Congress, an economic activity, which, when aggregated, would have a substantial effect on the price of health-care insurance. United States v. South-Eastern Underwriters Association, 322 U.S. 533 (1944) (holding that the Commerce Clause gave Congress the authority to regulate insurance).
5. Critics maintained that the withdrawal of all Medicaid funding given to a state was coercive and therefore violated the limits placed on the spending power.
6. National Federation of Independent Business v. Sebelius, 132 S. Ct. 2566 (2012).
7. Ibid., 2600.
8. Roberts was joined by the Court's more conservative members: Justices Antonin Scalia, Antony Kennedy, Clarence Thomas, and Samuel Alito. *Sebelius*, 132 S. Ct. at 2585–2594.

The Supreme Court generally referred to the minimum coverage by its commonly used name, the "individual mandate."

9. The Court examined its previous Commerce Clause jurisprudence, noting that even in *Wickard v. Filburn*, there was some preexisting economic activity—for example, the fact that the wheat farmer there was already placing a good deal of his grown wheat on the open market. *Sebelius*, 132 S. Ct. at 2590–2591. The Court dismissed the government's argument that individuals were already participating in the market for health care, if not in the market for insurance, simply because they might someday need health care.

10. Ibid., 2600.

11. Justices Scalia, Kennedy, Thomas, and Alito issued a strong dissenting opinion. Ibid., 2642–2656. They found it determinative that the act had itself characterized the payment as a penalty rather than a tax. Since the payment was not a tax, they argued, it could not be enacted under the authority of the Taxing and Spending Clause.

12. Ibid., 2608.

13. The Court found that "in this case, the financial 'inducement' Congress has chosen is much more than 'relatively mild encouragement'—it is a gun to the head." However, despite this constitutional infirmity, the remainder of the Medicaid provisions could be saved. Ibid., 2604–2608.

14. Ibid. Justices Scalia, Kennedy, Thomas, and Alito agreed that the Medicaid expansion was unconstitutional as written because of the coercive use of the spending power. However, they disagreed that the Medicaid provisions could be saved. Only Congress, not the Court, they argued, could fix the constitutional deficiency.

15. Romney took this position even though, as governor of Massachusetts, he had signed into law the Massachusetts scheme that served as the model for the Affordable Care Act. Romney maintained that only the states, not the federal government, had the authority to enact individual mandates into law.

16. A lawsuit against the president by members of Congress was not without precedent. In 1999, members of Congress sued President Clinton for alleged violations of the War Powers Act relating to his decision to use American military force against Yugoslavia. The U.S. Court of Appeals for the District of Columbia Circuit concluded that the congressional representatives did not have standing to file the lawsuit and affirmed its dismissal by the lower court. Campbell v. Clinton, 203 F.3d 19 (D.C. Cir. 2000).

17. King v. Burwell, 135 S.Ct. 2480 (2015).

18. President Obama based the authority to implement these orders on prior legislation enacted by Congress and his duty in Article II to "take Care that the Laws be faithfully executed." While many Republican members of Congress protested that Obama's actions were unconstitutional, these challenges never gained traction.

19. Secretary of Homeland Security, Janet Napolitano, issued a memorandum that same day, instructing officials within her department to exercise prosecutorial discretion when handling removal, or deportation, cases for illegal immigrants who fit certain criteria. Janet Napolitano, memorandum to David V. Aguilar, Alejandro Mayorkas, and John Morton, "Exercising Prosecutorial Discretion with Respect to Individuals Who Came to the United States as Children," June 15, 2012, www.dhs.gov/xlibrary/assets/s1-exercising-prosecutorial-discretion-individuals-who-came-to-us-as-children.pdf.

20. Arizona v. United States, 132 S.Ct. 2492, 2498 (2012).

21. Paul Stanley, "Legal Scholar Says Obama's Executive Orders Are Misuse of Power," *Christian Post*, June 19, 2012, www.christianpost.com/news/legal-scholar-says-obamas-executive-orders-are-misuse-of-power-76896/.

22. History books, they noted, were filled with many federal statutes that presidents had chosen not to enforce because the executives deemed the statutes unconstitutional. An example was President Jefferson's decision not to enforce the Alien and Sedition Acts.

23. Similarly, the National Rifle Association and its advocates in Congress responded with outrage in late 2012 when the president issued twenty-three executive actions aimed at curbing gun violence after the tragic shooting at Sandy Hook Elementary School in Connecticut. Critics accused President Obama of attempting to usurp Congress's authority and trying to undermine the protections of the Second Amendment. J. K. Trotter, "Obama's 23 Executive Actions on Gun Violence," *Atlantic Wire*, January 16, 2013, www.theatlanticwire.com/politics/2013/01/obama-executive-actions-gun-list/61075/; Chris Good, "Former AG Says Obama Risks Impeachment over Gun Control," *ABC News Online*, January 16, 2013, http://abcnews.go.com/blogs/politics/2013/01/former-ag-says-obama-risks-impeachment-over-gun-control/.

24. Jo Becker, "How the President Got to 'I Do' on Same-Sex Marriage," *New York Times*, April 16, 2014.

25. United States v. Windsor, 133 S.Ct. 2675 (2013). Members of Congress were forced to mount a defense of DOMA because the Obama administration refused to do so.

26. Hollingsworth v. Perry, 133 S.Ct. 2652 (2013).

27. Obergefell v. Hodges, 135 S.Ct. 2584 (2015).

28. By the beginning of Obama's last full year of his first term, the Senate had not approved any of his nominations to the National Labor Relations Board, because Senate Republicans believed the nominees were overly protective of unions. In addition, the Senate balked at approving a head for the Consumer Financial Protection Bureau, which had not had a leader in place since Congress had established it in 2008. In declaring in January 2012 that he would make recess appointments, Obama said: "When Congress refuses to act and as a result hurts the economy and puts people at risk, I have an obligation as president to do what I can without them. I will not stand by while a minority in the Senate puts party ideology ahead of the people they were elected to serve." Jim Puzzanghera and Lisa Mascaro, "Obama Bypassing Senate to Appoint Richard Cordray Consumer Chief," *Los Angeles Times*, January 4, 2012, http://articles.latimes.com/2012/jan/04/business/la-fi-obama-cordray-20120104. Subsequently, during Obama's second term, the Senate confirmed his nominees to the National Labor Relations Board and his nominee to head the Consumer Financial Protection Bureau.

29. In these sessions, which were begun by Senate Majority Leader Harry Reid, (D-NV), at least one member of the Senate was present, called the Senate into formal session, and then after a few moments, when no one brought any business before the Senate, declared the session over.

30. Lawfulness of Recess Appointments During a Recess of the Senate Notwithstanding Periodic Pro Forma Sessions, 36 Op. O.L.C. 1, 1 (2012), quoting Jack L. Goldsmith III (assistant attorney general, Office of Legal Counsel), memorandum to Alberto R.

Gonzales (counsel to the president), "Re: Recess Appointments in the Current Recess of the Senate," February 20, 2004, 1.

31. Pocket Veto Case, 279 U.S. 655 (1929). The Court's decision was issued shortly after Herbert Hoover assumed the presidency. See Chapter 31, "Herbert Hoover."

32. NLRB v. Canning, 133 S.Ct. 2861 (2013) (mem.).

33. NLRB v. Canning, 134 S.Ct. 2550 (2014).

34. Ibid., 8, 2558. The Court noted that presidents had made "thousands of intra-session recess appointments." Ibid., 2560. For instance, FDR appointed Dwight Eisenhower a permanent major general during an intrasession recess, and George H. W. Bush appointed Alan Greenspan chairman of the Federal Reserve Board during such a recess.

35. Ibid., 2560–2561.

36. Ibid., 2567.

37. Justice Scalia, concurring only in the judgment (joined by Justices Thomas and Alito), took sharp issue with the majority's logic. In Scalia's view, the "plain, original meaning of the constitutional text" would militate in favor of a narrow interpretation of the president's recess appointment power. Scalia would have limited the exercise of that power strictly to the "intermission between two formal legislative sessions" and only to fill vacancies that "happen during the Recess." Ibid., 2606 (Scalia J. concurring in the judgment). Scalia claimed that the majority's opinion would allow the recess appointment power to become "a weapon to be wielded by future Presidents against future Senates." Ibid., 2592.

38. In the wake of this tragedy, multicount indictments were brought against thirty-four defendants who were accused of having been involved in the illegal trafficking of firearms.

39. Staff of Senate Committee on the Judiciary and Staff of House Oversight and Government Reform Committee, *Joint Report on the Department of Justice's Operation Fast and Furious*, 112th Cong. (July 26, 2011).

40. Sharyl Attkisson, "Attorney General Eric Holder grilled by Congress on ATF 'Gunwalker' Controversy," *CBS News Online*, May 3, 2011, www.cbsnews.com/8301-31727_162-20059360-10391695.html.

41. U.S. Department of Justice, Office of Legal Counsel, "Letter for the President from Eric H. Holder, Jr., Attorney General, Re: Assertion of Executive Privilege over Documents Generated in Response to Congressional Investigation into Operation Fast and Furious," 36 Op. O.L.C. 1., June 19, 2012, www.justice.gov/sites/default/files/olc/opinions/2012/06/31/ag-ff-exec-pr. (hereinafter cited OLC Letter). The OLC Letter referenced an opinion from the Office of Legal Counsel, suggesting that "executive privilege may properly be asserted in response to a congressional subpoena seeking internal Department of Justice documents generated in the course of the deliberative process." It also pointed to precedents from prior presidents invoking executive privilege to protect documents produced as part of a deliberative process within the executive branch. These included President Clinton's claim of executive privilege to justify his refusal to turn over documents to congressional committees investigating firings in the White House Travel Office and his decision to grant clemency to sixteen members of a

Puerto Rican terrorist group, as well as President George W. Bush's invocation of executive privilege to withhold documents from committees investigating his firings of several U.S. attorneys and communications regarding the Environmental Protection Agency. The OLC Letter asserted that producing the documents would not "further a legislative function of Congress," and found that the attorney general and the department had made "extraordinary efforts to accommodate" the committee and fulfill their constitutional obligations, and the inspector general was already conducting an internal investigation into the matter, which reduced the urgency of the committee's needs.

42. Representative Issa relied on a D.C. Circuit court opinion holding that executive privilege "should not extend to staff outside the White House in executive branch agencies." Ibid.

43. Seventeen Democrats—mostly from conservative districts—voted in favor of the citation, and two Republicans voted against it.

44. Although many experts construed the contempt citation primarily as a symbolic act, the House steamed forward to enforce the citation. The deputy attorney general announced, on the same day as the House vote, that he would refuse to enforce it because Holder had done nothing illegal. James Cole (deputy attorney general) to John Boehner (Speaker of the U.S. House of Representatives), June 28, 2012. The Supreme Court had twice declared that the House and Senate both possessed inherent authority to enforce contempt citations. Anderson v. Dunn, 19 U.S. (6 Wheat.) 204 (1821); McGrain v. Daugherty, 273 U.S. 135 (1927). Morever, Congress had censured President Grover Cleveland's attorney general, Augustus Garland, for failing to cooperate in an investigation. Nonetheless, in this case, the House chose to avoid a messy court battle at this stage.

45. Morton Rosenberg and Todd B. Tatelman, *Congress's Contempt Power: Law, History, Practice, and Procedure*, order code RL 34097 (Washington, DC: Congressional Research Service, Report for Congress, July 24, 2007), 15. See Committee on the Judiciary v. Miers, 558 F. Supp. 2d. 53, 78 (D.D.C. 2008) (Bates, J.) (stating the belief that the "exercise of Congress's inherent contempt power through arrest and confinement of a senior executive official would provoke an unseemly constitutional confrontation that should be avoided").

46. Peter Bergen, "The New Story of the Death of Osama bin Laden," *CNN*, February 12, 2013, www.cnn.com/2013/02/12/opinion/bergen-osama-bin-laden-shooter/ index.html. Bin Laden's remains were flown to a U.S. aircraft carrier, where they were positively identified; the body was then buried at sea.

47. Robert Burns, "AP Source: DNA IDs bin Laden, Wife Named Him in Raid," *USA Today Online*, May 2, 2011, http://usatoday30.usatoday.com/news/washington/2011–05–02-osama-bin-laden-dna_n.htm.

48. Obama had similarly declared that he had the constitutional power to launch a military strike against Syria, although he ultimately asked Congress for approval first. Karen DeYoung, "Obama's Decision to Turn to Congress on Syria Triggers Debate," *Washington Post*, September 4, 2013, www.washingtonpost.com/world/national-security/obamas-decision-to-turn-to-congress-on-syria-decision-is-fodder-for-debate/2013/09/04/e59aace6–14ca-11e3-a100–66fa8fd9a50c_story.html.

49. "Counterterrorism Strategy Initiative," *New America Foundation*, accessed February 12, 2013, http://counterterrorism.newamerica.net/dashboard. In addition, there were

forty-eight U.S. drone strikes in Pakistan from 2004 to 2009 under President Bush. Some watchdog organizations estimate that the strikes have killed up to forty-five hundred people, including over a thousand civilians. "Covert War on Terror: The Data," *Bureau of Investigative Journalism*, accessed February 13, 2013, www.thebureauinvestigates.com/category/projects/drone-data/.

50. When asked why sixteen-year-old Abdulrahman al-Awlaki was killed two weeks after his father in a separate drone strike, senior Obama adviser Robert Gibbs stated that the teenager "should have [had] a far more responsible father." Connor Friedersdorf, "How Team Obama Justifies the Killing of a 16-Year-Old American," *Atlantic*, October 24, 2012, www.theatlantic.com/politics/archive/2012/10/how-team-obama-justifies-the -killing-of-a-16-year-old-american/264028

51. Scott Shane and Charlie Savage, "Report on Targeted Killings Whets Appetite for Less Secrecy," *New York Times*, February 6, 2013, national edition, A11.

52. U.S. Department of Justice, "Attorney General Eric Holder Speaks at Northwestern University School of Law," March 5, 2012, www.justice.gov/iso/opa/ag/speeches/2012/ ag-speech-1203051.html.

53. Josh Gernstein, "Obama: U.S. Seeks Due Process in Drone Strikes," *Politico*, September 7, 2013, www.politico.com/blogs/under-the-radar/2012/09/obama-us-seeks-due-process-in-drone-strikes-134889.html.

54. U.S. Department of Justice, *Department of Justice White Paper: Lawfulness of Lethal Operation Directed Against a U.S. Citizen Who Is a Senior Operational Leader of Al-Qa'ida or An Associated Force*, accessed May 27, 2015, http://msnbcmedia.msn.com/i/msnbc/ sections/news/020413_DOJ_White_Paper.pdf; Jane Mayer, "Torture and Obama's Drone Program," *New Yorker*, February15, 2013, www.newyorker.com/online/blogs/ newsdesk/2013/02/torture-and-obamas-drone-program.html.

55. In similar fashion, when Edward Snowden, a former National Security Agency contactor, leaked classified documents that revealed the existence of agency surveillance programs aimed at collecting phone metadata and other information about Americans in 2014, the public outcry over what many perceived to be a blatant disregard of First and Fourth Amendment protections by the government was such that President Obama was called on to propose reforms to the programs.

56. Barack Obama, "Remarks by the President in Address to the Nation on Immigration," The White House, November 20, 2014, www.whitehouse.gov/the-press-office/2014/11/20/remarks-president-address-nation-immigration.

57. Barack Obama, "Statement by the President on Cuba Policy Changes," The White House, December 17, 2014, www.whitehouse.gov/the-press-office/2014/12/17/ statement-president-cuba-policy-changes.

58. "An Open Letter to the Leaders of the Islamic Republic of Iran," *New York Times*, March 9, 2015, www.nytimes.com/interactive/2015/03/09/world/middleeast/document-the-letter-senate-republicans-addressed-to-the-leaders-of-iran.html?_r=0. President Obama eventually conceded that Congress had a role in any final agreement the administration reached with Iran and indicated that he would not object to legislation providing Congress the opportunity to review it.

# Conclusion

*An Evolving American Presidency*

KEN GORMLEY

The "energy" that the framers envisioned in the American presidency is not evident in the sparse text contained in Article II of the Constitution. Nor does it leap from the pages of the presidential-powers cases handed down by the Supreme Court over the past two centuries. Even reading a thick biography of each president would not tell the full story.

The complete picture only comes to light by tying together threads that span across presidencies. The foregoing chapters, when read together, illuminate remarkable images that would otherwise be obscured by a web of interrelated events. President Gerald Ford might not have pardoned Richard M. Nixon during the Watergate crisis if it were not for the exercise of the pardon power by President Woodrow Wilson in 1914, resulting in the Supreme Court's pronouncement in *Burdick v. U.S.*, which held that acceptance of a presidential pardon generally amounts to an admission of guilt. Once the dots are connected, it becomes clear that events that shaped the presidencies during the founding period are tied to the pre–Civil War period, or to the Progressive era, or to modern times, creating a web of interconnected events that tell a rich, remarkable story.

To be sure, certain foundational principles help shape the presidency within the nation's broader constitutional framework. As texts on the presidency commonly note, the principles of *separation of powers* (the allocation of powers among the three branches of government) and *federalism* (the distribution of powers between the federal and state governments) are regularly implicated as chief executives vie for power under the Constitution. There are dozens of examples of these principles at work in the foregoing chapters. For instance, George Washington tested the boundaries of presidential power in relation to Congress (separation of powers) in issuing the Neutrality Proclamation in 1793. President Andrew Jackson emphasized the sanctity of state authority (federalism) in vetoing bills that sought to recharter the national bank.

These foundational principles flow from the structure of the Constitution itself. They run throughout the story line as American presidents bring to life the nation's fundamental charter. Yet there is much more to understanding the story: Certain provisions in the Constitution have taken shape over time, creating a sturdy set of guideposts for present and future presidents. There also exist intricate threads that connect presidencies like a woven fabric; untangling these threads reveals hidden themes and clues about the direction that the American presidency will likely take as it continues to evolve.

While an exhaustive summary of these intersections would double the size of this volume, certain connections are important to highlight. This chapter seeks to arrange the puzzle pieces to construct a fresh look at issues that have linked the great array of American presidencies discussed in the preceding chapters, leading readers (hopefully) to new areas of exploration and discovery.[1]

## The Presidential Arena

None of the vast powers of the chief executive becomes relevant, of course, until an individual withstands the process of being elected or succeeding to the presidency. Identifying the rules that govern those rare individuals who enter and exit the presidential arena is a good way to start organizing the stories of forty-four presidents, before discussing the powers that they can wield. Consequently, one very important group of constitutional provisions on display in the foregoing chapters relates to the selection, removal, and replacement of presidents.

## *Election and Succession*

The constitutional provisions dealing with the election of presidents and the transfer of power have adapted over time, producing a surprisingly stable system of government. George Washington, in voluntarily stepping down after two terms in office, established an informal precedent that served the country well for many decades. Ulysses S. Grant flirted with running for a third nonconsecutive term, but lacked the support to do so. FDR won an unprecedented third and fourth term in the midst of World War II, dying just months after his fourth inauguration. The Twenty-Second Amendment was then added in 1951 to formally limit presidents to two elected terms, to avoid a repeat of the FDR model. Yet most presidents followed Washington's lead voluntarily. This has distinguished the American presidency from monarchies, dictatorships, and other forms of governance in which chief executives have maintained power indefinitely or as long as they could cling to it.

The Twelfth Amendment, added in 1804, provided for the separate election of president and vice president. Among other things, this amendment eliminated the awkward situation of having a president paired with a vice president of a different party (as was the case when President John Adams was forced to endure having his archrival, Thomas Jefferson, serve as his vice president). The Twelfth Amendment also allowed the president to avoid being stuck with a vice president who was a political liability. Jefferson quickly took advantage of this provision in 1804, dumping his vice president Aaron Burr (who had shot and killed former Secretary of Treasury Alexander Hamilton in a duel earlier that year) and selecting a new running mate—Governor George Clinton of New York—who was more compatible with his own political philosophy and comportment in office. Thus, the Twelfth Amendment improved the system for selecting executive leaders.

Moreover, the peaceful transfer of power that has taken place when American presidents have sought reelection and failed—starting with John Adams's loss to Thomas Jefferson in the famous "Revolution of 1800"—created a model that further shored up the stability of the system for electing chief executives, in a distinctly American fashion.

### CONTESTED ELECTIONS

A few highly contested elections have tested the foundations of the scheme constructed by the framers. The contested election of 1824, in which John Quincy Adams struck a "corrupt bargain" with House Speaker

Henry Clay of Kentucky, haunted Adams for his entire term until he was ushered out of office. The wildly disputed Hayes-Tilden election of 1876 threw the selection of the president into the lap of Congress, wreaking political havoc and forcing Congress to pass the Electoral Count Act of 1887, which established clearer rules to resolve disputed elections under the Twelfth Amendment. Ironically, the most recent instance of a hotly contested election—the Bush-Gore presidential race of 2000—never provided Congress an opportunity to test the mechanism created in the aftermath of the Hayes-Tilden election. When the Supreme Court injected itself into the matter by deciding *Bush v. Gore* and delivering a victory to Republican George W. Bush, it took the matter away from Congress and moved it into the judicial realm. The Court's action only fueled the fires of partisan disharmony, damaging the Court's own reputation in the process.[2]

In the end, however, the history of stability that has defined the process of electing presidents and transferring power, even under the most difficult circumstances, has been a key component of America's constitutional resilience.

## DEATH IN OFFICE

The Constitution creates various mechanisms to replace presidents in the case of death, incapacity, and infirmity. These provisions have led to a swirl of activity throughout American history.

Originally, the Constitution was unclear about what the precise title or role of the vice president should be in the case of the president's death in office. Article II, Section 1, Clause 6, stated only that in the case of the president's death or removal from office, "the Powers and Duties of the said Office . . . shall devolve on the Vice President." When President William Henry Harrison died in office after only thirty-one days, congressional foes of Vice President John Tyler sought to diminish his role by treating him as the "Vice President, now exercising the duties of President." Yet Tyler persevered. After he was sworn in as chief executive, he established the *Tyler precedent*, thus ensuring that a vice president actually becomes president in these circumstances. The Twenty-Fifth Amendment in 1967, after the assassination of President John F. Kennedy, formalized this constitutional interpretation: "In case of the removal of the President from office or of his death or resignation, the Vice President shall become President."

Over the course of forty-four presidencies, eight presidents have died in office: William Henry Harrison, Zachary Taylor, Abraham Lincoln, James A. Garfield, William McKinley, Warren G. Harding, Franklin D.

Roosevelt, and John F. Kennedy. Interestingly, the successors of these chief executives have been plagued by a curse of their own: none has won more than a single term in office on his own.

## IMPEACHMENT AND CENSURE

Several presidents have been subjected to efforts to impeach, censure, or remove them from office. Over the course of two centuries, none of these efforts has succeeded. Indeed, most efforts have never moved beyond political blustering and posturing.

John Adams, the second president, found himself threatened by censure or impeachment by Congress for his role in the Thomas Nash affair. Representative John Marshall (who later became chief justice) vigorously defended Adams in the chambers of Congress, extinguishing the effort to reprimand or remove him. Impeachment charges were drawn up against President John Tyler, in the House of Representatives, for his vigorous (some said reckless) use of the presidential veto power; yet, these efforts died on the vine before ever getting to the relevant congressional committee. President Andrew Johnson was the first president in American history to be actually impeached by the House of Representatives. He was charged with defying the Tenure of Office Act and other alleged misdeeds during the roiling period of Reconstruction. However, Johnson escaped conviction by one vote in the Senate, completing his term in office intact.

President Richard Nixon was teetering on the edge of impeachment for his Watergate misdeeds when he resigned from office and received a pardon from his successor, President Gerald R. Ford. While Nixon managed to circumvent the looming impeachment process, his legacy as president was forever damaged by that stamp of infamy. President William Jefferson Clinton became the second president in American history to be impeached in the House of Representatives; he was impeached, by a strict party-line vote, for allegedly lying under oath about an affair with former intern Monica Lewinsky. Yet Clinton prevailed; he was conclusively acquitted in the Senate, with the House Managers or prosecutors failing to come close to the two-thirds vote required for conviction.

At times, Congress has sought to punish, reprimand, or otherwise weaken presidents or their surrogates through the censure mechanism. Some censure votes have been aimed at the president himself; some have been aimed at his top cabinet members. The Senate censured Andrew Jackson for firing his treasury secretary and for removing federal deposits from the national bank;

however, several years later, the Senate expunged its censure of Jackson after he successfully protested that action. President Grover Cleveland's attorney general, Augustus Garland, was censured by Congress for refusing to turn over documents relating to the president's appointment of a new U.S. attorney in Alabama. Most recently, President Barack Obama's attorney general, Eric Holder, was held in contempt by the House of Representatives, largely by a party-line vote, for failing to turn over documents in the Fast and Furious investigation. In the end, President Obama invoked executive privilege and threw a wet blanket over that effort, causing the contempt proceedings to fizzle out. Thus, the censure mechanism, which appears nowhere in the Constitution, has generally proven to be an ineffective tool.

## The Presidential Tool Kit

Once presidents are elected and ensconced in office, their principal powers flow directly from the language of the Constitution. However, because these powers are spelled out in different places throughout the document, one cannot develop a clear picture of presidential authority unless one organizes the powers into logical groups. By studying the foregoing chapters to understand how American presidencies interface with the Constitution, one can identify clusters of power that form the core of the chief executive's authority. The resulting presidential tool kit consists, generally, of three components: basic functions that are essential to running the executive branch of government; functions that flow from the president's unusual role in the legislative process; and crucial functions relating to foreign affairs and commanding the military.

### *Basic Executive Functions*

#### OVERSEEING THE EXECUTIVE BRANCH

The job of overseeing the executive branch of government is one of the primary functions of the chief executive under the Constitution. It flows primarily from Article II, Section 1, which states: "The executive Power shall be vested in a President of the United States" (the *Vesting Clause*). This provision, coupled with Article II, Section 3, Clause 4, which states that the president shall "take Care that the Laws be faithfully executed" (the *Take Care Clause*), creates an important set of instruments in the presidential tool kit, particularly on the domestic front. Taken together, these sweeping commands empower the president to run an entire branch of government and to ensure that the laws enacted by Congress are implemented faithfully.

President George Washington was the first chief executive to develop these broadly stated powers. Initially, he sought to utilize the Supreme Court as a sort of advisory council to aid him in making important executive decisions. When Chief Justice John Jay rebuffed that effort, Washington turned to advisers within his own administration—which he dubbed his cabinet—thus solidifying the authority of that group for future presidents. President Franklin D. Roosevelt took dramatic steps to enhance the powers of the chief executive, establishing the Brownlow Committee to propose sweeping new managerial powers. This led to the Reorganization Act of 1949 and the creation of the Executive Office of the President, which allowed for the issuance of executive orders by the president and otherwise restructured and expanded the office of chief executive.

President Benjamin Harrison invoked the Take Care Clause of Article II to protect Supreme Court Justice Stephen Field, who had been the subject of a death threat. President Reagan invoked the same clause to fire air traffic controllers who had engaged in strikes in defiance of federal law. Thus, the president's role as overseer of the executive branch has brought with it vast authority, which has expanded dramatically as the nation itself has grown.

### APPOINTMENT AND REMOVAL OF KEY OFFICIALS

Another important aspect of the president's executive powers relates to appointment and removal of principal and inferior officers (Article II, Section 2, Clause 2). Initially, the power of *appointment* served as a major vehicle to reward loyal supporters and to manage a sprawling federal bureaucracy. President Andrew Jackson famously pushed this power to new limits through overt political patronage. The heated debate over patronage came to a head with the assassination of President James Garfield by a disgruntled office seeker; this led to the enactment of massive civil service reforms—including the creation of a nonpolitical Civil Service Commission—during the presidency of Chester A. Arthur. (Ironically, Arthur himself had been the beneficiary of patronage in New York.)

Battles have frequently erupted, as well, over the presidential *removal* power. President Andrew Jackson fired his treasury secretary without first consulting Congress, and stood his ground. Of course, the passage of the

Tenure of Office Act in 1867 constitutes one of the most dramatic attempts by Congress to curb the removal power of presidents without the advice and consent of the Senate. It led to the impeachment of President Andrew Johnson the following year, before it was repealed in 1887 at the urging of President Grover Cleveland. Several decades later, President Woodrow Wilson removed a postmaster without the advice and consent of the Senate, and this executive action was later upheld by the Supreme Court. Yet when FDR tried to remove an appointed member of the Federal Trade Commission (FTC) without congressional approval, before the expiration of that appointee's term, the Court disallowed this action, finding that the function of the FTC commissioner was not executive in nature but quasi-judicial or quasi-legislative, or both. Thus, even after the death of the Tenure of Office Act, removal issues linger.

The *recess appointment* provision of Article II, Section 2, Clause 3, gives presidents a certain degree of latitude to side-step the advice and consent provision when the Senate is not in session. Yet that provision is not a blank check. The Supreme Court in 2014 clipped the wings of President Barack Obama when he sought to bypass that constitutional language to deal with an obstinate Senate that was dragging its feet on his appointments. Drawing on the *Pocket Veto Case* from the Hoover era, which discussed the definition of *adjournment*, the Court found that the recess in question was too short (and thus technically not a recess) to justify bypassing the normal requirement of obtaining advice and consent from the Senate.

Thus, the American presidency is filled with examples of presidents and Congress battling over the scope of the chief executive's power to appoint or remove federal officers, particularly when the action occurs without the express permission of Congress. Power struggles between the two branches, undoubtedly, will continue in future cycles of American history.

### REPRIEVES AND PARDONS:
### A SWEEPING POWER

Another important executive function can be found in Article II, Section 2, Clause 1, relating to the power to grant reprieves and pardons. President George Washington first used this power to pardon rebels engaged in the Whiskey Rebellion, to calm the new nation after that insurgence. President Abraham Lincoln tapped into this power liberally to commute the sentences of Native Americans involved in the Sioux Uprising and deserters in the Union Army who agreed to return to duty. President Andrew Johnson issued a sweeping pardon to former Confederate officers after the Civil War, to unify the nation after that prolonged period of bloodshed. President Warren Harding commuted the sentence of socialist leader Eugene Debs, to end the period of governmental zeal in punishing alleged subversives during the World War I era. President Calvin Coolidge pardoned a bootlegger during Prohibition, to signal his administration's disapproval of harsh punishment relating to alcohol sales after the adoption of the Eighteenth Amendment. President Gerald Ford ended the long national nightmare of Watergate by pardoning former President Richard Nixon of all crimes he might have committed in that scandal. And President Jimmy Carter, fulfilling a campaign promise, granted unconditional pardons to those who had evaded the draft during the Vietnam War.

As the chief executive, the American president has ultimate authority to determine how and when laws should be executed. Thus, the Constitution gives the president wide latitude to determine when those convicted of crimes should receive mercy or leniency, for the greater good of the nation.

### SAFEGUARDING PRESIDENTIAL POWERS: EXECUTIVE PRIVILEGE

More than one president has invoked the notion of executive privilege to ward off perceived intrusions by other branches of government that threaten to hamper the exercise of his executive powers. The success rate has been mixed. President Richard Nixon unsuccessfully invoked an absolute notion of executive privilege to keep the Watergate special prosecutor and grand jury away from his secret White House tapes during the Watergate affair, claiming that releasing the material invaded the confidentiality that necessarily surrounds executive decision making and violated separation of powers. Nixon lost that battle in *U.S. v. Nixon*, which held that executive privilege is limited and must give way, when necessary for the fair administration of justice. Similarly, President Bill Clinton unsuccessfully sought to postpone (until after he left office) his deposition in the sexual harassment lawsuit filed by Paula Jones: In *Clinton v. Jones*, the Supreme Court concluded that no constitutional privilege or immunity—even temporary in nature—existed to halt a pending civil case against a president, unrelated to his or her official duties. Several years later, however, President George Bush and Vice President Dick Cheney successfully invoked executive privilege to prevent the disclosure of names of members of that administration's energy task force, convincing the Supreme Court that such a disclosure might reveal sensitive materials and impinge on presidential confidentiality.

It is undeniable that the president's powers as head of the executive branch are wide-ranging. They constitute the central source of his or her authority in the constitutional system. For that reason, the concept of executive privilege protects the sphere of confidentiality surrounding the chief executive, to a certain extent. Yet this zone of privilege is not unbounded; the Constitution ensures that it is held in check by Congress and the courts.

## POLICY-MAKING ROLE:
### THE POWER OF THE BULLY PULPIT

One of the most striking functions of the American presidency, as that office has evolved, is the chief executive's ability to articulate and implement far-reaching policies for the nation. This authority is nowhere expressly set forth in the Constitution. Yet it is strongly implied in the president's power as the unitary executive in the constitutional system.[3] It also flows from the president's role as principal spokesperson for the country in the realm of foreign affairs. Certain presidents throughout American history have been extremely effective in using this bully pulpit to advance their policy agendas.

Expansionism has occurred in the United States largely through presidents' assertion of power and spearheading of their own initiatives. President Thomas Jefferson led the drive for the Louisiana Purchase, knowing that nothing in the Constitution gave him the express power to do so: Jefferson referred to the Louisiana Purchase as a "treaty" to give himself cover, then pressed Congress to approve the purchase (and his actions) for the good of the nation. President James Monroe issued the Principles of 1823—otherwise known as the Monroe Doctrine—and ended up shaping America's foreign policy for the next two centuries. This was true even though the Monroe Doctrine was never codified in a treaty or statute and never approved by Congress. President James Polk articulated his vision of Manifest Destiny, declaring that the country needed to pursue an expansionist policy to open up more land for agriculture; by the end of Polk's presidency, the United States had annexed Texas and acquired huge tracts of additional territory. After Congress declared war on Spain, President William McKinley added the Philippines, Puerto Rico, Guam, and Hawaii, believing that these foreign territories were important for America's security and commerce; McKinley used the White House bully pulpit to lead the nation down the path of supporting this imperialist vision. And President Theodore Roosevelt, who was convinced that a Latin American canal was essential to U.S. trade interests, pushed through the Panama Canal project by dint of his strong willpower, dramatically shaping America's role in that part of the globe for the next century.

In a different way, Abraham Lincoln brilliantly tapped into the hidden powers of the presidency. Most notably, in delivering the famous Gettysburg Address, he recast the justification for the Civil War as a battle for the basic democratic principles of equality and freedom, reshaping the entire debate over the war. Similarly, Theodore Roosevelt used his influence to advance the Progressive agenda, including an environmental conservationist initiative and a crusade against abuses by big business. President William Howard Taft used his office to press Congress for a constitutional amendment to make federal income taxes lawful; his efforts led to a resolution proposing the Sixteenth Amendment, which was ratified in 1913. President Woodrow Wilson, at first wary of women's suffrage, became an ardent spokesman in favor of women's right to vote after witnessing the key role played by females in assisting the war effort during World War I; Wilson's strong support led to the ratification of the Nineteenth Amendment in 1920. President Franklin D. Roosevelt leveraged his popularity and credibility with the American public to accomplish sweeping policy changes in the United States through his New Deal program, to pull the country out of the Great Depression.[4] And President Barack Obama, a latecomer when it came to endorsing same-sex marriage, ultimately refused to enforce the Defense of Marriage Act and used his second inaugural address to openly embrace the legal recognition of same-sex marriage, helping to change the national dialogue on that subject on a grand scale.

Over time, the role of American presidents as shapers of national and international policy has become a key function of that high office. Presidents have used this power to push through bold initiatives and to achieve significant advances, often with nothing but the presidential bully pulpit to accomplish changes that forever impact the nation.

### *Legislative Function: The Chief Executive's Unusual Role*

Strongly tied to the chief executive's implicit power as a policy maker is the president's express role under the Constitution in shaping legislation. Although the function is often overlooked or misunderstood, the president has a formal role in the legislative process. This is different from the president's role in the tug-of-war that routinely occurs between the executive and legislative branches, as each branch protects its own turf in carrying out the separation-of-powers principle. Several provisions of the Constitution expressly give the president a role in how laws are introduced, approved, and interpreted. This is a uniquely American feature of the president's constitutional power.

## LAUNCHING LEGISLATIVE INITIATIVES

Article II, Section 3, begins by stating that "from time to time" the president shall give Congress information concerning the "State of the Union" and recommend to Congress "such Measures as he shall judge necessary and expedient." Spurred forward by these commands, presidents throughout history have proposed significant legislation and even drafted bills for Congress's consideration. President Benjamin Harrison worked with Congress to produce the Sherman Anti-Trust Act of 1890. The Kennedy and Johnson administrations drafted versions of civil rights legislation that ended up being instrumental in Congress's enacting of the Civil Rights Act of 1964 and the Voting Rights Act of 1965. President George W. Bush and his administration were deeply involved in drafting the USA Patriot Act in the aftermath of the terrorist attack of 9/11. And President Barack Obama and others in his administration took a lead role in conceiving of, and shepherding through Congress, the Affordable Care Act, using the president's loosely defined authority in the Constitution to advance this major, albeit controversial, legislative initiative.

Ever since the presidency of Dwight D. Eisenhower, the White House has maintained an Office of Legislative Affairs, which serves as a liaison with members of Congress and their staffs in pursuing joint enterprises. Thus, while the president's central role is to oversee the executive branch, he or she also plays a direct, constitutionally mandated role in the legislative process.

## CONVENING SPECIAL SESSIONS

The Constitution even gives the president power to convene special sessions of Congress on "Extraordinary Occasions" (Article II, Section 3). At various moments in history, presidents have utilized this provision, typically in times of urgency or emergency. Examples abound: Thomas Jefferson called Congress into session to ratify the Louisiana Purchase in

1803, and President James Madison convened Congress in special session at the outset of the War of 1812. President Franklin Pierce convened a special session of Congress in 1856 to force the legislature to allocate funds for the army. In 1929, President Herbert Hoover called Congress into session to address the serious recession in the farm economy. During the election of 1948, President Harry Truman famously invoked this provision, calling the "Do Nothing Congress" back into session and challenging it to pass legislation implementing pieces of the Republican Party platform.[5] Thus, the Constitution gives the president a direct vehicle for spurring Congress to action when he or she believes such action is necessary.

## VETO POWER: THE PRESIDENT'S CHECK

One of the most potent tools that the president has at his or her disposal, when it comes to the legislative process, is exercising the veto power. Article I, Section 7, Clause 2, of the Constitution—in setting forth the process by which legislation is enacted—specifically gives the chief executive power to return a bill unsigned, thus throwing the ball back to Congress. Congress can then try to override the presidential veto or abandon the bill and go back to the legislative drawing board.

The chief executive's breadth of authority in exercising veto power has grown, rather than diminished, over time. President George Washington purposely took a cautious approach in vetoing legislative acts; he did not wish to appear to be usurping Congress's power or to be repeating the sins of the British monarchy. During his eight years as president, Washington exercised his veto power only twice. Other early presidents took the position that the veto power was limited to situations in which they determined that a legislative bill was flatly unconstitutional, rather than objectionable for political reasons. Yet this cautious approach soon melted away. Presidents Andrew Jackson and John Tyler made robust use of the veto power to check Congress on major pieces of legislation with which they disagreed, including the reauthorization of the national bank. Soon, it became clear that there was virtually no limit on the number of vetoes or the justification for using such vetoes.

President Grover Cleveland used the veto power more than all of his predecessors combined—170 times in the first term and 414 times in the second term. President Richard Nixon sought to take the veto authority to new heights, impounding funds allocated for the Clean Water Act to thwart its implementation, after Congress overrode his veto of that act.

This action prompted the passage of the Impoundment Control Act of 1974 to curb future presidents from thwarting the will of Congress in this fashion. Federal courts largely held against Nixon's impoundment actions; one Supreme Court case struck down his withholding of funds for the Clean Water Act.[6]

Thus, the president's veto power has grown steadily over time. Indeed, this power is virtually absolute. The only check Congress has over it, in modern times, is to use the constitutional mechanism afforded to the legislature by the framers: Congress must muster a two-thirds vote in each chamber to override the president's veto.

## PRESENTMENT CLAUSE

A related aspect of the legislative process in which the president and the Congress have occasionally butted heads, particularly in modern times, relates to the Presentment Clause contained in Article I, Section 7, Clause 2. This provision states that before a bill can become law, it must be "presented to the President" to give the chief executive an opportunity to exercise a veto. President Ronald Reagan won a Presentment Clause battle in *INS v. Chadha*, when he prevented Congress from exercising a one-house veto of decisions of the Immigration and Naturalization Service relating to the deportation of noncitizens, without first sending the matter back to the president: The Supreme Court concluded that this violated the Presentment Clause. In *Clinton v. City of New York*, during the presidency of Bill Clinton, the Supreme Court nullified the Line Item Veto Act, which would have given the president the power to strike portions of legislation (including appropriations) he disliked while leaving the rest of the legislation intact. The Supreme Court concluded that the line-item veto mechanism violated the Constitution's Presentment Clause: It would improperly permit a chief executive to invalidate portions of duly enacted laws without going through the entire process anew.[7]

## SIGNING STATEMENTS: AN EXECUTIVE IMPRINT?

Presidents—particularly in the past few decades—have also tried to leave an imprint on the legislative process by appending *signing statements* to bills they approve, explaining their reasons for signing legislation in an effort to graft these statements onto the legislative history of congressional enactments. President Ronald Reagan used signing statements extensively, as did his Republican successors, presidents George H. W. Bush and George

W. Bush. Even Democratic President Barack Obama, despite questioning the use of presidential signing statements as a senator, has continued the trend, although not as robustly. It remains unclear how much weight or precedential value presidential signing statements have after a bill becomes law. Yet they constitute another executive thumbprint on the complex, interactive legislative process.

In sum, even though the president and Congress occupy separate spheres in the American system of government, the Constitution gives the president a number of formal and informal roles in the making and enacting of laws. These roles ensure that the president cannot be boxed entirely out of Congress's law-making enterprise; after all, it is the president, ultimately, who has the constitutional duty of enforcing the end product of Congress's work.

## Foreign Affairs and Military Command Powers

The president's authority in foreign affairs, acting as commander in chief, and in quelling domestic violence, has evolved in such a way that American presidents are typically at the apex of their power in this realm.

### LEAD ROLE IN FOREIGN AFFAIRS

Then-Congressman (later Chief Justice) John Marshall, who argued that the president was the "sole organ" in implementing foreign policy, successfully defended President John Adams when Adams turned over to Great Britain one of its citizens charged with murder, pursuant to the Jay Treaty. In doing so, Marshall established early on that matters of foreign affairs and issues abroad—while not within the exclusive domain of the chief executive—fell within the joint realm of the president and Congress.

President James Monroe took this power to a new height when he issued the Monroe Doctrine, which helped define America's role in the world and solidified the president's function as chief spokesperson regarding foreign policy. President William McKinley gathered up foreign possessions after the Spanish-American War, underscoring his preeminence as the nation's leader on the international front and creating a new brand of imperialistic presidency. Presidents Woodrow Wilson and Franklin D. Roosevelt wielded enormous power abroad in leading the country's efforts during the two World Wars. President John F. Kennedy took dramatic steps to exert his authority during the Cuban Missile Crisis, exercising his foreign policy authority to its utmost. And Jimmy Carter, who had been politically crippled by the Iran hostage crisis, was still able to utilize his foreign policy influence to establish a claims tribunal to resolve a political standoff with Iran.

### COMMANDER IN CHIEF: SHARED WARTIME POWERS

The Constitution states that Congress is empowered to "declare War" (Article I, Section 8, Clause 11). Yet it also states that the president is the "Commander in Chief" of the army and navy (Article II, Section 2, Clause 1). This results in the two branches of government sharing, or vying for, authority in this area. Numerous presidents have launched military action without first consulting Congress. James Polk began the Mexican-American War without involving Congress until after blood had been shed. William McKinley sent troops into China to quell the Boxer Rebellion without first seeking Congress's permission. Woodrow Wilson armed vessels and moved the country into World War I with Germany, without congressional authorization. President Harry Truman committed troops in Korea unilaterally. President Nixon secretly bombed Cambodia and committed troops to Southeast Asia, provoking Congress to pass the War Powers Resolution to reel him in. Thereafter, presidents have found ways to circumvent that statute, presumably under the theory that Congress never possessed constitutional authority to restrict the president's power so broadly in the first place. Yet there is often a delicate dance between the two branches of government when it comes to the War Powers Resolution: For instance, in early 1991, Congress authorized President George H. W. Bush to use force against Iraq if he reported that diplomatic efforts had failed; Bush thereafter gave such a report to Congress and launched Operation Desert Storm.

New technology has facilitated the expansion of presidents' commander-in-chief powers. President William McKinley conducted the Spanish-American War remotely from the White House, thanks to the invention of telephones and telegraphs. President George H. W. Bush helped to redefine warfare during Operation Desert Storm, using cruise missiles, stealth bombers, and modern computerized technology that decimated the opposition before it could respond. After 9/11, President George W. Bush invented a completely new method of doing battle in the war on terrorism, using national security tools, including the monitoring of emails and phone calls, as a means of waging war against a new brand of enemy. President Barack Obama, more recently, used drones for the targeted killing of suspected terrorists abroad, employing dramatic advances in technology to redefine the way America would fight enemies in other parts of the globe.

The commander-in-chief powers have been invoked by presidents for a wide variety of purposes, beyond committing military troops in foreign wars. President Zachary Taylor used his commander-in-chief powers to halt the effort by Narciso López and Southern "filibusters" (private mercenaries) to seize Cuba to make it a haven for slavery. President Abraham Lincoln invoked these same powers to issue the Emancipation Proclamation, to suspend the writ of habeas corpus, and to convene military tribunals during the Civil War. President Franklin D. Roosevelt used his commander-in-chief authority to evacuate Japanese American citizens from the West Coast and to move them to internment camps after the bombing of Pearl Harbor. (In 1988, the United States publicly apologized for this action and compensated individuals of Japanese descent and their families who had suffered because of these actions.) President Harry S. Truman summoned his powers as commander in chief to fire General MacArthur for defying him, after the general sought to expand the Korean War into China. President George W. Bush relied on these powers to justify employing "enhanced interrogation techniques" (some called it torture), to set up a detention camp in Guantanamo Bay to house prisoners beyond America's shores, and to create secret an NSA data collection program as part of a war on terror. (Not all of these efforts, in the end, met with success in the courts.)

### QUELLING DOMESTIC VIOLENCE

A type of authority often associated with commander-in-chief powers—but quite distinct from it—relates to the president's ability to quell domestic violence. The Preamble of the Constitution states that the government should "insure domestic Tranquility, [and] provide for the common defence." Article IV, Section 4, provides that the United States must guarantee to every state "a Republican Form of Government" and goes on to state that the legislative or executive branch, or both branches, must protect states against "invasion" and "domestic Violence." Relying on this language, presidents have sometimes used military force (including calling in state militias) to deal with domestic disturbances.

President Andrew Jackson issued his Proclamation of Nullification that led to the Force Bill, which authorized him to use military force against

South Carolina after that state defied a federal tariff. President John Tyler declared that he was prepared to call in militias from two states to quell the Dorr Rebellion in Rhode Island and was upheld by the Supreme Court in asserting that authority. President James Buchanan ordered twenty-five hundred troops—nearly one-third of the U.S. Army at that time—to oust Brigham Young as governor in Utah and to quell a purported Mormon uprising.

In more recent times, in 1957, President Dwight Eisenhower called in the National Guard to Central High School in Little Rock, Arkansas, to enforce the integration command of *Brown v. Board of Education*. President John F. Kennedy sent in troops to enroll James Meredith at Ole Miss and to confront Governor George Wallace in Alabama when Wallace blocked African American students from enrolling at the University of Alabama.

Thus, the president can wield enormous military power not only as commander in chief (which is generally linked to foreign affairs), but also on the domestic front, a power that flows from distinct sources in the Constitution.

## Connecting Threads

As the prior section highlights, the Constitution provides presidents with a tool kit in order to handle their constitutional duties as chief executive. Yet over time, presidents have had to confront an expansive array of problems that are not spelled out in the Constitution. They have done so by plunging themselves into events and being swept along by the currents of history, using their own ingenuity and judgment to stay afloat. The chapters of this book make visible a variety of broad "themes" that connect presidencies over time, quite distinct from the formal powers that define the office in the text of the Constitution. Some of these recurrent themes are particularly worth highlighting. Not only do they allow readers to map out important points of intersection among forty-four distinct chief executives, but they also provide a context for understanding why individual presidents behave as they do, and provide clues as to where the currents of history will likely take future American presidents, as they confront issues that are simultaneously new and part of the inevitable cycle of recurring historical events.

## Race: A Haunting Theme

If one were required to identify a single subject that has consistently dominated the story of American presidents and the Constitution, from the beginning of the nation until modern times, it would be race. Indeed, this dark, self-destructive theme jumps off the pages of the preceding chapters more so than any other theme does. The framers of the Constitution had largely ducked the issue of slavery, although it was unmistakably present in the document.

The infamous Three-Fifths Clause in Article I, Section 2, Clause 3, of the Constitution gave Southern slave-owning states a shrewd advantage for nearly a century. By stating that slaves were considered three-fifths persons for purposes of determining the number of representatives in Congress, Southern states amassed more representatives and won more electors in the Electoral College, while keeping blacks enslaved in the process. Another part of the Constitution provided that the slave trade could not be ended by Congress for twenty years, that is, until 1808 (Article I, Section 9). Moreover, slaves held in one state and escaping into another had to be "delivered up" to their owners, ensuring that slaves would remain private property of their white owners for the indefinite future (Article IV, Section 2, Clause 3). Presidents George Washington, Thomas Jefferson, and other early chief executives were themselves slave owners. Thus, the issue of race and slavery was impressed into the nation's constitutional fabric from its inception. Moreover, the Three-Fifths Clause kept Southern states in control for nearly a hundred years. It was not until the Fourteenth Amendment was ratified in 1868 that this odious provision was nullified.

In the decades before the Civil War, the slavery issue dominated most others. President James Monroe backed the Missouri Compromise of 1820, by which Missouri was free to determine if it would permit slaves, while slavery was prohibited in the rest of the Louisiana Territory. President Martin Van Buren sought to influence the courts in the *Amistad* case, unsuccessfully arguing that Africans who had staged a revolt on that ship constituted the property of Spain and should be returned to Cuba as slaves. (Former President John Quincy Adams, who had become an ardent abolitionist while serving in Congress, represented the Africans and won their freedom.) President Zachary Taylor had a plan to end the growing friction between North and South; tragically, Taylor died in office before he could ever implement his plan. Instead, President Millard Fillmore helped to push through the Compromise of 1850, which included the notorious Fugitive Slave Act of 1850 and unleashed new friction between North and South, culminating in the Kansas-Nebraska Act (during the presidency of Franklin Pierce) and "Bleeding Kansas."

The assassination of President Abraham Lincoln was a culminating event in the battle over the race issue at the conclusion of the Civil War, placing a pall over the country and making clear that the conflict was not over. Lincoln's successor, President Andrew Johnson, tried to veto the Civil Rights Act of 1866 (Congress overrode his veto); Johnson then urged states to reject the Fourteenth Amendment and sought to restore Confederate leaders to positions of authority in the South. President Ulysses S. Grant tried to advance the newly adopted Fourteenth and Fifteenth Amendments—yet he was largely frustrated by the Supreme Court's decisions of the Dreadful Decade, during which time Reconstruction efforts collapsed and the country turned its attention to more worldly economic interests.

Even after Reconstruction, the race issue continued to demand executive attention. President Grover Cleveland served as chief executive when *Plessy v. Ferguson* established in 1896 the harsh "separate but equal" doctrine—a decision he favored. President Dwight D. Eisenhower held office when the Supreme Court handed down its historic decision in *Brown v. Board of Education* (1954), which undid *Plessy*, yet Ike encouraged the Court to move slowly in *Brown II*, hoping to give Southern states latitude to end their segregationist ways in a "gradualist" fashion. In an ironic twist, however, Eisenhower was forced to send troops into Little Rock to maintain order at Central High School. Similarly, President John F. Kennedy and his brother, Attorney General Robert Kennedy, both of whom had proceeded cautiously on volatile race issues, were compelled to send Justice Department officials and troops into Mississippi and Alabama to enforce the Supreme Court's *Brown* decision in those Deep South states. The Kennedy administration went on to win several key civil rights cases in the Supreme Court on narrow grounds, as it struggled to get civil rights legislation adopted by Congress. That only occurred, however, after JFK's tragic assassination, which enabled President Lyndon B. Johnson to push through the Civil Rights Act of 1964 and the Voting Rights Act of 1965, largely as a tribute to the slain president.

President Jimmy Carter ushered in a new, proactive era, advocating for affirmative action to give boosts to minorities in higher education and employment and paving the way for the Supreme Court's landmark decision in the *Bakke* case. Three decades later, however, the Supreme Court handed down rulings limiting the scope of affirmative action in higher education. Ironically, this took place while President Barack Obama—the first African American president in the nation's history—took up residence in the White House.

And in a chilling reminder of the Missouri Compromise of 1820 and the Kansas-Nebraska Act that spawned Bleeding Kansas and the Civil War, President Barack Obama was forced to dispatch his own attorney general to Ferguson, Missouri, in the summer of 2014. Eric Holder's task was to quell race riots that erupted after an unarmed black teenager was shot to death by a white police officer, a sobering reminder that violence over race issues was not a relic of the Civil War period.

The issues of race, slavery, desegregation, affirmative action, and equal protection for all citizens have haunted the United States since its inception, revealing a nation with a dual personality.[8] More so than any other thread that ties together the evolving story of American presidents and the Constitution, the subject of race has overshadowed all others.

### The Commerce Clause

Another conspicuous thread relates to the Commerce Clause contained in Article I, Section 8, Clause 3, of the Constitution. Although this provision relates to a *congressional* power, it has played an important role in the initiatives of many American presidents.

The framers deliberately gave Congress broad powers under this provision, largely because the legislature's inability to regulate interstate commerce under the Articles of Confederation had rendered the legislative branch nearly impotent during that era. The Supreme Court's decision in *McCulloch v. Maryland* (1819), during the presidency of James Monroe, shored up Congress's ability to create a national bank by declaring that the states could not tax it out of existence. *McCulloch* articulated an extremely broad, almost unbounded concept of congressional authority under the Commerce Clause. In the late nineteenth century, however the Court adopted a crabbed view of the Commerce Clause, standing in the way of efforts by Congress and several presidents to break up powerful corporate trusts and monopolies. In *U.S. v. E.C. Knight* (1895), during the presidency of William McKinley, the Court prohibited Congress from using the

Sherman Act to regulate a trust in the sugar refining industry, concluding that the production of sugar involved merely manufacture, not commerce, and holding that it was beyond Congress's reach.

Yet the Court eventually went full circle, embracing an extraordinarily broad interpretation of Congress's powers under the Commerce Clause during Franklin D. Roosevelt's presidency. When FDR threatened to pack the Court with additional justices to push through his New Deal legislation, the Court abruptly approved several sweeping New Deal initiatives pursuant to Congress's power under the Commerce Clause.[9] In *Wickard v. Filburn* (1942), the Court went so far as to uphold the Agricultural Adjustment Act, which imposed quotas on the amount of wheat farmers could produce for private consumption, even though the wheat was not meant for shipment in interstate commerce. The Court concluded that Congress had sweeping power under the Commerce Clause and could even regulate a local farmer's wheat production "if it exerts a substantial effect on interstate commerce."

In creating their civil rights strategies, Presidents John F. Kennedy and Lyndon B. Johnson took advantage of this generous interpretation of Congress's power under the Commerce Clause. Both presidents avoided the rigid Reconstruction-era precedent under the Fourteenth Amendment's Equal Protection Clause, instead premising major civil rights bills on Congress's powers under the Commerce Clause. This approach culminated in LBJ's pushing through the Civil Rights Act of 1964—the most significant piece of civil rights legislation in the nation's history—which the Supreme Court upheld as a valid exercise of Congress's Commerce Clause powers.[10]

More recently, President Barack Obama succeeded in navigating through Congress the Affordable Care Act, which relied heavily on the legislature's power under the Commerce Clause. Although the Supreme Court's ruling on that controversial statute restricted Congress's power under the Commerce Clause, in one respect, it nonetheless underscored the potency of that constitutional provision in modern times. In *National Federation of Independent Business v. Sebelius* (2012), the Court drew a line in the sand, concluding that Congress lacked the authority under the Commerce Clause to enact the controversial individual-mandate provision of the act—because it amounted to *compelling* individuals to purchase health insurance coverage and to engage in commerce. Yet the Court went on to uphold the provision under Congress's broad taxing power. Moreover, the overall structure of the Affordable Care Act, by which Congress regulated the sprawling health-care industry, was clearly premised on a recognition that, in today's world, health care has become an interstate business and Congress can regulate it utilizing the legislature's enormous powers under the Commerce Clause. Indeed, that assumption was explicitly recognized by the Court when it upheld the statute.[11] In the end, the enactment of the Affordable Care Act turned out to be another de facto victory for the Commerce Clause.

Thus, the Commerce Clause has been an engine by which Congress and American presidents, working in tandem, have forged important legislative initiatives throughout many periods of American life.

### National Security versus Free Speech and Privacy

Numerous presidents have elevated national security to an urgent priority, often at the expense of citizens' free speech and privacy rights. This tension has animated the office of the presidency from the earliest days; it has reached a crescendo in modern times. President John Adams supported the Alien and Sedition Acts to punish dissenters and political dissidents during the Quasi-War with France. President James Monroe, perhaps the first "national security" president, established a broad power to speak for the nation in the realm of foreign affairs: In articulating the Monroe Doctrine, he laid the groundwork for future presidents to broaden their power in this domain. With the arrival of World War I, President Woodrow Wilson utilized the Espionage Act of 1917 and the Alien Act of 1918 to censor and prosecute opponents of the war, including conscientious objectors. Wilson's actions led to the Supreme Court's decision in *Schenck v. U.S.* (1919), establishing the restrictive "clear and present danger" test that allowed the government to wield a heavy hand in prosecuting alleged subversive speech, notwithstanding the guarantee of free speech embodied in the First Amendment.

President Warren Harding was deeply troubled by the government's prosecution of citizens who had opposed the U.S. war effort or expressed views contrary to the government. In a powerful, symbolic move, Harding commuted the ten-year prison sentence of Socialist Party of America leader Eugene V. Debs, who had been convicted under the Espionage Act for delivering an antiwar speech in Canton, Ohio. Yet the "clear and present danger" test persisted in various forms until decades later, permitting the governmental restriction of citizen speech deemed subversive. It was not until the aftermath of the infamous period of McCarthyism in the late 1950s, during the Eisenhower presidency, that the Supreme Court, in *Yates v. U.S.*, finally signaled its abandonment of that restrictive test, which had served to chill free speech.

During the post–World War II years of Harry S. Truman's presidency, the United States took major steps toward becoming a "national security state," with the passage of the National Security Act of 1947 and the creation of the National Security Council and the Central Intelligence Agency. (The formation of the United Nations—forged in 1942 by President Franklin D. Roosevelt and British Prime Minister Winston Churchill, along with representatives of twenty-six countries—was another step in this process.) Once again, however, the strong emphasis on national security was used to bolster efforts by Congress and the executive branch to restrict free speech and free press in the name of protecting the country.

A half century later, after the terrorist attacks of September 11, 2001, President George W. Bush swiftly secured the passage of the USA Patriot Act and established the Department of Homeland Security in 2002, creating a new unparalleled national security state. Bush also launched a secret NSA program, authorizing widespread, warrantless governmental wiretapping and collection of emails and phone calls (including those of American citizens) in the quest to root out terrorists. In carrying out this unprecedented data-gathering initiative, the Bush administration bypassed the judicial and legislative branches, concealing its actions in the name of national security. These efforts were so far-reaching that, once they became public, many Americans came to fear that their Fourth Amendment privacy rights were being threatened on an ongoing basis by their own government. In response, Congress amended the Foreign Intelligence Surveillance Act (FISA) to strike a more careful balance between the president, Congress, and the courts, particularly where the constitutional rights of citizens were affected.

President Barack Obama continued his own secret programs to pursue the war on terror, authorizing the mining, collection, and retention of details from the Verizon phone records of millions of Americans in the process. President Obama also confronted something completely new: the disgorgement of massive amounts of classified military information through WikiLeaks dumps, as American citizens such as Private First Class Bradley (later Chelsea) Manning and Edward Snowden made use of new technology to release unprecedented amounts of classified information into the public domain. The Obama administration vowed to prosecute these actions to the fullest extent under the Espionage Act, while Snowden (who fled to Moscow) declared his First Amendment right to make this information available around the globe.

The American presidency has repeatedly collided with First and Fourth Amendment rights as chief executives and Congress have sought to protect national security. In most cases, the interests of national security have won out—particularly during times of war and other crises. These recurring examples stand as a sober warning that the free speech and privacy rights of American citizens are often circumscribed by the exigencies confronting the country at specific moments in its history; moreover, times of fear and danger often produce an environment in which presidents and Congress can wield greater power than ever.

## Gender: The Forgotten Struggle

While issues relating to race have regularly consumed the attention of a large percentage of American presidents, a relatively small amount of attention has been paid to the issue of gender equality. The subject of voting, for instance, provides a vivid illustration. The U.S. Constitution, as originally drafted, did not even address the question of voting rights, leaving the matter to the states. Most states did not allow women to vote; indeed, New Jersey and several other states initially gave that right to females and then revoked it. During the presidency of Ulysses S. Grant, the Supreme Court concluded that the Privileges or Immunities Clause of the newly ratified Fourteenth Amendment did not require a state to admit women to practice law (*Bradwell v. Illinois*, 1872). The Court also held that this clause did not guaranty women the right to vote in state elections.

It was not until President Woodrow Wilson witnessed the great contributions of females during World War I that he eventually became a supporter of women's suffrage and helped to propel the ratification of the Nineteenth Amendment in 1920. The right to vote was designed to open up a whole panoply of other rights to women in the United States; however, that did not happen so swiftly.

Presidents as early as Harry Truman and Dwight D. Eisenhower favored passage of an Equal Rights Amendment (ERA) to the Constitution, expressly forbidding discrimination based on gender in a broader context. By the late 1970s, the movement to ratify the ERA had picked up considerable steam. President Jimmy Carter signed a bill extending the ratification period by three years, strongly endorsing the ERA's adoption. Yet the effort fizzled out—partly because *Frontiero v. Richardson* (1973) and other landmark cases created a higher standard of scrutiny for classifications based on gender under the Equal Protection Clause. Moreover, the *Roe v. Wade* decision (1973) injected the contentious abortion issue into the debate over the proposed amendment. By 1989, President George H. W. Bush had declared that the ERA was "unnecessary." It never made a comeback.

Similarly, it took nearly two hundred years before women were able to assume major roles in public service. It was not until the presidency of Ronald Reagan, in 1981, that the first female justice—Sandra Day O'Connor—was appointed to the U.S. Supreme Court. In 1993, the first female attorney general of the United States—Janet Reno—was sworn in during the presidency of Bill Clinton.

Occasionally, First Ladies have assumed the status of quasi-public figures by virtue of being married to chief executives. Dolley Madison—wife of President James Madison—was the first First Lady to take on a significant public persona, entertaining guests and helping to found a home for orphaned girls in Washington, D.C., thus beginning the long-running tradition of First Ladies' sponsoring projects of importance. Eleanor Roosevelt, the wife of President Franklin D. Roosevelt, was a powerful figure during her husband's presidency and, after his death, became U.S. representative to the United Nations, an organization that her husband had helped establish. Jackie Kennedy captivated the nation as a proponent of the arts and in spearheading an historic preservation effort of the White House. In 2001, former First Lady Hillary Rodham Clinton was elected to the U.S. Senate from New York and thereafter was appointed secretary of state (2009) under President Barack Obama, establishing herself as the first former First Lady to become an internationally renowned public official in her own right.

In sum, the issue of gender equality—and the role of women in the American system of government—has been surprisingly dormant throughout most of the nation's history. Only in recent years have presidents begun paying regular attention to this issue, in terms of appointments and other matters. This gradual but steady shift likely serves as a bellwether for more positive change during future presidencies.

### Special Prosecutors: Policing Modern Presidents

Particularly in modern times, chief executives must be aware that forces outside Congress or the judicial branch are watching to see if they have mishandled the powers in their presidential tool kit. Beginning with Watergate, the appointment of special prosecutors and independent counsels to investigate alleged criminal conduct on the part of presidents—and their closest advisers—has added a new layer of risk to the job of serving as chief executive in the United States.

The first special prosecutors were appointed to investigate the Teapot Dome scandal during the presidency of Warren Harding; the stress from that criminal investigation likely contributed to Harding's death in office. Atlee Pomerene and Owen Roberts (later a justice on the Supreme Court) investigated that scandal and unearthed a scheme of bribery and corruption at high levels of the executive branch, although President Harding was never directly implicated in wrongdoing. During the Watergate scandal, Archibald Cox became the archetype for a modern, principled special prosecutor, standing up to President Richard Nixon in subpoenaing key White House tapes that ultimately proved Nixon's culpability in the Watergate cover-up. (When Nixon fired Cox in the infamous Saturday Night Massacre, a firestorm of public protest led to the appointment of a new special prosecutor, Leon Jaworski, and the ultimate unraveling of the Nixon presidency.)

Every president since Richard Nixon has been haunted, in some fashion, by the ghosts of Watergate. President Gerald Ford was ushered out of office in part for pardoning Nixon and for frustrating the work of the Special Prosecutor's Office as it investigated Nixon's crimes. Jimmy Carter signed into law an Independent Counsel Law as part of the Ethics in Government Act (1978); this piece of legislation created a separation-of-powers nightmare for later presidents. Carter himself was the subject of a special-prosecutor investigation relating to alleged financial irregularities on his family's peanut farm.[12] Presidents Ronald Reagan and George H. W. Bush were swept up in the Iran-Contra investigation that left a blot on their respective presidencies. President Bill Clinton was the target of a multifaceted independent-counsel investigation that led to impeachment proceedings and nearly toppled his presidency. With the nation exhausted from that onslaught of scandals and investigations, Congress allowed the independent-counsel statute to expire in 1999. Nonetheless, President George W. Bush was forced to allow the appointment of a special prosecutor, overseen by the Department of Justice, to investigate the alleged improprieties of his vice president's close adviser, I. Lewis "Scooter" Libby.[13] And President Barack Obama, although he became the first president in modern times to avoid a full-blown independent-counsel investigation during his presidency, endured regular calls by political foes for the appointment of special prosecutors to investigate his actions.

Thus, the Watergate affair during the Nixon presidency created a new, unprecedented role for special prosecutors in policing presidents and their closest advisers in the executive branch. While the Independent Counsel Law has faded out of existence, the culture of special prosecutors has attached itself to the office of president in modern times, creating an ever-present threat of criminal exposure and, in extreme cases, the potential for removal from office if a president makes a fatal misstep.

## Shaping the Supreme Court

Presidents have interacted with, and tried mightily to shape, the Supreme Court since the beginning of the nation. In selecting the six original Supreme Court justices, President Washington sought geographic diversity and avoided overt politics in making his appointments, largely because organized political parties did not yet exist. Yet that tradition did not last long; subsequent presidents increasingly made their picks based upon political considerations in filling vacancies on the Court. President John Adams, for example, selected as his final judicial appointment John Marshall—an ardent Federalist like himself—to serve as chief justice. Marshall went on to shape the nation's jurisprudence in profound ways, accomplishing Adams's political goal.[14]

The relationship between presidents and the Supreme Court has sometimes been volatile. President Andrew Jackson openly defied the Court after its controversial decision in *Worcester v. Georgia* (1832), in which the Court held that the federal government, not the states, had exclusive authority over Native American affairs. In response, Jackson purportedly declared: "[Chief Justice] John Marshall has made his decision; now let him enforce it!" When the Supreme Court ruled that President Abraham Lincoln could not suspend the writ of habeas corpus during the Civil War, in *Ex Parte Merryman*, he simply ignored that decision. President Theodore Roosevelt was so irate at the Court and at his own appointee, Justice Oliver Wendell Holmes, after the Court's decision in *Lochner v. New York*, which meddled in his Progressive initiatives, that he waged an unsuccessful campaign to permit the recall of judges and justices. President Franklin D. Roosevelt went a step further, unveiling a bold proposal to pack the Court with additional justices to rein in recalcitrant jurists, until the Court capitulated and upheld key pieces of FDR's New Deal legislation.[15]

Dating back to the presidency of George Washington, presidents have learned a lesson when they have tried to nominate a justice whom Congress found offensive: Washington selected John Rutledge (via a recess appointment) to serve as chief justice in 1795, when John Jay stepped down to become governor of New York. After Rutledge gave a speech condemning the Jay Treaty with England, the Senate swiftly rejected this nominee and forced Washington to pick a new chief justice. Similarly, Congress thwarted President John Tyler in his final nomination to the High Court, riled by Tyler's then-unprecedented use of the veto power. The Senate dragged its feet and adjourned without taking action on the last nominee, leaving Tyler's successor to fill the seat as a final slap in the face of the outgoing president.

In modern times, increasingly, politics has entered into the judicial appointment process. Some presidents have seen great successes, while others have seen colossal failures flowing from their efforts to shape the Court. With the appointment of Chief Justice Warren Burger and later Justice William H. Rehnquist, President Richard Nixon put a conservative stamp on the Court that lasted for decades. President Ronald Reagan triggered one of the bloodiest battles in judicial appointment history when he nominated Judge Robert Bork (Nixon's controversial solicitor general and attorney general) for the Court. After a vicious partisan battle, the Senate shot down the nomination and set a new, aggressive tone for waging political warfare over a president's judicial nominees. Yet Reagan also hit a home run when he appointed the first female justice—Sandra Day O'Connor—who had a profound impact on the Court for decades. Indeed, Reagan reshaped the entire federal judiciary in a conservative mold with his systematic approach to selecting jurists who shared his political philosophy.

President George H. W. Bush unleashed an unexpected uproar when he nominated Judge Clarence Thomas for the High Court to replace the first African American justice, Thurgood Marshall; allegations of sexual harassment surfaced during Thomas's confirmation hearings, because of testimony from a former EEOC lawyer, Anita Hill. Yet Thomas survived the confirmation hearing in a dramatic standoff with Senate Democratic accusers and ended up further solidifying the conservative majority on the Court.

President Barack Obama appointed the first Hispanic to the Court—Justice Sonia Sotomayor. As of 2016, however, President Obama never had the opportunity to shift the Court's five-to-four conservative majority by replacing any of the justices in the majority, a goal that eluded him during his two-term presidency.

### After the White House: Post-Presidential Roles

Many presidents have not finished shaping the country after their time in the White House; some have continued to exert substantial influence during their post-presidential years. Indeed, some presidents' activities after leaving the White House have significantly shaped their legacies as public figures, even more so than their time as chief executives.

President John Quincy Adams, after losing his bid for a second term in the White House, was elected to the U.S. House of Representatives, where he served for seventeen years. It was here that Adams became a leading opponent of slavery, battling to end slavery in the District of Columbia, representing the escaped Africans in the *Amistad* case, and even fighting off efforts by fellow members of Congress to censure him for his antislavery positions. President John Tyler, ever devoted to the Southern cause in the years leading up to the Civil War, left office and was later elected to the Confederate House of Representatives. The only president with that dubious distinction, Tyler died before he was able to take his seat as a representative of the Confederacy, yet that mark has remained stamped on his record forever. President Andrew Johnson, Abraham Lincoln's successor who sought to thwart the congressional Republicans' efforts at Reconstruction, left office in ignominy after he narrowly escaped impeachment. Johnson then unsuccessfully ran for both the U.S. House of Representatives and the U.S. Senate from Tennessee. The state legislature finally selected him to serve in the Senate on the fifty-fourth ballot in January 1875, when he reportedly declared: "Thank God for the vindication." Johnson died shortly after this victory, however, having served in the U.S. Senate for only a few months.

President William Howard Taft became the first chief executive to be appointed chief justice of the United States, serving with distinction in that role for nearly a decade. Taft's record as chief justice arguably outshone his record as chief executive and elevated his place in American history. President Jimmy Carter, widely viewed as one of the most ineffective presidents of modern times, went on to become a renowned advocate for human rights and an international mediator, winning the Nobel Peace Prize and becoming one of the most effective former presidents in the nation's history. President Bill Clinton, having fended off multiple criminal investigations and prevailed in his impeachment trial while in office, went on to become a global philanthropist, an international ambassador of goodwill, and a wildly popular elder statesman. Clinton was largely credited with winning a second term for President Barack Obama by delivering a rousing speech at the Democratic Convention. Of equal significance, Clinton's spouse—Hillary Rodham Clinton—went on to become a U.S. senator from New York, secretary of state, and two-time presidential candidate (2008 and 2016), becoming the first former First Lady in American history to achieve such distinction as a public figure in her own right. This is unmistakable evidence that presidents' spouses will increasingly—in future eras—help to shape the legacy of the presidents themselves. They may even leave independent marks on history that equal (or outshine) those of their spouses.

## A Living History

The American presidency—as it interfaces with the Constitution—has not finished evolving, not by a long shot. As the forty-four chapters of this book illustrate, the energy that the framers of the Constitution pumped into the novel office of the chief executive continues to bring life to the American presidency in unexpected ways, as new eras appear and recede into history. Each time a new president takes office, he or she inherits a rich body of experience and precedent; he or she must draw upon that valuable storehouse in riding out unexpected gusts, gales, and tsunamis, keeping the ship of state steady and creating a fresh set of markers for future occupants of the office. At the same time, each president must wrestle with unplanned events, in order to shape his or her own legacy. As the framers' unfinished sketch of the American presidency continues to emerge through the energetic performance of the individuals thrust into this high office at specific moments in history, the story will continue to gain new layers of texture and sharp detail. This book now awaits unwritten chapters, as the story of American presidents and the Constitution continues to evolve and expand in unforeseen directions, taking paths that would have surprised and heartened the nation's founders.

## NOTES

1. Unless otherwise indicated, all material referenced in this chapter derives from the earlier chapter associated with the relevant president.
2. If the Supreme Court had left the disputed Florida electoral votes to Congress as set forth in the Twelfth Amendment, the result would have most likely been the same. Because the House of Representatives was controlled by a Republican majority, that body almost certainly would have selected Bush as president. Yet, if Congress had been free to follow the mechanism set forth in the Twelfth Amendment, partisan uproar would have probably been far less intense.
3. For an excellent discussion of the unitary executive model, see Louis Fisher, "The Unitary Executive and Inherent Executive Power," *University of Pennsylvania Journal of Constitutional Law* 12 (2010): 569.
4. President George H. W. Bush pushed hard for an amendment to the Constitution banning flag burning after the Supreme Court held that this was a form of political speech protected by the First Amendment. Although Bush failed, if he had won a second term in office, he might have succeeded, particularly in light of the outpouring of patriotic sentiment that followed the Gulf War.
5. Train v. City of New York, 420 U.S. 35 (1975).
6. Nixon's holding on to funds resulted in the passage of the Impoundment Control Act of 1974, to curb future presidents from thwarting the will of Congress by impounding funds in this fashion.
7. Legislative and committee vetoes continued in an "underground" fashion even after this decision, because these vetoes benefited both the legislative and the executive branches in certain instances by providing a swift way to reverse the decisions of executive agencies without going through the full legislative process. Louis Fisher, "The Legislative Veto: Invalidated, It Survives," *Law and Contemporary Problems* 55 (1993): 273.
8. This issue was not limited to former slaves of African origin. During the presidency of Chester A. Arthur, the Supreme Court, in Elk v. Wilkins, 112 U.S, 94 (1884), held that Native Americans were not citizens of the United States, with the meaning of the Fourteenth Amendment.

9. These included the ability to require collective bargaining in the steel industry pursuant to the National Labor Relations Act, in NLRB v. Jones & Laughlin Steel Corp., 301 U.S. 1 (1937), with the Court declaring that the manufacture of steel bore a "close and substantial relation" to interstate commerce.

10. Heart of Atlanta Motel and Katzenbach v. McClung, 379 U.S. 294 (1964).

11. The majority opinion by Chief Justice Roberts, in numerous places, emphasizes that the individual mandate was unconstitutional because it compelled individuals to engage in commerce rather than merely regulating commerce. By implication, the chief justice suggested that the power to regulate the health-care industry was valid under the Commerce Clause: "Given its expansive scope, it is no surprise that Congress has employed the commerce power in a wide variety of ways to address the pressing needs of the time. But Congress has never attempted to rely on that power to compel individuals not engaged in commerce to purchase an unwanted product." National Federation of Independent Business v. Sebelius, 132 S. Ct. 2566, 2586 (2012). Even Justice Scalia, who vigorously dissented in arguing that Congress lacked authority to adopt the individual mandate, seemed to acknowledge that Congress had the power to regulate the health-care industry, generally, under the Commerce Clause: "Congress has set out to remedy the problem that the best health care is beyond the reach of many Americans who cannot afford it. It can assuredly do that, by exercising the powers accorded to it under the Constitution. The question in this case, however, is whether the complex structures and provisions of the Patient Protection and Affordable Care Act (Affordable Care Act or ACA) go beyond those powers. We conclude that they do." Ibid., 2566, 2642–2643.

12. The Carter peanut-farm investigation took place before the passage of the Independent Counsel Law.

13. Libby was charged with making false statements to federal agents who were investigating a leak of the covert identity of CIA official Valerie Plame. Libby was ultimately convicted on multiple felony counts.

14. One exception was President Franklin Pierce, who avoided politics and patronage scrupulously, going so far as to consult with the sitting justices before nominating Justice Archibald Campbell.

15. Congress has sometimes altered the number of justices by statute. It raised the number from six to seven in 1807 and from seven to nine in 1837. During the presidency of Andrew Johnson in 1866, Congress reduced the number of justices from nine to seven, to prevent Johnson from furthering his own Reconstruction agenda by appointing another member to the Court. When Ulysses S. Grant became president, Congress regained confidence in the chief executive and, in 1869, returned the number of justices to nine, where it has remained ever since.

# ACKNOWLEDGMENTS

The editor would like to express particular gratitude to his special adviser, Joy Gobos McNally, a fabulous lawyer and legal scholar, who poured her abundant time and talent into this project, bringing it to an otherwise unattainable level of excellence. She coordinated the contributions of forty-four authors and made sure that each chapter went through numerous revisions and fit neatly into the larger historical picture. (Additionally, many thanks to her husband, Mark McNally, and their son, Evan McNally, who endured two years' worth of presidential mania as this book project galloped to a conclusion.) Frank Stoy, another special adviser, enthusiastically assisted in enlisting authors and in revising early drafts; his work was invaluable, and his contributions were extensive. An early research assistant, Devin Misour, helped to get the project under way and used his considerable organizational skills to keep it on track. Student research assistants Lauren Gailey, Lindsay Fouse, and David Frantz did excellent work in gathering valuable nuggets of research material and in helping to ready the manuscript for publication. Additional research assistants include Marcus Graham, Ryan Hemminger, David Cardone, Elizabeth Lamm, Timothy Relich, and other Duquesne Law School students who pushed this project forward with infectious enthusiasm, eager to see the book in print. Joel Fishman did a remarkable job tracking down hard-to-locate books and other historical material relating to the presidents. Also, special thanks to June Devinney, who did much of the typing and editing during the numerous revisions of these book chapters, as well as Kathy Koehler and Jill Chadwick, who provided valuable assistance.

Special thanks to Clara Platter, the talented editor at NYU Press who recognized the value of this book project early on and made it richer through her creative leadership; as well as to Constance Grady, the excellent editorial assistant at NYU Press who worked tirelessly to bring this project to fruition. Additionally, my thanks to Dorothea Stillman Halliday, our skilled managing editor; Charles B. Hames, our creative design and production manager; Patty Boyd, who (as usual) did a phenomenal job in her role as copy editor; and Robert Swanson, who prepared the index. As well, Mary Beth Jarrad (marketing and sales director), Betsy Steve (senior publicist), Edith Alston (editing specialist), and Mindy Basinger Hill (jacket designer) were invaluable members of the team at NYU Press.

Professor Akhil Reed Amar at Yale Law School and Louis Fisher, Scholar in Residence at the Constitution Project, read drafts of the manuscript and enhanced the book immeasurably; each of them is a remarkable constitutional expert with a vast knowledge of the American presidency—we were fortunate to have such insightful and brilliant readers.

Additionally, nearly forty historians, political scientists, and experts in particular presidencies gave generously of their time and talent to read drafts of individual chapters. Their expert comments added immensely to the richness and accuracy of the finished book. These prominent experts include Henry J. Abraham, Michael Les Benedict, Michael J. Birkner, Alan Brinkley, Harold H. Bruff, Brian J. Cook, Byron W. Danes, Chris Edelson, James W. Ely, Jr., Garrett Epps, David Farber, Paula S. Fass, Louis Fisher, Burt W. Folsom, Jr., Joyce S. Goldberg, John R. Greene, Michael F. Holt, William F. LaFeber, William E. Leuchtenburg, Marc W. Kruman, Gerard N. Magliocca, F. Thorton Miller, Keith W. Olson, Lynn Hudson Parsons, William D. Pederson, Allan Peskin, James P. Pfiffner, Richard M. Pious, Daniel Preston, Stephen G. Rabe, Thomas C. Reeves, Leo P. Ribuffo, Mark J. Rozell, Steven E. Schier, Bruce J. Schulman, Matthew M. Schousen, Peter M. Shane, David Stebenne, Michael J.C. Taylor, Gil Troy, and Frank J. Williams.

It is only through the collaborative work of dozens of preeminent scholars and enthusiastic students that this special book project was able to come to fruition. The editor of this volume is deeply grateful to all of them.

# ABOUT THE CONTRIBUTORS

SALADIN M. AMBAR is Assistant Professor of Political Science at Lehigh University. He is a former fellow of the Miller Center of Public Affairs at the University of Virginia and is the author of *How Governors Built the Modern American Presidency*.

WILLIAM D. BADER is a member of the Connecticut and Federal Bars. Mr. Bader is the author of highly acclaimed legal publications, including *Unknown Justices of the United States Supreme Court*, co-authored with Frank J. Williams, former Chief Justice of the Rhode Island Supreme Court; "Some Thoughts on Blackstone, Precedent, and Originalism" in the *Vermont Law Review*; and "Saint Thomas More: Equity and the Common Law Method," in the *Duquesne Law Review*.

JOHN Q. BARRETT is Professor of Law at St. John's University. He has served as an Elizabeth S. Lenna Fellow and board member at the Robert H. Jackson Center in Jamestown, New York. Professor Barrett is a nationally recognized expert on Justice Robert H. Jackson and the presidents of Jackson's era; he has written several books and articles on Justice Jackson and the U.S. Supreme Court.

MICHAEL LES BENEDICT is Professor Emeritus in the History Department at the Ohio State University. He is the author of *The Impeachment and Trial of Andrew Johnson* and *A Compromise of Principle: Congressional Republicans and Reconstruction*. He has also written a widely used textbook on American constitutional history, *The Blessings of Liberty*; a companion *Sources in American Constitutional History*; and a reader in Reconstruction history, *The Fruits of Victory: Alternatives in Restoring the Union, 1865–1877*.

JOHN L. BULLION is Professor of History at the University of Missouri. Professor Bullion has written several books on the presidency of Lyndon Johnson, including *In the Boat with LBJ* (2001); and *Lyndon B. Johnson and the Transformation of American Politics (2008).*

JEFFREY CROUCH is Assistant Professor of American Politics at American University. Dr. Crouch is the Reviews and Book Editor for *American University's Congress & the Presidency Journal* and is the author of *The Presidential Pardon Power.*

RICHARD V. DAMMS is Associate Professor of History at Mississippi State University. Professor Damms's research interests include the Cold War and the Eisenhower presidency. He is the author of *The Eisenhower Presidency, 1953–1961.*

RICHARD J. ELLIS is Mark O. Hatfield Professor of Politics at Willamette University. Professor Ellis has written extensively on the American presidency, including *The Development of the American Presidency; Judging Executive Power: Sixteen Supreme Court Cases That Have Shaped the American Presidency; Debating the Presidency: Conflicting Perspectives on the American Executive* (ed., with Michael Nelson); *Founding the American Presidency;* and *Dilemmas of Presidential Leadership: From Washington Through Lincoln* (with Aaron Wildavsky).

JONATHAN L. ENTIN is Associate Dean for Academic Affairs and Professor of Law and Political Science at Case Western Reserve University School of Law. Prior to teaching, he practiced at the law firm of Steptoe & Johnson LLP and clerked for then-Judge Ruth Bader Ginsburg on the U.S. Court of Appeals for the District of Columbia Circuit.

PAUL FINKELMAN is Senior Fellow at the Penn Program on Democracy, Citizenship, and Constitutionalism at the University of Pennsylvania and Scholar in Residence at the National Constitution Center. He is the author of more than two hundred scholarly articles and over forty books, including *Race and Liberty in the Age of Jefferson; A March of Liberty: A Constitutional History of the United States,* 2 vols. (co-authored with Melvin Urofsky); and *An Imperfect Union: Slavery, Federalism and Comity.* His scholarship has been cited in multiple U.S. Supreme Court decisions.

Louis Fisher is Scholar in Residence at the Constitution Project. For decades, Dr. Fisher served at the Library of Congress with the Congressional Research Service as Senior Specialist in Separation of Powers and with the Law Library as Specialist in Constitutional Law. He is the author of twenty books, including *President and Congress*; *Presidential Spending Power*; *Constitutional Conflicts Between Congress and the President*; *Presidential War Power*; and *The Politics of Executive Privilege*.

Michael J. Gerhardt is Samuel Ashe Distinguished Professor in Constitutional Law and Director of the Center for Law and Government at the University of North Carolina School of Law. He is the author of several books, including *The Power of Precedent*; *The Federal Impeachment Process: A Constitutional and Historical Analysis*; *The Federal Appointments Process*; and *The Forgotten Presidents*.

James N. Giglio is Distinguished Professor Emeritus in the History Department at Missouri State University. Professor Giglio specializes in the presidencies of Harry Truman and John F. Kennedy and has written several books on the two presidents, including *The Presidency of John F. Kennedy*; *Debating the Kennedy Presidency* (with Stephen G. Rabe); and *Truman in Cartoon and Caricature* (with Greg Thielen).

Ken Gormley is the newly appointed President of Duquesne University, where he previously served as Dean and Professor of Law. Gormley is the author of *The Death of American Virtue: Clinton vs. Starr*, a nonfiction work that covers the Clinton-Starr saga from Whitewater through the failed impeachment of President Clinton, as well as *Archibald Cox: Conscience of a Nation*, the biography of the Watergate special prosecutor. He has also written extensively on various American presidents, including Harry S. Truman, John F. Kennedy, Lyndon B. Johnson, Richard M. Nixon, Gerald R. Ford, and others.

Mark A. Graber is Associate Dean for Research and Faculty Development and Professor of Law and Government at University of Maryland Francis King Carey School of Law. Professor Graber is recognized as a leading scholar on constitutional law and politics and is the author of *Dred Scott and the Problem of Constitutional Evil*.

LORI COX HAN is Professor of Political Science at Chapman University. Professor Han is the author of several books, including *Presidents and the American Presidency*, and *A Presidency Upstaged: The Public leadership of George H. W. Bush*. She is also Editor of *New Directions in the American Presidency*.

GARY HART is a retired U.S. Senator and Senior Strategic Advisor and Independent Consultant at McKenna Long & Aldridge LLP. Prior to entering private practice, Senator Hart was Scholar in Residence and Wirth Chair Professor at the School of Public Affairs at the University of Colorado Denver and was a Distinguished Fellow at the Center for Strategic and International Studies. He is the author of *The Presidency of James Monroe*.

THOMAS A. HORROCKS is an Independent Scholar. Dr. Horrocks was the Director of the John Hay Library at Brown University and previously served as the Assistant Librarian of Houghton Library for Collections at Harvard University. He is the author of *President James Buchanan and the Crisis of National Leadership*.

JOHN W. JOHNSON is Professor of History at University of Northern Iowa. Professor Johnson's scholarship includes twentieth-century American history and American legal and constitutional history.

SCOTT KAUFMAN is Professor of History and Co-Director of the Robert E. McNair Center for Government and History at Francis Marion University. Professor Kaufman has written several books on the presidency of Jimmy Carter, including *Plans Unraveled: The Foreign Policy of the Carter Administration*; *Rosalynn Carter: Equal Partner in the White House*; *The Presidency of James Earl Carter Jr.* (co-edited with Burton Kaufman); and *The Companion to Gerald R. Ford and Jimmy Carter*.

RALPH KETCHAM is Professor Emeritus at the Departments of History, Public Affairs, and Political Science at Maxwell School of Syracuse University. Professor Ketcham is the author of *James Madison: A Biography*; and *The Madisons at Montpelier: Reflections on the Founding Couple*.

BENJAMIN A. KLEINERMAN is Associate Professor of Constitutional Democracy at James Madison College, Michigan State University.

Professor Kleinerman is the author of *The Discretionary President: The Promise and Peril of Executive Power*.

STANLEY KUTLER (deceased) was Professor Emeritus in the History Department at the University of Wisconsin–Madison. Professor Kutler wrote and edited several books on the Nixon administration, including *Abuse of Power: The New Nixon Tapes*; *The Wars of Watergate: The Last Crisis of Richard Nixon*; *The American Inquisition*; and *The Supreme Court and the Constitution* (editor). Professor Kutler was a Guggenheim Fellow, holder of the Garibaldi Chair in Political Science at the University of Bologna, Distinguished Exchange Scholar (National Science Foundation) for China, Fulbright 40th Anniversary Distinguished Lecturer in Peru, Bicentennial Professor at Tel Aviv University, and Fulbright Lecturer in Japan.

JOHN F. MARSZALEK is Giles Distinguished Professor Emeritus at Mississippi State University and the Executive Director and Managing Editor of the Ulysses S. Grant Association's Ulysses S. Grant Presidential Library. Professor Marszalek is a noted specialist on the Civil War era, the Jacksonian Period, and race relations, and he has written thirteen books on that period.

WILLIAM D. PEDERSON is American Studies Endowed Chair in Liberal Arts, Professor of Political Science, and Director of the International Lincoln Center at Louisiana State University. Professor Pederson is a nationally recognized expert on the presidency, particularly those of Abraham Lincoln and Franklin D. Roosevelt. He has also edited over thirty books on the presidency.

BARBARA A. PERRY is White Burkett Miller Professor of Ethics and Institutions at the University of Virginia's Miller Center, where she is Director of Presidential Studies and Co-chair of the Presidential Oral History Program. Her books include *The Supremes: An Introduction to the United States Supreme Court Justices*, 2nd ed.; *Jacqueline Kennedy: First Lady of the New Frontier*; and *Freedom and the Court: Civil Rights and Liberties in the United States*, 8th ed. (with Henry J. Abraham).

JOSEPH F. RISHEL is Professor Emeritus in the History Department at Duquesne University. Most recently, he published *Pittsburgh Remembers World War II*.

JAMES D. ROBENALT is a partner in the Business Litigation practice group, Thompson Hine LLP in Cleveland. Mr. Robenalt is also the author of several books on the American presidency, including *Presidency in the Twentieth Century: Linking Rings, W. W. Durbin, and the Magic and Mystery of America*; and *The Harding Affair: Love and Espionage During the Great War*.

FRANCINE SANDERS ROMERO is Associate Dean of the College of Public Policy and Associate Professor of Public Administration at the University of Texas. Dr. Romero is the author of *Presidents from Theodore Roosevelt Through Coolidge, 1901–1929: Debating the Issues in Pro and Con Primary Documents*.

MICHAEL A. ROSS is Associate Professor of History at the University of Maryland. He serves on the editorial board of the *Journal of Supreme Court History* and is the author of *Justice of Shattered Dreams: Samuel Freeman Miller and the Supreme Court During the Civil War Era*.

DAVID MARKS SHRIBMAN is Executive Editor and Vice President of the *Pittsburgh Post-Gazette*. Mr. Shribman was previously with the *Boston Globe*, serving as Assistant Managing Editor, Columnist, and Washington Bureau Chief. He was awarded the Pulitzer Prize in Journalism in 1995 for his coverage of Washington and American politics. He has a nationally syndicated column, *My Point*, and is the author of *I Remember My Teacher*.

CLIFF SLOAN is a partner at Skadden, Arps, Slate, Meagher & Flom LLP. He served as the Special Envoy for Guantanamo Closure at the U.S. State Department. Previously, Mr. Sloan worked for several nationally known media outlets and served as Associate Counsel in the Office of Independent Counsel for Iran-Contra, Assistant to the Solicitor General, and Associate Counsel to the President of the United States. He is also co-author of *The Great Decision: Jefferson, Adams, Marshall, and the Battle for the Supreme Court* (with David McKean).

ALLAN B. SPETTER is Professor Emeritus at the History Department at Wright State University and a Consulting Editor with the Miller Center of the University of Virginia, which specializes in presidential scholarship. Dr. Spetter served as Executive Secretary-Treasurer of the Society for Historians of American Foreign Relations. His writings include *The Presidency of Benjamin Harrison* (co-authored with Homer E. Socolofsky).

MOSHE SPINOWITZ is an associate at Skadden, Arps. Prior to joining the firm, Mr. Spinowitz served as a Law Clerk to Judge Michael Boudin on the U.S. Court of Appeals for the First Circuit, and Justice Antonin Scalia on the U.S. Supreme Court.

ROBERT J. SPITZER is Distinguished Service Professor and Chair of the Political Science Department at the State University of New York Cortland. Dr. Spitzer is also the Editor of the SUNY Press book series on American constitutionalism. His books include *The Presidency and Public Policy: The Four Arenas of Presidential Power, The Presidential Veto: Touchstone of the American Presidency, President and Congress: Executive Hegemony at the Crossroads of American Government*; and *The Presidency and the Constitution: Cases and Controversies* (with Michael A. Genovese).

KENNETH W. STARR is President of Baylor University. Prior to Baylor, Judge Starr served as the Duane and Kelly Roberts Dean and Professor of Law at Pepperdine University. Prior to entering academia, Judge Starr served as Solicitor General of the United States and U.S. Circuit Judge for the District of Columbia Circuit; he was appointed Independent Counsel for five investigations, including Whitewater. Judge Starr is also the author of *First Among Equals: The Supreme Court in American Life*.

DONALD GRIER STEPHENSON JR. is Charles A. Dana Professor of Government at Franklin & Marshall College. Professor Stephenson has written extensively on constitutional law, American government, and the U.S. Supreme Court, including the textbook *American Constitutional Law: Introductory Essays and Selected Cases*.

THOMAS C. SUTTON is Professor and Chair of Political Science at Baldwin-Wallace College. Dr. Sutton has written on the important Supreme Court cases decided during the Gilded Age and on the history of the vice presidency during that period.

FRANK J. WILLIAMS is former Chief Justice of the Rhode Island Supreme Court and former Appellate Judge on the U.S. Court of Military

Commissions Review. Chief Justice Williams is also a noted presidential scholar and author of *Judging Lincoln*; *James Madison: Philosopher, Founder, and Statesman* (with John R. Vile and William D. Pederson); and *Abraham Lincoln, Esq.: The Legal Career of America's Greatest President* (with Roger Billings).

DALE E. P. YURS was a graduate student in History at the University of Northern Iowa, where he worked with Professor John W. Johnson on projects involving the American presidency.

# PHOTO CREDITS

1. George Washington, by Gilbert Stuart, courtesy Library of Congress; superimposed against 1777 U.S. flag, courtesy Wikimedia Commons.
2. John Adams, second president of the United States, by Gilbert Stuart, courtesy Library of Congress; superimposed against 1795 U.S. flag, courtesy Wikimedia Commons.
3. Thomas Jefferson, by Albert Newsam, courtesy Library of Congress; superimposed against 1795 U.S. flag, courtesy Wikimedia Commons.
4. James Madison, by Gilbert Stuart, courtesy Library of Congress; superimposed against 1795 U.S. flag, courtesy Wikimedia Commons.
5. James Monroe, by Gilbert Stuart, courtesy Library of Congress; superimposed against 1795 U.S. flag, courtesy Wikimedia Commons.
6. John Quincy Adams, by George Peter Alexander Healy, courtesy Library of Congress; superimposed against 1822 U.S. flag, courtesy Wikimedia Commons.
7. Andrew Jackson, courtesy Library of Congress; superimposed against 1822 U.S. flag, courtesy Wikimedia Commons.
8. Martin Van Buren, courtesy Library of Congress; superimposed against 1836 U.S. flag, courtesy Wikimedia Commons.
9. William Henry Harrison, by Charles Fenderich from a painting by W. H. Franquinet, courtesy Library of Congress; superimposed against 1837 U.S. flag, courtesy Wikimedia Commons.
10. John Tyler, courtesy Library of Congress; superimposed against 1837 U.S. flag, courtesy Wikimedia Commons.
11. James K. Polk, courtesy Library of Congress; superimposed against 1837 U.S. flag, courtesy Wikimedia Commons.
12. Zachary Taylor, by Matthew B. Brady, courtesy Library of Congress; superimposed against 1848 U.S. flag, courtesy Wikimedia Commons.
13. Millard Fillmore, by J. C. Buttre, courtesy Library of Congress; superimposed against 1848 U.S. flag, courtesy Wikimedia Commons.

14. Franklin Pierce, by Matthew B. Brady and Levin C. Handy, courtesy Library of Congress; superimposed against 1851 U.S. flag, courtesy Wikimedia Commons.

15. James Buchanan, by Matthew B. Brady, courtesy Library of Congress; superimposed against 1851 U.S. flag, courtesy Wikimedia Commons.

16. Abraham Lincoln, by J. C. Buttre, courtesy Library of Congress; superimposed against 1859 U.S. flag, courtesy Wikimedia Commons.

17. Andrew Johnson, by Matthew B. Brady and Levin C. Handy, courtesy Library of Congress; superimposed against 1863 U.S. flag, courtesy Wikimedia Commons.

18. Ulysses S. Grant, by Matthew B. Brady and Levin C. Handy, courtesy Library of Congress; superimposed against 1867 U.S. flag, courtesy Wikimedia Commons.

19. Rutherford B. Hayes, by Matthew B. Brady and Levin C. Handy, courtesy Library of Congress; superimposed against 1867 U.S. flag, courtesy Wikimedia Commons.

20. James A. Garfield, by Matthew B. Brady and Levin C. Handy, courtesy Library of Congress; superimposed against 1877 U.S. flag, courtesy Wikimedia Commons.

21. Chester A. Arthur, by Charles Milton Bell, courtesy Library of Congress; superimposed against 1877 U.S. flag, courtesy Wikimedia Commons.

22. Grover Cleveland, courtesy Library of Congress; superimposed against 1877 U.S. flag, courtesy Wikimedia Commons.

23. Benjamin Harrison, by the Pach Brothers Firm, courtesy Library of Congress; superimposed against 1877 U.S. flag, courtesy Wikimedia Commons.

24. Grover Cleveland, courtesy Library of Congress; superimposed against 1891 U.S. flag, courtesy Wikimedia Commons.

25. William McKinley, courtesy Library of Congress; superimposed against 1896 U.S. flag, courtesy Wikimedia Commons.

26. Theodore Roosevelt, by the Pach Brothers Firm, courtesy Library of Congress; superimposed against 1896 U.S. flag, courtesy Wikimedia Commons.

27. William Howard Taft, courtesy Library of Congress; superimposed against 1908 U.S. flag, courtesy Wikimedia Commons.

28. Woodrow Wilson, courtesy Library of Congress; superimposed against 1912 U.S. flag, courtesy Wikimedia Commons.

29. Warren G. Harding, courtesy Library of Congress; superimposed against 1912 U.S. flag, courtesy Wikimedia Commons.

30. Calvin Coolidge, courtesy Library of Congress; superimposed against 1912 U.S. flag, courtesy Wikimedia Commons.

31. Herbert Hoover, courtesy Library of Congress; superimposed against 1912 U.S. flag, courtesy Wikimedia Commons.

32. Franklin D. Roosevelt, courtesy Library of Congress; superimposed against 1912 U.S. flag, courtesy Wikimedia Commons.

33. Harry S. Truman, courtesy Library of Congress; superimposed against 1912 U.S. flag, courtesy Wikimedia Commons.

34. Dwight D. Eisenhower, by Fabian Bachrach, courtesy Library of Congress; superimposed against 1912 U.S. flag, courtesy Wikimedia Commons.

35. John F. Kennedy, courtesy Library of Congress; superimposed against 1960 U.S. flag, courtesy Wikimedia Commons.

36. Lyndon B. Johnson, courtesy Library of Congress; superimposed against 1960 U.S. flag, courtesy Wikimedia Commons.

37. Richard M. Nixon, courtesy Library of Congress; superimposed against 1960 U.S. flag, courtesy Wikimedia Commons.

38. Gerald R. Ford, courtesy Library of Congress; superimposed against 1960 U.S. flag, courtesy Wikimedia Commons.

39. Jimmy Carter, by Karl Schumacher, courtesy Library of Congress; superimposed against 1960 U.S. flag, courtesy Wikimedia Commons.

40. Ronald Reagan, courtesy Library of Congress; superimposed against 1960 U.S. flag, courtesy Wikimedia Commons.

41. George H. W. Bush, by David Valdez, courtesy Library of Congress; superimposed against 1960 U.S. flag, courtesy Wikimedia Commons.

42. William Jefferson Clinton, courtesy Library of Congress; superimposed against 1960 U.S. flag, courtesy Wikimedia Commons.

43. George W. Bush, by Eric Draper, courtesy Library of Congress; superimposed against 1960 U.S. flag, courtesy Wikimedia Commons.

44. Barack Obama, by Pete Souza, courtesy Library of Congress; superimposed against 1960 U.S. flag, courtesy Wikimedia Commons.

# INDEX

*Ableman v. Booth*, 180n6

Abortion, 499–500

*Abrams v. United States*, 375

Abu Ghraib prison, 598

Acheson, Dean, 432

Act of war, 470n12

Adams, Abigail, 9, 36, 41, 43–44, 55

Adams, Charles F., 179n2

Adams, John, 8, 9, 26, 28, 45n18, 45n21, 49, 50, 51, 52–55, 58, 68, 91, 104, 364, 625, 637, 645, 650; censure threatening, 40–41; impeachment of, 40–41, 627; overview of, 34–44; reelection of, 41–43; XYZ Affair influencing, 37. See also *Marbury v. Madison*; Quasi-War

Adams, John Quincy, 44, 78–79, 84–85, 98n17, 98n19, 99n29, 104, 105, 121, 133, 138–39, 183, 238n27, 625–26; on federal government, 93; in House of Representatives, 652; in 1824 election, 92–93; overview of, 89–97; political career beginnings, 90–92; removal and, 93–94; tariff issue, 94–95

Addington, David, 597–98

*Adkins v. Children's Hospital*, 349–50

Advice and consent, 28–29, 528–29, 630. See also *Myers v. United States*

Affirmative action, 524–28, 534n21, 642–43

Affordable Care Act. See Patient Protection and Affordable Care Act

Afghanistan, 594–95, 600, 614

AFL-CIO. See American Federation of Labor and Congress of Industrial Organizations

African Americans, 300, 303, 318, 576. See also Affirmative action; Desegregation; Fifteenth Amendment; Segregation

Africans. See *Amistad* Case

Agnew, Spiro T., 500, 509, 510

Agricultural Adjustment Act (1938), 417, 485n26, 644. See also *Wickard v. Filburn*

Agricultural Adjustment Act of 1933, 415

Aguilar, David V., 618n19

Aguinaldo, Emilio, 321

Air traffic controllers. See Professional Air Traffic Controllers Organization strike

Alabama, 467–68, 479, 485n17, 628, 640, 642

*Alabama* Claims, 217–18, 224n22

Alabama National Guard, 467

Alexander Macomb House, 14n30

Alien Act of 1918, 363–64, 645

Alien and Sedition Acts, 38, 51, 52–53, 64, 364, 369n30, 377, 619n22, 645

Alito, Samuel, 617n8, 618n11, 618n14

Allen, William, 133

Al-Qaeda, 594–95. See also Bin Laden, Osama

Altgeld, John Peter, 310

Amar, Akhil Reed, 8, 107

American Federation of Labor and Congress of Industrial Organizations (AFL-CIO), 545–46

American Historical Association, 592

American Indians. See Native Americans

American Jewish Committee, 526

American Jewish Congress, 526

American Protective League (APL), 373, 381

American Railway Union, 310–11

American Revolution, 49, 54, 72n3, 76–77, 90

American Sugar Refining Company. See *United States v. E.C. Knight Co.*

American System agenda, 141

American Tobacco, 345–46

*Amistad* case, 96, 99n29, 119–21, 641
Amistad Committee, 121
*Anderson v. Dunn*, 621n44
Annexation, 79, 112, 144–45, 150–55, 156, 156n12, 327n23, 632, 637
Anti-Catholicism, 302
Anti-Defamation League, 526
Anti-Federalists, 19
Anti-Masonic Party, 174
Anti-Moiety Act (1874), 285n3
Antiquities Act, 334
APL. *See* American Protective League
Appointments, 53–55, 65–66, 269–70, 279–80, 281, 629–30. See also *Marbury v. Madison*; Recess appointment; Supreme Court, U.S.
Arizona, 348, 351, 353n18
Arkansas, 452–54, 571–72, 576, 582n6, 582n14, 585n42, 640, 642
Arkansas National Guard, 453, 640
Arkansas Supreme Court, 580
Armed neutrality, 361–62
Army, U.S., 162, 169, 170n1, 170n2, 310, 446, 640
Army of Northern Virginia, 218
Arthur, Chester, 271, 272–73, 285n3, 285n4, 286n10, 286n12, 286n13, 286n22, 287n23, 629; appointments of, 279–80; civil rights during, 282–84; executive powers of, 279–80; legislative leadership of, 280–82; overview of, 276–85; Supreme Court during administration of, 282–84, 654n8
Arthur, Ellen Herndon, 277
Arthur, William, 277
Article I, 6–7, 20, 22, 106, 259, 314n11; on habeas corpus, 225n30; Section 2, 91, 232, 352n14, 369n22; Section 3, 235–36; Section 4, 404n7; Section 7, 94, 400, 404n13, 576, 635, 636; Section 8, 50, 71n2, 178, 300, 301, 302, 322–23, 352n14, 643–45; Section 9, 225n30, 327n30, 352n14, 600–601, 604n37; on vice president, 44n3. *See also* Commerce Clause; General Welfare Clause; Necessary and Proper Clause; Presentment Clause; Three-fifths Clause; Veto power
Article II, 1–3, 22, 31n14, 135n16, 363, 430, 436, 618n18; on appointment, 270, 281;

on legislative function, 634; on salary, 132–33; Section 1, 131, 256, 264n4, 273, 349, 389, 492, 626, 628–29; Section 2, 27, 270, 281, 378–79, 381, 511–12, 518n13, 611, 630; Section 3, 304, 398, 438n10, 628–29, 634; Section 4, 578; Section 9, 132; on vice president, 44n3, 147n7, 273, 626. *See also* Advice and consent; Impeachment; Pardon Power; Recess appointment; Succession Clause; Take Care Clause; Vesting Clause
Article III, 54, 225n36, 338
Article IV: Fugitive Slave Clause of, 164–65, 171n10; Section 2, 164–65; Section 3, 80; Section 4, 140, 230, 259, 639
Articles of Confederation, 4, 5, 63, 643
Article VI, 66, 180n6. *See also* Supremacy Clause
Article XI, 235
Ashcroft, John, 597
*Ashcraft v. Tennessee*, 404n10
Ashmun, George, 154
Assassinations: of Ford, G., 516, 520n26, 583n17; of Garfield, J., 271–73, 274n1, 275n22, 278–80, 286n10, 629; of Kennedy, J. F., 134, 469, 476, 509, 642; of Lincoln, A., 223, 241, 642; of McKinley, W., 325–26
Atchison, David Rice, 190
Atlanta, Georgia, 478–79
Atlanta campaign, 222
Atom bomb, 563
Attorney General, 457n24, 486n33, 495, 576, 613–14, 648
Auchincloss, Louis, 332–33
AUMF Resolution. *See* Authorization for Use of Military Force Resolution
Austin, Texas, 167
Authorization for Use of Military Force (AUMF) Resolution, 594–95, 597, 600
Al-Awlaki, Abdulrahman, 622n50
Al-Awlaki, Anwar, 615, 616
Axson, Ellen Louise. *See* Wilson, Ellen

Baby Ruth candy bar, 292, 295n9
*Baker v. Carr*, 464
Bakke, Allan and *Bakke* Case. See *University of California Board of Regents v. Bakke*

Balanced Budget Act of 1997, 575
Balanced Budget and Emergency Deficit
 Control Act, 544–45, 552n25
Baldwin, Henry, 145
Baltimore & Ohio Railroad, 258
Bank of the United States, 206n8
Banks, 50, 64, 71n2, 107–8, 113n15, 113n17,
 117–19, 124n12, 141–42, 624, 643. *See also*
 National Bank
Barkley, Alben, 419
Barnett, Ross, 466
Battle of Bunker Hill, 90
Battle of Fallen Timbers, 128–29
Battle of Gettysburg, 218
Battle of New Orleans, 69, 105
Battle of Nile, 39
Beauregard, P. G. T., 214–15
Becker, Benton, 11–12, 512
Bee, Thomas, 40
Beef Trust, 341n25
Belgium, 69, 186, 397
Belknap, William W., 244
Bell, Griffin, 526–27, 533n17
Berlin Wall, 567
Bethlehem, Pennsylvania, 45n18
Bicameralism, 552n14, 552n17, 552n25
Bill of Rights, 48, 58n1, 64, 77, 364
Bills, 107–8, 111, 138, 140, 168–69, 231, 293,
 302, 303, 391–92, 394n19, 404n13, 484n14,
 485n17, 552n18, 639–40; bank, 141–42;
 farm, 397
Bin Laden, Osama, 594–95, 600, 614–16,
 621n46
Birmingham, Alabama, 467, 479, 485n17
Bituminous Coal Conservation Act, 415
Black, Hugo, 416, 420, 463, 471n31
Black Codes, 230
Black Hawk War, 216
Blackmun, Harry, 499, 569n26
Black Sea, 205n7
Black Tuesday, 399
Blaine, James G., 271, 272, 284, 291–92
Blair, Henry W., 302
Blair, John, 25
Blair Education Bill, 302
Blatchford, Samuel, 282
Bleeding Kansas, 642. *See also* Kansas-
 Nebraska Act

Blockade, 219, 221
Blockaders, 261
Block grants, 551n8
Blythe, Virginia Cassidy. *See* Clinton,
 Virginia
Boehner, John, 621n44
Bolívar, Simón, 129
Bolivia, 418–19. *See also* Gran Chaco War
Bolshevik Revolution, 372
Bonaparte, Napoléon, 52, 68, 92
Booth, John Wilkes, 223
Bootlegger, 388–89, 631
Border Patrol, 613
Border Ruffians, 190, 191
Bork, Robert H., 510–11, 549, 554n41, 555n52,
 651
Boston Massacre, 35
Botts, John Minor, 143
Boumediene, Lakhdar, 600–601
*Boumediene v. Bush*, 600–601, 604n37
Bouvier, Jacqueline. *See* Kennedy,
 Jacqueline
*Bowsher v. Synar*, 544–45, 552n24
Boxer Rebellion, 324, 638
Bradbury, James, 183
Bradley, Joseph, 256
*Bradwell v. Illinois*, 246, 647
Brady, John R., 272
Branches, 551n4
Brandeis, Louis, 366–67, 392, 394n24,
 405n17, 492, 542
*Brandenburg v. United States*, 456n12
Brazil, 339
Breckinridge, John C., 197, 202
Brennan, William Joseph, 458n42, 561, 565–
 66, 569n26
Brewer, David, 305, 310–11
Breyer, Stephen, 532, 576, 583n19, 584n29,
 591, 602n5, 612
Bribes, 509, 649
Bricker, John, 429, 446
Brinkley, Douglas, 520n26
Britain. *See* Great Britain
British, 8, 35, 40–41, 78–79, 148n21. *See also*
 Monroe Doctrine
*Bromley v. McCaughn*, 352n14
Brown, Henry, 305, 327n30
Brown, John, 190

Brownell, Herbert, 448, 451, 452–53
Brownlow, Louis, 414–15
Brownlow Committee, 414–15, 629
Brown's Indian Queen Hotel, 132–33
*Brown v. Board of Education I*, 447–49, 642
*Brown v. Board of Education II*, 449–52,
    453–54, 457n26, 458n42, 640, 642
Bryan, William Jennings, 319, 324, 325,
    326n15, 344
Buchanan, Elizabeth, 195
Buchanan, James, 105, 114n34, 145, 179,
    184–85, 186, 205n4, 205n6, 205n7, 206n8,
    206n9, 206n10, 207n22, 214, 262, 640;
    *Dred Scott v. Sandford* and, 197–99;
    Kansas handled by, 201–2; Mormon
    uprisings faced by, 199–201; overview of,
    194–204; secession influencing, 202–3
Buchanan, Pat, 569n28
Buckner, Simon Bolivar, 241
Buffalo, New York, 325
Buffalo World's Fair, 325
Bullion, J. W., 484n6
Bull Moose Party. *See* Progressive Party
Bully pulpit, 632–34
*Burdick v. United States*, 11–12, 364–65, 512,
    519n14, 623
Bureau of Indian Affairs, 287n30
Bureau of Investigation. *See* Federal Bureau
    of Investigation
Burger, Warren, 499, 502, 541, 543–44, 549,
    651
Burnett, John D., 292–93
Burns, Anthony, 189
Burr, Aaron, 42–43, 51, 56–57, 583n17, 625
Bush, Barbara, 559
Bush, Dorothy Walker, 558
Bush, George H. W., 97n1, 362, 534n29,
    541, 547, 567n4, 568n20, 569n28, 572, 573,
    582n14, 620n34, 636, 638, 648, 649, 654n4;
    overview of, 557–67; political speech and,
    564–66; Supreme Court shaped by, 560–
    62, 652. *See also* Flag burning; Persian
    Gulf War
Bush, George W., 12, 97n1, 425n34, 504n3,
    562, 566, 602n3, 602n9, 602n10, 602n15,
    603n19, 603n23, 615, 620n41, 621n49,
    631–32, 634, 637, 638–39, 646, 650,
    654n2; executive privilege and, 592–93;

interrogation used by, 597–98; 9/11 influ-
    encing, 593–601; overview of, 589–601;
    presidential papers and, 592; signing
    statements of, 599, 637; Supreme Court
    limiting, 599–601; war power limits,
    599–601. *See also* Energy task force;
    National Security Agency; Patriot Act;
    Torture
Bush, Jeb, 566, 591
Bush, Laura, 590
Bush, Prescott, 558
*Bush v. Gore*, 591, 602n3, 602n5, 626, 654n2
Butchers, 249n16
Butler, Pierce, 384n47, 415
Butler, William O., 179n2
Butterfield, Alexander, 500
Bybee, Jay S., 598
Byrnes, James E., 448

Cabinet, 22–24, 27, 40, 45n21, 147n8, 197,
    424n22, 509–10, 576
Calhoun, John, 78, 145, 153, 169
California, 152, 165, 166, 168, 169, 171n15, 176,
    188, 221, 259, 351n9, 492–93, 540–41
Cambodia, 515, 638
Campbell, Archibald, 655n14
Campbell, John, 187, 189, 192, 193n21,
    206n15, 314n14
Campbell, Parson, 76
*Campbell v. Clinton*, 585n45, 618n16
Canada, 68, 129, 177–78, 519n14
Cannon, Joseph, 340
Card, Andy, 597
Cardozo, Benjamin N., 402, 492
Carnegie, Andrew, 299, 319
Carter, James Earl, Sr., 522
Carter, Jimmy, 516–17, 519n14, 532n4, 533n6,
    533n8, 533n17, 534n31, 535n32, 541, 585n40,
    631, 642–43, 648, 649, 653, 655n12; as affir-
    mative action proponent, 524–28; claims
    tribunal, 530–31, 638; overview of, 521–32;
    Taiwan treaty terminated by, 528–29. *See
    also* Iran Hostage Crisis
Carter, Lillian, 522
Carter, Rosalynn, 522
Cass, Lewis, 163, 179n2, 184–85, 206n10
Catholicism, 463–64
Catholics, 206n12, 302

Catron, James, 198
Catron, John, 187
Censure, 40–41, 96, 108–10, 138, 293, 627–28
Census, 404n8
Central High School, 453–54, 576, 640, 642
Central Intelligence Agency (CIA), 429, 502, 515–16, 598, 646, 655n13
CFPB. *See* Consumer Financial Protection Bureau
Chadha, Jagdish, 542–44, 552n21, 552n24
Chapultepec, 184
Charleston, South Carolina, 203, 215
Chase, Chevy, 513
Chase, Salmon P., 216, 228, 235, 246
Chase, Samuel, 55
Checks and balances, 5, 10
Chemical weapons, 603n17
Cheney, Dick, 590, 631–32
*Cheney v. U.S. District Court for Dist. of Columbia*, 593, 602n10
*Cherokee Nation v. Georgia*, 114n36
Cherokee people, 112, 115n37
Chicago, Illinois, 268–69, 310, 376, 419, 483, 606
*Chicago Sun Times*, 439n31
Chief executive, 6–7, 13n3, 19, 27–28, 628–33. *See also* Legislative function
Chief justice, 29
Chief of staff, 509–10
China, 280, 432, 504, 528–29, 638, 639
Chinese Exclusion Law, 280
Chinese immigrants, 280
Chinese students, 225n27
Church, 58n2
Church, Frank, 515, 530
Church of England, 73n21
Church of Jesus Christ of Latter-Day Saints, 199–201, 640
CIA. *See* Central Intelligence Agency
Circuit riding, 32n18, 59n24
Civilians, drones killing, 621n49
Civil Liberties Act (1988), 425n43
Civil rights, 243–44, 282–84, 465–69, 477–79, 484n12, 484n14, 485n17, 644. *See also* Affirmative action
Civil Rights Act of 1866, 231–32, 254, 642
Civil Rights Act of 1875, 244, 282–83
Civil Rights Act of 1957, 457n26, 465, 475

Civil Rights Act of 1964, 477–79, 480, 485n20, 526, 527–28, 634, 642, 644
*Civil Rights Cases*, 282–83, 485n20
Civil Rights Commission, 457n24
Civil Rights Division, 457n24
Civil Service Commission, 242–43, 286n22, 287n23
Civil Service Reform Act, 553n29
Civil service reforms, 110, 270–71, 273–74
Civil suit, 583n16, 583n18, 583n19
Civil War, 12, 51, 170, 179, 190, 192, 203–4, 224n22, 226n39, 226n41, 255–56, 290–91, 352n15, 519n14, 595, 630–31, 642, 651; Gettysburg Address, 218; laws of war written during, 216–18, 222. *See also* Compromise of 1850; Gettysburg Address; Lincoln, Abraham
Claims tribunal, 530–31, 638
*Clapper v. Amnesty Intl. USA*, 603n23
Clark, Tom, 436, 478–79, 486n27
Clarke, John, 370n48
Classified information, 646–47
Clay, Henry, 80, 84, 92–93, 94, 95, 98n17, 105, 107, 108–9, 130, 132, 134n12, 141–42, 145, 162, 163, 164, 168–69, 170n3, 171n6, 171n15, 176, 192n2, 625–26
Clean Water Act, 495, 635
Clear and present danger test, 375, 447, 645–46
Clemens, Samuel, 321
Cleveland, Frances, 292, 294, 295n7, 295n9
Cleveland, Grover, 263, 273, 284, 295n7, 295n8, 295n9, 295n10, 298–99, 304, 314n17, 314n19, 318, 359, 360, 436, 628, 630, 642; executive powers and, 295n10, 295n12, 309–11; federal income taxes and, 311–12; overview of, 288–94, 308–13; Pullman Strike influenced by, 309–11; removal influenced by, 292–93; second term of, 308–13; segregation approval of, 312; Supreme Court during, 311–12; vetoes and, 293–94, 296n15, 635. See also *Debs v. United States*
Cleveland, Ruth, 292, 295n9
Clifford, Nathan, 265n20
Clinton, George, 56, 625
Clinton, Hillary, 571, 572–73, 575, 576–77, 578, 579, 581, 648, 653

Clinton, Roger, 571

Clinton, Virginia, 571

Clinton, William Jefferson, 391, 554n48, 566, 582n6, 582n13, 582n14, 583n17, 584n22, 584n32, 585n42, 585n45, 617n1, 618n16, 620n41, 648, 649–50, 653; domestic successes of, 575–76; impeachment of, 492, 577–80, 627; independent-counsel law expiration caused by, 580–81; overview of, 570–82. See also *Clinton v. City of New York*; *Clinton v. Jones*; Foster, Vince; Lewinsky, Monica; Starr, Kenneth; Whitewater

*Clinton v. City of New York*, 576, 636

*Clinton v. Jones*, 520n26, 573–74, 577, 580, 581, 583n16, 583n18, 583n19, 584n32

Coal mines, 426n49

Cold War, 85, 87n19, 455, 467, 522, 567. *See also* Cuban Missile Crisis; Korean War; Red Scare; Vietnam War

Cole, James, 621n44

Coleman, Ann, 195–96

Colfax, Louisiana, 246–47

Collective bargaining, 655n9

Combatants of Civil War, 226n37

Comey, James, 597

Commander in chief, 2, 12, 638–39

Commerce Clause, 178, 264n15, 314n11, 424n29, 468, 471n37, 476, 477–79, 485n20, 485n26, 608, 617n4, 643–45, 655n11. See also *National Federation of Independent Business v. Sebelius*; *United States v. E.C. Knight Co.*

Commerce Committee, 285n4

Commission for Relief, 397

Committee for Unemployment Relief, 399

Committee of Detail, 4–5, 29

Committee on Banking and Currency, 274n8

Committee on Manufactures, 95

Communist Party USA, 447

Compromise of 1820. *See* Missouri Compromise of 1820

Compromise of 1850, 174, 176–77, 179, 182, 188, 642

Compromise of 1877, 256–57, 262–63

Comptroller general, 552n25

Confederacy, 106, 186, 214–15, 221, 224n22, 225n23, 519n14

Confederate Army, 314n14

Confederate House of Representatives, 146, 652

Confederate officers, 630–31

Congress, 2–3, 6, 20–22, 24, 25, 33n30, 45n21, 49, 51, 71n2, 95–96, 109, 113n15, 113n17, 122–23, 148n30, 153, 170n1, 170n2, 171n5, 196, 213–14, 229–32, 233, 245, 254, 265n19, 267, 286n22, 300, 341n25, 352n15, 369n22, 425n32, 425n43, 430, 514–16, 518n2, 552n18, 602n5, 604n34, 613–14, 618n16, 619n23, 619n25, 621n43, 621n44, 622n58, 635, 638, 655n15; adjournment, 630; as bicameral body, 552n17; chambers of, 552n17; elections, 295n3; on flag burning, 569n27; health-care industry regulated by, 655n11; meeting date of, 404n7; popular sovereignty influencing, 193n21; slavery interfered with by, 98n28, 193n21; special prosecutor envisioned by, 554n40; special sessions of, 634–35. *See also* Censure; Commerce Clause; Continental Congress; Impeachment; Tenure of Office Act

Congressional Black Caucus, 526, 527

Congressional Budget and Impoundment Control Act (1974), 504n2

Congress of the Confederation, 19

Conkling, Roscoe, 269–70, 271, 272, 273, 275n18, 277–78, 282, 285n4, 286n7

Connally, John, 509

Connecticut, 147n14, 176–77, 619n23

Connecticut Compromise, 6

Connor, Bull, 467

Conservation, 334, 346

Constitution, 1–12, 19, 63, 81, 98n19, 321–23, 373–76

Constitutional construction, 69

Constitutional Convention, 3–8, 19, 29, 49, 63, 70, 71n2, 104

Consumer Financial Protection Bureau (CFPB), 611, 619n28

Containment policy, 215

Contempt citation, 613–14, 621n43, 621n44

Contested elections, 92–93, 625–26

Continental Army, 19, 76–77

Continental Congress, 9, 18, 63, 104

Contract Clause, 66

Contra rebels. *See* Iran Contra Affair

Cooley, Aaron, 178

*Cooley v. Board of Port Wardens of Philadelphia*, 178

Coolidge, Calvin, 380, 381, 393n2, 397, 612, 631; executive powers and, 388–91; legislative powers and, 388–91; overview of, 385–93; Supreme Court influenced by, 391–92

Coolidge, Calvin, Jr., 387

Coolidge, Grace Anna, 393n1

Cooper, James, 142

Cooper, John Milton, Jr., 360, 363

Cooper Union address, 193n21

*Cooper v. Aaron*, 453

Copland, Aaron, 225n26

Corbin, Paula. *See* Jones, Paula

Corrupt bargain, 93, 94, 95, 105

Cotton, 95

Cotton, Tom, 616–17

Cotton Letter, 616–17

Council of Censors, 14n24

Council of revision, 7

Court of Appeals for District of Columbia Circuit, U.S., 618n16

Court packing, 220–21, 341n33, 415–18, 484n7, 644, 651

Courts martial, 225n36

Covered jurisdictions, 486n33

Cox, Archibald, 464, 468–69, 471n37, 484n12, 485n20, 500, 501, 505n8, 547, 549, 585n40, 649

Cox, James, 373

Coxe, Tench, 5

Cranch, William, 132

Crawford, William H., 92–93

Creek people, 28, 77–79

Crittenden (senator), 171n6

Cronin, Thomas, 29

C-SPAN, 439n31

Cuba, 12, 96, 121, 165–66, 184, 185–86, 327n22, 327n23, 616, 639. *See also* Guantanamo Bay, Cuba; Havana, Cuba; Spanish-American War

Cuban Missile Crisis, 85, 462–63, 470n12, 637–38

Culver and Parker, 277

Cumming, Alfred, 200

Cummings, Homer S., 415–16

*Cunningham v. Neagle*, 304

Curtis, Benjamin, 177, 178, 180n7, 180n8, 187

Curtiss Company, 295n9

Custis, Martha Dandridge. *See* Washington, Martha

Cutler, Lloyd, 530

Czolgosz, Leon, 325–26

Dakota War. *See* Sioux Uprising

Daley, Richard, 493

Dallas, George Mifflin, 206n9

Dames & Moore, 534n31

*Dames & Moore v. Regan*, 531, 534n31

Dana, Francis, 90

Darrow, Clarence, 310

Daugherty, Harry, 377–79

Daugherty, Mally S., 390–91

Davis, James, 260

Davis, Jefferson, 162, 165, 185, 186, 189, 192, 215, 358

Davis, John W., 405n16

Davis, Nancy. *See* Reagan, Nancy

Day, William, 336–37, 394n19

Days, Drew, III, 527

D-day, 445

Dean, John, 500

Death of presidents, 129–34, 626–27. *See also* Assassinations

Debs, Eugene, 309–11, 313n4, 314n11, 360, 374–76, 377–79, 381, 382n11, 383n12, 384n49, 456n11, 631, 645

*Debs v. United States*, 375, 383n12

Decision of 1789, 109

Declaration of Independence, 44, 48, 49, 58n2, 217, 218, 223

Defense of Marriage Act (DOMA), 610–11, 619n25, 633

Delano, Sara, 410

*DeLima v. Bidwell*, 322

*Dellums v. Bush*, 563

Democratic Convention, 184–85, 419, 483, 653

Democratic National Committee. *See* Watergate

Democratic Party, 157n35, 183–84, 295n3, 465–66. *See also* Democrats

Democratic-Republicans, 36, 50, 64, 94, 144–45. *See also* Adams, John Quincy; Jefferson, Thomas; Madison, James; Monroe, James

Democrats, 148n30, 168, 171n8, 190–91, 242, 256, 291, 578, 579, 615, 621n43. *See also* Buchanan, James; Carter, Jimmy; Cleveland, Grover; Clinton, William Jefferson; Free-Soil Party; Jackson, Andrew; Johnson, Andrew; Johnson, Lyndon B.; Kennedy, John F.; Northern Democrats; Obama, Barack; Pierce, Franklin; Polk, James K.; Roosevelt, Franklin Delano; Southern Democrats; Truman, Harry S.; Van Buren, Martin; Wilson, Woodrow

*Dennis v. United States*, 456n11

Dent, Julia. *See* Grant, Julia

Department of Commerce, 525

Department of Foreign Affairs, 32n23

Department of Homeland Security, 595, 602n15, 646

Department of Justice, U.S., 374, 457n24, 466, 484n12, 526–27, 543, 547, 549, 550, 552n14, 552n24, 580, 596–97, 642. *See also* Holder, Eric

Department of State. *See* State Department, U.S.

Department of the Interior, 380

Department of the Navy, 379–80

Dependent Pension Bill (1887), 293

Deposits (banks), 108–10

Depression of 1893, 299, 305

Desegregation, 449–50, 455–56, 457n21, 642. See also *Brown v. Board of Education I*; *Brown v. Board of Education II*; Central High School; *Plessy v. Ferguson*; University of Alabama; University of Mississippi

Deserters, 225n41, 630

Detainee Treatment Act (2005), 599, 604n34

Dewey, John, 327n22, 430

Dewey, Thomas, 429

DeWitt, John, 425n41

Dingley Act, 322

Direct taxes, 352n14

Discrimination, 471n37

Doheny, Edward L., 380

Dole, Bob, 575, 576

DOMA. *See* Defense of Marriage Act

Domestic violence, 639–40

Dominican Republic, 242

Do Nothing Congress, 430, 635

"Don't ask, don't tell" policy, 576

*Dooley v. United States*, 322–23, 327n30

Dorr, Thomas, 139–41

Dorr Rebellion, 139–41, 640

Dorsey, Stephen, 270

Double jeopardy, 585n43

Doud, Mamie. *See* Eisenhower, Mamie

Douglas, Stephen A., 176, 184–85, 189–90, 201, 202, 213

Douglas, William O., 429, 435, 486n30, 509

Douglass, Frederick, 257

*Downes v. Bidwell*, 322

Draft, 498

Draft dodgers, 382n4, 519n14, 571, 631. See also *Debs v. United States*; *In re Debs*

Dreadful Decade, 245–47, 642

*Dred Scott v. Sandford*, 177, 187, 193n21, 197–99, 206n15, 213, 219, 230

Drones, 614–16, 621n49, 622n50, 639

Drug cartels, 613–14

Duane, William, 108

Due Process Clause, 249n17, 337, 350, 392, 600, 610, 615

Dukakis, Michael, 559, 564, 568n21

Dunn, Oscar J., 244

Dushkin, George M., 292–93

Eaton, Dorman, 287n23

Economic legislation, 213–14

Edmunds Act (1882), 262

*Edwards v. United States*, 400

EEOC. *See* Equal Employment Opportunity Commission

Ehrlichmann, John, 500

Eichman, Shawn, 565

Eighteenth Amendment, 387, 398, 631

Eisenhower, Dwight D., 171n4, 403, 405n20, 437, 457n26, 493, 496, 620n34, 634, 640, 642, 646, 648; Little Rock crisis influenced by, 452–54; McCarthy during presidency of, 446–47; overview of, 443–56; Red Scare during presidency of, 446–47. See also *Brown v. Board of Education I*; *Brown v. Board of Education II*

Eisenhower, Mamie, 444, 455

Elections, 92–93, 108–9, 255–57, 263, 264n4, 264n6, 295n3, 353n19, 602n5, 625–26

Electoral College, 6–7, 44n4, 92–93, 232, 255, 566

Electoral Count Act, 602n5, 626

Electoral votes, 264n6

Elk, John, 283–84

*Elk v. Wilkins*, 283–84, 654n8

Ellsberg, Daniel, 504n4

Ellsworth, Oliver, 26

Ely, James W., 333

Emancipation Proclamation, 204, 214–16, 217, 221, 229

Embargo, 57

Emerson, John, 197–99

Enemy combatants, 604n35

Energy task force, 592–93, 602n10, 631–32

Enforcement Act (1870), 250n22

*Engel v. Vitale*, 463

Enhanced interrogation techniques, 598, 639

Enumerated powers, 50, 58

Equal Employment Opportunity Commission (EEOC), 484n14, 561, 562

Equal protection, 249n16, 610

Equal Protection Clause, 392, 448, 464, 471n37, 484n12, 485n20, 526, 591, 644, 648

Equal Rights Amendment (ERA), 524, 533n8, 648

ERA. *See* Equal Rights Amendment

Era of Good Feelings, 77, 87n16

Espionage Act of 1917, 363–64, 373–75, 381, 384n49, 645, 647

Establishment Clause, 58n2, 463

Ethics in Government Act, 531, 547, 649

Europe, 86, 215

Evarts, William M., 235

Everett, Edward, 225n25

Excelsior Hotel, 582n13

Excise taxes, 352n14

Executive branch, 114n23, 122–23, 124n22, 628–29. *See also* Removal

Executive departments, Washington, G., creating, 27

Executive Office of the President, 629

Executive orders, 111, 334, 346, 426n49, 609–11, 616, 618n18, 619n23; 8773, 421; 9066, 420; 11905, 515–16

Executive powers, 31n14, 46n24, 109–10, 279–80, 295n10, 295n12, 309–11, 388–91, 429–30, 435–36, 514–16, 518n2, 545–46, 562–64, 593–601, 638–39; domestic violence, 639–40; presidential tool kit, safeguarding, 631–32; removal, 93–94, 114n23, 292–93, 334–35. *See also* Appointments; Signing statements; Veto power

Executive privilege, 502, 505n8, 516, 574, 583n16, 583n17, 583n18, 592–93, 613, 621n42, 628, 631–32

*Ex Parte Garland*, 512, 518n13

*Ex Parte Grossman*, 388–89

*Ex Parte Merryman*, 220, 651

*Ex Parte Milligan*, 221–22, 225n36, 268

*Ex Parte Quirin*, 425n34, 604n35

*Ex Parte Vallandigham*, 222, 226n39

Export clause, 327n30

Extramarital affairs, 578. *See also* Clinton, William Jefferson; Lewinsky, Monica

FAA. *See* Federal Aviation Administration

Fair Employment Practices Commission, 484n14

Fall, Albert, 379–80

Farm bill, 397

Farmers, 299, 326n14

Fast and Furious Operation investigation, 613–14

Faubus, Orval E., 452–54

FBI. *See* Federal Bureau of Investigation

Federal appellate courts, 59n24

Federal Aviation Administration (FAA), 553n28, 553n34. *See also* Professional Air Traffic Controllers Organization strike

Federal Bureau of Investigation (FBI), 364, 502, 577

Federal commissioners, 188–89

Federal funding, of higher education, 463–64

Federal government, Adams, J. Q., on, 93. See also *Worcester v. Georgia*

Federal income taxes, 311–12, 314n17, 347–48, 352n15

Federalism, 14n32, 105–6, 262, 624

Federalism Five, 550, 555n55

*The Federalist* No. 37 (Madison, J.), 113n3

*The Federalist* No. 47 (Madison, J.), 4, 5

*The Federalist* No. 48 (Madison, J.), 5

*The Federalist* No. 69 (Hamilton), 5, 31n14

*The Federalist* No. 70 (Hamilton), 5, 412

*The Federalist* No. 75 (Hamilton), 24

*The Federalist* No. 76 (Hamilton), 26

*The Federalist Papers* (Hamilton, Madison, J., and Jay), 63, 69–70, 113n3

Federalist Party, 38–40, 64, 65, 196

Federalists, 19, 36, 37, 38–40, 42–43, 50, 67. *See also* Adams, John; Adams, John Quincy

Federal judiciary, 549–50, 555n54

Federal Power Commission, 400–401

Federal ratio, 6–7

Federal Reserve Board, 620n34

Federal Trade Commission (FTC), 425n32, 630. See also *Humphrey's Executor v. United States*

Ferguson, Missouri, 617n2, 643

*Fernandez v. Wiener*, 352n14

Fessenden, William Pitt, 183

Field, Stephen J., 221, 249n17, 265n20, 303–4, 305, 629

Fifteenth Amendment, 243–44, 246, 250n22, 254, 305, 486n36, 642

Fifth Amendment, 11. See also *Burdick v. United States*; Due Process Clause

Filburn, Roscoe, 485n26

Filibusters, 165–66, 171n13, 639

Fillmore, Abigail, 174, 179

Fillmore, Millard, 133, 170, 172n18, 179n1, 179n2, 188, 200, 206n12, 273, 642; Compromise of 1850 supported by, 176–77; overview of, 173–79; Supreme Court during administration of, 177–78

Fillmore, Nathaniel, 174

Fillmore, Phoebe, 174

Final judgments, 124n22

Firearms trafficking, 620n38

First Amendment, 51, 262, 384n49, 447, 505n5, 622n55, 647. *See also* Establishment Clause; Flag burning; Patriot Act; *Schenck v. United States*

First Congress, 109

First Lady, 423n4, 648

First National Bank, 50, 64, 70

FISA. *See* Foreign Intelligence Service Act

Fisher, Louis, 361

*Fisher v. Univ. of Tex. at Austin*, 534n21

Fiske, Robert, 573, 575

Flag burning, 564–66, 569n27, 654n4

Flag Protection Act of 1989, 565

Fleischer, Ari, 594

Fletcher, Robert, 66–67

*Fletcher v. Peck*, 66–67, 72n14, 73n19, 91

Florida, 257, 566, 591, 602n3, 602n5, 654n2

Florida campaign, 77–79

Floridas, 22, 52, 86n2, 105, 162

Flowers, Gennifer, 582n14

Folger, Charles J., 291

Folsom, Frances. *See* Cleveland, Frances

Folsom, Oscar, 295n7

Foraker Act, 322, 327n30

Force Act, 282

Force Bill, 111, 138, 140, 639–40

Forcible obstructions, 314n8

Ford, Betty, 517

Ford, Gerald R., 11–12, 500, 503, 518n2, 518n12, 518n13, 519n14, 520n22, 523, 541, 583n17, 592, 623, 627, 631, 649; Congress influencing, 514–16; executive privilege relied on by, 516; intelligence oversight during presidency of, 515–16; overview of, 507–17; War Powers Resolution binding, 514–15. *See also* Nixon pardon

Ford's Theater, 223

Foreign affairs, 418–19, 637–39, 637–40

Foreign Intelligence Service Act (FISA), 596–97, 603n23, 646

Foreign policy, 335, 361–63. *See also* Sole-organ doctrine

Forsyth, John, 120

Fortas, Abe, 482–83

Fort Bridger, 200

Fort Donelson, 241

Fort Harrison, 162

Fort McHenry, 259

Fort Sumter, 203, 215

Foster, Vince, 572–73, 574

Founding Fathers, 369n39, 541

Four Horsemen, 384n47, 415

Fourteen Points for Peace, 362–63

Fourteenth Amendment, 232, 235, 243, 249n16, 249n17, 254, 283, 468, 471n37, 477–78, 484n12, 485n20, 486n30, 499–500, 602n3, 641, 642, 647, 654n8. *See also* Due Process Clause; Equal Protection Clause

Fourth Amendment, 394n24, 622n55, 646, 647. *See also* Patriot Act

Framers, 147n8

France, 22–24, 26, 27, 29, 37, 38–40, 43, 45n18, 57, 64, 77, 445, 645. *See also* Louisiana Purchase; Paris, France

Frankfurter, Felix, 434–35, 457n21

Franklin, Benjamin, 49

Fraud, 270, 500, 572, 575

Freedmen's Bureau, 231

Freedmen's Bureau Bill, 231

Freedom fighters, 225n26

Freedom Riders, 466

Free Exercise Clause, 58n2

Free Hungarian Radio, 225n26

Free-Soilers, 191. *See also* Van Buren, Martin

Free-Soil Party, 163

Free speech, 384n49, 456n12, 645–47. *See also* Espionage Act of 1917; *Schenck v. United States; Sedition Acts; Yates v. U.S.*

Fremont, John C., 179, 206n12, 277

French, 21, 45n21. *See also* Monroe Doctrine

French Constitution, 218

French Revolution, 91

Fries, John, 45n18

Fries's Rebellion, 45n18

Fromme, Lynette, 516, 583n17

*Frontiero v. Richardson*, 584n29, 648

FTC. *See* Federal Trade Commission

Fugitive Slave Act of 1793, 164–65, 171n11

Fugitive Slave Act of 1850, 172n18, 174, 176–77, 179, 277, 642

Fugitive Slave Clause, 164–65, 171n10

Fugitive Slave Law of 1850, 187

Fugitive Slave Laws, 168–69, 171n10, 188–89

Fulbright, J. William, 571

Fuller, Melville W., 311, 314n14, 314n15, 314n19, 323–24, 341n26

Gadsden Purchase, 185, 187

Gag rule, 96, 98n28, 119–20, 183

Gallatin, Albert, 65, 70

Garfield, Abram, 267

Garfield, Eliza, 267

Garfield, Harry, 272

Garfield, James, 247, 274n1, 274n8, 275n18, 275n22, 278–80, 285, 318, 629; assassination of, 271–73, 274n1, 275n22, 278–80, 286n10, 629; overview of, 266–74; succession of, 271–73

Garfield, Lucretia, 272

Garland, Augustus, 292–93, 628

Garrison, Arthur H., 426n49

Gays, 576. *See also* Same-sex marriage

Gender, 647–49

General Electric, 540

General Orders No. 100, 217–18. *See also* Lieber, Francis; Lincoln's Code

General Welfare Clause, 302

Genêt, Edmond, 91

Geneva Conventions, 217

George III (king), 4

Georgia, 66–67, 115n37, 411, 422, 428

German Americans, 363

Germany, 368n15, 405n20, 425n34. *See also* World War I

Gerry, Elbridge, 37, 39–40

Gettysburg Address, 218, 225n26, 633

Gibbs, Robert, 622n50

G.I. Bill of Rights, 413

Gilded Age. *See* Arthur, Chester; Cleveland, Grover; Garfield, James; Harrison, Benjamin; Hayes, Rutherford B.; McKinley, William

Giles, William B., 72n10

Gingrich, Newt, 584n22

Ginsburg, Douglas, 549–50

Ginsburg, Ruth Bader, 532, 576, 584n29

Gipp, George, 540

Glen Echo Amusement Park, 468–69

Glidden, Charles, 317

Goldberg, Arthur, 486n30

Goldman, Emma, 325

Goldsmith, Jack, 591
Goldwater, Barry, 171n9, 493, 503, 528–29, 540
*Goldwater v. Carter*, 528–29
Gómez, Máximo, 319–20
Gonzales, Alberto, 597
Goodhue, Grace Anna. *See* Coolidge, Grace Anna
Gore, Al, 8, 572, 579, 591, 654n2. See also *Bush v. Gore*
Governors' Conference (1910), 360
Graham, Christopher, 177–78
Gramm-Rudman-Hollings Act, 544–45, 552n25
Gran Chaco War, 418–19
Grant, Hannah Simpson, 240
Grant, Jesse R., 240
Grant, Julia, 240–41
Grant, Ulysses S., 33n30, 171n4, 179, 234, 248n2, 256, 260, 270, 271, 273, 275n22, 278, 286n22, 344, 576, 625, 642, 647, 655n15; civil rights and, 243–44; legislation and, 243–44; overview of, 239–48; Supreme Court appointments, 245–47
*Gratz v. Bollinger*, 534n21
Gray, Horace, 282
Great Britain, 22–24, 26, 27, 32n19, 57, 62–63, 64, 196, 224n22, 460–61, 542, 600, 637. *See also* War of 1812; World War I
Great Depression, 388, 392–93, 396, 398, 399, 402. *See also* New Deal
Greater Houston Ministerial Association, 461–62
Great Plains. *See* Kansas-Nebraska Act
Great Railroad Strike of 1877, 254, 258–60
Great Society, 555n58
Greeley, Horace, 271
Greenbacks, 274n8
Greene, John Robert, 520n22, 559
Greenspan, Alan, 620n34
Gregory, John M., 287n23
Grenada, 534n29
Grier, Robert, 198–99, 221, 245
Griswold, Erwin N., 405n16
Groesbeck, Alexander J., 405n16
Grossman, Philip, 388–89
*Grutter v. Bollinger*, 534n21
Guam, 321

Guantanamo Bay, Cuba, 12, 598, 599, 600–601, 604n34, 639
Guarantee Clause, 230
Guiteau, Charles, 267, 271–72, 274n1, 275n22, 278–79, 286n10
Gulf of Tonkin incident, 481–82
Gulf War. *See* Persian Gulf War
Gun violence, 619n23
Gun-walking, 613–14. *See also* Fast and Furious Operation investigation
*Gurleski v. United States*, 519n14

Habeas corpus, 219, 220, 221, 225n30, 244, 259, 600–601, 604n34, 604n37, 651
Hague Conventions, 217
Haig, Alexander, 502, 513
Haldeman, H. R., 500, 502, 509
Hale, John P., 183–84
Half-Breeds, 268, 286n7
Halleck, Henry W., 217
Halpin, Maria, 291
Hamby, Alonzo L., 438n14
Hamdan, Salim Ahmed, 600
*Hamdan v. Rumsfeld*, 600
Hamdi, Yaser, 599–600
*Hamdi v. Rumsfeld*, 599–600
Hamilton, Alexander, 5, 8, 22–24, 26, 27, 29, 30, 31n14, 37, 39, 43, 50, 63, 64, 69–70, 113n3, 171n7, 412
*Hampton v. U.S.*, 353n23
Hanna, Mark, 318–19, 324–25
Harding, Warren G., 349, 382n1, 383n20, 383n30, 384n47, 384n49, 386, 390–91, 397, 631, 645, 649; Constitution and, 373–76; dissent and, 377–79; overview of, 371–81; Supreme Court shaped by, 376–77, 384n47; war and, 377–79. *See also* Teapot Dome Scandal
Harlan, John Marshall, II, 336, 447, 458n42
*Harper vs. Virginia Board of Elections*, 486n36
Harris (sheriff), 282
Harrison, Anna, 126
Harrison, Benjamin, 127, 294, 629, 634; Blair Education Bill supported by, 302; Lodge Elections Bill and, 303; overview of, 297–305; Sherman Anti-Trust Act and, 300–302; Supreme Court and, 303–4, 305

Harrison, William, 123, 134n12, 138, 147n5, 147n8, 156n8, 163; cabinet of, 147n8; death of, 129–34; inaugural address of, 127; Jacksonians on, 127; overview of, 126–34; on slavery, 128; in War of 1812, 129; Whigs persuading, 127

Hartford Convention, 67, 68

Harvard model, 527–28. See also *University of California Board of Regents v. Bakke*

Havana, Cuba, 120

Hawaii, 321–22, 401, 419, 606. *See also* Pearl Harbor, Hawaii

Hawley-Smoot tariff law, 398

Hawthorne, Nathaniel, 183

Hay, George, 57

Hayes, Rutherford B., 97n1, 263n1, 264n4, 264n6, 272, 278, 285n4, 286n7, 317; moonshiners influenced by, 260–61; overview of, 253–63; on polygamy, 261–62; railroad strikes broken by, 254, 258–60; Reconstruction abandoned by, 257–58

Hayes-Tilden Election, 255–57, 264n4, 264n6, 602n5, 626

*Head Money Cases*, 352n14

Health-care industry, Congress regulating, 655n11

Health-care reform, 607–9, 617n3, 617n4, 617n8, 618n9, 618n11, 618n13, 618n14, 618n15

Hearst, William Randolph, 320, 327n21

*Heart of Atlanta Motel vs. United States*, 478–79, 486n27, 486n30

Helvidius. *See* Madison, James; Pacificus-Helvidius Debates

Hemings, Sally, 48–49

Henry, Lou. *See* Hoover, Lou

Henry, Patrick, 49, 63

Herndon, Ellen Lewis. *See* Arthur, Ellen Herndon

Herndon, William H., 154–55

Hersh, Seymour, 515–16

Higher education, federal funding of, 463–64

High Federalists, 39–40, 45n18

Hill, Anita, 562, 652

Hirabayashi, Gordon, 420

*Hirabayashi v. U.S.*, 420

Hiroshima, Japan, 429

Hitler, Adolf, 460–61

HIV/AIDS. *See* Human immunodeficiency virus/acquired immunodeficiency syndrome

Hoban, James, 42

Hoes, Hannah. *See* Van Buren, Hannah

Holder, Eric, 613–14, 615, 617n2, 621n43, 621n44, 628, 643

*Hollingsworth v. Perry*, 610–11

Holmes, Oliver Wendell, 336–37, 341n26, 364, 375, 383n12, 392, 394n24, 401, 651

Homeland Security Act of 2002, 595

Homestead Act, 214

Homestead Steel Strike, 299, 323

Homosexuality, 205n4, 576. *See also* Same-sex marriage

Hood, James, 467

Hoover, Herbert, 364, 378, 387, 404n8, 404n9, 405n17, 412, 532, 630, 635; Great Depression influenced by, 396, 398, 399; overview of, 395–403; Supreme Court influenced by, 399–402

Hoover, Hulda, 396

Hoover, J. Edgar, 382n9

Hoover, Jesse, 396

Hoover, Lou, 396

Hostage crisis, 529–31

House, Edward M., 362

House Committee on un-American Activities, 493

House Foreign Affairs Committee, 505n8

House Judiciary Committee, 205n6, 578

House of Representatives, U.S., 6–7, 20, 51, 64, 137, 150, 174, 295n3, 404n8, 461, 493, 505n8, 509, 552n17, 602n5, 609, 652, 654n2; contempt citations enforced by, 621n44; on flag burning, 569n27. *See also* Censure; Impeachment

House Oversight Committee, 613

Hughes, Charles Evans, 361, 387, 401, 416–17

Human immunodeficiency virus/acquired immunodeficiency syndrome (HIV/AIDS), 581

Humphrey, Hubert, 461, 494

*Humphrey's Executor v. United States*, 418, 425n32

Hungary, 225n26

Hunger strikes, 366

Hussein, Saddam, 362, 562–64, 578, 595
Hyde, Henry, 578, 579
*Hylton v. United States*, 32n22, 55

Illegal immigrants, 609–10
Illinois, 212–13, 216, 268–69, 493, 606–7. *See also* Chicago, Illinois
Immigrants, 351, 609–10
Immigration and Nationality Act, 543
Immigration and Naturalization Service (INS). See *INS v. Chadha*
Immigration quotas, 280, 404n8
Impeachment, 40–41, 114n23, 142–44, 148n30, 234–36, 292, 492, 495–96, 577–80, 585n43, 627–28, 652
Imperial presidency, 514
Implied powers, 45n21, 152, 300
Impoundment, 494–96, 504n2, 635
Impoundment Control Act of 1974, 496, 504, 514, 636, 654n6
Inaugural address, 105–6, 127, 132–33, 222, 279
Inchon, Korea, 432
Income tax, 305, 311–12, 314n17, 347–48, 352n15, 500
Independent counsel, 554n48, 567n4, 573, 580–81. See also *Morrison v. Olson*; Special prosecutors; Starr, Kenneth; Walsh, Lawrence E.
Independent-counsel law, 547–48, 580–81, 649, 650, 655n12
Indian Removal Act (1830), 114n36
Indian Territory, 284
Indian tribes, 114n36
Indirect taxes, 352n14
Individual mandates, 607–8, 617n8, 618n15, 655n11
Industrial Workers of the World (IWW), 373, 382n5
Inferior officers, 281
Inherent powers, 418–19, 430, 433–36
*In re Debs*, 310–11, 314n11, 374–76
INS. See *INS v. Chadha*
*Insular Cases*, 322, 327n27
Insurgency, 321
Insurrection, 139–41
*INS v. Chadha*, 542–44, 552n21, 552n24, 636
Integration, 485n17

Intelligence oversight, 515–16
Intelligible principle, 353n23
Internal improvements, 69–70, 93, 106–7, 110, 141, 206n12
International arbitration, 217–18
International Emergency Economic Powers Act, 530, 531, 535n32
International Military Tribunal, 405n20
Internment camps, 425n43, 639
Interrogation, 597–98
Interstate commerce, 178, 259, 310–11, 655n9. *See also* Commerce Clause
Interstate Commerce Commission, 301
Iran, 616–17, 622n58. *See also* Iran Hostage Crisis; Iranian-U.S. Claim Tribunal
Iran Contra Affair, 547–48, 560, 567n4, 573, 649
Iran Hostage Crisis, 529–31, 534n27, 534n31, 638
Iranian-U.S. Claim Tribunal, 530–31, 638
Iraq, 578, 595, 598, 603n17, 603n18. *See also* Persian Gulf War
Ironclad Amnesty Oath, 230
Issa, Darrell, 613, 621n42
IWW. *See* Industrial Workers of the World

Jackson, Andrew, 69, 76, 77–79, 92–93, 95, 98n23, 113n13, 113n17, 114n34, 114n36, 115n37, 115n38, 121, 127, 138, 140, 144, 163, 182, 192n2, 196, 205n7, 206n8, 219, 286n22, 438n6, 610, 627–28, 629, 635, 639–40, 650–51; National Bank destroyed by, 108–10; on nullification, 110–12; overview of, 103–12; vetoes of, 106–8, 113n10, 624
Jackson, Howell E., 305
Jackson, Rachel, 105
Jackson, Robert, 416, 421, 434, 435–36, 535n32
Jacksonians, 94, 95, 105, 127
Jamaica, 40
James, William, 411–12
Japan, 429, 563
Japanese, 401, 429, 431, 461, 558
Japanese Americans, 419–20, 425n41, 425n43, 639
Javits, Jacob, 530
Jaworski, Leon, 501
Jay, John, 4, 25–26, 29, 63, 69–70, 72n3, 113n3, 629, 651

Jay Treaty, 26, 41, 64, 72n3, 77, 637, 651
Jefferson, Martha, 48
Jefferson, Peter, 48
Jefferson, Thomas, 20, 21, 22–24, 27, 29, 30, 33n30, 42–43, 44, 58n1, 58n6, 63, 64–65, 66–67, 70, 72n5, 73n16, 73n17, 73n19, 76, 79–80, 83–84, 87n19, 104, 430, 494, 520n26, 619n22, 625, 632, 634–35; overview of, 47–58; second term of, 56–58; as Secretary of State, 50; as vice president, 50–51. *See also* Alien and Sedition Acts; Louisiana Purchase; *Marbury v. Madison*
Jeffersonian Republicans, 23
Jennings, Lizzie, 285n2
Jesuits, 302
Johnsen, Dawn E., 550, 555n58
Johnson, Andrew, 97n1, 179, 238n20, 241, 245, 254, 273, 292, 334, 519n14, 630–31, 642, 652–53, 655n15; impeachment of, 234–36, 292, 492, 627; overview of, 227–36; Reconstruction dealt with by, 228–32, 233–36; Tenure of Office Act obeyed by, 233
Johnson, Lyndon B., 469, 486n32, 486n35, 495, 497, 504n4, 509, 515, 524, 634, 642; civil rights during presidency of, 477–79, 644; overview of, 473–83; in political arena, 475; problems faced by, 482–83; as vice president, 476; Vietnam War during presidency of, 481–82. *See also* Civil Rights Act of 1964; Voting Rights Act of 1965
Johnson, Sam Ealy, 474
Johnson, William, 81
*Johnson v. Eisentrager*, 604n35
Joint Committee on Reconstruction, 231
Jones, Joseph, 76
Jones, Paula, 582n13, 583n16, 584n32. See also *Clinton v. Jones*
Jones, Stephen, 582n13
Judges' Bill, 391–92, 394n19
Judicial activism, 555n50, 555n52
Judicial ethics, 438n14
Judicial-recall provision, 348, 351
Judicial review, 32n22, 53–55
Judicial Watch, 602n10
Judiciary Act (1789), 25, 115n37, 205n6, 391

Judiciary Act (1801), 53
Judiciary Act (1925), 391–92

Kansas, 193n21, 201–2, 206n11, 444, 455, 553n28
Kansas-Nebraska Act, 182, 189–92, 196–97, 642
Katzenbach, Nicholas, 467, 480
*Katzenbach v. Morgan*, 486n36
*Katzenbach vs. McClung*, 478, 479, 486n27, 486n30
Keen, W. W., 315n24
Kellogg-Briand Pact of 1928, 388
Kendall, Amos, 122–23, 125n23
Kendall, David, 581
*Kendall v. United States*, 122–23, 125n28
Kennedy, Anthony, 550, 569n26, 610, 617n8, 618n11, 618n14
Kennedy, Edward M., 531–32, 549
Kennedy, Jacqueline, 461, 648
Kennedy, Joe, Jr., 460–62
Kennedy, John F., 134, 455, 471n37, 475, 476, 477, 478, 479, 481, 484n14, 485n17, 493, 496–97, 504n4, 509, 583n18, 634, 637–38, 640, 642; civil rights during presidency of, 465–69, 484n12, 644; overview of, 459–69; race in presidency of, 465–69; reapportionment tackled by, 464–65; religious issues of, 463–64. *See also* Cuban Missile Crisis
Kennedy, Joseph P., 460–61
Kennedy, Robert, 464, 465, 466, 468, 471n37, 475, 476, 484n12, 485n20, 642
Kent, William, 346
Kentucky, 162, 177–78
Kentucky Resolutions, 51
Kenya. See *INS v. Chadha*
Keyserling, Leon, 424n12
Khmer Rouge, 515
Khrushchev, Nikita, 438n12, 462–63
*Kidd v. Pearson*, 314n19
Kim Il Sung, 431, 438n12
King, Dorothy, 508
King, Leslie Lynch. *See* Ford, Gerald R.
King, Martin Luther, Jr., 467, 468, 480
King, Samuel Ward, 140
King, William R., 205n4
*King v. Burwell*, 609

Kissinger, Henry, 516
Kleindienst, Richard, 500
Know-Nothing Movement, 179
Know-Nothing Party, 206n12
Knox, Henry, 21
*Knute Rockne, All American*, 540
Korean War, 12, 431–33, 437, 638, 639
Korematsu, Fred T., 420
*Korematsu v. United States*, 420, 425n43
Kortright, Elizabeth. *See* Monroe, Elizabeth K.
Kosovo, 585n45
*Ku Klux Case. See U.S. v. Harris*
Ku Klux Klan, 244, 246–47, 282
Ku Klux Klan Act, 246–47
Kuwait. *See* Persian Gulf War

La Follette, Robert M., 360
Lamar, L. Q. C., 314n14, 314n19
Land Grant College Act, 213–14, 413
Latin America. *See* Monroe Doctrine
Lawrence, Kansas, 191
Laws of war, 216–18, 222, 226n37, 226n39
League of Nations, 362–63, 367, 369n22, 412, 431, 497
Lebanon, 534n29
Lecompton constitution, 201–2
Lee, Charles, 37
Lee, Robert E., 162, 165, 186, 218, 223, 241
Legal Defense and Educational Fund, 466
Legislation, 21, 213–14, 243–44, 280–82, 505n8
Legislative branch, 5, 21–22
Legislative function, 633–37
Legislative initiatives, 634
Legislative powers, 388–91, 634, 636
Legislative veto, 542–44, 552n12, 552n14, 552n21, 654n7
*The Lemmon Slave Case*, 277, 285n2
Leo XIII (pope), 320
Leutze, Emmanuel, 76–77
Lewinsky, Monica, 576–80, 627
*Lewis v. Lewis*, 213
Libby, I. Lewis, 650, 655n13
Library of Congress, 57
Lieber, Francis, 217–18
Liliuokalani (queen), 321–22

Kleburg, Richard, 474
Lincoln, Abraham, 12, 114n34, 154–56, 170n3, 179, 191, 193n21, 195, 202, 203, 204, 225n25, 226n39, 226n41, 228, 229, 268, 377, 411–12, 413, 434, 436, 595, 601, 630, 633, 639, 651; assassination of, 223, 241, 642; inaugural address of, 222; laws of war influenced by, 216–18; legislation influenced by, 213–14; overview of, 211–23; Sioux Uprising faced by, 216; Supreme Court confronted by, 219–22. *See also* Emancipation Proclamation; Gettysburg Address
Lincoln, Mary Todd, 223
Lincoln, Robert Todd, 269, 272
Lincoln-Douglas debates, 193n21, 213
*Lincoln Portrait*, 225n26
Lincoln's Code, 216–18. *See also* General Orders No. 100; Lieber, Francis
Line Item Veto Act, 576, 636
Liquor smuggling, 394n24
Literacy tests, 351, 486n33
Little Rock, Arkansas, 452–54, 576, 582n14, 585n42, 640, 642
*Little v. Barreme*, 43
Livingston, Bob, 578
Livingston, Edward, 38, 40–41, 66–67
Livingston, Robert, 86n2
Local self-government, 257, 260–62
*Lochner v. New York*, 337–38, 341n33, 417, 651
Lodge, Henry Cabot, 303, 325, 362–63, 461
Lodge Elections Bill, 303
Log Cabin and Hard Cider campaign, 128
Lome, Depuy de, 320
Longfellow, Henry Wadsworth, 183
López, Narciso, 165–66, 639
Lott, Trent, 579
Louisiana, 22, 73n16, 86n2, 156, 162, 163, 166, 245–47, 257, 594. *See also* Battle of New Orleans
Louisiana Purchase, 51–52, 77, 85, 86n2, 91, 206n11, 430, 632, 634–35
Louisiana Territory, 56
Louis XVI (king), 22
Lunch counters, protests, 468–69
*Luther v. Borden*, 140–41, 220
Lyon, James, 130

MacArthur, Douglas, 76, 432–33, 444, 639
Maclay, William, 28
Madariaga, Salvador de, 84
Madison, Dolley, 65, 70, 73n23, 648
Madison, James, 4, 5, 8, 13n3, 19, 23–24, 31n14, 50, 51, 53, 58n1, 71n2, 72n10, 73n15, 73n16, 73n21, 73n24, 74n30, 76, 82, 91, 104, 113n3, 124n22, 162, 217, 352n15, 551n4, 635; as father of Constitution, 63; as ineffective, 65–67; as influential, 64–65; overview of, 61–71; political leadership of, 65–67; as statesman, 64–65. *See also* War of 1812
Madison Guaranty Savings & Loan, 572
Mails, 259, 264n15, 310–11
Maine. *See* Missouri Compromise of 1820
Maine-Quebec border, 148n21
Malone, Vivian, 467
Mammoth Oil Company, 380
Manchuria, 431
Manifest Destiny, 151, 632
Manila, Philippines, 327n22
Manning, Chelsea, 647
Manson, Charles, 516
Marbury, William, 53–55
*Marbury v. Madison*, 3, 32n22, 52–55, 59n24, 65, 501
March on Washington for Jobs and Freedom, 468
Marcy, William L., 185
Marines, U.S., 515
*Marion Star*, 383n20
Marshall, George C., 444–45
Marshall, John, 3, 26, 37, 41, 42, 43, 46n24, 54, 56, 65, 66–67, 71, 73n15, 73n16, 73n19, 74n30, 76, 81–82, 87n16, 87n18, 112, 114n36, 115n37, 219, 322, 391, 501, 583n17, 627, 650–51
Marshall, Thurgood, 482, 552n25, 561, 569n26, 652
Marshall Court, 112
Marshall Plan, 429
Marti, José, 319–20
Martial law, 111, 140
Maryland, 220, 468–69, 500, 509
Mason, George, 77
Mason, John Y., 186
Mason, Samson, 142

Massachusetts, 35, 90–91, 96, 97, 147n14, 176–77, 386, 392, 461, 618n15. *See also* Dukakis, Michael
Mathews, Henry, 259
*Mayaguez* incident, 515, 517, 520n22, 529
Mayorkas, Alejandro, 618n19
Maysville Road Veto, 106–7, 113n13
McCain, John, 599, 601, 607
McCarthy, Joseph, 391, 446–47, 646
McClung, Ollie, 479
McCree, Wade, 526–27
*McCulloch v. Maryland*, 50, 81–82, 107, 643
McCullough, David, 437n1
McDougal, Jim, 572–73, 575, 577, 582n7, 583n17
McDougal, Susan, 572, 575, 584n21, 585n42
*McGrain v. Daugherty*, 390–91, 621n44
McHenry, James, 37, 42, 45n21
McIntosh, Catherine, 179
McKeon, John, 133
McKinley, Ida, 326n8
McKinley, Katie, 326n8
McKinley, William, 12, 263, 326n13, 326n15, 327n21, 327n22, 334, 563, 632–33, 637, 638, 643–44; African Americans advocated for by, 318; overview of, 316–26; reelection of, 324–25; Spanish-American War testing, 319–21; on territories, 321–23; trusts confronted by, 323–24
McNamara, Robert, 504n4
McReynolds, James, 370n48, 394n19, 415, 416, 424n22, 425n35
Medal of Freedom, 566
Medicaid, 608, 617n5, 618n13, 618n14
Meese, Edwin, 546
Mellon, Andrew, 387, 388
Meredith, James, 466–67, 640
Merritt, Edwin, 285n4
Merryman, John, 220
Mexican American War, 79, 152–55, 156, 165–66, 167–69, 170n3, 184, 368n15, 638
Mexican drug cartels, 613–14
Mexico, 155, 162, 185, 361, 368n15
Michigan, 176–77
Middle West, 326n13
Midnight appointments, 53–55
Midnight judges, 53–55
Midwest, 326n13

Military, 576, 646–47
Military command powers, 637–40
Military Commissions Act of 2006, 600–601
Military-industrial complex, 455
Military tribunals, 12, 225n36, 226n37, 226n39, 425n34, 600–601, 604n35
Militias (state), 147n14
Milk sickness, 212
Miller, Merle, 436
Miller, William Henry Harrison, 304
*Minor v. Happersett*, 246, 365
Minton, Sherman, 436
*Miranda v. Arizona*, 404n10
Mississippi, 642
*Mississippi v. Johnson*, 238n20
Missouri, 258, 617n2, 643. See also *Dred Scott v. Sandford*
Missouri Compromise of 1820, 79–80, 92, 137, 167, 206n11, 641. See also *Dred Scott v. Sandford*; Kansas-Nebraska Act
Missouri Question, 79–80
Mitchell, John, 500
Mitchell, William D., 400, 405n16
Moieties, 285n3
Mondale, Walter, 527, 547
Monroe, Elizabeth, 76
Monroe, Elizabeth K., 86
Monroe, James, 70, 86n2, 87n16, 87n18, 92–93, 106, 113n11, 137, 182, 520n26, 583n17, 632, 637, 641, 645; Constitution invoked by, 81; Florida campaign and, 77–79; Jackson, A., and, 77–79; Missouri question and, 79–80; overview of, 75–86; Supreme Court and, 81–82. See also Missouri Compromise of 1820
Monroe, Spence, 76
Monroe Doctrine, 82–85, 92, 335, 632, 637, 645
Montesquieu, Charles-Louis de Secondat, 13n5
Montgomery Ward & Company, 426n49
Monticello, 44, 50, 57, 58n2, 58n6
Moody, William, H., 336–37, 338
Moonshiners, 260–61
Morgan, David, 546
Morgenthau, Henry, 419
Mormons, 199–201, 261–62, 640

Morrill Act. *See* Land Grant College Act
Morris, Robert, 9
*Morrison v. Olson*, 548, 573
Morton, John, 618n19
Morton, Levi, 269
Mount Vernon, 19, 29
Murder, 260–61, 637
*Murphy v. Ford*, 512, 518n13
Murray, Eli Huston, 262
Murray, William Vans, 45n20
*Myers v. United States*, 125n25, 295n10, 349, 389, 425n32

NAACP. *See* National Association for the Advancement of Colored People
Nagasaki, Japan, 429
Napoleonic Wars, 57, 65
Nash, Thomas, 40–41, 627
National Association for the Advancement of Colored People (NAACP), 361, 405n20, 449–50, 466, 526
National Bank, 50, 64, 70, 108–10
National Commission on Law Observance & Enforcement, 398
National debt, 274n8
National defense, 21
National deficit, 568n20
*National Federation of Independent Business v. Sebelius*, 608, 618n9, 644–45, 655n11
National highway system, 106–7
National Industrial Recovery Act, 415
National Labor Convention, 244
National Labor Relations Act (NLRA), 424n29, 655n9
National Labor Relations Board (NLRB), 611, 619n28
National Park Service, 334
National Prohibition Act, 388–89
National Republicans, 94
National Rifle Association (NRA), 619n23
National Road, 81
National security, 645–47
National Security Act of 1947, 429, 602n15, 646
National Security Agency (NSA), 596–97, 622n55, 639
National Security Council, 429, 646
National security state, 363–64, 646

Native Americans, 20, 77–79, 105, 129, 147n5, 216, 242, 283–84, 287n30, 393n2, 630. See also *Elk v. Wilkins*; *Worcester v. Georgia*

NATO. *See* North Atlantic Treaty Organization

Navy, U.S., 166, 379–80, 522, 558, 614

Neagle, David, 304

Nebraska, 206n11, 287n30

Necessary and Proper Clause, 50, 118, 300, 485n26

Nelson, Horatio, 39

Nelson, Samuel, 145

Netherlands, 91

Neutrality Act (1794), 24, 165

Neutrality Proclamation of 1793, 22–24, 29, 91, 362, 624

New Deal, 341n33, 384n47, 401, 402, 412–15, 414–15, 422, 424n29, 471n37, 484n7, 485n20, 555n58, 609, 633, 644, 651

New England, 67, 68

New England Emigrant Aid Society, 190

New Jersey, 358, 359–60, 382n4, 647

New journalists, 295n8

New Mexico, 152, 167, 169, 172n18, 175, 176, 348, 351, 353n18

New Orleans, Louisiana. *See* Battle of New Orleans

New York, 4, 25, 56, 68, 117, 118, 147n14, 163, 166, 174–75, 179, 277–78, 286n7, 290–91, 317, 382n4. *See also* Buffalo, New York

New York City, 9, 86, 247, 277, 299, 303, 327n21, 332, 493, 593–95

*New York City Tribune*, 11–12, 364

New York Constitution, 7

New York Custom House, 277–78, 280

*New York Journal*, 327n21

New York Regents, 463

*New York Times*, 368n9, 496–97, 504n4

*New York Times Co. v. United States*, 497, 505n5, 505n6

Nicaragua. *See* Iran Contra Affair

9/11 attacks, 593–601, 614, 646

Nineteenth Amendment, 366, 373, 633, 647

Ninth Amendment, 193n21, 206n15

Nixon, Richard M., 11–12, 134, 365, 437, 445, 455, 462, 504n4, 505n8, 506n25, 509, 510–13, 515, 517, 518n2, 518n12, 518n13, 519n14, 547, 549, 580, 583n17, 592, 623, 627, 631, 635–36, 638, 649–50, 654n6; overview of, 491–504; Supreme Court of, 499–500, 651; Twenty-Sixth Amendment signed by, 498–99; Vietnam War inherited by, 496–99. *See also* Impoundment; Nixon pardon; Pentagon Papers; *Roe v. Wade*; *United States v. Nixon*; War Powers Resolution; Watergate

Nixon, Thelma Pat, 493

Nixon, Tricia, 493

Nixon pardon, 503, 510–13, 517, 518n12, 518n13, 623, 631

*Nixon v. Fitzgerald*, 583n16

NLRA. *See* National Labor Relations Act

NLRB. *See* National Labor Relations Board

*NLRB v. Canning*, 612

*NLRB v. Jones & Laughlin Steel Corp.*, 417, 424n29, 655n9

Nobel Peace Prize, 532, 653

No Child Left Behind, 593–94

Noncombatants, 226n37

No new taxes, pledge, 560

Noriega, Manuel, 534n29

Normandy, France, 445

North, Oliver, 547

North American Aviation, 420–21, 426n49, 435

North Atlantic Treaty Organization (NATO), 429, 445, 595

North Carolina, 244

Northern Democrats, 168, 190–91, 199

*Northern Securities Co. v. United States*, 336–37

Northern Whigs, 177

North Korea. *See* Korean War

North Vietnam. *See* Vietnam War

Northwest Ordinance, 177–78, 180n9

Northwest Territory, 178

NRA. *See* National Rifle Association

NSA. *See* National Security Agency

Nuclear war, 470n12

Nullification, 51, 98n23, 110–12, 180n6, 206n8, 639–40

Nuremberg, Germany, 405n20

Obama, Barack, 12, 504n3, 566, 581, 597, 601, 602n9, 603n23, 617n2, 617n3, 619n25, 619n28, 621n48, 622n50, 622n55, 622n58, 628, 630, 633, 634, 637, 639, 643, 644–45, 646–47, 648, 650, 652, 653; bin Laden killed by, 614–16, 621n46; executive orders used by, 609–11, 616, 618n18, 619n23; overview of, 605–17; recess appointments made by, 611–13. *See also* Holder, Eric; Patient Protection and Affordable Care Act; Same-sex marriage

Obama, Michelle, 606

Obamacare. *See* Patient Protection and Affordable Care Act

*Obergefell v. Hodges*, 611

Obstruction of mails, 264n15, 310–11

O'Connor, Sandra Day, 549, 550, 569n26, 600, 648, 651

Office of Independent Counsel, 578, 581

Office of Legal Counsel (OLC), 470n12, 585n43, 591, 598, 611–12, 620n41

Office of Legal Policy, 549, 555n54, 555n58

Office of Legislative Affairs, 634

Office of Price Administration, 493

Office of Solicitor General, 526–27

Ohio, 171n8, 176–78, 254, 263, 267

OLC. *See* Office of Legal Counsel

OLC Letter, 620n41

Old Guard, 339

Ole Miss. *See* University of Mississippi

Olmstead, Roy, 394n24

*Olmstead v. United States*, 394n24

Olney, Richard, 314n19

Omnibus Bill, 168–69

Omnibus Budget Reconciliation Act of 1990, 560

101st Airborne Division, 453

*Oneida*, 313

O'Neill, Thomas, 532n4

One person, one vote, 464–65

Operation CHAOS, 515–16

Operation Desert Shield, 562

Operation Desert Storm, 563, 567, 638

Operation Fast and Furious, 613–14. *See also* Fast and Furious Operation investigation; Gun-walking

Oregon, 151, 221, 264n4, 264n6, 396

Oregon Territory, 85

*Oregon v. Mitchell*, 498

Ostend Manifesto, 186

Oswald, Lee Harvey, 469

Pacific Ocean, 155

Pacific Railway Act, 214

Pacificus-Helvidius Debates, 23–24, 31n14

Pahlavi, Mohammed Reza, 529

Paine, Elijah, 277

Pakistan, 12, 614–16, 621n49

Palmer, A. Mitchell, 375, 382n9

Palmer Raids, 382n9

Panama, 534n29

Panama Canal, 335, 633

Panamanian revolution, 335

Pan American Petroleum Company, 380

Panic of 1837, 117–19, 129

Panic of 1873, 243

Panic of 1893, 309–11, 313, 318, 324

Paraguay, 418–19. *See also* Gran Chaco War

Parchment barriers, 55n4

Pardon power, 11–12; Adams, J., using, 45n18; Buchanan, J., using, 200; Bush, G. H. W., using, 547, 567n4; Carter, J., using, 533n6, 631; Coolidge, C., using, 388–89, 631; draft dodger, 533n6, 631; Ford, G., using, 503, 510–13, 517, 518n12, 518n13, 623, 631; Harding, W.'s, use of, 378–79, 384n49, 631; Jefferson, T., using, 53, 377; Johnson, A., using, 229–30, 630–31; Lincoln, A., using, 216, 225n41, 377, 630; Nixon, R., use of, 503, 510–13, 517, 518n12, 518n13, 623, 631; in presidential tool kit, 630–31; Vietnam War, 533n6; Washington, G., using, 630; Wilson, W., using, 364–65, 374–75, 623

Pardons, 519n14

Paris, France, 49, 58n1, 90, 403

Paris Peace Conference, 397

Parker, John J., 401, 405n20

PATCO Strike. *See* Professional Air Traffic Controllers Organization strike

Patient Protection and Affordable Care Act, 607–9, 617n3, 617n4, 617n8, 618n9, 618n11, 618n15, 634, 644–45, 655n11

Patriot Act, 596–97, 603n23, 634, 646

Patronage, 110, 269–71, 273–74, 286n7, 286n22, 629. *See also* Pendleton Act; Stalwarts; Tammany Hall

Paul, Alice, 533n8

Paulding, James, 125n28

*Paulding v. Decatur*, 125n28

Peace Convention, 146

Peanut warehouse (Carter), 531, 585n40, 649, 655n12

Pearl Harbor, Hawaii, 401, 419, 639

Peck, John, 66–67

Peckham, Rufus W., 314n14, 335, 337, 341n26

Pendergast, Tom, 428–29

Pendleton, George Hunt, 280–81

Pendleton Act, 273, 280–82, 285, 286n22, 318

Pennsylvania, 4–5, 14n24, 45n18, 124n22, 205n5, 585n37, 594. *See also* Philadelphia, Pennsylvania

Pentagon, 593–95

Pentagon Papers, 496–97, 504n4

Pepper, George Wharton, 405n16

Perkins, Frances, 413

Permanent Committee on Investigations, 446–47

Perot, H. Ross, 566

Persian Gulf War, 362, 562–64, 566, 567, 638, 654n4

Personal liberty laws, 164–65, 176–77

Peterson, William, 223

Pfiffner, James (professor), 599

Philadelphia, Pennsylvania, 36, 258. *See also* Constitutional Convention

Philippines, 321, 327n22

Phillips, Samuel F., 282–83

Pickering, Timothy, 37, 40, 42, 45n20

Pierce, Barbara. *See* Bush, Barbara

Pierce, Benjamin, 182, 185

Pierce, Franklin, 179, 192n2, 192n4, 196, 199, 206n11, 314n14, 635, 655n14; fugitive slaves influenced by, 188–89; Kansas-Nebraska Act signed by, 189–92; overview of, 181–92

Pierce, Jane, 185

Pike, Otis, 515–16

Pike Committee, 515–16

Pinchot, Gifford, 334

Pinckney, Charles, 37, 42, 65

Pinckney, Cotesworth, 98n28

Pinckney, Thomas, 36

Pinkerton guards, 299

Pious, Richard, 143

Plame, Valerie, 655n13

Platt, Tom, 269–70, 328n38

Platt Amendment, 327n23

Pledge of Allegiance, 564

*Plessy v. Ferguson*, 246, 312, 458n42, 642

Pocahontas, 368n12

Pocket veto, 113n10, 393n2

*The Pocket Veto Case*, 393n2, 612, 630

Poli, Robert E., 553n32

Policy-making role of president, 632–33

Political question doctrine, 220

Political speech, 564–66

Polk, James K., 115n38, 123, 145, 156n12, 162, 167, 177, 183, 184, 192n4, 196, 206n9, 638; bully pulpit used by, 632; in House of Representatives, U.S., 150; overview of, 149–56; on reelection, 156n9, 157n35; Spot Resolutions influencing, 154–56; Whigs denied by, 151. *See also* Mexican American War

*Pollock v. Farmers' Loan and Trust Company*, 311–12, 347, 352n15

Poll taxes, 480, 486n36

Polygamy, 261–62

Pomerene, Atlee, 380, 649

Poore, Benjamin Perely, 193n18

Popular sovereignty, 189–91, 193n21, 201, 206n15, 262

Populists, 299

Posse Comitatus Act (1879), 261

Postmasters, 630. See also *Kendall v. United States*; *Myers v. United States*

Post Office, 270

Post-presidential roles, 652–53

Potter, David, 168

Powell, Colin, 598

Powell, Lewis F., 499, 501–2, 527–28, 549

Powers, Abigail. *See* Fillmore, Abigail

POWs. *See* Prisoners of war

Prayer in public schools, 463

Preamble, 639

Presentment Clause, 543, 552n14, 552n18, 552n25, 576, 636

Presidency, 289–90, 415, 514, 623–54

President, 44n4, 135n16, 147n8, 438n10, 458n37, 520n26
Presidential papers, 518n12, 592. *See also* Watergate
Presidential power. *See* Executive powers
Presidential Recordings and Materials Preservation Act of 1974, 513
Presidential Records Act (1978), 506n25, 513
Presidential removal power. *See* Removal
Presidential tool kit, 628–40
Presidents, 506n25, 534n26, 552n18, 583n16, 585n43
*Prigg v. Pennsylvania*, 164–65
Principal officer, 27
Principles of 1823. *See* Monroe Doctrine
Prior restraint, 505n5, 505n6
Prisoners of war (POWs), 425n34
Privacy, 645–47
Private discrimination, 471n37
Privileges or Immunities Clause, 647
Prize Cases, 221
Proclamation of Neutrality. *See* Neutrality Proclamation of 1793
Proclamation on Nullification, 110–12, 639–40
Professional Air Traffic Controllers Organization (PATCO) strike, 545–46, 553n26, 553n29, 553n32, 553n34, 629
Progressive Movement, 333, 336–37, 340, 346, 360, 633
Progressive Party, 339, 348–49, 360
Progressive Republicans, 339
Prohibition, 387, 388–89
Public accommodations, 484n14, 485n17, 486n27
*Public Papers of Reagan*, 555n52
Public schools, prayer in, 463
Public Works Employment Act, 525
Puerto Rico, 321, 322–23, 327n22, 327n30
Pulitzer, Joseph, 320, 327n21
Pullman Strike, 309–11
Pupil Placement Law, 454
Putnam, James, 35

Al-Qaeda, 594–95. *See also* Bin Laden, Osama
Quarantine, 470n12

Quasi-War, 38–40, 43, 645
Quitman, John A., 166
Quotas. *See* Affirmative action

Race, 372, 465–69, 522, 523, 641–43. *See also* African Americans; Civil rights; Ferguson, Missouri
Racial divisions, 617n2
Radical Reconstruction, 254
Radical Republicans, 268
Railroad strikes, 254, 258–60, 264n15, 309–11
Randolph, Edmund, 6, 21–22, 109
Rasul, Shafig, 600
*Rasul v. Bush*, 600, 604n34
Ray, Robert, 580–81
Reagan, John Edward, 540
Reagan, Nancy, 540, 550, 551n1
Reagan, Nelle Wilson, 540
Reagan, Patricia, 551n1
Reagan, Ronald, 530–31, 532, 534n29, 534n31, 552n21, 552n24, 553n32, 553n34, 555n50, 559–61, 573, 629, 648, 649; federal judiciary reshaped by, 549–50, 555n54; independent-counsel law impacting, 547–48; overview of, 539–51; signing statements of, 546, 636. *See also* Balanced Budget and Emergency Deficit Control Act; *INS v. Chadha*; Iran Contra Affair; Legislative veto; Professional Air Traffic Controllers Organization strike
Reagan, Ronald Prescott, 551n1
Reapportionment, 464–65
Rebellion, 139–41, 640
Recall election, 353n19
Recess appointment, 285n4, 611–13, 620n34, 620n37, 630
*Reconcentrados* (resettlement camps), 320
Reconstruction, 228–32, 233–36, 238n21, 254, 257–58, 471n37, 485n20, 642, 655n15. *See also* Grant, Ulysses S.
Reconstruction Acts, 233–34, 238n20
Reconstruction Amendments, 247, 248
Records, 506n25, 518n12
Recount, 591, 602n3, 602n5, 654n2
Redeemers, 257–58
Red Scare, 386, 446–47
Reed, Stanley F., 416, 436

Reeder, Andrew H., 191

Reelection, 41–43, 108–9, 156n9, 157n35, 207n22, 324–25, 532

Refugees, 166

Rehnquist, William, 495, 499, 548, 549, 550, 569n26, 579–80, 651

Rehnquist Court, 550, 555n55, 555n58

Reid, Harry, 619n29

Religious issues, of Kennedy, J. F., 463–64

Relocation, 419–20

Removal, 93–94, 109–10, 114n23, 292–93, 334–35, 389–90, 629–30

Removal Act (1830), 105

Reno, Janet, 573, 576, 585n43, 648

Reorganization Act of 1949, 414–15, 629

Reparations, 425n43

Reprieves, 630–31

Republican government, 71n2

Republican National Committee, 270

Republican National Convention (1880), 268–69

Republican National Convention (1988), 568n20

Republican parties, 238n21

Republican Party, 64, 191, 199, 206n12, 248n2, 277, 339, 376, 569n28

Republicans, 40–41, 65–66, 94, 233–36, 242, 256, 257, 291–92, 339, 573, 578–79, 602n5, 615, 621n43. See also Arthur, Chester; Bush, George H. W.; Bush, George W.; Coolidge, Calvin; Eisenhower, Dwight D.; Ford, Gerald R.; Garfield, James; Grant, Ulysses S.; Harding, Warren G.; Harrison, Benjamin; Hayes, Rutherford B.; Hoover, Herbert; Lincoln, Abraham; McKinley, William; Nixon, Richard M.; Reagan, Ronald; Roosevelt, Theodore; Taft, William Howard

Reservations (Native American), 284

Resettlement, of Native Americans, 105

Resettlement camps (*reconcentrados*), 320

Revenue Act (1861), 352n15

Revenue collectors, 260–61

Revenue law, 265n19

Revised Statutes of United States, 264n14, 265n19

Revolution, 43–44, 49, 51, 54, 72n3, 76–77, 90, 91, 335, 372, 625

Revolutionary War. *See* American Revolution

*Reynolds v. Sims*, 465

*Reynolds v. United States*, 262

Rhode Island, 139–41, 176–77, 640

Richards, Ann, 590

Richardson, Elliot, 501

Right to vote, 283–84, 303, 365–66, 369n39, 484n14, 486n36, 498–99, 647–48

Rio Grande, 167. *See also* Mexican American War

Riots, 310–11, 372, 467–68. *See also* Ferguson, Missouri

River of Doubt, 339

Roads, 81

Roaring Twenties, 386–87

Robards, Rachel Donelson. *See* Jackson, Rachel

Robbins, Jonathan. *See* Nash, Thomas

Roberts, John, 608, 617n8, 655n11

Roberts, Owen J., 380, 401, 417, 649

Roberts Commissions, 401

Robertson, William H., 269, 280

Robinson, Joseph T., 416, 417

Robinson, Michelle. *See* Obama, Michelle

Rockefeller, John D., 300–302, 319

Rockefeller, Nelson, 510, 515

*Roe v. Wade*, 499–500, 648

Roman Catholic Church, 261, 302

Romney, Mitt, 609, 618n15

Roosevelt, Archie, 340

Roosevelt, Eleanor, 410, 411, 423n4, 648

Roosevelt, Franklin Delano, 10–11, 33n30, 341n33, 384n47, 402, 405n20, 423n4, 423n6, 424n29, 425n32, 425n41, 434, 435, 436, 460, 471n37, 542, 595, 620n34, 630, 633, 637, 639, 648, 651; Brownlow Committee of, 414–15, 629; foreign affairs influencing, 418–19; North American Aviation seized by, 420–21, 426n49, 435; overview of, 409–23; relocation of, 419–20; Supreme Court plan of, 415–18, 484n7, 644; third term of, 419, 625. *See also* New Deal

Roosevelt, James, 410

Roosevelt, Kermit, 338

Roosevelt, Quentin, 340
Roosevelt, Theodore, 33n30, 296n15, 306n9, 319, 324–25, 327n22, 328n38, 341n33, 344–46, 348–49, 350, 360, 410–11, 412, 416, 419–20, 583n18, 633, 651; conservation advanced by, 334, 346; foreign policy of, 335; overview of, 331–40; removal argued for by, 334–35; Sherman Anti-Trust Act and, 336–37. See also *Lochner v. New York*
Roosevelt Corollary, 335
Rosecrans, William S., 268
Rough Rider regiment, 325, 327n22
Round Island, 166
Ruckelshaus, William, 501
Rules Committee, 274n8
Rush, Richard, 68
Russia, 83, 90, 91–92, 185, 196, 205n7
Rutledge, John, 6, 25–26, 651
Ryan, Thelma Pat. *See* Nixon, Thelma Pat

St. Louis, Missouri, 258
Salary, 132–33, 285n3
Salt Lake City, Utah, 199–200
Same-sex marriage, 609–11, 610–11, 619n25, 633
Sandy Hook Elementary School, 619n23
Sanford, Edward T., 384n47, 401
Sanford, John, 197–99
Santa Fe, New Mexico, 167, 175
Santo Domingo, 242
Sarasota, Florida, 593–94
Sargent, Nathan, 130–31
*Saturday Night Live*, 513
Saturday Night Massacre, 501, 505n8, 547, 549
Savings-and-loan fraud, 572, 575
Sawyer, Charles, 434
Saxton, Ida. *See* McKinley, Ida
Scalia, Antonin, 549, 550, 569n26, 617n8, 618n11, 618n14, 620n37, 655n11
Schenck, Charles T., 364
*Schenck v. United States*, 364, 375, 645
Schlesinger, Arthur M., 84
Scott, Dred, 197–99
Scott, Tom, 254
Scott, Winfield, 155, 171n5, 171n9, 185, 220
Screen Actors Guild, 540, 545–46
Secession, 202–3

Second Amendment, 619n23
Secondary boycott, 310–11
Second Bank of United States, 108–10
Second Continental Congress, 49
Second Seminole War, 162
Secretary of state, 50, 64–65, 77, 78–79, 82
Secretary of war, Monroe, J., as, 77
Section 643, 265n19
Section 5297, 264n14
Sedition Acts, 38, 42, 53, 364, 373–74, 375, 381, 384n49
Segregation, 312, 361, 468–69, 642. See also *Brown v. Board of Education I*; *Brown v. Board of Education II*; *Plessy v. Ferguson*; University of Alabama; University of Mississippi
Seminole people, 77–79
Seminole Wars, 105
Senate, U.S., 2, 6, 22, 26, 27–28, 91, 183, 192n2, 236, 295n3, 304, 378, 383n25, 383n30, 446–47, 505n8, 552n17, 607, 619n28, 619n29, 652–53; contempt citations enforced by, 621n44; on flag burning, 569n27; lawyers, 405n16. *See also* Advice and consent; Appointments; Censure; Impeachment; Recess appointment
Senate Judiciary Committee, 417, 458n42, 562, 580
Senatorial courtesy, 269
Separate but equal, 449–50, 458n42. See also *Plessy v. Ferguson*
Separation of church and state, 58n2, 261–62, 463
Separation of powers, 10, 13n5, 14n31, 21–24, 438n14, 574, 624, 649. *See also* Independent counsel
September 11th (9/11), 593–601, 614, 646
Sequestration, 544–45, 552n25
Serurier, Charles, 73n24
Servicemen's Readjustment Act of 1944, 413
Seventeenth Amendment, 350
Seventieth Indiana Regiment, 298
Severalty law, 284
Seward, William, 190, 215
Sexual harassment, 562, 574, 652
Sexuality, 205n4
Seymour, Horatio, 242
Shanksville, Pennsylvania, 594

Shays' Rebellion, 4, 147n14
Sherman, William Tecumseh, 222, 298
Sherman Anti-Trust Act, 300–302, 305, 306n9, 310, 314n19, 336–37, 345–46, 634, 644
Shiloh, 241
Shiras, George, 305
*Shurtleff v. United States*, 334–35
Sierra Club, 602n10
Signing statements, 148n29, 504n3, 546, 599, 636–37
Silver letter, 309
Sinclair, Harry F., 380
Sino-American treaty, 528–29
Sioux Uprising, 216, 630
Sirica, John J., 501
Sixteenth Amendment, 311–12, 347–48, 350, 352n15, 633
Skelton, Martha. *See* Jefferson, Martha
Slacker raids, 382n4
*Slaughterhouse Cases*, 245–46, 249n16, 249n17
Slavery, 70–71, 95–96, 98n28, 119–20, 128, 156n12, 167–69, 176, 183–84, 185–86, 193n21, 196, 219, 285n2, 639, 641–42, 652; filibus-tering and, 165–66; states determining matters of, 206n15. *See also Amistad* case; Emancipation Proclamation; Mis-souri Compromise of 1820; Three-fifths Clause
Slaves, 6–7, 48–49, 77–79, 171n10, 188–89, 277, 654n8
Smith, Abigail. *See* Adams, Abigail
Smith, Alfred E., 393, 461
Smith, George Otis, 400–401, 405n16
Smith, Jess, 391
Smith, Joseph, 199
Smith, Robert, 72n10
Smith, Rosalynn. *See* Carter, Rosalynn
Smith, Samuel, 72n10
Smith, William French, 541, 544, 547, 549
Smith Act, 447, 456n11
Smoking-gun tape, 502, 503
Smuggling, 394n24
Snowden, Edward, 622n55, 647
Sobeloff, Simon E., 450
Socialist Party of America. *See* Debs, Eugene
Social security, 424n11

Social Security Act of 1935, 413
Sole-organ doctrine, 41, 369n20, 419, 425n35, 637
Solomon Islands, 461
Somalia, 614–16
Sorensen, Ted, 467–68
Soulé, Pierre, 186, 189
Souter, David, 561
South, 230, 247, 263n1, 642
South America. *See* Monroe Doctrine
South Carolina, 71, 202, 203, 215, 244, 257, 640. *See also* Calhoun, John; Charleston, South Carolina; Force Bill
*South Carolina v. Katzenbach*, 480–81, 486n36
Southeast Asia. *See* Vietnam War
Southern Democrats, 199, 255–57
Southerners, 165–66, 168, 189–90, 242, 457n26, 458n42, 486n27
Southern Manifesto, 452
Southern Whigs, 177
South Korea. *See* Korean War
South Vietnam. *See* Vietnam War
Sovereignty, 14n33, 189–91, 193n21, 201, 206n15, 262
Soviet Union, 431, 522, 567. *See also* Cuban Missile Crisis
Spain, 120–21. *See also* Cuba; Spanish-American War
Spanish, 22, 78–79, 120–21, 327n22. *See also* Monroe Doctrine
Spanish-American War, 12, 319–21, 327n21, 563, 632–33, 637, 638
Special Division of U.S. Court of Appeals for District of Columbia Circuit, 554n40
Special Forces, U.S., 529–30
Special prosecutors, 554n40, 554n41, 649–50
Special Prosecutor's Office, 649
Special sessions, 634–35
Specie Circular order, 118–19
Specter, Arlen, 585n37
Speech, freedom of, 363–64, 384n49, 505n5, 505n6, 564–66, 654n4. *See also* Espionage Act of 1917; Free speech; *Schenck v. United States*; Sedition Acts; *Yates v. U.S.*
Speer, Elizabeth. *See* Buchanan, Elizabeth
Spencer, John C., 145
Spending Clause, 608

Spoils system, 109–10, 279, 286n22

Spot Resolutions, 154–56

Spotty Lincoln. *See* Lincoln, Abraham

*Springer v. United States*, 352n15

Square Deal, 336–37

Stalin, Josef, 431, 438n12

Stalwarts, 268, 271, 280, 286n7, 286n10. *See also* Conkling, Roscoe

Standard Oil, 300–302

*Standard Oil Company v. U.S.*, 345–46

Stanford University, 396, 403

Stanton, Edwin, 217, 223, 234, 235–36, 241, 334

*Star of the West*, 203

Starr, Kenneth, 565, 575, 576–78, 580, 584n21

Star Route Frauds, 270

Starr Report, 578

State Department, U.S., 32n23, 72n10, 85

State nullification, 51

State of the Union, 2, 579

States, 14n33, 58n2, 114n36, 147n14, 205n6, 206n15, 265n20, 348, 542, 551n8. *See also* Missouri Compromise of 1820

States' rights, 187, 232

Statute for Religious Freedom, 63

St. Clair, Arthur, 20

St. Clair, James, 501–2

Steel industry, 655n9

*Steel Seizure Case*, 433–36, 437, 574

Steimer, Mollie, 364

*Stein v. New York*, 404n10

Stephens, Alexander, 153, 170n3

Stevens, John Paul, 552n25, 569n26, 574, 583n18

Stevens, Thaddeus, 254

Stevenson, Adlai, 325, 437, 445

Stewart, Potter, 458n42, 549

Stone, Geoffrey R., 364

Stone, Harlan F., 392, 394n24, 420, 425n35

Story, Joseph, 67, 73n21, 121, 131, 164–65

Strader, Jacob, 177–78

*Strader v. Graham*, 177–78, 180n9

Strict scrutiny, 392

Strikes, 254, 258–60, 264n15, 299, 309–11, 323, 366, 545–46, 553n26, 553n29, 553n32, 553n34

Strong, William, 261

*Stuart v. Laird*, 59n24

Substantive due process, 337–38

Subversive speech, 363–64

Succession, of Garfield, J., 271–73

Succession Clause, 492

Suffrage. *See* Right to vote

*Sugar Trust* Case. See *United States v. E.C. Knight Co.*

Suicide (Vince Foster), 572–73, 574

Sumter County Board of Education, 523

Sun Belt, 522

Supremacy Clause, 66, 72n14, 180n6, 261

Supreme Court, U.S., 11–12, 24–26, 28–29, 32n18, 43, 50, 53, 67, 81–82, 87n16, 91, 112, 122–23, 124n22, 145–46, 177–78, 180n9, 186–87, 205n6, 219–22, 238n20, 245–47, 249n17, 282–84, 303–4, 305, 306n9, 311–12, 314n8, 322–23, 334–35, 336–37, 345–46, 347, 366–67, 376–77, 384n47, 389–90, 391–92, 399–402, 415–18, 424n29, 448–49, 450–51, 452, 455, 458n42, 482–83, 484n7, 485n20, 499–500, 505n5, 505n6, 534n21, 535n32, 549–50, 555n55, 555n58, 560–62, 583n16, 599–601, 602n3, 604n35, 617n4, 617n8, 618n9, 618n13, 618n14, 629, 630, 636, 642, 643–45, 650–52, 653, 654n8, 655n14, 655n15; on balanced budget law, 552n25; on contempt citations, 614, 621n44; on desegregation, 457n21; on equal protection, 249n16; on executive privilege, 631–32; sole-organ doctrine jettisoned by, 369n20, 419, 425n35, 637; on unreasonable search and seizure, 394n24; on wiretapping, 394n24, 603n23. *See also* Court packing; Judicial review

Surratt, Mary, 223

Sutherland, George, 46n24, 384n47, 394n19, 415, 418–19

*Swift & Co. v. United States*, 341n25

Symmes, Anna. *See* Harrison, Anna

Sympathetic strike, 310–11

Syngman Rhee, 431

Syria, 621n48

Taft, Helen, 383n17

Taft, Robert, 431–32

Taft, William Howard, 295n10, 314n14, 338–39, 351n9, 353n18, 353n28, 360, 379, 381, 383n17, 383n30, 389, 391–92, 394n19, 394n24, 401, 617n1, 633, 653; conservation

of, 346; on income tax, 347–48; overview
of, 343–51; Progressive agenda of, 346;
states opposed by, 348; trusts battled
against by, 345–46

Taft-Hartley Act, 433–35, 436

Taiwan, 528–29

Take Care Clause, 304, 545, 628–29

Taliban, 594, 595

Tammany Hall, 291

Tammany Hall Democrats, 291

Taney, Roger, 108, 122–23, 131, 178, 180n9,
187, 198–99, 213, 216, 219–21

Tapes. *See* Watergate

Targeted killings, 614–16, 639

Tariffs, 94–95, 98n23, 142–43, 205n7, 314n17,
322–23, 397

Taxes, 45n18; direct, 352n14; excise, 352n14;
federal, 311–12, 314n17, 347–48, 352n15;
fraud, 500; income, 305, 311–12, 314n17,
347–48, 352n15, 500; indirect, 352n14; poll,
480, 486n36; whiskey, 260–61

Taxing and Spending Clause, 608, 618n11

Taylor, Zachary, 133, 152–53, 155, 157n35,
170n1, 170n3, 171n4, 171n5, 171n6, 174, 175,
179n2, 184, 206n10, 639, 641–42; filibus-
tering halted by, 165–66; fugitive-slave
issue and, 164–65; overview of, 161–70;
slavery influenced by, 167–69; Texas dealt
with by, 167

Teapot Dome Scandal, 379–80, 390, 391,
649

Tecumseh, 127

Tehran, Iran. *See* Iran Hostage Crisis

Tejas, 167

Teller Amendment, 327n23

Tenements, 299

*Tennesee v. Davis*, 261, 265n20

Tennessee Coal, Iron and Railroad Company, 346

Tenth Amendment, 193n21, 206n15, 555n54

Tenure of Office Act, 233, 235, 292–93, 334,
627, 630

TerHorst, Jerald, 511

*Terrett v. Taylor*, 73n21

Territories, 167–69, 321–23. *See also*
Annexation

Terrorism. *See* September 11th

Terry, David, 303–4

Texas, 79, 112, 144–45, 150–55, 156, 156n12, 167,
168–69, 170, 172n18, 175, 176, 188, 444, 469,
474, 475, 632

*Texas v. Johnson*, 564–66, 569n26

*Texas v. White*, 243

Thacher, Thomas D., 405n16

Third Virginia Regiment, 76–77

Thirteenth Amendment, 215–16, 230–31,
243, 259, 282–83

Thoman, Leroy, 287n23

Thomas, Clarence, 561–62, 617n8, 618n11,
618n14, 652

Thomas, Norman, 383n20

Thomas Nash affair, 40–41, 627

Thompson, Smith, 81, 145

Thornberry, Homer, 482

Three-fifths Clause, 6–7, 91, 232, 641

Tiananmen Square, 225n27

Tidewater area, 368n12

Tilden, Samuel, 255–57, 264n4. *See also*
Hayes-Tilden Election

Tippecanoe. *See* Harrison, William

Tippecanoe Creek, 127, 129

Tocqueville, Alexis de, 500

Todd, Dolley Payne. *See* Madison, Dolley

Tolls, 81

Topeka, Kansas, 191

Torture, 597–99, 601, 604n31

Tower, John, 548

Transcontinental railroad, 189, 214

Transcontinental Treaty, 83

Treason, 56

Treasury Department, 11–12, 280, 534n31

Treaties, 27–28, 32n19, 72n3, 383n25; of Fort
Wayne, 127; of Ghent, 92; of Guadalupe
Hidalgo, 155; law, 446; of Paris, 320–21; of
Peace (1783), 72n14; of 1795, 120–21; Sino-
American, 528–29; with Taiwan, 528–29;
Transcontinental, 83; of Versailles, 378.
*See also* Jay Treaty

Tripp, Linda, 577

Truman, Bess, 437

Truman, Harry S., 12, 76, 402–3, 405n20,
422, 423n4, 438n6, 438n14, 439n31, 444,
448, 528, 548n38, 563, 574, 583n18, 602n15,
635, 638, 639, 646, 648; Korean War
entered by, 431–33; overview of, 427–37.
See also *Steel Seizure Case*

Truman, Virginia, 428
Truman Doctrine, 429
Trumbull, Lyman, 243
Trusts, 300–302, 306n9, 323–24, 345–46
Tucker, Jim Guy, 575
Turkey, 463
Twain, Mark. *See* Clemens, Samuel
Tweed, William M., 291
Twelfth Amendment, 44n4, 56, 59n10, 92–93, 98n17, 131, 255, 591, 625, 654n2. *See also* Electoral Count Act
Twentieth Amendment, 404n7
Twenty-Fifth Amendment, 133–34, 509
Twenty-First Amendment, 398
Twenty-Fourth Amendment, 480
Twenty-Second Amendment, 33n30, 425n36, 454, 458n37, 548n38, 625
Twenty-Seventh Congress, 148n30
Twenty-Sixth Amendment, 498–99
Two-term tradition, 33n30, 425n36
Tyler, John, 127, 128, 129–34, 147n8, 147n10, 148n38, 273, 627, 635, 640, 652; annexation and, 144–45; impeachment of, 142–44, 148n30, 627; overview of, 136–46; second term of, 144–45; Supreme Court nominations of, 145–46, 651; Texas and, 144–45; vetoes used by, 141–44, 651. *See also* Dorr Rebellion
Tyler Precedent, 129–34

Underwood, Thomas J., 128–29
Uniformity Clause, 322–23
Union, 225n23, 225n36
Union Army, 225n41, 630
Union Navy, 221
United Nations (UN), 422, 423n4, 431, 432, 438n14, 446
United States (U.S.), 87n19, 224n22, 405n16
United States Code, 457n30, 504n2
*United States Code Congressional and Administrative News*, 546
United States Supreme Court. *See* Supreme Court, U.S.
*United States v. Addyston Pipe and Steel Co.*, 328n24
*United States v. American Tobacco Company*, 345–46
*United States v. Branscum*, 583n17

*United States v. Burr*, 583n17
*United States v. Carolene Products*, 392
*United States v. Cruikshank*, 246–47
*United States v. Curtiss-Wright Export Corporation*, 46n24, 362, 369n20, 418–19, 425n35
*United States v. E.C. Knight Co.*, 306n9, 312, 314n19, 323–24, 643–44
*United States v. Eichman*, 565–66, 569n26
*United States v. Fromme*, 520n26, 583n17
*United States v. Great Britain*, 224n22
*United States v. Harris*, 282, 283
*United States v. McDougal*, 583n17
*United States v. Midwest Oil Co*, 351n9
*United States v. Nixon*, 502–3, 516, 520n26, 583n17, 593, 602n10, 631
*United States v. Reese*, 250n22
*United States v. Smith*, 400–401, 405n16, 405n17
*United States v. South-Eastern Underwriters Association*, 617n4
*United States v. The Amistad*, 96, 99n29, 119–21, 641
*United States v. Windsor*, 610–11, 619n25
United Steelworkers of America. *See* *Steel Seizure Case*; *Youngstown Sheet and Tube Co. v. Sawyer*
University of Alabama, 452, 467–68, 640
*University of California Board of Regents v. Bakke*, 525–28, 534n21, 643
University of Michigan, 534n21
University of Mississippi, 466–67, 471n31, 640
Unlawful cohabitation, 262
Unreasonable search and seizure, 394n24
Uprisings, 199–201, 216, 225n26, 630, 640
USA Patriot Act. *See* Patriot Act
USS *Carl Vinson*, 614
USS *Maddox*, 481–82
USS *Maine*, 320
USS *San Jacinto*, 558
U.S. Steel, 346
Utah, 176, 199–201, 261–62, 640

Van Buren, Hannah, 117
Van Buren, Martin, 105, 107–8, 112, 115n38, 124n12, 125n23, 129, 163, 171n8, 179n2, 641; Congress and, 122–23; executive branch

and, 122–23; overview of, 116–24; Panic of 1837 influencing, 117–19; Supreme Court and, 122–23. See also *Amistad* case

Van Devanter, Willis, 390, 394n19, 415, 417

Venezuela, 225n26

Vesting Clause, 23–24, 349, 628–29. See also *Myers v. United States*

Veterans, World War I, 399

Vetoes: Cleveland, G., changing, 296n15; Jackson, A., approach to, 106–8, 113n10, 624; Justice Department on, 552n14; legislative, 542–44, 552n12, 552n14, 552n21, 654n7; Nixon, R., approach to, 505n8, 635–36; pocket, 113n10, 393n2; Reagan, R., attacking, 542–44; Roosevelt, T., using, 296n15; Tyler, J., approach to, 141–44, 651

Veto power, 2–3, 7; Adams, J. Q., on, 94–95; Bush, G. H. W., using, 560; Cleveland, G., using, 293–94, 635; Coolidge, C., using, 387; Ford, G., using, 514; Hayes using, 263; Jefferson, T., on, 20; Johnson, A., using, 231–32; in legislative function, 635–36; Madison, J., using, 69; overview of, 635–36; in presidential tool kit, 635–36; Taft, W., using, 351; Washington, G.'s, approach to, 20, 635

Vice presidents, 3, 35–36, 44n3, 44n4, 50–51, 147n7, 147n8, 147n10, 273, 476, 500, 506n25, 625, 626, 627

Vietnam War, 481–82, 483, 495, 496–99, 515, 519n14, 522, 631, 638. See also Pentagon Papers; War Powers Resolution

Vinson, Fred, 416, 434, 436, 448

Virginia, 6, 18, 48, 51, 58n2, 62–63, 64, 70, 72n14, 73n21, 77, 104, 137, 171n15, 368n12

Volstead Act, 388–89

Votes, 313n4, 369n39

Voting, 250n22, 287n30, 464–65, 486n32, 486n33, 633. See also Right to vote

Voting Rights Act of 1965, 479–81, 634, 642

Wage Stabilization Board, 433

Wagner, Robert F., 413, 424n12

Wagner Act. See National Labor Relations Act

*Wag the Dog*, 584n34

Walker, Robert, 201

Wallace, George, 467, 640

Wallace, Henry, 429

Wallace, Virginia. *See* Truman, Virginia

Walsh, Lawrence E., 548, 560

Walsh, Thomas J., 380

War, presidents and, 2, 216–18, 377–79, 562–64, 599–601, 603n17, 603n18; laws of, 216–18, 226n37, 226n39; ships, 224n22; on Terror, 12, 425n34, 597, 604n27, 638–39, 646–47. *See also* Afghanistan; Civil War; Iraq; Korean War; Mexican American War; Persian Gulf War; Vietnam War; War of 1812; World War I; World War II

War Crimes Act, 597–98

War Department, 20

*Ware v. Hylton*, 72n14

War Hawks, 67

War Labor Disputes Act, 426n49, 435

Warner Brothers Studio, 540

War of 1812, 8, 57, 67–70, 82, 91–92, 105, 111, 129, 635

War Powers Act. *See* War Powers Resolution

War Powers Resolution, 437, 496, 497–98, 504, 514–15, 517, 529–30, 534n26, 534n29, 568n18, 585n45, 618n16, 638

Warren, Earl, 448–49, 455, 457n21, 458n42, 482, 486n27, 499

Warren Commission, 509

Warren Court, 448–49, 450–51, 499, 555n58, 561

Washington, D.C., 9, 68, 82, 98n28, 171n15, 176, 188, 220, 223, 255–57, 271–72, 367, 532n4, 593–95, 648. *See also* Watergate

Washington, George, 4, 7–8, 9, 13n3, 14n30, 32n19, 33n30, 35, 39, 45, 49, 50, 54, 64, 72n3, 76–77, 104, 163, 182, 519n14, 624, 625, 635; advice and consent, sought by, 27–28; cabinet of, 22–24, 27; Congress's relationship with, 20–22; executive departments made by, 27; overview of, 17–30; Senate seeking of, 27–28; Supreme Court of, 24–26, 28–29, 629, 650, 651. *See also* Jay Treaty; Neutrality Proclamation of 1793

Washington, Martha, 18

Washington, William, 76–77

*Washington Post*, 496–97, 504n4

Washington State, 393n2

Waterboarding, 598

Watergate, 11–12, 134, 391, 495–96, 500–504, 505n8, 511–13, 514, 517, 522, 531, 580, 583n17, 627, 631, 649–50
Wayne, Anthony, 128–29
Wayne, James M., 221
Ways and Means Committee, 318
Weapons of mass destruction (WMD), 595, 603n17
Webster, Daniel, 84, 110, 140–41, 142, 148n21, 176, 177
Webster, Fletcher, 129, 131, 132
Weinberger, Caspar W., 547, 567n4
Welch, Laura. See Bush, Laura
Wellington (duke), 68
Wells, Lesley B., 382n11
West Coast, 419–20, 639
West Coast Hotel Co. v. Parrish, 341n33, 417
Western Division, 162
West Publishing Company, 546
West Virginia, 258, 259
Weyler, Valeriano, 320
Wheelchair, 423n6
Wherry, Kenneth, 431–32
Whig Convention, 163
Whigs, 107–8, 118, 124n12, 127, 138, 148n30, 151, 156n8, 157n35, 171n6, 171n8, 177, 182, 206n10, 289–90. See also Adams, John Quincy; Clay, Henry; Fillmore, Millard; Harrison, William; Taylor, Zachary; Tyler, John
Whiskey Rebellion, 171n7, 519n14, 630
Whiskey tax, 260–61
White, Byron, 569n26
White, Edward Douglass, 314n14, 341n26, 383n30
White, William Allen, 380
White Citizens' Councils, 452
White House, 9, 82, 512–13, 648
White supremacy, 261
Whitewater, 554n48, 572–73, 574, 575, 582n7
Whittaker, Charles E., 458n42
Wickard v. Filburn, 417, 479, 485n26, 618n9, 644
Wickersham, George W., 398
Wickersham Commission, 398
Wiggins, Charles, 503
WikiLeaks, 646–47
Wilkinson, James, 57

Willkie, Wendell, 419
Wilmot, David, 168
Wilmot Proviso, 168, 169
Wilson, Edith, 367, 368n12
Wilson, Ellen, 359, 361
Wilson, James, 4–5, 6, 25, 63
Wilson, Joseph Ruggles, 358
Wilson, Woodrow, 1, 11–12, 30, 289, 293, 312–13, 325, 339–40, 348–49, 369n30, 379, 382n11, 389, 397, 424n22, 425n32, 436, 497, 512, 617n1, 630, 637, 638, 645, 647; academic leadership of, 359; foreign policy of, 361–63; overview of, 357–68; pardon power used by, 364–65, 374–75, 623; Progressive agenda of, 360; right to vote supported by, 365–66; subversive speech restrictions of, 363–64; women supported by, 365–66. See also League of Nations
Windom, William, 269
Wiretaps, 394n24, 596–97, 603n23
Wisconsin, 176–77, 259
Wise, Henry A., 133
WMD. See Weapons of mass destruction
Wolcott, Oliver, Jr., 37
Women, rights of, 250n22, 365–66, 633, 647–48
Wood, Gordon S., 19
Woodbury, Levi, 177, 183
Woodrow, Janet, 358
Worcester v. Georgia, 112, 114n36, 115n37, 650–51
Workhouse, 382n11
World Trade Center, 593–95
World War I, 339–40, 361–64, 368n15, 382n5, 382n11, 383n25, 397, 399, 444, 633. See also Debs, Eugene; In re Debs; Wilson, Woodrow
World War II, 401, 414, 423, 426n49, 429, 444–45, 460–61, 462, 493, 498, 540, 558, 563. See also Roosevelt, Franklin Delano
Wormley House Hotel, 257
Worth, William J., 165
Wren, Christopher, 483
Wright, Susan Webber, 577, 580, 582n14, 584n21, 585n42
Writ of certiorari, 391–92
Writ of error, 391
Writ of habeas corpus. See Habeas corpus

Writ of mandamus, 125n23, 125n28
Wyman, Jane, 540, 551n1
Wyoming, 351n9, 379–80

XYZ Affair, 37

Yalu River, 432
*Yates v. U.S.*, 447, 456n11, 646
Yazoo Land Act, 66–67
Year of Woman, 562
Yellow journalism, 292, 327n21

Yemen, 614–16
Yoo, John, 597–98
Young, Brigham, 199–201, 640
Young Hickory. *See* Polk, James K.
Young Indians, 170n3
*Youngstown Sheet and Tube Co. v. Sawyer*,
    426n49, 434–36, 535n32
Yugoslavia, 618n16

Zimmerman telegram, 361, 368n15
*Zivotofsky v. Kerry*, 46n24, 369n20, 425n35